PASCAL

Problem Solving and Program Design

FOURTH EDITION

PASCAL

Problem Solving and Program Design

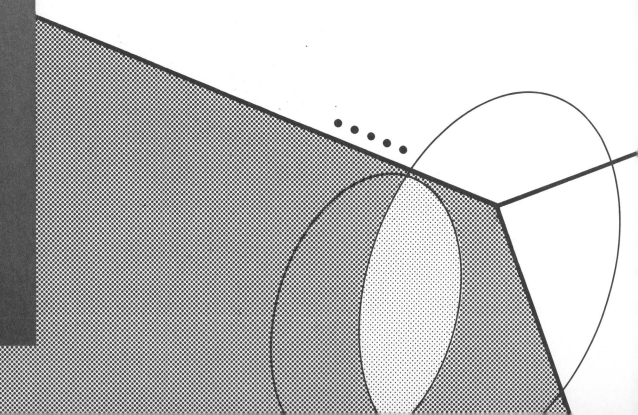

ADDISON-WESLEY PUBLISHING COMPANY
Reading, Massachusetts   Menlo Park, California   New York
Don Mills, Ontario   Wokingham, England   Amsterdam   Bonn
Sydney   Singapore   Tokyo   Madrid   San Juan   Milan   Paris

4th Edition

Elliot B. Koffman

Temple University

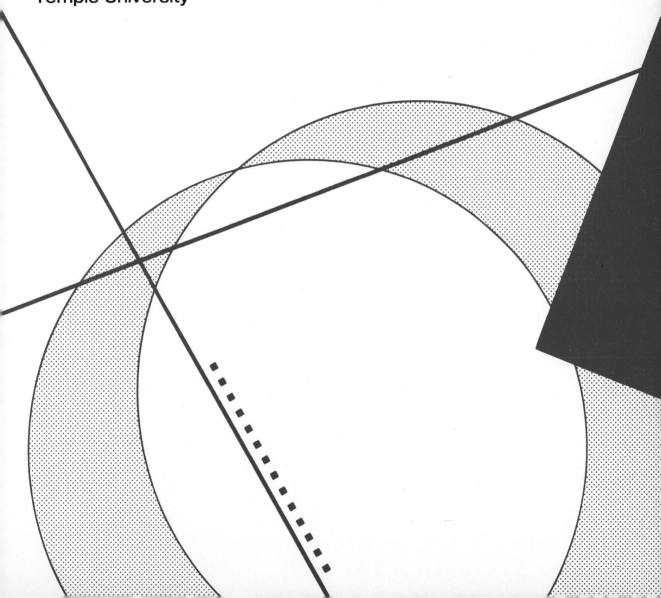

Lynne Doran Cote, Sponsoring Editor
Loren Hilgenhurst Stevens, Production Supervisor
Nancy Benjamin, Production Editor
Joyce C. Weston, Text Design
Joseph Vetere, Technical Art Consultant
Tech-Graphics, Illustrations
Trish Gordon, Manufacturing Supervisor
Sharon Elwell-Smizter Design, Cover Design
Peter M. Blaiwas, Cover Art Director

Library of Congress Cataloging-in-Publication Data

Koffman, Elliot B.
    Pascal : problem solving and program design / Elliot B. Koffman.
—4th ed.
      p.   cm.
    Includes index.
    ISBN 0-201-52710-3
    1. Pascal (Computer program language)   I. Title.
QA76.73.P2K624   1992
005.13′3—dc20   91-3247
                                    CIP

1 2 3 4 5 6 7 8 9 10—DO—9594939291

To those who have filled my life with love—

My wife, Caryn; my children, Richard, Deborah, and Robin; my father, Edward; and my mother-in-law, Enid Jackson

In loving memory of my mother, Leah, and my father-in-law, Mitchell Jackson

Preface

This is a textbook for a first course in problem solving and program design using the Pascal language. It assumes no prior knowledge of computers or programming. High school algebra is sufficient mathematics background for most of the material in this book. A limited knowledge of discrete mathematics, however, is desirable for certain sections.

My goal in revising this book has been to update the content and organization in accordance with the most recent computer science curricula recommendations. The last edition closely followed the recommendations of the ACM Computing Curricula Task Force for CS1[1] and CS2[2], which I chaired. Many of the changes in this edition have been influenced by the recent report of the ACM/IEEE-CS Joint Curriculum Task Force[3].

This new edition provides more emphasis on problem solving, software engineering, abstraction, and computing theory. There is also less emphasis on the spiral approach than in previous editions. To accomplish these changes, the first twelve chapters have been heavily revised.

Problem Solving

The connection between good problem-solving skills and effective software development is established early in Chapter 1 with a new section that discusses the art and science of problem solving. Chapter 1 also introduces a methodology for software development based on the systems approach to problem solving consisting of five phases: specify the problem, analyze the problem, design the solution, implement the solution, test the solution. The software development method is used in Chapter 2 to solve the first case study and is applied consistently to all the case studies in the text.

Chapter 3 continues the emphasis on problem solving by discussing top-down design, divide-and-conquer, solution by analogy, and generalizing a so-

---

1. Recommended Curriculum for CS1, Koffman, E., Miller, P., and Wardle, C., Communications of the ACM 27, 10 (Oct. 1984), 998–1001.

2. Recommended Curriculum for CS2, Koffman, E., Stemple, D., and Wardle, C., Communications of the ACM 28, 8 (Aug. 1985), 815–818.

3. Computing Curricula 1991, Report of the ACM/IEEE-CS Joint Curriculum Task Force, Tucker, A.B. (editor), 1991, ACM Press and IEEE Computer Society Press.

lution. An important section of this chapter demonstrates how a Pascal program can be derived by editing the documentation that results from systematically following the software development method.

Software Engineering

Many aspects of software engineering are covered in the book. Program style issues are discussed throughout in special displays. The concept of a program as a sequence of control structures is introduced early in Chapter 3. There are sections in several chapters that discuss algorithm tracing, program debugging, and testing.

Chapter 9 is a new chapter on software engineering. This chapter discusses the system/software life cycle (SLC), prototyping, and programming teams. There is in-depth coverage of all phases of the SLC, including more discussion of informal techniques for program testing (e.g., glass-box versus black-box testing, integration testing, structured walkthroughs) and formal methods for program verification, including a discussion of assertions and loop invariants. This chapter also reviews procedural abstraction and introduces data abstraction. It concludes with a discussion of professional ethics.

Procedural Abstraction

Although there is no universal agreement on when to introduce procedures and procedure parameters, most educators agree on the following points: procedures should be introduced as early as feasible, procedures should never process global data (side-effects), and procedure parameters are difficult for students to understand. The approach taken in the text is to discuss the importance of program modularization and reusability in Chapter 3 by introducing structure charts, procedures without parameters, and the standard functions of Pascal. Sections 3.5 and 3.6 motivate the use of procedures as program-building blocks by showing some applications of procedures without parameters (for example, displaying long lists of user instructions, drawing diagrams). Section 3.7 discusses the need for parameters and the limitations of procedures without parameters, thereby providing a foundation for the later study of parameters. Section 3.8 shows how to use Pascal's predefined functions.

Chapter 6 completes the study of procedures and functions, covering all aspects of parameter lists. The chapter begins by discussing procedures with only value parameters, then user-defined functions with value parameters, and, finally, procedures with both value and variable parameters. An optional section at the end of the chapter introduces recursive functions.

Some instructors prefer to cover procedures with and without parameters together. You can easily rearrange the sequence of topic coverage to do this. If you want to wait until Chapter 6 to cover procedures with and without parameters, you can defer sections 3.5–3.7 until then. Conversely, if you want to cover procedure parameters earlier, you can cover section 6.1 (value parameters) right after Chapter 3. You can cover sections 6.2–6.4 (user-defined functions, variable parameters, syntax of parameter lists) after completing the first two sections of Chapter 4 (Boolean expressions and the `if` statement).

The software engineering chapter (Chapter 9) introduces data abstraction, providing the first example of an abstract data type (ADT). Data abstraction and ADTs are used throughout the remainder of the text. The ADTs appearing in Chapters 11 and 12 have been extensively revised and improved.

Reduced Emphasis on the Spiral Approach

Comments from many previous users of the textbook indicated that the majority of instructors prefer to discuss both Pascal control structures for selection (`if` and `case`) at the same time. For this reason, Chapter 4 has been revised to cover the Boolean data type and the `if` and `case` control structures. Similarly, all three control structures for repetition (`while`, `for`, and `repeat`) are covered together in Chapter 5.

The coverage of files also reflects the desire to reduce spiraling. The essentials of file usage are discussed in Chapter 2, so that student programs can read data files prepared by the instructor. Chapter 8 provides complete coverage of text files, and Chapter 15 covers binary files.

Interviews with Computer Scientists

A new feature of this edition is a collection of interviews with several notable computer scientists (for example, Peter Denning, Patrick Winston, Adele Goldberg, C. J. Date, and others), which are placed throughout the text. These interviews alert beginning students to the breadth of the subject area, providing them with a description of issues of concern in several fields of computer science (for example, artificial intelligence, operating systems, databases, user interfaces) and some idea of the background preparation needed for success in these fields.

Increased Coverage of Theoretical Concepts

As recommended by the curriculum committee report, there is increased coverage of theoretical topics. Chapter 7 introduces numerical computation and iterative approximations, including Newton's method. Chapter 9 provides a discussion of program verification, focusing on assertions and loop invariants. Chapter 10 introduces searching and sorting an array, followed by a discussion of algorithm analysis and big-O notation.

Pedagogical Features

We employ several pedagogical features to enhance the usefulness of this book as a teaching tool. Some of these features are discussed below.

End-of-Section Exercises: Most sections end with a number of self-check exercises. These include exercises that require analysis of program fragments as well as short programming exercises. Answers to selected self-check exercises appear at the back of the book; answers to the rest of the exercises are provided in the instructor's manual.

End-of-Chapter Exercises: Each chapter ends with a set of quick-check exercises with answers. There are also chapter review exercises whose solutions appear in the instructor's manual.

End-of-Chapter Projects: Approximately one-third of the programming projects are new to this edition. Most chapters have one or two special programming project pairs where the second project in the pair requires a modification to the solution of the first project in the pair. The program disk (described below) contains a solution to the first project in each pair, which students can modify to solve the follow-up project. All project solutions appear in the instructor's manual.

Examples and Case Studies: The book contains a large number and variety of programming examples. Whenever possible, examples contain complete programs or procedures rather than incomplete program fragments. Each chapter contains one or more substantial case studies that are solved following the software development method. This edition contains several new case studies.

Syntax Display Boxes: The syntax displays describe the syntax and semantics of each new Pascal feature and provide examples. There are also several syntax diagrams in the body of the text; an appendix contains a complete collection of syntax diagrams.

Program Style Displays: The program style displays discuss issues of good programming style.

Error Discussions and Chapter Review: Each chapter ends with a section that discusses common programming errors. A chapter review includes a table of new Pascal constructs.

Program Disk

There is a disk that contains all of the programs, procedures, functions, and ADTs introduced in the book. For case studies, all procedures and functions are incorporated in a single program file. There are also solutions to selected programming projects on the disk. The disk can be processed by an IBM personal computer or compatible computer. The icon

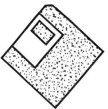

Directory: CHAP2
File: METRIC.PAS

appears alongside each program module or project indicating the name of the disk directory (e.g., CHAP2) and file (e.g., METRIC.PAS) containing the program. The book may be purchased with or without the disk.

xi
Preface

Laboratory Manual

A new feature of this edition is a laboratory manual, including a program disk. This manual provides support for laboratories based on the first thirteen chapters of the book. A number of laboratory exercises test a student's understanding of new concepts and provide additional practice in their application.

Coverage of Advanced Topics

Depending on their students' ability and background, instructors may cover anywhere from eleven to thirteen chapters in a one-semester course. The remainder of the book provides a good reference to topics normally covered in the second semester and, in some cases, may be used as the text for a second-semester course. There is certainly sufficient material for a two-quarter sequence. Advanced topics covered include:

recursion (Chapter 13)
sets and strings (Chapter 14)
binary files (Chapter 15)
stacks and queues (Chapter 16)
pointers and linked lists (Chapter 17)
ordered lists and trees (Chapter 18)
searching and sorting (Chapters 10, 12, and 19)
analysis of algorithms (Chapters 10, 18, and 19)

Appendixes and Supplements

Separate appendixes cover Pascal language elements, syntax diagrams, character codes, and additional Pascal features not described in the main body of the book. New to this edition are appendixes that describe how to use Turbo Pascal units and Vax Pascal modules to implement abstract data types. There is also an appendix on using Turbo Pascal.

An instructor's manual is available for this edition. Other supplements include transparency masters and a computerized test bank. Use the reference numbers below to order these supplements from your Addison-Wesley sales representative.

Instructor's Manual: 0-201-52711
Transparency Masters: 0-201-52713
Program Disk (if purchased separately): 0-201-52712 (3½″ disk)
                                        0-201-52612 (5¼″ disk)
Computerized Test Bank: 0-201-56560

Acknowledgments

Many people participated in the development of this book. I am especially grateful to Bruce Maxim (University of Michigan, Dearborn) who provided several new programming projects and new self-check exercises. Bruce also wrote the Turbo Pascal Appendix and revised the instructor's manual for this edition. The original instructor's manual was prepared by Keith Pierce (University of Minnesota, Duluth).

The principal reviewers were most essential in suggesting improvements and finding errors. They include: Pierre Balthazard, University of Arizona; Robert Christiansen, University of Iowa; John Goda, Georgia Institute of Technology; Anil Mehra, Colorado State University; Anne W. Oney, De Anza College; Keith Pierce, University of Minnesota; James C. Pleasant, East Tennessee State University; Michael C. Stinson, Central Michigan University; and Robert Strader, Stephen F. Austin State University. Besides reviewing the text, Professor Pleasant helped with the section on software verification.

We are also grateful to the many teachers who participated in telephone interviews or completed course surveys for Addison-Wesley's market research department. The information this research provided helped to shape the book's organization and pedagogy. They include: Dean R. Andrews, Texas State Technical College; Daniel J. Barrett, University of Massachusetts; John M. Barton, Freed-Hardeman University; George A. Benjamin, Muhlenberg College; Susan Bonzi, Syracuse University; Bill Boyd, Rhodes College; Linda D. Brinkerhoff, Erie Community College; John F. Buck, Indiana University; Allen R. Burns, Rutgers University; Mae M. Carpenter, Georgia College; Kan V. Chandras, Fort Valley State College; Darrah Chavey, Beloit College; Thomas G. Clarke, North Carolina A & T State University; Michael Erickson, Wichita State University; Susan Gauch, Northeastern University; Jarrell C. Grout, Stephen F. Austin State University; Stan Gurak, University of San Diego; Ron Johnson, Evangel College; Mike Liljegren, Illinois College; Slawomir J, Marcinkowski, Syracuse University; William Moy, University of Wisconsin; Michael G. Murphy, University of Houston; David A. Nelson, Muhlenberg College; James Nolen, Baylor University; James L. Noyes, Wittenberg University; Ed Rang, University of Wisconsin; Brian Ridgely, Alma College; Patricia Shelton, North Carolina A & T State University; Robert G. Strader, Stephen F. Austin State University; Vicci Varner, University of Texas; Leila L. Wallace, Geneva College; and Stephen Weiss, University of North Carolina.

The personnel at Addison-Wesley responsible for the production of this book worked diligently to meet a very demanding schedule. My editor, Peter Shepard, was closely involved in all phases of this project, starting with the initial market research. He did an excellent job of coordinating the writing and reviewing process and trying to keep me on schedule. Loren Hilgenhurst Stevens supervised the design and production of the book, while Nancy Benjamin coordinated the conversion of the manuscript to a finished book.

Philadelphia, PA   E.B.K.

Contents

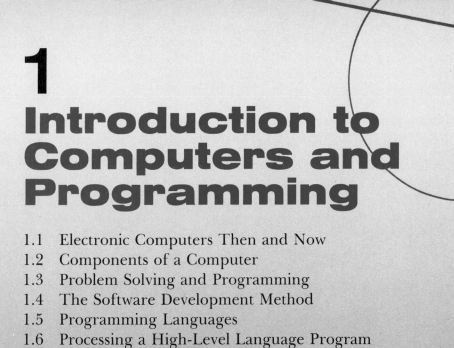

1
Introduction to Computers and Programming

From the 1940s until today—a period of only 50 years—the computer's development has spurred the growth of technology into realms only dreamed of at the turn of the century. It has also changed the way we live and how we do business. Today, we depend on computers to process our paychecks, send rockets into space, build cars and machines of all types, and help us do our shopping and banking. The computer program's role in this technology is essential; without a list of instructions to follow, the computer is virtually useless. Programming languages allow us to write those programs, and thus to communicate with computers.

You are about to begin the study of computer science using one of the most versatile programming languages available today: the Pascal language. This chapter introduces you to the computer and its components and to the major categories of programming languages.

1.1 Electronic Computers Then and Now

It is difficult to live in today's world without having some contact with computers. Computers are used to provide instructional material in schools, print transcripts, send out bills, reserve airline and concert tickets, play games, and help authors write books. Several kinds of computers cooperate in dispensing cash from an automatic teller machine; "embedded" or "hidden" computers help control the ignition, fuel system, and transmission of modern automobiles; at the supermarket, a computer device reads the bar codes on packages to total your purchases and help manage the store's inventory. Even microwave ovens have special-purpose computers built into them.

Computers were not always so pervasive in our society. Just a short time ago, computers were fairly mysterious devices that only a small percentage of the population knew much about. Computer know-how spread when advances in *solid-state electronics* led to cuts in the size and the cost of electronic computers. In the mid-1970s, a computer with the computational power of one of today's personal computers would have filled a 9-by-12-foot room and cost $100,000. Today, an equivalent personal computer (see Fig. 1.1) costs less than $3,000 and sits on a desktop.

If we take the literal definition for *computer* as "a device for counting or computing," then we could consider the abacus to be the first computer. The first electronic digital computer was designed in the late 1930s by Dr. John Atanasoff at Iowa State University. Atanasoff designed his computer to perform mathematical computations for graduate students.

The first large-scale, general-purpose electronic digital computer, called the ENIAC, was built in 1946 at the University of Pennsylvania. Its design was funded by the U.S. Army, and it was used to compute ballistics tables, predict the weather, and make atomic energy calculations. The ENIAC weighed 30 tons and occupied a 30-by-50-foot space (see Fig. 1.2).

Although we are often led to believe otherwise, computers cannot reason

Figure 1.1   IBM Personal Computer with Mouse

Figure 1.2   The ENIAC Computer (Photo Courtesy of Unisys Corporation)

as we do. Basically, computers are devices that perform computations at incredible speeds (more than one million operations per second) and with great accuracy. However, to accomplish anything useful, a computer must be *programmed*, that is, given a sequence of explicit instructions (a *program*) to perform.

To program the ENIAC, engineers had to connect hundreds of wires and arrange thousands of switches in a certain way. In 1946, Dr. John von Neumann, of Princeton University, proposed the concept of a *stored-program computer*: a program stored in computer memory rather than set by wires and switches. Von Neumann knew programmers could easily change the contents of computer memory, so he reasoned that the stored-program concept would greatly simplify programming a computer. Von Neumann's design was a success and is the basis of the digital computer as we know it today.

Brief History of Computing

Table 1.1 lists some of the important milestones along the path from the abacus to modern-day computers and programming languages. The entries before 1890 list some of the earlier attempts to develop mechanical computing devices. In 1890, the first special-purpose computer that used electronic sensors was designed; this invention eventually led to the formation of the computer-industry giant called IBM (International Business Machines).

As we look down the table from 1939 onward, we see a variety of new computers introduced. The computers listed before 1975 were all very large general-purpose computers, called *mainframes*. The computers listed after 1975 are all smaller computers.

A number of milestones in the development of programming languages and environments are also listed in Table 1.1, including FORTRAN (1957), CTSS (1965), Pascal (1971), and VisiCalc (1978).

We often use the term *first generation* to refer to electronic computers that used vacuum tubes (1939–1958). The *second generation* began in 1958 with the changeover to transistors. The *third generation* began in 1964 with the introduction of integrated circuits. The *fourth generation* began in 1975 with the advent of large-scale integration.

Categories of Computers

Modern-day computers are classified according to their size and performance. The three major categories of computers are microcomputers, minicomputers, and mainframes.

Many of you have seen or used *microcomputers*, such as the IBM PC (see Fig. 1.1). Microcomputers are also called *personal computers* or *desktop computers* because they are used by one person at a time and are small enough to fit on a desk. The smallest general-purpose microcomputers are often called *laptops* because they are small enough to fit into a briefcase and are often used on one's lap. The largest microcomputers, called *workstations* (see Fig. 1.3), are commonly used by engineers to produce engineering drawings and to assist in the design and development of new products.

Date	Event
2000 BC	The abacus is first used for computations.
1642 AD	Blaise Pascal creates a mechanical adding machine for tax computations. It is unreliable.
1670	Gottfried von Leibniz creates a more reliable adding machine that adds, subtracts, multiplies, divides, and calculates square roots.
1842	Charles Babbage designs an analytical engine to perform general calculations automatically. Ada Augusta (a.k.a. Lady Lovelace) is a programmer for this machine.
1890	Herman Hollerith designs a system to record census data. The information is stored as holes on cards, which are interpreted by machines with electrical sensors. Hollerith starts a company that will eventually become IBM.
1939	John Atanasoff, with graduate student Clifford Berry, designs and builds the first electronic digital computer. His project was funded by a grant for $650.
1946	J. Presper Eckert and John Mauchly design and build the ENIAC computer. It used 18,000 vacuum tubes and cost $500,000 to build.
1946	John von Neumann proposes that a program be stored in a computer in the same way that data are stored. His proposal (called "von Neumann architecture") is the basis of modern computers.
1951	Eckert and Mauchly build the first general-purpose commercial computer, the UNIVAC.
1957	An IBM team led by John Backus designs the first successful programming language, FORTRAN, for solving engineering and science problems.
1958	The first computer to use the transistor as a switching device, the IBM 7090, is introduced.
1958	Seymour Cray builds the first fully transistorized computer, the CDC 1604, for Control Data Corporation.
1964	The first computer using integrated circuits, the IBM 360, is announced.
1965	The CTSS (Compatible Time-Sharing System) operating system is introduced. It allows several users to simultaneously use or share a single computer.
1971	Nicklaus Wirth designs the Pascal programming language as a language for teaching structured programming concepts.
1975	The first microcomputer, the Altair, is introduced.
1975	The first supercomputer, the Cray-1, is announced.
1976	Digital Equipment Corporation introduces its popular minicomputer, the VAX 11/780.
1977	Steve Wozniak and Steve Jobs found Apple Computer.
1978	Dan Bricklin and Bob Frankston develop the first electronic spreadsheet, called VisiCalc, for the Apple computer.
1981	IBM introduces the IBM PC.
1982	Sun Microsystem introduces its first workstation, the Sun 100.
1984	Apple introduces the Macintosh, the first widely available computer with a "user-friendly" graphical interface using icons, windows, and a mouse device.

Figure 1.3 SUN Microsystems SPARCstation 370 (Photo Courtesy of Sun Micro-systems, Inc.)

Minicomputers are the next larger variety of computers. They generally operate at faster speeds than microcomputers and can store larger quantities of information. Minicomputers can serve several different users simultaneously. The computer you will use to solve problems for the course you are taking might well be a minicomputer, for example, a VAX computer from Digital Equipment Corporation. A small- or medium-size company might use a mini-computer to perform payroll computations and to keep track of its inventory. Engineers often use minicomputers to control a chemical plant or a production process.

The largest computers are called *mainframes.* A large company would have one or more mainframes at its central computing facility for performing busi-ness-related computations. Mainframes are also used as "number crunchers" to generate solutions to systems of equations that characterize engineering or scientific problems. A mainframe can solve in seconds equations that might take hours to solve on a minicomputer or even days on a microcomputer. The largest mainframes are called *supercomputers* and are used to solve the most complex systems of equations.

In the late 1950s, mainframe computers could perform only 50 instructions per second. Now it is not uncommon to have much smaller workstations that can perform over 20 million instructions per second. Obviously, there have been tremendous changes in the speed and size of computers in a relatively short time.

1.2 Components of a Computer

Despite large variations in cost, size, and capabilities, modern computers are remarkably similar to each other in a number of ways. Basically, a computer consists of the components shown in Fig. 1.4. The arrows connecting the components show the direction of information flow. These computer components are called the *hardware*.

All information that is to be processed by a computer first must be entered into the computer's *main memory* via an *input device*. The information in main memory is manipulated by the *central processor,* and the results of this manipulation are stored in main memory. Information in main memory can be displayed through an *output device. Secondary memory* is often used for storing large quantities of information in a semipermanent form.

Figure 1.4 Components of a Computer

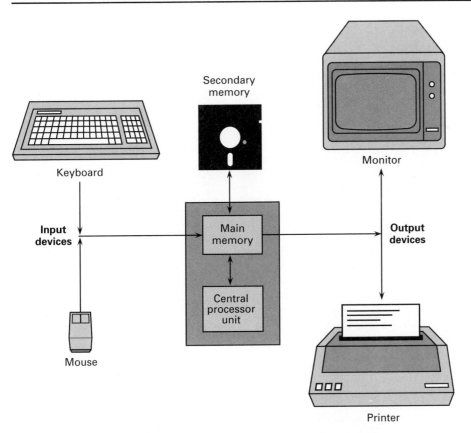

Computer Memory

A computer's main memory stores information of all types: instructions, numbers, names, lists, even pictures. Picture a computer's memory as an ordered sequence of storage locations called *memory cells*. To be able to store and then *retrieve*, or access, information, we must have some way to identify the individual memory cells. Each memory cell has a unique *address* associated with it. The address indicates the cell's relative position in memory. The sample computer memory in Fig. 1.5 consists of 1,000 memory cells, with addresses 0 through 999. (Most computers have memories that consist of millions of individual cells.)

The information stored in a memory cell is called its *contents*. Every memory cell always contains some information, although we may have no idea what that information is. Whenever new information is placed in a memory cell, any information already there is destroyed and cannot be retrieved. In Fig. 1.5, the contents of memory cell 3 are the number −26, and the contents of memory cell 4 are the letter H.

The memory cells shown in Fig. 1.5 are actually aggregates, or collections, of smaller units called *bytes*. A byte is the amount of storage required to store a single character. The number of bytes in a memory cell varies from computer

Figure 1.5 A Computer Memory with 1,000 Cells

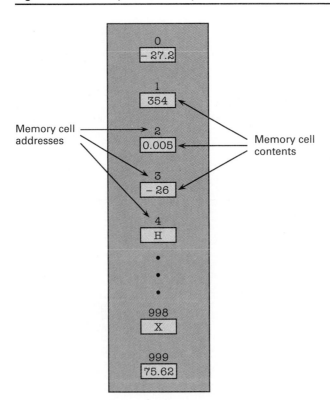

to computer. A byte is an aggregate of even small units of storage called *bits*, which are single binary digits (0 or 1). There are generally eight bits to a byte.

Each value is represented by a particular pattern of zeroes and ones. To store a value, the computer sets each bit of a selected memory cell to 0 or 1, thereby destroying what was previously in that bit. To retrieve a value from a memory cell, the computer copies the pattern of zeroes and ones stored in that cell to another storage area, the *memory buffer register,* where the bit pattern can be processed. The copy operation does not destroy the bit pattern currently in the memory cell.

The process just described is the same regardless of the kind of information—character, number, or program instruction—stored in a memory cell.

Central Processor Unit

The *central processor unit* (CPU) performs the actual processing and manipulation of information stored in memory. The CPU also retrieves information from memory. This information can be data or instructions for manipulating data. The CPU can also store the results of those manipulations back in memory for later use.

The *control unit* within the CPU coordinates all activities of the computer by determining which operations should be carried out and in what order. The control unit then transmits coordinating control signals to the computer components.

Also found within the CPU are the *arithmetic-logic unit* (ALU) and special storage locations called *registers*. The ALU consists of electronic circuitry to perform arithmetic operations (that is, addition, subtraction, multiplication, and division) and to make comparisons. The control unit copies the next program instruction from memory into the instruction register in the CPU. The ALU then performs the operation specified by the next instruction on data that are copied from memory into registers, and the computational results are copied to memory. The ALU can perform each arithmetic operation in about a millionth of a second. The ALU can also compare data stored in its registers (for example, which value is larger? are the values equal?); the operations that are performed next depend on the comparison results.

Input and Output Devices

Input and output (I/O) devices enable us to communicate with the computer. Specifically, I/O devices provide us with the means to enter data for a computation and to observe the results of that computation.

A common I/O device used with large computers is the computer terminal. A *computer terminal* is both an input and an output device. A terminal consists of a *keyboard* (used for entering information) and a *monitor* (used for displaying information). A computer terminal has no capability to do any local processing, so it is often called a *dumb terminal.*

Sometimes microcomputers are connected to larger computers and can be used as terminals. Because a microcomputer can also do local processing, a microcomputer connected to another computer is called a *smart terminal*.

A computer keyboard is similar to a typewriter keyboard except that it has some extra keys for performing special functions. On the IBM PC/AT–style keyboard shown in Fig. 1.6, the 12 keys in the top row labeled F1 through F12 are *function keys*. The function performed when you press one of these keys depends on the program that is executing.

Most personal computers are equipped with *graphics capability* (see Fig. 1.3), which enables the output to be displayed as a two-dimensional graph or picture. With some graphics devices, the user can communicate with the computer by using a mouse to move an electronic pointer.

The only problem with using a monitor as an output device is that it leaves no written record of the computation. Once the image disappears from the monitor screen, it is lost. If you want *hard-copy output,* you have to send your computational results to an output device called a *printer* (see Fig. 1.7).

Secondary Storage

Most computers have only a limited amount of main memory. Consequently, *secondary storage* provides additional data storage capability on most computer systems. For example, a *disk drive,* which stores data on a disk, is a common secondary storage device for today's personal computers (Fig. 1.7).

There are two kinds of disks: *hard disks* and *floppy disks.* A computer may have one or more drives of each kind. A hard disk normally cannot be removed from its drive, so the storage area on a hard disk is ofen shared by all the users of a computer. However, each computer user may have his or her own floppy disks that can be inserted into a disk drive as needed. Hard disks can store

Figure 1.6   Keyboard for the IBM PC/AT

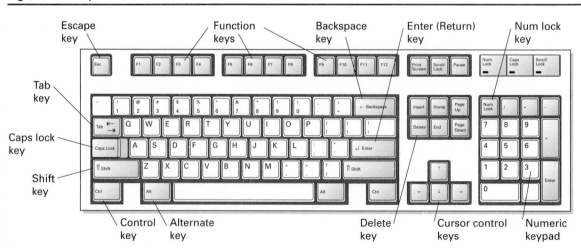

Figure 1.7   Printer (on Left) and Inserting a Floppy Disk into a Disk Drive

much more data than can floppy disks and operate much more quickly, but they are also much more expensive.

Information stored on a disk is organized into aggregates called *files*. The data for a program can be stored in a *data file* beforehand rather than being entered at the keyboard while the program is executing. Results generated by the computer can be saved as *output files* on disk. Most of the programs that you write will be saved as *program files* on disk.

Main Memory versus Secondary Memory

Main memory is much faster and more expensive than secondary memory. You must transfer data from secondary memory to main memory before they can be processed. Data in main memory are *volatile* and disappear when you switch off the computer. Data stored in secondary memory are *permanent* and do not disappear when the computer is switched off.

Computer Networks

Often several microcomputers in a laboratory are interconnected as a network of microcomputers (called a *local area network*) so that they can share the use of a large hard disk and high-quality printers. The microcomputers in the network can also access common programs and data stored on the disk.

Self-Check

1. What are the contents of memory cells 0 and 999 in Fig. 1.5? What memory cells contain the letter X and the fraction 0.005?
2. Explain the purpose of the arithmetic-logic unit, memory, the central processor, and the disk drive and disk. What input and output devices do you use with your computer?

1.3 Problem Solving and Programming

We mentioned earlier that a computer cannot think; therefore, to do any useful work, a computer must be provided with a *program,* that is, a list of instructions. Programming a computer is a lot more involved than simply writing a list of instructions. Problem solving is a crucial component of programming. Before we can write a program to solve a particular problem, we must consider carefully all aspects of the problem and then develop and organize its solution.

The Art and Science of Problem Solving

To succeed in academics or in the real world, you must be able to solve problems. Problem-solving ability is a combination of art and science. The art of problem solving is the transforming of a description of a problem into a form that permits a mechanical solution. A relatively straightforward example of this process is the transformation of an algebra word problem into a set of algebraic equations, which can then be solved for one or more unknowns.

In the real world, this process is more difficult because problem descriptions are often incomplete, imprecise, or ambiguous. The successful problem solver must be able to ask the right questions to clarify the problem and obtain any information missing from the problem statement. Next, the problem solver must analyze the problem and extract its essential features, identifying what is provided (the problem inputs) and what is required (the problem outputs). The problem solver must also be able to determine whether any constraints or simplifying assumptions can be applied to facilitate the problem solution. Often we cannot solve the most general case of a problem; we must make some realistic assumptions that limit or constrain the problem so that it can be solved.

The science part of problem solving involves knowledge of the problem environment, knowledge of the formulas or equations that characterize the environment, and the ability to apply and manipulate those formulas. Using this knowledge, the problem solver develops a series of steps whose successful completion will lead to the problem solution. Once the solution is obtained, the problem solver must verify its accuracy by comparing the computed results with observed results.

Planning and Checking Your Programs

Like most programming students, at first you will probably spend a great deal of time in the computer laboratory entering your programs. You will spend more time later removing the errors that inevitably will crop up in your programs.

It is tempting to rush to the computer laboratory and start entering your program as soon as you have some idea of how to write it. Resist this temptation. Instead, think carefully about the problem and its solution before you write any program instructions. When you have a potential solution in mind, plan it out beforehand (using either paper and pencil or a word processor) and modify it if necessary before you write the program.

Once you have written the program out, *desk check* your solution by carefully performing each instruction much as the computer would. To desk check a program, simulate the result of each program instruction using sample data that are easy to manipulate (for example, small whole numbers). Compare these results with the expected results and make any necessary corrections to your program. Only then should you go to the computer laboratory and enter your program. A few extra minutes spent evaluating the proposed solution using the process summarized in Fig. 1.8 may save hours of frustration later.

In this text, we stress a methodology for program solving and programming that has proved useful in helping students learn to program. This technique is described next.

Figure 1.8 Programming Strategy

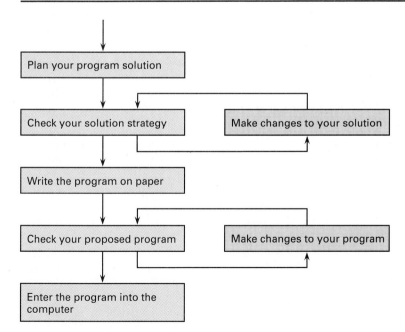

1.4 The Software Development Method

Students in many subject areas receive instruction in specific problem-solving methods. For example, business students are encouraged to follow a *systems approach* to problem solving; engineering and science students are encouraged to follow the *engineering and scientific method.* Although these problem-solving methods are associated with very different fields of study, their essential ingredients are quite similar.

Software engineers are involved with the design and implementation of reliable software systems. The title emphasizes that programmers, like engineers, are concerned with developing practical, reliable solutions to problems. However, the programmer's product is a software system rather than a physical system. Software engineers and software developers use the following *software development method* for solving programming problems.

1. **Requirements specification.** State the problem and gain a clear understanding of what is required for its solution. This sounds easy, but it can be the most critical part of problem solving. A good problem solver must be able to recognize and define the problem precisely. If the problem is not totally defined, you must study the problem carefully, eliminating the aspects that are unimportant and zeroing in on the root problem.
2. **Analysis.** Identify problem inputs, desired outputs, and any additional requirements or constraints. Identify what information is supplied as problem data and what results should be computed and displayed. Also, determine the required form and units in which the results should be displayed (for example, as a table with specific column headings).
3. **Design.** Develop a list of steps (called an *algorithm*) to solve the problem, then verify that the algorithm solves the problem as intended. Writing the algorithm is often the most difficult part of the problem-solving process. Once you have the algorithm, you should verify that it is correct before proceeding further.
4. **Implementation.** Implement the algorithm as a program, which requires knowledge of a particular programming language. Each algorithm step must be converted into a statement in that programming language.
5. **Testing and verification.** Test the completed program and verify that it works as expected. Don't rely on just one test case—run the program several times using different sets of data.

The first three steps in the software development method are critical; if they are not done properly, you will either solve the wrong problem or produce an awkward, inefficient solution. To perform these steps successfully, you must read the problem statement carefully before you attempt to solve the problem. You may need to read each problem statement two or three times. The first time, you should get a general idea of what is being asked. The second time, you should try to answer these questions: What information should the solution provide? What data do I have to work with? The answer to the first question will tell you the desired results, or the *problem outputs.* The answer to the second question will tell you the data provided, or the *problem inputs.* It may be helpful to underline the phrases in the problem statement that identify the inputs and outputs.

As already indicated, the design phase is often the most difficult part of the problem-solving process. When you write an algorithm, you should first list the major steps of the problem that need to be solved (the *subproblems*). Don't try to list each and every step imaginable; instead, concentrate on the overall strategy. Once you have a list of the subproblems, you can attack each one individually, in this way adding detail, or *refining the algorithm.* The process of solving a problem by breaking it up into its smaller subproblems is called *divide and conquer* and is a basic strategy for all kinds of problem-solving activities.

The software development method can be used with any programming language; indeed, only the implementation phase really requires detailed knowledge of a language or a particular computer. In industry, the testing phase is often carried out by individuals who do not know programming but who specialize in developing good tests of programs.

1.5 Programming Languages

Programming languages fall into three broad categories: machine, assembly, and high-level languages. *High-level languages* are more popular with programmers than the other two language categories. One reason for their popularity is that they are much easier to use than machine and assembly languages. Another reason is that a high-level language program is *portable,* which means that it can be used without modification on many different types of computers. An assembly language or a machine language program, on the other hand, can be used on only one type of computer.

Some common high-level languages are FORTRAN, BASIC, COBOL, C, Pascal, and Ada. Each language was designed with a specific purpose in mind. FORTRAN is an acronym for FORmula TRANslation, and its principal users are engineers and scientists. BASIC (Beginners All-purpose Symbolic Instructional Code) was designed to be easily learned and used by students. COBOL (COmmon Business Oriented Language) is used primarily for business data-processing operations. C combines the power of an assembly language with the ease of use and portability of a high-level language. Pascal was designed for teaching structured programming. Ada is a language based on Pascal and is used by the U.S. Department of Defense.

Each of these high-level languages has a *language standard* that describes the grammatical form (*syntax*) of the language. Every high-level language instruction must conform to the syntax rules specified in the language standard. These rules are precise—no allowances are made for instructions that are *almost* correct.

An important feature of high-level languages is that they allow us to write program instructions that resemble everyday language. We can reference data stored in memory using easily understood descriptive names, like Name and Rate, rather than the numeric memory cell addresses discussed in Section 1.2. We can also use familiar symbols to describe operations that we want performed. For example, in several high-level languages the instruction

```
Price := Cost + Profit;
```

means add Cost to Profit and store the result in Price. Cost, Profit, and Price are called *variables*.

In *assembly language,* we can also use descriptive names to reference data; however, we must specify the operations to be performed on the data more explicitly. In an assembly language, the high-level language instruction above might be written as

```
LOAD Cost
ADD Profit
STORE Price
```

Machine language is the native tongue of a computer. Each instruction in machine language is a *binary string* (a string of zeroes and ones). You may be familiar with the use of binary numbers to represent decimal integers (for example, binary 11011 corresponds to decimal 27). In an analogous way, a binary string can be used to indicate an operation to be performed and the memory cell or cells that are involved. The assembly language instructions above could be written in a machine language as

```
0010 0000 0000 0100
0100 0000 0000 0101
0011 0000 0000 0110
```

Obviously, what is easiest for a computer to understand is most difficult for a person to understand and vice versa.

A computer can understand only programs that are written in machine language. Consequently, each instruction in an assembler program or a high-level language program must first be translated into machine language. The next section discusses the steps required to process a high-level language program.

Exercises for Section 1.5

Self-Check

1. What do you think these high-level language statements mean?

   ```
   X := A + B + C;    X := Y/Z;    D := C - B + A;    X := X + 1;
   ```

2. Which high-level language was designed for teaching programming? Which was designed for business applications? Which was designed for translating scientific formulas?
3. Which type of language has instructions such as ADD X? Which type has instructions that are binary numbers?

1.6 Processing a High-Level Language Program

Before the computer can process a high-level language program, the programmer must enter the program at the terminal. The program is stored on disk as a file called the program file or *source file* (see Fig. 1.9). The programmer uses an editor program to enter the program and to save it as a source file.

Once the source file is saved, it can be translated into machine language. A *compiler* program processes the source file and attempts to translate each statement.

One or more statements in the source file may contain a *syntax error,* which means that the statement does not correspond exactly to the syntax of the high-level language. In that case, the compiler causes an error message to be displayed on your monitor screen and no object file is created. Syntax errors are discussed in more detail in Section 2.9.

At this point, you can correct your source file and have the compiler process it again. If there are no more errors, the compiler creates an *object file,* which is your program translated into machine language. This object file and any additional object files (for example, programs for input and output operations) that may be needed by your program are combined into a *load file* by the *linker* program. Finally, the *loader* program places the load file into memory, ready for execution. The editor, compiler, linker, and loader programs are part of your computer system. This process is shown in Fig. 1.9.

Executing a Program

To execute a program, the CPU must examine each program instruction in memory and send out the command signals required to carry out the instruction. Normally, the instructions are executed in sequence; however, as we will discuss later, it is possible to have the CPU skip over some instructions or execute some instructions more than once.

During execution, data can be entered into memory and manipulated in some specified way. There are program instructions that are used for entering or reading a program's data (called *input data*) into memory. After the input data are processed, instructions for displaying or printing values in memory can be executed to display the program results. The lines displayed by a program are called the *program output.*

Let's use the situation illustrated in Fig. 1.10—executing a payroll program stored in memory—as an example. The first step of the program enters into memory data that describe the employee's hours and pay rate. In step 2, the program manipulates the employee data and stores the results of the computations in memory. In the final step, the computational results are displayed as payroll reports or employee payroll checks.

Figure 1.9 Preparing a Program for Execution

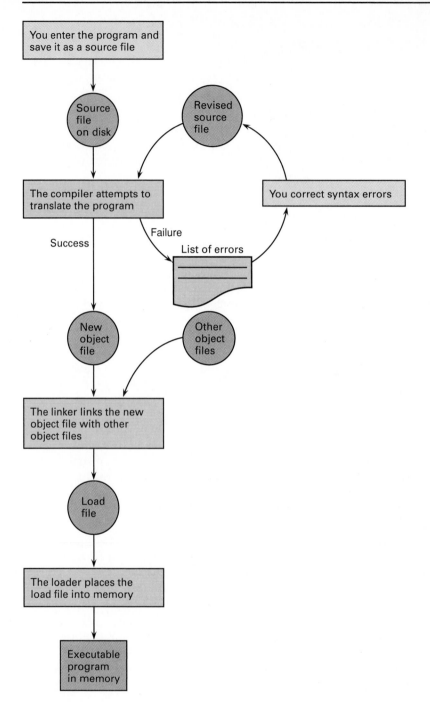

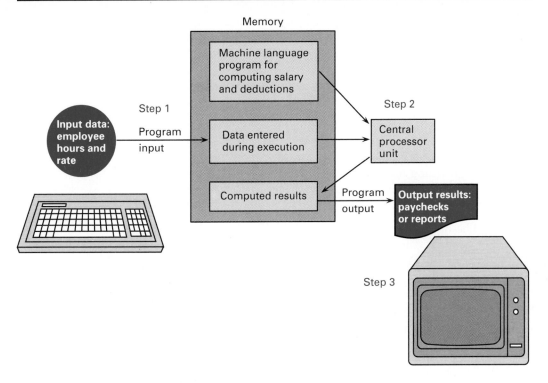

Exercises for Section 1.6

Self-Check

1. What is the role of a compiler? What is a syntax error? In which file would a syntax error be found?
2. What is the source file? An object file? A load file? Which do you create and which does the compiler create? Which does the linker create and which is processed by the loader? What do the compiler, linker, and loader programs do?

1.7 Using the Computer

The mechanics of entering a program as a source file and translating and executing it differ from system to system. Although we cannot give specific details for a particular computer system, we describe the general process in this section.

Operating Systems

Some of you will be using a *timeshared computer*. Universities often use timeshared computers for instructional purposes. In a timeshare environment, many users are connected by terminals to one central computer, and all users share the central facilities.

Others of you will be using a personal computer, which is a smaller, desktop computer used by one individual at a time. Regardless of what type of computer you use, you will need to interact with a supervisory program, called the *operating system,* within the computer. In timeshared computers, the operating system allocates the central resources among many users. Some operating system tasks are as follows:

* validating user identification and account number (timeshared system)
* making the editor, compiler, or linker programs available to users
* allocating memory and processor time
* providing input and output facilities
* retrieving needed files
* saving new files

The operating system for a personal computer performs all but the first task.

Each computer has its own special *control language* for communicating with its operating system. Although space does not allow us to provide the details here, we will discuss the general process. Your instructor will provide the specific commands for your system.

Booting or Logging-On

Before you can use a personal computer, you first need to boot the computer. *Booting* a personal computer involves inserting the operating system disk into the appropriate disk drive and switching on the computer. The operating system may prompt you for the date and time. Once booted, the operating system displays a prompt (for example, A>) to indicate that it is ready to accept commands. Figure 1.11 demonstrates booting an IBM Personal Computer using MS-DOS (the Microsoft® operating system); the computer user enters the characters that are in color; the other characters are those that the operating system displays.

Before you can use a timeshared computer, you must *log on,* or connect, to the computer. To log on, you enter your account name and password (given to

Figure 1.11   Booting a Personal Computer

```
MS-DOS Version 3.0

Current date is Tue 1-01-1980
Enter new date: 4-05-91

Current time is 0:01:43.53
Enter new time: 10:30

A>
```

you by your instructor). For security reasons, your password is not displayed. Figure 1.12 demonstrates this process for the Digital Equipment Corporation™ VAX computer. The computer user enters the characters that are in color; the other characters are those that the operating system displays. The timeshared operating system shown (VMS Version 4.5) displays the symbol $ as a prompt.

Figure 1.12 Logging on to a Computer

```
Username: Koffman
Password: Madaket

              CIS Department Vax-11/780 VMS V5.1

      Last interactive login on Friday, 29-April-1991 10:20

$
```

Creating a Program or File

Once you have booted your personal computer or logged on to a timeshared computer, you can begin to create your program. In most cases, you will use a special program called an *editor* to enter your Pascal program. After accessing the editor, you can start to enter a new Pascal program. If you want a record of the program once it is entered, you must save it as a permanent file on disk; otherwise, your program will disappear when your session with the editor is over. Follow these steps to create and save a program file:

1. Log on to a timeshared computer or boot a personal computer.
2. Access the editor program and indicate that you are creating a new file.
3. Enter each line of the program file.
4. Name your program file (if not named in step 2) and save it as a permanent file in secondary memory.
5. Exit from the editor.

Once you have created your program and you are satisfied that each line is entered correctly, you can attempt to compile, link, and execute the program. On some systems, you must give three separate commands; on other systems, one command, such as RUN, initiates this sequence of operations.

If your program will not compile because it contains syntax errors, you must edit, or correct, the program. Follow these steps to correct and reexecute a program file:

1. Reaccess the editor program and retrieve your program file.
2. Correct the statements containing syntax errors.
3. Save your edited program file.
4. Compile, link, and execute the new program file.

CHAPTER REVIEW

This chapter described the basic components of a computer: main and secondary memory, the CPU, and input and output devices. Remember these important facts about computers:

- A memory cell is never empty, but its initial contents may be meaningless to your program.
- The current contents of a memory cell are destroyed whenever new information is placed in that cell.
- Programs must be copied into the memory of the computer before they can be executed.
- Data cannot be manipulated by the computer until they are first stored in memory.
- A computer cannot think for itself; you must use a programming language to instruct it in a precise and unambiguous manner to perform a task.
- Programming a computer can be fun—if you are patient, organized, and careful.

We reviewed the history of computing and discussed the four generations of computers. We also described the different categories of computers: microcomputers, minicomputers, and mainframes. A computer's size and performance capability determine its category.

This chapter discussed problem solving and its importance in programming. We described the software development method, which stresses a careful, organized approach to solving programming problems. The five steps of the software development method are requirements specification, analysis, design, implementation, and testing and verification.

We also described the three different categories of programming languages—machine, assembler, and high-level—and explained their differences. A high-level language source program is translated into a machine-language object file by a compiler, linked with other object files by a linker, and finally loaded into memory by a loader. We discussed how to use a computer and its operating system to accomplish the tasks of entering a new program and running it on a computer.

✓ Quick-Check Exercises

1. The _____ translates a(n) _____ language program into _____.
2. After a program is executed, all program results are automatically displayed. True or false?
3. Specify the correct order for these four operations: execution, linking, translation, loading.
4. A high-level language program is saved on disk as a(n) _____ file or a(n) _____ file.
5. The _____ finds syntax errors in the _____ file.
6. A machine language program is saved on disk as a(n) _____ file.
7. The _____ program is used to create and save the source file.
8. The _____ creates the load file.
9. The _____ program is used to place the _____ file into memory.
10. Computers are becoming (more/less) expensive and (bigger/smaller) in size.

11. The first large-scale, general-purpose electronic computer was called the _____. It (was/was not) a stored-program computer.

Answers to Quick-Check Exercises

1. compiler, high-level, machine language
2. false
3. translation, linking, loading, execution
4. source, program
5. compiler, source
6. object
7. editor
8. linker
9. loader, load
10. less, smaller
11. ENIAC, was not

Review Questions

1. List at least three kinds of information stored in a computer.
2. List two functions of the CPU.
3. List two input/output devices and two secondary storage devices.
4. A computer can think. True or false?
5. List the three categories of programming languages.
6. Give three advantages of programming in a high-level language such as Pascal.
7. What processes are needed to transform a Pascal program to a machine language program that is ready for execution?
8. What are three characteristics of a structured program?
9. What is the difference between the requirements specification phase and the analysis phase of the software development method?
10. In which phase of the software development method is the algorithm for solution developed?

INTERVIEW
David A. Patterson

David A. Patterson is Professor of Computer Science at the University of California, Berkeley. An author and active consultant, Patterson led the design and implementation of RISC I, a 45,000 transistor microprocessor that was likely the first VLSI reduced instruction set computer. He is currently working on developing input/output systems to match the increasingly higher performance of new processors.

Looking back on your own experience as a student, what influenced you to choose computer science as a profession? Why computer architecture?

I was a mathematics major as an undergraduate and the math class I was planning to take was cancelled. I took a computer class instead. I found I loved the reality of the problem solving and the rapid change of ideas in computer science more than the abstraction and stability of higher mathematics. Serendipity played a role in my choice of computer architecture as well. As a graduate research assistant in computer software, I became the father of two sons about the time the research grant ran out. While I finished my Ph.D, my advisor helped get me a job at Hughes Aircraft Company, where we designed computers. Hence I learned software in academia and hardware in industry. My dissertation combined hardware and software, leaving my options open when I got a "real" job. U.C. Berkeley wanted me to work in computer architecture, so my path was set.

What are your impressions of the state of computer architecture education today? Do you think students majoring in computer science receive enough of a background in architecture?

Computer architecture education today is in the middle of a revolution—from a more historical or descriptive list of possible problem solutions to a foundation that teaches how to quantitatively evaluate the cost/performance of different options in different situations. I believe this is a transition that all systems fields will need to go through if computer science is to mature as a discipline. Obviously, it is better to learn the quantitative approach.

Where do you see the exciting research being done in computer architecture today?

The processor-centric approach to doing research in computer architecture is now reaping the harvest of neglect: computers are becoming input/output

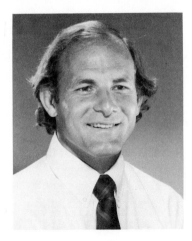

bound. Hence I believe the most exciting areas in computer architecture today revolve around I/O, particularly communication and storage. The possibility of using fast networks to allow thousands of desktop computers to act in concert as a supercomputer could change the industry. Taking advantage of the advances in magnetic tape (such as those used in video cameras) or optical disks (like those used in CD players) offers the opportunity to store 1000 times the data we can today. Such a large quantitative change will bring about a qualitative change in our society. For example, all books on a college campus could be stored on-line, requiring the same space and cost as a mini-computer. Imagine what would happen if any student with a TV screen and a telephone could get any book in several seconds!

My thesis is that a factor of 1000 increase in the storage capacity available on most local area networks will have a much greater impact than a factor of 1000 increase in processing speed for a gaggle of scientists.

The complexity of architectures seems to be ever increasing. What do you think fuels the need for more powerful and efficient machines?

Architecture complexity goes in cycles, and we recently just reset to simplicity as a result of the Reduced Instruction Set Computer (RISC) movement.

Complexity comes from the desire to get greater performance from a mature technology. As new technologies emerge, the rewards of simplicity inspire the return to simpler styles of computers.

Do you think the much discussed international competition (the United States versus Japan, for example) in the creation of supercomputers is overblown?

The international competition over the lead in traditional supercomputers is, to my way of thinking, like a competition to produce the world's fastest car. Even though it may be possible to build a few exotic cars that go as fast as a slow jet, it is clear that jets offer much greater speed and distance. The jets of computer architecture are parallel computers, with the effective top speed being a function of the number of processors you buy and the parallelism of the problem being solved. This is clearly the important competition, although not everyone may realize it.

The opportunity to become technological heros is available for people who know their three A's: Architecture, Algorithms, and Applications. These will be the people who can take advantage of the potential of parallel computers to solve problems important to society hundreds or thousands of times faster than today's most expensive computer.

What major developments do you foresee occurring in architecture in the 1990s?

Massively parallel computers will be established as the fastest computers in the land in the 1990s, washing away traditional supercomputers built by Cray, Convex, and NEC. For example, I believe we have already crossed the "Teraflops Threshold." A teraflops computer can calculate 10^{12} ("tera") FLoating point arithmetic operations per second ("FLOPS"), which is about 1000 times faster than today's supercomputers. Suppose you had an important computation that takes 10^{17} operations today and you have the choice of buying today's supercomputer and dedicating it to that computation or waiting and buying a teraflops machine and then starting the computation. Crossing the "Teraflops Threshold" means you get your answer sooner if you wait for the teraflops machine than if you started today. My view is that we have already crossed that threshold.

Terabytes (10^{12} bytes) are the flip side of teraflops—computers that will be connected to hundreds of terabytes via high speed networks. If copyrights and royalties can be resolved to the benefit of authors, publishers, and society, this technology will revolutionize the availability of information in all forms: books, libraries, magazines, mail, newspapers, and so on.

2
Problem Solving and Pascal

Programming is a problem-solving activity. If you are a good problem solver, you would likely be a good programmer. One important goal of this book is to help you improve your problem-solving ability. We believe that it is beneficial to approach each programming problem systematically and consistently. This chapter shows you how to apply the software development method to solve programming problems.

This chapter also introduces Pascal, which is a high-level, general-purpose programming language developed in 1971 by Professor Nicklaus Wirth of the Federal Institute of Technology (ETH) at Zürich, Switzerland. (A general-purpose programming language is one that can be put to many different applications.) Currently, Pascal is the most popular programming language for teaching programming concepts partly because its syntax is relatively easy to learn. Another reason for Pascal's popularity is that efficient Pascal compilers are available for almost all computers.

Pascal facilitates the writing of *structured programs*—programs that are relatively easy to read, understand, and keep in good working order—which is now accepted as standard programming practice. For this reason, Pascal is also widely used in industry. Another good reason for studying Pascal is that it was the basis for the design of the programming language Ada, the official language approved by the U.S. Department of Defense for software development.

To ensure that a Pascal program written on one computer will execute on another, a *language standard* describes all Pascal language constructs and specifies their syntax. This text follows the standard for Pascal approved by the American National Standards Institute (ANSI) and the International Standards Organization (ISO).

This chapter describes Pascal statements for performing computations and statements for entering data and displaying results. Besides introducing problem solving and Pascal, this chapter describes how to run Pascal programs interactively and in batch mode. In interactive programming, the program user enters data during program execution; in batch mode, the user must prepare a data file before program execution begins.

2.1 Applying the Software Development Method

In this textbook we provide case solutions for a number of programming problems, following the software development method outlined in Section 1.4. We begin each case study with a statement of the problem. As part of the problem analysis, we identify the data requirements for the problem, indicating the problem inputs and the desired outputs. Next, we develop and refine the initial algorithm. Finally, we implement the algorithm as a Pascal program. We provide a sample run of the program and discuss how to perform a more complete test of the program.

We walk you though a sample case study next. In this example, we provide a running commentary on the process so you will be able to apply it to other situations.

29

2.1 Applying the
Software
Development Method

Case Study: Converting Units of Measurement

Problem

You work in a store that imports fabric. Most of the fabric you receive is measured in square meters; however, the store's customers want to know the equivalent amount in square yards. You need to write a program that performs this conversion.

Analysis

The first step in understanding this problem is to determine what you are being asked to do. It should be clear that you must convert from one system of measurement to another, but are you supposed to convert from square meters to square yards, or vice versa? The problem states that you receive fabric measured in square meters, so the problem input is *fabric size in square meters.* Your customers want to know the *equivalent amount in square yards,* which must be your problem output. To write the program, we need to know the relationship between square meters and square yards. By examining a metric table, we find that 1 square meter equals 1.196 square yards.

The data requirements and relevant formulas are summarized below. The name SqMeters identifies the memory cell that will contain the problem input, and the name SqYards identifies the memory cell that will contain the program result, or the problem output.

Data Requirements

Problem Inputs
Sq Meters   {the fabric size in square meters}

Problem Outputs
SqYards   {the fabric size in square yards}

Relevant Formulas
1 square meter equals 1.196 yards

Design

Next, we try to formulate the algorithm that we must follow to solve the problem. We begin by listing the three major steps, or subproblems, of the algorithm.

Algorithm

1. Read the fabric size in square meters.
2. Convert the fabric size to square yards.
3. Display the fabric size in square yards.

Now, we must decide whether any steps of the algorithm need further refinement or whether they are perfectly clear as stated. Step 1 (reading data) and step 3 (displaying a value) are basic steps and require no further refinement. Step 2 is fairly straightfoward, but it might help to add some detail.

Step 2 Refinement

2.1 The fabric size in square yards is 1.196 times the fabric size in square meters.

The complete algorithm with refinements is shown below. The algorithm resembles an outline for a term paper. The refinement of step 2 is numbered as step 2.1 and is indented under step 2. We list the complete algorithm with refinements to show you how it all fits together.

Algorithm with Refinements

1. Read the fabric size in square meters.
2. Convert the fabric size to square yards.
    2.1 The fabric size in square yards is 1.196 the fabric size in square meters.
3. Display the fabric size in square yards.

Implementation

To implement the solution, we must write the algorithm as a Pascal program. To do this, we must first tell the Pascal compiler about the problem data requirements, that is, what memory cell names we are using and what kind of data will be stored in each memory cell. Next, we convert each algorithm step into one or more Pascal statements. If an algorithm step has been refined, we must convert the refinements into Pascal statements. You will be able to do this yourself as you learn more about Pascal.

Figure 2.1 shows the Pascal program along with a sample execution (the last three lines of the figure). For easy identification, the first and last lines of the program are in color, as are the input data typed in by the program user in the sample execution. Don't worry about understanding the details of this program yet. We give an overview of the main points of the program here and go into more detail later in the chapter.

One thing you might notice in Fig. 2.1 is a number of lines containing text enclosed in braces, such as

```
{Converts square meters to square yards.}
```

In Pascal, braces denote a program comment. A program *comment* is like a parenthetical remark in a sentence; its purpose is to provide supplementary

Figure 2.1   Metric Conversion Program

```
program Metric (Input, Output);
{Converts square meters to square yards.}

  const
    MetersToYards = 1.196;    {conversion constant}

  var
    SqMeters,                 {input — fabric size in meters}
    SqYards    : Real;        {output — fabric size in yards}

begin
  {Read the fabric size in square meters.}
  WriteLn ('Enter the fabric size in square meters >');
  ReadLn (SqMeters);

  {Convert the fabric size to square yards.}
  SqYards := MetersToYards * SqMeters;

  {Display the fabric size in square yards.}
  WriteLn ('The fabric size in square yards is ', SqYards)
end.


Enter the fabric size in square meters >
2.00
The fabric size in square yards is      2.392000E+00
```

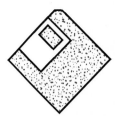

Directory: CHAP2
File: METRIC.PAS

information to the person reading the program. Program comments are ignored by the Pascal compiler and are not translated into machine language.

A program consists of two parts: the *declaration part* and the *program body*. The declaration part tells the compiler what memory cells are needed in the program and is based on the problem data requirements identified earlier during the problem analysis. Memory cells are needed for storing the variables SqMeters and SqYards and the conversion constant MetersToYards (value is 1.196).

The program body begins with the line

```
begin
```

The *program body* contains the Pascal *statements*, which are translated into machine language and later executed.

In the program body, each statement that begins with the word WriteLn causes a line of program output to be displayed. The first such line

```
WriteLn ('Enter the fabric size in square meters >');
```

displays the first output line in the sample execution, which asks the user to type in a value in meters. The next line,

```
ReadLn (SqMeters);
```

reads the data value typed by the program user (2.00) into the memory cell named SqMeters. The program statement

```
SqYards := MetersToYards * SqMeters;
```

computes the equivalent fabric size in square yards by multiplying the size in square meters by 1.196; the product is stored in the memory cell SqYards.

Finally, the program statement

```
WriteLn ('The fabric size in yards is ', SqYards)
```

displays a message *string* and the value of SqYards. The value of SqYards is displayed as a real number using scientific notation (2.392000E+00). The value printed is equivalent to 2.392×10^0, or 2.392, as will be explained later. The last program line is

```
end.
```

Some punctuation symbols appear in Fig. 2.1. Commas separate items in a list, a semicolon appears at the end of several lines, and the last line contains a period. We give guidelines for the use of these symbols later.

Testing

The last three lines of Fig. 2.1 show a sample run of this program, but how do we know that the program result is correct? You should always examine program results carefully to make sure that they make sense. In this run, a fabric size of 2.00 square meters is converted to 2.392 square yards, as it should be. To verify that the program works properly, we should enter a few more test values of square meters. We don't need to try more than a few test cases to verify that a simple program like this is correct.

Exercises for Section 2.1

Self-Check

1. List the five steps of the software development method.
2. What would the data requirements and formulas look like for a computer program that converts a weight in pounds to a weight in kilograms?

2.2 An Overview of Pascal

The rest of this chapter describes some basic features of the Pascal programming language. We base our discussion on the program in Fig. 2.1 and the program in the next example.

■ Example 2.1

Figure 2.2 contains a Pascal program and a sample execution of that program (the last four lines of the figure). The program displays a personalized message to the program user.

Figure 2.2   Printing a Welcoming Message

```
program Hello (Input, Output);
{Displays the user's nickname.}

  var
    Letterl, Letter2, Letter3 : Char;    {three letters}

begin
    WriteLn ('Enter a 3-letter nickname and press return >');
    ReadLn (Letterl, Letter2, Letter3);
    WriteLn ('Hello ', Letterl, Letter2, Letter3, '.');
    WriteLn ('We hope you enjoy studying Pascal!')
end.

Enter a 3-letter nickname and press return >
Bob
Hello Bob.
We hope you enjoy studying Pascal!
```

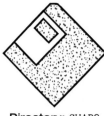

Directory: CHAP2
File: HELLO.PAS

The program line that starts with var and the line underneath it identify the names of three memory cells (Letterl, Letter2, Letter3) that will be used to store each letter of the nickname. The program instruction

```
    ReadLn (Letterl, Letter2, Letter3);
```

reads the three letters Bob (typed by the program user) into the three memory cells listed, with one letter per cell. The next line,

```
    WriteLn ('Hello ', Letterl, Letter2, Letter3, '.');
```

displays Bob after the message string 'Hello '. The string '.' causes a period to be printed after the third letter. Finally, the last program line displays the last line shown in the sample execution.

One of the advantages of Pascal is that it lets us write programs that resemble everyday English. At this point, you probably can read and understand the two sample programs, even though you do not know how to write your own programs. In the following sections, you'll learn more details about the Pascal programs in Figs. 2.1 and 2.2.   ■

Reserved Words and Identifiers

Each line of the programs in Figs. 2.1 and 2.2 satisfies the syntax rules for the Pascal language. Each line contains several different elements, such as reserved words, standard identifiers, special symbols, and names for memory cells. Let's look at the first three categories. *Reserved words,* which appear all in lowercase, have special meanings in Pascal and cannot be used for other purposes. The reserved words in Figs. 2.1 and 2.2 are

```
program, const, var, begin, end
```

Standard identifiers also have special meanings, but they can be used by the programmer for other purposes—however, we don't recommend this practice. The standard identifiers in Figs. 2.1 and 2.2 are

```
Real, Char, ReadLn, WriteLn, Input, Output
```

Some symbols (e.g., =, *, and :=) have special meanings in Pascal. Appendix A contains a complete list of these special symbols, as well as lists of reserved words and standard identifiers.

What is the difference between a reserved word and a standard identifier? Although you cannot use a reserved word as the name of a memory cell in your program, it is permissible to use a standard identifier. However, once you use a standard identifier to name a memory cell, the Pascal compiler no longer associates any special meaning with that identifier. For example, you could decide to use WriteLn as the name of a memory cell, but then you would not be able to use WriteLn for its normal purpose (to display program output). Because standard identifiers thus lose a valuable purpose, we don't recommend this practice.

The other identifiers appearing in the programs in Figs. 2.1 and 2.2 are described in more detail next.

PROGRAM
STYLE

The Use of Uppercase and Lowercase in Pascal Programs

Throughout the text, issues of good programming style are discussed in displays such as this one. These displays provide guidelines for improving the appearance and readability of programs. Most programs will be examined or studied by someone other than the programmers. A program that follows consistent style conventions is easier to read and understand than one that is sloppy or inconsistent. Although these conventions make it easier for humans to understand programs, they have no effect whatsoever on the computer.

In the programs in this text, reserved words always appear in lowercase, while identifiers are in mixed uppercase and lowercase. The first letter of each identifier is capitalized. If an identifier consists of two or more "words" pushed together (e.g., ReadLn is an abbreviation for Read Line), the first letter of each word is capitalized. We recommend that you follow this convention in your programs so it will be easy to distinguish reserved words from other identifiers.

The compiler does not differentiate between uppercase and lowercase. This means that you could write the reserved word const as CONST or the standard identifier ReadLn as READLN. However, according to our convention, const and ReadLn would be the preferred forms.

Since it is preferable not to redefine a standard identifier, many computer scientists emphasize this practice by writing standard identifiers in the same way as reserved words (i.e., all lowercase). If your instructor prefers that you adopt this convention, you should write the standard identifier ReadLn as readln.

Exercises for Section 2.2

Self-Check

1. Why shouldn't you use a standard identifier as the name of a memory cell in a program? Can you use a reserved word instead?
2. Do you think you could write a program that uses ReadLn as the name of a memory cell for storing a data value and WriteLn as the name of a memory cell for storing a program result?

2.3 Declarations in Pascal Programs

How do we tell the Pascal compiler what identifiers will be used in a program? One way is a *program heading,* such as

```
program Hello (Input, Output);
```

The program heading, beginning with the reserved word program, identifies the name of the program (Hello) and also tells the compiler where the input data will come from (file Input) and where output data will be written to (file Output). Input and Output are standard identifiers that represent the normal input and output devices for your computer system. For most of you, Input represents the keyboard and Output represents the monitor screen.

We tell the Pascal compiler the names of memory cells used in a program through constant declarations and variable declarations. The *constant declaration*

```
const
    MetersToYards = 1.196;
```

specifies that the identifier MetersToYards will be used as the name of the memory cell that always contains the number 1.196; the identifier Meters-ToYards is called a *constant.* Only data values that never change (e.g., the number of square yards in a square meter is always 1.196) should be associated with identifiers that are constants. Instructions that attempt to change the value of a constant cannot appear in a Pascal program.

The memory cells used for storing a program's input data and its computational results are called *variables* because the values stored in variables may change (and usually do) as the program executes. The *variable declaration*

```
var
    Letter1, Letter2, Letter3 : Char;
```

in Fig. 2.2 gives the names of three memory cells used for storing individual characters. The variable declaration

```
var
  SqMeters;                  {input - fabric size in meters}
  SqYards    : Real;         {output - fabric size in yards}
```

in Fig. 2.1 gives the names of two memory cells used to store real numbers (e.g., 30.0, 562.57). The variable names listed above are also identifiers.

In a variable declaration, the identifier (for example, Real, Integer, or Char) appearing to the right of the symbol : tells the Pascal compiler the *data type* (for example, a real number, an integer, or a character) of the information stored in a particular variable. A variable that is used for storing an integer value (a number without a decimal point) has data type Integer. Data types will be discussed in more detail in Section 2.6.

You have quite a bit of freedom in selecting the identifiers that you use in a program. The syntactic rules for identifiers are as follows:

1. An identifier must always begin with a letter.
2. An identifier must consist only of letters or digits.
3. A Pascal reserved word cannot be used as an identifier.

Some valid and invalid identifiers are listed below:

> *Valid identifiers*
> Letterl, Letter2, Inches, Cent, CentPerInch, Hello
>
> *Invalid identifiers*
> lLetter, const, var, Two*Four, Cent_Per_Inch, Joe's

Although these syntactic rules do not place a limit on the length of an identifier, some Pascal compilers use only a portion of an identifier (say, the first eight characters). These compilers would consider the identifiers Consonantl and Consonant2 to be the same identifier (Consonan); consequently, these identifiers could not be declared together in a program translated by such a compiler.

The identifier Cent_Per_Inch is invalid according to the Pascal language standard. However, many Pascal compilers allow the the underscore symbol _ in identifiers and would consider Cent_Per_Inch to be valid. Even if this is so on your computer, to ensure portability of your programs, we recommend that you avoid using the underscore symbol.

Pascal requires a declaration for every identifier used in a program unless that identifier is a standard identifier. Identifiers that are not standard identifiers are called *user-defined identifiers*. The reserved words and identifiers used in Figs. 2.1 and 2.2 are listed in Table 2.1.

Syntax Displays for Declarations

This section introduced the program heading, constant declarations, and variable declarations; the syntactic forms of Pascal language elements are summa-

Reserved Words	Standard Identifiers	User-Defined Identifiers
program, var, const, begin, end	Input, Output, Char, Real, ReadLn, WriteLn	Hello, Letter1, Letter2, Letter3, MetersToYards, SqMeters, SqYards, Metric

rized in the syntax displays below. Each display describes the syntactic form of
a language element and provides an example.

SYNTAX
DISPLAY

Program Heading

Form: program *pname* (Input, Output);
Example: program Hello (Input, Output);
Interpretation: The name of the program is indicated by *pname*. The input
data will be read from data file Input; the output results will be written
to data file Output.

SYNTAX
DISPLAY

Constant Declaration

Form: const
          constant = *value*;
Example: const
          Pi = 3.14159;
Interpretation: The specified *value* is associated with the identifier *constant*.
The *value* associated with *constant* cannot be changed. More than one
constant declaration may follow the word const. A semicolon appears at
the end of each constant declaration.
Note: The constant declarations must come first in a Pascal program.

SYNTAX
DISPLAY

Variable Declaration

Form: var
          variable list : *type*;
Example: var
          X, Y   : Real;
          Me, You : Integer;
Interpretation: A memory cell is allocated for each variable (an identifier)
in *variable list*. The data *type* (Real, Integer, etc.) to be stored in each
variable is specified between the colon and the semicolon. Commas separate the identifiers in *variable list*. More than one list of variables may be
declared after the word var.

Choosing Identifier Names

It is important to pick meaningful names for identifiers, so their use is easier to understand. For example, the identifier `Salary` would be a good name for a variable used to store a person's salary, whereas the identifier `S` or `Bagel` would be a bad choice.

As mentioned already, Pascal places no restriction on the length of an identifier. However, it is difficult to form meaningful names with fewer than three letters. On the other hand, typing errors become more likely when identifiers are too long. A reasonable rule of thumb is to use names that are between 3 to 10 characters in length.

If you mistype an identifier, the compiler will usually detect the mistake as a syntax error and display an *undefined identifier* error message during program translation. Mistyped identifiers sometimes resemble other identifiers, so it is best to avoid picking names that are similar to each other. Make sure you do not choose two names that are identical except for their use of case because the compiler will not be able to distinguish between them.

Exercises for Section 2.3

Self-Check

1. Why should the value of pi (3.14159) be stored in a constant?
2. Which comes first, the constant declarations or the variable declarations?
3. Indicate which of the following identifiers are Pascal reserved words, standard identifiers, valid identifiers, and invalid identifiers.

```
end    ReadLn   Bill    program   Sue's   Rate   Start
begin  const    XYZ123  123XYZ    ThisIsALongOne  Y=Z
Prog#2  'MaxScores'
```

Programming

1. Write a program heading and constant and variable declarations for a program named `Mine` that has the variables `Radius`, `Area`, and `Circumf` (all type `Real`) and the constant `Pi` (3.14159).

2.4 Executable Statements

One of the main functions of a computer is to perform arithmetic computations and display the results of those computations. These operations are specified by the *executable statements* that appear in the program body (following the reserved word `begin`). Each executable statement is translated by the Pascal compiler into one or more machine language instructions, which are copied to the object file and later executed. (Declarations, which describe the meaning and the purpose of each user-defined identifier to the Pascal compiler, are not translated into machine language instructions and do not appear in the object file.)

Programs in Memory

Before we examine each kind of executable statement in detail, let's see what computer memory looks like after a program has been loaded into memory and after that program executes. Figure 2.3 shows the metric conversion program loaded into memory and the program memory area before execution of the program body. The question mark in memory cells SqMeters and SqYards indicates that these variables are undefined (value unknown) before program execution begins. During program execution, the data value 2.00 is read into the variable SqYards. After the statement

```
SqYards := MetersToYards * SqMeters;
```

executes, the variables are defined as shown in Fig. 2.3b.

Figure 2.3 Memory Before and After Execution of a Program

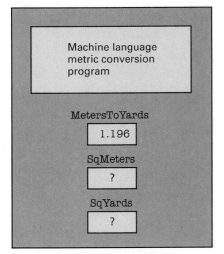

a. Memory before Execution

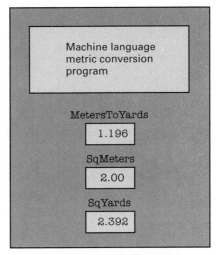

b. Memory after Execution

Assignment Statements

Assignment statements are used in Pascal to perform computations. The assignment statement

```
SqYards := MetersToYards * SqMeters;
```

in Fig. 2.1 assigns a value to the variable SqYards. In this case, SqYards is being assigned the result of the multiplication (* means multiply) of the constant MetersToYards by the variable SqMeters. Valid information must be stored in both MetersToYards and SqMeters before the assignment statement is executed. As shown in Fig. 2.4, only the value of SqYards is affected by the assignment statement; MetersToYards and SqMeters retain their original values.

Figure 2.4 Effect of SqYards := MetersToYards * SqMeters;

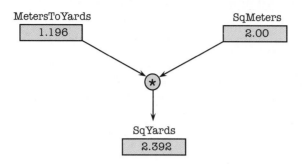

In Pascal, the symbol := is the *assignment operator* and should be read "becomes," "gets," or "takes the value of" rather than "equals." The : and the = must be adjacent with no intervening space. The general form of an assignment statement is shown in the next display.

SYNTAX
DISPLAY

Assignment Statements (Arithmetic)

Form: *result* := *expression*
Example: X := Y + Z + 2.0
Interpretation: The variable specified by *result* is assigned the value of *expression*. The previous value of *result* is destroyed. *Expression* can be a single variable, a single constant, or a combination of variables, constants, and the arithmetic operators listed in Table 2.2. *Expression* must be assignment compatible (described next) with the variable specified by *result*.

Table 2.2 Some Arithmetic Operators

Arithmetic Operator	Meaning
+	Addition
−	Subtraction
*	Multiplication
/	Real division

The real-division operator / always yields a real number as its result. Section 2.6 will introduce a division operator that yields an integer as its result.

An expression is *assignment compatible* with a result variable if both are the same data type or if the expression is type Integer and the result variable is type Real. This means that a type Real expression can be assigned only to a type Real variable, but a type Integer expression can be assigned to either a type Integer or a type Real variable. We will have more to say about assignment statements and expression types in Section 2.6.

■ Example 2.2
In Pascal, you can write assignment statements of the form

```
Sum := Sum + Item
```

where the variable Sum is used on both sides of the assignment operator. This is obviously not an algebraic equation, but it illustrates a common programming practice. This statement instructs the computer to add the current value of the variable Sum to the value of Item; the result is saved temporarily and then stored back into Sum. The previous value of Sum is destroyed in the process, as illustrated in Fig. 2.5; the value of Item, however, is unchanged. ■

Figure 2.5 Effect of Sum := Sum + Item

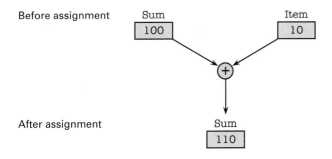

■ Example 2.3
In Pascal, you can also write assignment statements with an expression part that consists of a single variable or constant. The statement

```
NewX := X
```

instructs the computer to copy the value of X into NewX. The statement

```
NewX := -X
```

instructs the computer to get the value of X, negate that value, and store the result in NewX. For example, if X is 3.5, NewX is −3.5. Neither of the assignment statements above changes the value of X. ■

Input/Output Operations

Data can be stored in memory in three different ways: associated with a constant, assigned to a variable, or read into a variable. We have already discussed the first two methods. The third method, reading data into a variable, is necessary if you want the program to manipulate different data each time it executes. Reading data into memory is called an *input operation*.

As it executes, a program performs computations and assigns new values to variables. These program results can be displayed to the program user by an *output operation*.

All input/output operations in Pascal are performed by special program units called *input/output procedures*. The input/output procedures are supplied as part of the Pascal compiler, and their names are standard identifiers. This section discusses how to use the input procedure ReadLn and the output procedures Write and WriteLn.

The ReadLn Procedure

In Pascal, a *procedure call statement* is used to call or activate a procedure. Calling a procedure is analogous to asking a friend to perform an urgent task. You tell your friend what to do (but not how to do it) and wait for your friend to report back that the task is finished. After hearing from your friend, you can go on and do something else.

In Fig. 2.1, the procedure call statement

```
ReadLn (SqMeters);
```

calls procedure ReadLn (pronounced "read line") to read data into the variable SqMeters. Where does procedure ReadLn get the data it stores in variable SqMeters? It reads the data from the standard input device (Input). In most cases, the standard input device is the keyboard; consequently, the computer will attempt to store in SqMeters whatever information the program user types at the keyboard. Since SqMeters is declared as type Real, the input operation will proceed without error only if the program user types in a number. The program user should press the key labeled Return or Enter after typing the number. The effect of the ReadLn operation is shown in Fig. 2.6.

Figure 2.6 Effect of ReadLn (SqMeters);

Example 2.1 reads a person's nickname. Each person using the program may have a different nickname, so the procedure call statement

```
ReadLn (Letter1, Letter2, Letter3);
```

calls the ReadLn procedure to enter data into each of the three variables. Since these variables are declared as type Char, one character will be stored in each variable. Case is important for character data, so the letters B and b have different representations in memory. Again, the program user should press the Return key after typing in the three characters. Figure 2.7 shows the effect of this ReadLn statement when the letters B, o, and b are entered.

The number of characters read by the ReadLn procedure depends on the type of the variable in which the data will be stored. Only one character is read for a type Char variable; for a type Real variable, the program continues to

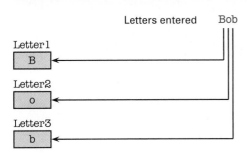

read characters until it reaches one that cannot be part of the number (usually indicated by a blank) or until the Return key is pressed.

How do we know when to enter the input data and what data to enter? Your program should print a prompting message, or prompt, that informs you what data to enter and when. Each character entered by the program user is *echoed* on the screen.

The ReadLn Procedure

Form: ReadLn (*input list*)

Example: ReadLn (Age, FirstInitial)

Interpretation: The ReadLn procedure reads into memory data typed at the keyboard during program execution. The program user must enter one data item for each variable specified in *input list*. Commas separate the variable names in *input list*.

The order of the data must correspond to the order of the variables in *input list*. Insert one or more blank characters between numeric data items. Do not insert any blanks between consecutive character data items unless the blank character is one of the data items being read. Press the Return or Enter key after all data items have been entered.

The WriteLn Procedure

To see the results of a program execution, we must have some way of specifying what variable values should be displayed. In Fig. 2.1, the procedure call statement

```
WriteLn ('The fabric size in square yards is ', SqYards)
```

calls the WriteLn (pronounced "write line") procedure to display a line of program output containing two items: the string literal 'The fabric . . . is ' and the value of SqYards. A *string literal* (or *string*) is a sequence of characters enclosed in apostrophes; the characters inside the apostrophes are printed but the apostrophes are not. The `WriteLn` procedure displays the line

```
The fabric size in square yards is     2.392000E+00
```

Unless directed otherwise, most Pascal compilers use Pascal scientific notation to display a real value. The number `2.392000E+00` is 2.3920 expressed in Pascal scientific notation. In normal scientific notation, 2.3920×10^0 means "multiply 2.3920 by 1." Since you cannot enter or display superscripts with Pascal, the letter `E` is used to indicate scientific notation (sometimes called *floating-point notation*).

In Fig. 2.2, the procedure call statement

```
WriteLn ('Hello ', Letter1, Letter2, Letter3, '.');
```

displays the line

```
Hello Bob.
```

In this case, three variable values are printed between the strings `'Hello '` and `'.'`.

Finally, the statements

```
WriteLn ('Enter the fabric size in square meters >');
WriteLn ('Enter a 3-letter nickname and press return >');
```

displays prompts for data in Figs. 2.1 and 2.2, respectively. A prompt can also describe the format of the data expected. You should always display a prompt just before a call to procedure `ReadLn` to remind the program user to enter data. It is important to precede each `ReadLn` operation with a `WriteLn` that prints a prompt; otherwise, the program user may have no idea that the program is waiting for data or what data to enter.

The *cursor* is a moving place marker that indicates the next position on the screen where information will be displayed. After a `WriteLn` procedure is executed, the cursor is advanced to the start of the next line on the screen.

WriteLn Without an Output List

The statements

```
WriteLn ('The fabric size in square yards is ', SqYards);
WriteLn;
WriteLn ('Metric conversion completed')
```

display the lines

```
The fabric size in square yards is     2.392000E+00

Metric conversion completed
```

The second `WriteLn` has no output list and causes the blank line in the middle of the program output. Execution of a `WriteLn` always causes the cursor to advance to the next line. If nothing is printed on the current line, a blank line appears in the program output.

The Write Procedure

Pascal provides a second output procedure, Write, that is similar to WriteLn in all respects except that the cursor is not advanced to the start of the next line after Write is finished executing. This means that if we use the following procedure call statements for data entry

```
Write ('Enter the fabric size in square meters >');
ReadLn (SqYards);
```

the Write statement will display the prompt and advance the cursor to the screen position just after the symbol >. Then the program user can type in the data value at the end of that line:

```
Enter the fabric size in square meters >2.00
```

The statement pair

```
Write ('The fabric size in square yards is ');
WriteLn (SqYards);
```

would display the same output line as the single statement

```
WriteLn ('The fabric size in square yards is ', SqYards);
```

It is generally more convenient to use the latter form.

Exercises for Section 2.4

Self-Check

1. Show the output displayed by the following program lines when the data entered are 5 and 7:

```
WriteLn ('Enter two integers>');
ReadLn (M, N);
M := M + 5;
N := 3 * N;
WriteLn ('M = ', M);
WriteLn ('N = ', N);
```

2. a. Write the following numbers in normal decimal notation:

   103E−4   1.2345E+6   123.45E+3

   b. Write the following numbers in Pascal scientific notation:

   1300   123.45   0.00426

3. Show the contents of memory before and after the execution of the program lines in exercise 1.

4. Show the output displayed by the following lines.

```
Write ('My name is: ');
WriteLn ('Doe, Jane');
WriteLn;
Write ('I live in ');
Write ('Ann Arbor, MI ');
WriteLn ('and my zip code is ', 48109);
```

Programming

1. Write statements that ask the user to type three numbers and read the three user responses into First, Second, and Third.

2. Write a statement that displays the value of X as indicated in the following line:

   The value of X is _____

3. Write a program that asks the user to enter the radius of a circle and then computes and displays the circle's area and circumference. Use the formulas

   Area = Pi × Radius × Radius
   Circumference = 2 × Pi × Radius

   where *Pi* is the constant 3.14159.

2.5 The General Form of Pascal Programs

The programs shown so far in this text have the general form described in Fig. 2.8. Each program begins with a program heading that identifies the name of the program.

Every identifier used in a program must be declared exactly once in the declaration part of a program, unless it is a standard identifier. The reserved words `const` and `var` may appear at most once and in the order shown in Fig. 2.8. All constant declarations come after `const` and all variable declarations after `var`. More than one constant may be declared, and there may be more than one variable list. Commas separate identifiers in a variable list, and a semicolon ends each declaration.

Figure 2.8 The General Form of a Pascal Program

```
program Name (Input, Output);
  const
    constant = value;
            .
            .
            .
    constant = value;                          declaration part
  var
    variable list : type;
            .
            .
            .
    variable list : type;

begin
  statement;
      .
      .                                         program body
      .
  statement
end.
```

The reserved word `begin` signals the start of the program body. The program body contains statements that are translated into machine language and eventually executed. The statements we have looked at so far perform computations and input/out operations. The last line in a program is

```
end.
```

Semicolons are used to separate Pascal statements. A semicolon is not needed before the first statement in a sequence nor after the last statement. Consequently, a semicolon should not appear after the reserved word `begin`. Although we don't recommend it, most Pascal compilers allow a semicolon after the last statement in a program. If present, this semicolon has the effect of inserting an "empty statement" between the last actual statement and the program terminator `end`.

A Pascal statement can extend over more than one line. For example, the variable and constant declarations in Fig. 2.2 start on one line and finish on the next. A statement that extends over more than one line cannot be split in the middle of an identifier, a reserved word, a number, or a string.

Also, we can write more than one statement on a line. For example, the line contains a statement that displays a prompt message and a statement that reads the data requested. A semicolon separates the two statements; another semicolon should occur at the end of the line if more statements follow. We recommend that you place only one statement on a line.

PROGRAM
STYLE

The Use of Blank Spaces

The consistent and careful use of blank spaces can significantly enhance the style of a program. A blank space is required between words in a program line (for instance, between `program` and `Hello` in Fig. 2.2).

The compiler ignores extra blanks between words and symbols. You may insert space to improve the style and appearance of a program. As shown in Fig. 2.1, you should always leave a blank space after a comma and before and after operators such as `*`, `−`, and `:=`. Remember to indent each line of a program except for the first and last lines and the line `begin` and to write the reserved words `const`, `var`, and `begin` on lines by themselves so they stand out. All lines except the first and last lines of the program and the line `begin` are indented two or more spaces. Finally, use blank lines between sections of the program.

We take all these measures for the sole purpose of improving the style—and hence the clarity—of our programs. Stylistic issues have no effect whatever on the meaning of the program as far as the computer is concerned; however, they can make it easier for people to read and understand the program.

Be careful not to insert blank spaces where they do not belong. For example, there cannot be a space between the characters `:` and `=` when they form the assignment operator `:=`. Also, the identifier `StartSalary` cannot be written as `Start Salary`.

Comments in Programs

The programs in Figs. 2.1 and 2.2 contain some English phrases enclosed in braces; these phrases are program comments. Programmers use comments to make a program easier to understand by describing the purpose of the program (see the first comment lines in Figs. 2.1 and 2.2), the use of identifiers (see the comments in the variable declarations), and the purpose of each program step (see the comments in the program bodies). Comments are an important part of the *documentation* of a program because they help others read and understand the program. The compiler, however, ignores comments and they are not translated into machine language.

As shown in Fig. 2.1, a comment can appear by itself on a program line, at the end of a line after a statement, or embedded in a statement. In the following variable declarations, the first comment is embedded in the declaration, while the second one follows the declaration.

```
var
   SqMeters,                    {input - fabric size in meters}
   SqYards    : Real;           {output - fabric size in yards}
```

We will document the use of most variables in this way. The next displays describe the syntax and the use of comments.

Comments

Form: {*comment*}

Example: {This is a comment}
              (* and so is this *)

Interpretation: A left brace indicates the start of a *comment;* a right brace indicates the end of a *comment.* Alternatively, the symbol pairs (* and *) may be used to mark the beginning and the end of a comment, respectively. Comments are listed with the program but are otherwise ignored by the Pascal compiler.

Note: It is not permissible to place one comment inside another.

Using Comments

Comments make a program more readable by describing the purpose of the program and the use of each identifier. For example, the comment in the following declaration

```
var
   SqMeters,                {input - fabric size in meters}
```

describes the use of variable SqMeters.

   You should also place comments within a program body to describe the purpose of each section of the program. Generally, you will include one comment in the program body for each major algorithm step. A comment within the program body should describe what the step does rather than simply restate the step in English. For example, the comment

```
{Convert the fabric size to square yards.}
SqYards := MetersToYards * SqMeters;
```

is more descriptive and hence preferable to

```
{Multiply MetersToYards by SqMeters and save the result in SqYards.}
SqYards := MetersToYards * SqMeters;
```

Before you implement each step in the initial algorithm, you should write a comment that summarizes the purpose of the algorithm step.

   Each program should begin with a header section that consists of a series of comments specifying

- the programmer's name
- the date of the current version
- a brief description of what the program does

If you write the program for a class assignment, you should also list the class identification and your instructor's name, as shown next.

```
program FirstAssignment (Input, Output);
{
 Programmer: William Bell     Date completed: May 9, 1992
 Instructor: Joe Joseph       Class: CS1

 This program reads a value in square meters and converts
 it to square yards.
}
```

Exercises for Section 2.5

Self-Check

1. What is wrong with the following comments?

   ```
   {This is a comment? *)
   (* How about this one {it seems like a comment} doesn't it *)
   ```

2. What is the purpose of including comments in a computer program?
3. Correct the syntax errors in the following program and rewrite it so it follows our style conventions. What does each statement of your corrected program do? What values are printed?

   ```
   program SMALL (INPUT, output)   VAR X, Y, X , real:
   BEGIN Y = 15.0,
   Z:= -Y + 3.5; Y + z =: x;
   writeln (x; Y; z);    end;
   ```

2.6 Data Types and Expressions

An *abstraction* is a model or a simplification of a physical object. We frequently use abstractions in problem solving and programming. For example, in problem solving we sometimes make simplifying assumptions that enable us to solve a limited version of a more general problem. In programming, *abstraction* is the process of focusing on what we need to know, ignoring irrelevant details.

Real Data Type

A *data type* is a set of values and a set of operations on those values. A *standard data type* in Pascal is a data type that is predefined (for example, Real, Integer, Char). In Pascal, we use the standard data type Real as an abstraction for the real numbers (in the mathematical sense). The data type Real is an abstraction because it does not include all real numbers. Some real numbers are too large or too small, and some real numbers cannot be represented precisely because of the finite size of a memory cell (more on this in Chapter 7). However, we can certainly represent enough of the real numbers in Pascal to carry out with sufficient accuracy most of the computations we wish to perform.

The normal arithmetic operators (+, − *, and /) for real numbers can be performed on type `Real` objects in Pascal. The assignment operator (`:=`) is another operator that can be used with type `Real` objects. We can also use the standard procedures `ReadLn`, `WriteLn`, and `Write` with type `Real` objects.

Objects of a data type can be variables, constants, or literals. A *literal* is a value that appears directly in a program. A type `Real` literal is a number that begins with a digit and contains a decimal point followed by at least one digit (e.g., `0.112`, `456.0`, `123.456`). A type `Real` literal may have a *scale factor*, which is the capital letter E followed by an optional sign and an integer (e.g., `0.112E3`, `456.0E–2`). A scale factor can also follow a string of digits without a decimal point (e.g., `123E6` and `123.0E6` are equivalent `Real` literals). A scale factor means multiply the number before the letter E by 10 raised to the power appearing after the letter E (e.g., `0.112E3` is 112.0, `456.0E–2` is 4.56). A `Real` literal may be preceded by a + or − sign when it appears in a program. Table 2.3 shows examples of valid and invalid `Real` literals.

Table 2.3 Valid and Invalid Real Literals

Valid Real Literals	Invalid Real Literals
`3.14159`	`150` (no decimal point)
`0.005`	`.12345` (no digit before.)
`12345.0`	`16.` (no digit after.)
`15.0E–04` (value is 0.0015)	`–15E–0.3` (0.3 invalid exponent)
`2.345E2` (value is 234.5)	`12.5E.3` (.3 invalid exponent)
`12E+6` (value is 12000000.0)	`.123E3`(.123 invalid Real)
`1.15E–3` (value is 0.00115)	

The last valid literal in the table, `1.15E–3`, has the same value as 1.15×10^{-3} in normal scientific notation, where the exponent $^{-3}$ causes the decimal point to be moved left three digits. A positive exponent causes the decimal point to be moved to the right (the + sign can be omitted when the exponent is positive).

Integer Data Type

Another standard data type (or data abstraction) in Pascal is type `Integer`, which is used to represent the integer numbers (for example, −77, 0, 999, +999). Because of the finite size of a memory cell, not all integers can be represented. On each system, the predefined constant `MaxInt` is the largest possible integer. You can use the statement

```
WriteLn (MaxInt);
```

to display that value. Normally, the smallest integer is −MaxInt−1.

Real and Integer data types differ in one basic way: a type Real object represents a number with a decimal point and a fractional part, whereas a type Integer object represents only a whole number. For this reason, type Integer objects are more restricted in their use. We often use them to represent a *count* of items (for example, the number of children in a family) because a count must always be a whole number.

The data type of the object stored in a particular memory cell determines how the bit pattern (or *binary string*) in that cell is interpreted. For example, a bit pattern that represents a type Real object is interpreted differently from a bit pattern that represents a type Integer object. But this is a detail that we do not need to be concerned with to use these data types in Pascal.

We can use the arithmetic operators listed earlier and the assignment operator with type Integer operands. Two additional operators, div (integer division operator) and mod (modulus operator), can be used with type Integer operands. We discuss these operators next.

Operators div and mod

The integer division operator, div, computes the integral part of the result of dividing its first operand by its second. For example, the value of 7 / 2 is 3.5, and the value of 7 div 2 is the integral part of this result, or 3. Similarly, the value of 299 / 100 is 2.99, and the value of 299 div 100 is the integral part of this result, or 2. Both operands of div must be integers, and the div operation is undefined when the divisor (the second operand) is zero. Table 2.4 shows some examples of the div operator.

Table 2.4 Examples of the div Operator

```
 3 div 15 = 0       3 div −15 =  0
15 div  3 = 5      15 div  −3 = −5
16 div  3 = 5      16 div  −3 = −5
17 div  3 = 5     −17 div   3 = −5
18 div  3 = 6     −18 div  −3 =  6
```

It is interesting to compare the values of the expressions 6 / 2 and 6 div 2. The value of 6 / 2 is the real number 3.0, whereas the value of 6 div 2 is the integer 3. Although these two results are equivalent in a mathematical sense, they are not the same in Pascal and are stored in memory as different binary strings.

The modulus operator, mod, returns the *integer remainder* of the result of dividing its first operand by its second. For example, the value of 7 mod 2 is 1 because the integer remainder is 1. The left side of the following diagram shows the effect of dividing 7 by 2 using long division: we get a quotient of 3 (7 div 2) and a remainder of 1 (7 mod 2). The diagram on the right shows that 299 mod 100 is 99 because we get a remainder of 99 when we divide 299 by 100.

```
7 div 2                          299 div 100
    ↓                                  ↓
    3 R1 ← 7 mod 2                    2 R99 ← 299 mod 100
 2√7                            100√299
    6                                200
    1                                 99
```

The magnitude of M mod N must always be less than the divisor N, so if M is positive, the value of M mod 100 must be between 0 and 99. The mod operation is undefined when N is zero or negative. Table 2.5 shows some examples of the mod operator. By comparing the second and third columns, you can see that −M mod N is equivalent to −(M mod N).

Table 2.5 Examples of the mod Operator

3 mod 5 = 3	5 mod 3 = 2	−5 mod 3 = −2
4 mod 5 = 4	5 mod 4 = 1	−5 mod 4 = −1
5 mod 5 = 0	15 mod 5 = 0	−15 mod 5 = 0
6 mod 5 = 1	15 mod 6 = 3	−15 mod 6 = −3
7 mod 5 = 2	15 mod 7 = 1	−15 mod −7 is undefined
8 mod 5 = 3	15 mod 8 = 7	15 mod 0 is undefined

The formula

```
M = (M div N) * N + (M mod N)
```

defines the relationship between the operators div and mod for a dividend of M and a divisor of N. By plugging in values for M, N, M div N, and M mod N, we can see that this formula holds for the two long division examples discussed earlier. In the first line below, M is 7 and N is 2; in the second line, M is 299 and N is 100.

```
  7 = (7 div 2) * 2 + (7 mod 2) = 3 * 2 + 1 = 7
299 = (299 div 100) * 100 + (299 mod 100) = 2 * 100 + 99 = 299
```

Using Integer Objects

The following case study gives an example of manipulating type Integer objects in Pascal.

Case Study: Finding the Value of a Coin Collection

Problem

Your little sister has been saving nickels and pennies for quite a while. Because she is getting tired of lugging her piggy bank with her whenever she goes to the store, she would like to trade in her collection for dollar bills and some change. To do this, she would like to know the value of her coin collection in dollars and cents.

Analysis

To solve this problem, we first must be given the count of nickels and the count of pennies in the collection. From those counts, we can then determine the total value of the collection in cents. Once we have that figure, we can do an integer division using 100 as the divisor to get the dollar value; the remainder of this division will be the loose change that she should receive. In the data requirements, we list the total value in cents (`TotalCents`) as a *program variable* because it is needed as part of the computation process, but is not a required problem output.

Data Requirements

Problem Inputs
```
Nickels : Integer {the count of nickels}
Pennies : Integer {the count of pennies}
```

Problem Outputs
```
Dollars : Integer {the number of dollars she should receive}
Change : Integer {the loose change she should receive}
```

Additional Program Variables
```
TotalCents : Integer {the total number of cents}
```

Relevant Formulas

1 dollar equals 100 pennies
1 nickel equals 5 pennies

Design

The algorithm is straightforward and is displayed next.

Initial Algorithm

1. Read in the count of nickels and pennies.
2. Compute the total value in cents.
3. Find the value in dollars and loose change.
4. Display the value in dollars and loose change.

Steps 2 and 3 may need refinement. Their refinements follow.

Step 2 Refinement
2.1   `TotalCents` is 5 times `Nickels` plus `Pennies`.

Step 3 Refinement
3.1   `Dollars` is the integer quotient of `TotalCents` and 100.
3.2   `Change` is the integer remainder of `TotalCents` and 100.

Implementation

The program is shown in Fig. 2.9. The statement

```
TotalCents := 5 * Nickels + Pennies;
```

implements algorithm step 2.1. The statements

```
Dollars := TotalCents div 100;
Change := TotalCents mod 100;
```

use the mod and div operators to implement algorithm steps 3.1 and 3.2.

Figure 2.9   Finding the Value of a Coin Collection

```
program Coins (Input, Output);
{Determines the value of a coin collection.}

  var
    Pennies,                {input — count of pennies}
    Nickels,                {input — count of nickels}
    Dollars,                {output — number of dollars}
    Change,                 {output — loose change}
    TotalCents : Integer; {total cents}

begin
  {Read in the count of nickels and pennies}
  Write ('Number of nickels >');
  ReadLn (Nickels);

  Write ('Number of pennies >');
  ReadLn (Pennies);

  {Compute the total value in cents}
  TotalCents := 5 * Nickels + Pennies;

  {Find the value in dollars and change.}
  Dollars := TotalCents div 100;
  Change := TotalCents mod 100;

  {Display the value in dollars and change.}
  WriteLn;
  Write ('Your collection is worth ', Dollars, ' dollars');
  WriteLn (' and ', Change, ' cents.')
end.

Number of nickels >30
Number of pennies >77

Your collection is worth     2 dollars and      27 cents.
```

Directory: CHAP2
File: COINS.PAS

Testing

To test this program, try running it with a combination of nickels and pennies that yields an exact dollar amount with no change left over. For example, 35 nickels and 25 pennies should yield a value of 2 dollars and no cents. Then increase and decrease the amount of pennies by one (26 and 24 pennies) to make sure that these cases are also handled properly.

Type of an Expression

The data type of each variable must be specified in its declaration, but how does Pascal determine the data type of an expression? The data type of an expression depends on the type of its operands. For example, the expression

```
Ace + Bandage
```

is type `Integer` if both `Ace` and `Bandage` are type `Integer`; otherwise, it is type `Real`. The expression

```
Ace / Bandage
```

is type `Real` because the `Real` division operator, `/`, always generates a type `Real` result. A Pascal expression is type `Integer` only if *all* its operands are type `Integer` and *none* of its operators is `/`. A Pascal expression is type `Real` if *any* of its operands is type `Real` or *any* of its operators is `/`.

A *mixed-type expression* is one that has both `Integer` and `Real` operands. Normally, we try to avoid mixing data types in an expression. The data type of a mixed-type expression must be `Real`.

Mixed-Type Assignment Statement

When an assignment statement is executed, the expression is first evaluated and then the result is assigned to the variable listed to the left of the assignment operator (`:=`). Either a type `Real` or a type `Integer` expression may be assigned to a type `Real` variable. Thus, if `M` and `N` are type `Integer` and `X` and `Y` are type `Real`, all the following assignment statements are valid:

```
M := 3;
N := 2;
X := M / N;       {assigns 1.5 to X}
Y := M div N;     {assigns 1.0 to Y}
```

In the last statement, the expression `M div N` evaluates to the integer 1. This value is converted to type `Real` (1.0) before it is stored in `Y`.

Pascal does not allow a type `Real` expression to be assigned to a type `Integer` variable because the fractional part of the expression cannot be represented and will be lost. This means that each of the following assignment statements is invalid if `Count` is a type `Integer` variable:

```
Count := 3.5;          {invalid; assignment of a real number to Integer}
Count := Count + 1.0;       {invalid; 1.0 is Real, so result is Real}
Count := Count / 2;         {invalid; result of division is Real}
```

Expressions with Multiple Operators

In our programs so far, most expressions have involved a single operator; however, expressions with multiple operators are common in Pascal. To understand and write expressions with multiple operators, we must know the Pascal rules for evaluating expressions. For example, in the expression X + Y / Z, is + performed before /, or vice versa? Is the expression X / Y * Z evaluated as (X / Y) * Z or as X / (Y * Z)? Verify for yourself that the order of evaluation does make a difference by substituting some simple values for X, Y, and Z. In both these expressions, the / operator is evaluated first; the reasons are explained in the Pascal rules for expression evaluation, which follow. These rules are based on standard algebraic rules.

Rules for Expression Evaluation

a. All parenthesized subexpressions must be evaluated separately. Nested parenthesized subexpressions must be evaluated inside out, with the innermost subexpression evaluated first.
b. *The operator precedence rule.* Operators in the same subexpression are evaluated in the following order: *, /, div, and mod first; + and – last.
c. *The left associative rule.* Operators in the same subexpression and at the same precedence level (such as + and –) are evaluated left to right.

Knowledge of these rules will help you understand how Pascal evaluates expressions. Use parentheses as needed to specify the order of evaluation. Often it is a good idea in complicated expressions to use extra parentheses to document clearly the order of operator evaluation. For example, the expression

```
X * Y * Z + A / B - C * D
```

can be written in a more readable form using parentheses:

```
(X * Y * Z) + (A / B) - (C * D)
```

■ Example 2.4

The formula for the area of a circle $a = \pi r^2$ may be written in Pascal as

```
Area := Pi * Radius * Radius
```

where Pi is the constant 3.14159. Figure 2.10 shows the *evaluation tree* for this formula. In this tree, arrows connect each operand with its operator. The order

Figure 2.10 Evaluation Tree for Area : = Pi * Radius * Radius

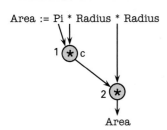

of operator evaluation is shown by the number to the left of each operator; the letter to the right of the operator indicates which evaluation rule applies. ∎

■ Example 2.5

The formula for the average velocity, v, of a particle traveling on a line between points p_1 and p_2 in time t_1 to t_2 is

$$v = \frac{p_2 - p_1}{t_2 - t_1}$$

This formula can be written and evaluated in Pascal as shown in Fig. 2.11. ∎

Figure 2.11 Evaluation Tree for V := (P2 − P1) / (T2 − T1)

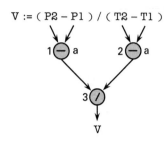

■ Example 2.6

Consider the expression

        Z − (A + B div 2) + W * Y

containing integer variables only. The parenthesized subexpression (A + B div 2) is evaluated first (rule a) beginning with B div 2 (rule b). Once the value of B div 2 is determined, it can be added to A to obtain the value of (A + B div 2). Next, the multiplication operation is performed (rule b), and the value for W * Y is determined. Then the value of (A + B div 2) is subtracted from Z (rule c). Finally, that result is added to W * Y. (See Fig. 2.12.) ∎

Figure 2.12 Evaluation Tree for Z − (A + B div 2) + W * Y

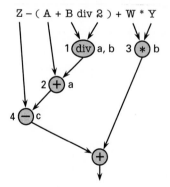

Writing Mathematical Formulas in Pascal

There are two problem areas in writing a mathematical formula in Pascal: one concerns multiplication and the other concerns division. Multiplication often can be implied in a mathematical formula by writing the two items to be multiplied next to each other, for example, $a = bc$. In Pascal, however, you must always use the * operator to indicate multiplication, as in

```
A := B * C
```

The other difficulty arises in formulas that involve division. We normally write the numerator and the denominator on separate lines:

$$m = \frac{y - b}{x - a}$$

In Pascal, however, all assignment statements must be written in a linear form. Consequently, parentheses are often needed to separate the numerator from the denominator and to clearly indicate the order of evaluation of the operators in the expression. The above formula would be written in Pascal as

```
M := (Y - B) / (X - A)
```

■ Example 2.7

This example shows several mathematical formulas rewritten in Pascal.

Mathematical Formula	Pascal Expression
1. $b^2 - 4ac$	B * B - 4 * A * C
2. $a + b - c$	A + B - C
3. $\dfrac{a + b}{c + d}$	(A + B) / (C + D)
4. $\dfrac{1}{1 + x^2}$	1 / (1 + X * X)
5. $a \times -(b + c)$	A * (-(B + C))

The points illustrated in these examples can be summarized as follows:

- Always specify multiplication explicitly by using the operator * where needed (1, 4).
- Use parentheses when required to control the order of operator evaluation (3, 4).
- Never write two arithmetic operators in succession; they must be separated by an operand or an open parenthesis (5). ■

Unary Minus

The fifth Pascal expression in Example 2.7 uses a unary minus to negate the value of (B + C) before performing the multiplication. The *unary minus* has only one operand and has the same precedence as the subtraction operator.

Char Data Type

The third standard data type in Pascal is type Char. We have already seen (Fig. 2.2) that type Char variables can be used to store any single character value. A type Char literal appearing in a Pascal program must be enclosed in apostrophes (for example, 'A'); however, you don't type apostrophes around character data entered at a terminal. When the ReadLn procedure reads character data into a type Char variable, the next character you enter at the terminal is stored in that variable. The blank character, which you enter by pressing the space bar, is written in a program as the literal ' '.

■ Example 2.8

The program in Fig. 2.13 first reads and echoes three characters entered at the keyboard. Next, it prints them in reverse order enclosed in asterisks. Each character is stored in a variable of type Char; the character value '*' is associated with the constant Border.
The line

```
        WriteLn (Border, Third, Second, First, Border)
```

displays the three characters in reverse order. As shown in the program output, each character value is printed in a single print position. The second character read in the sample run of Fig. 2.13 is a blank.   ■

Figure 2.13   Program for Example 2.8

Directory: CHAP2
File: REVERSE.PAS

```
program Reverse (Input, Output);
{Reads 3 characters and displays them in reverse order.}

   const
     Border = '*';                      {encloses 3 characters}

   var
     First, Second, Third : Char; {input/output — 3 characters}
begin
   Write ('Enter 3 characters >');
   ReadLn (First, Second, Third);
   WriteLn (Border, Third, Second, First, Border)
end.

Enter 3 characters >EBK
*KBE*
```

In Fig. 2.13, the string literal 'Enter 3 characters > ' is displayed as a prompt. In this example and in other earlier examples, we use strings as prompts and to clarify program output. Only single characters, not strings, can be stored in type Char variables; we will see how to process strings later in the text.

Boolean Data Type

The fourth standard data type in Pascal is type `Boolean` (named after the mathematician George Boole). `True` and `False` are the only two values associated with this data type. The identifier `Cloudy` is declared a type `Boolean` variable by the declaration

```
var
   Cloudy : Boolean;
```

The assignment statement

```
Cloudy := True;
```

assigns the Boolean value `True` to `Cloudy`. We will see how to use Boolean expressions (expressions that evaluate to `True` or `False`) in Chapter 4.

Ordinal Types

The data types `Integer`, `Boolean`, and `Char` have one property in common that is not shared by data type `Real`. We can list all the values of these types that can be represented in a particular version of Pascal. We cannot, however, list all of the values of type `Real` that may be represented. For example, if we attempt to list all the real numbers and we have 3.14, 3.15 in our list, someone could say we left out 3.141, 3.142, and so on. If we include those numbers, someone could say we left out 3.1411, 3.1412, and so on. A data type whose values can all be listed is called an *ordinal type*.

Exercises for Section 2.6

Self-Check

1. Indicate which of the following literal values are legal in Pascal and which are not. Identify the data type of each valid literal value.

   ```
       15    'XYZ'    '*'    $    25.123    15.    −999    .123    'x'
   "X"    '9'    '−5'    True    'True'
   ```

2. a. Evaluate the following expressions with 7 and 22 as operands.

   ```
        22 div 7      7 div 22      22 mod 7      7 mod 22
   ```

   Repeat the exercise for these pairs of integers:
   b. 15, 16   c. 3, 23   d. −4, 16

3. Given the declarations

   ```
   const
     Pi =    3.14159;
     MaxI =  1000;

   var
     X, Y : Real;
     A, B, I : Integer;
   ```

   indicate which of the following statesments are valid and find the value of each valid statement. Also indicate which statements are invalid and why. Assume that A is 3, B is 4, and Y is −1.0.

a. I := A mod B

b. I := (990 − MaxI) div A

c. I := A mod Y

d. X := Pi * Y

e. I := A / B

f. X := A / B

g. X := A mod (A / B)

h. I := B div 0

i. I := A mod (990 − MaxI)

j. I := (MaxI − 990) div A

k. X := A / Y

l. I := Pi * A

m. X := Pi div Y

n. X := A div B

o. I := (MaxI − 990) mod A

p. I := A mod 0

q. I := A mod (MaxI − 990)

4. Draw evaluation trees for the following expressions:

```
1.8 * Celsius + 32.0
(Salary − 5000.00) * 0.20 + 1425.00
```

5. Assume that you have the following variable declarations:

```
var
  Color, Lime, Straw, Yellow, Red, Orange : Integer;
  Black, White, Green, Blue, Purple, Crayon : Real;
```

Evaluate each of the following statements given these values: Color is 2, Black is 2.5, Crayon is −1.3, Straw is 1, Red is 3, Purple is 0.3E+1.

a. White := Color * 2.5 / Purple

b. Green := Color / Purple

c. Orange := Color div Red

d. Blue := (Color + Straw) / (Crayon + 0.3)

e. Lime := Red div Color + Red mod Color

f. Purple := Straw / Red * Color

6. Let A, B, C, and X be the names of four type Real variables and let I, J, and K be the names of three type Integer variables. Each of the following statements contains a violation of the rules for forming arithmetic expressions. Rewrite each statement so it is consistent with the rules.

a. X := 4.0 A * C

b. A := AC

c. I := 2 * −J

d. K := 3(I + J)

e. X := 5A / BC

f. I := 5J3

Programming

1. Write an assignment statement that might be used to implement the following equation in Pascal.

$$q = \frac{kA(T_1 − T_2)}{L}$$

2. Write a program that stores the values 'X', '0', 1.345E10, and True in separate memory cells. Your program should read the first three values as data items; use an assignment statement to store the last value.

3. Extend the program in Fig. 2.9 to handle dimes and quarters as well as nickels and pennies.

2.7 Formatting Program Output

In the sample program output shown so far, all real numbers were printed in Pascal scientific notation. Consequently, we had little control over the appearance, or the format, of each output line. This section explains how to specify the format of an output item.

Formatting Integer Values

It is fairly easy to specify the format of integer values displayed by a Pascal program. All that we need to do is add the symbols :n to an integer output list item, where n specifies the number of digits to be displayed (*field width*). For example, the lines

```
Write ('Your collection is worth ', Dollars :1, ' dollars');
WriteLn (' and ', Change :2, ' cents.')
```

indicate that one digit will be used to display the value of Dollars and two digits will be used to display the value of Change (a number between 0 and 99). If Dollars is 7 and Change is 8, the program output would be

```
Your collection is worth 7 dollars and  8 cents.
```

In this line, notice that there is an extra space before the value of Change (8). The reason is that the format specification :2 allows space for two digits to be printed. If the value of Change is between 0 and 9, a single digit is displayed *right-justified,* preceded by one blank space. We can use the format symbols :2 to display any output value between –9 and 99. For negative numbers, the minus sign is included in the count of digits displayed.

Table 2.6 shows how two integer values are printed using different format specifications. In this table, the character □ represents a blank character. The seventh line shows that the width specification may be a variable (or even an expression) that has an integer value. The last two lines show that when a width of 1 is used, the number is printed with no blanks preceding it, and the number of print columns used varies with the size of the number (i.e., the display field expands as needed).

Formatting Real Values

To describe the format specification for a Real value, we must indicate both the total field width needed and the desired number of decimal places. The

Table 2.6   Printing 234 and −234 Using Different Formats

Value	Format	Printed Output
234	:4	□234
234	:5	□□234
234	:6	□□□234
−234	:4	−234
−234	:5	□−234
−234	:6	□□−234
234	:Len	□□□234 (if Len is 6)
234	:1	234
−234	:1	−234

total field width should be large enough to accommodate all digits before and after the decimal point. We should also leave a display column for the decimal point and, for negative numbers, a minus sign.

If X is a type Real variable whose value will be between −99.9 and 999.9, we could use the output list item X :5:1 to display the value of X accurate to one decimal place. Table 2.7 shows different values of X displayed using this format specification. The values displayed in Table 2.7 are rounded to one decimal place, and all values are displayed right-justified in five columns.

Table 2.7   Displaying X Using Format Specification :5:1

Value of X	Output Displayed
−99.42	−99.4
0.123	□□0.1
−9.53	□−9.5
−25.55	−25.6
99.999	100.0
999.43	999.4

Table 2.8 shows some real values that were printed using other format specifications. As shown in the table, it is possible to use a format specification of the form :n for real values. In this case, the real value is printed in scientific notation using a total of n print positions.

Table 2.8   Formatting Real Values

Value	Format	Printed Output
3.14159	:5:2	□3.14
3.14159	:4:2	3.14
3.14159	:3:2	3.14
3.14159	:5:1	□□3.1
3.14159	:5:3	3.142
3.14159	:8:5	□3.14159
3.14159	:9	3.142E+00

Value	Format	Printed Output
0.1234	:4:2	0.12
−0.006	:4:2	−0.01
−0.006	:9	−6.00E−03
−0.006	:8:5	−0.00600
−0.006	:8:3	□□−0.006

PROGRAM
STYLE

Eliminating Leading Blanks

As shown in Tables 2.6 through 2.8, a number that requires fewer display columns than are specified by the format field width is displayed with leading blanks. To eliminate extra leading blanks, choose a format that will display the smallest value expected without leading blanks. If the actual value requires more display columns, the field width will expand to accommodate it. Thus, a format of :1 displays any integer value without leading blanks (for example, 29397 :1 is displayed as 29397). A format of :3:1 displays any real number accurate to one decimal place without leading blanks (for example, 99397.567 :3:1 is displayed as 99397.6); similarly, a format of :4:2 displays any real number accurate to two decimal places without leading blanks.

Formatting Strings

A string value is always printed right-justified in its field. Therefore, blank spaces will precede a string if the field in which it is printed is wider than the string. If *field width* is too small to accommodate a string value, the number of characters displayed will be equal to *field width*. Table 2.9 illustrates these points.

Table 2.9 Printing String Values Using Formats

String	Format	Printed Output
'*'	:1	*
'*'	:2	□*
'*'	:3	□□*
'ACES'	:1	A
'ACES'	:2	AC
'ACES'	:3	ACE
'ACES'	:4	ACES
'ACES'	:5	□ACES

Exercises for Section 2.7

Self-Check

1. Show the output lines for the following statements:

```
Write (-99 :4);
WriteLn ('Bottles' :8);
WriteLn ('-99' :4, -99 :8:2);
```

2. Correct the following statement:

```
WriteLn ("Joe's salary is ", Salary :2:10)
```

3. Show how the value -15.564 (stored in X) would be printed using these formats:

```
X :8:4   X :8:3   X :8:2   X :8:1   X :8:0   X :8
```

4. Assuming X (type Real) is 12.335 and I (type Integer) is 100, show the output lines for the following statements. For clarity, use the symbol □ to denote a blank space.

```
WriteLn ('X is ' :10, X :6:2, 'I is ' :4, I :5);
Write ('I is ' :10, I :1);
WriteLn ('X is ' :10, X :2:1);
```

Programming

1. If the variables A, B, and C are 504, 302.558, and -12.31, respectively, write a statement that will display the following line (for clarity, □ denotes a blank space).

```
□□504□□□□□302.56□□□□-12.3
```

2. Write a series of statements that will display a three-line heading consisting of your name, your school, and its city and state. Each line should be approximately centered on the computer screen or the printed page.

2.8 Interactive Mode, Batch Mode, and Data Files

There are two basic modes of computer operation: batch mode and interactive mode. The programs that we have written so far are intended to be run in interactive mode. In *interactive mode,* the program user can interact with the program and enter data while the program is executing. In *batch mode,* all data must be supplied beforehand, and the program user cannot interact with the program while it is executing. Batch mode is optional on most computers.

If you use batch mode, you must prepare a batch data file before you execute your program. On a time-shared system or a personal computer, a batch data file is created and saved in the same way as a program file or a source file.

Figures 2.14 and 2.15 show two versions of the metric conversion program rewritten as batch programs. In Fig. 2.14, we assume that the system file `Input` is associated with a batch data file instead of the keyboard. In most systems, this can be done relatively easily through *input-output redirection* using operating system commands. For example, in the UNIX® and MS-DOS® operating systems, you could instruct your program to take its input from file `MyData` instead of the keyboard by placing the symbols `<MyData` at the end of the command line that causes your compiled and linked program to execute. If you normally used the command line

    Metric

to execute this program, your new command line would be

    Metric <MyData

Figure 2.14 Batch Version of Metric Conversion Program

Directory: CHAP2
File: METRICBA.PAS

```
program MetricBatch (Input, Output);
{Converts square meters to square yards.}

   const
     MetersToYards = 1.196;      {conversion constant}

   var
     SqMeters,                   {input – fabric size in meters}
     SqYards    : Real;          {output – fabric size in yards}
begin
  {Read the fabric size in square meters.}
  ReadLn (SqMeters);
  WriteLn ('The fabric size in square meters is ', SqMeters :3:1);

  {Convert the fabric size to square yards.}
  SqYards := MetersToYards * SqMeters;

  {Display the fabric size in square yards.}
  WriteLn ('The fabric size in square yards is ', SqYards :4:2)
end.

The fabric size in square meters is 2.0
The fabric size in square yards is 2.39
```

Echo Prints versus Prompts

In Fig. 2.14, the statement

    ReadLn (SqMeters);

reads the value of SqMeters from the first (and only) line of the data file. Because the program input comes from a data file, there is no need to precede this statement with a prompt. Instead we follow the `ReadLn` with the statement

```
WriteLn ('Fabric size in square meters is ', SqMeters :3:1);
```

which *echo prints,* or displays, the value just read into `SqMeters`. This statement provides a record of the data manipulated by the program; without it, we would have no easy way of knowing what value was read. Whenever you convert an interactive program to a batch program, make sure you replace each prompt with an echo print that follows the `ReadLn` statement.

Output Redirection

You can also redirect program output to a disk file instead of to the screen. Then you could send the output file to the printer (using an operating system command) to obtain a hard copy of the program output. In UNIX or MS-DOS, you would use `>MyOutput` to redirect output from the screen to the file `My-Output`. These symbols should also be placed on the command line, which causes your program to execute. The command line

```
Metric >MyOutput
```

executes the compiled and linked code for the metric conversion program, reading program input from the keyboard and writing program output to the file `MyOutput`. However, it would be difficult to interact with this program because all program output, including any prompts, are sent to the output file. It would be better to use the command line

```
Metric <MyData >MyOutput
```

which reads program input from the data file `MyData` and sends program output to the output file `MyOutput`.

Preview of Text Files (Optional)

This section previews the use of text files as data files in Pascal. A complete treatment of this topic is discussed in Chapter 8. Skip this section if you will not be using data files until then.

A batch program reads its data from a data file that is created and saved beforehand with an editor program. The process used to create a text file is the same as that used to create a program file (steps 2 through 5 on page 21). The metric conversion program in Fig. 2.15 reads its data from the data file `InData` instead of the system file `Input`.

Figure 2.15 Metric Conversion Program Using the File InData

```
program MetricFile (InData, Output);
{Converts square meters to square yards.}
```

```
const
   MetersToYards = 1.196;      {conversion constant}

var
   InData : Text;              {input - data file}
   SqMeters,                   {input - fabric size in meters}
   SqYards    : Real;          {output - fabric size in yards}

begin
   {Read the fabric size in square meters.}
   Reset (InData);
   ReadLn (InData, SqMeters);
   WriteLn ('The fabric size in square meters is ', SqMeters :3:1);

   {Convert the fabric size to square yards.}
   SqYards := MetersToYards * SqMeters;

   {Display the fabric size in square yards.}
   WriteLn ('The fabric size in square yards is ', SqYards :4:2)
end.


The fabric size in square meters is 2.0
The fabric size in square yards is 2.39
```

Directory: CHAP2
File: METRICFI.PAS

In Fig. 2.15, the program heading

```
program MetricFile (InData, Output);
```

identifies InData as the name of the data file instead of the system file Input. The declaration

```
var
   InData : Text;      {input - data file}
```

indicates that InData has data type Text (a standard identifier) and is, therefore, a text file. The statement

```
Reset (InData);
```

prepares the file InData so that it can be read. Finally, the statement

```
ReadLn (InData, SqMeters);
```

reads a data value from the first (and only) line of the file InData. The sample output shown in Fig. 2.15 is generated when the file InData contains the line

```
2.0
```

Internal and External File Names

The program in Fig. 2.15 uses InData as the name of the data file being processed. InData is called the *internal name* of the data file. The data file may be stored under a different name on disk (its *external name*). The Pascal system does not know the file's external name unless you specify it. Specifying a file's external name is system-dependent; check with your instructor.

Some systems allow the use of an extended form of the `Reset` procedure. On these systems, the procedure call statement

```
Reset (InData, 'DataFile'); {prepare external file 'DataFile'}
```

may associate the internal name `InData` with the external name `DataFile`.

Exercises for Section 2.8

Self-Check

1. Explain the difference in placement of `WriteLn` statements used to display prompts and `WriteLn` statements used to echo data. Which are used in interactive programs? In batch programs?
2. How are input data provided to an interactive program? To a batch program?

Programming

1. Rewrite the program in Fig. 2.9 as a batch program. Assume data are read from the file `InData`.
2. Redo programming exercise 1, this time assuming that the data are read from the file `MyData`.

2.9 Common Programming Errors

One of the first things you will discover in writing programs is that a program rarely runs correctly the first time it is submitted. Murphy's Law, "If something can go wrong, it will," seems to be written with the computer programmer or programming student in mind. In fact, errors are so common that they have their own special name—*bugs*; the process of correcting them is called *debugging a program*. To alert you to potential problems, we provide a section on common errors at the end of each chapter.

When the compiler detects an error, the computer displays an *error message*, which indicates that you have made a mistake and what the cause of the error might be. Unfortunately, error messages are often difficult to interpret and are sometimes misleading. However, as you gain experience, you will become more proficient at understanding them.

There are two basic categories of error messages: syntax error messages and run-time error messages. *Syntax errors*, or *compilation errors*, are detected and displayed by the compiler as it attempts to translate your program. If a statement has a syntax error, it cannot be translated and your program will not be executed.

Run-time errors are detected by the computer and are displayed during execution of a program. A run-time error occurs as a result of the user directing the computer to perform an illegal operation, such as dividing a number by zero or manipulating undefined or invalid data. When a run-time error occurs, the computer stops executing your program and prints a diagnostic message that indicates the line where the error occurred. Sometimes the computer prints values of all variables as well.

Syntax Errors

Figure 2.16 shows a compiler listing of the metric conversion program. A *compiler listing* is a listing printed by the compiler during program translation that shows each line of the source program (preceded by a line number) and any syntax errors detected by the compiler. Errors are indicated by five asterisks and are summarized at the bottom of the compiler listing. The program contains the following syntax errors:

- missing semicolon after the program heading (line 1)
- use of : instead of = in the constant declaration (line 5)
- missing semicolon after the WriteLn statement (line 12)
- assignment statement with transposed variable and expression part (line 16)
- missing declaration for variable SqYards (lines 16 and 19)

Figure 2.16 Compiler Listing of a Program with Syntax Errors

```
 1 program Metric (Input, Output)
 2 {Converts square meters to square yards.}
 3
 4    const
*****        ^14
 5      MetersToYards : 1.196;       {conversion constant}
*****                    ^16,50
 6
 7    var
 8      SqMeters : Real;             {input - fabric size in meters}
 9
10 begin
11    {Read the fabric size in square meters.}
12    WriteLn ('Enter the fabric size in square meters >')
13    ReadLn (SqMeters);
*****        ^6
14
15    {Convert the fabric size to square yards.}
16    MetersToYards * SqMeters := SqYards;
*****                  ^59           ^104
17
18    {Display the fabric size in square yards.}
19    WriteLn ('The fabric size in square yards is ', SqYards)
*****                                                ^104
20 end.


   6:  illegal symbol
  14:  ";" expected
  16:  "=" expected
  50:  error in constant
  59:  error in variable
 104:  identifier not declared
```

The actual formats of the listing and the error messages produced by your compiler may differ from those in Fig. 2.16. In this listing, whenever an error is detected, the compiler prints a line with five asterisks, a caret symbol (^), and one or more numbers. The caret points to the position in the line above where the error was detected. Each number is a preassigned code for an error; the codes and their meanings are listed following the program.

To understand how this works, look at the first error in the program, which was detected after the reserved word const in line 4 was processed by the compiler. At this point the compiler recognized that a semicolon is missing (after the program heading) and indicated this by printing error code 14 (";" ex-pected). In this case, the position of the caret is misleading, because the compiler could not detect the error until it started to process the constant declaration. There is also a missing semicolon after line 12; however, the compiler prints error code 6 (illegal symbol) after it processes the standard identifier ReadLn in line 13.

Two error codes are printed after line 5 to indicate an incorrect symbol (: instead of =). The transposed assignment statement in line 16 is detected as error code 59 (error in variable); the compiler is looking for the variable in the assignment statement and detects an error when it reaches the asterisk.

An identifier not declared syntax error occurs if the compiler cannot find the declaration for an identifier referenced in the program body. This can happen because the programmer forgot the declaration or mistyped the name of the identifier. In Fig. 2.16, omission of the declaration for the variable SqYards causes the display of error code 104 (identifier not declared) after lines 16 and 19.

One syntax error often leads to the generation of multiple error messages. For example, forgetting to declare variable SqYards will cause an error message to be printed each time SqYards is used in the program. For this reason, it is often a good idea initially to concentrate on correcting the errors in the declaration part of a program and then recompile rather than attempt to fix all the errors at once. Many later errors will disappear once the declarations are correct.

Syntax errors are often caused by the improper use of apostrophes with strings. Make sure you always use an apostrophe, not a double quotation mark, to begin and end a string. Also, a string must begin and end on the same line.

Another common syntax error is a missing apostrophe or an extra apostrophe in a string. If an apostrophe is missing at the end, the compiler will assume that whatever follows is part of the string.

The following string contains an extra apostrophe:

```
WriteLn ('Enter Joe's nickname:');
```

The compiler will assume that the apostrophe used to indicate possession (Joe's) is terminating the string. This string must be entered as

```
WriteLn ('Enter Joe''s nickname:');
```

Two consecutive apostrophes inside a string indicate an apostrophe as a punctuation mark.

When using comments, you must be very careful to enclose them in { and

} or (* and *). If the opening { is missing, the compiler will attempt to process the comment as a Pascal statement, which should cause a syntax error. If the closing } is missing, the comment will simply be extended to include the program statements that follow it. If the comment is not terminated, the rest of the program will be included in the comment, and a syntax error such as incomplete program will be printed.

Run-Time Errors

Figure 2.17 shows an example of a run-time error. The program compiles successfully but contains no statement assigning a value to the variable X before the assignment statement

```
Z := X + Y;
```

is executed. The error messages after the program listing indicate the cause of the error ("undefined variable"), the location of the error (line 8), and the values of all variables in program TestError at the time of the error (X and Z are undefined).

Figure 2.17 A Program with a Run-Time Error

```
1   program TestError (Input, Output);
2
3     var
4       X, Y, Z : Real;
5
6   begin
7       Y := 5.0;
8       Z := X + Y;
9       WriteLn (X, Y, Z)
10  end.


Program terminated at line 8 in program TestError
Undefined variable in expression

                    --- TestError ---

X = UNDEFINED                    Y = 5.000000E+00
Z = UNDEFINED
```

Another common run-time error is "division by zero," which occurs if the program attempts to divide one variable by another variable that has a value of zero. Another common error, "arithmetic overflow," is detected when a program attempts to store a number that is too large in a variable.

As we indicated earlier, debugging a program can be time-consuming. The best approach is to plan your program carefully and desk check it to eliminate bugs before running the program. If you are not sure of the syntax for a particular statement, look it up. If you follow this approach, you will save yourself much time and trouble.

CHAPTER REVIEW

In this chapter, you saw how to use the Pascal programming language to perform some fundamental operations. You learned how to instruct the computer to read information into memory, perform some simple computations, and print the results of the computation. All of this was done using symbols (punctuation marks, variable names, and special operators such as *, −, and +) that are familiar, easy to remember, and easy to use. You do not have to know very much about your computer to understand and use Pascal.

The remainder of this text introduces more features of the Pascal language and provides rules for using those features. You must remember throughout that the rules of Pascal, unlike the rules of English, are precise and allow no exceptions. The compiler will be unable to translate Pascal instructions that violate these rules. Remember to declare every identifier used as a variable or constant and to separate program statements with semicolons.

New Pascal Constructs

Table 2.10 describes the new Pascal constructs introduced in this chapter.

Table 2.10   Summary of New Pascal Constructs

Construct	Effect
Program Heading `program Payroll (Input, Output);`	Identifies `Payroll` as the name of the program and `Input` and `Output` as the names of data files.

Constant Declaration
`const`
  `Tax = 25.00;`
  `Star = '*';`
	Associates the constant `Tax` with the real value `25.00` and the constant `Star` with the type `Char` value `'*'`.

Variable Declaration
`var`
  `X, Y, Z : Real;`
  `Me, It  : Integer;`
	Allocates memory cells `X`, `Y`, and `Z` for storage of real numbers and `Me` and `It` for storage of integers.

Assignment Statement `Distance := Speed * Time`	Assigns the product of `Speed` and `Time` as the value of `Distance`.
ReadLn Procedure `ReadLn (Hours, Rate)`	Enters data into the variables `Hours` and `Rate`.
Write Procedure `Write ('Net = ', Net :4:2)`	Displays the string `'Net = '` followed by the value of `Net` printed in a field of four or more columns and rounded to two decimal places.

Construct	Effect
WriteLn Procedure `WriteLn (X, Y)`	Displays the values of X and Y and advances the cursor to the next line.
Reset Procedure (Optional) `Reset (InData)`	Prepares the file InData for reading.
ReadLn with File (Optional) `ReadLn (InData, X, Y)`	Reads values of X and Y from a line of the file InData.

✓ Quick-Check Exercises

1. What value is assigned to X by the following statement?

   ```
   X := 25.0 * 3.0 / 2.5
   ```

2. What value is assigned to X by the following statement, assuming X is 10.0?

   ```
   X := X – 20.0
   ```

3. Show the exact form of the output line displayed when X is 3.456:

   ```
   WriteLn ('Three values of X are ', X :4:1, '*', X :5:2, '*', X :6:3);
   ```

4. Show the exact form of the output line when N is 345:

   ```
   WriteLn ('Three values of N are ', N :4, '*', N :5, '*', N :1);
   ```

5. Indicate which data type you would use to represent the following items: number of children at school, a letter grade on an exam, the average number of school days absent each year.
6. In which step of the software development method are the problem inputs and outputs identified?
7. How does `WriteLn` differ in its effect from `Write`?
8. If procedure `ReadLn` is reading two numbers, what character is typed after the first number? What is typed after the second number?
9. If procedure `ReadLn` is reading two characters, what character is typed after the first character? What is typed after the second character?
10. How does the computer determine how many data values to enter when a `ReadLn` operation is performed?
11. How does the program user determine how many data values to type in when a `ReadLn` operation is performed?
12. The compiler listing shows what kind of errors (syntax or run-time)?

Answers to Quick-Check Exercises

1. `30.0`
2. `–10.0`
3. `Three values of X are  3.5* 3.46* 3.456`
4. `Three values of N are  345*  345*345`

5. Integer, Character, Real
6. analysis
7. WriteLn causes subsequent output to be displayed on a new line.
8. a blank, the Return key
9. the second character, the Return key
10. by the number of variables in the input list
11. from reading the prompt
12. syntax errors

Review Questions

1. What type of information should be specified in the program header section comments?
2. Check the variables that are syntactically correct:

```
Income _____        Two Fold _____
1time  _____        C3PO     _____
const  _____        Income#1 _____
Tom's  _____        item     _____
```

3. What is illegal about the following declarations and statement?

```
const
  Pi = 3.14159;
var
  C, R : Real;

begin
  Pi := C / (2 * R * R);
```

4. What computer action is required by the following statement?

```
var Cell : Real;
```

5. If the average size of a family is 2.8 and this value is stored in the variable FamilySize, provide the Pascal statement to display this fact in a readable way (leave the cursor on the same line).
6. Write the data requirements, necessary formulas, and algorithm for programming project 6.
7. List the four standard data types of Pascal.
8. Convert the following program statements to read and echo data in batch mode.

```
Write ('Enter three numbers separated by spaces');
ReadLn (X, Y, Z);
WriteLn ('Enter two characters');
ReadLn (Ch1, Ch2);
```

9. Write an algorithm that allows for the input of an integer value, doubles it, subtracts 10, and displays the result.

Programming Projects

1. Write a program to convert a temperature in degrees Fahrenheit to degrees Celsius.

   Problem input
     Fahrenheit : Integer {temperature in degrees Fahrenheit}

Problem output
```
Celsius : Real {temperature in degrees Celsius}
```

Relevant formula

Celsius = (5/9) × (*Fahrenheit* − 32)

2. Write a program to read two data items and print their sum, difference, product, and quotient.

Problem inputs
```
X, Y : Integer {two items}
```

Problem outputs
```
Sum : Integer {sum of X and Y}
Difference : Integer {difference of X and Y}
Product : Integer {product of X and Y}
Quotient : Real {quotient of X divided by Y}
```

3. Write a program to read in the weight (in pounds) of an object and compute and print the weight in kilograms and grams. (Hint: 1 pound is equal to 0.453592 kilogram or 453.59237 grams.)

4. Write a program that prints your first initial as a block letter. (Hint: Use a 6 × 6 grid for the letter and print six strings. Each string should consist of asterisks (*) interspersed with blanks.)

5. If a human heart beats on the average of once a second, how many times does the heart beat in a lifetime of 78 years? (Use 365.25 for days in a year.) Rerun your program for a heart rate of 75 beats per minute.

6. Write a program that reads in the length and the width of a rectangular yard and the length and the width of a rectangular house situated in the yard. Your program should compute the time required to cut the grass at the rate of 2 square meters a second.

7. Write a program that reads in the numerators and the denominators of two fractions. Your program should print the numerator and the denominator of the fraction that represents the product of the two fractions. Also, print the percent equivalent of the resulting product.

8. Redo project 7, only this time compute the sum of the two fractions.

9. The Pythagorean theorem states that the sum of the squares of the sides of a right triangle is equal to the square of the hypotenuse. For example, if two sides of a right triangle have lengths 3 and 4, then the hypotenuse must have a length of 5. The integers 3, 4, and 5 together form a Pythagorean triple. There is an infinite number of such triples. Given two positive integers, m and n, where $m > n$, a Pythagorean triple can be generated by the following formulas:

Directory: CHAP2
File: PROJ2_7.PAS

$side1 = m^2 - n^2$
$side2 = 2mn$
$hypotenuse = m^2 + n^2$

Write a program that reads in values for m and n and prints the values of the Pythagorean triple generated by the above formulas.

INTERVIEW
Adele Goldberg

Adele Goldberg is President and CEO of ParcPlace Systems. Parc-Place Systems provides a broad range of products and services based on object-oriented technologies, including development tools for Smalltalk and for C++, that serve the applications development needs of corporate programmers. Previously, Goldberg was a research laboratory manager at Xerox PARC, where she wrote several books on the Smalltalk-80 system (Smalltalk-80: The Language, *with David Robson, and* Small-talk-80: The Interactive Programming Environment) *and led the effort to design, implement, and distribute the Smalltalk-80 development system on standard microprocessors.*

What influenced you to become a computer scientist?

I received a bachelor's degree in mathematics from the University of Michigan, where my degree work had been mostly theoretical. However, I worked as a programmer at the Center for Research on Learning and Teaching at the University and I also worked in an IBM business office in Chicago. There I had the opportunity to teach myself about programming IBM unit record equipment. After seeing what kind of work was available, and seeing opportunities in the application of computing to education, I decided to obtain more advanced training. I attended graduate school in Information Sciences at the University of Chicago and arranged to do my doctoral research at Stanford University in the Institute for Mathematical Studies in the So-

cial Sciences (IMSSS). My degree studies were in artificial intelligence, notably the incorporation of mechanical theorem provers into a system I designed for teaching proof construction in a course on symbolic logic. My particular long-term interests were, and still are, in the use of computers to augment both formal and informal learning.

How did your interests in learning lead you to the Smalltalk development team?

My interests in the use of computer technology for learning naturally led me to consider accessibility issues—that is, in order to be truly beneficial, tools taught in the classroom should be accessible wherever and whenever the person thinks of using them. Timesharing systems, such as the one I used in graduate school, tend to institutionalize learning because the tools that the students rely on are only available within the confines of the school itself. When I met Alan Kay, I immediately resonated with his ideas for the Dynabook, a personal computer that would have the same portability and ease of use as a printed book. The vision of the Dynabook incorporated the vision of a system structure in which people would find immediately usable applications but would also be able to easily learn how to specify applications and uses of their own invention. I joined Xerox Palo Alto Research Center in 1973, shortly after the start of the Smalltalk project. All of the people involved in the Small-talk project were, at one time or another, invited into the Dynabook project by Alan, who was looking for people to tackle the software and hardware issues associated with creating a truly personalizable and accessible system. Creating a language that would be easy enough to be accessible by almost anyone, yet powerful enough to allow the user to customize the system, was part of the challenge.

Smalltalk, the first uniformly object-oriented language, revolutionized programming for the personal computer in the 1980s. How was the language developed?

Smalltalk is based on ideas gleaned from the Simula language and from early work on visual programming, such as Sutherland's sketch pad. The earliest versions of Smalltalk were highly influenced by the tales of success from MIT with the Logo Project. We started out with the notion of a single language that would be learnable by children as well as adults, although I found that this spectrum was better understood as a series of tightly re-

lated languages. The Smalltalk system evolved gradually over the years, with an interesting research cycle: we would design and implement the language along with the user interface and development tools, reimplement any known applications, invent and implement new applications, then determine what was hard and what was easy to implement and why. We would then modify the language system design and repeat the cycle. The vision of the language remained the same, but its embodiment changed—because of new ideas about usage and how to learn, but also because of new technologies.

What is object-oriented programming, and to what do you attribute its popularity?

Object-oriented technology is a study of behavior, how to organize or classify behavior, and how to assign those behaviors to groups of objects. My early work with the Smalltalk project focused on determining design factors that contributed to learnability. This included devising pedagogical techniques, setting up special resource centers, and teaching. I typically taught students in the 10–13 year range. I observed that they learned to program fastest by using example programs, and extending and customizing them as needed. This is one of the basic concepts behind object programming. An object is the basic system component, or building block, and lends itself to customization or extension, making it unnecessary for a

programmer to start from scratch with every application.

An object consists of some private memory and a set of operations. It responds to a set of messages that specify which of its operations should be carried out. Messages may request an operation, but do not specify how it should be carried out. This not only minimizes interdependence between system components, but makes it possible for a user to employ an object without knowing the details of its internal implementation. This model of communicating objects applies to the most primitive objects as well as the high-level interaction between the computer and user in the Smalltalk system, and was important to us as we worked toward a powerful but very accessible system.

The modularity of object-oriented systems is a key reason for their popularity today. The value of modularity becomes apparent when designing and implementing large applications. As long as the message interface upon which other objects depend is not destroyed, components may be redesigned, tested, and implemented without disrupting the program's operation. The other reason is the somewhat inaccurate belief that you can't have a graphical interactive application unless you use an object-oriented style of implementation.

What advice would you give a student majoring in computer science today?

I would like students to understand that studies in computer science cannot be treated in isolation from a vision of how technology can be put to work to improve some aspect of work, education, or recreational life. We study programming languages, we invent new technologies for hardware and software, we study mathematics and psychology, and we study the introduction of technology into large and small organizations. And all of these studies are directed at applying our knowledge of the foundations of computing science to improve our ability to employ the computer as a tool.

3

Top-Down Design with Procedures and Functions

This chapter continues our discussion of problem solving. We introduce top-down design and show you how to develop a program starting from its system documentation. We also demonstrate how to solve a new problem by extending the solution to a problem that has already been solved.

We then discuss the importance of structured programming and why it is practiced. We describe the three types of control structures used in structured programming. Next we show you how to use a structure chart to represent the relationship between a problem and its subproblems. We introduce an important system structure, the procedure, that allows implementation of the solution to a subproblem as a separate program entity.

Finally, we discuss another system structure, the function, and describe how the use of functions and procedures enables us to reuse code that has already been tested and debugged. We also introduce the predefined functions of Pascal and explain how to use them to perform mathematical computations.

3.1 Top-Down Design and Program Development

We have been following an approach to solving programming problems—the software development method—that consists of five phases:

1. requirements specification
2. analysis
3. design
4. implementation
5. testing and verification

In the requirements specification phase, we determine precisely what problem we are expected to solve and what the program solution is supposed to do. This may require further clarification from your instructor or the person posing the problem.

In the analysis phase, we study the completed problem specification and attempt to identify the problem inputs and the desired outputs. We also list any formulas or relationships that might be relevant to the problem solution.

The design phase entails writing an algorithm that lists the major subproblems. Using a process called "divide and conquer," we solve these subproblems separately. We add solution details or refinements to the initial algorithm as required to clarify the solution.

During the implementation phase we write, or *code,* the refined algorithm in Pascal. The data requirements identified in the analysis phase form the basis of the declaration part of the program; the refined algorithm forms the basis for the program body.

Finally, we test and debug the program. After all obvious errors are removed, we run the program several times with a variety of test data to ensure that the program works properly. We check the program results against computations done by hand or using a calculator.

The approach to algorithm development followed in the design phase is called *top-down design*. This means that we start with the most abstract formulation of a problem and work down to more detailed subproblems. This chapter describes several ways to facilitate and enhance the top-down approach to programming. We begin by showing one way to move more efficiently from the analysis and design phase to the program code.

Developing a Program from Its System Documentation

Carefully following the software development method generates important system documentation before we even begin to code a program. This *system documentation* summarizes our intentions and thought processes as we develop the program data requirements and algorithm.

Program documentation is also provided inside a program itself in the form of comments. Comments describe the purpose of each program variable and also precede and explain each major algorithm step in the program body.

If you follow the software development method, you can use the system documentation that is developed as a starting point in coding your program. For example, for the metric conversion problem in Chapter 2, you can begin by duplicating the problem data requirements (part of the analysis phase) in the program declaration part (see Fig. 3.1). Then you can edit those lines to conform to the Pascal syntax for constant and variable declarations, thereby completing the declaration part of the program (see Fig. 3.2).

To develop the program body, use the initial algorithm, written as a list of comments, as a framework for the program. Then move each algorithm refinement under the algorithm step that it refines. Figure 3.3 shows the program framework you would have after this step; notice that the constant Meters-ToYards has been added to the declaration part. After the refinements are in place in the program body, you can begin to write actual Pascal statements. Place the Pascal code for an unrefined step directly under that step. For a step that is refined, either edit the refinement to change it from English to Pascal or replace it with Pascal code (see Fig. 3.4). We illustrate this entire process in the next case study.

Figure 3.1 Program with Unedited Declaration Part

```
program Metric (Input, Output);
{Converts square meters to square yards}

 problem inputs
   SqMeters    {the fabric size in square meters}
 problem outputs
   SqYards     {the fabric size in square yards}

begin

end.
```

Figure 3.2   The Declaration Part After Editing

```
program Metric (Input, Output);
{Converts square meters to square yards}

   var
     SqMeters,              {input — fabric size in square meters}
     SqYards   : Real;      {output — fabric size in square yards}

begin

end.
```

Figure 3.3   Using the Refined Algorithm as the Program's Framework

```
program Metric (Input, Output);
{Converts square meters to square yards}

   const
     MetersToYards = 1.196;                  {conversion constant}

   var
     SqMeters,              {input — fabric size in square meters}
     SqYards   : Real;      {output — fabric size in square yards}

begin
   {1.  Read the fabric size in square meters.}

   {2.  Convert the fabric size to square yards.}
       {2.1  The fabric size in square yards is 1.196 times the
             fabric size in square meters.}

   {3.  Display the fabric size in square yards.}

end.
```

Figure 3.4   Final Edited Program

```
program Metric (Input, Output);
{Converts square meters to square yards}

   const
     MetersToYards = 1.196;                  {conversion constant}

   var
     SqMeters,              {input — fabric size in square meters}
     SqYards   : Real;      {output — fabric size in square yards}

begin
   {Read the fabric size in square meters.}
   WriteLn ('Enter the fabric size in square meters >');
   ReadLn (SqMeters);
```

```
{Convert the fabric size to square yards}
SqYards := MetersToYards * SqMeters;

{Display the fabric size in square yards.}
  WriteLn ('The fabric size in square yards is ', SqYards)
end.
```

Case Study: Finding the Area and Circumference of a Circle

Problem
Read in the radius of a circle and compute and print its area and circumference.

Analysis
Clearly the problem input is the circle's radius. Two outputs are requested: the circle's area and circumference. These variables should be type `Real` because the inputs and outputs may contain fractional parts.

From our knowledge of geometry, we know the relationship between a circle's radius and its area and circumference; these formulas are listed below, along with the data requirements. Notice that we have written the English description of each variable as a Pascal comment to make it easier to produce the declaration part of our solution program.

Data Requirements

Problem Constant
```
    Pi = 3.14159;
```

Problem Inputs
```
    Radius : Real   {radius of a circle}
```

Problem Outputs
```
    Area : Real     {area of a circle}
    Circum : Real   {circumference of a circle}
```

Relevant Formulas
area of a circle $= \pi \times radius^2$
circumference of a circle $= 2\pi \times radius$

Design
Once you know the problem inputs and outputs, you should list the steps necessary to solve the problem. It is important that you pay close attention to the order of the steps. The initial algorithm follows.

Initial Algorithm

1. Read the circle radius.
2. Find the area.
3. Find the circumference.
4. Print the area and the circumference.

Algorithm Refinements

Next, we should refine any steps that do not have an obvious solution (steps 2 and 3).

> ### Step 2 Refinement
> 2.1   Assign Pi * Radius * Radius to Area.
>
> ### Step 3 Refinement
> 3.1   Assign 2 * Pi * Radius to Circum.

Implementation

Figure 3.5 shows the Pascal program so far. The program body consists of the initial algorithm and its refinements.

Figure 3.5   Outline of Program Circle

```
program Circle (Input, Output);
{Finds and prints the area and circumference of a circle}

   const
     Pi = 3.14159;

   var
     Radius,        {input  - radius of a circle}
     Area,          {output - area of a circle}
     Circum : Real; {output - circumference of a circle}

begin
   {1.  Read the circle radius.}

   {2.  Find the area.}
        {2.1  Assign Pi * Radius * Radius to Area.}

   {3.  Find the circumference.}
        {3.1   Assign 2 * Pi * Radius to Circum.}

   {4.  Print the area and the circumference.}

end.
```

To write the final program, we must convert the refinements (steps 2.1 and 3.1) to Pascal, write Pascal code for the unrefined steps (steps 1 and 4), and delete the step numbers from the comments. Figure 3.6 shows the final program.

Figure 3.6 Finding the Area and the Circumference of a Circle

```
program Circle (Input, Output);
{Finds and prints the area and circumference of a circle}

   const
     Pi = 3.14159;

   var
     Radius,        {input  - radius of a circle}
     Area,          {output - area of a circle}
     Circum : Real; {output - circumference of a circle}

begin
  {Read the circle radius.}
  Write ('Enter radius> ');
  ReadLn (Radius);

  {Find the area.}
  Area := Pi * Radius * Radius;

  {Find the circumference.}
  Circum := 2.0 * Pi * Radius;

  {Print the area and circumference.}
  WriteLn ('The area is ', Area :4:2);
  WriteLn ('The circumference is ', Circum :4:2)
end.

Enter radius> 5.0
The area is 78.54
The circumference is 31.42
```

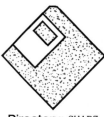

Directory: CHAP3
File: CIRCLE.PAS

Testing

The sample output in Fig. 3.6 provides a good test of the solution because it is relatively easy to compute by hand the area and the circumference for a radius value of 5.0. The radius squared is 25.0, so the value of the area appears correct. The circumference should be 10 times Pi, which is also an easy number to compute by hand.

Exercises for Section 3.1

Self-Check

1. Describe the problem inputs and outputs and the algorithm for computing an employee's gross salary given the hours worked and the hourly rate.
2. Write a program outline from the algorithm you developed in exercise 1. Use Fig. 3.5 as a model for your outline.

Programming

1. Add refinements to the program outline that follows and write the final Pascal program.

```
program SumAndAverage (Input, Output);
{Finds and prints the sum and average of two numbers}

  var
    One, Two,        {input - numbers to process}
    Sum,             {output - sum of One and Two}
    Average : Real; {output - average of One and Two}

begin
  {1. Read two numbers.}
  {2. Compute sum of numbers.}
  {3. Compute average of numbers.}
  {4. Print sum and average.}
end.
```

2. Write a complete Pascal program for self-check exercise 1.

3.2 Extending a Problem Solution

Quite often the solution to one problem turns out to be the basis for the solution to another problem. For example, we can easily solve the next problem by building on the solution to the previous problem.

Case Study: Finding the Most Pizza for Your Money

Problem
You and your college roommates frequently order a late-night pizza snack. Many pizzerias in the area deliver to dormitories. Since you are on a tight budget, you want to know which pizza is the best value.

Analysis
To find which pizza is the best value, we must be able to do a meaningful comparison of pizza costs. One way to do this is to compute the unit price of each pizza. The *unit price* of an item is obtained by dividing the total price of that item by a measure of its quantity. A good measure of quantity would be the pizza weight, but pizzas are not sold by weight—they are sold by size (diameter) measured in inches. Consequently, the best we can do is to use some meaningful measure of quantity based on pizza diameter. One such measure is pizza area. So for our purposes, we will define the unit price of a pizza as its price divided by its area.

The following data requirements list a pizza's size and price as problem inputs. Although the problem statement does not ask us to display the pizza's area, we are listing it as a problem output because the pizza's area will give us some idea of how many friends we can invite to share our pizza. The radius (one-half the diameter) is listed as a program variable because we need it to compute the pizza's area, but it is not a problem input or output.

Data Requirements

Problem Constant
```
Pi = 3.14159;
```

Problem Inputs
```
Size : Real {diameter or size of a pizza}
Price : Real {price of a pizza}
```

Problem Outputs
```
UnitPrice : Real {unit cost of a pizza}
Area : Real {area of a pizza}
```

Program Variables
```
Radius : Real {radius of a pizza}
```

Relevant Formulas

$area\ of\ a\ circle = \pi \times radius^2$
$radius\ of\ a\ circle = diameter/2$
$unit\ price = total\ price/area$

Design

As we have already mentioned, we are basing the solution to the pizza problem on the solution to the case study in Section 3.1 (finding the area and the circumference of a circle). The initial algorithm here is similar to the one shown earlier. The step that computes the circle's circumference (step 3) has been replaced with one that computes the pizza's unit price.

Initial Algorithm

1. Read in the pizza's diameter and price.
2. Compute the pizza's area.
3. Compute the pizza's unit price.
4. Display the unit price and the area.

The algorithm refinements follow. The refinement of Step 2 shows that we must compute the pizza's radius before we can compute its area.

Step 2 Refinement
2.1   Assign Diameter / 2 to Radius.
2.2   Assign Pi * Radius * Radius to Radius.

Step 3 Refinement
3.1   Assign Price / Area to UnitPrice.

Implementation

Figure 3.7 shows the Pascal program. We will write this program the same way as before: by editing the data requirements to develop the program declaration part and by using the initial algorithm with refinements as a starting point for the program body.

Figure 3.7 Pizza Program

Directory: CHAP3
File: PIZZA.PAS

```
program Pizza (Input, Output};
{Computes the unit price of a pizza}

   const
      Pi = 3.14159;

   var
      Diameter,          {input — diameter or size of a pizza}
      Price,             {input — price of a pizza}
      UnitPrice,         {output — unit cost of a pizza}
      Area,              {output — area of a pizza}
      Radius : Real;     {radius of a pizza}

begin
   {Read in the pizza diameter and price.}
   Write ('Size of pizza in inches >');
   ReadLn (Diameter);
   Write ('Price of pizza $');
   ReadLn (Price);

   {Compute the pizza area.}
   Radius := Diameter / 2;
   Area := Pi * Radius * Radius;

   {Compute the pizza unit price.}
   UnitPrice := Price / Area;

   {Display the area and unit price.}
   WriteLn;
   Write ('The pizza unit price is $', UnitPrice :4:2, ' per square inch');
   WriteLn (' per square inch.');
   WriteLn ('The pizza area is ', Area :3:1, ' square inches.')
end.

Size of pizza in inches >9.0
Price of pizza $7.45

The pizza unit price is $0.12 per square inch
The pizza area is 63.6 square inches.
```

Testing

To test this program, run it with a few different pizza sizes. You can verify that the program is working correctly by multiplying the unit price and the area. The product should equal the price of the pizza.

Self-Check

1. What changes are required to extend the payroll algorithm described in self-check exercise 1 Section 3.1 to allow for overtime hours to be paid at 1.5 times an employee's normal hourly rate when computing his or her gross salary? Assume that overtime hours are entered separately.

Programming

1. Write a complete Pascal program for the revised payroll algorithm developed in self-check exercise 1.

3.3 Structured Programming and Control Structures

Structured programming is a disciplined approach to programming that results in programs that are easy to read and understand and less likely to contain errors. The emphasis is on following accepted program style guidelines (such as using meaningful names for identifiers) to write code that is adequately documented with comments and that is clear and readable. Obscure tricks and programming shortcuts are strongly discouraged. Government organizations and industry are strong advocates of structured programming because structured programs are much more cost effective in the long term.

Program maintenance involves modifying a program to remove previously undetected bugs and to keep it up to date as government regulations or company policies change. It is not uncommon to maintain a program for five years or more, often after the programmers who originally coded it have left the company or moved on to other positions.

Control Structures

Structured programming utilizes *control structures* to control the flow of statement execution in a program. The control structures of a programming language enable us to combine individual Pascal statements into a single program entity with one entry point and one exit point. We can then write a program as a sequence of control structures rather than as a sequence of individual statements (see Fig. 3.8).

Compound Statements

The three categories of control structures are: sequence, selection, and iteration. So far, we have illustrated sequential control using compound statements in

Figure 3.8 A Program as a Sequence of Three Control Structures

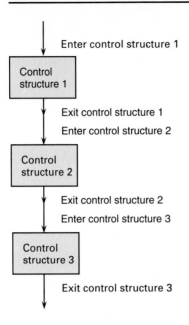

Pascal. A *compound statement* is a group of statements bracketed by `begin` and `end`:

```
begin
    statement₁;
    statement₂;
      .
      .
      .
    statementₙ
end
```

Control flows from *statement₁* to *statement₂*, and so on. A program body consists of a single compound statement. Later in this chapter, we introduce two system structures, procedures and functions, that also contain a body consisting of a single compound statement. The control structures for selection are described in Chapter 4 and the control structures for repetition in Chapter 5.

Motivation for Selection and Repetition Control Structures

In the last section, we extended the solution to one problem (find a circle's radius and circumference) into a second related problem (find the unit price of a pizza). We are not really finished yet because our goal was to be able to do a cost comparison of several pizzas with different prices and sizes to determine the best value.

One way to accomplish our larger goal is to run the program several different times, once for each pizza, and record the results. Then we can scan the list of results to determine which pizza has the lowest unit price.

A better solution would be to write a program that repeated the computation steps and compared unit prices, displaying as its final result the size and price of the pizza with the lowest unit price. Let's write an algorithm that will give us this improved solution.

Initial Algorithm for Improved Solution

1. For each pizza, read in a pizza's size and price and compute the unit cost. Compare the unit cost just computed with the previous unit costs and save the size and price of the pizza whose unit cost is the smallest so far.
2. Display the size and price of the pizza with the smallest unit cost.

The purpose of step 1 of the algorithm is to perform the cost computation for each individual pizza and somehow save the size and price of the pizza whose unit cost was the smallest. After all costs are computed, step 2 displays the size and price of the pizza that is the best buy.

We don't yet know how to do step 1 in Pascal because it involves the use of repetition and selection control structures. However, we can write a refinement of this step that will give you some idea of where we are heading in the next few chapters.

Step 1 Refinement

    1.1   Repeat the following steps for each pizza:
        1.2   Read in the next pizza size and price.
        1.3   Compute the unit price.
        1.4   If the new unit price is the smallest one so far, then save this pizza's size, price, and unit price.

Step 1.1 specifies the *repetition* of a group of steps: step 1.2 (read the data), step 1.3 (compute price), step 1.4 (compare price with smallest price so far). We repeat these steps as many times as necessary until all unit prices are computed and compared. Each time we compute a new unit price, step 1.4 compares it to the others, and the current pizza's size and price are saved if its unit price is smaller than any others computed so far. If the unit price is not the smallest so far, the current pizza's size and price are not saved. Step 1.4 is a *selection step* because it selects between two possible outcomes: a) save the pizza's data and b) do not save the pizza's data.

Exercises for Section 3.3

Self-Check

1. Why would a repetition step be used in an algorithm?
2. Show how the pizza algorithm and problem inputs described in Section 3.2 could be modified to allow the computation of the unit price of either a single circular pizza or a single square pizza.

3.4 Structure Charts

As mentioned earlier, one of the most fundamental ideas in problem solving is dividing a problem into subproblems and solving each subproblem independently of the others. In attempting to solve a subproblem at one level, we often introduce new subproblems at a lower level. The splitting of a problem into its related subproblems is analogous to the process of refining an algorithm. Each time we refine an algorithm step, we generate new refinements (subproblems) at a lower level. This section uses a case study to introduce a documentation tool that will enable you to keep track of the relationships between subproblems.

Case Study: Drawing Simple Diagrams

Problem
You would like to be able to draw some simple diagrams or figures on your printer or screen. Two examples are the diagram for a house and the stick figure of a person in Fig. 3.9.

Figure 3.9 House and Stick Figure

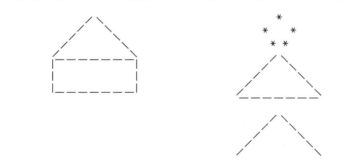

Analysis
The house figure consists of a triangle without its base on top of a rectangle. The stick figure consists of a shape that resembles a circle, a triangle, and a triangle without its base. We should be able to draw both figures using the following four basic graphical components:

- a circle
- a baseline
- parallel lines
- intersecting lines

Design

Let's focus on the stick figure of a person. We can divide the problem of drawing this figure into the following three subproblems.

Initial Algorithm

1. Draw a circle.
2. Draw a triangle.
3. Draw intersecting lines.

Algorithm Refinements

Since a triangle is not one of our basic components, we must refine step 2.

> ### Step 2 Refinement
> 2.1   Draw intersecting lines.
> 2.2   Draw a base.

We can use a diagram called a *structure chart* to show the relationship between the original problem and its subproblems. The structure chart corresponding to our initial algorithm is shown in Fig. 3.10.

Figure 3.10   Structure Chart for Drawing Stick Figure

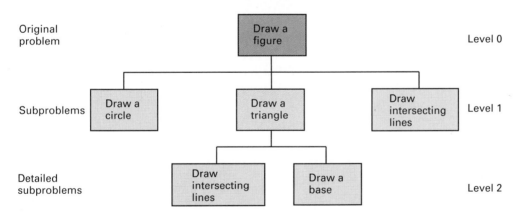

As we trace down the diagram, we go from an abstract problem to a detailed subproblem. The original problem is shown at the top, or level 0, of the structure chart. The major subproblems appear at level 1. The detailed subproblems that result from the refinement of a level-1 step are shown at level 2 and are connected to their level-1 subproblem. The structure chart shows that the solution to subproblem *Draw a triangle* (level 1) depends on the solutions to the detailed subproblems *Draw intersecting lines* and *Draw a base* (both level 2). Since the subproblem *Draw a circle* is not refined further, no level-2 subproblems are connected to it.

Structure charts are intended to show the structural relationship between subproblems. The algorithm (not the structure chart) shows the order in which we must carry out each step to solve the problem.

Exercises for Section 3.4

Self-Check

1. Draw the structure chart for the pizza problem in Section 3.2.
2. Draw the structure chart for the problem of drawing the house shown in Fig. 3.9.
3. Draw the structure chart for the problem of drawing a triangle and a rectangle with a circle between them.

3.5 Procedures

A structure chart proceeds from the original problem at the top level down to its detailed subproblems at the bottom level. We should follow this *top-down* approach when we code a program which we can do by using the procedure system structure.

A Pascal *procedure* is a grouping of program statements into a single program unit. Just like the Pascal `ReadLn` and `WriteLn` procedures, each Pascal procedure that we write can be activated through the execution of a procedure call statement. If we assume that we have procedures available that implement each of the level-2 subproblems in Fig. 3.10, we could use the following code fragment to implement the level-1 subproblem *Draw a triangle*:

```
{Draw a triangle.}
DrawIntersect;
DrawBase;
```

This code fragment contains two procedure call statements. During program execution, the procedure call statement

```
DrawIntersect;
```

causes the statements contained in the body of procedure `DrawIntersect` to be executed. You will see how to write procedure `DrawIntersect` in the next section.

Figure 3.11 shows the body of a program that draws a stick figure, assuming that the solution to each subproblem in Fig. 3.10 is implemented as a separate procedure. The program body (called the *main program*) implements our original algorithm. The program body begins with the code for step 1 (Draw a circle), which consists of a call to procedure `DrawCircle`. The code for step 2 (Draw a triangle) consists of calls to procedures `DrawIntersect` and `DrawBase`. The code for step 3 (Draw intersecting lines) consists of a second call to procedure `DrawIntersect`.

Figure 3.11 Main Program Body for Drawing a Stick Figure

```
begin {StickFigure}
  {Draw a circle.}
  DrawCircle;

  {Draw a triangle.}
  DrawIntersect;
  DrawBase;

  {Draw intersecting lines.}
  DrawIntersect
end. {StickFigure}
```

SYNTAX DISPLAY

Procedure Call Statement

Form: *pname*
Example: `DrawCircle`
Interpretation: The procedure call statement initiates the execution of procedure *pname*. After *pname* has finished executing, the program statement that follows the procedure will be executed.

Declaring Procedures

Just like other identifiers in Pascal, a procedure must be declared before it can be referenced in a program body. Figure 3.12 shows the declaration for procedure `DrawCircle`.

Figure 3.12 Procedure DrawCircle

```
procedure DrawCircle;
{Draws a circle}

begin {DrawCircle}
  WriteLn ('   *  ');
  WriteLn (' *   *');
  WriteLn ('  * * ')
end; {DrawCircle}
```

A procedure declaration begins with a *procedure heading*, which consists of the word `procedure` followed by the procedure name (an identifier) and a semicolon. A comment describing the purpose of the procedure comes next, followed by the *procedure body*. The procedure body always starts with `begin` and ends with `end;`. In Fig. 3.12, the procedure body contains the three `WriteLn` statements that cause the computer to draw a shape that resembles a circle. The procedure call statement

    DrawCircle

causes these `WriteLn` statements to execute.

In this text, the `begin` and `end` that bracket a procedure body are followed by a comment that identifies the procedure's name. The comment is added for clarity and is not required by Pascal. However, Pascal does require the semicolon that follows `end`.

Each procedure declaration may contain declarations for its own constants, variables, and even other procedures. These identifiers are considered *local* to the procedure; in other words, they can be referenced only within the procedure (more on this later).

Procedure Declaration

Form: procedure *pname*;
          local declarations
          begin
              procedure body
          end;

Example: procedure Skip3Lines;
            {Skips three lines}

            begin {Skip3Lines}
                WriteLn;
                WriteLn;
                WriteLn
            end;   {Skip3Lines}

Interpretation: The procedure *pname* is declared. Any identifiers that are declared in the *local declarations* are defined only during the execution of the procedure and can be referenced only within the procedure. The *procedure body* describes the data manipulation to be performed by the procedure.

Placement of Procedure Declarations in a Program

The three procedures called in Fig. 3.11 must appear in the declaration part of the program, just before the program body. It makes no difference which procedure is declared first; their order of execution is determined by the order of procedure call statements in the program body. Figure 3.13 shows the complete program with its procedures.

Figure 3.13 Program to Draw a Stick Figure

99

3.5 Procedures

```
program StickFigure (Output);
{Displays a stick figure}

   procedure DrawCircle;
   {Draws a circle}

   begin  {DrawCircle}
      WriteLn ('    *   ');
      WriteLn (' *    *');
      WriteLn ('   * * ')
   end; {DrawCircle}

   procedure DrawIntersect;
   {Draws intersecting lines}

   begin  {DrawIntersect}
      WriteLn ('  /\  ');
      WriteLn (' /  \ ');
      WriteLn ('/    \')
   end;  {DrawIntersect}

   procedure DrawBase;
   {Draws a base}

   begin {DrawBase}
      WriteLn ('-------')
   end;  {DrawBase}

begin  {StickFigure}
   {Draw a circle.}
   DrawCircle;

   {Draw a triangle.}
   DrawIntersect;
   DrawBase;

   {Draw intersecting lines.}
   DrawIntersect
end.  {StickFigure}
```

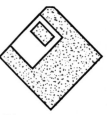

Directory: CHAP3
File: STICKFIG.PAS

Notice that it was not necessary to include the file Input in the program heading in Fig. 3.13. This is because the program does not read any input data.

Use of Comments in a Program with Procedures

Figure 3.13 includes several comments. Each procedure begins with a comment that describes its purpose. The begin and end that bracket each procedure body and the main program body are followed by a comment identifying that procedure or program. From now on throughout this text, the first and last lines of each procedure declaration are in color to help you locate each procedure in the program listing.

Relative Order of Execution of Procedures and the Main Program

In the stick figure problem, we wrote the main program body as a sequence of procedure call statements before we specified the details of all procedures. The next step is to provide the missing procedure declarations.

When we actually put the separate procedures and the main program body together in a complete program, the procedures appear in the declaration part of the program just before the program body. The compiler must translate the procedure declarations before it translates the main program body. When it reaches the end of each procedure body, the compiler inserts a statement that causes a *return* from the procedure back to the calling statement. In the main program body, the compiler translates a procedure call statement as a transfer of control to the procedure.

Figure 3.14 shows the main program body and the procedure `DrawCircle` of the stick figure program in separate areas of memory. Although the Pascal statements are shown in Fig. 3.14, the object code corresponding to each statement is actually stored in memory.

Figure 3.14   Flow of Control Between the Main Program and a Procedure

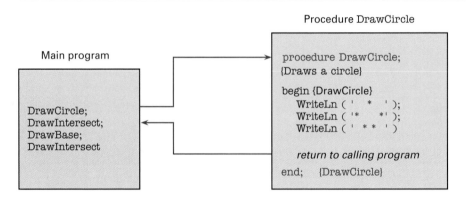

When we run the program, the first statement in the main program body is the first statement executed (the call to `DrawCircle` in Fig. 3.14). When the computer executes a procedure call statement, it transfers control to the procedure that is referenced (indicated by the colored line in Fig. 3.14). The computer allocates any memory that may be needed for the procedure's local data and then performs the statements in the procedure body. After the last statement in the procedure body is executed, control returns to the main program (indicated by the black line in Fig. 3.14), and the computer releases any memory that was allocated to the procedure. After the return to the main program, the next statement is executed (the call to `DrawIntersect` in Fig. 3.14).

Procedural Abstraction

One important advantage of procedures is that they allow us to remove from the main program the code that provides the detailed solution to a subproblem. Because these details are provided separately in the procedures and not in the main program, we can write the main program as soon as we have specified the initial algorithm and before we refine any of the steps. We should delay writing the procedure for an algorithm step until we have finished refining that step. This approach to program design, called *procedural abstraction,* enables us to defer implementation details and to write our program in logically independent sections, the same way we develop the solution algorithm.

Reuse of Procedures

Another advantage of using procedures is that procedures can be executed more than once in a program. For example, procedure DrawIntersect is called twice in Fig. 3.13. Each time DrawIntersect is called, the list of output statements shown in Fig. 3.13 is executed and a pair of intersecting lines is drawn. If we were not using procedures, the WriteLn statements that draw the lines would have to be listed twice in the program body, thereby increasing the main program's length and the chance of error.

Finally, once you have written and tested a procedure, you can use it in other programs or procedures. For example, the procedures we created for program StickFigure could easily be used in programs that draw other diagrams. We discuss the reuse of code in Section 3.8.

■ Example 3.1

Many diagrams contain triangles and rectangles. We can use procedures DrawIntersect, DrawParallel, and DrawBase to define two new procedures, DrawTriangle and DrawRectangle, as shown in Fig. 3.15. The comment in Fig. 3.15 reminds us that we must precede our two new procedures with declarations for the three procedures that they call. ■

Figure 3.15   Procedures DrawTriangle and DrawRectangle

```
{Insert procedures DrawIntersect, DrawParallel, and DrawBase.}

procedure DrawTriangle;
{Draws a triangle}

begin   {DrawTriangle}
  DrawIntersect;
  DrawBase
end;   {DrawTriangle}

procedure DrawRectangle;
{Draws a rectangle}
```

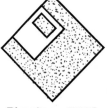

Directory: CHAP3
File: STICKFIG.PAS

```
begin  {DrawRectangle}
  DrawBase;
  DrawParallel;
  DrawBase
end;  {DrawRectangle}
```

Local Declarations in Procedures

Identifiers declared within a procedure are called *local identifiers* because they can be referenced only within that procedure. Figure 3.16 shows another version of procedure DrawCircle with a local constant named OutSymbol. The WriteLn statements in the procedure body display OutSymbol at various locations to draw a shape that resembles a circle. The advantage of using this local constant is that we can easily change the appearance of the circle just by changing the line that defines the value of OutSymbol. The circle displayed by this new procedure looks like this:

Figure 3.16 Procedure DrawCircle with a Local Constant

Directory: CHAP3
File: STICKFIG.PAS

```
procedure DrawCircle;
{Draws a circle}

  const
    OutSymbol = ' @ ';

begin  {DrawNewCircle}
  WriteLn (OutSymbol :4);
  WriteLn (OutSymbol :2, OutSymbol :4);
  WriteLn (OutSymbol :3, OutSymbol :2)
end; {DrawNewCircle}
```

Exercises for Section 3.5

Self-Check

1. Assume that you have procedures PrintH, Print I, PrintM, and PrintO, each of which draws a large block letter (for example, PrintO draws the block letter O). What is the effect of executing the following main program body?

```
begin {main}
  PrintH;
  PrintI;
  WriteLn;   WriteLn;   WriteLn;
  PrintM;
  PrintO;
  PrintM
end. {main}
```

1. Write a procedure named Skip5Lines that skips five blank lines.
2. Write procedure DrawParallel.
3. Write a main program to print HI HO in block letters using three procedures. First, provide a structure chart for this problem.
4. Write procedures PrintH, PrintI, PrintM, and PrintO.

3.6 Displaying User Instructions

We will limit the use of procedures for the time being because you do not yet know how to pass information into or out of a procedure. (We discuss this further in Section 3.7 and in Chapter 6). Until you have this ability, we will use procedures only to display multiple lines of program output, such as instructions to a program user, a title page, or a special message that precedes a program's results.

■ Example 3.2

The procedure Instruct in Fig. 3.17 displays instructions to a user of our earlier program that computes the area and the circumference of a circle (see Fig. 3.6). If procedure Instruct is placed in the declaration part of the original program, the new program body can begin with the procedure call statement

```
Instruct;
```

The rest of the program body consists of the executable statements shown earlier. Figure 3.18 shows the output displayed by calling procedure Instruct. The rest of the program output is the same as the output shown earlier.   ■

Figure 3.17 Procedure Instruct

```
procedure Instruct;
{Displays instructions to a user of program Circle}

begin {Instruct}
  WriteLn ('This program computes the area');
  WriteLn ('and circumference of a circle.');
  WriteLn;
  WriteLn ('To use this program, enter the radius of');
  WriteLn ('the circle after the prompt: Enter radius>');
  WriteLn;
  WriteLn ('The circumference will be computed in the');
  WriteLn ('same units of measurement as the radius. The');
  WriteLn ('area will be computed in the same units squared.');
  WriteLn
end; {Instruct}
```

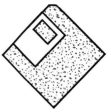

Directory: CHAP3
File: CIRCLEIN.PAS

Figure 3.18   Output Displayed by Procedure Instruct

```
This program computes the area
and circumference of a circle.

To use this program, enter the radius of
the circle after the prompt: Enter radius>

The circumference will be computed in the
same units of measurement as the radius. The
area will be computed in the same units squared.
```

Exercises for Section 3.6

Self-Check

1. Why is it better to place the user instructions in a procedure rather than to insert the WriteLn statements in the program body itself?

Programming

1. Write a procedure similar to Instruct for the pizza program shown in Fig. 3.7.
2. Rewrite the metric conversion program shown in Fig. 3.4 so that it includes a procedure that displays instructions to its user.
3. Show the revised program Circle with a call to Instruct.

3.7 Procedures as Program Building Blocks

Programmers use procedures like building blocks to construct large programs. When you were very young, you probably used alphabet blocks to demonstrate your potential as a budding architect. These blocks were big, with two smooth sides and two sides with "ribs." Unfortunately, you could not use a great many blocks to build a tower without having the tower topple over.

As you grew older, many of you started to play with Lego blocks (see Fig. 3.19). Instead of ribs, each plastic Lego block had one surface with little protrusions and one surface with little cups. By placing the protrusions into the cups, you could build rather elaborate structures.

What does all this have to do with programming? Well, procedures DrawCircle and DrawParallel are like alphabet blocks. You can write some cute little programs with these procedures, but they are not particularly useful. To be able to construct more interesting programs, we must provide procedures with protrusions and cups so they can be easily interconnected.

Figure 3.19 Lego Blocks

105

3.7 Procedures as
Program Building
Blocks

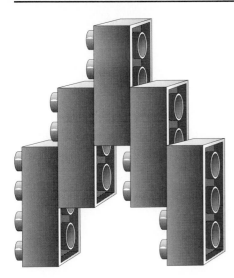

The parameters of a procedure fulfill this purpose. The procedure call statement

```
WriteLn ('The area is ', Area);
```

consists of two parts: the name of the Pascal procedure being called, `WriteLn`, and a parameter list enclosed in parentheses. The parameter list contains two parameters (a string and a variable name) separated by commas. Because it has a parameter list, procedure `WriteLn` is more versatile and, hence, more useful than procedure `DrawCircle`. Procedure `DrawCircle` can display only a circle shape, whereas procedure `WriteLn` can display whatever we want it to.

The parameters of a procedure are used to receive information passed into the procedure from the main program (or another procedure) or to return results computed by the procedure back to the main program (or another procedure). Parameters that receive information from the main program are called *input parameters;* parameters that return results to the main program are called *output parameters*. Figure 3.20 is a diagram of a procedure with inputs and outputs.

Figure 3.20 Procedure with Inputs and Outputs

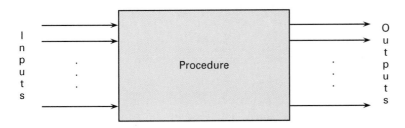

We provide a complete discussion of input and output parameters for procedures in Chapter 6. For the time being, we will only use procedures without parameters to display lengthy messages or instructions to program users. We will also continue to use the Pascal ReadLn, Write, and WriteLn procedures for data entry and display.

Exercises for Section 3.7

Self-Check

1. How does the use of procedure parameters make it possible to write larger, more interesting programs?
2. Why are WriteLn's parameters considered to be input parameters and ReadLn's parameters considered to be output parameters?

3.8 Functions and Reusability

Pascal provides another system structure, called a *function,* that is similar to a procedure and that can also be used as a program building block. Unlike procedures, all function parameters should be input parameters. A function has a single result, which is returned directly to the main program without the use of an output parameter. Figure 3.21 shows a function's inputs and its single output.

Figure 3.21 Function with Multiple Inputs and Single Output

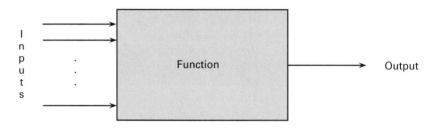

As an example, let's see how we might use a function named Sqrt that performs the square root computation. If X is 16.0, the assignment statement

        Y := Sqrt(X)

is evaluated as follows:

1. X is 16.0, so function Sqrt computes the square root of 16.0, or 4.0.
2. The function result, 4.0, is assigned to Y.

The expression part of this assignment statement is known as a *function designator* and consists of the function name, Sqrt, followed by the function *argument,* X, enclosed in parentheses.

A function can be thought of as a "black box" that is passed one or more input values and automatically returns a single output value. Figure 3.22 illustrates this for the call to function Sqrt. The value of X (16.0) is the function input, and the function result, or output, is the square root of 16.0 (result is 4.0).

Figure 3.22   Function Sqrt as a "Black Box"

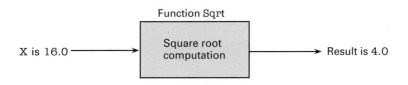

A function is called into execution by a function designator that is written in an expression. After the function executes, its result is substituted for the function designator. If W is 9.0, the assignment statement

```
Z := 5.7 + Sqrt(W)
```

is evaluated as follows:

1. W is 9.0, so function Sqrt computes the square root of 9.0, or 3.0.
2. The value of 5.7 and 3.0 are added together.
3. The sum, 8.7, is stored in Z.

The two calls to function Sqrt discussed so far have different arguments, X and W. We illustrate this feature of functions again in the next example.

■ Example 3.3

The program in Fig. 3.23 displays the square root of two numbers provided as input data (First and Second) and the square root of their sum. To do so, it must call the Pascal function Sqrt three times:

```
Answer := Sqrt(First);
Answer := Sqrt(Second);
Answer := Sqrt(First + Second);
```

For the first two calls, the function arguments are variables (First and Second). The third call shows that a function argument can also be an expression (First + Second). For all three calls, the result returned by function Sqrt is assigned to variable Answer. The program begins with a call to procedure Instruct, which displays some user instructions.

Figure 3.23   Program SquareRoots

```
program SquareRoots (Input, Output);
{Performs three square root computations}

  var
    First, Second,       {input — two data values}
    Answer : Real;       {output — a square root value}
```

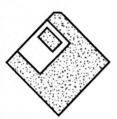

Directory: CHAP3
File: SQUARERO.PAS

```
Procedure Instruct;
{Displays user instructions}

begin {Instruct}
   WriteLn ('This program demonstrates the use of the ');
   WriteLn ('Pascal function Sqrt (square root).');
   WriteLn ('You will be asked to enter two numbers --');
   WriteLn ('the program will display the square root of ');
   WriteLn ('each number and the square root of their sum.');
   WriteLn
end;   {Instruct}

begin   {SquareRoots}
  {Display instructions.}
  Instruct;

  {Get first number and display its square root.}
  Write ('Enter the first number >');
  ReadLn (First);
  Answer := Sqrt(First);
  WriteLn ('The square root of the first number is',
          Answer :4:2);

  {Get second number and display its square root.}
  Write ('Enter the second number >');
  ReadLn (Second);
  Answer := Sqrt(Second);
  WriteLn ('The square root of the second number is',
          Answer :4:2);

  {Display the square root of the sum of both numbers.}
  Answer := Sqrt(First + Second);

  WriteLn ('The square root of the sum of both numbers is ',
          Answer :4:2)
end. {SquareRoots}


This program demonstrates the use of the
Pascal function Sqrt (square root).
You will be asked to enter two numbers --
the program will display the square root of
each number and the square root of their sum.

Enter the first number >9.0
The square root of the first number is 3.00
Enter the second number >16.0
The square root of the second number is 4.00
The square root of the sum of both numbers is 5.00
```

If you look closely at the program in Fig. 3.23, you will see that each statement contains a call to a Pascal procedure (Write, WriteLn, ReadLn, Instruct) or a Pascal function (Sqrt)—we have used Pascal procedures and function Sqrt as building blocks to construct a new program. ∎

Predefined Functions and Reusability

A primary goal of software engineering is to write error-free code. One way to accomplish this goal is to reuse whenever possible code that has already been written and tested. In software engineering, this feature is called *reusability*. Stated more simply, "Why reinvent the wheel?"

Pascal promotes reusability by providing several predefined functions, like Sqrt, that can be used to perform complicated mathematical computations. Table 3.1 lists the names and descriptions of some of these predefined functions.

Table 3.1 Some Predefined Mathematical Functions

Function	Purpose	Argument	Result
Abs(X)	Returns the absolute value of X	Real/Integer	Same as argument
ArcTan(X)	Returns the angle y in radians satisfying $X = \tan(y)$, where $-\pi/2 \leq y \leq \pi/2$	Real/Integer	Real (radians)
Cos(X)	Returns the cosine of angle X	Real/Integer (radians)	Real
Exp(X)	Returns e^x, where $e = 2.71828 \ldots$	Real/Integer	Real
Ln(X)	Returns the natural logarithm of X for $X > 0.0$	Real/Integer	Real
Round(X)	Returns the closest integer value to X	Real	Integer
Sin(X)	Returns the sine of angle X	Real/Integer (radians)	Real
Sqr(X)	Returns the square of X	Real/Integer	Same as argument
Sqrt(X)	Returns the positive square root of X for $X \geq 0.0$	Real/Integer	Real
Trunc(X)	Returns the integral part of X	Real	Integer

Except for Abs, Round, Sqr, and Trunc, each function in Table 3.1 returns (computes) a Real value regardless of its argument type (Real or Integer). The type of the result computed by Abs or Sqr is the same as the type of its argument.

The functions Round and Trunc require type Real arguments and always return type Integer values. These functions determine the integral part of a real-valued expression. Consequently, the expressions

```
Trunc(1.5 * Gross)
Round(Cents / 100)
```

have Integer values and may be assigned to Integer variables. Trunc simply *truncates,* or removes, the fractional part of its argument; Round *rounds* its argument to the nearest whole number. For example, Trunc(17.5) is 17, while Round(17.5) is 18; Trunc(-3.8) is -3, while Round(-3.8) is -4.

Most of the functions in Table 3.1 perform common mathematical computations. The arguments for `Ln` and `Sqrt` must be positive. The arguments for `Sin` and `Cos` must be expressed in radians, not degrees. `ArcTan` expresses its result in radians.

■ Example 3.4

We can use the Pascal functions `Sqr` and `Sqrt` to compute the roots of a quadratic equation in X of the form

$$AX^2 + BX + C = 0$$

The two roots are defined as

$$Root_1 = \frac{-B + \sqrt{B^2 - 4AC}}{2A}, \qquad Root_2 = \frac{-B - \sqrt{B^2 - 4AC}}{2A}$$

when the *discriminant* $(B^2 - 4AC)$ is greater than zero. If we assume that this is the case, we can use the following assignment statements to assign values to `Root1` and `Root2`:

```
{Compute two roots, Root1 and Root2, for Disc >0.0}
Disc := Sqr(B) - 4 * A * C ;
Root1 := (-B + Sqrt(Disc)) / (2 * A);
Root2 := (-B - Sqrt(Disc)) / (2 * A)
```

■

■ Example 3.5

If we know the length of two sides (B and C) of a triangle (see Fig. 3.24) and the angle between them in degrees (*Alpha*), we can compute the length of the thrid side (A) by using the formula

$$A^2 = B^2 + C^2 - 2BC \cos Alpha$$

To use Pascal's cosine function (`Cos`), we must express its argument angle in radians instead of degrees. To convert an angle from degrees to radians, we multiply the angle by $\pi/180$. If we assume that `Pi` represents the constant π, the following Pascal assignment statement computes the unknown side length:

```
A := Sqrt(Sqr(B) + Sqr(C) - 2 * B * C * Cos(Alpha * Pi / 180.0))
```

■

Figure 3.24   Triangle with Unknown Side A

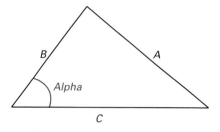

There is no exponentiation operator in Pascal, which means it is not possible to write u^v directly when u and v are type Real. However, the theory of logarithms tells us that

$$ln(u^v) = v \times ln(u)$$

and

$$z = e^{ln(z)}$$

where e is 2.71828. . . . So if we substitute u^v for z in the above equation, we get

$$u^v = e^{ln(u^v)} = e^{(v \times ln(u))}$$

This formula can be implemented in Pascal as ■

```
UToPowerV := Exp(v * Ln(u))
```

A Look at Where We Are Heading

Pascal also allows us to write our own functions. Let's assume that we have already written functions FindArea and FindCircum:

- Function FindArea(R), which returns the area of a circle with radius R
- Function FindCircum(R), which returns the circumference of a circle with radius R

We can reuse these functions in two programs shown earlier in this chapter (see Figs. 3.6 and 3.7). The program in Fig. 3.6 displays the area and circumference of a circle whose radius is provided as input data; Figure 3.25 shows a revised program that uses the two functions FindArea and FindCircum. The program in Fig. 3.25 contains the two assignment statements

```
Area := FindArea(Radius);
Circum := FindCircum(Radius);
```

The expression part of each assignment statement above is a function designator with argument Radius (the circle radius). The result returned by each function execution is stored in an output variable for the program (Area or Circum).

Figure 3.25   Finding Area and Circumference with Functions

```
program CircleFunction (Input, Output);
{Finds and prints the area and circumference of a circle using functions}

   const
     Pi = 3.14159;

   var
     Radius,         {input  - radius of a circle}
     Area,           {output - area of a circle}
     Circum : Real;  {output - circumference of a circle}
```

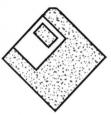

```
{Insert functions FindArea and FindCircum here.}

begin {AreaAndCircum}
  {Read the circle radius.}
  Write ('Enter radius> ');
  ReadLn (Radius);

  {Find the area.}
  Area := FindArea(Radius);

  {Find the circumference.}
  Circum := FindCircum(Radius);

  {Print the area and circumference.}
  WriteLn ('The area is ', Area :4:2);
  WriteLn ('The circumference is ', Circum :4:2)
end. {CircleFunction}
```

```
Enter radius> 5.0
The area is 78.54
The circumference is 31.42
```

The declaration part of Fig. 3.25 contains the comment

```
{Insert functions FindArea and FindCircum here.}
```

which reminds us to insert the functions that we are assuming have already been written and tested. Chapter 6 shows you how to write your own functions.

Besides the advantage of reusing "tried and true" code, using these two functions frees us from having to be concerned with the details of computing a circle's area or circumference when we write the main program. This is one way we can manage and reduce the complexity of writing programs.

Exercises for Section 3.8

Self-Check

1. Rewrite the following mathematical expressions using Pascal functions:

   a. $\sqrt{U + V} \times W^2$
   b. $\log_n (X^Y)$
   c. $\sqrt{(X - Y)^2}$
   d. $|XY - W/Z|$

2. Evaluate the following function designators:

   a. Trunc(-15.8)
   b. Round(-15.8)
   c. Round(6.8) * Sqr(3)
   d. Sqrt(Abs(Round(-15.8)))
   e. Round(3.5)
   f. Sqr(3.0)

1. Write statements that compute and display the absolute difference of the two variables X and Y. If $X > Y$, then the absolute difference is $(X - Y)$; if $Y > X$, then the absolute difference is $(Y - X)$. Use function Abs.
2. Using the Round function, write a Pascal statement to round any real value X to the nearest two decimal places. Hint: You will have to multiply the value by 100.0 before rounding.
3. Write a complete Pascal program that prompts the user for the Cartesian coordinates of two points, $(X1, Y1)$ and $(X2, Y2)$, and displays the distance between them computed by using the following formula:

$$distance = \sqrt{(X1 - X2)^2 + (Y1 - Y2)^2}$$

3.9 Common Programming Errors

Remember to declare each procedure used in a program. Procedure declarations *must* precede procedure calls; they are usually found in the declaration part of a program just after the variable declarations. For the time being, use procedures only to display messages or user instructions.

Syntax or run-time errors may occur when you use Pascal's predefined functions. Make sure that each function argument is the correct type. For example, the arguments for functions Round and Trunc should be type Real. If the argument for function Sqrt or Ln is negative, a run-time error will occur.

CHAPTER REVIEW

The first part of this chapter discussed more aspects of problem solving. We reviewed the top-down approach to solving problems and showed how to use the system documentation created by following the software development method as the framework for the final program. We also demonstrated how to extend the solution to one problem to form the basis of the solution for another problem. We then discussed how structure charts show relationships between different levels of subproblems or between algorithm steps and their refinements.

We discussed the importance of using structured programming techniques to write programs that are easy to read, understand, and maintain. We explained that structured programs consist of sequences of control structures and described the compound statement as a control structure for sequential execution.

We showed how to use a system structure, the procedure, to implement the solution to a subproblem as a separate program module. We also introduced Pascal's built-in functions and discussed how functions enable us to reuse code that has been previously written and tested.

New Pascal Constructs in Chapter 3

The new Pascal constructs introduced in this chapter are described in Table 3.2.

Table 3.2 Summary of New Pascal Constructs

Construct	Effect

Compound Statement
`begin {group}`
`  Write ('Enter x >');`
`  ReadLn (X);`
`  Positive := Abs(X);`
`  Root := Sqrt(Positive)`
`end {group}`
	The statements in the compound statement are executed in sequence.

Procedure Declaration
`procedure Display;`
`{Prints 3 lines}`
`   const`
`     Star = '*';`
 	
`begin {Display}`
`  WriteLn (Star);`
`  WriteLn (Star);`
`  WriteLn (Star)`
`end; {Display}`
	Procedure `Display` is declared and can be called to print three lines of asterisks. The local constant `Star` is defined only when `Display` is executing.

Procedure Call Statement `Display`	Calls procedure `Display` and causes it to begin execution.
Function Designator `Sqrt(X + Y)`	Calls function `Sqrt` to compute the square root of the expression `X + Y`.

✓ Quick-Check Exercises

1. The principle of reusability states that every procedure in your program must be used more than once. True or false?
2. Developing a program from its documentation means that every statement in the program has a comment. True or false?
3. Are `WriteLn`'s parameters input parameters or output parameters?
4. Each procedure is executed in the order in which it is declared in the main program. True or false?
5. How is a procedure executed in a program?
6. List the order of the declarations in a program.
7. What is a procedure parameter?

8. Explain how a structure chart differs from an algorithm.
9. Write this equation as a Pascal statement using functions Exp, Ln, and Sqr:

$$y = (e^{a \ ln \ b})^2$$

10. What does the following procedure do?

```
procedure Nonsense;
begin {Nonsense}
   WriteLn ('*****');
   WriteLn ('*   *');
   WriteLn ('*****')
end; {Nonsense}
```

11. What does the following program body do?

```
begin
   Nonsense;
   Nonsense;
   Nonsense
end.
```

Answers to Quick-Check Exercises

1. false
2. false
3. input
4. false
5. It is called into execution by a procedure call statement.
6. constants, variables, procedures
7. Parameters are used to receive information from the caller or to pass results back to the caller.
8. A structure chart shows the relationship between subproblems; an algorithm lists the sequence in which subproblems are performed.
9. Y := Sqr(Exp(A * Ln(B)));
10. It displays a rectangle.
11. It displays three rectangles on top of each other.

Review Questions

1. Describe what it means to extend a problem solution.
2. The diagram that shows the algorithm steps and their interdependencies is called a

   _____.

3. What are three advantages of using procedures?
4. When is a procedure executed and where must it appear in the main program?
5. Is the use of procedures a more efficient use of the programmer's time or the computer's time? Explain your answer.
6. How do functions differ from procedures?
7. Write a program that prompts the user for the two legs of a right triangle and makes use of the Sqr and Sqrt functions and the Pythagorean theorem to compute the length of the hypotenuse.
8. Write a program that draws a rectangle made up of asterisks. Use two procedures: DrawSides and DrawLine.
9. Draw a structure chart for the program described in review exercise 8.

Programming Projects

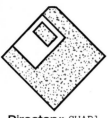

1. Write two procedures, one that displays a triangle and one that displays a rectangle. Use these procedures to write a complete Pascal program from the following outline.

```
program StackHouses (Input, Output);
begin
   {1. Draw triangle.}
   {2. Draw rectangle.}
   {3. Print 2 blank lines.}
   {4. Draw triangle.}
   {5. Draw rectangle.}
end;
```

2. Add the procedures from Fig. 3.13 to the ones for project 1. Use these procedures in a program that draws a rocket ship (triangle over rectangles over intersecting lines), a male stick figure (circle over rectangle over intersecting lines), and a female stick figure standing on the head of a male stick figure. Write procedure Skip5Lines and call it to place five blank lines between each drawing.

3. Write procedures to display your initials in block-letter form, then execute these procedures.

4. Write a computer program that computes the duration of a projectile's flight and its height above the ground when it reaches the target. As part of your solution, write and call a procedure that displays instructions to the program user.

   Problem constant
      G = 32.17   {gravitational constant}

   Problem input
      Theta   : Real   {input — angle (radians) of elevation}
      Distance : Real   {input — distance (ft) to target}
      Velocity : Real   {input — projectile velocity (ft/sec)}

   Problem output
      Time   : Real   {output — time (sec) of flight}
      Height   : Real   {output — height at impact}

   Relevant formulas
      time   = *distance/(velocity* × cos(*Theta*))
      height = *velocity* × *time* − (*g* × *time*^{2})/2

5. Four track stars entered the mile race at the Penn Relays. Write a program that will read in the race time in minutes (Minutes) and seconds (Seconds) for a runner and compute and print the speed in feet per second (FPS) and in meters per second (MPS). (Hints: There are 5,280 feet in one mile, and one kilometer equals 3,282 feet.) Test your program on the following times.

Minutes	Seconds
3	52.83
3	59.83
4	00.03
4	16.22

   Write and call a procedure that displays instructions to the program user.

6. A cyclist coasting on a level road slows from a speed of 10 miles per hour to 2.5 miles

per hour in one minute. Write a computer program that calculates the cyclist's constant rate of acceleration and determines how long it will take the cyclist to come to rest, given an initial speed of 10 miles per hour. (Hint: Use the equation

$$a = (v_f - v_i)/t$$

where a is acceleration, t is time interval, v_i is initial velocity, and v_f is final velocity.) Write and call a procedure that displays instructions to the program user.

7. In shopping for a new house, you must consider several factors. In this problem, the initial cost of the house, the estimated annual fuel costs, and the annual tax rate are available. Write a program that will determine the total cost of a house after a five-year period for each of the following sets of data. You should be able to inspect your program output to determine the best buy.

Initial House Cost	Annual Fuel Cost	Tax Rate
$67,000	$2,300	0.025
$62,000	$2,500	0.025
$75,000	$1,850	0.020

To calculate the house cost, add the initial cost to the fuel cost for five years, then add the taxes for five years. Taxes for one year are computed by multiplying the tax rate by the initial cost. Write and call a procedure that displays instructions to the program user.

8. A manufacturer wants to determine the cost of producing an open-top cylindrical container. The surface area of the container is the sum of the area of the base (π times the radius squared) plus the area of the side (2π times the radius times the height of the container). Write a program to read in the radius (Radius) of the base, the height (Height) of the container, the cost per square centimeter of the material (Cost), and the number of containers to be produced (Quantity). Calculate the cost of each container and the total cost of producing all the containers. Write and call a procedure that displays instructions to the user.

INTERVIEW
Peter J. Denning

Peter J. Denning is Associate Dean for Computing and Chair of the Computer Science Department at George Mason University. Previously, he was founding Director of and Research Fellow at the Research Institute for Advanced Computer Science (RIACS) at the NASA Ames Research Center. His primary research interests include computer systems architecture, parallel computation, operating systems, and performance modeling.

What influenced you to become a computer scientist?

I got there less by deliberative choice than by drift. From an early age, I was interested in science, especially astronomy and botany. By seventh grade, stimulated by a desire to build a completely automatic signal control system for my Lionel trains, I studied electricity. Shortly thereafter, stimulated by an interest in radio and telephone communications, I studied electronics. These pursuits left me with a wealth of relays from an old pinball machine, which made their way into two computers I designed and built for the Southern Connecticut Science Fair. One was an adding machine, the other a linear equation solver—and both prize-winners. By graduation, I had high momentum for studying electrical engineering with specialization in computers, which I did in college and graduate school.

What is a computer scientist?

If you asked me this a year ago, I would have given you the widely accepted definition: a computer scientist is a professional scientist who specializes in computers and the study of phenomena surrounding computers. But I have begun to question this definition. As I look at other professions, such as medicine and law, I see that they are made up of people, technologies, institutions, and practices that have emerged to take care of other people's recurrent concerns in given domains (such as health and law). The domain of recurrent and permanent concern that has given rise to the computing profession is information processing and communications. We have developed technologies (computers and networks), institutions (schools, professional societies, magazines, book publishers, etc.), and standards (programming languages, software engineering, databases, communication protocols, operating systems, etc.) to address these concerns.

So I now say it's the other way around. The concerns are not phenomena that surround the computers. The computers surround the concerns.

You have stated elsewhere that "computer science educators and researchers are experiencing an increasing sense of isolation." Why do you say this?

As long as computer scientists are convinced they are studying phenomena surrounding computers, they will not see the concerns of people in the world. They will propose new algorithms for shared memory management without checking whether anyone is buying computers with memory partitioned among distinct tasks. They will study formal methods for software design without learning how a customer has organized work.

I wouldn't conclude that the computer scientist isn't working on something important. What's missing is the practice of articulating the connection between one's work and the concerns of others.

Deep in the recesses of modern medical research laboratories you'll find scientists working on delicate, highly sophisticated experiments that only a few people in the whole world can understand technically. If you ask why they do it, you are likely to hear, "If our hypothesis is borne out, we will have the key to curing Alzheimer's disease." Until computer science researchers can similarly express the relevance of their work to others, outsiders may wonder how well connected computer science research and education are to real concerns.

You have written, "Computer science should embrace applications and computational science. The interaction between computing and other disciplines must be a mutual exchange, not simply a one-way process of passing out help on request." What role does computing education play in this?

I defined the computing profession as the people who devote their careers to taking care of the concerns of others in information processing and communications. (In saying this I intentionally imply that the computing and communications professions are coming together.) People in other disciplines are finding it impossible to be successful in their businesses without computing. They need the help of experts to design, install, and maintain computers and software to help them succeed in their work. In a similar way, computational science—the study of physical phenomena using very high-speed computation—needs the expertise of computer scientists for designing highly parallel algorithms, languages, and operating systems. Many computer scientists have convinced themselves that people in these other disciplines simply want better programmers. Computer scientists often call these other disciplines "applications," an appellation that hides opportunities for the advancement of computer science.

In truth, the people in those disciplines want partners who are willing to understand their problems and help solve them. A partnership will lead to the professional advancement of both the computer scientist and the other professional.

Computing education must include training in the basic skill of working with people from other disciplines.

In his 1968 Turing Lecture, R. W. Hamming said, "We must give a good deal of attention to broad training in the field. . . . We need to prepare our students for the year 2000 when many of them will be at the peak of their career. It seems to me to be more true in computer science than in many other fields that 'special-ization leads to triviality.' " What do you say to this?

Hamming saw early what many are coming to see today: if others judge that you are esoteric and specialized, they will conclude that you have nothing to offer them, and they will leave you alone. This is where the isolation comes from. I fully agree that a broad education is the only defense against excessive specialization and isolation.

One of the key elements of a broad education is the skill of learning to learn. This may sound like what we all came together to do in college. But most of college is spent on "instruction," which has been characterized as the transfer of a subset from the store of scientific knowledge into the porous minds of the students. I maintain that there is less learning taught than most people think in universities, and that there is a connection between our information-flow model of teaching and the complaints of our graduates and our employers that students are not adequately prepared for the jobs they take after graduation.

Learning to learn implies a practical understanding of the way we progress through different stages of competence in a domain, from beginner to expert. It requires the skill of organizing one's time to learn, the skill of reading books and literature, the skill of talking to others, the skill of writing notes and short papers articulating half-formed ideas. And most of all, it requires the skill of finding a teacher—someone more competent than you who is willing to make assessments about your progress, and is able to guide you to practices that will produce your own capability for action in the new domain.

We often hear and read about ethics in a range of professions—medicine, law, politics—and it appears that those professions have gone some distance toward articulating a code of ethical behavior. Is that true of computer science?

Indeed, many professions have articulated values and standards for the practice of their profession. The major societies in the computing profession—ACM, IEEE, and DPMA—have articulated codes of ethics, and many business executives articulated standards for responsible behavior in their organizations.

It's only been since 1985 that computers have exploded into a pervasive presence in business, first as stand-alone tools and now as ports to the worldwide network. Not until 1988 did computer break-ins and virus attacks become enough of a disruption to gain public attention. The ensuing debate has questioned whether young people are learning to be responsible citizens in a world of computers and networks, where fortunes can rise and fall on the integrity of information. In consequence, more organizations are promulgating codes of conduct, schools are paying more attention to the social network in which computer scientists will practice, and the professional societies are endorsing improved codes of ethics and fair information practice.

This is a period of transition. We will emerge with much clearer, shared understandings of responsible conduct in computers and networks.

How would you define a "socially responsible" computer scientist?

That's a good question. To begin with, we must remember that "responsibility" is an assessment made by others as a consequence of one's actions. We should therefore identify the kinds of actions that would lead others to characterize a person as responsible. In general, responsible people are those who, through their actions, lead others to characterize them as trustworthy, forthright, reliable, and honest.

To say that a person is responsible in a domain of action is to say that the person fulfills promises, honors commitments, and lives up to obligations in that domain. There are a number of dimensions along which a person can make commitments and incur obligations, most notably morality, formal contracts, informal everyday agreements, laws and regula-tions, standard practices, and declarations. In a given situation, a responsible computer scientist, or any responsible person, is aware of commitments and obligations along all these dimensions and organizes actions to be consistent with them all.

The responsible person is able to make well-grounded assessments of the consequences of actions on others. That person will anticipate negative consequences and take care of them. If an action results in unanticipated negative consequences, the person will take steps to undo or mitigate them.

The responsible manager takes care that people in the group orient their actions to fulfill the group's missions, and that each group member is growing and developing in his or her career.

Finally, responsible people are also educated on the history of the communities in which they live and work. Cultural background and historical traditions affect what actions are possible and how other people will react. One need not slavishly stick with traditions, but one needs to have one's eyes open when departing from traditions.

I include all of these elements in the dimensions of a socially responsible computer scientist.

4

Selection Structures: if and case Statements

This chapter shows you how to write algorithms and programs with steps that select from several courses of action. You will see two ways to do this in Pascal. The first technique is to use a Pascal `if` statement with a Boolean expression; the second approach is to use a `case` statement. This chapter provides many examples of `if` and `case` statements. It also introduces syntax diagrams and shows you how to use them to check the syntax of a Pascal construct.

We continue our study of problem solving and introduce one more problem-solving strategy: solution by analogy. We describe how to use data flow information in structure charts to provide additional system documentation. We also explain how to hand-check, or trace, the execution of an algorithm or program to ensure that it does what we expect it to.

4.1 Boolean Expressions

In all the algorithms illustrated so far, we executed each algorithm step exactly once in the order in which it appeared. Often, however, we are faced with situations in which we must provide alternative steps that may or may not be executed, depending on the input data. For example, the tax rate assessed by the Internal Revenue Service (IRS) depends on an individual's salary. Single persons who earn less than \$18,550 pay a tax rate of 15%, while those who earn between \$18,550 and \$44,900 pay a tax rate of 15% on the first \$18,550 and a tax rate of 28% on the rest. Consequently, an income tax program must be able to select the correct tax rate to use in a tax computation.

To accomplish this goal, a program must be able to determine whether the correct answer to the question "Is annual income less than \$18,550?" is "Yes" or "No." In Pascal, this is accomplished by evaluating a Boolean expression. Assuming that the taxable income is stored in the type `Real` variable `Income`, the Boolean expression corresponding to this question is

```
Income < 18500.00
```

There are only two possible values for a Boolean expression: `True` or `False`. If `Income` is less than `18500.00`, the Boolean expression above evaluates to `True`; if `Income` is not less than `18500.00`, the expression evaluates to `False`.

Most Boolean expressions, or *conditions*, that we use have one of these forms:

variable relational-operator variable
variable relational-operator constant

Relational operators are the familiar symbols < (less than), <= (less than or equal to), > (greater than), >= (greater than or equal to), = (equal to), or <> (not equal to). The two operands of a relational operator must be the same data type (both type `Boolean`, `Char`, `Integer`, or `Real`), or one may be type `Real` and the other type `Integer`. A *constant* may be a *literal constant* (e.g., 3, 4.5, 'X') or a constant identifier (e.g., Pi).

■ Example 4.1

Table 4.1 shows the relational operators and some sample conditions. Each condition is evaluated assuming the following variable values.

X   Power   MaxPow   Y   Item   MinItem   MomOrDad   Num   Sentinel
-5   1024   1024   7   1.5   -999.0   'M'   999   999

Table 4.1 Pascal Relational Operators and Sample Conditions

Operator	Condition	Meaning	Boolean Value
<=	X <= 0	X less than or equal to 0	True
<	Power < MaxPow	Power less than MaxPow	False
>=	X >= Y	X greater than or equal to Y	False
>	Item > MinItem	Item greater than MinItem	True
=	MomOrDad = 'M'	MomOrDad equal to 'M'	True
<>	Num <> Sentinel	Num not equal to Sentinel	False

■

Boolean Variables and Constants

The simplest Boolean expression is a Boolean variable or constant that can be set to either of the Boolean values, True or False. The statement

```
const
  Debug = True;
```

specifies that the Boolean constant Debug has the value True; the statement

```
var
  Switch, Flag : Boolean;
```

declares Switch and Flag to be Boolean variables—variables that may be assigned only the values True and False. Given these declarations, the following assignment statements are all valid.

```
Switch := Debug;      {Switch gets True}
Flag := False;        {Flag gets False}
Switch := Flag;       {Switch gets value of Flag}
```

After executing these statements, both Flag and Switch will have the value False.

Boolean Operators

A Boolean variable or constant is the simplest form of a Boolean expression (for example, Switch). As we discussed earlier, we can use the relational operators (<, =, >, and so on) to form simple Boolean expressions or conditions (e.g., Income < 18500.00).

We can use Boolean operators to form more complicated Boolean expressions. There are three Boolean operators: and, or, and not. These operators require type `Boolean` operands. Examples of Boolean expressions formed with these operators are

```
(Salary < MinSal) or (NumDepend > 5)
(Temp > 90.0) and (Humidity > 0.90)
WinningRecord and (not Probation)
```

The first Boolean expression determines whether an employee is eligible for special scholarship funds. It evaluates to `True` if either condition in parentheses is true. The second Boolean expression describes an unbearable summer day, with temperature and humidity both in the nineties. The expression evaluates to `True` only when both conditions are true. The third Boolean expression manipulates two Boolean variables (`WinningRecord`, `Probation`.) A college team for which this expression is true may be eligible for the postseason tournament.

The Boolean operators, which can be used only with Boolean expressions, are described in Tables 4.2, 4.3, and 4.4.

Table 4.2 The and Operator

operand1	operand2	operand1 and operand2
true	true	true
true	false	false
false	true	false
false	false	false

Table 4.3 The or Operator

operand1	operand2	operand1 or operand2
true	true	true
true	false	true
false	true	true
false	false	false

Table 4.4 The not Operator

operand1	not operand1
true	false
false	true

Table 4.2 shows that the and operator yields a true result only when both its operands are true. Table 4.3 shows that the or operator yields a false result only when both its operands are false. The not operator has a single operand; Table 4.4 shows that the not operator yields the *logical complement*, or negation, of its operand (that is, if `Switch` is `True`, `not Switch` is `False` and vice versa).

The precedence of an operator determines its order of evaluation. Table

4.5 shows the precedence of all operators in Pascal, including the relational operators.

125

4.1 Boolean
Expressions

Table 4.5 Operator Precedence

Operator	Precedence
not	Highest (evaluated first)
*, /, div, mod, and	
+, −, or	
< , <= , = , <> , >= , >, in	Lowest (evaluated last)

As you can see, the `not` operator has the highest precedence, followed by the multiplicative operators (including `and`), the additive operators (including `or`), and, last, the relational operators. The relational operator `in` is discussed in Section 7.4. Since the relational operators have the lowest precedence, they generally should be used with parentheses to prevent syntax errors.

■ Example 4.2

The expression

```
X < Min + Max
```

involving the real variables X, Min, and Max is interpreted correctly as

```
X < (Min + Max)
```

because + has higher precedence than <. However, the expression

```
Min <= X and X <= Max
```

causes the syntax error *invalid type of operands*. It is interpreted as

```
Min <= (X and X) <= Max
```

because and has higher precedence than <. This is an error because the type `Real` variable X cannot be an operand of the Boolean operator and.

The above error is quite common; however, you can easily avoid this error and similar ones by using parentheses freely. The use of parentheses as shown below would prevent a syntax error:

```
(Min <= X) and (X <= Max)
```

■

Testing for a Range of Values

Expressions similar to the preceding one are common in programming. If Min represents the lower bound of a range of values and Max represents the upper bound (Min is less than Max), the expression tests whether X lies within the range Min through Max, inclusive. In Fig. 4.1, this range of values is shaded. The expression is true if X lies within this range and false if X is outside the range.

Figure 4.1 Range of True Values for (Min <= X) and (X <= Max)

Min   Max

More Boolean Expressions

■ Example 4.3

The following Boolean expressions are all legal if X, Y, and Z are type Real and Flag is type Boolean. The value of each expression, shown in brackets, assumes that X is 3.0, Y is 4.0, Z is 2.0, and Flag is False.

1. `(X > Z) and (Y > Z)`   [True]
2. `(X + Y / Z) <= 3.5`   [False]
3. `(Z > X) or (Z > Y)`   [False]
4. `not Flag`   [True]
5. `(X = 1.0) or (X = 3.0)`   [True]
6. `(Z < X) and (X < Y)`   [True]
7. `(X <= Z) or (X >= Y)`   [False]
8. `(not Flag) or ((Y + Z) >= (X - Z))`   [True]
9. `not (Flag or ((Y + Z) >= (X - Z)))`   [False]

Expression 1 gives the Pascal form of the relationship "X and Y are greater than Z." It is often tempting to write this as

```
X and Y > Z
```

However, this is an illegal Boolean expression because the Real variable X cannot be an operand of the Boolean operator and. Similarly, expression 5 shows the correct way to express the relationship "X is equal to 1.0 or to 3.0."

Expression 6 is the Pascal form of the relationship Z < X < Y (i.e., "X is in the range Z (2.0) to Y (4.0)"). The boundary values, 2.0 and 4.0, are excluded from the range of X values that yield a result of True.

Expression 7 is true if the value of X lies outside the range bounded by Z and Y. In Fig. 4.2, the shaded areas represent the values of X that yield a True result. Both Y and Z are included in the set of values that yield a True result.

Figure 4.2 Range of True Values for (X <= Z) or (X >= Y)

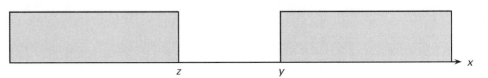

z   y

Finally, expression 8 is evaluated in Fig. 4.3; the values given at the beginning of Example 4.3 are shown above the expression. ■

Figure 4.3   Evaluation Tree for (not Flag) or ((Y + Z) >= (X − Z))

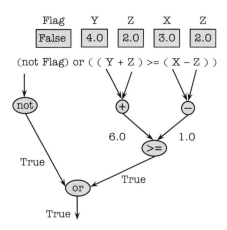

Boolean Assignment

We can write assignment statements that assign a Boolean value to a Boolean variable. If Same is type Boolean, the statement

```
Same := True
```

assigns the value True to Same. Since assignment statements have the general form

    variable := *expression*

we can use the statement

```
Same := (X = Y)
```

to assign the value of the Boolean expression (X = Y) to Same. The value of Same will be True when X and Y are equal; otherwise, Same will be False.

■ Example 4.4

The following assignment statements assign values to two Boolean variables, InRange and IsLetter. InRange gets True if the value of N is in the range −10 through 10; IsLetter gets True if Ch is an uppercase or a lowercase letter.

```
InRange := (-10 <= N) and (N <= 10);
IsLetter := (('A' <= Ch) and (Ch <= 'Z') or
             ('a' <= Ch) and (Ch <= 'z'))
```

The expression in the first assignment statement is True if N satisfies both of the conditions listed (N is greater than −10 and less than 10); otherwise, the expression is False. The expression in the second assignment statement uses the Boolean operators and and or. The subexpression on the first line is True if Ch is an uppercase letter; the subexpression on the second line is True if Ch is a lowercase letter. Consequently, IsLetter gets True if Ch is a letter; otherwise, IsLetter gets False. ∎

∎ Example 4.5

Either of the following assignment statements assigns the value True to Even (type Boolean) if N is an even number:

```
Even := not (Odd(N))        |        Even := (N mod 2) = 0
```

The statement on the left calls the Pascal function Odd, which returns True if N is an odd number and False if N is an even number. The not operator complements the value of the function result and assigns it to Even. Consequently, Even gets True if Odd(N) returns False (N is an even number). The expression on the right assigns a value of True to Even when the remainder of N divided by 2 is zero. (All even numbers are divisible by 2.) ∎

Reading and Writing Boolean Values

As you will see in the next section, Boolean expressions appear primarily in control structures, where they are used to determine the sequence in which Pascal statements are executed. We do not usually process Boolean data in the same way that we process numerical data. Consequently, we rarely read Boolean values as input data or display Boolean values as program results. If necessary, we can display the value of a Boolean variable using procedure Write or WriteLn; however, we cannot use procedure ReadLn to read in a Boolean variable. (We explain how to read a Boolean value in Chapter 7.) If Switch is False, the statement

```
WriteLn ('Value of Switch is ', Switch)
```

displays the line

```
Value of Switch is FALSE
```

Exercises for Section 4.1

Self-Check

1. Assuming X is 15.0 and Y is 25.0, what are the values of the following conditions?

    ```
    X <> Y      X < X      X >= (Y - X)      X = (Y + X - Y)
    ```

2. Evaluate each of the following expressions if A is 5, B is 10, C is 15, and Flag is True.
    a. (C = (A + B)) or not Flag
    b. (A <> 7) and (C >= 6) or Flag
    c. not (B <= 12) and (A mod 2 = 0)
    d. not ((A > 5) or (C < (A + B)))

3. Draw the evaluation tree for expression 9 of Example 4.3.

1. Write a Boolean expression for each of the following relationships.
   a. X is in the range −1.5 to 3.2.
   b. A is in the range 17 to 23, inclusive.
   c. Y is greater than X and less than Z.
   d. W is equal to 6 or not greater than 3.

2. Write the following Boolean assignment statements.
   a. Assign a value of True to Between if N is in the range −K and +K, inclusive; otherwise, assign a value of False.
   b. Assign a value of True to Uppercase if Ch is an uppercase-letter; otherwise, assign a value of False.
   c. Assign a value of True to Divisor if M is a divisor of N; otherwise, assign a value of False.

4.2 The if Statement

A Pascal programmer can use the if statement to select among several alternatives. An if statement always contains a Boolean expression. For example, the if statement

```
if Gross > 100.00 then
   Net := Gross − Tax
else
   Net := Gross
```

selects one of the two assignment statements listed. It selects the statement following then if the Boolean expression is true (i.e., Gross is greater than 100.00); it selects the statement following else if the Boolean expression is false (i.e., Gross is not greater than 100.00).

Figure 4.4 is a graphical description, called a *flowchart,* of the preceding if statement. A flowchart shows the step-by-step execution of a control statement or program fragment. A diamond-shaped box in a flowchart indicates a condition. There is always one path into a condition and two paths out (labeled True and False). A rectangular box indicates an assignment statement or a process.

Figure 4.4 shows that the condition (Gross > 100.00) is evaluated first. If the condition is true, the arrow labeled True is followed, and the assignment statement in the rectangle on the right is executed. If the condition is false, the arrow labeled False is followed, and the assignment statement in the rectangle on the left is executed.

More Examples of if Statements

The if statement above has two alternatives, but only one will be executed for a given value of Gross. Example 4.6 illustrates that an if statement can also have a single alternative that is executed only when the condition is true.

Figure 4.4 Flowchart of if Statement with Two Alternatives

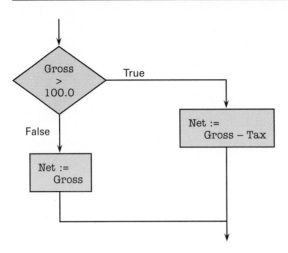

■ Example 4.6

The following if statement has one alternative, which is executed only when X is not equal to 0. It causes Product to be multiplied by X; the new value is saved in Product, replacing the old value. If X is equal to 0, the multiplication is not performed. Figure 4.5 is a flowchart of this if statement.

```
{Multiply Product by a nonzero X only}
if X <> 0.0 then
   Product := Product * X
```

■

Figure 4.5 Flowchart of if Statement with One Alternative

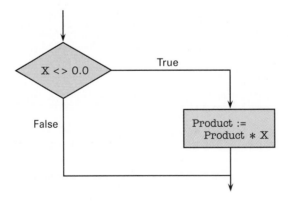

■ Example 4.7

The following statement has two alternatives. It displays either 'Hi Mom' or 'Hi Dad', depending on the character stored in the variable MomOrDad (type Char).

```
if MomOrDad = 'M' then
   WriteLn ('Hi Mom')
```

```
    else
       WriteLn ('Hi Dad')
```

■ Example 4.8

The following if statement has one alternative; it displays the message 'Hi Mom' only when MomOrDad has the value 'M'. Regardless of whether or not 'Hi Mom' is displayed, the message 'Hi Dad' is always displayed. The semicolon terminates the if statement and is needed to separate the if statement from the second call to procedure WriteLn.

```
if MomOrDad = 'M' then
   WriteLn ('Hi Mom');
WriteLn ('Hi Dad')
```

The next if statement is incorrect because the semicolon appears before the line else. The compiler will detect a syntax error when it reaches the line else because the semicolon terminates the if statement, and a new statement cannot begin with else.

```
if MomOrDad = 'M' then
   WriteLn ('Hi Mom');
else                    {error – new statement begins with else}
   WriteLn ('Hi Dad')
```

Syntax Displays for if Statements

The following display summarizes the forms of the if statement we have used so far. The next section illustrates the use of if statements and decision steps in solving problems.

SYNTAX
DISPLAY

---

if Statement (One Alternative)

Form: if *condition* then
              statement$_T$

Example: if X > 0.0 then
             PosProd := PosProd * X

Interpretation: If *condition* evaluates to True, then *statement*$_T$ is executed; otherwise, *statement*$_T$ is skipped.

SYNTAX
DISPLAY

---

if Statement (Two Alternatives)

Form: if *condition* then
              statement$_T$
          else
              statement$_F$

Example: `if X >= 0.0 then`
       `Write ('Positive')`
    `else`
       `Write ('Negative')`

Interpretation: If *condition* evaluates to True, then *statement*$_T$ is executed and *statement*$_F$ is skipped; otherwise, *statement*$_T$ is skipped and *statement*$_F$ is executed.

PROGRAM
STYLE

Format of the if Statement

In all the `if` statement examples in this text, *statement*$_T$ and *statement*$_F$ are indented. The word `else` is entered on a separate line, aligned with the word `if`. The format of the `if` statement makes its meaning apparent. We do this solely to improve program readability; the format makes no difference to the compiler.

Exercises for Section 4.2

Self-Check

1. What do the following statements display?

  a. `if 12 < 12 then`
      `WriteLn ('Never')`
    `else`
      `WriteLn ('Always')`

  b. `Var1 := 15.0;`
    `Var2 := 25.12;`
    `if Var2 <= 2 * Var1 then`
      `WriteLn ('O.K.')`
    `else`
      `WriteLn ('Not O.K.')`

2. What value is assigned to X for each of the following segments when Y is 15.0?

  a. `X := 25.0;`
    `if Y <> (X - 10.0) then`
      `X := X - 10.0`
    `else`
      `X := X / 2.0;`

  b. `if (Y < 15.0) and (Y >= 0.0) then`
      `X := 5 * Y`
    `else`
      `X := 2 * Y;`

Programming

1. Write Pascal statements to carry out the following steps.

  a. If `Item` is nonzero, then multiply `Product` by `Item` and save the result in

Product; otherwise, skip the multiplication. In either case, print the value of Product.

b. Store the absolute difference of X and Y in Z, where the absolute difference is (X − Y) or (Y − X), whichever is positive. Do not use the Abs function in your solution.

c. If X is 0, add 1 to ZeroCount. If X is negative, add X to MinusSum. If X is greater than 0, add X to PlusSum.

4.3 Syntax Diagrams

Until now we have used syntax displays to describe each new Pascal construct. The complete syntax of Pascal can also be described using special *syntax diagrams*. Syntax diagrams are sometimes called railroad diagrams because they resemble diagrams that show the track layout for a model railroad. We introduce syntax diagrams at this point because they enable us to describe succinctly the syntax of Pascal control structures.

As an example, let's study the syntax diagram for the *program* shown in Fig. 4.6. The diagram consists of a group of syntactic elements connected by arrows. The category of each syntactic element is indicated by its shape:

- Reserved words are enclosed in ovals.
- Special symbols (punctuation marks and operators) are enclosed in circles.
- Syntactic elements with their own syntax diagrams are enclosed in rectangles.

Figure 4.6   Syntax Diagram for Program

program

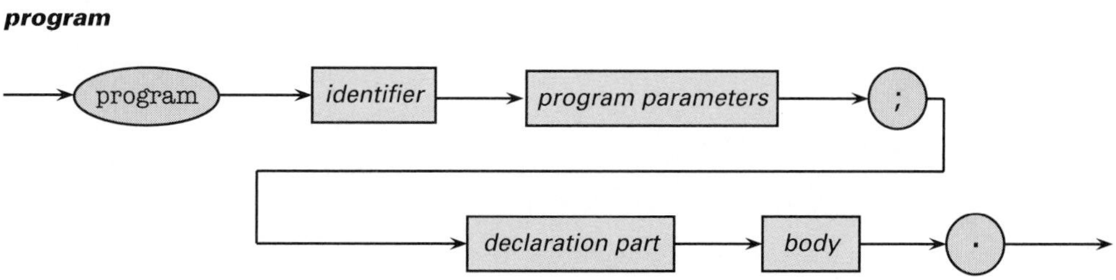

If we trace through the top row of Fig. 4.6 following the arrows, we see that a Pascal program begins with the reserved word program, an *identifier*, *program parameters*, and a semicolon. The program header

```
program First (Input, Output);
```

satisfies this part of the syntax diagram, provided that First is an *identifier* and (Input, Output) are *program parameters*. To determine whether this is true, we have to check the syntax diagrams for both these syntactic elements, which we will do next. The rest of the syntax diagram for *program* indicates that the semicolon should be followed by the syntactic elements *declaration part, body,* and the period symbol.

The syntax diagram for *identifier* (see Fig. 4.7) shows that an *identifier* may be a single *letter* (A-Z, a-z). We determine this by tracing the horizontal arrow at the top of the diagram from left to right. By tracing through the loops in the diagram, we see that the initial *letter* may be followed by one or more *letter* or *digit* (0-9) characters (for example, R2D2, First). This corresponds to our earlier definition of *identifier* (see Section 2.3).

Figure 4.7   Syntax Diagrams for *identifier* and *program parameters*

identifier

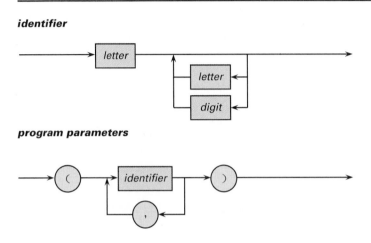

program parameters

The syntax diagram for *program parameters* (see Fig. 4.7) shows that *program parameters* consist of one or more *identifier* elements separated by the comma symbol and enclosed in parentheses. Each time we trace around the loop, we add a comma symbol and another *identifier* to the *program parameters*. Examples we have seen so far are (Output) and (Input, Output).

To complete the description of the syntax for a Pascal *program*, we must provide syntax diagrams for the syntactic elements *declaration part* and *body*. The diagram for *declaration part* is provided in Appendix B, along with the other syntactic elements of Pascal. The syntax diagram for *body* (see Fig. 4.8) shows that a program *body* is a *compound statement,* or a sequence of one or more *statement* elements separated by semicolons and bracketed by begin and end.

Figure 4.8   Syntax Diagrams for *body* and *compound statement*

body

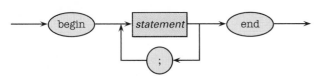

You can use syntax diagrams to verify that a program statement is correct before you enter it. If a syntax error occurs during debugging, you can refer to the appropriate syntax diagram to determine the correct form of the element that is incorrect. Appendix B contains all Pascal syntax diagrams.

Exercises for Section 4.3

Self-Check

1. Which of these identifiers satisfies the syntax diagram that follows?

   Ace   R2D2   R245   A23B   A1c   B34d5c   A23cd

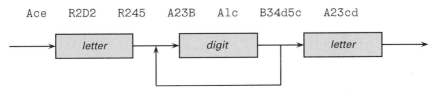

2. Draw a syntax diagram that might be used to describe Real-like numeric literals that begin with a digit, end with a digit, and contain a single decimal point somewhere in between.

4.4 if Statements with Compound Statements

Figure 4.9 shows the syntax diagram for an if statement. Two paths lead from the leftmost arrow to the rightmost arrow. We define an if statement with one alternative by tracing the horizontal path at the top of the diagram. We define an if statement with two alternatives by tracing the path that leads down and through the reserved word else.

Figure 4.9 Syntax Diagram for an if Statement

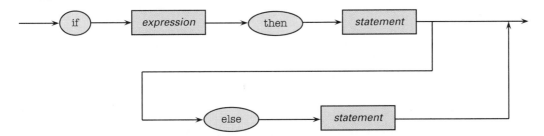

The *statement* following the word then or else may be a single executable statement or a compound statement. Some of the statements that can be used are assignment statements, procedure call statements, and other if statements.

More Examples of if Statements

This section provides examples of if statements with compound statements following then or else.

■ Example 4.9

Suppose you manage a clothing boutique and are planning a spring sale. You could use the following if statement to compute the discounted price of an item. The statement first determines the discount by multiplying the item price and the discount rate (a fraction); next, it deducts the discount from the item price. The compound statement is not executed when the discount rate is 0.

```
if DiscRate <> 0.0 then
   begin
      Discount := Price * DiscRate;    {Compute discount amount}
      Price := Price - Discount        {Deduct discount from price}
   end {if}
```
■

■ Example 4.10

Later chapters show the usefulness of being able to order a pair of data values in memory so that the smaller value is stored in one variable (say, X) and the larger value in another (say, Y). The if statement in Fig. 4.10 rearranges any two values stored in X and Y so that the smaller number will always be in X and the larger number will always be in Y. If the two numbers are already in the proper order, the compound statement will not be executed.

Figure 4.10   if Statement to Order X and Y

```
if X > Y then
   begin {switch X and Y}
      Temp := X;                    {Store old X in Temp}
      X := Y;                       {Store old Y in X}
      Y := Temp                     {Store old X in Y}
   end {if}
```

The variables X, Y, and Temp should all be the same data type. Although the values of X and Y are being switched, an additional variable, Temp, is needed to store a copy of one of these values.

Table 4.6 is a step-by-step simulation of the execution of this if statement when X is 12.5 and Y is 5.0. The table shows that Temp is initially undefined (indicated by ?). Each line of the table shows the part of the if statement that is being executed, followed by its effect. If any variable gets a new value, its new value is shown on that line. The last value stored in X is 5.0, and the last value stored in Y is 12.5.
■

Statement Part	X	Y	Temp	Effect
	12.5	5.0	?	
if X > Y then				12.5 > 5.0 is true.
Temp := X;			12.5	Store old X in Temp.
X := Y;	5.0			Store old Y in X.
Y := Temp		12.5		Store old X in Y.

■ Example 4.11

As manager of a clothing boutique, you may want to keep records of your checking transactions. In the following statement, the true task processes a transaction (TransAmount) that represents a check you wrote as payment for goods received (in which case, TransType is 'C'); the false task processes a deposit made into your checking account. In either case, an appropriate message is printed and the account balance (Balance) is updated. Both the true and false statements are compound statements.

```
if TransType = 'C' then
  begin  {check}
    Write ('Check for $', TransAmount :4:2);
    Balance := Balance – TransAmount    {Deduct check amount}
  end  {check}
else
  begin  {deposit}
    Write ('Deposit of $', TransAmount :4:2);
    Balance := Balance + TransAmount    {Add deposit amount}
  end  {deposit and if}
```

The semicolons in the if statement separate the individual statements in each alternative. A common error would be to insert a semicolon after the first end (end; {check}), which would terminate the if statement prematurely. An unexpected symbol error message would be displayed when the compiler tried to translate the rest of the if statement (beginning with else). ■

PROGRAM
STYLE

Writing if Statements with Compound True or False Statements

Each if statement in this section contains at least one compound statement bracketed by begin and end. Each compound statement is indented. The purpose of the indentation is to improve our ability to read and understand the if statement; indentation is ignored by the Pascal compiler.

    The comment after each end helps to associate the end with its corresponding begin. The comments are not required either but are included to improve program readability.

Semicolons are required between the individual statements within a compound statement. Semicolons should not appear before or after the reserved words then, else, or begin. A semicolon may appear after an end that terminates the entire if statement.

Exercises for Section 4.4

Self-Check

1. In the following statement, insert semicolons where needed to avoid syntax errors and indent to improve readability.

```
if X > Y then
begin
X := X + 10.0
WriteLn ('X Bigger')
end
else
WriteLn ('X Smaller')
WriteLn ('Y is ', Y)
```

2. What would be the effect of removing the bracketing begin and end in exercise 1?
3. What would be the effect of placing a bracketing begin and end around the last two lines in exercise 1?
4. Correct the following if statement:

```
if Num1 < 0 then
   begin
      Product := Num1 * Num2 * Num3;
      WriteLn ('Product is ', Product :1)
   end;
else
   Sum := Num1 + Num2 + Num3;
   WriteLn ('Sum is ', Sum :1);
```

5. What syntax diagrams would be used to validate the following if statement? Provide the label of every syntax diagram that desribes an element of this statement.

```
if X > 0 then
   begin
      X := 25.0;
      WriteLn ('Positive')
   end;
```

Programming

1. Write an if statement that computes the average of a set N numbers whose sum is Total when N is greater than 0 and that prints an error message when N is not greater than 0. The average should be computed by dividing Total by N.
2. Write an interactive program that contains a compound if statement and that can be used to compute the area of a rectangle (*area* = *base* × *height*) or a triangle (*area* = 1/2 × *base* × *height*) after prompting the user to type the first character of the figure name (R or T).

4.5 Decision Steps in Algorithms

In the problem that follows, you will see how to write a payroll program that can compute an employee's gross pay and net pay after deductions.

Case Study: Payroll Problem

Problem

Write a payroll program that computes an employee's gross pay. The program should also compute net pay using the following criterion to determine the amount to be deducted from the employee's gross salary for Social Security tax: if an employee earns more than $100.00 in a week, deduct a tax of $25.00; otherwise, deduct no tax.

Analysis

To compute gross pay, we must know the hours worked and the hourly rate (the problem inputs). After reading these data, we can compute gross pay by finding their product. Next, we can compute the employee's net pay by subtracting any tax deduction from gross pay.

Data Requirements

Problem Constants
```
TaxBracket = 100.00   {maximum salary without a tax deduction}
Tax = 25.00           {amount of tax withheld}
```

Problem Inputs
```
Hours : Real    {hours worked}
Rate : Real     {hourly rate}
```

Problem Outputs
```
Gross : Real    {gross pay}
Net : Real      {net pay}
```

Relevant Formulas

gross pay = hourly rate × hours worked
net pay = gross pay − deductions

Design

The initial algorithm follows, and the structure chart is shown in Fig. 4.11. We have added *data flow* information to the structure chart, which shows the inputs and outputs of each individual algorithm step. The structure chart shows that the step "Enter data" provides values for Hours and Rate as its outputs (data flow arrow points up). Similarly, the step "Compute gross pay" uses Hours and

Case Study: Payroll Problem, continued

`Rate` as its inputs (data flow arrow points down) and provides `Gross` as its output. We discuss the relevance of the data flow information after we complete the problem solution.

Figure 4.11 Structure Chart for Payroll Problem

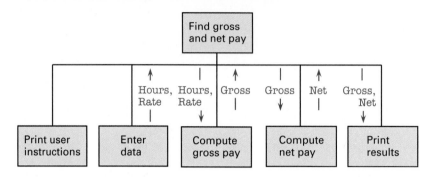

Initial Algorithm

1. Display user instructions.
2. Enter hours worked and hourly rate.
3. Compute gross pay.
4. Compute net pay.
5. Print gross pay and net pay.

Algorithm Refinements

Now let's write the refinement of algorithm step 4 as a *decision step*.

> *Step 4 Refinement*
> 4.1 if Gross > TaxBracket then
>   Deduct a tax of $25
>   else
>   Deduct no tax

This decision step is expressed in *pseudocode,* which is a mixture of English and Pascal used to describe algorithm steps. In the pseudocode for a decision step, we use indentation and the reserved words `if`, `then`, and `else` to show the logical structure of the decision step. The decision step condition can be written in English or Pascal; similarly, the `True` and `False` tasks can be written in English or Pascal.

Implementation

The program is shown in Fig. 4.12. It begins with a multiple-line comment that explains the program's purpose. Rather than surround each line of the comment with braces, we place the opening brace on a separate line before the comment and the closing brace on a separate line after the comment.

Figure 4.12 Program for Payroll Problem

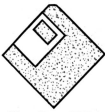

Directory: CHAP4
File: PAYROLL.PAS

```
program Payroll (Input, Output);
{
 Computes and prints gross pay and net pay given an hourly
 rate and number of hours worked.  Deducts a tax of $25 if
 gross salary exceeds $100; otherwise, deducts no tax.
}
  const
    TaxBracket = 100.00;   {maximum salary for no deduction}
    Tax = 25.00;           {tax amount}

  var
    Hours, Rate,           {input - hours worked, hourly rate}
    Gross, Net  : Real;    {outputs - gross pay, net pay}

  procedure InstructPay;
  {Displays user instructions}

  begin {InstructPay}
    WriteLn ('This program computes gross and net salary.');
    WriteLn ('A tax amount of $', Tax :4:2, ' is deducted');
    WriteLn ('for an employee who earns more than $',
             TaxBracket :4:2);
    WriteLn;
    WriteLn ('Enter hours worked and hourly rate');
    WriteLn ('on separate lines after the prompts.');
    WriteLn
    WriteLn ('Press Return after typing each number.');
  end; {InstructPay}


begin {Payroll}
  InstructPay;               {Display user instructions.}

  {Enter Hours and Rate}
  Write ('Hours worked> ');
  ReadLn (Hours);
  Write ('Hourly rate> ');
  ReadLn (Rate);

  {Compute gross salary.}
  Gross := Hours * Rate;

  {Compute net salary.}
  if Gross > TaxBracket then
    Net := Gross - Tax      {Deduct a tax amount}
  else
    Net := Gross;           {Deduct no tax}

  {Print Gross and Net.}
  WriteLn ('Gross salary is $', Gross :4:2);
  WriteLn ('Net salary is $', Net :4:2)
end.  {Payroll}
```

```
This program computes gross and net salary.
A tax amount of $25.00 is deducted
for an employee who earns more than $100.00
```

```
Enter hours worked and hourly rate
on separate lines after the prompts.
Press Return after typing each number.

Hours worked> 40.0
Hourly rate> 5.0
Gross salary is $200.00
Net salary is $175.00
```

The program begins by calling procedure InstructPay to display the user instructions (the first six lines of program output). After the input data are read, the if statement

```
if Gross > TaxBracket then
   Net := Gross — Tax     {Deduct a tax amount}
else
   Net := Gross;          {Deduct no tax}
```

implements the decision step (step 4). The comments on the right are embedded in the if statement. The semicolon in the last line separates the if statement from the output statements that follow.

Testing

To test this program, you should run it with at least two sets of data. One data set should yield a gross salary greater than $100.00, and one should yield a gross salary less than $100.00. You should also test the program with a data set that yields a gross salary that is exactly $100.00.

PROGRAM
STYLE

Using Constants to Enhance Readability and Maintenance

The constants TaxBracket and Tax appear in the preceding if statement and in Fig. 4.12. We could just as easily have placed the constant values (100.00 and 25.00) directly in the if statement. The result would have been

```
if Gross > 100.00 then
   Net := Gross — 25.00     {Deduct a tax amount}
else
   Net := Gross;            {Deduct no tax}
```

However, the use of constants rather than constant values provides two advantages. First, the original if statement is easier to understand because it uses the descriptive names TaxBracket and Tax rather than numbers, which have no intrinsic meaning. Second, a program written with constants is much easier to maintain than one written with constant values. For example, if we want to use different constant values in the Payroll program in Fig. 4.12, we need to change only the constant declaration. However, if we had inserted constant values directly in the `if` statement, we would have to change the `if` statement and any other statements that manipulate the constant values.

Note that the constants also appear in two `WriteLn` statements in procedure `InstructPay`. It is perfectly permissible to reference program constants in a procedure body.

Adding Data Flow Information to Structure Charts

In Fig. 4.11, we added data flow information to the structure chart showing the inputs and outputs of each individual algorithm step. Data flow information is an important part of system documentation. It shows what program variables are processed by each step and the manner in which those variables are processed. If a step gives a new value to a variable, then the variable is considered an *output of the step*. If a step displays a variable's value or uses a variable in a computation without changing its value, the variable is considered an *input to the step*. For example, the step "Compute net pay" processes variables `Gross` and `Net`. This step uses the value of `Gross` (its input) to compute `Net` (its output).

Figure 4.11 shows that a variable may have different roles for different subproblems in the structure chart. When considered in the context of the original problem statement, `Hours` and `Rate` are problem inputs (data supplied by the program user). However, when considered in the context of the subproblem "Enter data," the subproblem's task is to deliver values for `Hours` and `Rate` to the main program; thus, they are considered outputs from this step. When considered in the context of the subproblem "Compute gross pay," the subproblem's task is to use `Hours` and `Rate` to compute a value of `Gross`, so they are considered inputs to this step. In the same way, the role of the variables `Gross` and `Net` changes as we go from step to step in the structure chart (see self-check exercise 1).

Case Study: Finding the First Letter

Problem
Read three letters and find and display the one that comes first in the alphabet.

Analysis
From our prior experience with conditions and decision steps, we know how to use the relational operator `<` to compare two numbers to see which one is smaller. In Pascal, we can also use this operator to determine whether one letter precedes another in the alphabet. For example, the condition `'A' < 'F'` is true because `A` precedes `F` in the alphabet. Since we have no direct way to compare three items, our strategy will be to do a sequence of pairwise comparisons. We will start by comparing the first two letters and finding the smaller of that pair.

Next, we can compare that result to the third letter and find the smaller of that pair. The result of the second comparison will be the smallest of all three letters.

Data Requirements

Problem Inputs
```
Ch1, Ch2, Ch3 : Char {three letters}
```

Problem Outputs
```
AlphaFirst : Char {the alphabetically first letter}
```

Design
The initial algorithm follows. Figure 4.13 shows the structure chart that corresponds to the algorithm.

Figure 4.13 Structure Chart for Finding Alphabetically First Letter

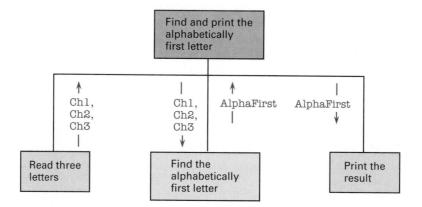

Initial Algorithm

1. Read three letters into Ch1, Ch2, and Ch3.
2. Save the alphabetically first letter of Ch1, Ch2, and Ch3 in AlphaFirst.
3. Display the alphabetically first letter.

Algorithm Refinements
You can perform step 2 by first comparing Ch1 and Ch2 and saving the alphabetically first letter in AlphaFirst; this result can then be compared to Ch3. The refinements of step 2 follow.

Step 2 Refinement
2.1   Save the alphabetically first of Ch1 and Ch2 in AlphaFirst.
2.2   Save the alphabetically first of Ch3 and AlphaFirst in AlphaFirst.

Step 2.1 Refinement
2.1.1 if Ch1 precedes Ch2 then
       2.1.2 AlphaFirst gets Ch1
    else
       2.1.3 AlphaFirst gets Ch2

Step 2.2 Refinement
2.2.1 if Ch3 precedes AlphaFirst then
       2.2.2 AlphaFirst gets Ch3

Figure 4.14 is a structure chart that shows the relationship between step 2 and its refinements. The double-headed arrow on the far right indicate that AlphaFirst is an input to this step and that, because its value may be changed by this step, AlphaFirst is also an output.

Figure 4.14 Structure Chart for Step 2 of First-Letter Problem

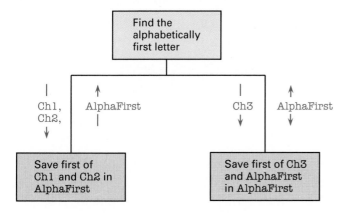

Implementation
Program FirstLetter is shown in Fig. 4.15. The if statement with two alternatives saves either Ch1 or Ch2 in AlphaFirst. The if statement with one alternative stores Ch3 in AlphaFirst if Ch3 precedes the value already in AlphaFirst. Later in the chapter, you will see that if statements with more than two alternatives are also possible in Pascal.

Figure 4.15 Finding the Alphabetically First Letter

```
program FirstLetter (Input, Output);
{Finds and displays the alphabetically first letter}

   var
      Ch1, Ch2, Ch3,                  {three letters read}
      AlphaFirst     : Char;          {alphabetically first letter}
```

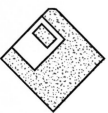

Directory: CHAP4
File: FIRSTLET.PAS

```
begin  {FirstLetter}
   {Read three letters.}
   Write ('Enter any three letters> ');
   ReadLn (Ch1, Ch2, Ch3);

   {Save the alphabetically first of Ch1 and Ch2 in AlphaFirst.}
   if Ch1 < Ch2 then
      AlphaFirst := Ch1              {Ch1 comes before Ch2}
   else
      AlphaFirst := Ch2;             {Ch2 comes before Ch1}

   {Save the alphabetically first of Ch3 and AlphaFirst.}
   if Ch3 < AlphaFirst then
      AlphaFirst := Ch3;            {Ch3 comes before AlphaFirst}

   {Display result.}
   WriteLn (AlphaFirst, ' is the first letter alphabetically')
end. {FirstLetter}


Enter any three letters> EBK
B is the first letter alphabetically
```

Testing

To test this program, you should make sure that it works when the "smallest"
letter is in any of the three positions. The next section describes the four cases
that should be tested. You should also see what happens when one of the letters
is repeated, and when one or more of the letters is lowercase.

Using Functions

The program in Fig. 4.15 is an example of where functions could be used to
improve the structured programming process by facilitating top-down design
and thereby generating more concise, readable code. Let's assume we have a
function named `GetFirst` that returns the alphabetically first of its two type
`Char` arguments. Rather than use the `if` statements in the main program to
compare `Ch1` and `Ch2` and then `Ch3` and `AlphaFirst`, we can call function
`GetFirst` to do this:

```
{Save the alphabetically first of Ch1 and Ch2 in AlphaFirst}
AlphaFirst := GetFirst(Ch1, Ch2);

{Save the alphabetically first of Ch3 and AlphaFirst}
AlphaFirst := GetFirst(Ch3, AlphaFirst)
```

These two assignment statements would replace the two `if` statements that
appear in Fig. 4.15, resulting in a much shorter and more readable program.
The first call to `GetFirst` returns the smaller of `Ch1` and `Ch2`, which is saved
in `AlphaFirst`. The second call to `GetFirst` returns the smaller of `Ch3` and the
current value of `AlphaFirst`, which is also saved in `AlphaFirst`. After both
statements execute, `AlphaFirst` contains the smallest of all three letters, as

required. Of course, function `GetFirst` must contain an `if` statement that compares its arguments, and `GetFirst` must be inserted in the program declaration part. We will write this function in Section 6.2.

Exercises for Section 4.5

Self-Check

1. Explain the use of variables `Gross` and `Net` for each step in Fig. 4.11.
2. Draw a structure chart for the pizza problem in Section 3.2 showing the relationship between the main program and its four subproblems. Add data flow information to this structure chart. Discuss how the role of the variable representing pizza area (a problem output) changes for each subproblem.

Programming

1. Modify the structure chart and program for the first letter problem to find the first of four letters.
2. Write a structure chart and program to find the alphabetically last of three letters.

4.6 Tracing an Algorithm

A critical step in the design of an algorithm or program is to verify that it is correct before you spend extensive time entering or debugging it. Often a few extra minutes spent in verifying the correctness of an algorithm will save hours of testing time later.

One important technique, a hand trace or desk check, consists of a careful, step-by-step simulation on paper of how the computer would execute the algorithm or program. The results of this simulation should show the effect of each step's execution using data that are relatively easy to process by hand. In Section 4.4, we simulated the execution of an `if` statement that switches the values of two variables. Next, we simulate the execution of the refined algorithm for the first-letter problem.

Refined Algorithm

1. Read three letters into `Ch1`, `Ch2`, and `Ch3`.
2. Save the alphabetically first of `Ch1`, `Ch2`, and `Ch3` in `AlphaFirst`.
    2.1 Save the alphabetically first of `Ch1` and `Ch2` in `AlphaFirst`.
        2.1.1 `if Ch1 precedes Ch2 then`
                2.1.2 `AlphaFirst gets Ch1`
            `else`
                2.1.3 `AlphaFirst gets Ch2`
    2.2 Save the alphabetically first of `Ch3` and `AlphaFirst` in `AlphaFirst`.
        2.2.1 `if Ch3 precedes AlphaFirst then`
                2.2.2 `AlphaFirst gets Ch3`
3. Display the alphabetically first letter.

Table 4.7 shows a trace of the algorithm for the data string THE. Each step is listed at the left in the order of its execution. If a program step changes the value of a variable, then the table shows the new value. The effect of each step is described at the far right. For example, the table shows that the statement

```
ReadLn (Ch1, Ch2, Ch3);
```

stores the letters T, H, and E in the variables Ch1, Ch2, and Ch3.

Table 4.7 Trace of Program in Figure 4.15

Algorithm Step	Ch1 ?	Ch2 ?	Ch3 ?	AlphaFirst ?	Effect
1. Read three letters	T	H	E		Reads the data.
2.1.1 if Ch1 precedes Ch2					'T' < 'H' is False.
2.1.3 AlphaFirst gets Ch2				H	'H' is first so far.
2.2.1 if Ch3 precedes AlphaFirst					'E' < 'H' is True.
2.2.2 AlphaFirst gets Ch3				E	'E' is first.
3. Display AlphaFirst					Prints E is the first letter ...

The trace in Table 4.7 clearly shows that the alphabetically first letter, E, of the input string is stored in AlphaFirst and printed. To verify that the algorithm is correct, you would need to select other data that cause the two conditions to evaluate to different combinations of their values. Since there are two conditions and each has two possible values (True or False), there are two times two, or four, different combinations that should be tried. (What are they?) An exhaustive desk check of the algorithm would show that it works for all of these combinations.

Besides the four cases discussed above, you should verify that the algorithm works correctly for unusual data. For example, what would happen if all three letters or a pair of letters were the same? Would the algorithm still provide the correct result? To complete the desk check, you would need to show that the algorithm handles these special situations properly.

In tracing each case, you must be careful to execute the algorithm exactly as the computer would execute it. Often programmers assume that a particular step will be executed and don't explicitly test *each* condition and trace *each* step. A trace performed in this way is of little value.

Exercises for Section 4.6

Self-Check

1. Provide sample data and traces for the remaining three cases of the first-letter problem:

a. Case 1, both conditions are True.
b. Case 2, first condition is True, second is False.
c. Case 3, both conditions are False.
2. Consider two special cases of the first-letter problem. Determine the value of the conditions when
   a. Two of the three letters are the same.
   b. All three letters are the same.
3. Trace the payroll program in Fig. 4.12 when
   a. Hours is 30.0 and Rate is 5.00.
   b. Hours is 20.0 and Rate is 4.00.

4.7 More Problem-Solving Strategies

Often what appears to be a new problem turns out to be a variation of one you have already solved. Consequently, an important skill in problem solving is the ability to recognize that a problem is similar to one solved earlier. As you progress through this course, you will start to build up a library of programs and procedures. Whenever possible, you should try to adapt or reuse parts of successful programs.

Modifying a Problem Solution

An experienced programmer usually writes programs that can be easily changed or modified to fit other situations. For one reason or another, programmers (and program users) often wish to make slight improvements to a program after having used it. If the original program is designed carefully from the beginning, the programmer will be able to accommodate changing specifications with a minimum of effort. As you will find by working through the next problem, it may be possible to modify one or two control statements rather than rewrite the entire program.

Case Study: Computing Overtime Pay

Problem
We want to modify the payroll program so that employees who work more than 40 hours a week are paid double for all overtime hours worked.

Analysis
This problem is a modification of the payroll problem solved in Fig. 4.12. Employees who work more than 40 hours are to be paid one rate for the first 40 hours and a higher rate for the extra hours over 40. Employees who work

40 hours or less are to be paid the same rate for all hours worked. We can solve this problem by replacing step 3 ("Compute gross pay") in the original algorithm with a decision step that selects either a straight pay computation or a computation with overtime pay.

Data Requirements

Problem Constants
```
TaxBracket = 100.00   {maximum salary without a tax deduction}
Tax = 25.00           {amount of tax withheld}
MaxHours = 40.0       {maximum hours without overtime pay}
OvertimeRate = 2.0    {double pay for overtime}
```

Problem Inputs
```
Hours : Real    {hours worked}
Rate : Real     {hourly rate}
```

Problem Outputs
```
Gross : Real    {gross pay}
Net : Real      {net pay}
```

Relevant Formulas
regular pay = *hourly rate* × *hours worked*
overtime pay = *hours over* MaxHours × OvertimeRate × *hourly rate*
net pay = *gross pay* − *deductions*

Design
The critical change to the algorithm involves modifying step 3 of the algorithm. The algorithm is repeated here followed by a new refinement for step 3.

Initial Algorithm

1. Display user instructions.
2. Enter hours worked and hourly rate.
3. Compute gross salary, including any overtime pay.
4. Compute net salary.
5. Print gross salary and net salary.

Algorithm Refinements

Step 3 Refinement
```
3.1  if no overtime hours were worked then
        3.2  Gross gets Hours * Rate
     else
        begin
           3.3  Compute the gross pay for regular hours.
           3.4  Add the pay for overtime hours to gross pay.
        end
```

Implementation

To write the program, we first replace the assignment statement in Fig. 4.12 that computes gross pay,

```
{Compute gross pay}
Gross := Hours * Rate;
```

with the `if` statement

```
{Compute gross pay including any overtime pay}
if Hours <= MaxHours then
  Gross := Hours * Rate
else
  begin {overtime}
    Gross := MaxHours * Rate;
    Gross := Gross + (Hours - MaxHours) * OvertimeRate * Rate
  end {overtime}
```

If the condition Hours <= MaxHours is true, there is no overtime pay, so gross pay is computed as before; otherwise, Gross is computed in two steps. The first step computes the pay for the regular hours only; the second step adds the pay for any overtime hours (Hours – MaxHours) to the value just computed.

More Problem Solving: Solution by Analogy

Sometimes a new problem is simply an old one presented in a new guise. Each time you face a problem, you should try to determine whether you have solved a similar problem before and, if so, adapt the earlier solution. This problem-solving strategy requires a careful reading of the problem statement to detect requirements similar to those of earlier problems that may be worded differently.

Case Study: Computing Insurance Dividends

Problem

Each year an insurance company sends out dividend checks to its policyholders. The basic dividend rate is a fixed percentage (4.5%) of the policyholder's paid premium. If the policyholder has made no claims, the dividend rate for that policy is increased by a bonus rate (0.5%). Write a program to compute dividends.

Analysis

This problem is quite similar to the modified payroll problem. Just as there was a bonus pay rate for workers with overtime hours, there is a bonus dividend for policyholders with no claims. We must first read in the input data (the number of claims and the premium). We then use a decision step to select either the basic dividend computation or the computation with a bonus dividend.

Data Requirements

Problem Constants
```
BasicRate = 0.045      {the basic dividend rate of 4.5%}
BonusRate = 0.005      {the bonus dividend rate of 0.5%}
```

Problem Inputs
```
Premium : Real         {premium amount}
NumClaims : Integer    {number of claims}
```

Problem Outputs
```
Dividend : Real        {dividend amount}
```

Design
The initial algorithm and structure chart (see Fig. 4.16) follow.

Figure 4.16 Structure Chart for Insurance Dividend Problem

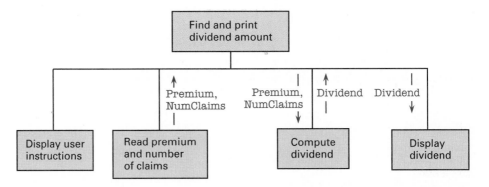

Initial Algorithm

1. Display user instructions.
2. Enter premium amount and number of claims.
3. Compute dividend, including a bonus dividend when earned.
4. Print total dividend.

Algorithm Refinements
The refinement of step 3 in this problem is similar to the refinement of step 3 in the modified payroll problem.

Step 3 Refinement
3.1 if the basic dividend applies then

      3.2 Dividend gets Premium * BasicRate

```
    else
       begin
```
          3.3   Compute the basic dividend.
          3.4   Add the bonus dividend to the basic dividend.
```
       end
```

Implementation

The complete program is shown in Fig. 4.17. The basic dividend rate, 4.5%, is written as the decimal fraction 0.045, and the bonus rate, 0.5%, is written as the decimal fraction 0.005. Because Pascal has no % operator, decimal fractions are required. All real numbers must begin with a digit; therefore, the zero in front of the decimal point is required for a real value less than 1.0. The `if` statement at the end of the program displays an extra message to policyholders who receive a bonus dividend.

Figure 4.17   Insurance Company Dividend Program

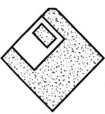

Directory: CHAP4
File: COMPDIVI.PAS

```pascal
program CompDividend (Input, Output);
{Finds and prints the insurance dividend}

   const
      BasicRate = 0.045;       {basic dividend rate 4.5%}
      BonusRate = 0.005;       {bonus dividend rate 0.5%}

   var
      NumClaims : Integer;     {input  - number of claims}
      Premium,                 {input  - premium amount}
      Dividend : Real;         {output - dividend amount}


   procedure InstructDividend;
   {Displays user instructions}

   begin {InstructDividend}
      WriteLn ('This program displays an insurance policy dividend.');
      WriteLn ('The basic dividend is ',
               BasicRate :5:3, ' times the premium.');
      WriteLn ('A bonus dividend of ',
               BonusRate :5:3, ' times the premium is paid');
      WriteLn ('for policies with no claims against them.');
      WriteLn
   end; {InstructDividend}


begin {CompDividend}
   InstructDividend;                    {Display user instructions.}

   {Enter Premium and NumClaims.}
   Write ('Premium amount  > $');
   ReadLn (Premium);
   Write ('Number of claims> ');
   ReadLn (NumClaims);
```

```
{Compute dividend using bonus rate when earned.}
if NumClaims <> 0 then
  Dividend := Premium * BasicRate
else
  begin {bonus}
    Dividend := Premium * BasicRate;        {basic dividend}
    Dividend := Dividend + Premium * BonusRate   {plus bonus}
  end; {bonus}

{Print total dividend.}
WriteLn ('Total dividend is $', Dividend :4:2);
if NumClaims = 0 then
  WriteLn ('This includes a bonus dividend for zero claims!')
end.
```

This program displays an insurance policy dividend.
The basic dividend is 0.045 times the premium.
A bonus dividend of 0.005 times the premium is paid
for policies with no claims against them.

Premium amount > $1200.00
Number of claims> 0
Total dividend is $60.00
This includes a bonus dividend for zero claims!

Exercises for Section 4.7

Self-Check

1. Revise the pizza problem from Section 3.2 so that the user can compute the unit price of either a circular or a square pizza. Give the algorithm with refinements.
2. Draw a structure chart for the revised pizza problem, including data flow information.

Programming

1. Provide the complete program for the overtime pay problem.
2. Write the program for the revised pizza problem in self-check exercise 1.

4.8 Nested if Statements and Multiple-Alternative Decisions

Until now, we have used if statements to implement decisions involving up to two alternatives. In this section, you will see how the if statement can be used to implement decisions involving several alternatives.

A nested if statement occurs when the True or False statement of an if statement is itself an `if` statement. A nested `if` statement can be used to implement decisions with several alternatives, as shown in the next examples.

■ Example 4.12

The following nested `if` statement has three alternatives. It causes one of three variables (NumPos, NumNeg, or NumZero) to be increased by 1 depending on whether X is greater than zero, less than zero, or equal to zero, respectively.

```
{increment NumPos, NumNeg, or NumZero depending on X}
if X > 0 then
  NumPos := NumPos + 1
else
  if X < 0 then
    NumNeg := NumNeg + 1
  else  {X = 0}
    NumZero := NumZero + 1
```

The execution of this `if` statement proceeds as follows: the first condition (X > 0) is tested; if it is true, NumPos is incremented and the rest of the `if` statement is skipped. If the first condition is false, the second condition (X < 0) is tested; if it is true, NumNeg is incremented; otherwise, NumZero is incremented. It is important to realize that the second condition is tested only when the first condition is false.

The flowchart in Fig. 4.18 illustrates the execution of this statement. This diagram shows that one and only one of the statements in a rectangular box will be executed. Table 4.8 traces the execution of this statement when X is −7.

■

Figure 4.18 Flowchart of Nested if Statement in Example 4.12

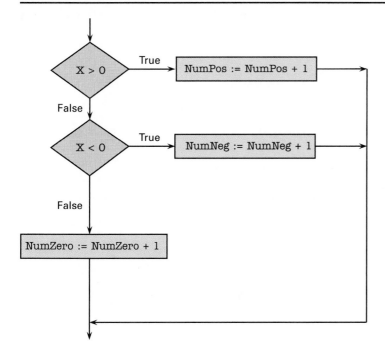

Table 4.8 Trace of if Statement in Example 4.12 for X = −7

Statement Part	Effect
if X > 0 then	−7 > 0 is false.

else if X < 0 then
    NumNeg := NumNeg + 1
	−7 < 0 is true;
	    add 1 to NumNeg.

PROGRAM
STYLE

Nested if Statements versus a Sequence of if Statements

Beginning programmers sometimes prefer to use a sequence of if statements rather than a single nested if statement. For example, the previous
if statement rewritten as a sequence of if statements would look like this:

```
if X > 0 then
   NumPos := NumPos + 1;
if X < 0 then
   NumNeg := NumNeg + 1;
if X = 0 then
   NumZero := NumZero + 1;
```

Although the sequence is logically equivalent to the original, it is not nearly
as readable or as efficient. Unlike the nested if statement, the sequence
does not show clearly that one and only one of the three assignment
statements is executed for a particular X. With respect to efficiency, in the
sequence of if statements, all three of the conditions are always tested. In
the nested if statement, only the first condition is tested when X is positive.

Writing a Nested if Statement as a Multiple-Alternative Decision

Nested if statements can become quite complex. If there are more than three
alternatives and indentation is not consistent, it may be difficult to determine
the if to which a given else belongs. (In Pascal, this is always the closest if
without an else.) It is easier to write the nested if statement in Example 4.12
as the *multiple-alternative decision* described in the next syntax display.

SYNTAX
DISPLAY

Multiple-Alternative Decision

Form: if *condition*$_1$ then
                 statement$_1$
             else if *condition*$_2$ then

```
            statement₂
                .
                .
                .
        else if conditionₙ then
            statementₙ
        else
            statementₑ
```

Example: `{increment NumPos, NumNeg, or NumZero depending on X}`
```
if X > 0 then
    NumPos := NumPos + 1
else if X < 0 then
    NumNeg := NumNeg + 1
else  {X = 0}
    NumZero := NumZero + 1
```

Interpretation: The conditions in a multiple-alternative decision are evaluated in sequence until a true condition is reached. If a condition is true, the statement following it is executed and the rest of the multiple-alternative decision is skipped. If a condition is false, the statement following it is skipped and the next condition is tested. If all conditions are false, then *statement*ₑ following the last `else` is executed.

Writing a Multiple-Alternative Decision

In a multiple-alternative decision, the word `else` and the next condition appear on the same line. All the words `else` align, and each *dependent statement* is indented under the condition that controls its execution.

Order of Conditions

Often the conditions in a multiple-alternative decision are not *mutually exclusive;* in other words, more than one condition may be true for a given data value. If this is the case, then the order of the conditions becomes important because only the statement sequence following the first true condition is executed.

■ Example 4.13

Suppose you want to match exam scores to letter grades for a large class of students. Grades are based on exam scores, as follows:

Exam Score	Grade Assigned
90 and above	A
80–89	B
70–79	C
60–69	D
below 60	F

The following multiple-alternative decision prints the letter grade assigned according to this table. If you had an exam score of 85, the last three conditions would be true if evaluated; however, a grade of B would be assigned because the first true condition is `Score >= 80`.

```
{correct grade assignment}
if Score >= 90 then
   Write ('A')
else if Score >= 80, then
   Write ('B')
else if Score >= 70 then
   Write ('C')
else if Score >= 60 then
   Write ('D')
else
   Write ('F')
```

The order of conditions can also have an effect on program efficiency. If we know that low exam scores are much more likely than high scores, it would be more efficient to test first for scores below 60, next for scores between 60 and 69, and so on (see Programming exercise 1 at the end of this section).

It would be incorrect to write the decision as shown below. All passing exam scores (60 or above) would be incorrectly categorized as a grade of D because the first condition would be true and the rest would be skipped.

```
{incorrect grade assignment}
if Score >= 60 then
   Write ('D')
else if Score >= 70 then
   Write ('C')
else if Score >= 80 then
   Write ('B')
else if Score >= 90 then
   Write ('A')
else
   Write ('F')
```
∎

∎ Example 4.14

You could use a multiple-alternative `if` statement to implement a *decision table* that describes several alternatives. For instance, let's say you are an accountant setting up a payroll system for a small firm. Each line of Table 4.9 indicates an employee's salary range and a corresponding base tax amount and tax percentage. Given a salary, you can calculate the tax by adding the base tax for that salary range and the product of the percentage of excess and the amount of salary over the minimum salary for that range.

For example, the second line of the table specifies that the tax due on a salary of $2,000.00 is $225.00 plus 16% of the excess salary over $1,500.00 (i.e., 16% of $500.00, or $80.00). Therefore, the total tax due is $225.00 plus $80.00, or $305.00.
∎

Table 4.9 Decision Table for Example 4.14

Range	Salary	Base Tax	Percentage of Excess
1	0.00– 1,499.99	0.00	15%
2	1,500.00– 2,999.99	225.00	16%
3	3,000.00– 4,999.99	465.00	18%
4	5,000.00– 7,999.99	825.00	20%
5	8,000.00–15,000.00	1425.00	25%

The `if` statement in Fig. 4.19 implements the tax table. If the value of Salary is within the table range (0.00 to 15,000.00), exactly one of the statements assigning a value to Tax will be executed. A trace of the `if` statement for Salary = 2000.00 is shown in Table 4.10. You can see that the value assigned to Tax, 305.00, is correct.

Figure 4.19 if Statement for Table 4.9

```
if Salary < 0.0 then
   WriteLn ('Error!  Negative salary $', Salary :10:2)
else if Salary < 1500.00 then              {first range}
   Tax := 0.15 * Salary
else if Salary < 3000.00 then              {second range}
   Tax := (Salary − 1500.00) * 0.16 + 225.0
else if Salary < 5000.00 then              {third range}
   Tax := (Salary − 3000.00) * 0.18 + 465.00
else if Salary < 8000.00 then              {fourth range}
   Tax := (Salary − 5000.00) * 0.20 + 825.00
else if Salary <= 15000.00 then            {fifth range}
   Tax := (Salary − 8000.00) * 0.25 + 1425.00
else
   WriteLn ('Error!  Too large salary $', Salary :10:2)
```

Table 4.10 Trace of if Statement in Fig. 4.19 for Salary = $2000.00

Statement Part	Salary 2000.00	Tax ?	Effect
if Salary < 0.0			2000.0 < 0.0 is false.
else if Salary < 1500.00			2000.0 < 1500.0 is false.
else if Salary < 3000.00			2000.0 < 3000.0 is true.
Tax := (Salary − 1500.00)			Evaluates to 500.00.
* 0.16			Evaluates to 80.00.
+ 225.00		305.00	Evaluates to 305.00.

Validating the Value of Variables

It is important to validate the value of a variable before performing computations, so you do not use invalid or meaningless data. Instead of computing an incorrect tax amount, the `if` statement in Fig. 4.19 prints an error message if the value of `Salary` is outside the range covered by the table (0.0 to 15,000.00). The first condition detects negative salaries; an error message is printed if `Salary` is less than zero. All conditions evaluate to `False` if `Salary` is greater than 15,000.00, and the alternative following `else` displays an error message.

Nested if Statements with More Than One Variable

The nested `if` statements so far have all involved testing the value of a single variable; consequently, we have been able to write each nested `if` statement as a multiple-alternative decision. If several variables are involved in the decision, we will not always be able to use a multiple-alternative decision. Example 4.15 shows a situation in which we can use a nested `if` statement as a "filter" to select data that satisfy several different criteria.

■ Example 4.15

The Department of Defense would like a program that identifies single males between the ages of 18 and 26, inclusive. One way to do this is to use a nested `if` statement that sets a Boolean variable `AllMet` to `True` if all criteria are satisfied. In the following nested `if` statement, we assume that all variables have initial values and that the Boolean variable `Single` has been set previously to indicate whether the individual is single (`Single` is `True`) or not (`Single` is `False`).

```
{Set AllMet to True if all criteria are met.}
AllMet := False;              {criteria not met yet}
if Single then
   if (Gender = 'M') then
      if Age >= 18 then
         if Age <= 26 then
            AllMet := True;   {criteria are all met}
```

The Boolean flag `AllMet` is initialized to `False`. The assignment statement at the end of the `if` statement executes and resets `AllMet` to `True` only when all the conditions listed above it are `True`.

Another approach to solving this problem is to write a Boolean expression that represents the logical and of all the individual conditions that must be true. This expression appears on the right side of the following Boolean assignment. The `if` statement following the Boolean assignment displays an appropriate message based on the value assigned to `AllMet`.

```
{Set AllMet to True if all criteria are met.}
AllMet := Single and (Gender = 'M') and
          (Age >= 18) and (Age <= 26);
```

```
{Display the result of the filtering operation.}
if AllMet then
   WriteLn ('Current person satisfies the criteria.')
else
   WriteLn ('All criteria are not satisfied.')
```

■ Example 4.16

You have just had a meeting with your parents to discuss your options for next year. Your parents told you that you could apply to an Ivy League school if you get your SAT scores above 1300 and you earn more than $2000 over the summer. If your SAT scores are not over 1300 but you still earn over $2000 this summer, then your parents suggest you apply to a state university and live at the dorm. If you cannot earn the necessary $2000, your parents would like you to commute to a local community college. The following nested if statement summarizes the decision process you should follow; the flowchart in Fig. 4.20 diagrams it.

```
if Earnings > 2000.00 then
   if SAT > 1300 then
      WriteLn ('Apply to Ivy League')
   else
      WriteLn ('Apply to state university')
else
   WriteLn ('Apply to community college')
```

Figure 4.20 Flowchart of College Decision Process

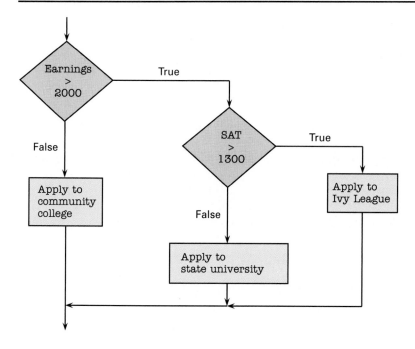

To verify that this nested if statement is correct, it would be necessary to trace its execution for all possible combinations of SAT scores and summer earnings. It is clear that the rightmost rectangle is entered only when both conditions are true. The leftmost rectangle is always entered when the condition involving earnings is false. The rectangle in the middle is entered when the condition involving earnings is true, but the condition involving SAT scores is false.

We could also use the following multiple-alternative decision to implement this decision structure.

```
if (Earnings > 2000.00) and (SAT > 1300) then
   WriteLn ('Apply to Ivy League')
else if (Earnings > 2000.00) then
   WriteLn ('Apply to state university')
else
   WriteLn ('Apply to community college')
```

The first condition is true if both summer earnings and SAT scores are large enough. The second condition is tested only when the first condition fails, so it can be true only when earnings are sufficient but SAT scores are too low. Note that it is not necessary to test the value of SAT in the condition following else if. Finally, the else clause executes when summer earnings are also too low.

It usually does not matter whether you use the nested if statement shown first or the multiple-alternative decision structure shown above to implement a decision like the one diagrammed in Fig. 4.20. In the next section, we discuss when it is important to use a nested if statement instead of a multiple-alternative decision.

Short-Circuit Evaluation of Boolean Expressions

When evaluating Boolean expressions, we often employ a technique called *short-circuit evaluation*. This means that we can stop evaluating a Boolean expression as soon as its value can be determined. For example, if the value of Single is False, then the Boolean expression

```
Single and (Gender = 'M') and
(Age >= 18) and (Age <= 26)
```

must be False regardless of the value of the other conditions (i.e., False and (. . .) must always be False). Consequently, there is no need to evaluate the other conditions when Single is False.

Your Pascal compiler probably does not use short-circuit evaluation. This means that it may continue to evaluate a Boolean expression even after its value is determined. This can lead to execution errors, as shown next.

■ Example 4.17
If X is 0, the if condition

```
if (X <> 0.0) and (Y / X > 5.0) then
```

is False because (X <> 0.0) is False, and False and (. . .) must always be False. Consequently, there is no need to evaluate the subexpression (Y / X > 5.0) when X is 0. However, if this expression is evaluated, a division by zero run-time error will occur because the divisor X is 0.

Because of the possibility of error, the `if` condition above should be split:

```
if (X <> 0.0) then
   if (Y / X > 5.0) then
```

The first condition *guards* the second and prevents the latter from being evaluated when X is 0.

Be wary of short-circuit evaluation and avoid writing Boolean expressions that rely on it. Even if your compiler happens to use *short-circuit evaluation,* a run-time error may result when the program is compiled and executed on another computer. ∎

Exercises for Section 4.8

Self-Check

1. Trace the execution of the nested `if` statement in Fig. 4.19 for Salary = 13500.00.
2. What would be the effect of reversing the order of the first two conditions in the `if` statement of Fig. 4.19?
3. Evaluate the following expressions, with and without short-circuit evaluation, if X = 6 and Y = 7.
   a. (X > 5) and (Y div X <= 10)
   b. (X <= 10) or (X / (Y − 7) > 3)

Programming

1. Rewrite the `if` statement for Example 4.13 using only the relational operator < in all conditions.
2. Implement the following decision table using a nested `if` statement. Assume that the grade point average is within the range 0.0 through 4.0.

Grade Point Average	Transcript Message
0.0–0.99	Failed semester—registration suspended
1.0–1.99	On probation for next semester
2.0–2.99	(no message)
3.0–3.49	Dean's list for semester
3.5–4.0	Highest honors for semester

3. Implement the decision table from programming exercise 2 without using a nested `if` statement.
4. Write a Pascal program that reads a person's age, gender, and marital status (use letters to indicate the second and third criteria). The program should display a message indicating whether the individual meets the criteria described in Example 4.15.

4.9 The case Statement

The `case` statement can also be used in Pascal to select one of several alternatives. It is especially useful when the selection is based on the value of a single variable or a simple expression (called the *case selector*). The case selector may be an ordinal type (type `Integer`, `Boolean`, or `Char`, but not type `Real`). In Chapter 7, you will encounter other data types that can be used as case selectors.

■ Example 4.18

The `case` statement

```
case MomOrDad of
  'M', 'm' : WriteLn ('Hello Mom – Happy Mother''s Day');
  'D', 'd' : WriteLn ('Hello Dad – Happy Father''s Day')
end;  {case}
```

behaves the same way as the following `if` statement when the character stored in MomOrDad is one of the four letters listed (M, m, D, or d).

```
if (MomOrDad = 'M') or (MomOrDad = 'm') then
  WriteLn ('Hello Mom – Happy Mother''s Day')
else if (MomOrDad = 'D') or (MomOrDad = 'd') then
  WriteLn ('Hello Dad – Happy Father''s Day')
```

The message displayed by the `case` statement depends on the value of the case selector MomOrDad (type Char). If the case selector value is `'M'` or `'m'`, the first message is displayed. If the case selector value is `'D'` or `'d'`, the second message is displayed. The lists `'M'`, `'m'`, and `'D'`, `'d'` are called *case labels*. ■

■ Example 4.19

The following `case` statement computes the gross pay earned for a particular day, where the value of DayNumber indicates whether the day is a Saturday (DayNumber is 7), a Sunday (DayNumber is 1), or a weekday (DayNumber is 2 through 6). The worker is paid time and a half during the weekend. Of course, the values of DayNumber, DailyRate, and Hours must be defined before the `case` statement executes.

```
{Compute gross pay for a particular day}
case DayNumber of
  1, 7  : begin{1, 7}
            WeekendRate := 1.5 * DailyRate;
            Gross := Hours * WeekendRate
          end; {1, 7}
  2, 3, 4, 5, 6 : Gross := Hours * DailyRate
end {case}
```

One common error is using a string such as `'Saturday'` or `'Sunday'` as a case label. This causes a syntax error such as `identifier expected` or `illegal character in identifier`. It is important to remember that only ordinal values (that is, single characters, integers, or Boolean values) may appear in case labels.

The syntax display for the `case` statement follows; Fig. 4.21 shows its syntax diagram. ■

case statement

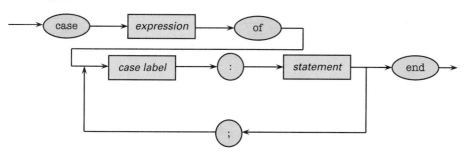

case label

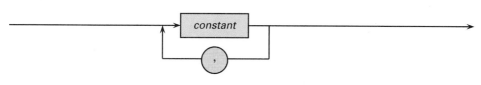

case Statement

Form:
```
case selector of
    label₁ : statement₁;
    label₂ : statement₂;
        .
        .
        .
    labelₙ : statementₙ
end
```

Example:
```
case N of
    1, 2 : WriteLn ('Buckle my shoe');
    3, 4 : WriteLn ('Shut the door');
    5, 6 : WriteLn ('Pick up sticks')
end {case}
```

Interpretation: The *selector* expression is evaluated and compared to each of the case labels. Each $label_i$ is a list of one or more possible constants, separated by commas. Only one $statement_i$ will be executed; if the selector value is listed in $label_i$, $statement_i$ is executed. Control is then passed to the first statement following the case end. Each $statement_i$ may be a single or a compound Pascal statement.

Note 1: If the value of the selector is not listed in any case label, an error message is printed and program execution stops.

Note 2: A particular selector value may appear in at most one case label.

Note 3: The type of each constant in a case label value must correspond to the type of the selector expression.

Note 4: Any ordinal data type is permitted as the selector type.

As indicated in note 1 of the case statement display, a case expression out of range error message is printed during execution if the selector value does not appear in any case label. Consequently, all possible values of the selector must be listed in exactly one case label. If no action is to be performed for a particular case label, this is indicated by placing the semicolon, or end (for the last case), immediately following the colon.

Each *statement*ᵢ except the last one should be followed by a semicolon; the last statement is followed by the word end. Note that there is no corresponding begin for a case statement.

Guarding a case Statement

We often guard a case statement with an if statement to prevent the occurrence of a case expression out of range error. The if statement in Fig. 4.22 guards the case statement nested inside it. The case statement executes only when the value of DayNumber is in the range 1 through 7, as required; an error message is printed when DayNumber is invalid. Note that there is no semicolon after the end {case}. (Why?)

Figure 4.22   A Guarded case Statement

```
{Compute gross pay for a particular day}
if (DayNumber >= 1) and (DayNumber <= 7) then
  case DayNumber of
    1, 7  : begin {1, 7}
              WeekendRate := 1.5 * DailyRate;
              Gross := Hours * WeekendRate
            end; {1, 7}
    2, 3, 4, 5, 6  : Gross := Hours * DailyRate
  end {case}
else
  WriteLn (DayNumber :1, ' is an invalid day number')
```

otherwise Clause (Non-Standard)

As an alternative to guarding a case statement with an if statement, some compilers provide the otherwise clause as a means of avoiding a case expression out of range error. The otherwise clause in the case statement of Fig. 4.23 executes and displays an error message if the value of DayNumber does not match any of the case labels.

Figure 4.23   case with otherwise

```
{Compute gross pay for a particular day}
case DayNumber of
  1, 7  : begin {1, 7}
            WeekendRate := 1.5 * DailyRate;
            Gross := Hours * WeekendRate
          end; {1, 7}
```

```
  2, 3, 4, 5, 6  : Gross := Hours * DailyRate
otherwise
  WriteLn (DayNumber :1, ' is an invalid day number')
end {case}
```

Comparison of Nested if Statements and the case Statement

You can use nested `if` statements, which are more general than a `case` statement, to implement any multiple-alternative decision. A `case` statement, however, is more readable and should be used whenever practical. Case labels that contain type `Real` values or strings are not permitted.

   You should use the `case` statement when each case label contains a reasonably sized list of values (10 or fewer). However, if the number of values in a case selector is large or there are large gaps in those values, use a nested `if` statement. You should also use nested `if` statements when a `case expression out of range` error is possible because a large number of values require no action to be taken.

Type Boolean case Selectors

Although `case` statements may contain type `Boolean` case selectors, this rarely happens. The following `case` and `if` statements are equivalent; however, the `if` statement is preferable.

```
case X = Y of
   True  : WriteLn ('Equal');
   False : WriteLn ('Unequal')
end {case}
```
```
if X = Y then
   WriteLn ('Equal')
else
   WriteLn ('Unequal')
```

Exercises for Section 4.9

Self-Check

1. Write an `if` statement that corresponds to the following `case` statement:

```
case X > Y of
   True  : WriteLn ('X greater');
   False : WriteLn ('Y greater or equal')
end
```

2. Can the nested `if` statement examples from Section 4.8 be rewritten using `case` statements? If not, why not?
3. Why would you want to guard a `case` statement in standard Pascal?

Programming

1. Write a `case` statement that prints a message indicating whether `NextCh` (type `Char`) is an operator symbol (+, −, *, =, <, >, /), a punctuation mark (comma, semicolon, parenthesis, brace, bracket), or a digit. Your statement should print the category selected.

2. Write a nested `if` statement that is equivalent to the `case` statement described in programming exercise 1.
3. Guard the `case` statement described in programming exercise 1.

4.10 Common Programming Errors

You can use the Boolean operators, `and`, `or`, and `not`, only with Boolean expressions. In the expression

```
Flag and (X = Y)
```

the variable `Flag` must be type `Boolean`. The statement would be invalid without the parentheses unless X and Y were type `Boolean`.

Be careful with the use of semicolons inside an `if` statement. Use semicolons only to separate the statements of a compound statement within an `if` statement. A semicolon is needed after the `if` statement when more statements follow. Semicolons must not be used before or after the reserved words `then` or `else` in an `if` statement. If you use a semicolon just before `else`, the compiler will terminate the `if` statement and incorrectly assume that the `else` begins a new statement.

Don't forget to bracket a compound statement used as a `True` task or a `False` task with `begin` and `end`. If the `begin-end` bracket is missing, only the first statement will be considered part of the task, which can lead to a syntax error. In the following example, the `begin-end` bracket around the `True` task is missing. The compiler assumes that the semicolon at the end of the assignment statement terminates the `if` statement, which may lead to a `;` expected syntax error (at the end of the first `WriteLn` statement). If you insert a semicolon at the end of the `WriteLn` statement, you may get an `unexpected symbol` syntax error (the reserved word `else`). Of course, the correct thing to do is to bracket the compound statement with `begin` and `end`.

```
if X > 0 then
   Sum := Sum + X;
   WriteLn ('Greater than zero')
else
   WriteLn ('Less than zero');
```

When writing a nested `if` statement, try to select the conditions so that you can use the multiple-alternative format shown in Section 4.8. If the conditions are not mutually exclusive (i.e., more than one condition may be true), the most restrictive condition should come first.

When using a `case` statement, make sure the case selector and labels are of the same ordinal type (`Integer`, `Char`, or `Boolean`, but not `Real`). Remember that only lists of values may be used as case labels and that no value may appear in more than one case label. If the selector evaluates to a value not listed in any of the case labels, an error diagnostic may occur and your program may stop. For this reason, it is often wise to guard the `case` with an `if` statement. This way you can ensure that the case executes only when the if condition is True. Don't forget to terminate a case statement with an end {case}; there is no matching begin.

CHAPTER REVIEW

In this chapter, we discussed how to represent decision steps in an algorithm (using pseudocode) and how to implement them in Pascal using if and case statements. We also introduced the Boolean operators (and, or, not) and explained how to use them to write Boolean expressions.

You learned how to describe the syntax of Pascal using syntax diagrams. To avoid syntax errors, you should refer to the appropriate syntax diagrams if you are unsure of the form of a statement (see Appendix B). If the compiler detects a syntax error that you do not understand, refer again to the syntax diagram to determine the cause of the error.

We continued our discussion of problem solving and demonstrated how to solve a new problem by making an analogy to an earlier problem. We also showed how to add data flow information to structure charts to improve system documentation. You saw that a variable processed by a subproblem is classified as an input or an output based on how it is used by that subproblem—the same variable may be an input to one subproblem and an output from another.

You also saw how to use traces to verify that an algorithm or a program is correct. You can discover errors in logic by carefully tracing an algorithm or program. Tracing an algorithm or program before typing in the program will save you time in the long run.

A second selection structure, the case statement, was introduced in this chapter as a convenient means of implementing decisions with several alternatives. We discussed how to use the case statement to implement decisions that are based on the value of a variable or simple expression (the case selector). The case selector can be type Integer, Char, or Boolean, but not type Real.

New Pascal Constructs

The new Pascal constructs introduced in this chapter are described in Table 4.11.

Table 4.11   Summary of New Pascal Constructs

Construct	Effect
if Statement	

One Alternative
`if X <> 0.0 then`
`   Product := Product * X`
	Multiplies Product by X only if X is nonzero.

Two Alternatives
`if X >= 0.0 then`
`   WriteLn (X :12:2, ' is positive')`
`else`
`   WriteLn (X :12:2, ' is negative')`
	If X is greater than or equal to 0.0, display ' is positive'; otherwise, display the message ' is negative'.

Table 4.11, *continued*

Construct	Effect

Several Alternatives
```
if X < 0.0 then
  begin
    WriteLn ('negative');
    AbsX := -X
  end
else if X = 0.0 then
  begin
    WriteLn ('zero);
    AbsX := 0.0
  end
else
  begin
    WriteLn ('positive');
    AbsX := X
  end
```

One of three messages is printed, depending on whether X is negative, positive, or zero. AbsX is set to represent the absolute value or magnitude of X.

case Statement
```
case NextCh of
  'A', 'a' : WriteLn ('Excellent');
  'B', 'b' : WriteLn ('Good');
  'C', 'c' : WriteLn ('O.K.');
  'D', 'd', 'F', 'f' :
              begin
                Write ('Poor, student is');
                WriteLn (' on probation')
              end
end {case}
```

Prints one of four messages based on the value of NextCh (type Char). If NextCh is 'D', 'd' or 'F', 'f', the student is put on probation.

✓ Quick-Check Exercises

1. An if statement is a control statement for _____.
2. What is a compound statement?
3. A case statement is often used instead of _____.
4. What values can a Boolean expression have?
5. The relational operator <> means _____.
6. A hand trace is used to verify that a(n) _____ is correct.
7. A(n) _____ is used to verify that a program statement is grammatically correct.
8. Correct the syntax errors in the following statement:

   ```
   if X > 25.0 then
     begin
       Y := X;
     else
       Y := Z
     end;
   ```

9. What value is assigned to Fee by the following if statement when Speed is 75?

```
if Speed > 35 then
   Fee := 20.0
else if Speed > 50 then
   Fee := 40.00
else if Speed > 75 then
   Fee := 60.00
```

10. Answer exercise 9 for the following if statement. Which if statement is correct?

```
if Speed > 75 then
   Fee := 60.0
else if Speed > 50 then
   Fee := 40.00
else if Speed > 35 then
   Fee := 20.00
```

11. What output line(s) are displayed by the following statements when Grade is 'I'? When Grade is 'B'? When Grade is 'b'?

```
case Grade of
   'A' : Points := 4;
   'B' : Points := 3;
   'C' : Points := 2;
   'D' : Points := 1;
   'E', 'I' ,'W' : Points := 0
end;

if ('A' <= Grade) and (Grade <= 'D') then
   WriteLn ('Passed, points earned = ', Points)
else
   WriteLn ('Failed, no points earned');
```

12. Explain the difference between the statements on the left and the statements on the right. For each, what is the final value of X if the initial value of X is 0?

```
if X >= 0 then            if X >= 0 then
   X := X + 1                X := X + 1;
else if X >= 1 then       if X >= 1 then
   X := X + 2;               X := X + 2;
```

Answers to Quick-Check Exercises

1. selection or decision-making
2. a statement bracketed by begin and end
3. nested if statements or a multiple-alternative if statement
4. True and False
5. not equal
6. algorithm
7. syntax diagram
8. Remove begin and end and the first semicolon.
9. 20.00 (first condition is met)
10. 40.00; the one in exercise 10
11. when Grade is 'I':
       Failed, no points earned
    when Grade is 'B':

```
       Passed, points earned = 3
   when Grade is 'b':
       a case expression out of range error occurs
```

12. A nested `if` statement is on the left; a sequence of `if` statements is on the right. X becomes 1 on the left; X becomes 3 on the right.

Review Questions

1. A decision in Pascal is actually an evaluation of a(n) _____ expression.

2. How does a relational operator differ from a Boolean operator?

3. What is short-circuit Boolean evaluation? Why should its use be discouraged?

4. Trace the following program fragment and indicate which procedure will be called if a data value of 27.34 is entered.

```
WriteLn ('Enter a temperature> ');
ReadLn (Temp);
if Temp > 32.0 then
   NotFreezing
else
   IceForming
```

5. Write a nested `if` statement to display a message that indicates the educational level of a student based on his or her number of years of schooling: 0-None, 1 through 5-Elementary School, 6 through 8-Middle School, 9 through 12-High School, > 12-College. Print a message to indicate bad data as well.

6. How can syntax diagrams aid a new user in becoming comfortable with an unfamiliar programming language?

7. Given the following syntax diagram, circle the words under the diagram that are valid.

words

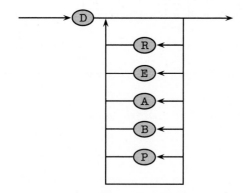

PEAR   BREAD   DREAR   DEADEN   DAD   DRAB

8. Write a guarded `case` statement to select an operation based on the value of Inventory. Increment `TotalPaper` by `PaperOrder` if Inventory is 'B' or 'C'; increment

TotalRibbon by 1 if RibbonOrder is 'E', 'F', or 'D'; increment TotalLabel by LabelOrder if Inventory is 'A' or 'X'. Do nothing if Inventory is 'M'.

9. Write the six pairs of words that satisfy the syntax diagram for *thing*.

Chapter Review

thing

stuff

10. In the syntax diagram for the case statement (see Fig. 4.21), to what syntactic element would DayNumber in Fig. 4.22 correspond? Answer the same question for the symbols 1, 7 and the symbols 2, 3, 4, 5, 6.

Programming Projects

1. Write procedures to draw a square and a triangle. Write a program that reads a letter S or T and based on that letter draws either a square or a triangle.
2. Add procedures to draw a circle and a line to programming project 1. Revise the main program to read three letters chosen from the set C (for Circle), L (for Line), S (for Square), and T (for Triangle) into three type Char variables. Next, your program should draw the three figures indicated. For example, if the data line is CLT, the program should draw a circle, a line, and a triangle. Use a separate case statement to draw each of the three figures. Each type Char variable should be used as a case selector.
3. While spending the summer as a surveyor's assistant, you decide to write a program that transforms compass headings in degrees (0 to 360) to compass bearings. A compass bearing consists of three items: the direction you face (north or south), an angle between 0 and 90 degrees, and the direction you turn before walking (east or west). For example, to get the bearing for a compass heading of 110.0 degrees, you would first face due south (180 degrees) and then turn 70.0 degrees east (180.0 − 110.0). Be sure to check the input for invalid compass headings.
4. Write a program that reads in a room number, its capacity, and the size of the class enrolled so far and prints an output line showing the classroom number, capacity, number of seats filled and available, and a message indicating whether the class is filled. Call a procedure to display the following headings before the output line.

`Room  Capacity  Enrollment  Empty seats  Filled/Not Filled`
Display each part of the output line under the appropriate heading. Test your
program with the following classroom data:

Room	Capacity	Enrollment
426	25	25
327	18	14
420	20	15
317	100	90

5. Write a program that will determine the additional state tax owed by an employee.
The state charges a 4% tax on net income. Determine net income by subtracting a
$500 allowance for each dependent from gross income. Your program will read gross
income, number of dependents, and tax amount already deducted. It will then
compute the actual tax owed and print the difference between tax owed and tax
deducted followed by the message 'SEND CHECK' or 'REFUND', depending on whether
the difference is positive or negative.

6. The New Telephone Company has the following rate structure for long-distance
calls:

   • Any call started after 6:00 p.m. (1800 hours) but before 8:00 a.m. (0800 hours) is
   discounted 50%.
   • Any call started after 8:00 a.m. (0800 hours) but before 6:00 p.m. (1800 hours) is
   charged full price.
   • All calls are subject to a 4% federal tax.
   • The regular rate for a call is $0.40 per minute.
   • Any call longer than 60 minutes receives a 15% discount on its cost (after any other
   discount is subtracted and before tax is added).

   Write a program that reads the start time for a call based on a 24-hour clock
   and the length of the call. The gross cost (before any discounts or tax) should be
   printed followed by the net cost (after discounts are deducted and tax is added). Use
   a procedure to print instructions to the program user.

7. Write a program that will calculate and print out bills for the city water company.
The water rates vary depending on whether the bill is for home use, commercial use,
or industrial use. A code of H means home use, C means commercial use, and I
means industrial use. Any other code should be treated as an error.

   The water rates are computed as follows:

   Code H: $5.00 plus $0.0005 per gallon used
   Code C: $1,000.00 for the first 4 million gallons used and $0.00025 for each ad-
            ditional gallon
   Code I: $1,000.00 if usage does not exceed 4 million gallons; $2,000.00 if usage is
            more than 4 million gallons but does not exceed 10 million gallons; and
            $3,000.00 if usage exceeds 10 million gallons

   Your program should prompt the user to enter an Integer account number, code
   (type Char), and the gallons of water used expressed as a Real number. Your program
   should echo the input data and print the amount due from the user.

5

Repetition: while, for, and repeat Statements

So far we have covered Pascal control structures for sequence and selection. In this chapter, we discuss Pascal's control structures for repetition. You will see how to specify the repetition of a group of program statements (called a *loop*) using the while, for, and repeat statements.

We discuss the relative advantages of each of the three loop forms (while, for, and repeat) and determine when it is best to use each form. We also reexamine nested control structures, especially nested loops, and demonstrate how to use them.

5.1 Repetition in Programs: The while Statement

Just as the ability to make decisions is an important programming tool, so is the ability to specify the repetition of a group of operations. For example, a company has seven employees, and we want to perform the same gross pay and net pay computations for each employee. Rather than duplicate the steps seven times in a program, we can write them once and tell Pascal to repeat them.

The repetition of steps in a program is called a *loop*. The *loop body* contains the steps to be repeated. Pascal provides three control statements for specifying repetition. We examine the while statement first and then the for and repeat statements.

The while Statement

The program shown in Fig. 5.1 computes and displays the weekly pay for each of seven employees, assuming no overtime pay. The loop body (steps that are repeated) is the compound statement starting on the third line. The loop body reads an employee's payroll data and computes and displays that employee's gross pay. After seven weekly pay amounts are displayed, the last statement in Fig. 5.1 calls procedure WriteLn to display the message 'All employees processed'.

Figure 5.1   Loop to Process Seven Employees

```
CountEmp := 0;                    {no employees processed yet}
while CountEmp < 7 do             {test value of CountEmp}
  begin
    Write ('Hours> ');
    ReadLn (Hours);
    Write ('Rate > $');
    ReadLn (Rate);
    Pay := Hours * Rate;
    WriteLn ('Weekly pay is $', Pay :4:2);
    CountEmp := CountEmp + 1       {increment CountEmp}
  end; {while}

WriteLn ('All employees processed');
```

The three lines in color in Fig. 5.1 control the looping process. The first statement

```
CountEmp := 0;          {no employees processed yet}
```

stores an initial value of 0 in the variable CountEmp, which represents the count of employees processed so far. The next line evaluates the Boolean expression CountEmp < 7. If it is true, the compound statement representing the loop body is executed, causing a new pair of data values to be read and a new pay amount to be computed and displayed. The last statement in the loop body

```
CountEmp := CountEmp + 1     {increment CountEmp}
```

adds 1 to the value of CountEmp. After executing the last step in the loop body, control returns to the line beginning with while, and the Boolean expression is reevaluated for the next value of CountEmp.

The loop body is executed once for each value of CountEmp from 0 to 6. Eventually CountEmp becomes 7, and the Boolean expression will evaluate to False. When this happens, the loop body is not executed, and control passes to the WriteLn statement that follows the loop body.

The Boolean expression following the reserved word while is called the *loop repetition condition.* The loop is repeated when this condition is true. We say that the loop *is exited* when this condition is false.

The flowchart of the while loop in Fig. 5.2 summarizes our discussion so far about while loops. It shows that the condition in the diamond-shaped box is evaluated first. If it is true, the loop body is executed, and the process is repeated. The while loop is exited when the condition becomes false.

Figure 5.2 Flowchart of a while Loop

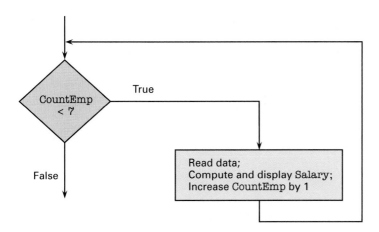

Make sure you understand the difference between the while statement in Fig. 5.1 and the if statement

```
if CountEmp < 7 then
   begin
      ...
   end; {if}
```

The compound statement after the reserved word `then` executes at most one time. In a `while` statement, the compound statement after the reserved word `do` may execute more than one time.

Syntax of the while Statement

In Fig. 5.1, the variable `CountEmp` is called the *loop-control variable* because its value determines whether the loop body is repeated. Three critical steps involve the loop-control variable `CountEmp`.

- `CountEmp` is set to an initial value of 0 (*initialized to* 0) before the `while` statement is reached.
- `CountEmp` is tested before the start of each loop repetition (called an *iteration* or a *pass*).
- `CountEmp` is updated (its value increased by 1) during each iteration.

Steps similar to these three steps (initialization, testing, and updating) must be performed for every `while` loop. If the first step is missing, the initial test of `CountEmp` will be meaningless. The last step ensures that we make progress toward the final goal (`CountEmp >= 7`) during each repetition of the loop. If the last step is missing, the value of `CountEmp` cannot change, so the loop will execute "forever" (an *infinite loop*). The syntax display for the `while` statement follows; Fig. 5.3 shows the syntax diagram.

SYNTAX
DISPLAY

The while Statement

Form: `while` *expression* `do`
                 statement

Example: `{Display N asterisks.}`
`CountStar := 0;`
`while CountStar < N do`
`   begin`
`      Write ('*');`
`      CountStar := CountStar + 1`
`   end {while}`

Interpretation: *expression* (a condition to control the loop process) is tested and if it is true, *statement* is executed and *expression* is retested. *statement* is repeated as long as (while) *expression* is true. When *expression* is tested and found to be false, the `while` loop is exited and the next program statement after the `while` statement is executed.

Notes: If *expression* evaluates to false the first time it is tested, *statement* will not be executed.

while statement

You must be careful with the placement of semicolons in a while statement. Make sure you do not place a semicolon after the word do. If you make this error, the Pascal compiler will execute what it assumes is an *empty statement* as your loop body. Such a "statement" will do nothing forever or until your patience or time limit expires.

Formatting the while Statement

For clarity, we indent the body of a while loop. If the loop body is a compound statement bracketed by begin and end, we terminate it with end {while}.

Exercises for Section 5.1

Self-Check

1. How many times is the following loop body repeated? What is printed during each repetition of the loop body?

```
X := 3;
Count := 0;
while Count < 3 do
  begin
    X := X * X;
    WriteLn (X);
    Count := Count + 1
  end {while}
```

2. Answer exercise 1 if the last statement in the loop is

```
Count := Count + 2
```

3. Answer exercise 1 if the last statement in the loop body is omitted.

Programming

1. Write a while loop that displays each integer from 1 to 5 on a separate line together with its square.
2. Write a while loop that displays each integer from –2 to 3 on a separate line. Display the values in the sequence –2, –1, 0, and so on.

5.2 Accumulating a Sum or a Product

Often we use loops to accumulate a sum or a product by repeating an addition or multiplication operation. The next example uses a loop to accumulate a sum.

■ Example 5.1

The program in Fig. 5.4 has a `while` loop similar to the loop in Fig. 5.1. Besides displaying each employee's weekly pay, it accumulates the total payroll (TotalPay) for a company. The assignment statement

```
TotalPay := TotalPay + Pay;          {add next pay}
```

adds the current value of Pay to the sum being accumulated in TotalPay. Figure 5.5 traces the effect of repeating this statement for the three values of Pay shown in the sample run.

Figure 5.4 Program to Compute Company Payroll

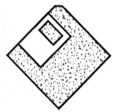

Directory: CHAP5
File: COMPANY.PAS

```
program CompanyPayroll (Input, Output);
{Computes the payroll for a company}

   var
      NumberEmp,                    {number of employees}
      CountEmp : Integer;           {current employee}
      Hours,                        {hours worked}
      Rate,                         {hourly rate}
      Pay,                          {weekly pay}
      TotalPay : Real;              {company payroll}

begin
   {Enter number of employees.}
   Write ('Enter number of employees >');
   ReadLn (NumberEmp);

   {Compute each employee's pay and add it to the payroll.}
   TotalPay := 0.0;
   CountEmp := 0;                            {start with first employee}
   while CountEmp < NumberEmp do
      begin
         Write ('Hours> ');
         ReadLn (Hours);
         Write ('Rate > $');
         ReadLn (Rate);
         Pay := Hours * Rate;
         WriteLn ('Pay is $', Pay :4:2);
         WriteLn;
         TotalPay := TotalPay + Pay;         {add next pay}
         CountEmp := CountEmp + 1
      end; {while}

   WriteLn;  WriteLn ('All employees processed');
   WriteLn ('Total payroll is ', TotalPay :4:2)
end. {CompanyPayroll}
```

```
Enter number of employees> 3
Hours> 5
Rate > $4.00
Pay is $20.00

Hours> 6
Rate > $5.00
Pay is $30.00

Hours> 1.5
Rate > $10.00
Pay is $15.00

All employees processed
Total payroll is $65.00
```

Figure 5.5 Accumulating Partial Sums

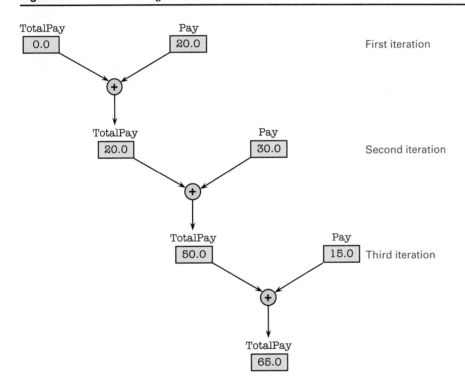

Prior to loop execution, the statement

```
TotalPay := 0.0;
```

initializes the value of TotalPay to 0. This step is critical; if it is omitted, the final sum will be off by whatever value happens to be stored in TotalPay when the program begins execution. ∎

Generalizing a Loop

The first loop in Fig. 5.1 has a serious deficiency in that it can be used only when the number of employees is exactly 7. The loop in Fig. 5.4 is much better because it can be used for any number of employees. That program begins by reading the total number of employees into variable NumberEmp. Before each execution of the loop body, the loop repetition condition CountEmp < NumberEmp compares the number of employees processed so far (CountEmp) to NumberEmp.

Accumulating Partial Products

In a similar way, we can use a loop to accumulate a product, as shown in the next example.

■ Example 5.2

The following loop computes and displays all products of its data items that are less than 10000. It computes each new partial product by repeated execution of the statement

```
Product := Product * Item   {Compute next product}
```

Figure 5.6 traces the change in the value of Product with each execution of the above statement. If the data items are 10, 500, and 3, the partial products 1, 10, and 5000 are displayed.

```
{Display partial products less than 10000.}
Product := 1;
while Product < 10000 do
  begin
    WriteLn (Product);            {Display partial product.}
    Write ('Enter next item> ');
    ReadLn (Item);
    Product := Product * Item   {Compute next product.}
  end {while}
```

Loop exit occurs when the value of Product is greater than or equal to 10000. Consequently, the last value assigned to Product (15000 in Fig. 5.6) is not displayed.

The loop in Fig. 5.6 differs from the other loops in this section. Its repetition condition involves a test of the variable Product. Besides controlling loop repetition, the variable Product also stores the result of the computation being performed in the loop. The other loops involve a test of a variable, CountEmp, that represents the count of loop repetitions. CountEmp is not directly involved in the computation being performed in those loops. We discuss these differences further in the next section.   ■

Exercises for Section 5.2

Self-Check

1. What output values are displayed by the following while loop for a data value of 5?

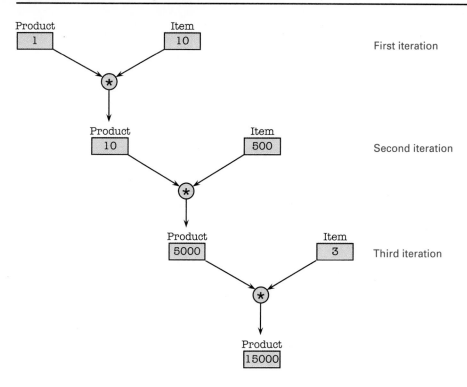

First iteration

Second iteration

Third iteration

```
WriteLn ('Enter an integer> ');
ReadLn (X);
Product := X;
Count := 0;
while Count < 4 do
   begin
      WriteLn (Product);
      Product := Product * X;
      Count := Count + 1
   end; {while}
```

2. What values are displayed if the call to `WriteLn` comes at the end of the loop instead of at the beginning?

3. What does the following segment display? Insert `begin` and `end` where needed and correct the errors. The corrected segment should read five numbers and display their sum.

```
Count := 0;
while Count <= 5 do
Count := Count + 1;
Write ('Next number> ');
ReadLn (NextNum);
NextNum := Sum + NextNum;
WriteLn (Count :1, ' numbers were added;');
WriteLn ('their sum is ', Sum:4:2)
```

4. How would the program in Fig. 5.4 need to be modified to display the average employee salary, in addition to the total payroll amount?

Programming

1. Write a program segment that computes $1 + 2 + 3 + \ldots + (N - 1) + N$, where N is a data value.

5.3 Counting Loops and Conditional Loops

The `while` loop in Fig. 5.4 is called a *counter-controlled loop* (or *counting loop*) because its repetition is controlled by a variable whose value represents a count. The counter-controlled loop in Fig. 5.4 follows this format:

Set *counter variable* to 0
`while` *counter variable* < *final value* `do`
   `begin`
     . . .
     increase *counter variable* by 1
   `end`

We use a counter-controlled loop when we can determine prior to loop execution exactly how many loop repetitions will be needed to solve our problem. This number should appear as the final value in the `while` condition. Section 5.5 shows how to use the `for` statement to implement counting loops.

Conditional Loops

In many programming situations, we cannot determine the exact number of loop repetitions that will be needed before loop execution begins. The number of repetitions may depend on some aspect of the data that is not known before the loop is entered, but that usually can be stated by a condition. For example, we may want to continue writing checks as long as our bank balance is positive, as indicated by the following pseudocode description.

`while` the balance is still positive `do`
   `begin`
     Read in the next transaction
     Update and print the balance
   `end`

The actual number of loop repetitions performed depends on the type of each transaction (deposit or withdrawal) and its amount.

■ Example 5.3

The program in Fig. 5.7 traces the progress of a hungry worm approaching an apple. Each time it moves, the worm cuts the distance between itself and the apple by its own body length until the worm is close enough to enter the apple. A `while` loop is the correct looping structure to use because we have no idea beforehand how many moves will be required.

Figure 5.7 Worm Bites Apple

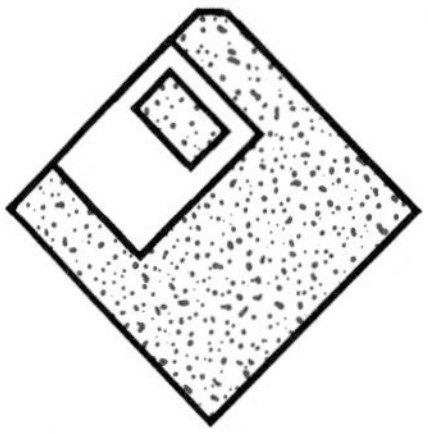

```
program WormApple (Input, Output);
{
  Prints distances between a worm and an apple.  With each move,
  the worm cuts the distance by its body length
  until it is close enough to enter the apple.
}
  const
    WormLength = 3.5;    {worm body length in inches}

  var
    InitialDist,         {starting distance of worm from apple}
    Distance : Real;     {distance between worm and apple}

begin {WormApple}
  Write ('Enter initial distance between worm and apple in inches >');
  ReadLn (InitialDist);

  {
  Cut the distance between the worm and the apple by the worm's
  body length until the worm is close enough to enter the apple.
  }
  Distance := InitialDist;
  while Distance >= WormLength do
    begin
      WriteLn ('The distance is ', Distance :4:2);
      Distance := Distance - WormLength       {reduce Distance}
    end; {while}

  {Print final distance before entering the apple.}
  WriteLn;
  Write ('The last distance before the worm enters ');
  WriteLn ('the apple is ', Distance :3:1)
end. {WormApple}

Enter initial distance between worm and apple in inches >12.0
The distance is 8.5
The distance is 5.0

The last distance before the worm enters the apple is 1.5
```

Let's take a close look at the `while` loop in Fig. 5.7. The assignment statement just before the loop initializes the variable `Distance` to the starting distance (`12.0`), which was previously read into `InitialDist`. Next, the loop header is reached and the *loop repetition condition* (or `while` condition)

```
Distance >= WormLength;
```

is evaluated. Since this condition is true, the loop body (through `end`) is executed. The loop body displays the value of `Distance`, and the statement

```
Distance := Distance - WormLength      {reduce Distance}
```

reduces the value of Distance, thereby bringing the worm closer to the apple. The loop repetition condition is then retested with the new value of Distance (8.5): 8.5 >= 3.5 is true, so the loop body displays Distance again, and Distance becomes 5.0. The loop repetition condition is tested a third time: 5.0 >= 3.5 is true, so the loop body displays Distance again, and Distance becomes 1.5. The loop repetition condition is tested again: 1.5 >= 3.5 is false, so loop exit occurs, and the statements following the loop end are executed.

It is important to realize that the loop is not exited at the exact instant that Distance becomes 1.5. If more statements appeared in the loop body after the assignment to Distance, they would be executed. Loop exit does not occur until the loop repetition condition is retested at the top of the loop and found to be false.

Just as in the counting loop in Fig. 5.4, three critical steps in Fig. 5.7 involve the loop-control variable (Distance):

- Distance is initialized to InitialDist before the loop header is reached.
- Distance is tested before each execution of the loop body.
- Distance is updated (reduced by 3.5) during each iteration.

Remember that similar steps must appear in every loop that you write. ■

Exercises for Section 5.3

Self-Check

1. What is the least number of times that the body of a while loop can be executed?
2. a. What is displayed by the following segment?

```
Sum := 0;
while Sum < 100 do
Sum := Sum + 5;
WriteLn (Sum :1);
```

   b. Rewrite the loop so that it prints all multiples of 5 from 0 through 100, inclusive.
3. a. What values are displayed if the data value in the sample run of the program in Fig. 5.7 is 9.45?
   b. What values would be displayed by this program if the order of the statements in the loop body were reversed?
4. a. How would you modify the loop in Fig. 5.7 so that it also determines the number of moves (CountMoves) made by the worm before it enters the apple?
   b. In your modified loop, which is the loop-control variable, Distance or CountMoves?

Programming

1. There are 9,870 people in a town whose population increases by 10% each year. Write a loop that determines how many years (CountYears) it would take for the population to go over 30,000.

5.4 Loop Design

It is one thing to be able to analyze the operation of a loop and another to design our own loops. We will attack this problem in two ways. One approach is to analyze the requirements for a new loop to determine what initialization, testing, and updating of the loop-control variable are needed. A second approach is to develop templates for loop forms that frequently recur and to use a template as the basis for a new loop. (We discuss loop templates later in this section.)

To gain some insight into the design of the loop needed for the worm problem, we study the comment in Fig. 5.7 that summarizes the goal of this loop.

```
{
 Cut the distance between the worm and the apple by the worm's
 body length until the worm is close enough to enter the apple.
}
```

To accomplish this goal, we must concern ourselves with loop control and loop processing. Loop control involves making sure that loop exit occurs when it is supposed to; loop processing involves making sure the loop body performs the required operations.

To help us formulate the necessary loop control and loop-processing steps, it is useful to list what we know about the loop. In this example, if `Distance` is the distance of the worm from the apple, we can make three observations:

1. `Distance` must be equal to `InitialDist` just before the loop begins.
2. `Distance` during pass i must be less than the value of `Distance` during pass $i - 1$ by the length of the worm.
3. `Distance` must be between zero and the worm's body length just after loop exit.

Statement 1 simply indicates that `InitialDist` is the starting distance of the worm from the apple. Statement 2 says that the distance of the worm from the apple must be cut by the worm's body length during each iteration. Statement 3 is derived from the fact that the worm must be close enough to enter the apple on its next move right after loop exit. Therefore, after loop exit, the worm's distance from the apple must be less than its body length. Because the worm has not yet entered the apple, the distance cannot be negative.

Statement 1 by itself tells us what initialization must be performed. Statement 2 tells us how to process `Distance` within the loop body (that is, subtract its body length). Finally, statement 3 tells us when to exit the loop. Since `Distance` is decreasing, loop exit should occur when `Distance` < `WormLength` is true. These considerations give us the following outline, which is the basis for the `while` loop shown in Fig. 5.7. The loop-repetition condition, `Distance >= WormLength`, is the opposite of the exit condition, `Distance < WormLength`.

1. Initialize `Distance` to `InitialDist`
2. while `Distance >= WormLength` do
   begin

```
    3. Display Distance
    4. Reduce Distance by WormLength
end {while}
```

while Loops with Zero Iterations

The body of a while loop is not executed if the loop-repetition test fails (evaluates to False) when it is first reached. To verify that you have the correct initialization steps, make sure that your program still generates the correct results for zero iterations of the loop body. If WormLength is greater than the value read into InitialDist (say, 0.4), the loop body in Fig. 5.7 would not execute, and the following lines would be correctly displayed.

```
Enter initial distance between worm and apple in inches> 0.4
The last distance before the worm enters the apple is 0.4.
```

Displaying a Table of Values

The next example illustrates how to use a loop to display a table of values.

■ Example 5.4

Your physics professor wants you to write a program that displays the effect of gravity on a free-falling object. Your instructor would like a table that shows the height of an object dropped from a tower for every second that it is falling.

Assuming t is the time of free fall, we can make the following observations about the height of an object dropped from a tower:

- At $t = 0.0$, the object height is the same as the tower height.
- While it is falling, the object height is the tower height minus the distance that it has travelled.
- Free fall ends when the object height is less than or equal to 0.0.

These considerations form the basis for the while loop shown in Fig. 5.8. The object height (Height) is initialized to the tower height (Tower). The while condition

```
Height > 0.0
```

ensures that loop exit occurs when the object hits the ground. Within the loop body, the assignment statement

```
Height := Tower - 0.5 * G * Sqr(T)
```

computes the object height, where distance travelled is represented by the formula

$$distance = \tfrac{1}{2}gt^2$$

and g is the gravitational constant.

The number of lines in the table depends on the time interval between lines (DeltaT) and the tower height (Tower), both of which are data values. During each loop iteration, the current elapsed time, t, and the current object height, Height, are displayed and new values are assigned to these variables. The message following the table is displayed when the object hits the ground.

■

Figure 5.8 Dropping an Object from a Tower

```pascal
program FreeFall (Input, Output);
{
  Displays the height of an object dropped
  from a tower until it hits the ground
}

  const
    G = 9.80665;        {gravitational constant for metric units}

  var
    Height,             {height of object}
    Tower,              {height of tower}
    T,                  {elapsed time}
    DeltaT : Real;      {time interval}

begin {FreeFall}
  {Enter tower height and time interval.}
  Write ('Tower height in meters> ');
  ReadLn (Tower);
  Write ('Time in seconds between table lines> ');
  ReadLn (DeltaT);  WriteLn;

  {Display object height until it hits the ground.}
  WriteLn ('Time' :10, 'Height' :10);
  T := 0.0;
  Height := Tower;
  while Height > 0.0 do
    begin
      WriteLn (T :10:2, Height :10:2);
      T := T + DeltaT;
      Height := Tower - 0.5 * G * Sqr(T)
    end; {while}

  {Object hits the ground.}
  WriteLn;
  WriteLn ('SPLATT!!!')
end. {FreeFall}

Tower height in meters> 100.0
Time in seconds between table lines> 1.0
      Time      Height
      0.00      100.00
      1.00       95.10
      2.00       80.39
      3.00       55.87
      4.00       21.55

SPLATT!!!
```

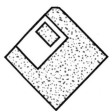

Directory: CHAP5
File: FREEFALL.PAS

Displaying a Table

The program in Fig. 5.8 displays a table of output values. Before the loop is reached, the statement

```
WriteLn ('Time' :10, 'Height' :10);
```

displays the two strings that appear in the table headings. Since a string is printed right-justified in its field, the rightmost character of the first string appears in column 10 and the rightmost character of the second string appears in column 20 (10 + 10).

Within the loop body, the statement

```
WriteLn (T :10:2, Height :10:2);
```

displays a pair of output values each time it is executed. The rightmost digit of the first number appears in column 10, and the rightmost digit of the second number appears in column 20. Therefore, a table consisting of two columns of numbers is displayed, and each column is right-aligned with its respective heading. Make sure that the field width (10, in this case) is big enough to accommodate the largest value that will be printed.

Working Backward to Determine Loop Initialization

It is not always so easy to come up with the initialization steps for a loop. In some cases, we must work backward from the results that we know are required in the first pass to determine what initial values will produce those results.

■ Example 5.5

Your 10-year-old cousin is learning the binary number system and has asked you to write a program that displays all powers of 2 that are less than a certain value (say, 10,000). Assuming that each power of 2 is stored in the variable Power, we can make two observations about the loop.

1. Power during pass i is 2 times Power during pass $i - 1$ (for $i > 1$).
2. Power must be between 10,000 and 20,000 just after loop exit.

Statement 1 derives from the fact that the powers of 2 are all multiples of 2; statement 2 from the fact that only powers less than 10,000 are to be displayed. From statement 1 we know that Power must be multiplied by 2 in the loop body. From statement 2 we know that the loop exit condition is Power >= 10000, so the loop repetition condition is Power < 10000. These considerations lead us to the following outline:

```
1. Initialize Power to ___
2. while Power < 10000 do
      begin
         3. Display Power
         4. Multiply Power by 2
      end
```

One way to complete step 1 is to ask what value should be displayed during the first loop repetition. The value of N raised to the power 0 is 1 for any number N. Therefore, if we initialize Power to 1, the value displayed during the first loop repetition will be correct.

1. Initialize Power to 1 ∎

Sentinel-Controlled Loops

Frequently, you will not know exactly how many data items a program will process before it begins execution. This may happen because there are too many data items to count beforehand or because the number of data items provided depends on how the computation proceeds.

One way to handle this situation is to instruct the user to enter a unique data value, called a *sentinel value,* as the last data item. The program then tests each data item and terminates when the sentinel value is read. The sentinel value should be carefully chosen and must be a value that could not normally occur as data.

■ Example 5.6

The following statements must be true for a sentinel-controlled loop that accumulates the sum (in Sum) of a collection of exam scores where each score is read into the variable Score. The sentinel score must not be included in the sum.

1. Sum is the sum of all scores read so far.
2. Score contains the sentinel value just after loop exit.

From statement 1 we know that we must add each score to Sum in the loop body and that Sum initially must be 0 for its final value to be correct. From statement 2 we know that loop exit must occur after the sentinel value is read into Score. These considerations lead to the following trial loop form:

Incorrect Sentinel-Controlled Loop
***

1. Initialize Sum to 0
2. while Score is not the sentinel do
    begin
        3. Read the next score into Score
        4. Add Score to Sum
    end

Since Score has not been given an initial value, the while condition in step 2 cannot be evaluated when the loop is first reached. Another problem is that after step 3 reads the sentinel value, step 4 adds the sentinel value to Sum before loop exit occurs. The solution to these problems is to read the first score as the initial value of Score before the loop is reached and to switch the order of the read and add steps in the loop body. The outline for this solution is shown next.

1. Initialize Sum to 0
2. Read the first score into Score
3. while Score is not the sentinel do
   begin
   4. Add Score to Sum
   5. Read the next score into Score
   end

Step 2 reads in the first score, and step 4 adds this score to 0 (initial value of Sum). Step 5 reads all remaining scores, including the sentinel. Step 4 adds all scores except the sentinel to Sum.

The initial read before the loop (step 2) is often called the *priming read*. This is analogous to the process of priming a pump, which is done by pouring a cup of water into the pump chamber before the pump can be used to draw water out of a well.

Figure 5.9 shows a Pascal program that codes this loop. The sentinel value used is −1, because all exam scores should be non-negative. The constant declaration

```
const
   Sentinel = -1;        {sentinel value}
```

associates the constant Sentinel with the sentinel value.

Figure 5.9   Using a Sentinel-Controlled Loop

Directory: CHAP5
File: SUMSCORE.PAS

```
program SumScores (Input, Output);
{Accumulates the sum of exam scores}

   const
      Sentinel = -1;           {sentinel value}

   var
      Score,                   {input - each exam score}
      Sum : Integer;           {output - sum of scores}

begin {SumScores}
   {Accumulate the sum.}
   Sum := 0;
   WriteLn ('When done, enter -1 to stop.');
   Write ('Enter the first score> ');
   ReadLn (Score);
   while Score <> Sentinel do
      begin
         Sum := Sum + Score;
         Write ('Enter the next score> ');
         ReadLn (Score)
      end; {while}

   {Display the sum.}
   WriteLn;
   WriteLn ('Sum of exam scores is ', Sum :1)
end. {SumScores}
```

```
When done, enter -1 to stop.
Enter the first score> 55
Enter the next  score> 33
Enter the next  score> 77
Enter the next  score> -1

Sum of exam scores is 165
```

Although it may look strange at first to see the statement

```
ReadLn (Score);
```

at two different points in the program, this is a perfectly good programming practice and causes no problems. The sample run shown in Fig. 5.9 processes the scores 55, 33, and 77. The sentinel value (−1) is the last data value entered, but it is not included in the sum.

It is usually instructive (and often necessary) to question what happens when there are no data items to process. In that case, the sentinel value should be entered as the "first score." Loop exit would occur right after the first (and only) test of the loop repetition condition, so the loop body would not be executed; in other words, it is a loop with zero iterations. Sum would retain its initial value of 0, which would be correct. ∎

Template for a Sentinel-Controlled Loop

Sentinel-controlled loops have the general form shown next.

1. Read the first value of *input variable*
2. while *input variable* is not equal to the sentinel do
   begin
   . . .
       Read the next value of *input variable*
   end

The sentinel value must be a value that would not be entered as a normal data item. For program readability, we usually store the sentinel value in a constant.

Loops Controlled by Boolean Flags

Boolean variables are often used as *program flags,* which signal whether or not a particular event occurs. The flag value should be False if the event has not occurred and True if it has occurred. A flag-controlled loop executes until the event being monitored occurs.

For example, let's assume we are reading various data characters typed at the keyboard, and we want to save the first digit character that is read. A Boolean variable, say DigitRead, could be used as a flag to monitor whether a digit character has been read.

Program Variable
```
DigitRead : Boolean    {program flag – value is True after
                        a digit character has been read;
                        otherwise, value is False.        }
```

Because no characters have been read before the data entry loop executes, we should initialize DigitRead to False. The while loop must continue to execute as long as DigitRead is False, because this means that the event "digit character read as data" has not yet occurred. Therefore, the loop repetition condition should be (not DigitRead), because this condition is True when DigitRead is False. Within the loop body, we will read each data item and set the value of DigitRead to True if that data item is a digit character. The while loop follows.

```
DigitRead := False;         {assume no digit character was read}
while (not DigitRead) do
  begin
    Write ('Enter another data character >');
    ReadLn (NextChar);
    DigitRead := ('0' <= NextChar) and (NextChar <= '9')
  end {while}
```

Inside the loop body, the assignment statement

```
DigitRead := ('0' <= NextChar) and (NextChar <= '9')
```

assigns a value of True to DigitRead if NextChar is a digit character (within the range '0' through '9'); otherwise, DigitRead remains False. If DigitRead becomes True, loop exit occurs; if DigitRead remains False, the loop continues to execute until a digit character is finally read.

Template for a Flag-Controlled Loop

The general form of a flag-controlled loop is shown next.

1. Initialize *flag* to False
2. while *flag* is still False do
     begin
       . . .
         Reset *flag* to True if event being monitored occurs
     end

The last step in the loop body updates the flag value, setting it to True after the first occurrence of the event being monitored.

Exercises for Section 5.4

Self-Check

1. Describe how it would be possible to "work backward" to determine the initial value of the loop variable required for programming exercise 3 of this section.

2. Why would it be incorrect to move the assignment statement in the sentinel-controlled loop of Fig. 5.9 to the end of the loop body?

Programming

1. Modify the counter-controlled loop in Fig. 5.4 so that it is a sentinel-controlled loop. Use a negative value of Hours as the sentinel.
2. Write a program segment that allows the user to enter values and prints out the number of positive values entered and the number of negative values entered. Use 0 as the sentinel value.
3. Write the while loop that displays all powers of an integer, n, less than a specified value, MaxPower. On each line of a table, show the power (0, 1, 2, . . .) and the value of the integer n raised to that power.
4. Write a loop that prints a table of angle measures along with their sine and cosine values. Assume that the initial and final angle measures (in degrees) are available in InitDeg and FinalDeg (type Real), respectively, and that the change in angle measure between table entries is given by StepDeg.
5. Write a flag-controlled loop that continues to read pairs of integers until it reads a pair with the property that the first integer in the pair is evenly divisible by the second.

5.5 The for Statement

So far, we have used the while statement to implement repetition in programs. Recall from Section 5.2 that a counter variable controls the repetition of a counter-controlled loop and that a counter-controlled loop has the following template:

```
Set counter to initial value
while counter <= final value do
   begin
      . . .
      increment counter to its next value
   end
```

Pascal provides another loop form, the for statement, that is more efficient for implementing counter-controlled loops. The pseudocode that follows describes a for statement that has the same behavior as the preceding while statement.

```
for counter := initial value to final value do
   begin
      . . .
   end
```

All manipulation of the counter is specified in the for statement header. These three operations are:

1. Initialize *counter* to *initial value*.
2. Test if *counter* <= *final value*.
3. Increment *counter* to its next value before each test.

■ Example 5.7

The following two statements behave in the same way.

```
{Print N blank lines}          {Print N blank lines}
Line := 1;                     for Line := 1 to N do
while Line <= N do                WriteLn
  begin
    WriteLn;
    Line := Line + 1
  end {while}
```

If Line is declared as an integer variable, the for statement on the right causes the WriteLn operation to be performed N times. The while loop implementation shown on the left is longer because of the assignment statements

```
Line := 1;
Line := Line + 1
```

which are needed to initialize and update the counter variable.   ■

■ Example 5.8

The for statement in Fig. 5.10 reads payroll data for seven employees and computes and displays each employee's weekly pay. Compare it with the while statement shown in Fig. 5.1.

Figure 5.10   for Loop to Process Seven Employees

```
for EmpNumber := 1 to 7 do
  begin
    Write ('Hours >');
    ReadLn (Hours);
    Write ('Rate  > $');
    ReadLn (Rate);
    Pay := Hours * Rate;
    WriteLn ('Weekly pay is $', Pay :4:2)
  end; {for}

WriteLn ('All employees processed')
```

You should read the first line of Fig. 5.10 as "for each value of EmpNumber from 1 to 7 do." There is no need to provide additional Pascal statements to set EmpNumber to an initial value or to update the value of EmpNumber; these two operations are automatically performed in a for loop.   ■

■ Example 5.9

Figure 5.11 shows a procedure, PrintI, that displays the letter I in block form. This procedure prints seven lines that contain asterisks in columns 4 and 5. A blank line is printed just before the return from the procedure.

Figure 5.11 Procedure PrintI

197

5.5 The for Statement

```
procedure PrintI;
{Prints the block letter I}

    var
      NextLine : Integer;   {Loop-control variable -
                                from 1 to 7             }

begin {PrintI}
  for NextLine := 1 to 7 do
    WriteLn ('    **');
  WriteLn
end; {PrintI}
```

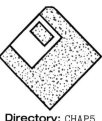

Directory: CHAP5
File: PRINTI.PAS

The for statement in Fig. 5.11 specifies that the counter variable NextLine should take on each of the values in the range 1 to 7 during successive loop repetitions. This means that the value of NextLine is 1 during the first loop repetition, 2 during the second loop repetition, and 7 during the last loop repetition. ∎

PROGRAM
STYLE

Counter Variables as Local Variables

In Fig. 5.11, the counter variable NextLine is declared as a local variable in procedure PrintI. All counter variables must be declared as local variables.

The counter variable may be referenced in the loop body, but its value cannot be changed. In the next example, you'll see a for statement for which the counter variable is referenced in the loop body.

∎ Example 5.10

The program in Fig. 5.12 uses a for loop to print a list of integer values and their squares and square roots. During each repetition of the loop body, the statements

```
Square := Sqr(I);
Root := Sqrt(I);
```

compute the square and square root of the counter variable I; then the values of I, Square, and Root are displayed. Table 5.1 traces the execution of the for loop. ∎

Figure 5.12 Table of Integers, Squares, and Square Roots

```
program Squares (Output);
{Displays a table of integers and their squares and square roots}

  const
    MaxI = 4;              {largest integer in table}
```

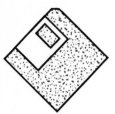

```
var
   I,                   {counter variable}
   Square : Integer;    {output - square of I}
   Root : Real;         {output - square root of I}

begin {Squares}
   {Prints a list of integers, their squares, and their square roots}
   WriteLn ('I' :10, 'I * I' :10, 'Square root' :15);
   for I := 1 to MaxI do
      begin
         Square := Sqr(I);
         Root := Sqrt(I);
         WriteLn (I :10, Square :10, Root :15:1)
      end {for}
end. {Squares}
```

```
       I     I * I    Square root
       1       1         1.0
       2       4         1.4
       3       9         1.7
       4      16         2.0
```

Table 5.1 Trace of Program in Figure 5.12

Statement	I	Square	Root	Effect
	?	?	?	
for I := 1, MaxI	1			Initialize I to 1.
Square := Sqr(I);		1		Assign 1 to Square.
Root := Sqrt(I);			1.0	Assign 1.0 to Root.
WriteLn ...				Print 1, 1, 1.0.
Increment and test I	2			2 <= 4 is true.
Square := Sqr(I);		4		Assign 4 to Square.
Root := Sqrt(I);			1.4	Assign 1.4 to Root.
WriteLn ...				Print 2, 4, 1.4.
Increment and test I	3			3 <= 4 is true.
Square := Sqr(I);		9		Assign 9 to Square.
Root := Sqrt(I);			1.7	Assign 1.7 to Root.
WriteLn ...				Print 3, 9, 1.7.
Increment and test I	4			4 <= 4 is true.
Square := Sqr(I);		16		Assign 16 to Square.
Root := Sqrt(I);			2.0	Assign 2.0 to Root.
WriteLn ...				Print 4, 16, 2.0.
Increment and test I	?			Exit loop.

The trace in Table 5.1 shows that the counter variable I is initialized to 1 when the for loop is reached. After each loop repetition, I is incremented by 1 and tested to see whether its value is still less than or equal to MaxI (4). If the test result is true, the loop body is executed again, and the next values of I, Square, and Root are printed. If the test result is false, the loop is exited.

I is equal to MaxI during the last loop repetition. After this repetition, the value of I becomes undefined (indicated by ? in the last table line), and the loop is exited. You should not reference the variable I again until it is given a new value.

Syntax of the for Statement

The syntax display of the for statement follows; Fig. 5.13 shows the syntax diagram. When writing a for statement, make sure that you do not place a semicolon after the word do. For example, the for statement

```
for I := -5 to 5 do;          {empty statement after do}
   WriteLn (I :1);
```

executes an empty statement 11 times. After loop exit, the value of I is considered undefined, so there is no way of knowing what will be displayed by the WriteLn statement. If the semicolon after do is removed, the for statement lists the integers from -5 through 5.

Figure 5.13   Syntax Diagram of the for Statement

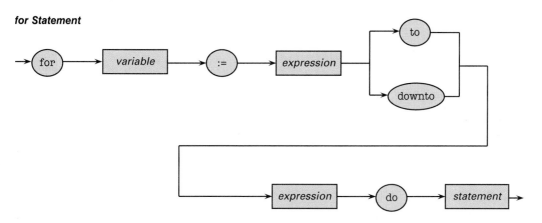

for Statement

The for Statement

Form: for *counter* := *initial* to *final* do
            statement

   for *counter* := *initial* downto *final* do
            statement

Example: for I := 1 to 5 do
            begin
               ReadLn (Indata, NextNum);
               Sum := Sum + NextNum
            end;

```
         for CountDown := 10 downto 0 do
            WriteLn (CountDown :2)
```
Interpretation: The *statement* that comprises the loop body is executed once for each value of *counter* between *initial* and *final*, inclusive. *initial* and *final* may be constants, variables, or expressions of the same ordinal type as *counter*.

Note 1: The value of *counter* cannot be modified in *statement*.

Note 2: The value of *final* is computed once, just before loop entry. If *final* is an expression, any change in the value of that expression will have no effect on the number of iterations performed.

Note 3: After loop exit, the value of *counter* is considered undefined.

Note 4: *statement* is not executed if *initial* is greater than *final*. (In the downto form, *statement* is not executed if *initial* is less than *final*.)

Changing Variables in Final Expressions

The for statement

```
ReadLn (K);
for I : = 0 to 3 * K − 1 do
   WriteLn (I + K);
```

contains the variable K in its *final expression*. This expression is evaluated when the for statement is entered. If the value read into K is 3, the *final expression* value is 8, so the loop body executes for values of I between 0 and 8, inclusive, and the WriteLn statement displays the nine integers in the range 3 through 11.

What happens if we change the value of K in the loop body? In the for statement

```
ReadLn (K);
for I := 0 to 3 * K − 1 do
   begin
      WriteLn (I + K);
      K := K + 1
   end; {for}
```

the value of K increases each time the loop body executes. If the same value is read into K as before, does this change the number of loop repetitions? The answer is "No"; the *final expression* is evaluated only once, and its value depends only on the initial value read into K. However, because the values of both I and K increase by 1 each time the loop body executes, the values displayed will change. If we read the value 3 into K again, the WriteLn statement will now display the nine odd integers in the range 3 through 19. Self-check exercise 2 at the end of this section asks you to trace the loop execution for yourself to confirm this result.

Type Char Counter Variables

The for loop can be used with other ordinal types besides Integer. The next example uses a counter variable of type Char.

■ Example 5.11
The following for loop prints each uppercase letter and its lowercase equivalent on a line (for example, Aa). (We describe functions Chr and Ord in Section 7.5.) The counter variable, Next, must be type Char.

```
for Next := 'A' to 'Z' do
   WriteLn (Next, Chr(Ord(Next) + 32))                    ■
```

Counting Down

The examples given so far use the reserved word to and increase the value of the counter variable after each loop repetition. If the reserved word downto is used instead, the value of the counter variable decreases after each loop repetition.

■ Example 5.12
A student wants a table showing the Fahrenheit temperature that corresponds to each integer Celsius (C) temperature from 5 degrees C downto −10 degrees C. She could use the following for loop:

```
for Celsius := 5 downto −10 do
   begin
      Fahrenheit := 1.8 * Celsius + 32;
      WriteLn (Celsius :10, Fahrenheit :15:1)
   end;  {for}                                             ■
```

Exercises for Section 5.5

Self-Check

1. a. Trace the following program segment:

```
J := 10;
for I := 1 to 5 do
   begin
      WriteLn (I, J);
      J := J − 2
   end; {for}
```

   b. Rewrite the preceding program segment so that it produces the same output but uses 0 as the initial value of I.

2. Trace both for loops in the subsection "Changing Variables in Final Expressions."

3. Write for loop headers that process all value of Celsius (type Integer) in the following ranges:

a. -10 through $+10$
b. 100 through 1
c. 15 through 50
d. 50 through -75

4. Which of the built-in Pascal data types can be used to declare `for` loop counter variables?

Programming

1. Write a program segment containing a `for` statement that computes the sum of the odd integers in the range 0 to 100, inclusive.
2. Redo programming exercise 1 from Section 5.2 using a `for` loop to compute the sum of the first N positive integers and compare this sum to the value computed using the formula

$$\frac{N(N + 1)}{2.0}$$

5.6 The repeat Statement

The `repeat` statement is used to specify a conditional loop that is repeated until its condition becomes true. Such a loop is called a *repeat-until* loop.

■ Example 5.13

Both program segments in Fig. 5.14 print the powers of 2 whose values lie between 1 and 1000.

Figure 5.14 while (*left*) and repeat (*right*) Statements

```
Power := 1;                          Power := 1;
while Power < 1000 do                repeat
  begin                                Write (Power :5);
    Write (Power :5);                  Power := Power * 2
    Power := Power * 2               until Power >= 1000
  end  {while}
```

The test used in the repeat–until loop (Power >= 1000) is the *logical complement*, or opposite, of the test used in the while loop. The loop body is repeated until the value of Power is greater than or equal to 1000. Since loop repetition stops when the condition is true, the test is called a *loop-termination test* rather than a loop-repetition test. (We discuss logical complements further in Section 7.3).

The syntax display for the repeat statement follows; Fig. 5.15 shows its syntax diagram. Note that there is no need for a begin–end bracket around the loop body because the reserved words repeat and until perform this function. ■

The repeat Statement (repeat-until Loop)

Form: `repeat`
       loop-body
    `until` *termination-condition*

Example: `repeat`
     `Write ('Enter a digit> ');`
     `Read (Ch)`
  `until ('0' <= Ch) and (Ch <= '9')`

Interpretation: After each execution of *loop body, termination-condition* is evaluated. If *termination-condition* is true, loop exit occurs and the next program statement is executed. If *termination-condition* is false, *loop-body* is repeated.

Figure 5.15 Syntax Diagram of the repeat Statement

repeat statement

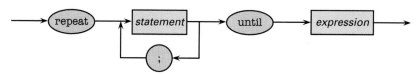

■ Example 5.14

The program in Fig. 5.16 uses a `repeat–until` loop to find the largest value in a sequence of data items. The variable `Item` is used to hold each data item, and the variable `LargestSoFar` is used to save the largest data value encountered. Within the loop, the `if` statement

```
if Item > LargestSoFar then
   Largest := Item              {save the new largest number}
```

redefines the value of `LargestSoFar` if the current data item is larger than all previous data values.

Figure 5.16 Finding the Largest Value

```
program Largest (Input, Output);
{Finds the largest number in a sequence of integer values}

const
  MinValue = –MaxInt;       {a very small integer}

  var
    Item,                   {each data value}
    LargestSoFar : Integer;   {largest value so far}

begin  {Largest}
  {Initialize LargestSoFar to a very small integer.}
  LargestSoFar := MinValue;
```

Directory: CHAP5
File: LARGEST.PAS

```
{Save the largest number encountered so far.}
WriteLn ('Finding the largest value in a sequence:');
repeat
  Write ('Enter an integer or ', MinValue :1, ' to stop> ');
  ReadLn (Item);
  if Item > LargestSoFar then
    LargestSoFar := Item          {save the new largest number}
until Item = MinValue;

  WriteLn ('The largest value entered was ', LargestSoFar :1)
end.  {Largest}
```

```
Finding the largest value in a sequence:
Enter an integer or -32767 to stop> -999
Enter an integer or -32767 to stop> 500
Enter an integer or -32767 to stop> 100
Enter an integer or -32767 to stop> -32767
The largest value entered was 500
```

The constant `MinValue`, which represents a very small integer value, serves two purposes in program `Largest`. By initializing `LargestSoFar` to `MinValue` before loop entry, we ensure that the condition `Item > LargestSoFar` will be true during the first loop repetition, so the first data item will be saved as the largest value so far. We are also using `MinValue` as a sentinel because it is unlikely to be entered as a data item for a program that is finding the largest number in a sequence. ∎

■ Example 5.15

A `repeat` statement is often used to control a *menu-driven program,* which prints a list of choices from which the program user selects a program operation. For example, the menu displayed for a statistics program might look like this:

```
1. Compute an average.
2. Compute a standard deviation.
3. Find the median.
4. Find the smallest and largest value.
5. Plot the data.
6. Exit the program.
```

The main control routine for such a program would follow the pseudocode below, where `ExitChoice` is the constant 6.

```
repeat
  Display the menu
  Read the user's choice
  Perform the user's choice
until choice is ExitChoice
```

The following program fragment (Fig. 5.17) implements this loop in Pascal. For each iteration, procedure `DisplayMenu` displays the menu and the user's choice is read. Procedure `DoChoice` is called with the actual parameter `Choice`, and the loop repeats if the user's choice is not `ExitChoice`. (You will see how to write procedures with parameters in the next chapter.) ∎

```
repeat
  DisplayMenu;                       {Display the menu choices}
  WriteLn ('Enter a number between 1 and ', ExitChoice :1);
  ReadLn (Choice);
  DoChoice (Choice)                  {perform the user's choice}
until Choice = ExitChoice
```

Review of for, while, and repeat Loops

Pascal contains three kinds of loops: for, while, and repeat. You should use
the for loop as a counting loop, that is, a loop for which the number of iterations
required can be determined at the beginning of loop execution. The loop-
control variable of a for loop must belong to an ordinal type (not Real).

The while and repeat loops are both conditional loops; their number of
iterations depends on whether the value of a condition is True or False. The
while loop is repeated as long as its loop-repetition condition is true; the repeat
loop is repeated until its loop-termination condition becomes true. It is relatively
easy to rewrite a repeat loop as a while loop by complementing the condition.
However, not all while loops can be written as repeat loops, because a repeat
loop will always execute at least once, whereas a while loop body may be skipped
entirely. For this reason, a while loop is preferred over a repeat loop unless
you are certain that at least one loop iteration must always be performed.

To illustrate the three loop forms, Fig. 5.18 presents a simple counting
loop. (The ellipses represent the loop body.) The for loop is the best to use in
this situation. The repeat loop must be nested in an if statement to prevent
it from being executed when StartValue is greater than StopValue. For this
reason, the repeat–until version of a counting loop is least desirable.

Figure 5.18 Comparison of the Three Loop Forms

```
for Count := StartValue to StopValue do
  begin
    . . .
  end   {for}


Count := StartValue
while Count <= StopValue do
  begin
    . . .
    Count := Count + 1
  end   {while}


Count := StartValue;
if StartValue <= StopValue then
  repeat
    . . .
    Count := Count + 1
  until Count > StopValue
```

In Fig. 5.18, Count, StartValue, and StopValue must all be the same ordinal type. The assignment statement

```
Count := Count + 1
```

is used in both the while and repeat loops to update the loop control-variable Count (not required in the for statement). Count will be equal to StopValue + 1 after the while or repeat loops are executed; Count will be equal to StartValue if these loops are skipped. The value of Count is considered undefined after loop exit in the for loop version and must be redefined before its next use.

Exercises for Section 5.6

Self-Check

1. What does the following while statement display? Rewrite it as a for statement and then as a repeat statement.

```
Num := 10;
while Num <= 100 do
  begin
    WriteLn (Num);
    Num := Num + 10
  end   {while}
```

2. What does the following for statement display? Rewrite it as a while statement and then as a repeat statement.

```
for N := 3 downto -1 do
  WriteLn (N, ' squared is ', Sqr(N))
```

3. When would you use a repeat–until loop rather than a while loop in a program?

Programming

1. Write a program fragment that skips over a sequence of positive integer values read as data until it reaches a negative value. Write two versions: one using repeat and one using while.
2. Write a program fragment that could be used as the main control loop in a menu-driven program for updating an account balance (W = withdrawal, D = deposit, Q = quit). Assume that procedures ProcessWithdrawal and ProcessDeposit already exist and are called with the actual parameter Balance. Prompt the user for a transaction code (W, D, or Q) and call the appropriate procedure.

5.7 Nested Loops

This section examines nested loops. You have seen examples of nested if statements in earlier programs. It is also possible to nest loops. Nested loops consist of an outer loop with one or more inner loops. Each time the outer loop is repeated, the inner loops are reentered, their loop-control parameters are reevaluated, and all required iterations are performed.

■ Example 5.16

Figure 5.19 shows a sample run of a program with two nested `for` loops. The outer loop is repeated three times (for I equals 1, 2, 3). Each time the outer loop is repeated, the statement

```
WriteLn ('Outer' :5, I :7);
```

displays the string `'Outer'` and the value of I (the outer loop-control variable). Next, the inner loop is entered, and its loop-control variable, J, is reset to 1. The number of times the inner loop is repeated depends on the current value of I. Each time the inner loop is repeated, the statement

```
WriteLn ('Inner' :7, J :10)
```

displays the string `'Inner'` and the value of J.

Figure 5.19 Program with Nested for Loops

```
program NestLoop (Output);
{Illustrates a pair of nested for loops}

   var
     I, J : Integer;              {loop-control variables}

begin  {NestLoop}
   WriteLn ('I' :12, 'J' :5);    {Print heading.}
   for I := 1 to 3 do
     begin  {outer loop}
       WriteLn ('Outer' :5, I :7);
       for J := 1 to I do
         WriteLn ('Inner' :7, J :10)
     end  {outer loop}
end.  {NestLoop}
```

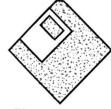

Directory: CHAP5
File: NESTLOOP.PAS

```
          I   J
Outer     1
   Inner      1
Outer     2
   Inner      1
   Inner      2
Outer     3
   Inner      1
   Inner      2
   Inner      3
```

The outer loop-control variable, I, is the loop parameter that determines the number of repetitions of the inner loop. Although this is perfectly valid, you cannot use the same variable as the loop-control variable of both an outer and inner `for` loop in the same nest. ■

■ Example 5.17

Program `Triangle` in Fig. 5.20 draws an isosceles triangle. The program contains an outer loop (loop-control variable Row) and two inner loops. Each time the outer loop is repeated, two inner loops are executed. The first inner loop prints the leading blank spaces; the second inner loop prints one or more asterisks.

Figure 5.20   Isosceles Triangle Program

Directory: CHAP5
File: TRIANGLE.PAS

```
program Triangle (Output);
{Draws an isosceles triangle}

  const
    NumLines = 5;                    {number of rows in triangle}
    Blank = ' ';  Star = '*';    {output characters}

  var
    Row,                         {loop control for outer loop}
    LeadBlanks,                {loop control for first inner loop}
    CountStars : Integer;    {loop control for second inner loop}

begin  {Triangle}
  for Row := 1 to NumLines do
    begin                                  {Draw each row.}
      for LeadBlanks := NumLines - Row downto 1 do
        Write (Blank);                 {Print leading blanks.}
      for CountStars := 1 to 2 * Row - 1 do
        Write (Star);                        {Print asterisks.}
      WriteLn                               {Terminate line.}
    end  {for Row}
end.  {Triangle}



    *
   ***
  *****
 *******
*********
```

The outer loop is repeated five times; the number of repetitions performed by the inner loops is based on the value of Row. Table 5.2 lists the inner loop-control parameters for each value of Row. As shown in Table 5.2, four blanks and one asterisk are printed when Row is 1, three blanks and three asterisks are pritned when Row is 2, and so on. When Row is 5, the first inner loop is skipped, and nine (2 * 5 - 1) asterisks are printed.   ■

Table 5.2   Inner Loop-Control Parameters

Row	LeadBlanks	CountStars	**Effect**
1	4 downto 1	1 to 1	Displays 4 blanks and 1 star
2	3 downto 1	1 to 3	Displays 3 blanks and 3 stars
3	2 downto 1	1 to 5	Displays 2 blanks and 5 stars

Row	LeadBlanks	CountStars	Effect
4	1 downto 1	1 to 7	Displays 1 blank and 7 stars
5	0 downto 1	1 to 9	Displays 0 blanks and 9 stars

■ Example 5.18

The program in Fig. 5.21 prints the addition table for integer values between 0 and 9. For example, the last table line shows the result of adding to 9 each of the digits 0 through 9. The initial for loop prints the table heading, which is the operator +, and the list of digits from 0 through 9.

The nested for loops are used to print the table body. The outer for loop (loop-control variable Addend1) first prints the current value of Addend1. In the inner for loop, each value of Addend2 (0 through 9) is added to Addend1, and the individual sums are printed. Each time the outer loop is repeated, 10 additions are performed; a total of 100 sums are printed. ■

Figure 5.21 Printing an Addition Table

Directory: CHAP5
File: ADDTABLE.PAS

```
program AddTable (Output);
{Prints an addition table}

   const
     MaxDigit = 9;                    {largest digit}

   var
     Addend1,                         {first addend}
     Addend2,                         {second addend}
     Sum      : Integer;              {sum of addends}
begin  {AddTable}
   {Print the table heading.}
   Write ('+');
   for Addend2 := 0 to MaxDigit do
     Write (Addend2: 3);             {Print each digit in heading.}
   WriteLn;                          {Terminate heading.}

   {Print the table body.}
   for Addend1 := 0 to MaxDigit do
     begin                          {Print each row of the table.}
       Write (Addend1 :1);          {Identify first addend.}
       for Addend2 := 0 to MaxDigit do
         begin
           Sum := Addend1 + Addend2;
           Write (Sum :3)            {Print sum of addends.}
         end;  {for Addend2}
       WriteLn                       {Terminate table row.}
     end {for Addend1}
end.  {AddTable}
```

```
+  0  1  2  3  4  5  6  7  8  9
0  0  1  2  3  4  5  6  7  8  9
1  1  2  3  4  5  6  7  8  9 10
2  2  3  4  5  6  7  8  9 10 11
3  3  4  5  6  7  8  9 10 11 12
4  4  5  6  7  8  9 10 11 12 13
5  5  6  7  8  9 10 11 12 13 14
6  6  7  8  9 10 11 12 13 14 15
7  7  8  9 10 11 12 13 14 15 16
8  8  9 10 11 12 13 14 15 16 17
9  9 10 11 12 13 14 15 16 17 18
```

Exercises for Section 5.7

Self-Check

1. What is displayed by the following program segments assuming M is 3 and N is 5?

   a.
   ```
   for I := 1 to N do
      begin
         for J := 1 to I do
            Write ('*');
         WriteLn
      end; {for I}
   ```

   b.
   ```
   for I := N downto 1 do
      begin
         for J := M downto 1 do
            Write ('*');
         WriteLn
      end; {for I}
   ```

2. Show the output printed by the following nested loops:

   ```
   for I := 1 to 2 do
      begin
         WriteLn ('Outer' :5, I :5);
         for J := 1 to 3 do
            WriteLn ('Inner' :7, I :3, J :3);
         for K := 2 downto 1 do
            WriteLn ('Inner' :7, I :3, K :3)
      end;  {for I}
   ```

Programming

1. Write a program that prints the multiplication table.
2. Write a nest of loops that causes the following output to be printed:

   ```
   1
   1 2
   1 2 3
   1 2 3 4
   1 2 3
   1 2
   1
   ```

5.8 Debugging and Testing Programs

In Section 2.8, we described the two general categories of error messages that you are likely to see: syntax errors and run-time errors. It is also possible for a program to execute without generating any error messages but still produce incorrect results. Sometimes the cause of a run-time error or the origin of incorrect results is apparent and the error can easily be fixed. However, often the error is not obvious and may require considerable effort to locate.

The first step in attempting to find a hidden error is to examine the program output to determine which part of the program is generating incorrect results. Then you can focus on the statements in that section to determine which one or ones are at fault. To help you locate problem areas, you may need to insert extra debugging statements that display intermediate results at different points in your program. You may also want to insert extra WriteLn statements to trace the values of certain critical variables during program execution. For example, if the loop in Fig. 5.9 is not computing the correct sum, you might want to insert an extra diagnostic WriteLn statement, as shown by the line in color in the following loop:

```
ReadLn (Score);
while Score <> Sentinel do
  begin
    Sum := Sum + Score;
    WriteLn ('***** score is ', Score, ' sum is ', Sum);
    Write ('Enter the next score> ');
    ReadLn (Score)
  end; {while}
```

The diagnostic WriteLn statement displays each partial sum that is accumulated and the current value of Score, along with a string of asterisks at the beginning of its output line. The asterisks make it easier to identify diagnostic output in the debugging runs and easier to locate the diagnostic WriteLn statements in the source program.

Be careful when you insert extra diagnostic WriteLn statements. Sometimes it will be necessary to add a begin-end bracket if a single statement inside an if or a while statement becomes a compound statement when a diagnostic WriteLn is added. If you insert a WriteLn statement after the last statement in the loop body, don't forget to separate the two statements with a semicolon.

Once it appears that you have located an error, you will want to take out the extra diagnostic statements. As a temporary measure, it is sometimes advisable to make the diagnostic statements comments by enclosing them in braces. If the same errors crop up again in later testing, it is easier to remove the braces than to retype the diagnostic statements. (You will see in the next chapter how to use a Boolean constant to turn diagnostic print statements off and on.)

Off-by-One Loop Errors

A fairly common error in programs with loops is a loop that executes one more time or one less time than it is supposed to. If a sentinel-controlled while loop performs an extra repetition, it may erroneously process the sentinel value along with the regular data.

If a while loop performs a counting operation, make sure that the initial and final values of the loop-control variable are correct. For example, the loop body below executes N + 1 times instead of N times. If your intention is to execute the loop body N times, change the while condition to Count < N.

```
Count := 0;
while Count <= N do
  begin
    Sum := Sum + Count;
    Count := Count + 1
  end;
```

Checking Loop Boundaries

You can get a good idea of whether a loop is correct by checking what happens at the *loop boundaries,* that is, the initial and final values of the loop-control variable. For a for loop, you should carefully evaluate the *initial expression* and the *final expression* to make sure that the values make sense. Then substitute these values everywhere the counter variable appears in the loop body and verify that you get the expected results at the boundaries. As an example, in the for loop

```
Sum := 0;
for I := K to N-K do
  Sum := Sum + Sqr(I);
```

check that the first value of the counter variable I is supposed to be K and that the last value is supposed to be N − K. Next, check that the assignment statement

```
Sum := Sum + Sqr(I);
```

is correct at these boundaries. When I is K, Sum gets the value of K squared. When I is N − K, the value of (N − K) squared is added to the previous Sum. As a final check, pick some small value of N and K (say, 3 and 1) and trace the loop execution to see that it computes Sum correctly for this case.

Using Debugger Programs

Many computer systems have *debugger programs* to help you debug a Pascal program. A debugger program lets you execute your program one statement at a time (*single-step execution*) so you can see the effect of each statement. You can select several variables whose values will be automatically displayed after each statement executes. This process allows you to trace the program's execution. Besides printing a diagnostic when a run-time error occurs, the debugger indicates the statement that caused the error and displays the values of the variables you selected.

You can also separate your program into segments by setting breakpoints at selected statements. A *breakpoint* is like a fence between two segments of a program. You can request the debugger to execute all statements from the last breakpoint up to the next breakpoint. When the program stops at a breakpoint, you can display selected variables and thus determine whether the program segment executed correctly. If a program segment executes correctly, you will want to execute through to the next breakpoint. If it does not, you may want to set more breakpoints within that segment or perhaps perform single-step execution through that segment.

Testing

After all errors have been corrected and the program appears to execute as expected, the program should be tested thoroughly to make sure that it works. In Section 4.6, we discussed tracing an algorithm and suggested that you provide enough sets of test data to ensure that all possible paths are traced. The same is true for a completed program. Make enough test runs to verify that the program works properly for representative samples of all possible data combinations.

Exercises for Section 5.8

Self-Check

1. For the `while` loop in the subsection entitled "Off-by-One Loop Errors," add debugging statements to show the value of the loop-control variable at the start of each repetition. Also, add debugging statements to show the value of Sum at the end of each loop repetition.
2. Do exercise 1 for the loop in the subsection "Checking Loop Boundaries."

5.9 Common Programming Errors

Beginners sometimes confuse `if` and `while` statements because both statements contain a condition. Make sure that you use an `if` statement to implement a decision step and a `while` statement to implement a conditional loop.

Be careful when you use tests for inequality to control the repetition of a `while` loop. For instance, the following loop is intended to process all transactions for a bank account `while` the balance is positive.

```
while Balance <> 0.0 do
   Update (Balance)
```

If the bank balance goes from a positive to a negative amount without being exactly `0.0`, the loop will not terminate; it will become an infinite loop. This loop would be safer:

```
while Balance > 0.0 do
   Update (Balance)
```

You should verify that the repetition condition for a `while` loop will eventually become false. If you use a sentinel-controlled loop, remember to provide a prompt that tells the program user what value to enter as the sentinel. Make sure that the sentinel value cannot be confused with a normal data item.

If the loop body contains more than one statement, remember to bracket it with `begin` and `end` (unless it is a `repeat-until` loop). Otherwise, only the first statement will be repeated, and the remaining statements will be executed when and if the loop is exited. The loop below will not terminate because the step that updates the loop-control variable is not considered part of the loop body. The program will continue to print the initial value of `Power` until it either exceeds its time limit or you instruct the computer to terminate its execution.

```
while Power <= 10000 do
   WriteLn ('Next power of N is ', Power :6);
   Power := Power * N;
```

Be sure to initialize to 0 a variable used for accumulating a sum by repeated addition, and to initialize to 1 a variable used for accumulating a product by repeated multiplication. Omitting this step will lead to results that are inaccurate.

The value of the counter variable in a `for` statement either increases by 1 (to form) or decreases by 1 (downto form) after each repetition. If `M` is greater than `N`, the following `WriteLn` statement will not execute because the initial value that would be assigned to `I` is larger than its final value.

```
for I := M to N do
   WriteLn (I, M, N);
```

Similarly, the `WriteLn` statement below will not execute because the initial value that would be assigned to `I` is smaller than its final value.

```
for I := N downto M do
   WriteLn (I, M, N);
```

A `repeat-until` loop always executes at least once. Use a `repeat` statement only if you are certain that there is no possibility of zero loop iterations; otherwise, use a `while` loop instead.

Be sure to trace each nest of loops carefully, checking the inner and outer loop-control variables. A loop-control variable in a `for` statement cannot be changed inside the loop body. It is also illegal to use the same loop-control variable in two `for` statements within the same nest.

CHAPTER REVIEW

This chapter examined the `while` statement and used it to repeat steps in a program. You learned how to implement counter-controlled loops, or loops where the number of repetitions required can be determined before the loop is entered. You also found that the while statement can be used when you do not know the exact number of repetitions required before the loop begins.

In designing a while loop, we need to consider both the loop-control and loop-processing operations that must be performed. Separate Pascal statements are needed for initializing and updating the loop-control variable that is tested in the loop repetition condition.

We also discussed a common technique for controlling the repetition of a while loop: using a special sentinel value to indicate that all required data have been processed. In this case, an input variable must appear in the loop-repetition condition. This variable is initialized when the first data value is read (the priming read), and it is updated at the end of the loop when the next new data value is read. Loop repetition terminates after the sentinel value is read.

We also introduced the for statement (for loop) and the repeat statement (repeat-until loop). We used the for statement to implement counting loops, in which the exact number of loop iterations could be determined before loop repetition begins. The counter variable may increase in value (to form) or decrease in value (downto form) after each loop iteration. Remember that the final value expression for the counter variable is evaluated when the loop is first reached and cannot be changed during loop execution.

We used the repeat statement to implement conditional loops. With the repeat statement, you can implement a loop that will always execute at least one time.

We also analyzed nested loops. Each time an outer loop is repeated, every inner loop of the nest is reentered and executed to completion.

New Pascal Constructs

The Pascal constructs introduced in this chapter are described in Table 5.3.

Table 5.3 Summary of New Pascal Constructs

Construct	Effect
while Statement	

<pre>Sum := 0;
while Sum <= MaxSum do
  begin
    Write ('Next integer> ');
    ReadLn (Next);
    Sum := Sum + Next
  end {while}</pre>
	A collection of input data items is read and their sum is accumulated in Sum. This process stops when the accumulated sum exceeds MaxSum.

for Statement	

<pre>for CurMonth := 3 to 9 do
  begin
    ReadLn (MonthSales);
    YearSales := YearSales +
               MonthSales
  end {for}</pre>
	The loop body is repeated for each value of CurMonth from 3 to 9, inclusive. For each month, the value of MonthSales is read and added to YearSales.

Table 5.3, *continued*

Construct	Effect
repeat Statement	

```
Sum := 0;
repeat
  ReadLn (NextInt);
  WriteLn (NextInt);
  Sum := Sum + NextInt
until NextInt = 0
```

Integer values are read and their sum is accumulated in Sum. The process terminates after the first zero is read.

✓ Quick-Check Exercises

1. A while loop is called a _____ loop.
2. It is an error if a while loop body never executes. True or false?
3. The priming step for a while loop is what kind of statement? When is it used?
4. The sentinel value is always the last value added to a sum being accumulated in a sentinel-controlled loop. True or false?
5. Which loop form (for, repeat, while)
    a. executes at least one time?
    b. is the most general?
    c. should be used to implement a counting loop?
    d. should be used in a menu-driven program?
6. What does the following segment display?

    ```
    Product := 1;
    Counter := 2;
    while Counter <= 5 do
      Product := Product * Counter;
      Counter := Counter + 1;
    WriteLn (Product)
    ```

7. What does the segment in exercise 6 display if the begin-end bracket is inserted where intended?
8. During the execution of the following program segment:

    ```
    for I := 1 to 10 do
      begin
        for J := 1 to I do
          Write (I * J);
        WriteLn
      end
    ```

    a. How many times does the Write statement execute?
    b. How many times does the WriteLn statement execute?
    c. What is the last value displayed?

Answers to Quick-Check Exercises
1. conditional
2. false
3. an input operation; in a sentinel-controlled loop

4. False—the sentinel should not be processed.
5. a. repeat   b. while   c. for   d. repeat
6. Nothing—the loop executes "forever."
7. the value of 1 * 2 * 3 * 4 * 5, or 120.
8. a. 1 + 2 + 3 + ... + 9 + 10, or 55   b. 10   c. 100

Review Questions

1. How does a sentinel value differ from a program flag as a means of loop control?
2. For a sentinel value to be used properly when reading in data, where should the input statements appear?
3. Write a program called Sum to sum and print a collection of payroll amounts entered at the terminal until a sentinel value of –1 is entered.
4. Hand trace the following program given these data:

```
4 2 8 4    1 4 2 1    9 3 3 1    -22 10 8 2    3 3 4 5

program Slopes (Input, Output);
   const
      Sentinel = 0.0;

   var
      Slope, Y2, Y1, X2, X1 : Real;

begin {Slopes}
   WriteLn ('Enter four numbers separated by spaces');
   WriteLn ('The last two numbers cannot be the same, but');
   WriteLn ('The program terminates if the first two are.');
   WriteLn ('Enter four numbers> ');
   ReadLn (Y2, Y1, X2, X1);
   Slope := (Y2 - Y1) / (X2 - X1);
   while Slope <> Sentinel do
      begin
         WriteLn ('Slope is ', Slope :5:2);
         WriteLn ('Enter four more numbers> ');
         ReadLn (Y2, Y1, X2, X1);
         Slope := (Y2 - Y1) / (X2 - X1)
      end {while}
end. {Slopes}
```

5. Rewrite the while loop in program Slope (review question 4) as a
   a. repeat-until loop
   b. flag-controlled loop
6. Consider the program segment.

```
Count := 0;
for I := 1 to N do
   begin
      Read (X);
      if X = I then
         Count := Count + 1
   end;
```

   a. Write a while loop equivalent to the for loop.
   b. Write a repeat-until loop equivalent to the for loop.

7. Explain where semicolons are needed within
   a. an if statement
   b. a case statement
   c. a while statement
   d. a for statement
   e. a repeat-until statement

Programming Projects

1. Write a program that will find the smallest, largest, and average value in a collection of N numbers, where the value of N is the first data item read.
2. Modify programming project 1 to compute and display both the range of values in the data collection and the variance of the data collection. To compute the variance, accumulate the sum of the squares of the data values (SumSquares) in the main loop. After loop exit, use the formula

   $$variance = sum\text{-}of\text{-}squares - (sum\text{-}of\text{-}data)^2 \,/\, N$$

   Finally, compute the standard deviation, s, which is a measure of how much the data values deviate from the average value. Use the formula

   $$s^2 = variance \,/\, (N - 1)$$

3. Bunyan Lumber Co. needs to create a table of the engineering properties of its lumber. The dimensions of the wood are given as the base and the height in inches. Engineers need to know the following information about lumber:

   $$cross\text{-}sectional\ area = base \times height$$
   $$moment\ of\ inertia = (base \times height^3)/12$$
   $$section\ modulus = (base \times height^2)/6$$

   The owner, Paul, makes lumber with base sizes 2, 4, 6, 8, 10, and 12 inches. The height sizes are 2, 4, 6, 8, and 10 inches. Produce a table with appropriate headings to show these values and the computed engineering properties. Do not duplicate a 2-by-6 board with a 6-by-2 board.
4. Write a program to read a collection of integer data items and find and print the index of the first and last occurrence of the number 12. Your program should print index values of 0 if the number 12 is not found. The index is the sequence number of the data item 12. For example, if the eighth data item is the only 12, then the index value 8 should be printed for the first and last occurrence.
5. a. Write a program to read in a collection of exam scores ranging in value from 1 to 100. Your program should count and print the number of outstanding scores (90–100), the number of satisfactory scores (60–89), and the number of unsatisfactory scores (1–59). It should also display the category of each score. Test your program on the following data:

63	75	72	72	78	67	80	63	75
90	89	43	59	99	82	12	100	

   b. Modify your program to display the average exam score (a real number) at the end of the run.
6. Write a program to process weekly employee time cards for all employees of an organization. Each employee will have three data items: an identification number, the

hourly wage rate, and the number of hours worked during a given week. Each employee is to be paid time-and-a-half for all hours worked over 40. A tax amount of 3.625 percent of gross salary will be deducted. The program output should show the employee's number and net pay. Display the total payroll and the average amount paid at the end of the run.

7. Suppose you own a beer distributorship that sells Piels (ID number 1), Coors (ID number 2), Bud (ID number 3) and Iron City (ID number 4) by the case. Write a program to
   a. read in the case inventory for each brand for the start of the week
   b. process all weekly sales and purchase records for each brand
   c. print out the final inventory

   Each transaction will consist of two data items. The first item will be the brand identification number (an integer). The second will be the amount purchased (a positive integer value) or the amount sold (a negative integer value). The weekly inventory for each brand (for the start of the week) will also consist of two items: the identification number and the initial inventory for that brand. For now, you may assume that you always have sufficient foresight to prevent depletion of your inventory for any brand. (Hint: Your data entry should begin with eight values representing the case inventory, followed by the transaction values.)

8. Revise programming project 7 to make it a menu-driven program. The menu operations supported by the revised program should be (E)nter Inventory, (P)urchase Beer, (S)ell Beer, (D)isplay Inventory, and (Q)uit Program. Negative quantities should no longer be used to represent goods sold.

9. Write a savings account transaction program that will process the following sets of data:

   Group 1

I	1234	1054.07
W		25.00
D		243.35
W		254.55
Z		

   Group 2

I	5723	2008.24
W		15.55
Z		

   Group 3

I	2814	128.24
W		52.48
D		13.42
W		84.60
Z		

   Group 4

I	7234	7.77
Z		

   Group 5

I	9367	15.27
W		16.12
D		10.00
Z		

Group 6

I	1134	12900.00
D		9270.00
Z		

The initial record in each group contains the code (I) along with the new account number and its initial balance. All subsequent transaction records show the amount of each withdrawal (W) and deposit (D) made for that account, followed by a sentinel value (Z). Display the account number and its balance after processing each record in the group. If a balance becomes negative, print an appropriate message and take whatever corrective steps you deem proper. If there are no transactions for an account, print a message stating so. A transaction code (Q) should be entered to quit program execution.

John K. Ousterhout is a Professor in the Department of Electrical Engineering and Computer Sciences at the University of California at Berkeley. His interests include operating systems, distributed systems, user interfaces, and computer-aided design. He is currently leading the development of Sprite, a network operating system for high-performance workstations, and Tcl/Tk, a new programming system for graphical user interfaces.

How did you become involved in the field of computing?

As an undergraduate I majored in physics. I had no exposure to computers until after my freshman year. I got a summer job in the Cyclotron laboratory at Michigan State University and had to learn Fortran to process experimental data. I guess you could say it was love at first byte. By my junior year I'd taken a few computer classes and realized that the thing I liked most about physics was playing with the computers in the lab. At that point it was too late to switch majors, but I took several more computer science classes and applied to graduate school in computer science.

Why do you think that studying operating systems is important?

In studying operating systems, students are exposed to several important concepts that may not be covered in any other computer science classes. For example, operating systems classes are often the first place that students learn about concurrency, how to manage several tasks all going on at about the same time. Networking and security may also be introduced, both of which are becoming more and more important in computer systems.

Is it better to study a single operating system in detail, or survey the principles common to many systems?

I think both approaches are useful. In studying a single system you get to see how all the different pieces fit together, but it's also useful to compare different approaches and examine the concepts without getting bogged down in the details of a single system.

What do you consider to be the major achievements in operating systems over the last decade?

I think the most important achievement was the development of techniques for dealing with networks: communication protocols, network file systems, and techniques that allow a networked collection of workstations to work together almost as if they were a single computer. Another major achievement was the development of a portable version of the UNIX operating system. It used to be that a new operating system had to be written from scratch for each new computer architecture. With UNIX it became possible to use the same system on many different kinds of computers. It only takes a few months of work to modify UNIX to run on a new hardware platform, at which point most existing applications can run on the new machine with no changes. This portability was one of the most important factors in the success of new RISC architectures: without it

INTERVIEW
John K. Ousterhout

the software development costs would probably have been too high for the new machines to survive.

What do you think will be the most important developments in operating systems over the next ten years?

I have a technology-centered view of the world; interesting developments in operating systems (and most other areas of computer science) stem from new developments in the basic computer technologies like processors and memories. For example, networking became an interesting issue only when computers were cheap enough for everyone to have one and networks like Ethernet were available to tie them together. Computer graphics became interesting when memory costs made it feasible to store one bit of information for each point on the screen. Over the next ten years I see machines getting 100 times faster than today's machines, networks getting 100 times faster, and computer storage becoming 100 times cheaper than today. This will make it cost-effective to use audio and video as an integral part of computer applications, and new operating system techniques will be needed to support this. Faster networks will make it possible for more computers to be more closely interconnected. I can imagine techniques being developed so that any computer in the United States can easily access information on any other computer in the country. Managing and communicating this information will present many interesting issues for operating system designers.

What impact did Berkeley UNIX have on the competitive field of operating systems? How do you see the UNIX world shaking out?

The Berkeley UNIX project built on the original UNIX work at Bell Laboratories to make the VAX version of UNIX much more powerful and widely used. In particular, Berkeley researchers developed key network support, virtual memory, and a new faster file system. Because of its portability and its success on the VAX, Berkeley UNIX became the natural choice for new hardware platforms like the 68000 series and the RISC architectures. I think that the Berkeley work played a key role in the overall success of UNIX.

Today there are several versions of UNIX floating around, some of which are based strongly on the Berkeley UNIX and some of which have only a few of the Berkeley features. I doubt that a single version will win out; instead, I see them gradually becoming more similar as the UNIX facilities become more standardized. Even today, the various UNIXes are similar enough for many programs to run unchanged on all the different flavors. Because of the power and portability of UNIX, I think UNIX-based workstations will take over a substantial portion of the market currently dominated by personal computers running the more primitive MS-DOS operating system.

What advice would you give to undergraduates planning to major in computer science?

I have two pieces of advice: stay broad, and learn to communicate. Rather than focusing on a narrow sub-specialty, I encourage students to take a broad variety of courses, including many outside computer science. The reason for this is that computer technology is evolving very rapidly. Most of what we know today will be obsolete in a few years. The only way to survive radical technology changes is to develop a very broad set of skills. If you get cubbyholed, you'll get left behind. Even courses that seem totally unrelated to computer science, such as art, literature, history, or finance, will broaden your perspective and contribute in subtle ways to your problem-solving abilities with computers.

Communication skills are also very important, both writing and speaking. It doesn't do any good to have a great idea if you can't explain it to other people and get them excited about it. I've found that people who can organize thoughts for communication are usually good at organizing computer software too.

6

Modular Programming

Chapter 3 introduced you to procedures; you learned how to use them to write separate program modules corresponding to the individual steps in a problem solution. We have not used procedures extensively because we have not yet discussed how to pass information between individual procedures or between procedures and the main program. So far, our procedures can only manipulate data that are stored locally.

Chapter 3 also introduced you to functions. A function is a module that returns a single result. You saw how to write expressions that call Pascal's predefined functions (for example, Sqr, Sqrt), and how functions can be used to facilitate structured design.

This chapter introduces a very important concept in programming: the use of parameters. In this chapter, you will see that parameters provide a convenient way to pass information between a main program and a procedure or a function. Parameters also make procedures and functions more versatile because they enable a module to manipulate different data each time it is called. For example, WriteLn (M) displays the value of its parameter, M; WriteLn (N) displays the value of its parameter, N.

Our goal throughout this course is to use procedures and functions as building blocks of larger program systems. As you progress through the course, your programming skills and your own personal *library* of procedures and functions will grow. You should be able to reuse procedures and functions written for earlier applications in new programs.

6.1 Introduction to Parameter Lists

We can make an analogy between a carefully designed program that uses procedures and functions and a stereo system. Each stereo component is an independent device that performs a specific operation. The stereo receiver and the compact disk (CD) player are "black boxes" that we connect together. We know the purpose of each component, but we have no idea what electronic parts are used inside each box or how they function; however, we do not need to know these technical details in order to use the stereo system.

Information in the form of electronic signals is sent back and forth between the stereo components over wires. If you look at the rear of a stereo receiver, you will find that some connection points, or plugs, are marked as inputs and others are marked as outputs. The wires attached to the input plugs carry electronic signals into the receiver, where they are processed. (These signals may come from a cassette deck, a tuner, or a CD player). New electronic signals generated by the receiver come out of the receiver from the output plugs and go to the speakers or back to the cassette deck for recording.

Currently, we know how to design the separate components (procedures) of a programming system, but we don't know how to pass data between the main program and a procedure. In this chapter, you will learn how to use *parameter lists* to provide communication paths between the main program and its modules (or between two modules).

Actual Parameter Lists

Each procedure call statement has two parts: a procedure name and an actual parameter list. In the procedure call statement

```
WriteLn (X, Y);
```

the *actual parameter list* is (X, Y). The two *actual parameters* are X and Y, whose values are passed into procedure WriteLn. We know that procedure WriteLn displays the values of X and Y.

In the procedure call statement

```
ReadLn (V, W);
```

the actual parameters are V and W. In this case, the procedure reads data values into these variables. The data type of each variable determines what kind of value is read.

The actual parameters are treated differently in these two procedure call statements. In the first call statement, the values of X and Y are passed into procedure WriteLn and the procedure displays these values. Since the procedure does not change the values of X and Y, they are considered *procedure inputs*. In the second call statement, the execution of procedure ReadLn changes the contents of V and W. Because ReadLn sends values back to the calling program, V and W are considered *procedure outputs*. Figure 6.1 is a block diagram of a procedure with input and output parameters.

Figure 6.1 Procedure with Inputs and Outputs

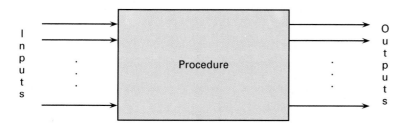

Formal Parameter Lists

The system procedures WriteLn and ReadLn differ from procedures that you will write in two important respects. For these two procedures, the number of actual parameters may vary from one call to the next, and the data type of a particular actual parameter (say, the first) may also vary from one call to the next. For each procedure that we write, the number of actual parameters must be the same each time that procedure is called, and the data type of a particular parameter must always be the same.

How do we tell the Pascal compiler the number of procedure parameters and the type of each parameter? The answer is through the formal parameter list.

Procedure `ReportSumAve` in Fig. 6.2 computes and displays the sum and the average of two type `Real` values that are passed into the procedure as procedure inputs. The *formal parameter list*

```
(Numl, Num2 {input} : Real)
```

tells the Pascal compiler the number of parameters being processed (two), the data type of each parameter (both type `Real`), and the names that we will use in place of the actual parameter names in the procedure body (`Num1` for the first parameter and `Num2` for the second). We use the *formal parameters*, `Num1` and `Num2`, in the procedure body to describe what we want done to the actual parameters. The actual parameters are not known when the procedure is written but are determined when the procedure call statement executes. The comment `{input}` identifies `Num1` and `Num2` as procedure inputs.

Figure 6.2 Procedure to Display a Sum and an Average

Directory: CHAP6
File: REPORTSU.PRO

```
procedure ReportSumAve (Numl, Num2 {input} : Real);
{
  Computes and displays the sum and average of Num1 and Num2.
  Pre : Num1 and Num2 are assigned values.
  Post: The sum and average value of Num1 and Num2 are
        computed and displayed.
}
  var
    Sum,                        {sum of Num1, Num2}
    Average : Real;             {average of Num1, Num2}

begin {ReportSumAve}
  Sum := Numl + Num2;
  Average := Sum / 2.0;
  WriteLn ('The sum is ', Sum :4:2);
  WriteLn ('The average is ', Average :4:2)
end; {ReportSumAve}
```

Parameter Correspondence

Procedure `ReportSumAve` begins with a lengthy comment that describes the procedure's operations. We will discuss this comment further at the end of this section.

There are two local variables declared in the procedure, `Sum` and `Average`. The statements

```
Sum := Numl + Num2;
Average := Sum / 2.0;
```

assign values to these local variables as follows: the sum of the values passed into parameters `Num1` and `Num2` is stored in `Sum` and their average is stored in `Average`. For the procedure call statement the formal parameter `Num1` is passed the value `6.5`, and the formal parameter `Num2` is passed the value `3.5`. The value assigned to `Sum` is `10.0`, and the value assigned to `Average` is `5.0`. These two values are displayed. The correspondence between the actual and the formal parameters is shown next:

Actual Parameter	*Formal Parameter*
6.5	Num1
3.5	Num2

For the procedure call statement

```
ReportSumAve (X, Y)
```

the value of `X` is passed to formal parameter `Num1`, and the value of `Y` is passed to formal parameter `Num2`.

Actual Parameter	*Formal Parameter*
X	Num1
Y	Num2

Figure 6.3 shows the main program data area and the procedure data area after this procedure call statement executes. The values `8.0` and `10.0` are passed into the formal parameters `Num1` and `Num2`, respectively. The local variables, `Sum` and `Average`, are initially undefined; the execution of the procedure body changes the values of these variables to `18.0` and `9.0`, respectively.

Figure 6.3 Data Areas After Call of ReportSumAve

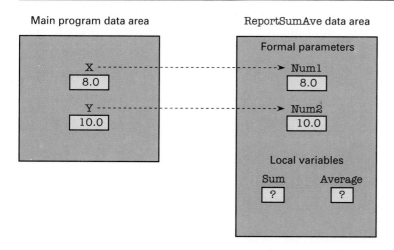

Procedure `ReportSumAve` can compute and display the sum and the average of any pair of type `Real` numbers. We can get the procedure to operate on a different pair of numbers simply by changing the parameter list. The procedure call statement

```
ReportSumAve (Y, X)
```

would generate the same results as the one above; however, formal parameter
Num1 would correspond to actual parameter Y and formal parameter Num2 would
correspond to actual parameter X.

Actual Parameter	Formal Parameter
Y	Num1
X	Num2

The Procedure Data Area

Each time a procedure call statement is executed, an area of memory is allocated
for storage of that procedure's data. Included in the procedure data area are
storage cells for any local variables or constants that may be declared in the
procedure. The procedure data area is always erased when the procedure
terminates; it is re-created empty (all values undefined) when the procedure is
called again.

Illegal Parameter Substitution Errors

The data type of each actual parameter must be assignment compatible (see
Section 2.4) with the data type of its corresponding formal parameter; otherwise,
an illegal parameter substitution syntax error occurs. How does the Pascal
compiler determine whether an actual parameter has a correct data type? The
Pascal compiler knows the required data type for each actual parameter because
a procedure's declaration must precede its first call. The formal parameter list
(in the procedure declaration) specifies the data type of each procedure parameter.

PROGRAM
STYLE

Choosing Formal Parameter Names

We have stated that the names used for formal parameters are arbitrary.
Although this is true, you should continue to follow the convention of
picking names that help to document the use of the formal parameter.
Remember that the correspondence between an actual and a formal parameter is determined solely by position in the parameter lists, regardless
of what names are used.

As we discussed earlier, one of the main reasons for having functions
and procedures is to facilitate the reuse of previously written and tested
modules in future programs. Try to pick formal parameter names that
are meaningful and generic rather than specific names tailored to a particular program application.

Preconditions and Postconditions

The multiple-line comment at the beginning of procedure `ReportSumAve` documents its operation. We use the commenting style below

```
{
    . . . comments . . .
}
```

for comments that extend over multiple lines.

The comment line

```
Pre : Num1 and Num2 are assigned values.
```

describes the condition that must be true before the procedure is called; this condition is known as a *precondition*. The lines

```
Post: The sum and average value of Num1 and Num2 are
      computed and displayed.
```

describe the condition that must be true after the procedure execution is completed; this condition is called a *postcondition*.

The use of explicit preconditions and postconditions provides valuable documentation to other programmers who might want to use the procedure. For example, the preconditions tell a programmer what must be done before the procedure is called. In this case, two data values must be assigned or read into the actual procedure parameters prior to calling `ReportSumAve`. The postconditions tell a programmer the effect of the procedure's execution on its parameters. In this case, their sum and average are computed and displayed.

You might say that the preconditions and the postconditions serve as an informal contract between the procedure and any program that uses it. The preconditions indicate any expectations the procedure may have with respect to its parameters. The postconditions tell what the procedure does and what will happen to its parameters if the precondition is met. All bets are off if the preconditions are not met; therefore, the calling program must ensure that all actual parameters satisfy the procedure preconditions before each call to a procedure.

Exercises for Section 6.1

Self-Check

1. What is the primary purpose of procedure parameters?
2. Consider the procedure `Cube`:

```
procedure Cube (N : Integer);
begin {Cube}
  Write (N :1, ' cubed is ');
  N := N * N * N;
  WriteLn (N :1)
end; {Cube}
```

a. What is displayed when the procedure call statement

```
Cube (3)
```

   executes?
b. If M is 5, what happens when the procedure call statement

```
Cube (M)
```

   executes?
c. What is the value of the actual parameter M after the procedure executes?
d. Where should M be declared and what should its data type be?
3. Write preconditions and postconditions for
   a. procedure Cube in self-check exercise 2.
   b. the procedure described in programming exercise 1.

Programming

1. Write a procedure that displays the absolute difference of its two formal parameters, X and Y (i.e., if X is larger, the absolute difference is X – Y; if Y is larger, the absolute difference is Y – X).

6.2 Functions: Modules That Return a Single Result

In Section 3.8, we introduced functions and discussed how functions return a single result to the program that calls them. We also showed how to call a function through a function designator in an expression. The expression part of the following assignment statement is a function designator that calls the predefined function Sqrt.

```
Z := Sqrt(X * Y)
```

Variable Z gets the function result after function exit occurs. Figure 6.4 is a block diagram of a function showing its inputs and its single output.

Figure 6.4 Function with Multiple Inputs and Single Output

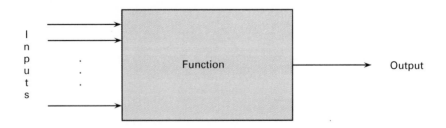

In Section 3.8, we discussed how we can simplify numeric computations by using Pascal's built-in functions in writing arithmetic expressions. We also showed how to use two of these functions, Exp and Ln, to raise a value to a

power. Because raising to a power is a relatively common operation, it would be useful to write our own library function that does this. Figure 6.5 shows function Exponent, which raises its first argument to the power indicated by its second argument.

Figure 6.5 Function Exponent

```
function Exponent (U, V : Real) : Real;
{
 Returns its first argument raised to the power specified
 by its second argument.
 Pre : U and V are defined.
 Post: Returns U raised to the power V.
}
begin {Exponent}
  if U = 0.0 then
    Exponent := 0.0
  else if U > 0.0 then
    Exponent := Exp(V * Ln(U))
  else
    Exponent := 1.0 / Exp(V * Ln(-U))
end; {Exponent}
```

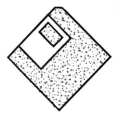

Directory: CHAP6
File: EXPONENT.FUN

The function heading indicates that Exponent has two type Real parameters (or arguments); the identifier following the colon tells us that Exponent returns a type Real result. Pascal defines a function result by assigning a value to the identifier that is the function name (Exponent in this case).

The if statement in the function body causes one of three assignment statements to execute, thereby defining the function result. If the value passed into U is 0, the assignment statement

```
Exponent := 0.0
```

sets the function result to 0. If the value passed into U is positive, the assignment statement

```
Exponent := Exp(V * Ln(U))
```

calls Pascal's built-in functions Exp and Ln to calculate the desired result and assign it to Exponent. The logarithm of a negative number is not defined, so the statement

```
Exponent := 1.0 / Exp(V * Ln(-U))
```

defines the function result when U is negative. This statement uses the algebraic relationship $V^U = 1 / V^{-U}$.

If we have a main program with three type Real variables, X, Y, and Z, the main program statement

```
Z := Exponent(X, Y)
```

calls Exponent to raise X to the power Y. Upon return from the function, the function result is substituted for the function designator and is assigned to Z.

Figure 6.6 shows the main program data area and the function data area

Figure 6.6 Data Areas After Function Call

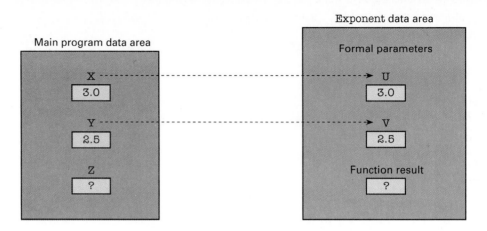

after the function call but before the function body begins execution. For the particular values of X and Y shown (3.0 and 2.5), the function execution defines the function result as 15.59. Figure 6.7 shows the program data area and the function data area after the function body finishes execution but before the function return. Notice that there is no connection between main program variable Z and the memory cell in Exponent's data area that represents the function result. The function result will be assigned to Z after the return to the main program.

Figure 6.7 Data Areas After Function Execution

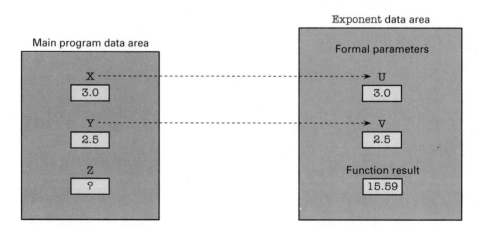

■ Example 6.1

In Section 4.5, we discussed how we might use a function named GetFirst in a program that finds the alphabetically first letter in a sequence of three letters. Function GetFirst returns the alphabetically smaller of its two arguments and is shown in Fig. 6.8.

```
function GetFirst (Char1, Char2 : Char) : Char;
{
 Returns the alphabetically smaller of its two arguments.
 Pre : Char1 and Char2 are defined.
 Post: If Char1 < Char2, returns Char1;
       otherwise, returns Char2.
}
begin {GetFirst}
  if Char1 < Char2 then
    GetFirst := Char1
  else
    GetFirst := Char2
end; {GetFirst}
```

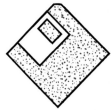

Directory: CHAP6
File: GETFIRST.FUN

The function heading tells us that GetFirst has two type Char parameters (Char1 and Char2) and returns a type Char result. The function body consists of an if statement that compares its parameter values. Each time the function is called, the if statement executes exactly one of the following assignment statements:

```
GetFirst := Char1    |    GetFirst := Char2
```

These statements define the function result by assigning a value (either Char1 or Char2) to the function name.

If Ch1, Ch2, and Ch3 are the main program variables being compared, we can call GetFirst using the assignment statement

```
{Save the alphabetically first of Ch1 and Ch2 in AlphaFirst}
AlphaFirst := GetFirst(Ch1, Ch2);
```

The actual parameters are Ch1 and Ch2, so the smaller of Ch1 and Ch2 is returned and stored in AlphaFirst. In the next call to GetFirst,

```
{Save the alphabetically first of Ch3 and AlphaFirst}
AlphaFirst := GetFirst(Ch3, AlphaFirst)
```

the actual parameters are Ch3 and AlphaFirst, so the smaller of Ch3 and the current value of AlphaFirst is returned and stored in AlphaFirst. The fact that the function result will be stored in AlphaFirst after the function return does not affect the function's execution. The final value of AlphaFirst will be the alphabetically first of Ch1, Ch2, and Ch3.

We will leave the trace of the first call to GetFirst as an exercise (self-check exercise 1). The parameter correspondence for the second call, Get-First(Ch3, AlphaFirst), follows:

Actual Parameter	*Formal Parameter*
Ch3	Char1
AlphaFirst	Char2

Figure 6.9 shows the main program data area and the function data area right after this function call, assuming main program variables Ch3 and AlphaFirst

contain C and A, respectively. Because C < A is false, function GetFirst executes the assignment statement

```
GetFirst := Char2
```

which defines the function result as A. This result is returned and substituted for the function designator in the main program statement that called the function. ∎

Figure 6.9 Data Areas After Second Function Call

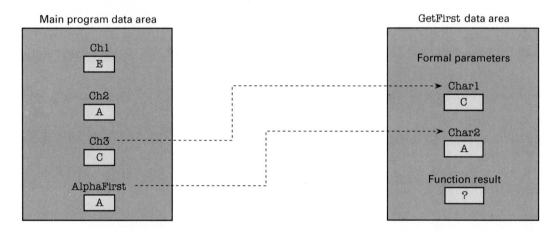

Function Declaration

Form:
```
function fname (formal parameters) : ftype;
    local declaration section
begin
    function body
end;
```

Example:
```
function InverseSum (X, Y : Real) : Real;
{Computes 1.0 divided by the sum of X, Y.}
   var
      SumXY : Real;  {local storage for the sum of X, Y}

begin {InverseSum}
   SumXY := X + Y;
   InverseSum := 1.0 / SumXY
end; {InverseSum}
```

Interpretation: The function *fname* is declared. The *formal parameters* are enclosed in parentheses. The identifiers declared in the *local declaration section* are local to the function and are defined only during the execution of the function. A formal parameter cannot be declared as a local identifier.

The *function body* describes the data manipulation to be performed by the function using the formal parameter names in the description. When a formal parameter is referenced during function execution, the value of the corresponding actual parameter is manipulated.

Function *fname* returns a single result of type *ftype* in the following way. Each time the function is called, a statement of the form

fname := *expression*

must execute. This statement defines the function result.

Note 1: The identifier *ftype* must be the name of a standard data type (Integer, Real, Boolean, or Char), a subrange type or enumerated type (described in Chapter 7), or a pointer type (described in Chapter 17).

Note 2: If there are no parameters, omit the *formal parameters* and the parentheses.

Function Designator

Form: *fname*(*actual parameters*)

Example: InverseSum(3.0, Z)

Interpretation: The *actual parameters* are enclosed in parentheses. When function *fname* is called into execution, the first actual parameter corresponds to the first formal parameter, the second actual parameter corresponds to the second formal parameter, and so on. A function designator must always appear within an expression; after execution, the function result replaces the function designator in that expression.

Note: If there are no parameters, omit the *actual parameters* and the parentheses.

Writing a Driver Program to Test a Function

In the next example, we will write a function that computes income tax owed and a small program whose sole purpose is to call and test that function. A program used to test the operation of a function or a procedure is called a *driver* program.

■ Example 6.2

Figure 4.19 contains an if statement used to determine the income tax due for a particular salary based on the tax table shown in Table 4.9. Since this table appears in many different programs, your accountant has decided to place it in function FindTax (Fig. 6.10). The assignment statement

```
MyTax := FindTax(MySalary);
```

calls function FindTax, passing the value of MySalary into input parameter

Salary. If the value passed into Salary is within the range of the table, the tax owed is computed and returned as the function result; otherwise, −1.0 is returned. ■

Figure 6.10   Driver Program with Function FindTax

Directory: CHAP6
File: DRIVER.PAS

```
program Driver (Input, Output);
{Tests function FindTax.}

   var
     MySalary,                          {input - salary}
     MyTax     : Real;                  {output - tax}

   function FindTax (Salary : Real) : Real;
   {
   Returns tax amount owed for a salary < $15000.
   Pre : Salary is assigned a value.
   Post: If Salary is within range, returns the tax owed;
         otherwise, returns -1.0.
   }
     const
       MaxSalary = 15000.00;    {Maximum salary for table}
       OutOfRange := -1.0;      {"Tax" for an out-of-range salary}

   begin  {FindTax}
     if Salary < 0.0 then
       FindTax := OutOfRange                  {Salary too small}
     else if Salary < 1500.00 then            {first range}
       FindTax := 0.15 * Salary
     else if Salary < 3000.00 then            {second range}
       FindTax := (Salary - 1500.00) * 0.16 + 225.00
     else if Salary < 5000.00 then            {third range}
       FindTax := (Salary - 3000.00) * 0.18 + 465.00
     else if Salary < 8000.00 then            {fourth range}
       FindTax := (Salary - 5000.00) * 0.20 + 825.00
     else if Salary <= MaxSalary then         {fifth range}
       FindTax := (Salary - 8000.00) * 0.25 + 1425.00
     else
       FindTax := OutOfRange                  {Salary too large}
   end;  {FindTax}


begin  {Driver}
  Write ('Enter a salary less than or equal to $15000.00> $');
  ReadLn (MySalary);
  MyTax := FindTax(MySalary);
  if MyTax >= 0.0 then
    WriteLn ('The tax on $', MySalary :4:2, ' is $', MyTax :4:2)
  else
    WriteLn ('Salary $', MySalary :4:2, ' is out of table range')
end.  {Driver}


Enter a salary less than or equal to $15000.00>  $6000.00
The tax on $6000.00 is $1025.00
```

Validating Input Parameters

The `if` statement in function `FindTax` tests for an invalid value of the input parameter `Salary` before performing the tax computation. All procedures and functions should validate their input parameters; there are no guarantees that the values passed to an input parameter will be meaningful.

Cohesive Modules

Function `FindTax` is concerned only with tax computation. It neither reads in a value for `Salary` nor displays the computed result. The result is returned to the calling program, which may display it or pass it on to a procedure that prints results. `FindTax` does not display an error message in the event that the value passed to `Salary` is out of range. It simply returns a special value (–1.0) to indicate this, and the calling program displays the error message.

Modules that perform a single operation are called *cohesive modules*. It is good programming style to write cohesive modules, which help to keep functions and procedures relatively compact and easy to read, write, and debug.

Writing Driver Programs to Test Modules

The main program body in Fig. 6.10 consists of a statement for data entry, an assignment statement with a function designator in its expression part, and an `if` statement to display the function result. The sole purpose of the program is to test the function `FindTax`. Such a program is called a driver program.

Experienced programmers often use driver programs to pretest functions and procedures. Generally, the small investment in time and effort required to write a short driver program pays off by reducing the total time spent debugging a large program system containing several modules.

Boolean Functions

We have discussed functions that return type `Real` or type `Char` results. We can also write functions that return type `Integer` or type `Boolean` results (Boolean functions). Boolean functions are sometimes used as conditions in `if` statements.

■ **Example 6.3**

You have written an algorithm that contains the following decision step. For the purposes of this example, we have no interest in the details of the three procedures called in the if statement, we just want to make sure that the correct procedure is called.

```
if Ch is a letter then
    Call procedure ProcessLetter
else if Ch is a digit character then
    Call procedure ProcessDigit
else
    Call procedure ProcessSpecial
```

There are many ways to implement this decision. One would be to use a case statement with separate case labels for letters, digits, and special characters. Another approach would be to write the following if statement, which uses functions IsLetter and IsDigit to determine whether Ch is a letter or a digit.

```
if IsLetter(Ch) then
   ProcessLetter (Ch)
else if IsDigit(Ch) then
   ProcessDigit (Ch)
else
   ProcessSpecial (Ch)
```

The function designator IsLetter(Ch) is a Boolean expression. It has a value of True if Ch is a letter and a value of False if Ch is not a letter. Similarly, the Boolean expression IsDigit(Ch) has a value of True if Ch is a digit character and a value of False otherwise.

Figure 6.11 shows functions IsLetter and IsDigit. Both functions consist of a single statement that assigns a Boolean value to the function name, thereby defining the function result. Boolean assignment statements were discussed in Section 4.1. ■

Figure 6.11 Functions IsLetter and IsDigit

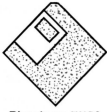

Directory: CHAP6
File: ISLETTER.FUN

```
function IsLetter (Ch : Char) : Boolean;
{
 Returns True when its argument is a letter; otherwise,
 returns False
}
begin {IsLetter}
   IsLetter := (('A' <= Ch) and (Ch <= 'Z')) or
               (('a' <= Ch) and (Ch <= 'z'))
end; {IsLetter}


function IsDigit (Ch : Char) : Boolean;
{
 Returns True when its argument is a digit character;
 otherwise, returns False
}
```

```
begin {IsDigit}
  IsDigit := ('0' <= Ch) and (Ch <= '9')
end; {IsDigit}
```

Exercises for Section 6.2

Self-Check

1. a. Show the main program data area and the function data area for the function designator `GetFirst(Ch1, Ch2)`.
   b. Trace the function execution.
2. Why is the `if` statement currently in `FindTax` better than the one sketched below?

```
if Salary < 0.0 then
  WriteLn (Salary :4:2, ' is out of range')  {Salary too small}
  ...
else
  WriteLn (Salary :4:2, ' is out of range')  {Salary too large}
```

3. What does the following function do?

```
function Hypot (X, Y : Real) : Real;
begin
  Hypot := Sqrt(Sqr(X) + Sqr(Y))
end;  {Hypot}
```

   Write a statement that calls this function with arguments `A` and `B` and stores the function result in `C`.
4. Write preconditions and postconditions for function `Hypot` shown in exercise 3.

Programming

1. Write a driver program that tests function `FindTax` for all values of `Salary` from `-400.00` to `15100.00` in increments of `500.00`.
2. Write a function that computes the absolute difference of its two arguments, where the absolute difference of A and B is $A - B$ if A is greater than B and $B - A$ if B is greater than A.
3. Write a function that raises a real number (X) to an integer power (N) by multiplying X by itself N times (use a `for` loop). Will your function work for negative values of X or N? Hint: To make your function work for negative values of N, use `Abs(N)` as the *final* expression in the `for` loop. Then use the fact that $X^N = 1 / X^{-N}$ to compute the correct result when N is negative.

6.3 Value Parameters and Variable Parameters

So far you know how to pass inputs into a procedure or a function and how to return a single result from a function. In this section, you will learn how to return one or more results from a procedure.

When a procedure call executes, the computer allocates memory space in the procedure data area for each formal parameter. The value of each actual input parameter is stored in the memory cell(s) allocated to its corresponding formal parameter. The procedure body can manipulate this value. Next, we will discuss how a procedure returns outputs to the program (or procedure) that calls it.

Procedure ComputeSumAve in Fig. 6.12 is similar to ReportSumAve. The differences are that ComputeSumAve has four parameters: two for input (Num1 and Num2) and two for output (Sum and Average). Procedure ComputeSumAve computes the sum and the average of its inputs but does not display them. Instead, these values are assigned to formal parameters Sum and Average and returned as procedure results to the calling program.

Figure 6.12   Procedure to Compute a Sum and an Average

Directory: CHAP6
File: COMPUTE.PRO

```
procedure ComputeSumAve (Num1, Num2 {input} : Real;
                         var Sum, Average {output} : Real);
{
  Computes the sum and average of Num1 and Num2.
  Pre : Num1 and Num2 are assigned values.
  Post: The sum and average of Num1 and Num2 are computed
        and returned.
}
begin {ComputeSumAve}
  Sum := Num1 + Num2;
  Average := Sum / 2.0
end; {ComputeSumAve}
```

To see how this works, assume that the main program declares X, Y, Sum, and Mean as type Real variables. The procedure call statement

```
ComputeSumAve (X, Y, Sum, Mean)
```

sets up the following parameter correspondence:

Actual Parameter	Formal Parameter
X	Num1
Y	Num2
Sum	Sum
Mean	Average

The values of X and Y are passed into the procedure when it is first called. These values are associated with formal parameters Num1 and Num2. The statement

```
Sum := Num1 + Num2;
```

stores the sum of the procedure inputs in the main program variable Sum (the third actual parameter). The statement

```
Average := Sum / 2.0
```

divides the value stored in the main program variable Sum by 2.0 and stores the quotient in the main program variable Mean (the fourth actual parameter). Figure 6.13 shows the main program data area and the procedure data area after the procedure call but before the procedure body begins execution; Figure 6.14 shows these data areas just after the procedure body finishes execution. The procedure execution sets the values of main program variables Sum and Mean to 18.0 and 9.0, respectively.

Figure 6.13 Data Areas After Procedure Call

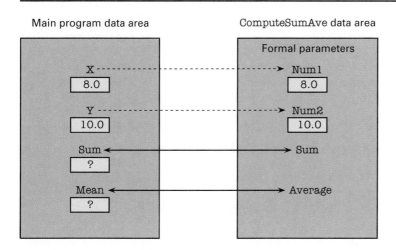

Figure 6.14 Data Areas After Procedure Execution

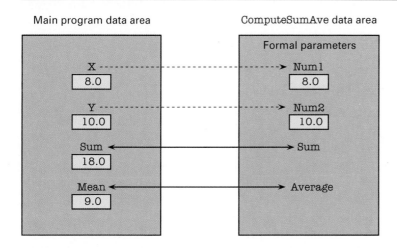

In Figure 6.12, the reserved word var precedes the declaration of formal parameters Sum and Average. This tells the compiler to treat them as *variable parameters*. The compiler stores the memory address of the actual variable that corresponds to each variable parameter in the procedure data area. Through this address, the procedure can access the actual variable in the calling program and change its value or use its value in a computation. In Fig. 6.13, this relationship is shown by a double headed arrow connecting each variable parameter with its corresponding actual parameter. Notice that the reserved word var appears only in the formal parameter list, not the actual parameter list.

Protection Afforded by Value Parameters

Figure 6.13 points out an important difference between formal parameters used as procedure inputs and those used as procedure outputs. Because they are not preceded by the reserved word var, formal parameters Num1 and Num2 are considered *value parameters*. As such, they have their own local storage cells in the procedure data area. The value passed into formal parameter Num1 is stored in the procedure data area at the time of the procedure call, and there is no further connection between formal parameter Num1 and its corresponding actual parameter. This is indicated by the broken line in Fig. 6.13.

The value of formal parameter Num1 or Num2 can be used in computations or even changed by the procedure body without affecting the corresponding actual parameter. For example, if we add the statement

```
Num1 := -5.0
```

to the end of procedure ComputeSumAve, the value of formal parameter Num1 will be changed to -5.0, but the value stored in the actual parameter X will still be 8.0.

By making an input parameter a value parameter, we protect its value and prevent it from being changed by the procedure's execution. If we forget to declare an output parameter as a variable formal parameter (a common source of error), then its value (not its address) will be stored locally, and any change to its value will not be returned to the calling program.

PROGRAM
STYLE

Writing Formal Parameter Lists

In Fig. 6.12, the formal parameter list

```
(Num1, Num2 {input} : Real;
 var Sum, Average {output} : Real);
```

is written on two lines to improve program readability. The value parameters are written on the first line with the comment {input} inserted to document their use as procedure inputs. The variable parameters are written on the second line with the comment {output}.

Generally, we will follow the practice shown in Fig. 6.12 in writing formal parameter lists. Input parameters will be listed first, and any output parameters will be listed last. The order of the actual parameters in the procedure call must correspond to the order of the formal parameters.

Passing Information Between Procedures

So far, you have seen two similar procedures, `ReportSumAve` and `Compute-`
`SumAve`, and you have learned how to pass information between a main program
and a procedure. Sometimes we need to pass information between procedures.
For example, we might want to pass the results returned by `ComputeSumAve` to
another procedure, say, `Correlate`, for further processing.

Let's assume that the main program variables `X` and `Y` are passed into
procedure `ComputeSumAve`. We can declare two more main program variables,
say `TempSum` and `TempAve`, to hold the procedure results. The procedure call
statements

```
ComputeSumAve (X, Y, TempSum, TempAve);
Correlate (TempSum, TempAve)
```

pass the outputs of `ComputeSumAve` (`TempSum` and `TempAve`) to `Correlate` for
further processing. Thus, we can use main program variables to facilitate the
exchange of information between procedures.

When to Use a Variable Parameter or a Value Parameter

You may be wondering how to decide when to use a variable parameter and
when to use a value parameter. Some rules of thumb follow:

- If information is to be passed into a procedure and does not have to be
  returned, or passed out of the procedure, then the formal parameter representing that information should ordinarily be a value parameter (e.g., `Num1`
  and `Num2` in Figs. 6.2 and 6.12). A parameter used in this way is called an
  input parameter.
- If information is to be returned to the calling program from a procedure,
  then the formal parameter representing that information must be a variable
  parameter (e.g., `Sum` and `Average` in Fig. 6.12). A procedure used in this way
  is called an *output parameter*.
- If information is to be passed into a procedure, perhaps modified, and a new
  value returned, then the formal parameter representing that information
  must be a variable parameter. A parameter used in this way is called an *input/
  output parameter*.

Although we make a distinction between output parameters and input/
output parameters, Pascal treats them in the same way. Both kinds of parameters
must be declared as variable parameters, so the address of the corresponding
actual parameter is stored in the procedure data area when the procedure is
called. For an input/output parameter, we assume there are some meaningful
data in the actual parameter before the procedure executes; for an output
parameter, we make no such assumption.

Passing Expressions to Value Parameters

You can use an assignment-compatible expression (or variable or constant) as an actual parameter corresponding to a value parameter. For example, the procedure call statement

```
ComputeSumAve (X + Y, 10.5, MySum, MyAve);
```

calls ComputeSumAve to compute the sum (returned in MySum) and the average (returned in MyAve) of the expression X + Y and the real number 10.5. However, only variables can correspond to variable parameters, so MySum and MyAve must be declared as type Real variables in the calling program. This restriction is imposed because an actual parameter corresponding to a variable parameter may be modified when the procedure executes; it is illogical to allow a procedure to change the value of either a constant or an expression.

Writing Functions as Procedures

Now that we know how to return results from a procedure, we can write a function as a procedure with a single var parameter. Figure 6.15 shows function Exponent from Fig. 6.5 rewritten as procedure ProcExponent. ProcExponent returns a single result through the var parameter Exponent. If the main program declares X, Y, and Z as type Real variables, you *could* use the procedure call statement

```
ProcExponent (X, Y, Z)
```

to save in Z the value of X raised to the power Y.

Figure 6.15   Procedure ProcExponent

Directory: CHAP6
File: PROCEXPO.PRO

```
procedure ProcExponent (U, V {input} : Real;
                               var Exponent {output} : Real);
{
 Returns through Exponent the value of U raised to the
 power V.
 Pre : U and V are defined.
 Post: Exponent has the value of U raised to the power V.
}
begin {ProcExponent}
   if U = 0.0 then
      Exponent := 0.0
   else if U > 0.0 then
      Exponent := Exp(V * Ln(U))
   else
      Exponent := 1.0 / Exp(V * Ln(-U))
end; {ProcExponent}
```

In general, however, you should avoid doing this and instead, use functions whenever a module computes and returns a single result. Use procedures for modules that return any other number of results. If a module performs input/output operations, it should be implemented as a procedure even when it returns only a single result. The exception would be a function that displays an error message for invalid data and otherwise returns a single result.

Software Engineering: Function Side Effects

Until now, we have written all functions using value parameters. This allows us to use an expression as a function argument. You may be wondering about using variable parameters with functions. If a function has a variable parameter, it would be possible to modify that parameter, thereby returning a second result when the function executes. A result returned in this way is called a function *side effect*. Function side effects are undesirable; it is difficult to debug programs that have them because they are not expected. Therefore, you should declare all function parameters as value parameters, to prevent function side effects.

Multiple Calls to a Procedure

Next, we will study two procedures that generally would be called more than once in a given program. Each procedure processes different data values each time it is called. The use of procedure parameters makes this possible.

■ Example 6.4

Procedure MakeChange (Fig. 6.16) can be used to determine the quantity of a particular denomination of bills or coins given as change. The input parameter ChangeDenom specifies the value of each change unit (for example, 10.00 for ten-dollar bills, 0.10 for dimes). The input/output parameter, ChangeNeeded, is passed the amount of change that must be made. The procedure determines how many units (NumUnits) of a particular change denomination should be dispensed. The value returned through ChangeNeeded is the amount of change remaining after the change is dispensed. For example, if the value passed into ChangeNeeded is 20.45 and ChangeDenom is 10.00, the value of Trunc(2.045), or 2, is returned through NumUnits and the value of (20.45 – 20.00) or 0.45 is returned through ChangeNeeded.

Figure 6.16 Procedure MakeChange

```
procedure MakeChange (ChangeDenom {input} : Real;
                      var ChangeNeeded {input/output} : Real;
                      var NumUnits {output} : Integer);
{
 Determines the number of units (NumUnits) of change of a
 particular denomination (ChangeDenom) to dispense when
 making change for amount ChangeNeeded.  Also returns the
 remaining amount of change left to make in ChangeNeeded.
 Pre : ChangeDenom > 0.0 and ChangeNeeded >= 0.0 .
 Post: NumUnits is the number of units of change to dispense
       and ChangeNeeded is reduced by the change amount given.
}
begin {MakeChange}
  NumUnits := Trunc(ChangeNeeded / ChangeDenom);
  ChangeNeeded := ChangeNeeded — (NumUnits * ChangeDenom)
end; {MakeChange}
```

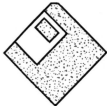

Directory: CHAP6
File: MAKECHAN.PRO

If the main program declares `Change` as type `Real` and `NumTens` as type `Integer`, the second statement below

```
Change := 20.45;
MakeChange (10.00, Change, NumTens);
WriteLn ('Number of tens is ', NumTens :1);
WriteLn ('Change left to dispense is ', Change :4:2);
```

calls `MakeChange` to determine how many ten-dollar bills to dispense in change and the amount of `Change` remaining. The `WriteLn` statements display the procedure results:

```
Number of tens is 2
Change left to dispense is 0.45
```

Figure 6.17 shows the main program data area and the procedure data area just after the procedure call; Figure 6.18 shows the main program data area

Figure 6.17 Data Areas After Call of MakeChange

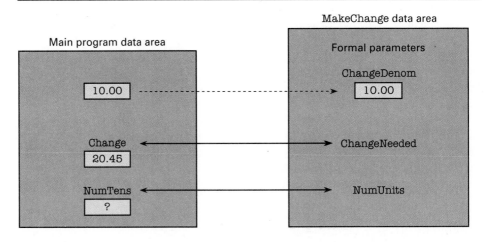

Figure 6.18 Data Areas After Execution of MakeChange

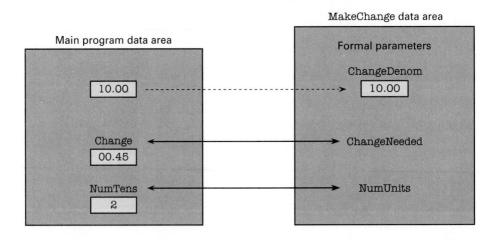

and the procedure data area just after the execution of procedure MakeChange. These figures show that the procedure execution updates the value of Change (from 20.45 to 0.45) and defines the value of NumTens as 2.

If the main program continued with the statements

```
MakeChange (0.10, Change, NumDimes);
WriteLn ('Number of dimes is ', NumDimes :1);
WriteLn ('Change left to dispense is ', Change :4:2);
```

where NumDimes is type Integer, the following lines would be displayed:

```
Number of dimes is 4
Change left to dispense is 0.05
```

Case Study: Sorting Three Numbers

Problem
In many real-life and programming situations, we want to arrange a set of data so that it follows some numerical or alphabetical sequence. In programming, this is called a *sorting* problem. You won't be able to solve this problem for large data sets yet; however, you can write a program that reads any three numbers into the variables Num1, Num2, Num3 and rearranges the data so that the smallest number is stored in Num1, the next smaller number in Num2, and the largest number in Num3.

Analysis
Rearranging a collection of data items so that the values are in either increasing or decreasing order is a special case of a sorting problem. Since we have only three items to be sorted, we will solve this special case now; the general sorting problem is a bit more complicated, so we will consider it later. We will follow an approach similar to the one used to find the smallest of three letters (Section 4.5) and develop a sequence of pairwise comparisons.

Data Requirements

Problem Inputs
Num1, Num2, Num3 : Real   {three numbers}

Problem Outputs
The three numbers stored in increasing order in Num1, Num2, Num3

Design

Initial Algorithm

1. Read the three numbers into Num1, Num2, and Num3.
2. Place the smallest number in Num1, the next smaller in Num2, and the largest number in Num3.
3. Print Num1, Num2, and Num3.

Algorithm Refinements

We can think of the variables Num1, Num2, Num3 as representing a list of consecutive storage cells. To perform step 2, we can compare pairs of numbers, always moving the smaller number in the pair closer to the front of the list (Num1) and the larger number closer to the end of the list (Num3). It should take three comparisons to sort the numbers in the list; one possible sequence of comparisons is shown here.

Step 2 Refinement

2.1 Compare Num1 and Num2 and store the smaller number in Num1 and the larger number in Num2.

2.2 Compare Num1 and Num3 and store the smaller number in Num1 and the larger number in Num3.

2.3 Compare Num2 and Num3 and store the smaller number in Num2 and the larger number in Num3.

Table 6.1 traces this refinement for the input sequence 8.0, 10.0, 6.0. The final order is correct.

Table 6.1 Trace of Step 2 Refinement for Data 8.0, 10.0, 6.0

Algorithm Step	Num1	Num2	Num3	Effect
	8.0	10.0	6.0	
2.1				Num1, Num2 are in order.
2.2	6.0		8.0	Switch Num1 and Num3.
2.3		8.0	10.0	Switch Num2 and Num3.

The structure chart for step 2 of this algorithm is shown in Fig. 6.19. The data flow information for step 2.1 shows that Num1 and Num2 are used as both inputs and outputs. Since steps 2.1, 2.2, and 2.3 perform the same operation on different data, it would be a waste of time and effort to write a different procedure for each step. We will use one procedure, Order, to order any pair of numbers.

Figure 6.19 Structure Chart for Step 2 of Sorting Problem

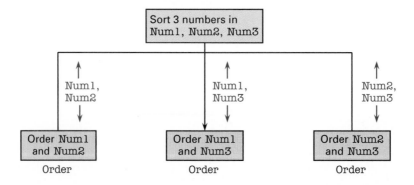

Implementation

The procedure call statement

```
Order (Num1, Num2);
```

can be used to perform step 2.1 of the algorithm: store the smaller number in
Num1 and the larger number in Num2. The complete program is shown in
Fig. 6.20. The main program body contains three statements that call procedure
Order:

```
Order (Num1, Num2);     {Order the data in Num1 and Num2.}
Order (Num1, Num3);     {Order the data in Num1 and Num3.}
Order (Num2, Num3);     {Order the data in Num2 and Num3.}
```

Since each of these statements contains a different actual parameter list, a
different pair of variables will be manipulated each time the procedure is called.

Figure 6.20   Program to Order Three Numbers

```
program Sort3Numbers (Input, Output);
{
  Reads three numbers and sorts them
  so that they are in increasing order
}
  var
    Num1, Num2, Num3 : Real;          {a list of three cells}


  procedure Order (var X, Y {input/output} : Real);
  {
    Orders a pair of numbers represented by X and Y so that the
    smaller number is in X and the larger number is in Y.
    Pre : X and Y are assigned values.
    Post: X is the smaller of the pair and Y is the larger.
  }
    var
      Temp : Real;            {copy of number originally in X}

  begin {Order}
    if X > Y then
      begin {Switch the values of X and Y}
        Temp := X;                    {Store old X in Temp.}
        X := Y;                       {Store old Y in X.}
        Y := Temp                     {Store old X in Y.}
      end {if}
  end;  {Order}


begin   {Sort3Numbers}
    WriteLn ('Enter 3 numbers to be sorted separated by spaces> ');
    ReadLn (Num1, Num2, Num3);

    {Sort the numbers}
    Order (Num1, Num2);     {Order the data in Num1 and Num2.}
    Order (Num1, Num3);     {Order the data in Num1 and Num3.}
    Order (Num2, Num3);     {Order the data in Num2 and Num3.}
```

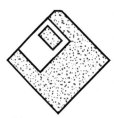

Directory: CHAP6
File: SORT3NUM.PAS

Case Study: Sorting Three Numbers, continued

```
     {Print the results}
     WriteLn ('The three numbers in order are:');
     WriteLn (Num1 :8:2, Num2 :8:2, Num3 :8:2)
end.  {Sort3Numbers}


Enter 3 numbers to be sorted separated by spaces>
8.0  10.0  6.0
The three numbers in order are:
   6.00    8.00   10.00
```

The body of procedure Order consists of the if statement from Fig. 4.10. The procedure heading contains the formal parameter list

```
(var X, Y {input/output} : Real)
```

which identifies X and Y as the formal parameters. X and Y are classified as input/output parameters because the procedure uses the current actual parameter values as inputs and may return new values.

The sequence of the actual parameters is important. The first actual parameter is paired with the first formal parameter, the second actual parameter is paired with the second formal parameter, and so on. If the first procedure call statement in Fig. 6.20 were written as

```
Order (Num2, Num1);
```

the smaller number would be stored in Num2 and the larger number in Num1, instead of the other way around.

Exercises for Section 6.3

Self-Check

1. Trace the execution of procedure MakeChange when ChangeNeeded is 5.56 and ChangeDenom is 5.00.
2. Show the output displayed by the following program in the form of a table of values for X, Y, and Z.

```
program Show (Output);

  var
    W, X, Y, Z : Integer;


  procedure SumDiff (Num1, Num2 : Integer;
                        var Num3, Num4 : Integer);
  begin {SumDiff}
    Num3 := Num1 + Num2;
    Num4 := Num1 - Num2
  end; {SumDiff}

begin  {Show}
```

```
      X := 5;  Y := 3;  Z := 7;  W := 9;
      WriteLn ('   X   Y   Z   W');
      SumDiff (X, Y, Z, W);
      WriteLn (X :4, Y :4, Z :4, W :4);
      SumDiff (Y, X, Z, W);
      WriteLn (X :4, Y :4, Z :4, W :4);
      SumDiff (Z, W, Y, X);
      WriteLn (X :4, Y :4, Z :4, W :4);
      SumDiff (Z, Z, X, Y);
      WriteLn (X :4, Y :4, Z :4, W :4);
      SumDiff (Y, Y, Y, W);
      WriteLn (X :4, Y :4, Z :4, W :4)
   end.   {Show}
```

    a. Show the program output.

    b. Write the preconditions and postconditions for procedure `SumDiff`.

3. Trace the execution of the following three procedure call statements:

```
   Order (Num3, Num2);
   Order (Num3, Num1);
   Order (Num2, Num1)
```

    a. Trace the execution of the three procedure call statements for the data sets `8.0, 10.0, 6.0`, and `10.0, 8.0, 6.0`.

    b. What is the effect of this sequence of procedure calls?

4. A procedure has four formal parameters: `W`, `X`, `Y`, and `Z` (all type `Real`). During execution, the procedure stores the sum of `W` and `X` in `Y` and the product of `W` and `X` in `Z`. Which parameters are inputs and which are outputs?

5. Is the module described in programming exercise 4 better implemented as a function or a procedure?

Programming

1. Write a main program that reads in an amount of change to make and calls procedure `MakeChange` with different parameters to determine the number of twenties, tens, ones, quarters, dimes, and pennies to dispense as change.

2. Write the procedure for self-check exercise 2.

3. Write a procedure that displays a table showing all powers of its first argument from zero through the power indicated by its second argument (a positive integer). The procedure should also return the sum of all values displayed. For example, if the first argument is `10` and the second argument is `3`, the procedure should display `1`, `10`, `100`, and `1000` and return `1111` as its result.

4. Write a procedure that raises its first parameter (type `Real`) to the power indicated by its second parameter (a positive integer). Use repeated multiplication. Return the result through the third parameter.

6.4 Syntax Rules for Parameter Lists

This section presents the syntax rules for procedure declarations and procedure call statements with parameters. The displays that follow summarize these rules.

Procedure Declaration (Procedure with Parameters)

Form:
```
procedure pname (formal parameters);
declaration section
begin
    procedure body
end;
```

Example:
```
procedure Highlight (Ch {input} : Char;
                     var NumStars {output} : Integer);
{
  Displays Ch between two asterisks and returns the
  numbers of asterisks printed.
  Pre : Ch is defined.
  Post: Returns 3 in NumStars if Ch = Border; otherwise,
        returns 2 in NumStars.
}
  const
    Border = '*';

begin {Highlight}
  Write (Border);  Write (Ch);  Write (Border);
  if Ch = Border then
    NumStars := 3
  else
    NumStars := 2
end; {Highlight}
```

Interpretation: The procedure *pname* is declared. The *formal parameters* are enclosed in parentheses. The identifiers declared in the *declaration section* are local to the procedure and are defined only during the execution of the procedure. A formal parameter cannot be declared as a local identifier in the *declaration section.*

The *procedure body* describes the data manipulation to be performed by the procedure using the formal parameter names in the description. For a variable parameter, the procedure manipulates the corresponding actual parameter; for a value parameter, a local memory cell is initialized to the actual parameter's value, and the procedure manipulates the local copy without altering the actual parameter.

Procedure Call Statement (Procedure with Parameters)

Form: *pname* (*actual parameters*)
Example: `Highlight ('A', NumAsterisks)`
Interpretation: The *actual parameters* are enclosed in parentheses. When procedure *pname* is called into execution, the first actual parameter is associated with the first formal parameter, the second actual parameter with the second formal parameter, and so on. For a value parameter, the actual parameter's value is saved in the procedure. For a variable parameter, the actual parameter's address is saved in the procedure.

Note: The actual parameters must satisfy the rules for parameter list correspondence discussed later in this section.

You must follow certain rules when writing parameter lists, as illustrated by this syntax diagram for a formal parameter list:

Formal Parameter List

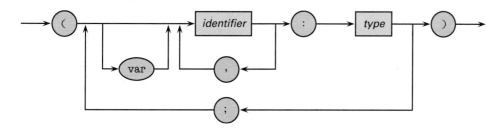

This diagram shows that a *formal parameter list* is always enclosed in parentheses. It consists of one or more lists of identifiers. Each list may be preceded by var. Identifiers are separated by commas, lists of identifiers are separated by semicolons, and each list must end with a colon followed by a data type name (e.g., Real or Char).

■ Example 6.5

Each of the two following parameter lists is printed on two or more lines to improve readability:

```
(Ch3 : Char;                (M, N, O : Integer;
 var X, Y, Z : Real)         var X, Y, Z : Real;
                                 A, B, C : Real)
```

In both lists, X, Y, Z are declared to be type Real variable parameters. Ch3 is a type Char value parameter; A, B, and C are type Real value parameters; and M, N, and O are type Integer value parameters.

This example points out a common error with formal parameter lists. In the list on the right, we indented A, B, and C. Students often think that the word var is implied by this indentation and that A, B, and C are also variable parameters. This is not correct! The word var must appear before each list of variable parameters.

The formal parameter list also determines the form of any actual parameter list that may be used to call the procedure. This form is determined during the translation of the program when the compiler processes the procedure declaration.

Later, when it reaches a procedure call statement, the compiler checks the actual parameter list for consistency with the formal parameter list. An actual parameter list may be a list of expressions, variables, or constants separated by commas. An actual parameter list and its corresponding formal parameter list must agree in **N**umber, **O**rder, and **T**ype (**NOT**), as described in the following rules. ∎

Rules for Parameter List Correspondence

1. Correspondence between actual and formal parameters is determined by position in their respective parameter lists. These lists must be the same size. The names of corresponding actual and formal parameters may be different.
2. For variable parameters, the types of corresponding actual and formal parameters must be identical. For value parameters, the actual parameter must be assignment compatible with its corresponding formal parameter (see Sections 2.4 and 7.7).
3. For variable parameters, an actual parameter must be a variable. For value parameters, an actual parameter may be a variable, a constant, or an expression.

∎ Example 6.6

A main program contains the following declarations:

```
var
  X, Y : Real;
  M : Integer;
  Next : Char;
```

and

```
procedure Test (A, B : Integer;
                var C, D : Real;
                var E : Char);
```

where only the heading for procedure `Test` is shown. Procedure `Test` has two value parameters (`A` and `B`) and three variable parameters (`C`, `D`, and `E`). Any of the following procedure call statements would be syntactically correct in the main program.

```
Test (M + 3, 10, X, Y, Next);
Test (M, MaxInt, Y, X, Next);
Test (35, M * 10, Y, X, Next);
```

The correspondence specified by the first parameter list is shown in Table 6.2. The last column in the table describes each formal parameter.

Table 6.2 Parameter Correspondence for Test (M + 3, 10, X, Y, Next)

Actual Parameter	Formal Parameter	Description
M + 3	A	Integer, value
10	B	Integer, value
X	C	Real, variable
Y	D	Real, variable
Next	E	Char, variable

Table 6.2 shows that an expression (e.g., M + 3) or a constant (e.g., 10) may be associated with a value parameter. All the procedure call statements in Table 6.3 contain syntax errors, as indicated.

Table 6.3 Invalid Procedure Call Statements

Procedure Call Statement	Error
Test (30, 10, M, X, Next)	Type of M is not Real.
Test (M, 19, X, Y)	Not enough actual parameters.
Test (M, 10, 35, Y, 'E')	Constants 35 and 'E' cannot correspond to variable parameters.
Test (M, 3.0, X, Y, Next)	Type of 3.0 is not Integer.
Test (30, 10, X, X + Y, Next)	Expression X + Y cannot correspond to a variable parameter.
Test (30, 10, C, D, E)	C, D, and E are not declared in the main program.

The last procedure call statement in Table 6.3 points out an error often made in using procedures. The actual parameter names (C, D, and E) are the same as their corresponding formal parameter names. However, since these names are not declared in the main program, they cannot appear in an actual parameter list used in the main program.

When writing relatively long parameter lists such as the ones above, you must be careful not to transpose two actual parameters; doing so will result in a syntax error if it violates a parameter correspondence rule. If no syntax is violated, the procedure execution will probably generate incorrect results. ■

Exercises for Section 6.4

Self-Check

1. Provide a table similar to Table 6.2 for the other correct parameter lists shown in Example 6.6.
2. Correct the syntax errors in the following formal parameter lists:

   ```
   (var A, B : Integer, C : Real)
   (VALUE M : Integer; var Next : Char)
   (var Account, Real; X + Y , Real)
   ```

3. Assuming the declarations

   ```
   const
     MaxInt = 32767;

   var
     X, Y, Z : Real;
     M, N : Integer;

   procedure Massage (var A, B : Real;
                      X : Integer);
   ```

which of the following are correct, which are incorrect, and if incorrect, why?

a. Massage (X, Y, Z);
b. Massage (X, Y, 8);
c. Massage (Y, X, N);
d. Massage (M, Y, N);
e. Massage (25.0, 15, X);
f. Massage (X, Y, M+N);
g. Massage (A, B, X);
h. Massage (Y, Z, M);
i. Massage (Y+Z, Y-Z, M);
j. Massage (Z, Y, X);
k. Massage (X, Y, M, 10);
l. Massage (Z, Y, MaxInt);

Programming

1. Redo programming exercise 4 for Section 6.3 assuming that the second parameter can be any integer value.

6.5 Stepwise Design with Functions and Procedures

Now that you can pass data into and out of procedures, you can make more use of procedures and functions in programming. From now on, many of the level-1 subproblems shown in a structure chart will be implemented as separate procedures or functions. If the solution to a subproblem cannot be written easily using just a few Pascal statements, it will be coded as a procedure or a function. In this section, you will see how to practice stepwise design of programs using procedures and functions. We will do this by considering the problem outlined next.

Case Study: General Sum-and-Average Problem

Problem

We have written earlier program fragments that found the sum or the product of a collection of data items. Accumulating a sum of data values is a problem that occurs again and again in programming. This problem involves writing a program that finds and displays the sum and the average of a list of real data values. We will use a modular approach so we can develop modules that can be reused when this problem surfaces again.

Analysis

Figure 5.4 shows a loop that computes the total payroll for a company. We can adapt this approach to compute the sum of a collection of data values. To compute an average, we divide a sum by the number of items considered, being careful not to perform this division if the number of items summed is 0.

Data Requirements

Problem Inputs

```
NumItems : Integer      {number of data items to be summed}
Item : Real             {each data item}
```

Problem Outputs

```
Sum : Real              {sum of data items}
Average : Real          {average of data}
```

Relevant Formulas

average = sum of data / number of data items

Design

Initial Algorithm

1. Read the number of items.
2. Compute the sum of the data.
3. Compute the average of the data.
4. Print the sum and the average.

Figure 6.21 shows the structure chart, which documents the data flow between the main problem and its subproblems. We will implement each step

Figure 6.21 Structure Chart with Data Flow Information

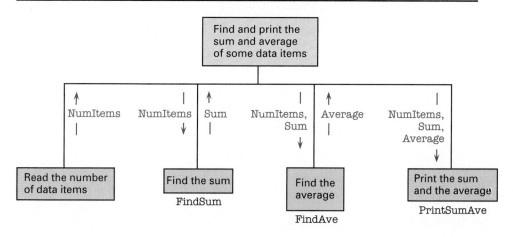

that has a nontrivial solution as a separate module. A label under a step denotes the name of the module that implements that step. Each step except the first is implemented in a separate module.

Figure 6.21 shows the data flow between the main program and each module. You will recall from Section 4.5 that all variables whose values are set by a module are considered module outputs (indicated by an arrow pointing out of the module). All variables whose values are used in a computation but are not changed by the module are considered module inputs (indicated by an arrow pointing into the module). Since the step "Read the number of data items" defines the value of the variable NumItems, NumItems is an output of this step. Module FindSum needs the value of NumItems to know how many data items to read and sum; consequently, NumItems is an input to module FindSum. The variable Sum is an output of module FindSum. Sum must be provided as an input to modules FindAve and PrintSumAve. The variable Average is an output of module FindAve and an input to module PrintSumAve.

Implementation

Once the data flow information has been added to the structure chart, we can write the main program before we even refine the algorithm. We can follow the approach described in Section 3.1 to write the main program. We begin by copying the data requirements into the program declaration part. All the variables that appear in the structure chart should be declared in the main program because they are used to store data passed to a module or results returned from a procedure. We will omit the declaration for variable Item because it does not appear in the structure chart; however, it must be declared later in module FindSum. Next, we move the initial algorithm into the program body, writing each algorithm step as a comment (see Fig. 6.22).

Figure 6.22   Outline of Program for General Sum and Average

```
program SumItems (Input, Output);
{Finds and prints the sum and the average of a list of data items}

   var
     NumItems : Integer;   {input — number of items to be added}
     Sum,                  {output — sum being accumulated}
     Average : Real;       {output — average of the data}

   {
    Insert declarations for procedures FindSum and PrintSumAve and
    function FindAve here.
   }

begin  {SumItems}
   {Read the number of items}

   {Compute the sum of the data}
```

```
{Compute the average of the data}

{Print the sum and average}

end.  {SumItems}
```

To complete the main program, we must implement each algorithm step *in-line* (as part of the main program code) or as a procedure or function call. We will implement the data entry step in-line because it consists of a simple `Write` (for a prompt) and a `ReadLn`. The structure chart shows `FindSum` and `FindAve` as modules that return a single result. We will implement `FindAve` as a function; however, we will implement `FindSum` as a procedure because `FindSum` must read each data item before adding it to the sum. We will implement `PrintSumAve` as a procedure with three input parameters.

The data flow information in Fig. 6.21 tells us the actual parameters to use in each procedure or function call. In the case of a function, it also tells us the name of the main program variable that will hold the function result. For example, the assignment statement

```
Average := FindAve(NumItems, Sum);
```

should be used to call `FindAve` and set the value of `Average`. We can determine that the procedure call statement

```
FindSum (NumItems, Sum);
```

should be used to call `FindSum` (`NumItems` is an input parameter and `Sum` is an output parameter). The procedure call statement

```
PrintSumAve (NumItems, Sum, Average)
```

should be used to call `PrintSumAve` (all input parameters). The final main program is shown in Fig. 6.23.

Figure 6.23 Main Program for General Sum-and-Average Problem

```
program SumItems (Input, Output);
{Finds and prints the sum and the average of a list of data items}

  var
    NumItems : Integer;   {input - number of items to be added}
    Sum,                  {output - sum being accumulated}
    Average : Real;       {output - average of the data}

  {
    Insert declarations for procedures FindSum and PrintSumAve and
    function FindAve here.
  }

begin  {SumItems}
  {Read the number of items}
```

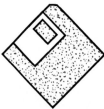

```
      Write ('How many items will be added? ');
      ReadLn (NumItems);

      {Compute the sum of the data}
      FindSum (NumItems, Sum);

      {Compute the average of the data}
      Average := FindAve(NumItems, Sum);

      {Print the sum and average}
      PrintSumAve (NumItems, Sum, Average)
end.  {SumItems}
```

Procedure FindSum

Now that the main program is complete, we can concentrate on its individual modules. We will begin with FindSum. In specifying the data requirements for FindSum, we should list the procedure inputs and outputs. We also need two local variables: one for storing each data item (Item) and one for loop control (Count).

Data Requirements

Procedure Inputs

NumItems : Integer   {number of data items to be summed}

Procedure Outputs

Sum : Real   {the sum of the data items}

Local Variables

Item : Real   {each data item}
Count : Integer   {count of data items summed}

In Section 5.2, we discussed accumulating a sum in a loop. We emphasized the need to initialize the sum to zero prior to loop entry. The loop-control steps must ensure that the correct number of data items are read and included in the sum being accumulated. Since we know the number of items to sum beforehand (NumItems), we can use a counting loop. These considerations lead to the algorithm for FindSum, shown next. The code for FindSum appears in Fig. 6.24.

Algorithm for FindSum

1. Read in the number of items to be summed
2. Initialize Sum to 0
3. for each value of Count from 1 to NumItems do
   begin
      4. Read in the next item
      5. Add it to Sum
   end

Figure 6.24 Procedure FindSum

```
procedure FindSum (NumItems {input} : Integer;
                   var Sum {output} : Real);
{
  Computes the sum of a list of NumItems data items.
  Pre : NumItems is assigned a value.
  Post: NumItems data items are read; their sum is stored in Sum.
}

  var
    Count : Integer;       {count of items added so far}
    Item  : Real;          {the next data item to be added}

begin {FindSum}
  {Read each data item and add it to Sum}
  Sum := 0.0;
  for Count := 1 to NumItems do
    begin
      Write ('Next number to be added> ');
      ReadLn (Item);
      Sum := Sum + Item
    end {for}
end; {FindSum}
```

Directory: CHAP6
File: SUMITEMS.PAS

Figure 6.25 shows the parameter correspondence specified by the procedure call statement

```
FindSum (NumItems, Sum);
```

assuming the value 10 is read into NumItems just before the procedure call. The local variables, Count and Item, are undefined when the procedure is called.

Figure 6.25 Parameter Correspondence for FindSum (NumItems, Sum)

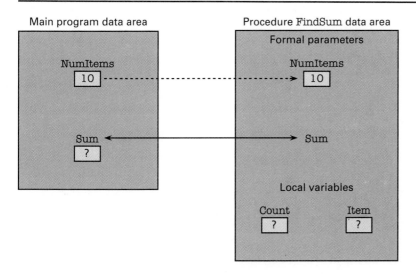

The procedure begins by initializing to 0 the main program variable Sum, which corresponds to variable parameter Sum. The for loop reads each data item into the local variable Item and adds it to the main program variable Sum. The loop exit and procedure return occur after 10 items have been added.

Function FindAve and Procedure PrintSumAve

Both FindAve and PrintSumAve are relatively straightforward. We list their data requirements and algorithms next. Both algorithms include a test of NumItems. If NumItems is not positive, it makes no sense to compute or display the average of the data items. Figure 6.26 shows function FindAve, and Fig. 6.27 shows procedure PrintSumAve.

Figure 6.26 Function FindAve

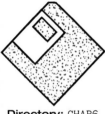

Directory: CHAP6
File: SUMITEMS.PAS

```
function FindAve (NumItems {input} : Integer;
                  Sum {input} : Real) : Real;
{
  Returns the average of NumItems data items with sum of Sum.
  Pre : NumItems and Sum are defined.
  Post: If NumItems is positive, returns Sum / NumItems;
        otherwise, returns zero.
}
begin  {FindAve}
  {Compute the average of the data}
  if NumItems > 0 then
    FindAve := Sum / NumItems
  else
    FindAve := 0.0
end;   {FindAve}
```

Figure 6.27 Procedure PrintSumAve

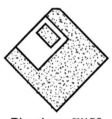

Directory: CHAP6
File: SUMITEMS.PAS

```
procedure PrintSumAve (NumItems {input} : Integer;
                       Sum, Average {input} : Real);
{
  Displays the sum and average of NumItems data items.
  Pre : NumItems, Sum, and Average are defined.
  Post: Displays Sum and also Average if NumItems > 0.
}
begin  {PrintSumAve}
  if NumItems > 0 then
    begin
      WriteLn ('The sum is ', Sum :4:2);
      WriteLn ('The average is ', Average :4:2)
    end
  else
    WriteLn ('Sum and average are not defined')
end;   {PrintSumAve}
```

Data Requirements for FindAve

Function Inputs

```
NumItems : Integer          {the number of data items}
Sum : Real                  {the sum of all data}
```

Function Output

The average of the data

Initial Algorithm for FindAve

1. if NumItems is positive then
  2. Set FindAve to Sum divided by NumItems
 else
  3. Set FindAve to 0

Data Requirements for PrintSumAve

Procedure Inputs

```
NumItems : Integer          {the number of data items}
Sum : Real                  {the sum of all data}
Average : Real              {the average of the data}
```

Initial Algorithm for PrintSumAve

1. if NumItems is positive then
  2. Display the sum and the average of the data

Testing

You must insert the function and procedure declarations in the declaration part of program SumItems (after the variable declarations) before you can run the program. In testing SumItems, you should make sure that the program displays the sum and the average correctly when NumItems is positive and displays a diagnostic when NumItems is zero or negative. Figure 6.28 shows a sample run.

Figure 6.28 Sample Run of SumItems

```
How many numbers will be added? 3
Next number to be added> 5.0
Next number to be added> 6.0
Next number to be added> −7.0
The sum is 4.00
The average is 1.33
```

When to Use a Function or Procedure in a Program System

The structure chart for the general sum-and-average program, shown in Fig. 6.21, contains four steps, and all but the first step are performed by separate modules. It was obvious that step 1 could be implemented using a Write and a ReadLn, so that step was written directly in the main program. We used a procedure (FindSum) for step 2 because its algorithm was relatively complicated. Even though steps 3 and 4 were relatively easy to implement, we used a function (FindAve) for step 3 and a procedure (PrintSumAve) for step 4 because their implementations were rather lengthy. You should follow this line of reasoning in determining whether to implement a step as a separate module. From this point on, your main program bodies will consist primarily of a sequence of procedure and function calls.

Multiple Declarations of Identifiers in a Program System

The identifiers Sum and NumItems are declared as variables in the main program and as formal parameters in the three modules called by the main program. Each function or procedure call in the main program associates the main program variable Sum with the formal parameter Sum, and the main program variable NumItems with the formal parameter NumItems. You may be wondering if this violates any rules of Pascal. It does not—the compiler is able to distinguish between the different uses of these two identifiers. We explain how this is done in Section 6.7.

Exercises for Section 6.5

Self-Check

1. Procedure FindSum returns a single value. Why do you think it was not implemented as a function?
2. Draw the main program data area and the function data area for the call to FindAve assuming that Sum is 100.0 and NumItems is 10.
3. Draw the main program data area and the procedure data area for the call to PrintSumAve.

6.6 Nested Procedures

Procedures FindSum and PrintSumAve are nested, or contained, in program SumItems. It is also possible for one procedure to be nested within another.

■ Example 6.7

Procedure Triangle in Fig. 6.29 uses procedure PrintStars to draw a triangle. The procedure parameter NumRows determines the number of lines in the triangle. The procedure call statement

```
Triangle (5)
```

assigns a value of 5 to NumRows and causes the following triangle to be drawn:

```
*
**
***
****
*****
```

Figure 6.29   Procedure Triangle

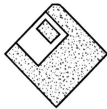

Directory: CHAP6
File: TRIANGLE.PRO

```
procedure Triangle (NumRows {input} : Integer);
{
  Prints a triangle by displaying lines of increasing length.
  The number of lines is determined by NumRows.
  Pre : NumRows is assigned a value.
  Post: A triangle is displayed.
  Requirements: Calls procedure PrintStars to display each line.
}
  var
    Row : Integer;               {loop control for Triangle}



  procedure PrintStars (NumStars : Integer);
  {
    Prints a row of asterisks.  The number of
    asterisks printed is determined by NumStars.
    Pre : NumStars is assigned a value.
    Post: A row of asterisks is displayed.
  }
    const
      Star = '*';                {symbol being printed}

    var
      CountStars : Integer;      {loop control for PrintStars}

  begin {PrintStars}
    {Print a row of asterisks}
    for CountStars := 1 to NumStars do
      Write (Star);
    WriteLn
  end; {PrintStars)


begin  {Triangle}
  {Print lines of increasing length}
  For Row := 1 to NumRows do
    PrintStars (Row)
end; {Triangle}
```

This example shows that a procedure may be declared inside another procedure and called by that procedure. In this case, the calling procedure (Triangle) passes information into procedure PrintStars each time it calls PrintStars. The for loop in the body of procedure Triangle repeatedly executes the procedure call statement

```
PrintStars (Row)
```

Each time `PrintStars` is called, the current value of `Row` (1 to `NumRows`) is passed into `NumStars`, and `PrintStars` displays a row of asterisks; the number of asterisks is determined by the value of `Row`. For example, the procedure call statement

```
PrintStars (5);
```

causes a line with five asterisks to be displayed.

Because procedure `PrintStars` is declared within procedure `Triangle`, `PrintStars` is considered a local identifier in `Triangle`. In the next section, you will see that local identifiers cannot be referenced outside the procedure in which they are declared. This means that `PrintStars` cannot be called directly by a main program or by any other procedures that we may write. This reduces the potential for reusing `PrintStars` and is a good reason to avoid nesting procedures. ∎

Exercises for Section 6.6

Self-Check

1. Why would you want to nest one procedure inside another?
2. What would be the disadvantage of including procedures `Triangle` and `Rectangle` (see programming exercise 1) in the same program? What action would you take if this were the case?

Programming

1. Write a procedure `Rectangle`, having parameters `Length` and `Width`, that displays a rectangle of `Width` lines, each of which has `Length` asterisks. Procedure `PrintStars` should be nested inside procedure `Rectangle`.
2. Rewrite program `Sort3Numbers` (Fig. 6.20) so that three calls to procedure `Order` in the main program are replaced by a single call to a procedure `Order3`, which has three input/output parameters. Procedure `Order` should be nested inside procedure `Order3`.

6.7 Scope of Identifiers

Each procedure in a nest of procedures has its own declaration part and its own body; this is also true for the main program. Figure 6.30 displays the organization of procedures in program `Nested`. Each box represents a procedure or program *block*. A block contains the module's formal parameter list, declaration part, and body. The name of the module is indicated just above the block.

Figure 6.30 shows procedures `Outer` and `Too` nested within the main program block. Procedure `Inner` is shown nested within the block for `Outer`.

Figure 6.30 Procedure Nesting

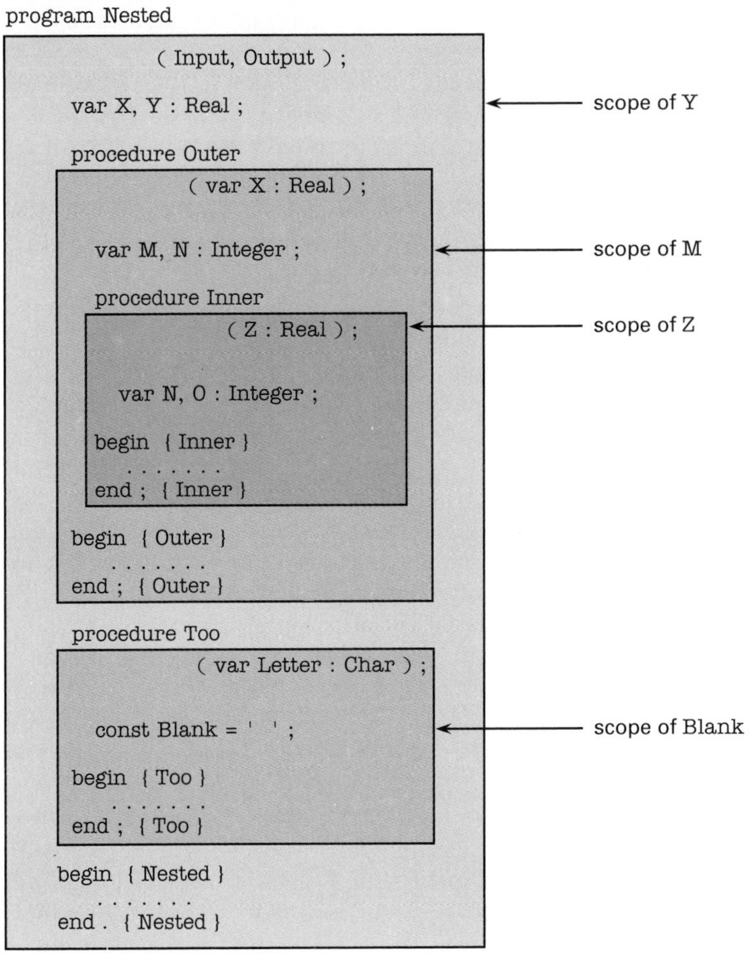

267

6.7 Scope of
Identifiers

program Nested

```
                    ( Input, Output ) ;

    var X, Y : Real ;                        ←——— scope of Y

    procedure Outer
                    ( var X : Real ) ;

        var M, N : Integer ;                 ←——— scope of M

        procedure Inner
                        ( Z : Real ) ;       ←——— scope of Z

            var N, O : Integer ;

        begin  { Inner }
            . . . . . . .
        end ;  { Inner }

    begin  { Outer }
        . . . . . . .
    end ;  { Outer }

    procedure Too
                    ( var Letter : Char ) ;

        const Blank = ' ' ;                  ←——— scope of Blank

    begin  { Too }
        . . . . . . .
    end ;  { Too }

    begin  { Nested }
        . . . . . . .
    end .  { Nested }
```

The statements in each procedure or function body written so far manipulate only local identifiers. Although we have not done so yet, it is possible in Pascal to reference identifiers that are not declared locally. The Pascal scope rules tell us where an identifier is *visible* and can be referenced.

Pascal Scope Rules

1. The scope of an identifier is the block in which it is declared. Therefore, an identifier declared in procedure P is visible in procedure P and all procedures enclosed in procedure P.
2. If identifier I declared in procedure P is redeclared in some inner procedure Q enclosed in P, then procedure Q and all its enclosed procedures are excluded from the scope of I declared in P.

According to rule 1, the *scope of an identifier* is the block in which it is declared. The scope of the parameter `Letter` and the constant `Blank` (see Fig. 6.30) is the block for procedure `Too`; therefore, `Letter` and `Blank` are visible only in procedure `Too`.

Because procedure `Inner` is nested in procedure `Outer`, the scope of an identifier declared in procedure `Outer` includes the block for procedure `Inner`. Therefore, an identifier declared in `Outer` (e.g., variable `M`) is visible in the body of either procedure.

Figure 6.30 shows the scope of formal parameter `Z` as the block for procedure `Inner` only. Formal parameter `Z` is not visible in the body of procedure `Outer` or procedure `Too` or in the main program body.

Rule 2 takes effect when there are multiple declarations of the same identifier. We discuss rule 2 in the next section.

Because all procedures are nested within the main program block, an identifier declared in the main program is visible anywhere in the program system. For this reason, main program variables are called *global variables*.

Although global variables can be referenced in procedures, it is a dangerous practice. If a procedure references a global variable, it is possible for the value of that variable to change when the procedure is executed (a phenomenon called a *side effect*). Often, no documentation exists to indicate that the procedure manipulates a global variable; consequently, it may be difficult to find the statement in a procedure that is responsible for assigning an incorrect or unexpected value to a global variable. If the statement

```
Y := Y + 3.5;     {Example of a side effect}
```

appears in any procedure in Fig. 6.30, it will cause a side effect (adding `3.5` to global variable `Y`) whenever that procedure is called.

The formal parameter list and the local declarations for a procedure explicitly document the data that will be manipulated. We will continue to manipulate only identifiers (including formal parameters) that are declared locally in a procedure. The only exceptions will be global constants and type identifiers (discussed in later chapters). It is permissible to reference a global constant in a procedure, because Pascal does not allow the value of a constant to be changed. Hence, there can be no side effect when a global constant is referenced. A global variable, however, should be passed as an actual parameter to any procedure that manipulates it.

Multiple Declarations of Identifiers

An identifier can be declared only once in a given procedure; however, the same identifier can be declared in more than one procedure. In Fig. 6.30, for example, `X` is declared as a global variable in the main program and as a formal parameter in procedure `Outer`. Consequently, when `X` is referenced in the program system, some question may arise in our minds as to which declaration takes precedence.

Scope rule 2 states that procedures `Outer` and `Inner` are excluded from the scope of global variable `X` because `X` is declared as a formal parameter of

Outer. Therefore, when X is referenced in the body of procedure Outer or procedure Inner, formal parameter X is manipulated. When X is referenced anywhere else in the program system, global variable X is manipulated.

If an identifier is not declared locally, then scope rule 2 requires the compiler to use the closest declaration in an outer block containing the point of reference. For example, if identifier N is referenced in procedure Inner or procedure Outer, the corresponding local declaration for identifier N is used. If identifier M is referenced in procedure Inner, where it is not declared locally, the declaration for variable M in procedure Outer is used. A reference to identifier M in either the main program body or procedure Too would cause an identifier not declared syntax error.

Table 6.4 shows the meaning of each valid reference to an identifier in the blocks of Fig. 6.30. Procedure names have been included with other identifiers in this table; they will be discussed later.

Table 6.4 Valid Identifier References for Figure 6.30

Block	Meaning of Each Identifier
Nested	Input, Output: parameters of Nested X, Y: global variables Outer, Too: procedures declared in Nested
Outer	X: parameter of Outer M, N: local variables Inner: local procedure Y: variable declared in Nested Outer, Too: procedures declared in Nested
Inner	Z: parameter of Inner N, O: local variables M: variable declared in Outer X: parameter of Outer Inner: procedure declared in Outer Y: variable declared in Nested Outer, Too: procedure declared in Nested
Too	Letter: parameter of Too Blank: local constant X, Y: global variables Outer, Too: procedures declared in Nested

Illustrating the Scope Rules

Next, we will look at an example that illustrates bad programming practice because identifier names are not meaningful and are unnecessarily redundant. Studying this example should help you master the Pascal scope rules.

■ Example 6.8

Figure 6.31 shows a procedure declared in a main program. W is declared as a variable in both the procedure and the main program; X is declared as a variable in the main program and as a parameter in the procedure; Y is declared as a variable in the main program only.

Figure 6.31 Program ScopeRules

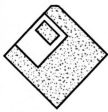

Directory: CHAP6
File: SCOPERUL.PAS

```
program ScopeRules (Output);
  var
    W, X, Y : Real;

  procedure Change (var X {input/output} : Real);
    var
      W, Z : Real;

  begin  {Change}
    W := 35.0;          {change local W}
    X := 6.0;           {change parameter X}
    Y := Y + 1.0;       {side effect – change global Y}
    Z := 3.0;           {change local Z}
    WriteLn ('W' :5, 'X' :5, 'Y' :5, 'Z' :5);
    WriteLn (W :5:1, X :5:1, Y :5:1, Z:5:1, ' in Change')
  end; {Change}


begin  {ScopeRules}
  W := 5.5;             {initialize global W}
  X := 2.0;             {initialize global X}
  Y := 3.0;             {initialize global Y}
  Change (W);           {update global W}
  WriteLn (W :5:1, X :5:1, Y :5:1, ' in ScopeRules' :19)
end.   {ScopeRules}

  W     X     Y     Z
35.0  6.0   4.0   3.0  in Change
 6.0  2.0   4.0        in ScopeRules
```

The main program begins by initializing global variables W, X, and Y. The initial values of the three main program variables are shown next.

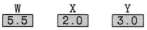

The procedure call statement

```
Change (W);
```

calls procedure Change with main program variable W corresponding to parameter X. In Change, the assignment statement

```
  X := 6.0;            {change parameter X}
```

stores 6.0 in the main program variable W, and the assignment statement

```
Y := Y + 1.0;      {side effect — change global Y}
```

increments the main program variable Y (a side effect). The other two assign-ment statements in Change affect its local variables W and Z only.

The second WriteLn statement in Change displays the values of its local identifiers (W, X, and Z) and the global variable Y just before the procedure return. The WriteLn statement in the main program displays the values of the three main program variables after the return.

```
  W          X          Y
┌─────┐   ┌─────┐   ┌─────┐
│ 6.0 │   │ 2.0 │   │ 4.0 │
└─────┘   └─────┘   └─────┘
```

Notice that main program variable X is unchanged and that the value of W is 6.0 (not 35.0).

It is interesting to consider what happens if X or Y is used as the actual parameter instead of W. That question is left as an exercise at the end of this section.   ■

Procedure Calls

Since procedure names are identifiers, the Pascal scope rules specify where a procedure can be referenced or called. In Fig. 6.30, procedures Outer and Too are global identifiers (declared in the main program), so they can be called anywhere. Procedure Inner is declared in procedure Outer, so it can be called only by procedure Outer or by Inner itself (called a *recursive procedure call;* see Section 6.10).

As things stand now, a call to Inner in the body of procedure Too or the main program body would cause an identifier not declared syntax error. If we declare procedure Inner in the main program instead of inside procedure Outer, then both the main program and procedure Too will be able to call Inner.

The Forward Declaration

In the preceding section, we implied that procedures Outer and Inner can call procedure Too because Too is a global identifier. However, since procedure Too is declared after procedure Outer, the Pascal compiler has no way of checking that a call to Too in procedure Outer (or Inner) is correct. Therefore, we must either change the order of procedures Outer and Too or provide a *forward declaration* for procedure Too if Too is called by procedure Outer. The first line below is a forward declaration:

```
procedure Too (var Letter : Char); Forward;

procedure Outer (var X : Real);
  . . .
end; {Outer}

procedure Too;
  . . .
end; {Too}
```

The heading for procedure Too comes first, followed by the complete declaration for procedures Outer and Too. The formal parameter list for procedure Too appears only in the forward declaration.

In most cases, you can avoid the use of forward declarations by paying close attention to the order of procedure declarations. The only exception is for *mutually recursive procedures,* or procedures that call each other.

Exercises for Section 6.7

Self-Check

1. Explain why variable N declared in procedure Outer cannot be referenced by the main program, procedure Inner, or procedure Too.
2. What would be the effect of executing the body of Inner as shown below?

```
begin  {Inner}
  X := 5.5;
  Y := 6.6;
  M := 2;
  N := 3;
  O := 4
end; {Inner}
```

3. If the statement sequence in exercise 2 appeared in a different block, some of the assignment statements would be syntactically incorrect. Identify the incorrect statements and indicate the effect of executing the others if the statement sequence appeared in procedure
   a. Outer
   b. Too
   c. Nested
4. Consider program ScopeRules shown in Fig. 6.31.
   a. What kind of error would occur if the assignment statement

   ```
   Z := 15.0;
   ```

   were inserted in the main program?
   b. Show the new values of W, X, and Y if X is the actual parameter in the call to procedure Change.
   c. What if Y is the actual parameter in the call to Change?
   d. What would be the effect of making formal parameter X a value parameter?

6.8 Problem Solving Illustrated

In this section, we demonstrate the top-down design process in solving a problem. The program solution is implemented in a stepwise manner starting at the top of the structure chart (with the main program). The problem solution makes extensive use of procedures with parameters.

Case Study: Balancing a Checkbook

Problem

You have just received a new personal computer and would like to write a program to help balance your checkbook. The program will read your initial checkbook balance and each transaction (check or deposit). It will print the new balance after each transaction and a warning message if the balance becomes negative. At the end of the session, the starting and final balances should be printed, along with a count of the number of checks and deposits processed.

Analysis

After the starting balance is read, each transaction wil be read and processed separately. We can use a simple code ('C' or 'D') to distinguish between checks and deposits. The transaction amount will be a real number. We will display the result of each transaction as it occurs, flagging transactions that cause the account balance to become negative. We will terminate processing transactions when the user enters a special code ('Q').

The starting balance must be available at the end, so we will save it in variable StartBal. We will use a different variable, CurBal, to keep track of the current balance; the final value of CurBal is a problem output. We must also enter and save the transaction data, including the type code and amount.

Data Requirements

Problem Inputs
```
StartBal : Real            {starting checkbook balance}
Transaction Data
    TranType : Char        {type of transaction}
    Amount : Real          {amount of transaction}
```

Problem Outputs
```
CurBal : Real              {current balance after each transaction}
NumCheck : Integer         {number of checks}
NumDep : Integer           {number of deposits}
```

Design

Initial Algorithm

1. Display the instructions and read the starting balance.
2. For each transaction, read the transaction, update and print the current balance, and increment the count of checks or deposits.
3. Print the starting and final balances and the number of checks and deposits processed.

Figure 6.32 shows the structure chart for this algorithm. The level-1 sub-problems will be written as procedures Initiate, Process, and Report. The data flow information shows that StartBal is read by Initiate and passed to

Process. Procedure Process defines the program results (CurBal, NumCheck, NumDep); these results are passed to Report and printed.

Figure 6.32 Structure Chart (Levels 0 and 1) for Checkbook Problem

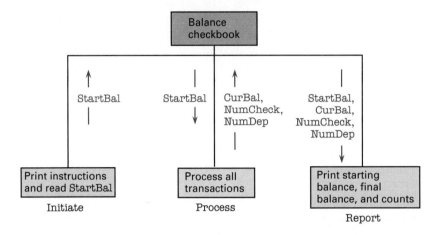

The variables shown in the structure chart should be declared in the main program, because each variable must be declared at the highest level in which it appears in the structure chart. Variables that are passed between the main program and a level-1 procedure must be declared in the main program.

Notice that the variables that represent the transaction data do not appear in the structure chart. They will be manipulated only by procedure Process and its subordinate procedures, so they do not have to be visible in the main program. They will be declared later as local variables in Process.

Implementation: Coding the Main Program

The data flow information from Fig. 6.32 is used to write the parameter lists in the main program, shown in Fig. 6.33. Procedures Initiate and Report consist of input/output statements only, so we write them now. Because procedure Process requires further refinement, we write it as a stub. The main program body consists of calls to its three level-1 procedures.

Figure 6.33 Checkbook-Balancing Program with Stub for Process

Directory: CHAP6
File: CHECKBOO.PAS

```
program CheckBook (Input, Output);
{
  Reads the starting balance for a checking account and processes
  all transactions.  Prints the new balance after each transaction
  is processed.  Also prints a count of the total number of checks
  and deposits processed.
}
  var
    StartBal,                            {input - starting balance}
```

```
  CurBal      : Real;                    {output - current balance}
  NumCheck,                              {output - number of checks}
  NumDep      : Integer;                 {output - number of deposits}


procedure Initiate (var {output} StartBal : Real);
{
  Displays the instructions and reads the starting balance.
  Pre : None
  Post: User instructions are displayed and StartBal is read in.
}
begin   {Initiate}
  WriteLn ('Balance your checking account!');
  WriteLn;
  WriteLn ('Enter C (Check), D (Deposit), or Q (Quit)');
  WriteLn ('after prompt C, D, or Q >');
  WriteLn;
  WriteLn ('Enter a positive number after prompt Amount $');
  WriteLn;
  Write ('Begin by entering your starting balance $');
  ReadLn (StartBal)
end;   {Initiate}


procedure Process (StartBal {Input} : Real;
                   var CurBal {output} : Real;
                   var NumCheck, NumDep {output} : Integer);
begin  {Process stub}
  WriteLn ('Procedure Process entered.');
  CurBal := 0.0;  NumCheck := 0;  NumDep := 0
end; {Process}


procedure Report (StartBal, CurBal {input} : Real;
                  NumCheck, NumDep {input} : Integer);
{
  Prints the starting and final balances and the count of checks
  and deposits.
  Pre : StartBal, CurBal, NumCheck, and NumDep are assigned values.
  Post: Program results are displayed.
}
begin {Report}
  WriteLn;
  WriteLn ('Starting balance was $', StartBal :10:2);
  WriteLn ('Final    balance is  $', CurBal :10:2);
  WriteLn ('Number of checks written: ', NumCheck :3);
  WriteLn ('Number of deposits made : ', NumDep :3)
end; {Report}


begin  {CheckBook}
  {Display user instructions and read StartBal}
  Initiate (StartBal);

  {Process each transaction}
  Process (StartBal, CurBal, NumCheck, NumDep);

  {Print starting and final balances and count of checks/deposits}
  Report (StartBal, CurBal, NumCheck, NumDep)
end. {CheckBook}
```

Case Study: Balancing a Checkbook, continued

Coding Process and Its Level-2 Procedures

Procedure Process performs step 2 of the algorithm, which is repeated below.

2. For each transaction, read the transaction, update and print the current balance, and increment the count of checks or deposits.

It is obvious that a loop is needed. Assuming that we do not know how many transactions will occur, we can use a sentinel-controlled while loop to compare the transaction code to a sentinel value. The loop properties follow:

1. CurBal is StartBal plus all transactions that are deposits and minus all transactions that are checks.
2. NumCheck is the count of checks so far.
3. NumDep is the count of deposits so far.
4. The transaction code is the sentinel just after loop exit.

These statements suggest the following refinement:

Algorithm for Process

1. Initialize NumCheck and NumDep to 0
2. Initialize CurBal to StartBal
3. Read the first transaction
4. while the transaction code is not the sentinel do
       begin
           5. Update CurBal and increment NumCheck or NumDep
           6. Display CurBal and the transaction
           7. Read the next transaction
       end

The structure chart for Process is shown in Fig. 6.34. Procedure

Figure 6.34 Structure Chart for Procedure Process

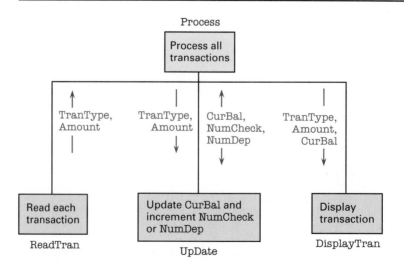

ReadTran performs steps 3 and 7 of the algorithm, UpDate performs step 5, and DisplayTran performs step 6. Two new variables, TranType and Amount (the transaction data), should be declared as local variables in procedure Process. Variables passed only between a level-1 and a level-2 procedure should be declared in the level-1 procedure. The identifiers CurBal, NumCheck, and NumDep are formal parameters of Process.

Local Variables for Process
```
TranType : Char          {the transaction type}
Amount : Real            {the transaction amount}
```

The three procedures subordinate to Process are fairly easy to write. One decision that we must make is how to handle invalid transaction codes. If we take care of them in the beginning (i.e., in procedure ReadTran), we will not have to be concerned about them in the remaining procedures. We will use the repeat statement (step 1 of the following algorithm) to ensure that ReadTran ignores any invalid transaction types (not 'C', 'D', or 'Q'). The data requirements for ReadTran follow.

Data Requirements for ReadTran
Procedure Inputs
  None

Procedure Outputs
```
    TranType : Char          {transaction type}
    Amount : Real            {transaction amount}
```

Algorithm for ReadTran

1. repeat
     2. Read TranType
   until TranType is 'C', 'D', or 'Q'
3. if TranType is not 'Q' then
     4. Read the transaction amount

Procedure Update must update the values of its three input/output parameters, CurBal, NumCheck, and NumDep, using the strategy outlined in the decision table (Table 6.5). We will implement this table using a case statement (not shown).

Table 6.5 Decision Table for Update

Condition	Desired Action
TranType = 'D'	Increment NumDep, add Amount to CurBal.
TranType = 'C'	Increment NumCheck, subtract Amount from CurBal.

Case Study: Balancing a Checkbook, continued

Data Requirements for Update

Input Parameters

TranType : Char	{transaction type}
Amount : Real	{transaction amount}

Input/Output Parameters

CurBal : Real	{current balance}
NumCheck : Integer	{number of checks}
NumDep : Integer	{number of deposits}

We will not discuss DisplayTran further, since its implementation is relatively straightforward. We could write ReadTran, Update, and DisplayTran as nested procedures inside procedure Process. It would be clearer, however, to write them as separate procedures at the same level. Because Process calls all three procedures, the declaration for Process must follow the declaration for its subordinate procedures. Figure 6.35 shows all four procedures; notice that we have added the line

Uses: ReadTran, Update, and DisplayTran

to the documentation section for Process.

Figure 6.35 Procedures for the Checkbook-Balancing Program

Directory: CHAP6
File: CHECKBOO.PAS

```
procedure ReadTran (var TranType {output} : Char;
                    var Amount {output} : Real);
{
  Reads each transaction.
  Pre : None
  Post: TranType and Amount are read in.
        Value returned through TranType is 'C', 'D', or 'Q'.
}
begin {ReadTran}
  WriteLn;
  repeat
    Write ('C, D, or Q >');
    ReadLn (TranType)
  until (TranType = 'C') or (TranType = 'D') or (TranType = 'Q');
  if TranType <> 'Q' then
    begin
      Write ('Amount $');
      ReadLn (Amount)
    end {if}
end; {ReadTran}


procedure UpDate (TranType {input} : Char;
                  Amount {input} : Real;
                  var CurBal {input/output} : Real;
                  var NumCheck, NumDep {input/output} : Integer);
{
  Updates CurBal and increments NumCheck for a check or
  NumDep for a deposit.
  Pre : TranType is 'C', 'D', or 'Q'.
```

```
       Post: CurBal is increased (deposit) or decreased (check) by
             Amount.  NumCheck or NumDep is increased by one.
}
begin {Update}
  case TranType of
    'C' : begin
             CurBal := CurBal - Amount;
             NumCheck := NumCheck + 1
          end; {Check}
    'D' : begin
             CurBal := CurBal + Amount;
             NumDep := NumDep + 1
          end; {Deposit}
    'Q' : {do nothing}
  end {case}
end; {Update}


procedure DisplayTran (TranType {input} : Char;
                       Amount, CurBal {input} : Real);
{
  Displays current transaction and balance.
  Pre : TranType is 'C', 'D', or 'Q'.
  Post: Transaction data are displayed.
}
begin {DisplayTran}
  case TranType of
    'C' : begin
             Write ('Check for  $', Amount: 12:2);
             WriteLn ('    Balance of $', CurBal :12:2);
             if CurBal < 0.0 then
                WriteLn ('Warning!  Your account is overdrawn.')
          end; {Check}
    'D' : begin
             Write  ('Depositing $', Amount :12:2);
             WriteLn ('    Balance of $', CurBal :12:2)
          end; {Deposit}
    'Q' : {do nothing}
  end {case}
end; {DisplayTran}


procedure Process (StartBal {input} : Real;
                   var CurBal {output} : Real;
                   var NumCheck, NumDep {output} : Integer);
{
  Processes each transaction.  Reads each transaction, updates and
  prints the current balance, and increments the count of checks or
  deposits.
  Pre : StartBal is assigned a value.
  Post: CurBal is StartBal plus deposits and minus withdrawals.
        NumCheck is the count of checks.
        NumDep is the count of deposits.
  Uses: ReadTran, Update, and DisplayTran
}
  var
    TranType : Char;        {transaction type (check or deposit)}
    Amount : Real;          {transaction amount}

begin  {Process}
  {Initialize counters to zero and CurBal to StartBal}
  NumCheck := 0;  NumDep := 0;  CurBal := StartBal;
```

Case Study: Balancing a Checkbook, continued

```
      {Read first transaction}
      Read (TranType, Amount);

      {Process each transaction until done}
      while TranType <> 'Q' do
        begin
          Update (TranType, Amount, CurBal, NumCheck, NumDep);
          DisplayTran (TranType, Amount, CurBal);
          ReadTran (TranType, Amount)
        end {while}
end; {Process}
```

Procedure DisplayTran contains a case statement that differentiates between checks and deposits. When TranType is 'C', an if statement executes
that detects an overdrawn account (CurBal is negative). Nothing happens in
procedures Update and DisplayTran when TranType is 'Q'. Don't forget to
include the end {case} for the case statements.

Testing

Before running this program, make sure you insert procedure Process and its
subordinate procedures in the main program (in place of the stub for Process).
A sample run of the checkbook-balancing program is shown in Fig. 6.36. When
you test this program, provide invalid as well as valid transaction types. Also
make sure that invalid transaction types are ignored.

Figure 6.36   Sample Run of Checkbook-Balancing Program

```
Balance your checking account!

Enter C (Check), D (Deposit), or Q (Quit)
after prompt C, D, or Q >

Enter a positive number after prompt Amount $

Begin by entering your starting balance $1000.00

C, D, or Q >D
Amount $100.00
Depositing $  100.00      Balance of $  1100.00

C, D, or Q >C
Amount $1200.00
Check for  $ 1200.00      Balance of $  -100.00
Warning!  Your account is overdrawn.

C, D, or Q >X
C, D, or Q >Q
```

```
Starting balance was $  1000.00
Final    balance  is $  -100.00
Number of checks written:   1
Number of deposits made :   1
```

Software Engineering: Stepwise Design

The program system for the checkbook problem is a good illustration of the stepwise design process. It uses procedures to implement each of the subproblems shown in the structure chart. Each of the procedures is clear and concise.

The main program at the bottom of Fig. 6.33 contains three procedure call statements. The second procedure call statement

```
Process (StartBal, CurBal, NumCheck, NumDep);
```

is used to process all transactions. Procedure Process calls procedures Read-Tran, Update, and DisplayTran to perform the read, update, and display operations, respectively. These level-2 procedures must be declared before procedure Process, or they could be nested within Process. We prefer to write them before Process because doing so makes Process more concise and readable.

The variables TranType and Amount are declared in Process (not the main program) because they are used only by Process and the level-2 procedures that Process calls. A variable should be declared in the highest level module that uses it and no higher. Process passes these variables as actual parameters to the level-2 procedures.

Avoiding Aliases

The procedures written for the checkbook-balancing program are a little different from others we have written in that there is little likelihood that they will be reused in other program systems. For this reason, we did not attempt to use generic names to represent the formal parameters in the procedures. In similar cases, you should consistently use the same formal parameter name to represent a particular data item in each module, rather than using different names, or *aliases,* for that data item. The use of aliases makes it more difficult to read and understand a program system that contains multiple modules.

Exercises for Section 6.8

Self-Check

1. Write the data requirements and algorithm for procedure `DisplayTran`.
2. Write the algorithm for procedure `Update`.
3. Why was it not necessary to guard the `case` statements in `Update` and `DisplayTran` to prevent a `case expression out of range` error?
4. If procedures `ReadTran`, `Update`, and `DisplayTran` were nested inside procedure `Process`, would it be necessary to use `TranType` and `Amount` as formal parameters? Explain your answer.

Programming

1. Rewrite the `case` statements in procedures `Update` and `DisplayTran` as `if` statements.
2. Modify the checkbook program so that a penalty amount of $15.00 is deducted for each overdrawn check and a count of overdrawn checks is maintained and printed next to each overdrawn check. Reset the count of overdrafts to zero whenever the balance becomes positive.

6.9 Debugging and Testing a Program System

Top-Down and Bottom-Up Debugging and Testing

As the number of statements in a program system grows, the possibility of error also increases. If we keep each module to a manageable size, the likelihood of error increases much more slowly. It is also easier to read and test each module. Finally, passing global variables to procedures through parameter lists minimizes the chance of harmful side effects, which are always difficult to locate.

In the last case study, we inserted a *stub* in the main program for a procedure (`Process`) that was not yet written. When a team of programmers is working on a problem, this is a common practice. Obviously not all modules will be ready at the same time. The use of stubs enables us to test and debug the main program flow and those modules that are available.

Each stub displays an identification message and assigns values to its output parameters to prevent execution errors caused by undefined values. We show the stub for procedure `Process` again in Fig. 6.37. If a program contains one or more stubs, the message printed by each stub when it is called provides a trace of the call sequence and allows the programmer to determine whether the flow of control within the main program is correct. The process of testing a main program in this way is called *top-down testing*.

When a module is completed, it can be substituted for its stub in the main program. However, we often perform a preliminary test of a new module first because it is easier to locate and correct errors when dealing with a single module rather than a complete program system. We can test a new module by

```
procedure Process (StartBal {input} : Real;
                    var CurBal {output} : Real;
                    var NumCheck, NumDep {output} : Integer);
begin {Process stub}
  WriteLn ('Procedure Process entered.');
  CurBal := 0.0;  NumCheck := 0;  NumDep := 0
end; {Process}
```

writing a short driver program similar to the driver program shown in Fig. 6.10 which is used to test function FindTax.

Don't spend a lot of time creating an elegant driver program, because you will discard it as soon as the new module is tested. A driver program should contain only the declarations and executable statements necessary to test a single module. A driver program should begin by reading or assigning values to all input parameters and to input/output parameters. Next comes the call to the module being tested. After calling the module, the driver program should display the module results. The driver program for function FindTax is repeated in Fig. 6.38.

Figure 6.38 Driver Program for Function FindTax

```
program Driver (Input, Output);
{Tests function FindTax.}

   var
     MySalary,                      {input – salary}
     MyTax     : Real;              {output – tax}

{Insert function FindTax here.}

begin {Driver}
  Write ('Enter a salary less than or equal to $15000.00>  $');
  ReadLn (MySalary);
  MyTax := FindTax(MySalary);
  if MyTax >= 0.0 then
    WriteLn ('The tax on $', MySalary :4:2, ' is $', MyTax :4:2)
  else
    WriteLn ('Salary $', MySalary :4:2, ' is out of table range')
end.  {Driver}
```

Once we are confident that a module works properly, it can be substituted for its stub in the program system. The process of separately testing individual modules before inserting them in a program system is called *bottom-up testing*.

By following a combination of top-down and bottom-up testing, a programming team can be fairly confident that the complete program system will be relatively free of errors when it is finally put together. Consequently, the final debugging sessions should proceed quickly and smoothly.

Debugging Tips for Program Systems

The following list gives suggestions for debugging a program system.

1. As you write the code, use comments to carefully document each module parameter and local identifier. Also use comments to describe the module operation.
2. Leave a trace of execution by printing the module name as you enter it.
3. Print the values of all input and input/output parameters upon entry to a module. Check that these values make sense.
4. Print the values of all module outputs after returning from a module. Hand-compute these values to verify that they are correct. For procedures, make sure that all input/output and output parameters are declared as variable parameters.
5. Make sure that a module stub assigns a value to each of its outputs.

It is a good idea to plan for debugging as you write each module rather than after the fact. Include the output statements required for tips 2 through 4 in the original Pascal code for the module. When you are satisfied that the module works as desired, you can remove the debugging statements. One way to remove the statements is to change them to comments by enclosing them in braces. If you have a problem later, you can remove the braces, thereby changing the comments back to executable statements.

Another approach to turning debugging statements on and off is to use a global Boolean constant (say, Debug), which is declared in the main program. The declaration

```
const
   Debug = True;        {turn debugging on}
```

should be used during debugging runs, and the declaration

```
const
   Debug = False;       {turn debugging off}
```

should be used during production runs. Within the main program body and its procedures, each diagnostic print statement should be part of an if statement with Debug as its condition. If procedure Process begins with the following if statement, the WriteLn statements will execute only during debugging runs (Debug is True), as desired.

```
if Debug then
   begin
      WriteLn ('Procedure Process entered');
      WriteLn ('Input parameter StartBal has value ', StartBal :4:2)
   end;   {if}
```

6.10 Recursive Functions (Optional)

In section 6.8, we stated that the Pascal scope rules allow a function or procedure to call itself. A module that calls itself is a *recursive* module. We describe one recursive function in this section; Chapter 13 provides a more extensive discussion of recursion.

We begin by describing a function that returns an integer value representing the factorial of its argument. The *factorial of N* is the product of all integers less than or equal to N and is written in mathematics as *N*!. Figure 6.39 shows one version of the factorial function.

Figure 6.39 Function Factorial

```
function Factorial (N : Integer) : Integer;
{
 Returns the product 1 * 2 * 3 * ... * N for N > 1;
 returns 1 when N is 0 or 1.
}
  var
    I,                        {loop control variable}
    ProductSoFar : Integer;   {accumulated product}
begin
  ProductSoFar := 1;          {initialize accumulated product}

  {Perform the repeated multiplication for N > 1}
  for I := 2 to N do
    ProductSoFar := ProductSoFar * I;

  {Define function result}
  Factorial := ProductSoFar
end; {Factorial}
```

Directory: CHAP6
File: FACTORIA.FUN

The local variable ProductSoFar is used to accumulate the partial product and is initialized to 1. The for statement in Fig. 6.39 performs the repeated multiplication when N is greater than 1. If N is 0 or 1, the for statement does not execute, so ProductSoFar remains 1. After loop exit, the last value of ProductSoFar is assigned to Factorial, thereby defining the function result.

You may be wondering why we need to introduce the local variable ProductSoFar. Would it be possible to accumulate the product directly in the function name and write the function body as shown below?

```
begin {Factorial}
  Factorial := 1;              {Initialize the function result}

  {Perform the repeated multiplication for N > 1}
  for I := 2 to N do
    Factorial := Factorial * I    {invalid recursive call}
end; {Factorial}
```

The answer is "No." The function body above contains an illegal use of the function name in the expression Factorial * I. Whenever the identifier Factorial appears in an expression, it is considered a function designator, so it must be followed by an argument.

Figure 6.40 shows function Factorial rewritten as a recursive function. A *recursive function* is one that calls itself. In Fig. 6.40, the if statement implements the following formulas, which form the recursive definition of *N*!:

$N! = N \times (N - 1)!$ for $N > 1$

$N! = 1$ for $N = 0$ or 1

When N is greater than 1, instead of executing a loop to perform repeated multiplication, as in Fig. 6.39, the statement

```
Factorial := N * Factorial(N-1)
```

executes, which is the Pascal form of the first formula above. The expression part of this statement contains a valid function designator, Factorial(N–1), which calls function Factorial with an argument that is 1 less than the current argument (called a *recursive call*). When N is less than or equal to 1, the statement

```
Factorial := 1
```

executes, stopping the chain of recursive calls and returning a result of 1.

Figure 6.40   Recursive Function Factorial

Directory: CHAP6
File: FACTORIA.FUN

```
function Factorial (N : Integer) : Integer;
{
  Returns the product 1 * 2 * 3 * ... * N for N > 1;
  returns 1 when N is zero or 1.
}
begin {Factorial}
  if N <= 1 then
    Factorial := 1
  else
    Factorial := N * Factorial(N-1)
end; {Factorial}
```

If the argument in the initial call to Factorial is 3, the following chain of recursive calls occurs:

```
Factorial(3) → 3 * Factorial(2) → 3 * (2 * Factorial(1))
```

The last call in the chain evaluates to 1, and the value of 3 * 2 * 1, or 6, is returned as the result of the original call.

Exercises for Section 6.9

Self-Check

1. Show the chain of recursive calls to function Mystery when M is 4 and N is 3. What do you think Mystery does?

```
function Mystery (M, N : Integer) : Integer;
begin {Mystery}
  if N = 1 then
    Mystery = M
  else
    Mystery = M * Mystery(M, N-1)
end;   {Mystery}
```

1. Write a function C(N, R) that returns the number of different ways R items can be selected from a group of N items. The mathematical formula for C(N, R) follows. Test C(N, R) using both the recursive and the nonrecursive versions of function Factorial.

$$C(N, R) = \frac{N!}{R!(N-R)!}$$

2. Write a recursive function that finds the greatest common divisor (GCD) of two integers. The GCD of two integers is the largest integer that divides them both. It is defined recursively as

GCD(M, N) is GCD(N, M) for M < N
GCD(M, N) is N when N is a divisor of M (M mod N is zero)
GCD(M, N) is GCD(N, M mod N) when N is not a divisor of M

6.11 Common Programming Errors

There are many opportunities for error when you use modules with parameter lists, so you must be extremely careful. The proper use of parameters is difficult for beginning programmers to master, but it is an essential skill. One obvious pitfall occurs in not ensuring that the actual parameter list has the same number of parameters as the formal parameter list. The syntax error number of parameters does not agree with declaration indicates this problem.

Each actual parameter must be assignment compatible with its corresponding formal parameter (for a value parameter) or the same data type (for a variable parameter). An actual parameter that corresponds to a variable formal parameter must be a variable. A violation of either of these rules will result in an illegal parameter substitution syntax error.

You should return a procedure result to the calling module by assigning a value to a variable parameter. Any value assigned to a value parameter is stored locally in the procedure and will not be returned. If your procedure seems to execute properly but does not return the expected result(s), it is possible that you forgot to declare an output or input/output parameter as a variable parameter.

Remember to return all function results by assigning a value to the function name. It is bad programming practice to return a second function result through a variable parameter (function side effect). It is also bad programming practice to directly manipulate a global variable in a procedure or function; all nonlocal variables should be passed to a module through its parameter list.

The Pascal scope rules determine where an identifier is visible and can be referenced. If an identifier is referenced outside its scope, an identifier not declared syntax error will result.

CHAPTER REVIEW

This chapter discussed the use of parameters for passing data to functions and procedures and from procedures. The parameter list provides a highly visible communication path between a module and its calling program. By using parameters, we can cause different data to be manipulated by a module each time we call it, making it easier to reuse the module in other program systems.

There are two types of parameters: value parameters and variable parameters. A value parameter is used only for passing data into a module. A variable parameter is used to return results from a procedure. The actual parameter that corresponds to a value parameter can be an expression or a constant; the actual parameter that corresponds to a variable parameter must be a variable.

We also discussed the scope of identifiers. An identifier is visible and can be referenced anywhere within the block that declares it. If one block is nested inside another and an identifier is declared in the outer block, then the identifier's meaning in the inner block is determined by its declaration in the outer block. If the identifier is declared in both blocks, then its meaning in the inner block is determined by its declaration in the inner block.

A global variable is one that is declared in the main program; a local variable is one that is declared in a procedure. A local variable is defined only during the execution of the procedure; its value is lost when the procedure is finished.

In the optional section, we discussed writing a recursive function, which is a function that calls itself. Chapter 13 covers this topic in detail.

New Pascal Constructs

The Pascal constructs introduced in this chapter are described in Table 6.6.

Table 6.6 Summary of New Pascal Constructs

Construct	Effect

Function Declaration
```function Sign (X : Real) : Char;```
```begin {Sign}```
``` if X > 0.0 then```
```   Sign := '+'```
``` else```
```   Sign := '-'```
```end; {Sign}```
	Returns a character value that indicates the sign ('+' or '-') of its type Real argument X.

Procedure Declaration
```procedure DoIt (X : Real;```
```   Op : Char;```
```   var Y : Real;```
```   var Sign : Char);```
	If Op is '+', returns X + X through Y; if Op is '*', returns X * X through Y. Returns a character value that indicates the sign ('+' or '-') of X through Sign.

Table 6.6, *continued*

Construct	Effect
``` begin {DoIt} case Op of '+' : Y := X + X; '*' : Y := X * X end; {case} if X > 0.0 then Sign := '+' else Sign := '-' end; {DoIt} ```	

Procedure Call Statement

`DoIt (-5.0, '*', Y, MySign)`	Calls procedure `DoIt`. `-5.0` is passed into `X`, `'*'` into `Op`, `25.0` is returned to `Y`, and `'-'` is returned to `MySign`.

✓ Quick-Check Exercises

1. The _____ parameters appear in the procedure call, and the _____ parameters appear in the procedure declaration.
2. Constants and expressions can correspond to formal parameters that are _____ parameters.
3. Formal parameters that are variable parameters must have actual parameters that are _____.
4. Formal parameters that are variable parameters must have actual parameters that are the _____ data type.
5. The data types of corresponding value parameters must be _____.
6. Which is used to test a procedure, a driver or a stub?
7. Which is used to test main program flow, a driver or a stub?
8. A(n) _____ occurs when a function assigns a value to one of its variable parameters or when a procedure changes a global variable.
9. What are the values of main program variables X and Y after the following program executes?

```
program Nonsense;
  var X, Y : Real;

  procedure Silly (X : Real);
    var Y : Real;
  begin
    Y := 25.0;
    X := Y
  end; {Silly}

begin {Nonsense}
  Silly (X)
end. {Nonsense}
```

10. Answer exercise 9 if parameter X of Silly is a variable parameter.
11. Answer exercise 9 if parameter X of Silly is a variable parameter and the local declaration for Y is removed from Silly.
12. Answer exercise 9 if parameter X of Silly is a variable parameter, Y is a local variable in Silly, and the procedure call statement is changed to

    Silly (Y)

13. Answer exercise 12 if the local declaration for Y is removed from Silly.
14. How does a function return its value?

Answers to Quick-Check Exercises
1. actual, formal
2. value
3. variables
4. same
5. assignment compatible
6. driver
7. stub
8. side effect
9. Both are undefined.
10. X is 25.0, Y is undefined.
11. Both are 25.0.
12. X is undefined, Y is 25.0.
13. X is undefined, Y is 25.0.
14. A function returns its single value by assigning a value to the function name.

Review Questions

1. Write the procedure heading for a procedure called Script that accepts three parameters passed to it. The first parameter is the number of spaces to print at the beginning of a line. The second parameter is the character to print after the spaces, and the third parameter is the number of times to print the second parameter on the same line.
2. Write a function called LetterGrade that has a parameter called Grade and that returns the appropriate letter grade using a straight scale (90–100 is an A, 80–89 is a B, and so on).
3. Why would you choose to make a formal parameter a value parameter rather than a variable parameter?
4. Explain the allocation of memory cells when a procedure is called.
5. Write the procedure heading for a procedure named Pass that will have two integer parameters. The first parameter should be a value parameter and the second a variable parameter.
6. Explain the use of a stub in refining an algorithm.
7. In the chart that follows, write Yes for each procedure on the right that can be referenced (called) by the procedure on the left and No for each procedure that is inaccessible.

```
program ProcScope;

    procedure A;

        procedure B;

            procedure C;
            ...

            end; {C}

            procedure D;
            ...

            end; {D}
        ...

        end; {B}
    ...

    end; {A}
    ...

end. {ProcScope}
```

| Calling | Callable Procedures | | | |
Procedure	A	B	C	D
A				
B				
C				
D				

8. List two reasons for implementing a module as a procedure rather than as a function.

Programming Projects

1. The assessor in your town has estimated the market value of all fourteen properties and would like you to write a program that determines the tax owed on each property and the total tax to be collected. The tax rate is 12.5 cents per dollar of assessed value. The assessed value of each property is 28% of its estimated market value. The market values are as follows:

$150,000	$148,000	$145,500	$167,000	$137,600	$147,100
$165,000	$153,350	$128,000	$158,000	$152,250	$148,000
$156,500	$143,700				

Directory: CHAP6
File: PROJ6_1.PAS

You need to write procedures that correspond to the following procedure headers as part of your solution.

```
procedure PrintInstructions;
{Displays instructions to the user}

procedure ProcessProperties (var TotalTax {output} : Real);
{Reads market values and computes taxes on all properties}

function ComputeTax (Market : Real) : Real;
{Computes tax on a property with market value Market}

procedure PrintSummary (TotalTax {input} : Real);
{Displays value of TotalTax}
```

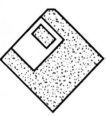

2. Revise programming project 1 assuming a 5% surcharge for all properties with market value over $150,000. Also, grant a 10% discount for senior citizens. You will need to enter a second data item for each property indicating whether its owner is a senior citizen. Write a separate procedure that reads and returns the current property market value and sets a Boolean parameter to True if the owner is a senior citizen.

3. The trustees of a small college are considering voting a pay raise for the 12 faculty members. They want to grant a 5.5% pay raise; however, before doing so, they want to know how much this will cost. Write a program that will print the pay raise for each faculty member and the total amount of the raises. Also, print the total faculty payroll before and after the raise. Test your program for the following salaries:

$32,500	$24,029.50	$36,000	$43,250
$35,500	$22,800	$30,000.50	$28,900
$43,780	$47,300	$44,120.25	$24,100

Refer to programming project 1 for a guide as to what procedures and functions will be needed.

4. Revise programming project 3 assuming that faculty earning less than $30,000 receive a 7% raise, faculty earning more than $40,000 receive a 4% raise, and all others receive a 5.5% raise. Write a new function that determines the raise percentage. Also, for each faculty member, print the raise percentage as well as the amount.

5. Patients who take many kinds of medication often have difficulty remembering when to take their medicine. Given the following set of medications, write a program that prints a table indicating what medication to take at any given hour. Use a counter variable Clock to go through a 24-hour day.

Medication	Frequency
Iron	0800, 1200, 1800
Antibiotic	Every 4 hours starting at 0400
Vitamin	0800, 2100
Calcium	1100, 2000

6. A monthly magazine wants a program that will print out renewal and cancellation notices to its subscribers. Using procedures when advisable, write a program that first reads in the current month number (1 through 12) and year. For each subscription processed, read in four data items: the account number, the month and the year the subscription started, and the number of years paid for the subscription.

Read in each set of subscription information and print a renewal notice if the current month is either the month prior to expiration or the month of expiration. A cancellation notice should be printed if the current month comes after the expiration month.

Sample input might be

```
10   91          for a current month of October 1991
1364   4   91   3   for account 1364, whose 3-year subscription
                 began in April 1991
```

7. The square root of a number N can be approximated by repeated calculation using the formula

```
NG = .5(LG + N / LG)
```

where NG stands for next guess and LG stands for last guess. Write a procedure that implements this process. The first parameter will be a positive real number, the second will be an initial guess of the square root, and the third will be the computed result.

The initial guess will be the starting value of LG. The procedure will compute a value for NG using the formula. The difference between NG and LG is checked to see whether these two guesses are almost identical. If so, the procedure is exited and NG is the square root; otherwise, the new guess (NG) becomes the last guess (LG), and the process is repeated (i.e., another value is computed for NG, the difference is checked, etc.).

For this program, the loop should be repeated until the magnitude of the difference is less than 0.005 (Delta). Use an initial guess of 1.0 and test the program for the numbers 4, 120.5, 88, 36.01, and 10,000.

8. It is a dark and stormy night. Secret agent 007 is behind enemy lines at a fuel depot. He walks over to a cylindrical fuel tank 20 feet tall and 8 feet in diameter. He opens a 2-inch-diameter circular nozzle. He knows that the volume of the fuel leaving the tank is

$$volume\ lost\ =\ velocity \times area\ of\ the\ nozzle \times time$$

and that

$$velocity\ =\ 8.02 \times \sqrt{height\ of\ fluid\ in\ the\ tank}$$

How long will it take to empty the tank?

Hint: Although this is really a calculus problem, we can simulate it with the computer and get a close answer. We can calculate the volume lost over a short period of time, say, 60 seconds, and assume that the loss of fluid is constant. We can then subtract the volume from the tank and determine the new height of the fluid inside the tank at the end of the minute. We can then calculate the loss for the next minute. This can be done over and over until the tank is dry. Print a table showing the elapsed time in seconds, the volume lost, and the height of the fluid. At the very end, convert the total elapsed seconds to minutes. The fluid height can be negative on the last line of the table.

7 Simple Data Types

S o far in your programming experience, you have used the four standard data types of Pascal: `Integer`, `Real`, `Char`, and `Boolean`. This chapter takes a closer look at these data types and introduces some new operators and operations that you can perform on them.

You'll also learn how to declare two new kinds of data types: subrange types and enumerated types. A *subrange type* is a limited range of values defined over another data type. To make large programs more readable, you can declare data types, called *enumerated types,* whose values you specify, depending on the problem domain.

All these data types—standard types, subrange types, and enumerated types—are *simple* or *scalar* data types, that is, only a single value can be stored in each variable. We also introduce sets, which can be used to store multiple values and show you how to use sets and the set membership operator `in` to simplify Boolean expressions.

In an optional section at the end of the chapter, we discuss how to evaluate a series and how to find a function root using iterative approximations. We use Newton's method to solve the latter problem.

7.1 Constants

Let's begin by reexamining the syntax for constants in Pascal. Figure 7.1 shows the syntax diagrams for a constant declaration. Each constant definition has the form

> *identifier* = *constant*

where *constant* may be a number, a previously defined constant identifier, a literal string, or the reserved word `nil`. (We discuss string values in Chapters 10 and 14 and `nil` in Chapter 17.)

■ Example 7.1

A sample constant declaration follows:

```
const
    Max = 100;
    Min = -Max;
    SpeedOfLight = 2.998E+5;
    Debug = True;
    Name = 'Alice';
```

The constant declaration for `Min` uses the previously defined constant `Max`. Because `Max` has the value 100, `Min` has the value −100. The constant `Speed-OfLight` is associated with a real value (299800.0) expressed in scientific notation. The Boolean constant `Debug` is associated with the Boolean value `True`. The constant `Name` is associated with the *literal string* `'Alice'`.

As mentioned earlier, there are two reasons for using constants. First, the name `SpeedOfLight` has more meaning to a reader of the program than the value 2.998E+5. Second, if we change the value of a constant in its declaration, we also change the value of that constant wherever it is referenced in the program. ■

Constant declaration

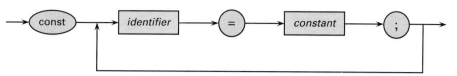

Constant

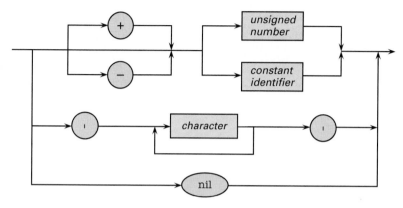

Exercises for Section 7.1

Self-Check

1. Which of the constants declared below are valid? Which are invalid?

```
const
   MinInt = -MaxInt;
   MaxLetter = 'Z';
   MinusZ = -MaxLetter;
   MaxSize = 50;
   MinSize = MaxSize - 10;
```

2. Why would you declare an identifier as a constant rather than as a variable?

7.2 Numeric Data Types: Real and Integer

The data types Integer and Real are used to represent numeric information. We used Integer variables as loop counters and to represent data, such as exam scores, that are whole numbers. In most other instances, we used type Real numeric data.

Differences Between Numeric Types

You may be wondering why it is necessary to have two numeric types. Can the data type `Real` be used for all numbers? The answer is yes, but on many computers, operations involving integers are faster than those involving real numbers. Less storage space is needed to store integers. Also, operations with integers are always precise, whereas there may be some loss of accuracy with real numbers.

These differences result from the way real numbers and integers are represented in your computer's memory. All data are represented in memory as *binary strings,* strings of 0s and 1s. However, the binary string stored for the integer 13 is not the same as the binary string stored for the real number 13.0. The actual internal representation is computer dependent, and real numbers often require more bytes of computer memory. Compare the sample integer and real formats shown in Fig. 7.2.

Figure 7.2 Integer and Real Formats

Figure 7.2 shows that positive integers are represented by standard binary numbers. If you are familiar with the binary number system, you know that the integer 13 is represented as the binary number 01101.

Real format is analogous to scientific notation. The storage area occupied by a real number is divided into two sections: the mantissa and the exponent. The *mantissa* is a binary fraction between 0.5 and 1.0 for positive numbers and between -0.5 and -1.0 for negative numbers. The exponent is a power of 2. The mantissa and the exponent are chosen so that the following formula is correct.

$$real\ number\ =\ mantissa\ \times\ 2^{exponent}$$

Because of the finite size of a memory cell, not all real numbers in the range of reals can be represented precisely. We talk more about this later.

Besides the capability of storing fractions, the range of numbers that may be represented in real format is considerably larger than for integer format. For example, on Control Data Corporation's Cyber series of computers, positive real numbers range in value from 10^{-294} (a very small fraction) to 10^{+322}, whereas the range of positive integers extends from 1 to approximately 10^{15}. In that computer, a real number requires twice the storage space of an integer.

The predefined constant `MaxInt` is the largest integer represented in your Pascal system. The range of integers extends from –MaxInt (or –MaxInt – 1 on some systems) through `MaxInt`.

Numeric Literals

A constant value appearing in an expression is called a literal. The data type of a numeric literal is determined in the following way. If the literal has a decimal point, it is considered type `Real`. A type `Real` literal may also have a decimal *scale factor*. For example, in the literal 2.998E+5, the scale factor is 10^5. A literal without a decimal point is considered type `Integer` unless it has a scale factor. For example, the literal 5E2 is considered type `Real` (value is 500.0) because it has a scale factor.

Review of Integer Division

In Section 2.6, we introduced two operators, `div` and `mod`, that could be used only with integer operands. The operator `div` yields the integer quotient of its first operand divided by its second; the operator `mod` yields the integer remainder of its first operand divided by its second (for example, 7 `div` 2 is 3, and 7 `mod` 2 is 1). The next example illustrates the use of these operators.

■ Example 7.2

Procedure `PrintDigits` in Fig. 7.3 prints each digit of its parameter `Decimal` in reverse order (e.g., if `Decimal` is 738, the digits printed are 8, 3, 7). This is accomplished by printing each remainder (0 through 9) of `Decimal` divided by 10; the integer quotient of `Decimal` divided by 10 becomes the new value of `Decimal`.

Figure 7.3 Printing Decimal Digits

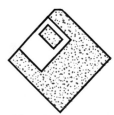

Directory: CHAP7
File: PRINTDIG.PRO

```
procedure PrintDigits (Decimal {input} : Integer);
{
  Prints the digits of Decimal in reverse order.
  Pre : Decimal is non-zero.
  Post: Each digit of Decimal is displayed, starting with the
        least significant one.
}
  const
    Base = 10;                       {number system base}

  var
    Digit : Integer;                 {each digit}

begin {PrintDigits}
  Decimal := Abs(Decimal);           {Make Decimal positive}
  {Find and print remainders of Decimal divided by Base.}
  while Decimal <> 0 do
    begin
      Digit := Decimal mod Base;     {Get next digit.}
      Write (Digit :1);
      Decimal := Decimal div Base    {Get next quotient.}
    end; {while}
  WriteLn
end; {PrintDigits}
```

The parameter Decimal is the loop-control variable. Within the while loop, the mod operator assigns to Digit the rightmost digit of Decimal; the div operator assigns the rest of the number to Decimal. The loop is exited when Decimal becomes 0. Because Decimal is a value parameter, the actual parameter value is not changed by the procedure execution.

Table 7.1 is a trace of the procedure execution for an actual parameter of 43. The digits 3 and 4 are displayed. ■

Table 7.1 Trace of Execution of PrintDigits (43)

Statement	Decimal	Digit	Effect
while Decimal <> 0 do	43		43 <> 0 is true.
Digit := Decimal mod Base		3	Next digit is 3.
Write (Digit :1)			Print 3.
Decimal := Decimal div Base	4		Quotient is 4.
while Decimal <> 0 do			4 <> 0 is true.
Digit := Decimal mod Base		4	Next digit is 4.
Write (Digit : 1)			Print 4.
Decimal := Decimal div Base	0		Quotient is 0.
while Decimal <> 0 do			0 <> 0 is false.
			Exit loop.

Numerical Inaccuracies

One of the problems in processing real numbers is that sometimes an error occurs in representing real data. Just as certain numbers cannot be represented exactly in the decimal number system (e.g., the fraction 1/3 is 0.333333 . . .), so some numbers cannot be represented exactly in real format. A *representational error* depends on the number of binary digits (bits) used in the mantissa: the more bits, the smaller the error.

The number 0.1 is an example of a real number that cannot be represented exactly in the binary number system. The effect of a small error is often magnified through repeated computations. Therefore, the result of adding 0.1 10 times is not exactly 1.0, so the following loop may fail to terminate on some computers.

```
Trial := 0.0;
while Trial <> 1.0 do
  begin
    . . .

    Trial := Trial + 0.1
  end {while}
```

If the loop repetition test is changed to Trial < 1.0, the loop may execute 10 times on one computer and 11 times on another. For this reason, it is best to use integer variables whenever possible in loop-repetition tests.

Other problems occur when very large and very small real numbers are manipulated. When a large number and a small number are added, the larger number may "cancel out" the smaller number, resulting in a *cancellation error*. If X is much larger than Y, then X + Y may have the same value as X (e.g., 1000.0 + 0.0001234 is equal to 1000.0 on some computers).

If two very small numbers are multiplied, the result may be too small to be represented accurately, so it will be represented as zero. This phenomenon is called *arithmetic underflow*. Similarly, if two very large numbers are multiplied, the result may be too large to be represented. This phenomenon, called *arithmetic overflow*, is handled in different ways by different Pascal compilers. (Arithmetic overflow can also occur when very large integer values are processed.)

■ Example 7.3

The program in Fig. 7.4 draws a sine curve. It uses the Pascal function Sin, which returns the trigonometric sine of its parameter, an angle expressed in radians. As an illustration of the numerical inaccuracy that may result when real computations are performed, examine the sine value displayed for the angles of 180 and 360 degrees. The actual sine should be zero; in both cases, the sine value computed is quite small (approximately 10^{-6}), but it is not zero. Because the value of the constant Pi is imprecise, the result of any computation involving Pi will have a small numerical error.

Figure 7.4 Plotting a Sine Curve

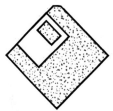

Directory: CHAP7
File: SINECURV.PAS

```
program SineCurve (Output);
{Plots a sine curve}

  const
    Pi = 3.14159;                    {constant Pi}
    Star = '*';                      {symbol being plotted}
    Scale = 20;                      {scale factor for plot}
    MinAngle = 0;                    {smallest angle}
    MaxAngle = 360;                  {largest angle}
    StepAngle = 18;                  {increment in degrees}

  var
    Theta,                           {angle in degrees}
    Indent : Integer;                {column of each *}
    Radian,                          {angle in radians}
    RadPerDegree : Real;             {radians per degree}

begin  {SineCurve}
  RadPerDegree := Pi / 180.0;
  WriteLn ('Theta', 'Sine curve plot' : 28);
  Theta := MinAngle;                 {initial value of Theta}
  while Theta <= MaxAngle do
    begin
      Radian := Theta * RadPerDegree;          {Compute radians.}
      Indent := 1 + Round(Scale * (1.0 + Sin(Radian)));
      Write (Theta :4, '|');
      Write (Star :Indent);                {Plot * in column Indent.}
      WriteLn (Sin(Radian) :20);           {Print sine value.}
      Theta := Theta + StepAngle;          {Get next angle.}
    end  {while}
end.  {SineCurve}
```

```
Theta                          Sine curve plot
   0|                   *                     0
  18|                      *        3.090168E-01
  36|                         *        5.877849E-01
  54|                          *         8.090166E-01
  72|                            *         9.510562E-01
  90|                             *         1.000000E+00
 108|                            *         9.510570E-01
 126|                          *         8.090180E-01
 144|                        *         5.877869E-01
 162|                     *        3.090194E-01
 180|                  *        2.621549E-06
 198|               *        -3.090146E-01
 216|             *        -5.877830E-01
 234|            *        -8.090152E-01
 252|          *        -9.510555E-01
 270|         *        -1.000000E+00
 288|         *        -9.510579E-01
 306|           *        -8.090194E-01
 324|            *        -5.877893E-01
 342|              *        -3.090214E-01
 360|                 *        -5.243099E-06
```

The while loop in Fig. 7.4 executes for values of Theta equal to 0, 18, 36, ... 360 degrees. For each Theta, the first assignment statement,

```
Radian := Theta * RadPerDegree;          {Compute radians.}
```

computes the number of radians corresponding to Theta. Then the variable Indent is assigned a value based on Sin(Radians):

```
Indent := 1 + Round(Scale * (1.0 + Sin(Radian)));
```

This value increases from 1 when Sin(Radian) is −1.0 to 41 (1 + Scale * 2.0) when Sin(Radian) is 1.0. Finally the statement

```
Write (Star :Indent);          {Plot * in column Indent.}
```

plots an asterisk somewhere in columns 1 through 41, as determined by the value of Indent. Recall that a string (or character) is printed right-justified in its field; the value of Indent determines the size of the output field. ∎

PROGRAM
STYLE

Checking Boundary Values

The discussion for Example 7.3 states that the value of Indent ranges from 1 to 41 as the sine value goes from −1 to 1. It is always a good idea to check the accuracy of these assumptions; you can usually do so by checking the boundaries of the range, as shown below.

```
Sin(Radian) is −1.0, Indent := 1 + Round(Scale * (1.0 +
                        (−1.0)))
```

```
                       Indent := 1 + Round(20 * 0.0)
                       Indent := 1

    Sin(Radian) is +1.0, Indent := 1 + Round (Scale * (1.0 + 1.0))
                       Indent := 1 + Round(20 * 2.0)
                       Indent := 41
```

Exercises for Section 7.2

Self-Check

1. How does cancellation error differ from representational error?
2. Assume that the program shown in Fig. 7.4 has been modified to plot the Pascal function Ln. Determine the range of values for Indent using the following assignment statement as X goes from 0.1 to 5.0.

```
Indent := 1 + Round(Scale * (1.0 + Ln(X)))
```

Programming

1. Write a Pascal program to determine the largest integer and the largest real number that can be used on your computer system.

7.3 The Boolean Data Type

We have used Boolean expressions as conditions in if, while, and repeat statements. In this section, we discuss how to read a Boolean value and how to complement a Boolean expression.

Reading and Writing Boolean Values

Procedure WriteLn displays Boolean values, but procedure ReadLn cannot be used to read a Boolean value. Procedure ReadLnBool (see Fig. 7.5) "reads" a Boolean value by assigning a Boolean value to output parameter BoolVal based on the next data character. The statement

```
BoolVal := (NextChar = 'T') or (NextChar = 't');
```

assigns True to BoolVal if the data character read into NextChar is T or t; otherwise, it assigns False to BoolVal.

Figure 7.5   Procedure ReadLnBool

```
procedure ReadLnBool (var BoolVal {output},
                          Success {output} : Boolean);
{
  Reads a Boolean value (represented by T or F) into BoolVal and
  sets the flag Success.
  Pre : None
```

```
          Post: BoolVal is set to True if T or t is read; otherwise,
                BoolVal is set to False.  Success is set to True only
                if one of the four characters T, t, F, or f is read.
}
  var
     NextCh : Char;               {a data character}

begin {ReadLnBool}
  ReadLn (NextCh);
  BoolVal := (NextCh = 'T') or (NextCh = 't');
  Success := BoolVal or (NextCh = 'F') or (NextCh = 'f')
end; {ReadLnBool}
```

Using a Boolean Parameter as a Flag

The second parameter of ReadLnBool is used as a flag to signal whether a valid data character was read. In ReadLnBool, the assignment statement

```
     Success := BoolVal or (NextCh = 'F') or (NextCh = 'f')
```

assigns True to Success if the character read was T, t, F, or f.

If the value returned in Success is False, the calling program should call ReadLnBool again. Assuming the calling program contains the variable declarations

```
     var
        NextBool,              {input – next Boolean data value}
        ReadDone : Boolean;    {flag – True if read succeeds;  }
                               {                otherwise, False}
```

the following repeat statement could be used to read a Boolean value into NextBool.

```
     repeat
        Write ('Enter T or F> ');
        ReadLnBool (NextBool, ReadDone)
     until ReadDone;
```

The repeat statement executes until procedure ReadLnBool sets ReadDone to True.

Complementing a Condition

Chapter 5 introduced two conditional loop forms: the while and the repeat. Figure 5.14 shows a while loop with condition Power < 1000 and an equivalent repeat statement with condition Power >= 1000. To convert from one conditional loop to the other, we need to know how to form the *complement* of a condition. We can complement a simple condition by changing the relational operator, as shown next.

Operator	*Operator in Complement*
<	>=
<=	>
>	<=
>=	<
=	<>
<>	=

For example, the complement of X <= Y is X > Y. Also, if an expression begins with not, removing the not forms its complement (e.g., the complement of not Flag is Flag).

DeMorgan's theorem explains how to complement a compound Boolean expression: write the complement of each individual Boolean expression and change each and to or and each or to and. Another way to complement a Boolean expression is to precede the entire expression with not. Table 7.2 shows the complements of some Boolean expressions.

DeMorgan's Theorem

not (*expression*₁ and *expression*₂) =
$$\text{(not } expression_1\text{) or (not } expression_2\text{)}$$

not (*expression*₁ or *expression*₂) =
$$\text{(not } expression_1\text{) and (not } expression_2\text{)}$$

Table 7.2 Complements of Some Boolean Expressions

Expression	Complement
1. (X >= 1) and (X <= 5)	(X < 1) or (X > 5)
2. (not Flag) or (X <= Y)	Flag and (X > Y)
3. Flag and (not Switch)	(not Flag) or Switch
4. (N mod M = 0) and Flag	(N mod M <> 0) or (not Flag)
5. (Next = 'A') or (Next = 'a')	(Next <> 'A') and (Next <> 'a')
6. (Next = 'A') or (Next = 'a')	not ((Next = 'A') or (Next = 'a'))

In Table 7.2, Flag is a Boolean variable, Next is type Char, and X, Y, M, and N are type Integer. In the complement of the expression on line 1, the relational operators are reversed (e.g., >= changed to <) and the operator and is changed to or. Lines 5 and 6 show two complements of the same expression. In line 6, the expression is complemented simply by preceding the entire condition with the Boolean operator not. Any Boolean expression can be complemented in this way.

Exercises For Section 7.3

Self-Check

1. Write the complements of the following conditions:
   a. `(X <= Y) and (X <> 15)`
   b. `(X <= Y) and (X <> 15) or (Z = 7.5)`
   c. `(X <> 15) or (Z = 7.5) and (X <= Y)`
   d. `Flag or not (X <> 15.7)`
   e. `not Flag and (X <= 8)`
2. Why does good programming style require that ReadLnBool be implemented as a procedure rather than as a function?

Programming

1. Write a `repeat` loop controlled by a Boolean flag that prompts the program user to enter an integer X in the range –K to +K, inclusive. Loop termination occurs after the user enters an appropriate value of X.
2. Write a procedure that has two integer input parameters, M and N, and one Boolean output parameter that is set to True when the value of M is a divisor of N and False otherwise.

7.4 Set Values in Boolean Expressions

Many of you have studied sets in a mathematics course. In mathematics, a set is represented by a list of *set elements* enclosed in curly braces. In Pascal, set elements are enclosed in square brackets. For example, the set of odd integers from 1 through 9 is written as {1, 3, 5, 7, 9} in mathematics and as [1, 3, 5, 7, 9] in Pascal. The order in which elements are listed in a set is immaterial; the Pascal set [9, 5, 7, 1, 3] is equivalent to [1, 3, 5, 7, 9].

■ Example 7.4

In procedure ReadLnBool (see Fig. 7.5), the statement

```
Success := BoolVal or (NextCh = 'F') or (NextCh = 'f')
```

assigns a value of True to Success if the value of NextCh is 'T', 't', 'F', or 'f'. The following assignment is equivalent:

```
Success := NextCh in ['T','t','F','f']
```

It uses the set membership operator in and the set whose members are the lowercase and uppercase forms of the letters t and f. The expression is True if NextCh is one of the values listed; otherwise, the expression is False. ■

Subrange Notation for Sets

The set ['0'..'9','+','-','E','.'] describes the set of characters that may appear in a real number. This set contains 14 elements. It is more convenient to use the *subrange notation* `'0'..'9'` to denote the 10 digit characters rather than list each character separately.

Set Values

Form:　　[*list-of-elements*]
Example: `['+', '-', '*', '/', '<', '>', '=']`
Interpretation: A set is defined whose set elements are the *list-of-elements* enclosed in brackets. The elements of a set must belong to the same ordinal type or to compatible ordinal types (defined in Section 7.7). Commas separate elements in the *list-of-elements*. A group of consecutive elements may be specified with subrange notation (i.e., *minval..maxval*, where *minval* and *maxval* are type-compatible expressions and *minval* is considered less than or equal to *maxval*.

Set Membership Operator in

Form:　　*element* in [*list-of-elements*]
Example: `NextCh in ['+','-','*','/','<','>','=']`
Interpretation: The set membership operator in describes a condition that evaluates to `True` when *element* is included in *list-of-elements*; otherwise, the condition evaluates to `False`. The data type of *element* must be compatible with the set elements. Operator in has the same precedence as the relational operators.

Test for Set Exclusion

The Boolean expression `not (NextCh in ['T','t','F','f'])` is `True` when `NextCh` is not a member of the indicated set. A common error is writing this expression as `NextCh not in ['T','t','F','f']`.

Exercises for Section 7.4

Self-Check

1. Which of the following sets are valid? Which are invalid? What are the elements of the valid sets?
   a. `[1, 3, 1..5]`
   b. `['1', '3', '1'..'5']`
   c. `[1, 3, '1'..'5']`
   d. `['1', '3', 'A'..'C']`
2. Write the complement of the following condition:

   `not Flag and (NextDigit in [1..9])`

3. Write a set that consists of the special characters used for punctuation in Pascal or to denote operators.
4. Write a Boolean expression that is equivalent to the one shown below and that does not contain a set.

```
X in [1..3, 5, 7]
```

7.5 Character Variables and Functions

Pascal provides a character data type that can store and manipulate individual characters such as those that make up a person's name, address, and other personal data. Character variables are declared using the data type `Char`. A type `Char` literal consists of a single character (a letter, a digit, a punctuation mark, or the like) enclosed in apostrophes. A character value may be assigned to a character variable or associated with a constant identifier, as shown next:

```
const
  Star = '*';

var
  NextLetter : Char;

begin
  NextLetter := 'A'
```

The character variable `NextLetter` is assigned the character value `'A'` by the assignment statement. A single character variable or value may appear on the right side of a character assignment statement. Character values can also be compared, read, and printed.

Using Relational Operators with Characters

Assuming `Next` and `First` are type `Char`, the Boolean expressions

```
Next = First
Next <> First
```

determine whether two character variables have the same or different values. Order comparisons can also be performed on character variables using the relational operators `<`, `<=`, `>`, and `>=`.

To understand the result of an order comparison, you must know something about the way characters are represented internally within your computer. Each character has its own unique numeric code; the binary form of this code is stored in a memory cell that has a character value. These binary numbers are compared by the relational operators in the normal way.

Three common character codes are shown in Appendix C. The digit characters are an increasing sequence of consecutive characters in all three codes.

For example, in ASCII (American Standard Code for Information Interchange), the digit characters '0' through '9' have code values of 48 through 57 (decimal). The following order relationship holds for the digit characters (i.e., '0' < '1', '1' < '2', and so on).

'0'<'1'<'2'<'3'<'4'<'5'<'6'<'7'<'8'<'9'

The uppercase letters are also an increasing sequence of characters, but they are not necessarily consecutive. In ASCII, the uppercase letters have the decimal code values 65 through 90. The following order relationship holds for uppercase letters.

'A'<'B'<'C' < ... <'X'<'Y'<'Z'

The lowercase letters are also an increasing, but not necessarily consecutive, sequence of characters. In ASCII, the lowercase letters have the decimal code values 97 through 122 and the following order relationship holds.

'a'<'b'<'c'< ... <'x'<'y'<'z'

In our examples and programs we will assume that the lowercase letters are included, and that the letters are consecutive characters.

In ASCII, the *printable characters* have codes from 32 (the code for a blank or space) to 126 (the code for the symbol ˜). The other codes represent nonprintable *control characters*. Sending a control character to an output device causes the device to perform a special operation such as returning the cursor to column 1, advancing the cursor to the next line, or ringing a bell.

The Ordinal Functions: Ord, Pred, and Succ

The data types Integer, Boolean, and Char are considered ordinal types (first discussed in Section 2.6). With ordinal data types, each value (except the first) has a unique predecessor; each value (except the last) has a unique successor. For example, the predecessor of 5 is 4; the successor of 5 is 6. The data type Real is not an ordinal type, because a real number such as 3.1415 does not have a unique successor. (Is its successor 3.1416 or 3.14151?)

The order or sequence of an ordinal data type is well defined. For example, −MaxInt (or −MaxInt − 1 on some systems) is the smallest integer, and the positive integers follow the sequence 1, 2, 3, . . . , MaxInt − 1, MaxInt. The order of the Boolean values is False, True.

The Pascal function Ord determines the *ordinal number*, or relative position, of an ordinal value in its sequence of values. If the parameter of Ord is an integer, the ordinal number returned is the integer itself. For all other ordinal values, the ordinal number of the first value in the sequence is 0, the ordinal number of the second value is 1, and so on. Thus, Ord(False) is 0 and Ord(True) is 1. If A and B belong to the same ordinal type and A < B is true, then Ord(A) < Ord(B) must also be true.

The Pascal function Pred returns the predecessor of its parameter, and the Pascal function Succ returns the successor. These functions, like Ord, can be used only with parameters that are ordinal types.

■ Example 7.5

Table 7.3 shows the results of using the `Ord`, `Succ`, and `Pred` functions with an integer or Boolean parameter. As shown in Table 7.3, one value in each ordinal type does not have a successor (`MaxInt`, `True`). The Boolean value that does not have a predecessor is `False`. The integer value that does not have a predecessor is system dependent and is either `–MaxInt` or `–MaxInt – 1`.

Table 7.3   Results of Some Ord, Succ, and Pred Functions

Parameter	Ord	Succ	Pred
15	15	16	14
0	0	1	−1
−30	−30	−29	−31
MaxInt	MaxInt	Undefined	MaxInt − 1
−MaxInt	−MaxInt	−MaxInt + 1	−MaxInt − 1 or undefined
False	0	True	Undefined
True	1	Undefined	False

Although you can use these functions with any of the ordinal types, they are most often used with type `Char` and the enumerated types, which are discussed in Section 7.8. The ordinal number of a character is based on the character set code used by Pascal and, therefore, is computer dependent.   ■

■ Example 7.6

Table 7.4 shows some results of the `Ord`, `Succ`, and `Pred` functions for ASCII.

Table 7.4   Results of Some Ord, Succ, and Pred Functions for ASCII

Parameter	Ord	Succ	Pred
C	67	D	B
7	55	8	6
y	121	z	x
Blank	32	!	Unprintable

The table shows that the digit `'7'` has the ordinal number 55 in ASCII. Regardless of the character code used, the expression

```
Ord('7') − Ord('0') = 7
```

will always be true because the digit characters must be in consecutive sequence.

Table 7.4 also shows that the character `'C'` has the ordinal number 67 in ASCII. Since the character `'D'` is the successor of the character `'C'`, it must have an ordinal number of 68. And since the letters are in consecutive sequence in ASCII, the Boolean expression

```
Ord('C') − Ord('A') = 2
```

is true. In ASCII, the lowercase letters follow the uppercase letters, and the difference in code values for both cases of the same letter is 32 (e.g., Ord('a') − Ord('A') is 32). ∎

The Function Chr

The function Chr returns a character as its result. The character returned is the one whose ordinal number is the function argument. Therefore, the result of the function reference Chr(67) is the character with ordinal number 67 (the letter C in the ASCII code).

If Ch is a type Char variable, the *nested function reference*

```
Chr(Ord(Ch))
```

has the same value as Ch. Therefore, the function Chr is the *inverse* of the Ord function for the characters.

∎ Example 7.7

Function LowerCase in Fig. 7.6 returns the lowercase form of an uppercase letter passed to its parameter NextChar. If NextChar does not contain an uppercase letter, LowerCase returns NextChar as its result.

Figure 7.6 Function LowerCase

```
function LowerCase (Ch : Char) : Char;
{
 Returns the lowercase form of its argument.
 Pre : None
 Post: Returns the lowercase equivalent of Ch if Ch is
       an uppercase letter; otherwise, returns Ch.
}
begin {LowerCase}
  if Ch in ['A'..'Z'] then
    LowerCase := Chr(Ord(Ch) − Ord('A') + Ord('a'))
  else
    LowerCase := Ch
end; {LowerCase}
```

Directory: CHAP7
File: LOWERCAS.FUN

If Ch has the value 'C', the Boolean expression is true, and the first assignment statement is evaluated as shown below (assuming the letters are consecutive characters).

```
LowerCase := Chr(Ord('C') − Ord('A') + Ord('a'))
             Chr(67 − 65 + 97)
             Chr(99) = 'c'
```

In the ASCII code, the value of Ord('a') − Ord('A') is 32, so we can write this assignment statement as

```
LowerCase := Chr(Ord(Ch) + 32)
```

∎

■ Example 7.8

A *collating sequence* is a sequence of characters arranged by ordinal number. The program in Fig. 7.7 prints part of a Pascal collating sequence. It lists the characters with ordinal numbers 32 through 90, inclusive. The sequence shown is for the ASCII code; the first character printed is a blank (ordinal number 32).

Figure 7.7 Printing Part of a Collating Sequence

Directory: CHAP7
File: COLLATE.PAS

```
program Collate (Output);
{Prints part of a collating sequence}

   const
     Min := 32;                    {smallest ordinal number}
     Max := 90;                    {largest ordinal number}

   var
     NextOrd : Integer;            {each ordinal number}

begin  {Collate}
   {Print characters Chr(32) through Chr(90)}
   for NextOrd := Min to Max do
     Write (Chr(NextOrd));         {Print next character.}
   WriteLn
end.  {Collate}


   !"#$%&'()*+,-./0123456789:;<=>?@ABCDEFGHIJKLMNOPQRSTUVWXYZ
```

The functions introduced in this section are summarized in Table 7.5. ■

Table 7.5 Functions for Ordinal Types

Function	Purpose	Argument	Result
Chr(N)	Returns the character whose ordinal number is N	Integer	Char
Ord(N)	Returns the ordinal number of its argument	Any ordinal type	Integer
Pred(N)	Returns the predecessor of its argument	Any ordinal type	Same as argument
Succ(N)	Returns the successor of its argument	Any ordinal type	Same as argument

Self-Check

1. Evaluate the following:
   a. Ord(True)
   b. Pred(True)
   c. Succ(False)
   d. Ord(True) – Ord(False)
2. Evaluate the following assuming the letters are consecutive characters.
   a. Ord('D') – Ord('A')   f. Ord('7') – Ord('6')
   b. Ord('d') – Ord('a')   g. Ord('9') – Ord('0')
   c. Succ(Pred('a'))   h. Succ(Succ(Succ('d')))
   d. Chr(Ord('C'))   i. Chr(Ord('A') + 5)
   e. Chr(Ord('C') – Ord('A') + Ord('a'))
3. Write a while loop equivalent to the following for loop:

   ```
   for Ch := 'A' to 'Z' do
     WriteLn (Ch, Ord(Ch));
   ```

Programming

1. Write a function UpperCase that returns as its value the uppercase equivalent of its character argument or, if there is none, prints the value of its argument.

7.6 Subrange Types

One of the most important features of Pascal is that it permits the declaration of new data types. Many of these data types are discussed in later chapters. This section focuses on new data types that are subranges of the ordinal types where a *subrange* defines a subset of the values associated with a particular ordinal type (the *host type*). Subranges both make a program more readable and enable Pascal to detect when a variable is given a value that is unreasonable in the problem environment.

■ Example 7.9

Type declarations begin with the reserved word type and are used to declare a new data type. The Pascal scope rules for identifiers (see Section 6.7) apply to names of data types. Two subrange types are declared next, as well as a variable of each new type.

```
type
  Letter = 'A'..'Z';
  DaysInMonth = 1..31;

var
  NextChar : Letter;
  InDay : DaysInMonth;
```

The first subrange, Letter, has the host type Char. Any character value from 'A' to 'Z', inclusive, can be stored in a variable of type Letter. The computer displays an error message and stops program execution if you attempt to store any other character in a variable of type Letter. For example, the assignment statement

```
NextChar := 'a'
```

should cause the run-time error value out of range, and stop program execution, because the character value 'a' is not included in data type Letter. Some Pascal compilers will detect this *range violation* as a syntax error during compilation.

DaysInMonth is a subrange with base type Integer. A variable of type DaysInMonth can be used to keep track of the current data, a value between 1 and 31, inclusive. The statement

```
ReadLn (InDay)
```

reads a data value into InDay (type DaysInMonth). A value out of range run-time error occurs if the data value is less than 1 or greater than 31. ■

SYNTAX
DISPLAY

Subrange Type Declaration

Form: type *subrange-type* = *minvalue* .. *maxvalue*;
Example: type LowCase = 'a' .. 'z';
Interpretation: A new data type named *subrange-type* is defined. A variable of type *subrange-type* can be assigned a value from *minvalue* through *maxvalue*, inclusive. The values *minvalue* and *maxvalue* must belong to the same ordinal type (called the host type), and Ord(*minvalue*) must be less than or equal to Ord(*maxvalue*).
Note: *minvalue* and *maxvalue* may be constant identifiers of the same data type.

The scope rules for a subrange type identifier are the same as for other Pascal identifiers. The operations that can be performed on a variable whose type is a subrange are the same as for the host type of the subrange. The host type is determined by the pair of values that defines the subrange; the ordinal number of the first value must be less than the ordinal number of the second value.

PROGRAM
STYLE

Reason for Using Subranges

You may be wondering why bother with subranges—they don't seem to provide any new capabilities. However, subranges do allow additional opportunity for your program to "bomb." If a user attempts to store an out-of-range value in a variable whose type is a subrange, program execution will stop. If `InDay` is type `Integer` (instead of `DaysInMonth`), the program will continue to execute regardless of what value is assigned to `InDay`. Assigning an overly large value (say, 1000) to `InDay` may cause a later statement to fail or the program to generate incorrect results. In the former case, the program user may have difficulty finding the statement that was actually at fault (i.e., the statement that assigned the out-of-range value). In the latter case, the program user may not even be aware that an error has occurred if the program executes in a normal manner. The use of subranges ensures the immediate detection of an out-of-range value.

The Order of Pascal Declarations

In standard Pascal, the `type` declarations must come between the constant declarations and the variable declarations in a Pascal block. The form of the declaration part for a standard Pascal block is summarized as follows:

> *constant declarations*
> *type declarations*
> *variable declarations*
> *procedure and function declarations*

Many compilers do not require strict adherence to this sequence. They follow the less restrictive rule that each identifier must be declared before its first use, which allows a programmer to mix declarations and to group related constant, type, and variable declarations to enhance readability, as shown next. Although we usually do not advocate the use of nonstandard features because it reduces portability, you should be aware that this capability exists. (We discuss this topic again in Section 9.5.)

```
{nonstandard declaration part}

const
  FirstLetter = 'A';
  LastLetter = 'Z';

type
  Letter = FirstLetter..LastLetter;

var
  NextChar : Letter;

type
  DaysInMonth = 1..31;

var
  InDay : DaysInMonth;
```

Exercises for Section 7.6

Self-Check

1. Which of the following subranges are illegal?

a. 1..MaxInt   f. 0..'9'
b. 'A'..'Z'   g. 15..−15
c. −15..15   h. 'ACE'..'HAT'
d. 'A'..'z'   i. 'a'..'Z'
e. −5.0..5.0   j. −MaxInt..−MaxInt + 5

2. Explain why using procedure ReadLnInt (described in programming exercise 1) would be safer than using ReadLn to read Integer subrange values into a program.

Programming

1. Write a procedure ReadLnInt that has input parameters Min and Max (type Integer) and output parameters N (type Integer) and Success (Boolean). Your procedure should prompt the user to enter a value for N and set Success to True if N is in the range Min to Max, inclusive; Success should be set to False otherwise.

7.7 Type Compatibility and Assignment Compatibility

Data types are considered *type compatible* if they are the same type, if one is a subrange of another (e.g., Letter and Char in Example 7.9), or if they are both subranges of the same host type. As an example, the data type Character declared below is considered the same type as Char, so Character, Char, and Letter are type compatible.

```
type
  Character = Char;
  Letter = 'A'..'Z';

var
  NextCh : Character;
```

Operands that are type-compatible can be manipulated by the same operator. For example, the expression

```
NextCh <> '3'
```

is syntactically correct as long as NextCh is type Char, Character, or Letter. On the other hand, the expression

```
NextCh <> 3
```

causes a syntax error because the integer 3 is not type compatible with NextCh.

The variable InDay declared in Example 7.9 can be manipulated like any type Integer variable. It can be used as an actual parameter that corresponds to a formal value parameter that is type Integer, type DaysInMonth, or any other subrange with host type Integer. However, the rules for correspondence of variable parameters are more restrictive (i.e., corresponding variable parameters must be the same type), so `InDay` can correspond only to a formal variable parameter that is type `DaysInMonth`.

An expression is considered *assignment compatible* with a variable if their types are type compatible. If the variable type is a subrange, the value of the expression must be within the allowable range. If a variable and an expression are assignment compatible, then the expression can be assigned to the variable without error.

Assuming the declarations

```
type
  Letter = 'A'..'Z';

var
  Next Ch : Letter;
  Ch : Char;
```

the assignment statement

```
NextCh := '3'
```

causes the syntax error `value to be assigned is out of bounds` because the constant value `'3'` is not assignment compatible with the variable `NextCh` (type `Letter`). If `Ch` is type `Char`, the assignment statement

```
NextCh := Ch
```

will compile, but it may cause a `value out of range` run-time error. This error occurs if the character stored in `Ch` is not an uppercase letter.

In Section 2.4, we mentioned that there is one exception to the rule that a variable and an expression must be type compatible to be assignment compatible. Recall that a type `Integer` expression is assignment compatible with a type `Real` variable. This means that a type `Integer` expression can be assigned to a type `Real` variable or that it can correspond to a value parameter that is type `Real`.

We discuss more issues of type compatibility and assignment compatibility in later chapters.

Exercises for Section 7.7

Self-Check

1. Assuming that `I` is type `0..10`, `J` is type `Integer`, and `K` is type `Real`, indicate whether each of the following expressions is assignment compatible with the variable on the left and whether any constraints are necessary to avoid an out-of-range error.
   a. `K := 3 * I + J`
   b. `I := 15`
   c. `J := Trunc(K) + 2 * I`
   d. `I := I div J`
   e. `I := I / J`
   f. `I := J mod 11`
   g. `J := 2 * K + 3`
2. Explain why a compiler cannot determine whether a `value out of range` error may occur at run time for a particular assignment statement.

7.8 Enumerated Types

This section introduces a feature of Pascal that improves the readability of large programs. In many programming situations, the standard data types and their values are inadequate. For example, in a budget program you might want to distinguish among the following categories of expenditures: entertainment, rent, utilities, food, clothing, automobile, insurance, miscellaneous. Although you could create an arbitrary code that associates entertainment with a character value of 'e', rent with a character value of 'r', and so on, Pascal allows you to create *enumerated types,* each with its own set of meaningful values.

For example, the enumerated type Expenses has eight possible values enclosed in parentheses:

```
type
   Expenses = (Entertainment, Rent, Utilities, Food,
               Clothing, Automobile, Insurance, Miscellaneous);

var
   ExpenseKind : Expenses;
```

The variable ExpenseKind (type Expenses) can contain any of the eight values. The following if statement tests the value stored in ExpenseKind.

```
if ExpenseKind = Entertainment then
   WriteLn ('Postpone until after your payday.')
else if ExpenseKind = Rent then
   WriteLn ('Pay before the first of the month!')
...
```

■ Example 7.10

The enumerated type Day has the values Sunday, Monday, and so on:

```
type
   Day = (Sunday, Monday, Tuesday, Wednesday,
          Thursday, Friday, Saturday);        {days of the week}
```

The values associated with an enumerated type must be identifiers; they cannot be numeric, character, or string literals (e.g., 'Sunday' cannot be a value for an enumerated type).

The scope rules for identifiers apply to enumerated types and their values. Each enumerated-type value is treated as a constant identifier in the block containing the type-declaration statement. The type declaration must precede any variable declaration that references it.   ■

Enumerated Type Declaration

Form: type *enumerated-type* = (*identifier-list*) ;

Example: type Class = (Freshman, Sophomore, Junior, Senior);

Interpretation: A new data type named *enumerated-type* is declared. The values associated with this type are specified in the *identifier-list.* Each value is defined as a constant identifier in the block containing the type-declaration statement.

Note: A particular identifier can appear in only one *identifier-list* in a given block.

An identifier cannot appear in more than one enumerated-type declaration. If type Day is already declared, the type declaration

```
type
   TDay = (Tuesday, Thursday);
```

is invalid because Tuesday and Thursday are associated with type Day.

Enumerated-Type Operators

Like the standard types Integer, Boolean, and Char, each enumerated type is considered an ordinal type, so the order relations of its values are fixed when the enumerated type is declared. For type Day, the first value in its list (Sunday) has ordinal number 0, the next value (Monday) has ordinal number 1, and so on. The only operators that can accompany ordinal types are the relational and assignment operators. The following order relations are all true:

```
Sunday < Monday
Wednesday <> Tuesday
Wednesday = Wednesday
Wednesday >= Tuesday
Entertainment < Rent
```

The order relation

```
Entertainment < Wednesday
```

would cause a syntax error because the values are associated with two different enumerated types.

The assignment operator can define the value of a variable whose type is an enumerated type. The variable declaration

```
var
   Today,                        {current day of the week}
   Tomorrow : Day;               {day after Today}
```

specifies that Today and Tomorrow are type Day; therefore, they can be assigned any of the values listed in the declaration for type Day. Consequently, the assignment statements

```
Today := Friday;
Tomorrow := Saturday;
```

assign the value Friday to variable Today and Saturday to variable Tomorrow. After the assignments, the following order relations are all true.

```
Today = Friday
Tomorrow = Saturday
Today < Tomorrow
Today <> Wednesday
Today >= Sunday
```

We can use functions Succ, Pred, and Ord (see Section 7.5) with enumerated types. Some examples are given next, assuming that Today is Friday and Tomorrow is Saturday.

```
Ord(Today) is 5
Ord(Tomorrow) is 6
Succ(Today) is Saturday
Pred(Today) is Thursday
Pred(Succ(Today)) is Friday
Succ(Tomorrow) is undefined
Pred(Tomorrow) is Friday
```

The next-to-last example is undefined because no value of type Day follows Saturday. Similarly, if Today is Sunday, the value of Pred(Sunday) is undefined. Succ or Pred operations leading to undefined results may cause a range error or an overflow error during program execution.

■ Example 7.11

The following if statement assigns the value of Tomorrow based on the value of Today (both type Day).

```
if Today = Saturday then
   Tomorrow := Sunday
else
   Tomorrow := Succ(Today)
```

Because the days of a week are cyclical, Tomorrow is set to Sunday when Today is Saturday. The last value (Saturday) in the enumerated type Day is treated separately because Succ(Today) is undefined when Today is Saturday.

Because enumerated types are ordinal types, we can use variables that belong to enumerated types as *counter* variables in for statements and as *case selectors* in case statements. The next two examples show a for statement and a case statement. ■

■ Example 7.12

The for loop in Fig. 7.8 reads the hours worked each weekday for an employee and accumulates the sum of the hours worked in WeekHours. Assuming that the counter variable Today is declared as the enumerated type Day, the loop executes for Today equal to Monday through Friday. During each iteration, the calls to Write, WriteDay, and WriteLn display a prompt such as

```
Enter hours for Monday>
```

where WriteDay (see programming exercise 3 at the end of this section) displays the day name (string 'Monday'). Next, each value read into DayHours is added to WeekHours. After loop exit, the final value of WeekHours is displayed. ■

Figure 7.8 Accumulating Hours Worked

321

7.8 Enumerated
Types

```
WeekHours := 0.0;
for Today := Monday to Friday do
  begin
    Write ('Enter hours for ');
    WriteDay (Today);
    Write ('> ');
    ReadLn (DayHours);
    WeekHours := WeekHours + DayHours
  end; {for}

WriteLn ('Total weekly hours are ', WeekHours :4:2)
```

Reading and Writing Enumerated Type Values

Enumerated types are defined by the programmer; thus, their values are not known in advance. The Pascal input/output procedures cannot read or write enumerated type values. However, you can write your own procedures for this purpose.

■ Example 7.13

Given the declarations

```
type
  Color = (Red, Green, Blue, Yellow);

var
  Eyes : Color;
```

the statement

```
Write (Ord(Eyes) :1)
```

can be used for diagnostic printing during debugging. It does not print the value of Eyes, but it does display the ordinal number of the value, that is, an integer from 0 (for Red) to 3 (for Yellow).

Procedure WriteColor in Fig. 7.9 prints a string that represents a value of type Color. If the value of Eyes is defined, the statement

```
WriteColor (Eyes)
```

displays the value of Eyes as a string. Make sure you understand the difference between the string 'Blue' and the constant identifier Blue.

Figure 7.9 Procedure to Print a Value of Type Color

```
procedure WriteColor (InColor {input} : Color);
{
    Displays the value of InColor.
    Pre : InColor is assigned a value.
    Post: The value of InColor is displayed as a string.
}
```

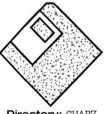

Directory: CHAP7
File: WRITECOL.PRO

```
begin {WriteColor}
  case InColor of
    Red    : WriteLn ('Red');
    Green  : WriteLn ('Green');
    Blue   : WriteLn ('Blue');
    Yellow : WriteLn ('Yellow')
  end {case}
end; {WriteColor}
```

We often use case statements, such as the one in Fig. 7.9, whose case labels are values associated with an enumerated type. Be careful not to use a string such as 'Red' as a case label. This causes a syntax error such as iden-tifier expected or illegal character in identifier. Remember that only ordinal values or constants (including enumerated constants) can appear in case labels.

It is slightly more difficult to read the value of an enumerated-type variable than it is to display it. The next example shows one method. ■

■ Example 7.14

Procedure ReadLnColor in Fig. 7.10 returns one value of type Color and one of type Boolean. If Eyes is type Color and ValidColor is type Boolean, the procedure call statement

```
ReadLnColor (Eyes, ValidColor)
```

attempts to read the value of Eyes and sets ValidColor to indicate the success (ValidColor is True) or failure (ValidColor is False) of this operation. ReadLnColor reads a single color value from each data line, ignoring all but the first letter on the line. If Black and Brown are added to the list of values for Color, it becomes necessary to read additional characters when the first letter read is B. We leave this as an exercise (see programming exercise 2). The procedure documentation indicates that ReadLnColor calls function LowerCase (see Fig. 7.6). ■

Figure 7.10   Procedure ReadLnColor

Directory: CHAP7
File: READLNCO.PRO

```
procedure ReadLnColor (var ItemColor  {output} : Color;
                       var ValidColor {output} : Boolean);
{
  Assigns a value to ItemColor based on an input character.  Sets
  ValidColor to indicate whether the assignment was made.
  Pre : None
  Post: ItemColor is defined if the character read is 'r', 'g',
        'b', 'y', or their uppercase forms.
        ValidColor is set to True if ItemColor is defined;
        otherwise, ValidColor is set to False.
  Uses: LowerCase (see Figure 7.6)
}
  var
    ColorChar : Char;           {first letter of color name}

begin  {ReadLnColor}
  Write ('Enter first letter of color> ');
```

```
ReadLn (ColorChar);
ColorChar := LowerCase(ColorChar);    {Convert to lowercase.}

{Assign the color value}
if ColorChar in ['r', 'g', 'b', 'y'] then
  begin {valid color}
    ValidColor := True;
    case ColorChar of
      'r' : ItemColor := Red;
      'g' : ItemColor := Green;
      'b' : ItemColor := Blue;
      'y' : ItemColor := Yellow
    end {case}
  end {valid color}
else
    ValidColor := False          {valid color was not read}
end; {ReadLnColor}
```

Subranges of Enumerated Types

We can declare subranges of enumerated types. The following declarations
specify that WeekDay (values Monday through Friday) is a subrange of type Day
and that variable SchoolDay is type WeekDay.

```
type
   Day = (Sunday, Monday, Tuesday, Wednesday,
          Thursday, Friday, Saturday);    {days of the week}
   WeekDay = Monday..Friday;              {weekdays only}

var
   SchoolDay : WeekDay;
```

The assignment statement

```
   SchoolDay := Monday;
```

is valid; however, the assignment statement

```
   SchoolDay := Sunday;
```

causes a constant out of range syntax error.

Why Use Enumerated Types?

At this point you may have a legitimate concern: is it worth using enumerated
types, considering that it is so much trouble to read and write their values?
Also, if we need to use a letter code to enter the value of an enumerated type
variable, why not use that code throughout the program? The fact is that
enumerated types in a program make that program considerably easier to read
and understand.

■ Example 7.15
The if statement

```
   if DayNum = 1 then
      PayFactor := 2.0       {double pay for Sunday}
```

```
else if DayNum = 7 then
   PayFactor := 1.5      {time and a half for Saturday}
else
   PayFactor := 1.0      {regular pay}
```

might appear in a payroll program without enumerated types if Sunday and Saturday are "coded" as the integers 1 and 7, respectively. If we use the enumerated type Day and the variable Today (type Day), we can write this statement as

```
if Today = Sunday then
   PayFactor := 2.0
else if Today = Saturday then
   PayFactor := 1.5
else
   PayFactor := 1.0
```

The latter form is obviously more readable because, instead of an obscure code, it uses values (Saturday and Sunday) that are meaningful to the problem. Consequently, the comments on the right in the top statement are not needed.

■

In a lengthy program, the extra overhead required to implement procedures for reading and writing the values associated with an enumerated type are insignificant. If these procedures are placed in your own library of modules (discussed in Chapter 9), it will be easy to reuse procedures that you have already written.

Another advantage of using enumerated types is that the creation of an enumerated type automatically limits the range of values that can be assigned to a variable. If we use an integer code, any integer value can be assigned unless we take the trouble to declare a subrange type. When we declare an enumerated type, we explicitly declare the set of values that can be assigned to a variable of that type. In the preceding example, any integer value can be assigned to variable DayNum; however, only one of the seven values listed in the declaration for enumerated type Day can be assigned to variable Today.

Exercises for Section 7.8

Self-Check

1. Evaluate each of the following function designators, assuming before each operation that Today (type Day) is Thursday.
   a. Ord(Monday)
   b. Ord(Today)
   c. Today < Tuesday
   d. Succ(Wednesday)
   e. Pred(Succ(Today))
   f. Succ(Today)
   g. Pred(Today)
   h. Today >= Thursday
   i. Pred(Sunday)
   j. Ord(Succ(Succ(Today)))
2. Indicate whether each of the following type declarations is valid or invalid. Explain what is wrong with each invalid type declaration.
   a. type Letters = ('A', 'B', 'C');
   b. type Letters = (A, B, C);
        TwoLetters = (A..B);

c. `type Letters = ('A'..'Z');`
d. `type Boolean = (True, False);`
e. `type Day = (Sun, Mon, Tue, Wed, Thu, Fri, Sat);`
   ` WeekDay = Mon..Fri;`
   ` WeekEnd = Sat..Sun;`
   ` TDay = (Tue, Thu);`

Programming

1. Declare an enumerated type `Month` and rewrite the following `if` statement, assuming that `CurMonth` is type `Month` instead of type `Integer`. Also, write the equivalent case statement.

```
if CurMonth = 1 then
  WriteLn ('Happy new year')
else if CurMonth = 6 then
  WriteLn ('Summer begins')
else if CurMonth = 9 then
  WriteLn ('Back to school')
else if CurMonth = 12 then
  WriteLn ('Happy Holidays');
```

2. Rewrite procedure `ReadLnColor` (see Fig. 7.10), assuming that `Black` and `Brown` are also values for enumerated type `Color`.
3. Write procedure `WriteDay` for enumerated type `Day`.

7.9 Iterative Approximations (Optional)

Numerical analysis is the field of study concerned with developing methods to use computers to solve computational problems in mathematics. Some examples of numerical methods include finding solutions to sets of equations, performing operations on matrices, finding roots of equations, and performing mathematical integration. This section contains two case studies that illustrate methods for iteratively approximating solutions to computational problems. You may wish to skip this material if you do not have the appropriate mathematical background.

Case Study: Approximating the Value of e

Problem

A number of mathematical quantities can be represented by a series approximation, where a series is represented by a summation of an infinite number of terms. We can use this technique to compute *e* (value is 2.71828 . . .), the base of the natural logarithms.

Analysis

We can get an approximation to the value of *e* by evaluating the series

$$1 + 1/1! + 1/2! + 1/3! + \ldots + 1/N! + \ldots$$

where *N*! is the factorial of *N*, as defined in Section 6.10 and repeated here:

$$N! = N \times (N - 1)! \quad \text{for } N > 1$$
$$N! = 1 \quad \text{for } N = 0 \text{ or } 1$$

This expression can be represented with *summation notation* as

$$\sum_{i=0}^{N} 1/i!$$

where the first term is obtained by substituting 0 for *i* (1/0! is 1/1), the second term is obtained by substituting 1 for *i* (1/1!), and so on. The larger the value of *N*, the more terms will be included in the series, resulting in increased accuracy. The value of *N* will be a problem input.

Data Requirements

Problem Input
N : Integer   {number of terms, N, in the sum}

Problem Output
E : Real   {approximate value of e}

Program Variables
IthTerm : Real   {ith term of the series}
I : Integer   {loop–control variable}

Design

We can use a counting loop to implement the summation formula.

Initial Algorithm

1. Read in the value of N.
2. Initialize E to 1.0.
3. Initialize the *i*th term to 1.0.
4. for each I from 1 to N do
    begin
        5. Compute the *i*th term in the series.
        6. Add the *i*th term to E.
    end
7. Print the value of E.

Implementation

The program is shown in Fig. 7.11. Inside the `for` loop, the statement

```
IthTerm := IthTerm / I;
```

computes the value of the *i*th term in the series by dividing the previous term by the loop-control variable I. The formula that follows shows that this division does indeed produce the next term in the series.

$$(1 / (I - 1)!) / I = 1 / (I \times (I - 1)!) = 1 / I!$$

Because 0! is 1, IthTerm must be initialized to 1.0. The statement

```
E := E + IthTerm;
```

adds the new value of IthTerm to the sum being accumulated in E. Trace the execution of this loop to satisfy yourself that IthTerm takes on the values 1/1!, 1/2!, 1/3!, and so on, during successive loop iterations.

Figure 7.11   Series Approximation to e

```
program ESeries (Output);
{Computes the value of e by a series approximation}

   var
     E,                    {value being approximated}
     IthTerm : Real;       {ith term in series}
     N,                    {number of terms in series}
     I   : Integer;        {loop-control variable}

begin {eSeries}
   Write ('Enter the number of terms in the series> ');
   ReadLn (N);

   {Compute each term and add it to the accumulating sum.}
   E := 1.0;              {initial sum}
   IthTerm := 1.0;        {first term}
   I := 1;
   while I <= N do
     begin
       IthTerm := IthTerm / I;
       E := E + IthTerm;
       I := I + 1
     end; {while}

   {Print the result.}
   WriteLn ('The approximate value of e is ', E :20)
end. {eSeries}


Enter the number of terms in the series> 15
The approximate value of e is      2.7182818284E+00
```

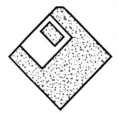

Directory: CHAP7
File: ESERIES.PAS

Testing

To determine whether this algorithm works, it is sufficient to run the program for a particular value of N and compare the result with e, which is 2.71828183. Obviously the value computed for N equals 15 is very close to the actual value. It would be interesting to see the effect of the value of N on the accuracy of the final computed result. Programming exercise 1 asks you to compute and display such a table.

Case Study: Newton's Method for Finding Roots

Problem

Your calculus instructor would like you to write a program that uses Newton's method for finding a root of an equation, $y = f(x)$, where k is a root if $f(k)$ equals 0. Newton's method starts with an initial guess for a root, x_0, and then generates successive approximate roots $x_1, x_2, \ldots, x_j, x_{j+1}, \ldots$ using the iterative formula

$$x_{j+1} = x_j - \frac{f(x_j)}{f'(x_j)}$$

where $f'(x_j)$ is the derivative of function f evaluated at $x = x_j$. The formula above generates a new guess, x_{j+1}, from a previous one, x_j. Newton's method terminates when successive guesses are sufficiently close in value, that is, when

$$|x_{j+1} - x_j| < epsilon$$

where *epsilon* is a very small constant (e.g., 0.00001).

Sometimes Newton's method will fail to converge to a root. In that case, the program should terminate after a large number of trials (say, 100).

Analysis

Figure 7.12 shows the geometric interpretation of Newton's method, where x_0, x_1, and x_2 represent successive guesses for the root. At each point x_j, the derivative, $f'(x_j)$, is the tangent to the curve, $f(x)$. The next guess for the root, x_{j+1}, is the point where the tangent crosses the x-axis.

From geometry, we get the equation

$$\frac{y_{j+1} - y_j}{x_{j+1} - x_j} = m$$

where m is the slope of the line between points (x_{j+1}, y_{j+1}) and (x_j, y_j). From Fig. 7.12, if (x_j, y_j) is a point on the curve, and (x_{j+1}, y_{j+1}) is the next point on the x-

Figure 7.12 Geometric Interpretation of Newton's Method

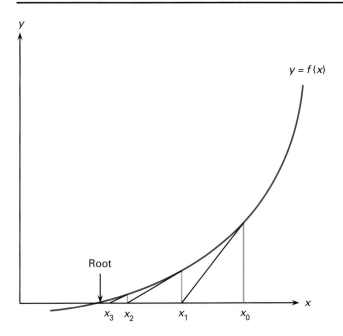

axis, then y_{j+1} is 0, y_j is $f(x_j)$, and m is $f'(x_j)$. By substituting and rearranging terms, we get

$$-f(x_j) = f'(x_j) \times (x_{j+1} - x_j)$$

which leads to the formula shown at the beginning of the case study. In the data requirements that follow, XLast corresponds to x_j and XNext corresponds to x_{j+1}.

Data Requirements

Problem Constants
```
Epsilon = 0.00001    {minimum distance between successive guesses}
MaxGuess = 100       {maximum number of guesses}
```

Program Outputs
```
XNext : Real         {next guess for a root}
NumGuess : Integer   {count of guesses}
```

Program Variables
```
XLast : Real         {last guess for a root}
```

Functions
```
F(X)                 {function whose root is being determined}
FPrime(X)            {derivative of function F(X)}
```

Design

The initial guess for the root is read into XNext. Inside a loop, we compute the next guess for the root value, XNext, from the last guess, XLast. The loop must continue to execute until the difference between successive guesses is less than Epsilon. The algorithm follows.

Algorithm for Newton's Method

1. Read the initial guess into XNext and set NumGuess to 1.
2. repeat
    3. Set XLast to the last guess, which is stored in XNext.
    4. Compute the next guess, XNext, from XLast by evaluating $f(\text{XLast})$ and $f'(\text{XLast})$.
    5. Increment NumGuess.
  until Abs(XNext − XLast) is less than Epsilon or
      NumGuess > MaxGuess
6. if a root was found then
    7. Display the root and the function value at the root.
8. Display the number of guesses.

Implementation

The program must contain declarations for function F(X), the function whose root is being computed, and function FPrime(X), the derivative of F(X). The program in Fig. 7.13 computes the root for the function

$$f(x) = 5x^3 - 2x^2 + 3$$

with the derivative

$$f'(x) = 15x^2 - 4x$$

Figure 7.13 Newton's Method

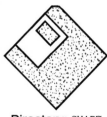

Directory: CHAP7
File: NEWTON.PAS

```
program Newton (Input, Output);
{Finds a root of an equation using Newton's method}

   const
      Epsilon = 0.00001;      {minimum distance between successive guesses}
      MaxGuess = 100;         {maximum number of guesses}

   var
      XLast : Real;           {last guess for a root}
      XNext : Real;           {next guess for a root}
      NumGuess : Integer;     {count of guesses}

   function F(X : Real) : Real;
   {The function whose root is being found}
   begin {F}
      {Insert function here.}
      F := 5 * X * X * X - 2 * X * X + 3
   end;   {F}
```

```
function FPrime(X : Real) : Real;
{The derivative of F(X)}
begin {FPrime}
   {Insert function derivative here.}
   FPrime := 15 * X * X - 4 * X
end;   {FPrime}

begin {Newton}
   {Read the initial guess into XNext and set NumGuess to 1.}
   Write ('Initial guess for a root>');
   ReadLn (XNext);
   NumGuess := 1;

   {Compute successive guesses.}
   repeat
      XLast := XNext;                          {XLast is last guess.}
      XNext := XLast - F(XLast) / FPrime(XLast);
      NumGuess := NumGuess + 1
   until (Abs(XNext - XLast) < Epsilon) or (NumGuess > MaxGuess);

   {Display the root and function value if a root was found.}
   if Abs(XNext - XLast) < Epsilon then
      begin
         WriteLn ('The approximate root is ', XNext);
         WriteLn ('The function value is ', F(XNext))
      end
   else
      WriteLn (NumGuess :1, ' guesses made')
end.   {Newton}


Initial guess for a root> 1.0
The approximate root is -7.2900142869E-01
The function value is -3.6379788071E-12
9 guesses made
```

Testing

The function value in Fig. 7.13 is sufficiently close to zero that we can feel confident that we have found a root. To test Newton's method, run the program on several mathematical functions and with several different starting points for each function. In most cases, Newton's method should find a solution relatively quickly.

You may find there are situations in which Newton's method does not work but cycles until `MaxGuess` guesses are made. At other times Newton's method will fail because `FPrime(XLast)` becomes 0 and a `division by zero` run-time error occurs. In those cases, you must try a different technique for finding function roots. One such technique (the bisection method) is described in programming project 6 at the end of this chapter.

Exercises for Section 7.9

Self-Check

1. Determine the output from program Newton (Fig. 7.13) if the initial guess for the root is 0.0, the value used for constant Epsilon is 0.1, and

$$f(x) = x^2 - 2x + 1$$
$$f'(x) = 2x - 2$$

Programming

1. Display a table that shows e and N for values of N between 3 and 15.
2. The value of e^x is represented by the series

$$1 + x + x^2/2! + x^3/3 + \ldots + x^n/n! + \ldots$$

Write a program to compute and print the value of this series for any x and n. Compare the result to Exp(x) and print a message 'O.K.' or 'Not O.K.', depending on whether the difference between these results exceeds 0.0001.

7.10 Common Programming Errors

You must take a good deal of care when working with complicated expressions. It is easy to inadvertently omit parentheses or operators. If an operator or a single parenthesis is omitted, a syntax error will be detected. If a pair of parentheses is omitted, the expression, although syntactically correct, will compute the wrong value.

Sometimes it is beneficial to break a complicated expression into subexpressions that are separately assigned to *temporary variables* and then to manipulate those temporary variables. For example, it is easier to write correctly the three assignment statements

```
Temp1 := Sqrt(X + Y);
Temp2 := 1 + Temp1;
Z := Temp1 / Temp2
```

than the single assignment statement

```
Z := Sqrt(X + Y) / (1 + Sqrt(X + Y))
```

which has the same effect. Using three assignment statements is also more efficient because the square root operation is performed only once; it is performed twice in the single assignment statement.

The only operators that can be used with type Char data are the relational operators. The Boolean expression

```
3 <> '3'          {incompatible operands}
```

is invalid because one of its operands is an integer and the other is a character value.

Make sure you use parentheses properly in compound Boolean expressions. The Boolean operators and, or, and not have higher precedence than the relational operators, so parentheses are required in expressions such as

```
(-5.0 <= X) and (X <= 5.0)
```

Also be careful when you use the set relational operator in. The Boolean expression on the left is correct, but the expressions on the right are incorrect.

Correct	*Incorrect*
not (X in [1..3])	not X in [1..3]
	X not in [1..3]

Syntax or run-time errors can occur when you use the built-in functions. The argument of the function Chr must be type Integer; the argument of the functions Ord, Succ, and Pred must be an ordinal type (not type Real). The results of the functions Succ, Pred, and Chr will be undefined for certain arguments.

Subranges can help you detect erroneous computations or data. If a value being assigned is outside the subrange, an out of range error occurs. The operations that can be performed on a variable with a subrange type are determined by the host type for that subrange. However, a variable whose type is a subrange type cannot correspond to a formal variable parameter whose type is the host type for that subrange.

When you are declaring enumerated types, remember that only identifiers can appear in the list of values for an enumerated type. Strings, characters, and numbers are not allowed. Make sure that the same constant identifier does not appear in more than one enumerated-type declaration in a given block. It is permissible for a given constant identifier to appear in more than one subrange-type declaration. Remember that no standard procedures are available to read or write the values of an enumerated type.

CHAPTER REVIEW

This chapter discussed the manipulation of simple data types, including the standard types (Boolean and Char) and programmer-defined subranges and enumerated types. We discussed the internal representation of simple types and discussed the differences between the numeric types, Integer and Real. We explained that real arithmetic is inherently less precise because not all real numbers can be represented exactly. We described other sources of numerical errors, such as cancellation errors and arithmetic overflow and underflow.

We introduced DeMorgan's theorem, which describes how to form the complement of a Boolean expression. We also introduced the set relational operator and explained how to use set values in Boolean expressions. We often use Boolean expressions with set values to guard a case statement and prevent its execution when the case selector value is not a case label.

We discussed the functions Pred, Succ, and Ord, which are used to manipulate ordinal data types. The function Chr, the inverse of Ord, finds the character corresponding to a given ordinal number.

We showed you how subrange declarations provide additional documentation for ordinal variables that have a restricted range of values. Run-time errors may occur if such variables are assigned out-of-range values.

You also saw how to declare enumerated types with a list of values tailored to a particular application. The use of enumerated types makes large programs more readable.

Finally, we discussed numerical analysis, which is the branch of mathematics and computer science concerned with developing techniques for mathematical computation. We demonstrated how to use iterative approximations to evaluate a series and to find the root of an equation.

New Pascal Constructs

The Pascal constructs introduced in this chapter are described in Table 7.6.

Table 7.6 Summary of New Pascal Constructs

Construct	Effect

Subrange Declaration
`type`
`  Digit =  '0'..'9';`
	A subrange of the characters is declared. This subrange (named `Digit`) consists of the character values `'0'` through `'9'`.

Enumerated Type Declaration
`type`
`  BColor = (Blue, Black,`
`    Brown);`
	An enumerated type `BColor` is declared with values `Blue`, `Black`, and `Brown`.

✓ Quick-Check Exercises

1. a. Evaluate the Boolean expression

       True and ((30 mod 10) in [0..3])

   b. Is the outer pair of parentheses required?
   c. What about the inner pair?
   d. Write the complement of the Boolean expression using DeMorgan's theorem.
2. Indicate which of the following can appear in a set value: a subrange of integers, a list of integers, a real value, a Boolean value, a type `Char` value, a string value, an enumerated-type value.
3. Explain how to use a set value to guard a `case` statement and prevent a `case value out of range` error.
4. In ASCII, what is the value of each of the following?
   a. `Chr(Ord('a'))`   c. `Chr(Ord('z') - 25)`
   b. `Chr(Ord('a') + 3)`   d. `Chr(Ord('z') - 32)`
5. What is the value of `Ord('9') - Ord('0')`? Is this answer the same for all Pascal compilers? What about `Ord('z') - Ord('a')`?

6. a. Can a variable whose type is a subrange type correspond to a formal variable parameter whose type is the host type?

   b. What if the formal parameter is a value parameter?

7. If two variables are type compatible, can one always be assigned to the other?

8. Under what condition can one variable be assigned to another when they are not type compatible?

9. What is wrong with the following enumerated-type declaration?

```
type Prime = (2, 3, 5, 7, 9, 11, 13);
```

10. Consider the enumerated type declaration

```
type Class = (Frosh, Soph, Jr, Sr);
```

   What is the value of
   a. Ord(Succ(Pred(Soph)))   b. Pred(Pred(Jr))

Answers to Quick-Check Exercises

1. a. True   b. Yes   c. not needed

   d. False or not ((30 mod 10) in [0..3])

2. a subrange of integers, a list of integers, a Boolean value, a type Char value, and an enumerated-type value.

3. A set value can be used in an if statement condition that permits the case statement to be executed only when the case selector matches one of the elements in the set. All case label values should appear in the set value.

4. a. 'a'   b. 'd'   c. 'a'   d. 'Z'

5. 9; yes; 25 on ASCII and CDC character sets but not on EBCDIC

6. a. no   b. yes

7. Yes, if they are the same type, or the variable getting a new value is the host type and the other is a subrange of that host. If the variable getting a new value is a subrange type, the new value must be in range.

8. A variable whose type is Integer or a subrange type whose host type is Integer can be assigned to a type Real variable.

9. Integers cannot appear as enumerated-type values.

10. a. 1   b. Frosh

Review Questions

1. What are the advantages of data type Integer over data type Real?

2. List and explain three computational errors that may occur in type Real expressions.

3. Write an enumerated type declaration for Fiscal as the months from July through June. Declare the subrange Winter as December through February.

4. Write procedures for reading and writing values for variables of enumerated type Season.

```
type Season = (Winter, Spring, Summer, Fall);
```

5. Write a for loop that runs from 'Z' to 'A' and prints only the consonants. Test each character against the set of vowels.

6. a. Write a case statement that tests if Today is a working day. Print either the message 'Workday' or 'Weekend'. Assume Today is type Day, an enumerated type that has the days of the week as its values.

   b. Is it necessary to guard this case statement?

7. Write an `if` statement that will write out `True` or `False` according to the following conditions: either `Flag` is `True` or `Color` is `Red`, or both `Money` is `Plenty` and `Time` is `Up`.

8. Write a statement to assign a value of `True` to the Boolean variable `Overtime` only if a worker's weekly `Hours` are greater than 40.

9. a. Write a Boolean expression using the `Ord` function that will determine whether the ordinal value for `'a'` is greater than the ordinal value for `'Z'`.

   b. What is the value of this expression in ASCII?

10. Write the Pascal statements necessary to enter an integer between 0 and 9, inclusive, and convert it to an equivalent character value (e.g., 0 to `'0'`, 1 to `'1'`) to be stored in a character variable `Num`.

11. Write a Pascal function with `Integer` argument N and `Real` argument X that returns as its value the first N terms of the series

$$x + 1/2\, x^2 + 1/3\, x^3 + 1/4\, x^4 + \ldots + 1/n\, x^n$$

Directory: CHAP7
File: PROJ7_1.PAS

Programming Projects

1. An integer N is divisible by 9 if the sum of its digits is divisible by 9. Recall how we used `mod` in procedure `PrintDigits` (Fig. 7.3) to reverse a number's digits and print them one at a time. Develop a program to determine whether the following numbers are divisible by 9.

   $N = 154368$
   $N = 621594$
   $N = 123456$

2. Redo programming project 1 by reading each digit of the number to be tested into the type `Char` variable `Digit`. Form the sum of the numeric values of the digits. **Hint:** The numeric value of `Digit` (type `Char`) is `Ord(Digit) - Ord('0')`.

3. A number is said to be *perfect* if the sum of its divisors (except for itself) is equal to itself. For example, 6 is a perfect number because the sum of its divisors (1 + 2 + 3) is 6. The number 8 is said to be *deficient* because the sum of its divisors (1 + 2 + 4) is only 7. The number 12 is said to be *abundant* because the sum of its divisors (1 + 2 + 3 + 4 + 6) is 16. Write a program that lists the factors of the numbers between 1 and 100 and classifies each number as perfect, deficient, or abundant.

4. Find out how to access the printer from a Pascal program running on your computer system. Write a program for generating a bar graph on the printer that summarizes the rainfall in Bedrock for one year. Include the average monthly rainfall and the maximum monthly rainfall during the year as part of the program output.

   Prompt the user for the amount rainfall for a particular month and instruct the computer to send an appropriate output line to the printer. Assume that no one month will have more than 14 inches of rainfall. Your graph should resemble the graph that follows:

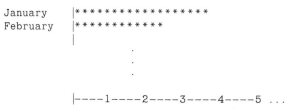

```
January     |* * * * * * * * * * * * * * *
February    |* * * * * * * * * * *
            |
                      .
                      .
                      .

            |----1----2----3----4----5 ...

            Inches of Rainfall
```

As part of your solution, write procedures that correspond to the procedure headers shown below.

```
procedure WriteMonth (Month {input} : Integer);
{Writes the string corresponding to the value of Month.}

GetMonthlyTotal (Month {input} : Integer;
                    var Inches {output},
                        MaxInches {input/output},
                        TotInches {input/output} : Real);
{
  User is prompted for Inches of rainfall during a Month.
  MaxInches and TotInches are updated so that they contain the
  maximum and the total inches of rainfall input so far.
}

procedure DrawBar (Month {input} : Integer;
                   Inches {input} : Real);
{
  Draws a bar whose length is computed from Inches and whose label is
  determined by the value of Month.
}

procedure DrawScaleLine;
{Draws scale and label at bottom of graph.}
```

5. The interest paid on a savings account is compounded daily. This means that if you start with *StartBal* (in dollars) in the bank, at the end of the first day you will have a balance of

$$StartBal \times (1 + Rate/365)$$

where *Rate* is the annual interest rate (0.10 if the annual rate is 10 percent). At the end of the second day, you will have

$$StartBal \times (1 + Rate/365) \times (1 + Rate/365)$$

and at the end of N days you will have

$$StartBal \times (1 + Rate/365)^N$$

dollars. Write a program that processes a set of data records, each of which contains values for *StartBal, Rate,* and *N*, and computes the final account balance.

6. The bisection method is another means of finding an approximate root for the equation f(X) = 0 on the interval XLeft to XRight, inclusive (assuming the function is continuous on this interval). The interval endpoints (XLeft and XRight) and the tolerance for the approximation (Epsilon) are entered by the user.

   The bisection method calls for the identification of an interval [XLeft, XRight] that is less than Epsilon in length over which f(X) changes sign (from positive to negative or vice versa). The midpoint (XMid = (XLeft + XRight)/2.0)) of the interval will be an approximation to the root of the equation when f(XMid) is very close to 0. Of course, if you find a value of XMid so that f(XMid) = 0, you have found a very good approximation of the root and the algorithm should stop.

   One way to detect a sign change is to examine the value of the products f(XLeft) * f(XMid) and f(XMid) * f(XRight). If one of the products is negative, then a sign change has occurred over that interval (either [XLeft, XMid] or [XMid, XRight]). If neither product is negative, there is no root in the interval [XLeft, XRight]. If the sign change occurs in the interval [XLeft, XMid], let XRight = XMid and repeat the process. Similarly, if the sign change occurs in the interval [XMid, XRight], let XLeft = XMid and repeat the process. Figure 7.14 shows an example of a root in the interval [XLeft, XMid].

Figure 7.14   Root in Interval [XLeft, XMid]

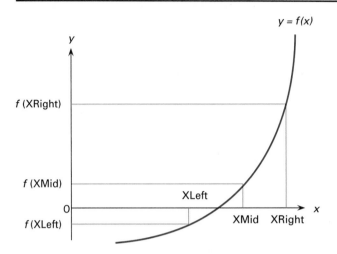

Write a program that uses the bisection method to determine an approximation to the equation

$$5x^3 - 2x^2 + 3 = 0$$

over the interval [-1, 1] using Epsilon = 0.0001.

7. We can approximate the area under the curve described by a function f by dividing the area into a number of rectangles and then accumulating the sum of all the rectangular areas. Figure 7.15 shows an example of the *midpoint method,* so named because the curve intersects each rectangle at its middle (as measured along the x-axis). The area of each rectangle is w (its width) times the function value at its midpoint. The area of the rectangle with left endpoint x_1 is $w * f(x_1 + w/2)$. If the interval $[a, b]$ is divided into n rectangles, the area under the curve is represented by the sum

$$Area = w \sum_{i=0}^{n-1} f(a + i * w + w/2)$$

where w is $(b - a)/n$ and the first rectangle begins at $x = a$, the second at $x = a + w$, the third at $x = a + 2w$, and so on.

Write a program that uses the midpoint approximation to find the area under the curve (the value of the definite integral) for the function

$$f(x) = -3x^2 + 2x + 4$$

over the interval [-2, 3]. Test your program using several different values of n. The larger n is, the better the approximation should be.

Figure 7.15 Midpoint Method   **339**

Chapter Review

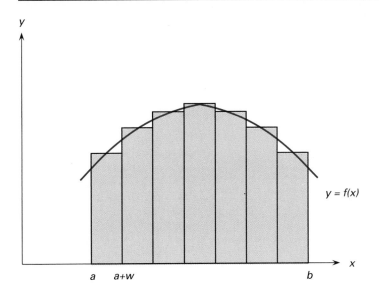

8. Experiments that are too expensive or too dangerous to perform are often simulated on a computer when the computer is able to provide a good representation of the experiment. Find out how to call the random-number generator (usually a function that returns a real value in the range 0 to 1) for your Pascal system. Write a program that uses the random-number generator to simulate the dropping of glass rods, which break into three pieces. The purpose of the experiment is to estimate the probability that the lengths of the three pieces are such that they might form the sides of a triangle.

   For the purposes of this experiment, you can assume that a glass rod always breaks into three pieces. If you use the line segment 0 to 1 (on the real number line) as a mathematical model of a glass rod, a random-number generator (function) can be used to generate two numbers between 0 and 1 that represent the coordinates of the breaks. The triangle inequality (the sum of the lengths of two sides of a triangle is always greater than the length of the third side) may be used to test the length of each piece against the lengths of the other two pieces.

   To estimate the probability that the pieces of a rod would form a triangle, you will need to repeat the experiment many times and count the number of times a triangle can be formed from the pieces. The probability estimate is the number of successes divided by the total number of rods dropped. Your program should prompt the user for the number of rods to drop and allow the experiment to be repeated.

INTERVIEW
James D. Foley

James Foley is Professor of Computer Science and Director of the new Graphics, Visualization, and Usability Center in the College of Computing at Georgia Institute of Technology. His interests include user interfaces and interactive computer graphics; his research focuses on building UIDE, the User Interface Design Environment.

How would you define "human-computer interaction"? Why is it important?

I would define it by analogy to person-to-person communication. People communicate back and forth using a combination of words, gestures, and facial expressions to represent information that they want to convey to each other. Human computer interaction addresses the ways in which humans and computers communicate. We have to tell the computer what we want and the computer has to tell us what information it has. Human-computer interaction looks at the language that encompasses this two-way communication: from the person to the computer and from the computer to the person.

The challenge is to design a language that makes it easy for the person to communicate to the computer and that enables the computer to respond in a form most understandable to people. Graphics plays an important part because graphical representations are often more understandable—that is, you can get information out of a chart of data, for example, more quickly than from a column of data.

Computer-human interaction is important in both an eco-nomic sense and a broader sense. In an economic sense, it is really the last frontier in the growth of the computer industry. The only thing keeping the computer industry growing is being able to do more and more things with computers. To get computers in the hands of more and more people, we need to find new forms of human-computer communication that will enable and facilitate new types of work.

In a broader sense, human-computer interaction strives to expand people's capabilities and intellectual leverage, so people can do their jobs more quickly, concentrate on the intellectually fulfilling parts of a job, and have access to more information more quickly.

What has influenced you the most in your own work?

I started out in graphics and came to realize that graphics was only an enabler—an important enabler, and one where research issues are plentiful—but the experience of building in-

teractive computer graphics systems and seeing the power they brought to people got me interested in human-computer interaction, as well as continuing my interest in computer graphics.

It seems the most dramatic achievements in computer science have occurred in the area of graphics. Can the gains made in the 80s be matched in the 90s, or has this field matured to the point where achievements will be more evolutionary than revolutionary?

Yes, the achievements will be more evolutionary than revolutionary. As you go from year to year now, the gains in realism are smaller than they used to be because we've done all the easy things. Making pictures more and more realistic is essentially becoming a matter of dealing with mathematical formulations of physics, of how light interacts with surfaces, and of modeling of objects. We know how to model things that are geometrically shaped and to some extent those that are probabilistically or randomly shaped, like the branching patterns of trees, and we're making progress on doing things that don't have nice mathematical formulations.

A question that I and others keep asking is "how realistic is realistic enough?" We sometimes get preoccupied with making pictures more and more realistic, but we may not always need the picture to be completely realistic. In fact, some studies have shown that realistic detail can sometimes get in the way of the message

to be conveyed. I think the biggest growth for graphics is not in making pictures more and more realistic but in finding creative new ways in which graphics can be used to leverage productivity.

For someone electing to concentrate in the area of graphics, how important is it to understand the underlying hardware principles?

It depends on what you want to do. It's analogous to whether you want to be a race car driver or an automobile designer. If you're the race car driver that would correspond to trying to get the most you can out of the current technology. You need to understand some of the underlying hardware in order to make it work as well as possible—which operations are fast and which are slow, how to organize the data so that access speeds are maximized, and so on. If you want to be an automobile designer, you need to understand the hardware very well. I think most people who study graphics are in the race car driver category.

What exciting things are being done today in the area of user interfaces?

Exciting things are going on in the area of virtual realities, creating 3D environments that appear to be real, behave realistically, and with which you interact realistically. Speech recognition is another exciting area, as are the gesture-based interfaces, or what's now called "pen computing." Pen comput-

ing allow users to use a stylus on a liquid crystal display as they would write on a piece of paper. All three developments are making the way we interact with computers more like the way we interact with the real world, so we need to learn less about the system and transfer the skills and knowledge we use in the real world to working with the computer.

What advice do you have for students who want to work in human-computer interaction?

If you want to study human-computer interaction, there are two computing systems that you have to understand: the one on the desk and the one in your head. You need to understand the input/output channels for the human processor, as it is sometimes called—the eyes, ears, hands, and fingers—and you need to understand these capabilities as well as the capabilities of the computer. That means studying psychology, particularly cognitive psychology and perceptual psychology, and human factors. I like to compare people who get involved in human-computer interaction to the "Renaissance man," because to do a good job of designing computer interfaces you have to have a breadth of understanding beyond computer science, understanding both the human processor and the application area for which you are designing, and be open to learning about a new discipline.

8

Input/Output and Text Files

This chapter covers some of the fine points of input and output in Pascal. It discusses how to read multiple data items of different types from a data line. It also provides a complete discussion of text files, or files of characters, and describes the Pascal functions and features for reading and writing text files.

8.1 Reading a Line of Characters

In this section, you will see how Pascal reads a line of characters. We will introduce one procedure, Read, and one function, EOLN, that can be used for this purpose.

The Read Procedure

So far we have used the ReadLn procedure to read data into a program. Pascal also provides the Read procedure for data entry. Unlike ReadLn, Read can continue to read data from the same data line during successive calls. We often use Read in a loop to read a sequence of data characters into a single input variable, as shown next.

■ Example 8.1

The program in Fig. 8.1 reads a sentence ending in a period and counts the number of blanks in that sentence. Each character entered after the prompting message is read into the variable Next and tested to see if it is a blank.

The statement

```
Read (Next)
```

which appears twice in the program, reads one character at a time from the data line because Next is type Char. The while loop exit occurs after the sentinel character ('.') is read. After loop exit, ReadLn advances the cursor to the start of the next line.   ■

Figure 8.1   Counting Blanks in a Sentence

Directory: CHAP8
File: BLANKCOU.PAS

```
program BlankCount (Input, Output);
{Counts the number of blanks in a sentence}
  const
    Blank = ' ';                     {character being counted}
    Sentinel = '.';                  {sentinel character}

  var
    Next  : Char;                    {next character in sentence}
    Count : Integer;                 {number of blank characters}

begin  {BlankCount}
  WriteLn ('Enter a sentence ending with a "', Sentinel, '" ');
  WriteLn ('and then press RETURN');
```

```
{Process each data character up to the sentinel.}
Count := 0;                          {Initialize Count.}
Read (Next);                         {Get first character.}
while Next <> Sentinel do
   begin
     if Next = Blank then
       Count := Count + 1;           {Increment blank count.}
     Read (Next)                     {Get next character.}
   end;  {while}
ReadLn;                              {Skip the RETURN.}

  WriteLn ('The number of blanks is ', Count :1)
end.  {BlankCount}


Enter a sentence ending with a "." and then press RETURN
There was an old woman who lived in a shoe.
The number of blanks is 9
```

Like the ReadLn statement, the Read statement causes input data to be stored in the variables specified in its input list. The statements

```
Read (Next)    |    ReadLn (Next)
```

cause one data character to be read into the character variable Next, but there is one important difference between them. After the ReadLn statement is executed, the computer automatically skips over any characters remaining on the current data line to the start of the next data line; any additional characters typed on the current data line are not processed. There is no skip to the next line after a Read statement is executed; therefore, any additional characters typed on the current line are processed by the next Read or ReadLn statement.

The following statement sequences are equivalent:

```
Read (Next);    |    ReadLn (Next)
ReadLn          |
```

The ReadLn statement skips over all characters on the current data line through the character that represents the Return key. We use the symbol <eoln> (for *End Of LiNe*) to denote the character that appears at the end of a data line when the Return key is pressed.

Read Procedure

Form: Read (*input-list*)

Example: Read (Next, N, X)

Interpretation: Data are entered into each variable specified in the *input-list*. There must be one data item for each variable in the *input-list*, and the order of the data must correspond to the order of the variables in the *input-list*. Insert one or more blank characters between numeric data items. Do not insert any extra blanks between consecutive character data items.

> The first character that follows the last one read will be processed when
> the next Read or ReadLn statement is executed. Press the Return key after
> you have entered all data items.
> **Note:** Read is system dependent. On some systems, data characters are
> processed as they are typed in; on others, the data characters are not
> processed until after the Return key is pressed, so you can edit the data
> line (using the Backspace key).

ReadLn Without an Input List

Form: ReadLn

Interpretation: Skips over any characters on the current data line that are
not read (through the <eoln>) without processing them.

The EOLN Function

In Fig. 8.1, we used a sentinel character (a period) to indicate the end of a
sentence. Since the Return key is used to terminate a line of data characters,
you may be wondering whether it is possible for a program to determine that
the next "character" to be processed is <eoln>. Pascal provides a function named
EOLN that returns True when the next data character is the <eoln>; otherwise,
EOLN returns False.

■ Example 8.2

The following while loop counts the number of blanks in a data line; it uses
the EOLN function for loop control.

```
{Process each input character up to the <eoln>.}
Count := 0;
while not EOLN do
  begin
    Read (Next);              {Get each character.}
    if Next <> Blank then
      Count := Count + 1
  end; {while}
ReadLn;                       {Skip the <eoln>.}
```

The while condition not EOLN is True when the result returned by function
EOLN is False. EOLN returns False when the next data character is not the
<eoln>. Therefore, the Read statement in the loop body reads all data characters
in the current data line. When the next character is <eoln>, not EOLN is False,
so loop exit occurs and the ReadLn statement executes, skipping over the
<eoln>.

We can substitute this loop for the one in Fig. 8.1 if we remove the priming
Read that precedes the loop body. A priming Read is not necessary when a

while loop uses the EOLN condition to test for the <eoln>. This test should be made before the first data character is read.

Although the <eoln> character is not actually read into Next in the preceding loop, a Pascal program can read this character. When this happens, Pascal stores the blank character in the variable receiving <eoln> as its data item. ∎

∎ Example 8.3

Sometimes you may want to read a number as a string of individual characters, thus enabling a program to detect and ignore possible data entry errors. Procedure ReadInt in Fig. 8.2 reads in a string of characters ending with <eoln> and ignores any character that is not a digit. It also computes and returns the value of the number (an integer) formed by the digits only. For example, if the characters $15,43AB2% are entered, the value returned through NumData will be 15432.

Figure 8.2 Reading a Number as a String of Characters

```
procedure ReadInt (var NumData {output} : Integer);
{
 Reads consecutive characters ending with <eoln>.  Computes
 the integer value of the digit characters, ignoring non-digits.
 Pre : None
 Post: Returns in NumData the numeric value of the digit
       characters read.  Advances to the next line.
}
  const
    Base = 10;                           {the number system base}

  var
    Next : Char;                         {each character read}
    Digit : Integer;    {the value of each numeric character}

begin  {ReadInt}
  {Accumulate the numeric value of the digits in NumData}
  NumData := 0;                          {Initial value is zero.}
  while not EOLN do
    begin
      Read (Next);
      if ('0' <= Next) and (Next <= '9') then
        begin {digit}
          Digit := Ord(Next) - Ord('0');      {Get digit value.}
          NumData := Base * NumData + Digit  {Add digit value.}
        end {digit}
    end; {while}
  ReadLn                                  {Skip <eoln>.}
end;  {ReadInt}
```

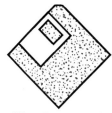

Directory: CHAP8
File: READINT.PRO

In Fig. 8.2, the statements

```
Digit := Ord(Next) - Ord('0');      {Get digit value}
NumData := Base * NumData + Digit    {Add digit value}
```

assign to Digit an integer value between 0 (for character value '0') and 9 (for character value '9'). The number being accumulated in NumData is multiplied by 10, and the value of Digit is added to it. Table 8.1 traces the procedure execution for the data characters 3N5<eoln>; the value returned is 35. ■

Table 8.1 Trace of Execution of Procedure ReadInt for 3N5<eoln>

Statement	Next	Digit	NumData	Effect
NumData := 0			0	Initialize NumData
while not EOLN do				EOLN is False, not EOLN is True
Read (Next)	3			Get character
if ('0'<=Next) and (Next<='9')				'3' is a digit
Digit := Ord(Next) − Ord('0')		3		digit value is 3
NumData := Base*NumData+Digit			3	NumData gets 3
while not EOLN do				EOLN is False, not EOLN is True
Read (Next)	N			Get character
if ('0'<=Next) and (Next<='9')				'N' is not a digit
while not EOLN do				EOLN is False, not EOLN is True
Read (Next)	5			Get character
if ('0'<=Next) and (Next<='9')				'5' is a digit
Digit := Ord(Next) − Ord('0')		5		digit value is 5
NumData := Base*NumData+Digit			35	NumData gets 10*3+5
while not EOLN do				EOLN is True, not EOLN is False
ReadLn				Skip <eoln>

Using ReadLn After a Loop End

After the loop in Fig. 8.2 is exited, the statement

```
ReadLn                              {Skip <eoln>.}
```

executes. You will often find a ReadLn statement right after the end of a loop that uses not EOLN as its loop repetition test. The purpose of this ReadLn is to skip over the <eoln> character that caused loop repetition to terminate. If the <eoln> is not skipped, the first character processed by the next Read or ReadLn will be the <eoln>, not the character at the start of the next data line. This can cause unexpected program results and/or lead to a run-time error.

Exercises for Section 8.1

Self-Check

1. Refer to program `BlankCount` (Fig. 8.1). In terms of the value computed for `Count`, would it make any difference if `not EOLN` were used as the `while` loop condition, rather than `Next <> Sentinel`?
2. Explain why `Read` might be preferred to `ReadLn` as a means of obtaining numeric data from the user of an interactive program.

Programming

1. Write a procedure that reads a real literal typed from the keyboard one character at a time and returns the number of digits to the left of the decimal point and the number of digits to the right of the decimal point.

8.2 Review of Batch Processing

Although we discussed batch processing and the use of data files in Section 2.8, all our example programs so far have been interactive. Interactive programs read all input data from the keyboard and display all outputs on the screen. This mode of operation is fine for small programs. However, as you begin to write larger programs, you will see that there are many advantages to using data files for program input and output.

You can create a data file using a text editor in the same way that you create a program file. Once the data file is entered in computer memory, you can carefully check and edit each line and then save the final data file as a permanent disk file. When you enter data interactively, you do not always have the opportunity to examine and edit the data. Also, the data is processed as it is entered—it is not saved permanently.

After the data file is saved on disk, you can instruct your program to read data from the data file rather than from the keyboard. Recall from Chapter 2 that this mode of program execution is called *batch processing*. Because the program data are supplied before execution begins, prompting messages are not required in batch programs. Instead, batch programs must contain display statements that echo print data values, thereby providing a record of the data that are read and processed in a particular run.

Besides giving you the opportunity to check for errors in your data, using data files provides another advantage. Because a data file can be read many times, during debugging you can rerun the program as often as you need to, without reentering the test data each time.

You can also instruct your program to write its output to a disk file rather than display it on the screen. When output is written to the screen, it disappears after it scrolls off the screen and cannot be retrieved. However, if program output is written to a disk file, you have a permanent copy of it. You can get a hard copy of a disk file by sending it to the printer, or you can use an operating system command such as

> TYPE *filename*

to list file *filename* on the screen.

Finally, you can use the output file generated by one program as a data file for another program. For example, a payroll program may compute employee salaries and write each employee's name and salary to an output file. A second program that prints employee checks could use the output of the payroll program as its data file.

Exercises for Section 8.2

Self-Check

1. List three advantages of writing your program output to a data file rather than simply displaying it on the computer screen.
2. a. For a computer program that handles the booking of airline reservations, would batch processing of data be preferable to interactive data processing? Explain your answer.
   b. What about a program for printing student transcripts at a university?

8.3 Text Files

Pascal can process two kinds of files: text files and binary files. We examine text files in this chapter and binary files in Chapter 15. A *text file* is a collection of characters stored under the same name in secondary memory (i.e., on a disk). A text file has no fixed size. To mark the end of a text file, the computer places a special character, called the *end-of-file* character (denoted as <eof>), following the last character in a text file.

As you create a text file using an editor program, you press the Return key to separate the file into lines. Each time you press this key, the <eoln> character is placed in the file.

The following lines represent a text file consisting of two lines of letters, blank characters, and the special characters . and !.

```
This is a text file!<eoln>
It has two lines.<eoln><eof>
```

Each line ends with the <eoln> character, and the <eof> character follows the last <eoln> in the file. For convenience in examining the file's contents, we have listed each line of the file (through <eoln>) as a separate line, although this would not be the case in the actual disk file. The disk file consists of a sequence of characters occupying consecutive storage locations on a *track* of the disk, as shown next.

```
This is a text file!<eoln>It has two lines.<eoln><eof>
```

This file would occupy 40 bytes of disk storage, including one byte for each

<eoln> and one byte for the <eof>. The first character of the second line (I) would follow directly after the last character of the first line (the <eoln> character).

The Keyboard and the Screen as Text Files

In interactive programming, Pascal uses the system files Input and Output to represent the keyboard and the screen, respectively. Both Input and Output are considered text files because their individual components are characters.

Normally we enter one line of data at a time at the keyboard, pressing the Return key to indicate the end of a data line. Pressing the Return key inserts the <eoln> character in system file Input. Normally in interactive programming, we use a sentinel value to indicate the end of data rather than attempting to place the <eof> character in system file Input (although the <eof> character could be used). No single key represents the <eof> character, so most systems use the Control key followed by a letter (e.g., in MS-DOS, Control Z).

Displaying characters on the screen is equivalent to writing characters to system file Output. We can use the Write or WriteLn procedure to write output characters to the screen. When we use the WriteLn procedure, an <eoln> character is added after the output characters are written (or displayed), moving the cursor to the start of the next line of the screen.

The EOF Function

The <eoln> and <eof> characters are different from the other characters in a text file because they mark the end of a line and the end of a file, respectively, and are not data characters. A program can read the <eoln> character into a type Char variable; however, the character value ' ' (blank or space) will be stored in that variable, and its value printed as a blank. If a program attempts to read the <eof> character, an attempt to read beyond end of file run-time error occurs.

Pascal provides two functions that enable us to determine whether the next character is <eoln> or <eof>. We have already discussed the function EOLN, which returns a value of True if the next character is the <eoln> character; the function EOF returns a value of True if the next character is the <eof> character.

SYNTAX
DISPLAY

EOLN Function

Form: EOLN(*filename*)

Interpretation: The function result is True if the next character to be processed in *filename* is the <eoln> character; otherwise, the function result is False.

Notes: If *filename* is omitted, it is assumed to be the system file Input. It is an error to call the EOLN function if EOF(*filename*) is True.

EOF Function

Form: EOF (*filename*)

Interpretation: The function result is True if the next character to be processed in file *filename* is the `<eof>` character; otherwise, the function result is False.

Notes: If *filename* is omitted, it is assumed to be the system file Input. If a Read operation is attempted when the value of EOF is True, an `attempt to read past the end of the input file` error occurs and the program stops.

Declaring a Text File

Before we can reference a text file in a program, we must declare it, just as with any other data object. For example, the declaration

```
var
   InData, OutData : Text;
```

identifies InData and OutData as variables of type Text. Text is the predefined data type for a text file; therefore, InData and OutData are the names of text files in any program containing the above declaration.

In addition, the program heading must include the names of all disk files being processed. So if program IODemo1 read all its data from file InData and displayed its output on the screen, you would use the program heading

```
program IODemo1 (InData, Output);
```

If program IODemo2 read all its input data from file InData and wrote its output to file OutData, you would use the program heading

```
program IODemo2 (InData, OutData);
```

It is possible for a program to read data from more than one input file or to write results to more than one output file. You would use the program heading

```
program IODemo3 (Input, InData, Output, OutData);
```

if some input data came from the keyboard and some from file InData, and some output was displayed on the screen and some written to file OutData. The file names can appear in any order in the program heading.

If you did not need to retain file OutData on disk after program IODemo3 finishes execution, you would omit its name from the program heading. A file that exists only during the execution of a program is called a *temporary file*.

To access a text file created by a Pascal program after the program finishes execution, we must know its *directory name,* which is the name used to identify it in the disk's directory. A disk's directory lists the names of all files stored on the disk. A file's directory name must follow whatever conventions apply on your particular computer system. For example, some systems limit a file name to eight characters, a period, and a three-letter extension. Many programmers use the extension `.DAT` or `.TXT` to designate a text file.

You need to communicate to the operating system the directory names of any files you are using so that the system knows the correspondence between file variables and directory names. This process is system dependent. Your instructor will give you the details for your particular system; we will show you some examples later in this section.

Preparing a File for Input or Output

Before a program can use a file, the file must be prepared for input or output. At any given time, a file can be used for input or for output, but not for both simultaneously. If a file is being used for input, its components can be read as data. If a file is being used for output, new components can be written to the file.

The procedure call statement

```
Reset (InData);
```

prepares file `InData` for input by moving its file-position pointer to the beginning of the file. The *file-position pointer* selects the next character to be processed in the file. After the `Reset` operation is performed, the next character to be read is always the first character in the file; the `Reset` operation must be done before any characters are read from file `InData`. The `Reset` operation fails if file `InData` was not previously saved on disk.

The procedure call statement

```
Rewrite (OutData);
```

prepares file `OutData` for output. If no file `OutData` is saved on disk, a file that is initially empty (i.e., `OutData` has no characters) is created. If a file `OutData` has already been saved on disk, its file-position pointer moves to the beginning of the file. Any program output replaces the old data associated with file `OutData`; all old data are lost. There is no need to prepare the system files `Input` or `Output` for processing.

You can read and process a file a second time in the same program run by performing the `Reset` operation again. A program can also read and echo print an output file that it creates by calling the `Reset` procedure with the newly created file as its parameter. The `Reset` operation prepares this file for input, and your program can then read data from that file.

Reset Procedure

Form: Reset (*infile*)

Interpretation: File *infile* is prepared for input, and the file-position pointer for *infile* is moved to the first file component. The Reset operation is automatically performed on system file Input, so Reset (Input) is not required.

Rewrite Procedure

Form: Rewrite (*outfile*)

Interpretation: File *outfile* is prepared for output, and *outfile* is initialized to an empty file. Any data previously associated with file *outfile* are lost. The Rewrite operation is automatically performed on system file Output, so Rewrite (Output) is not required.

Techniques for Specifying Directory Names

Some Pascal systems use an extended form of the Reset and Rewrite procedures to associate a file name used in a Pascal program with the file's directory name. For example, the procedure call statements

```
Reset (InData, 'InData.DAT');
Rewrite (OutData, 'OutFile.DAT');
```

specify that file variable InData corresponds to disk file InData.DAT and that file variable OutData corresponds to disk file OutFile.DAT. Note that this use of Reset and Rewrite is nonstandard and may not be supported on your system.

In Turbo Pascal, the Assign statement is used to associate a file variable with a disk file. The statements

```
Assign (InData, 'InData.DAT');
Assign (OutData, 'OutFile.DAT');
```

must precede the Reset or Rewrite statement.

In VAX Pascal, the Open statement is used for this purpose.

```
Open (InData, 'InData.DAT', Old);
Open (OutData, 'OutFile.DAT');
```

The parameter Old indicates that file InData.DAT was previously created.

Reading and Writing a Text File

You've learned how to declare a text file and how to prepare a text file for processing. All that remains is to find out how to instruct the computer to read data from an input file or to write program results to an output file.

If `NextCh` is a type `Char` variable, we know that the procedure call statement

```
Read (NextCh)
```

reads the next data character typed at the keyboard into `NextCh`. This is really an abbreviation for the procedure call statement

```
Read (Input, NextCh)
```

which has the same effect. The first parameter for a `Read` (or `ReadLn`) operation should be a file name. However, the file name may be omitted if it is file `Input`.

The statement

```
Read (InData, NextCh)
```

reads the next character from file `InData` into `NextCh`, where the next character is the one selected by the file-position pointer. The computer automatically advances the file-position pointer after each `Read` operation. Remember to prepare `InData` for input using `Reset` before the first `Read` operation.

In a similar manner, the procedure call statements

```
Write (Ch)
```

and

```
Write (Output, Ch)
```

display the value of `Ch` on the screen. The statement

```
Write (OutData, Ch)
```

writes the value of `Ch` to the end of file `OutData`. Remember to prepare `OutData` for output using `Rewrite` before the first `Write` operation.

■ Example 8.4

For security reasons, it is a good idea to have a backup, or duplicate, copy of a file in case the original is lost. Even though many operating systems provide a command that copies a file, we will write our own Pascal program to do this. Program `CopyFile` in Fig. 8.3 copies each character in file `InData` to file `OutData`. The program heading lists the three text files that are processed, including file `Output` (the screen).   ■

Figure 8.3 Copying a File

```
program CopyFile (Output, InData, OutData);
{Copies file represented by InData to file OutData}

   var
      InData,           {data file}
      OutData : Text;   {output file}

   procedure CopyLine (var Indata {input},
                           OutData {output} : Text);
   {
```

Directory: CHAP8
File: COPYFILE.PAS

```
    Copies a line of file InData to file OutData.
    Pre : InData is opened for input and OutData for output.
    Post: Next line of InData is written to OutData.
          The last character processed in InData is <eoln>;
          The last character written to OutData is <eoln>.
}
  var
    Next : Char;        {each data character}

begin {CopyLine}
  {Copy all data characters from InData to OutData.}
  while not EOLN(InData) do
    begin
      Read (InData, NextCh);
      Write (OutData, NextCh)
    end; {while}

  {Process the <eoln>. }
  ReadLn (InData);
  WriteLn (OutData)
end; {CopyLine}

begin {CopyFile}
  {Prepare the text files for input/output.}
  Reset (InData);
  Rewrite (OutData);

  {Copy each character from InData to OutData.}
  while not EOF(InData) do
    CopyLine (InData, OutData);

  {Display a message on the screen.}
  WriteLn (Output, 'Input file copied to output file.')
end. {CopyFile}

Input file copied to output file.
```

After `InData` and `OutData` have been prepared, the `while` loop in procedure `CopyFile` executes. This loop calls `CopyLine` to copy each line of the input file to the output file. The main program loop terminates when the `<eof>` character is reached.

Within `CopyLine`, the statements

```
Read (InData, NextCh);
Write (OutData, NextCh)
```

read the next character of the file `InData` into `NextCh` and write that character to file `OutData`. When the next character in `InData` is `<eoln>`, loop exit occurs and the statements

```
ReadLn (InData);
WriteLn (OutData)
```

execute. The data file, `InData`, is the only parameter in the call to `ReadLn`. Because `ReadLn` has no input list, it does not read any data but simply advances the file-position pointer for `InData` past the `<eoln>` character. The `WriteLn` procedure writes the `<eoln>` character to file `OutData`.

Figure 8.4 shows the result of executing this statement pair after reaching the end of the first line of file InData. The next character to process in file InData is in color. Part a) shows the situation just before executing this statement pair; part b) shows the situation just after.

Figure 8.4   Effect of First ReadLn and WriteLn

```
            File InData                          File OutData
This is a text file!<eoln>              This is a text file!
It has two lines.<eoln><eof>
```

a. Before ReadLn and WriteLn

```
            File InData                          File OutData
This is a text file!<eoln>              This is a text file!<eoln>
It has two lines.<eoln><eof>
```

b. After ReadLn and WriteLn

It is interesting to consider the effect of deleting either of the statements. If WriteLn (OutData) is deleted, the <eoln> character will not be written to file OutData whenever the end of a line is reached in file InData. Consequently, OutData will contain all the characters in file InData but on one line.

If ReadLn (InData) is deleted, the file-position pointer will not be advanced, and the <eoln> character will still be the next character to process. When CopyLine is called again, EOLN(InData) will still be True, so the while loop exit occurs immediately, and another <eoln> character is written to file OutData. This continues "forever," or until the program is terminated by the program user or its time limit is exceeded.

After each <eoln> character is processed, we return from CopyLine, and the main program loop calls function EOF to test whether more data lines are left to be copied. When the <eof> character is the next character to process, the EOF function returns True, so we exit the main loop. This is the situation after the second line from file InData has been read:

```
            File InData                          File OutData
This is a text file!<eoln>              This is a text file!<eoln>
It has two lines.<eoln><eof>            It has two lines.<eoln>
```

After loop exit, the statement

```
WriteLn (Output, 'Input file copied to output file.')
```

writes a message to file Output (the screen). After program CopyFile is finished, the computer automatically writes the <eof> character at the end of file Out-Data.

Default File Parameters

In Fig. 8.3, the text file InData is the file parameter in the calls to functions EOLN and EOF. A common error is forgetting to use a file parameter with EOLN or EOF. In that case, the system uses Input as the *default file parameter*. Similarly, if you forget to use a file parameter with Read/ReadLn or Write/WriteLn, the system uses Input or Output by default. Normally no error diagnostic is displayed, so the cause of the error is not obvious.

Explicit File Parameters versus Default Parameters

The last WriteLn statement in Fig. 8.3 contains an explicit reference to the file parameter Output, even though Output is the default file parameter. We recommend the use of an explicit file parameter for the sake of consistency in programs that process other text files. If you always use a file parameter in these programs, you are less likely to forget one that is needed. If you forget a file parameter, the default file (Input or Output) will be processed instead of the intended file.

Variable File Parameters

Procedure CopyLine has two variable parameters, InData and OutData. It may seem strange to declare file InData as variable, since this parameter represents an input file. However, Pascal requires all file parameters to be variable because it may not be possible to make a local copy of a very large file in memory.

Reading and Writing Numeric Data

When a value is being read into a type Char variable, only a single character is read regardless of what that character might be (e.g., a letter, a digit, a blank, the <eoln> character). Consequently, the file-position pointer is advanced one character position. When a value is being read into a numeric variable (type Integer or type Real), a group of characters is read, and the file-position pointer is advanced past all characters in the group.

When reading a numeric value, the computer skips over any leading blanks or <eoln> characters until it encounters a character that is neither a blank nor an <eoln> character. This character must be a sign or a digit; if it is not, an execution error such as non-digit found while reading number occurs, and the program stops. If the first character is valid, the computer continues reading characters until it encounters a character that cannot be part of the number; the terminating character should be a blank or an <eoln> character. The file-position pointer is advanced to the terminating character.

Although we have not done so in interactive programming, it is possible to read more than one number at a time or a mixture of numeric and character data. If several variables are listed in the parameter list for Read or ReadLn, then the computer reads data into each variable in the order in which the variable appears. The file-position pointer advances after each value is entered. When procedure Read is used, the file-position pointer advances to the first character that was not read. When ReadLn is used, the file-position pointer advances past any characters at the end of the current data line to the start of the next data line (i.e., past the next <eoln> character). Any characters skipped over in this way are not processed.

Table 8.2 shows several examples of Read and ReadLn statements and their effects. Assume that X is type Real, N is type Integer, C is type Char, and the first character processed is the first character in the file. The position of the file-position pointer after each Read operation is shown in color in the right column. The symbol □ denotes a blank character.

Table 8.2 Effect of Read/ReadLn

Statement and Effect	Next Character to Process
Read (InData, X, N, C) X is 1234.56, N is 789, C is ' '	1234.56□789□A345.67<eoln> W<eoln><eof>
Read (InData, X, N, C, C) X is 1234.56, N is 789, C is 'A'	1234.56□789□A345.67<eoln> W<eoln><eof>
ReadLn (InData, X, N, C) X is 1234.56, N is 789, C is ' '	1234.56□789□A345.67<eoln> W<eoln><eof>
Read (InData, X, C, N) X is 1234.56, C is ' ', N is 789	1234.56□789□A345.67<eoln> W<eoln><eof>
ReadLn (InData, X, C, N) X is 1234.56, C is ' ', N is 789	1234.56□789□A345.67<eoln> W<eoln><eof>
Read (InData, C, X, N) C is '1', X is 234.56, N is 789	1234.56□789□A345.67<eoln> W<eoln><eof>
ReadLn (InData, C, X, N) C is '1', X is 234.56, N is 789	1234.56□789□A345.67<eoln> W<eoln><eof>
ReadLn (InData, X, N); Read (InData, C); X is 1234.56, N is 789, C is 'W'	1234.56□789□A345.67<eoln> W<eoln><eof>
ReadLn (InData, X); ReadLn (InData, C); X is 1234.56, C is 'W'	1234.56□789□A345.67<eoln> W<eoln><eof>

Writing a numeric value to a file is similar to writing a numeric value to the screen. The computer writes the number as a sequence of digit characters. The character – precedes a negative number. The character . is inserted into a type Real value. You can specify the number of characters that represent a numeric value by using a format specification; otherwise, this specification is controlled by the Pascal system.

Read, ReadLn Procedures (for Text Files)

Form: Read   (*infile*, *input-list*)
             ReadLn (*infile*, *input-list*)

Example: Read (InData, X, Y, Z);
             ReadLn (InData, Ch1, Ch2)

Interpretation: A sequence of characters is read from file *infile* into the variables specified in *input-list*. The type of each variable in *input-list* must be Char, Integer, a subrange of Char or Integer, or Real. If the data type of a variable is Char, only a single character is read into that variable; if the data type of a variable is Integer or Real, a sequence of numeric characters is read, converted to a binary value, and stored in that variable. If Read is used, the file-position pointer for *infile* is advanced past the last character read. If ReadLn is used, the file-position pointer for *infile* is advanced to the start of the next line.

Notes: If *infile* is omitted, it is assumed to be the system file Input. File *infile* must first be prepared for input via Reset (*infile*), except when *infile* is Input. An error occurs if EOF(*infile*) is True before a Read operation is attempted.

Write, WriteLn Procedures (for Text Files)

Form: Write   (*outfile*, *output-list*)
             WriteLn (*outfile*, *output-list*)

Example: Write (MyResult, Salary);
             WriteLn (MyResult, Hours :3:1, ' $', Salary :4:2)

Interpretation: The characters specified by *output-list* are written to the end of file *outfile*. The type of each expression in *output-list* must be one of the standard data types (Boolean, Char, Integer, Real), a subrange of a standard data type, or a character string. If an expression is type Char, a single character is written to file *outfile*; otherwise, a sequence of characters may be written. If WriteLn is used, an <eoln> mark is written as the last character in *outfile*. The file-position pointer for *outfile* is at the end of the file.

Notes: If *outfile* is omitted, it is assumed to be the system file Output. File *outfile* must first be prepared for output via Rewrite (*outfile*), except when *outfile* is Output.

Self-Check

1. Let X be type `Real`, N type `Integer`, and C type `Char`. Indicate the contents of each variable after each `Read` operation is performed assuming that the file consists of the following lines and that the `Reset` operation occurs before each `Read`.

```
123 3.145 XYZ<eoln>
35 Z<eoln>
```

   a. `ReadLn (InData, N, X);  Read (InData, C)`
   b. `Read (InData, N, X, C);`
   c. `Read (InData, N, X, C, C);`
   d. `ReadLn (InData, N);  Read (InData, C);`
   e. `ReadLn (InData, X);  Read (InData, C, N);`
   f. `ReadLn (InData, C, N, X);  Read (InData, C);`
   g. `ReadLn (InData, C, C, C, X);  Read (InData, N);`
   h. `Read (InData, N, X, C, C, C, C, N);`
   i. `Read (InData, N, X, C, C, C, C);`
2. List the functions and procedures that can be used with variable identifiers of type `Text`.

Programming

1. Write a procedure that returns a count of the number of nonblank characters appearing on the current line of a data file.
2. Rewrite program `CopyFile` (Fig. 8.3) as a procedure with files `InData` and `OutData` as parameters.

8.4 Using Text Files

If one program writes its output to a disk file rather than to the screen, a second program may use that output file as its own data file. In this way, the two programs communicate with each other through the disk file. This section discusses an example of a program whose output file will be used as another program's data file.

Case Study: Preparing a Payroll File

Problem
Your company's accountant wants you to write two programs for processing the company's payroll. The first program is to read a data file consisting of employee salary data. The data for each employee are stored on two consecutive lines:

the first line is the employee's name, and the second line contains that employee's hours worked and hourly rate. A sample data file follows.

```
Peter Liacouras<eoln>
40.0 500.00<eoln>
Caryn Koffman<eoln>
20.0 10.00<eoln><eof>          ^z
```

The first program echoes each employee's name to an output file, followed by a line containing the employee's computed gross salary. It also computes and displays the total payroll amount. The output file corresponding to the preceding data file is shown next. The second line of the output file contains the product of the two values read from the second line of the data file.

```
Peter Liacouras<eoln>
20000.00<eoln>
Caryn Koffman<eoln>
200.00<eoln><eof>
```

The second program is to read the output file and print payroll checks based on the contents of that file. For example, the first check issued should be for $20,000.00 made out to Peter Liacouras.

Analysis
We will write the the first program now and leave the second one as a programming project (see programming project 1 at the end of this chapter). The program must copy each employee's name to the output file. It must also compute each employee's salary, copy it to the output file, and add it to the payroll total.

Data Requirements

Problem Inputs (from Data File InEmp)
```
NextCh : Char        {the letters in each employee's name}
Hours : Real         {each employee's hours worked}
Rate : Real          {each employee's hourly rate}
```

Problem Outputs (to Output File OutEmp)
```
NextCh : Char        {the letters in each employee's name}
Salary : Real        {each employee's salary}
```

Problem Output (to System File Output)
```
Payroll : Real       {the payroll total}
```

Design
The main program will prepare the files for input and output and call procedure ProcessEmp to process all employees and accumulate the total payroll. After ProcessEmp is finished, the main program will display the final payroll total.

Algorithm for Main Program
1. Prepare files InEmp and OutEmp.
2. Process all employees and compute payroll total.
3. Display the payroll total.

Algorithm Refinements
The algorithm for ProcessEmp follows. Step 3 of ProcessEmp is performed by procedure CopyLine (see Fig. 8.3). Figure 8.5 shows the structure chart.

Algorithm for ProcessEmp
1. Initialize payroll total to 0.0
2. while there are more employees do
    begin
        3. Read next employee's name from InEmp and write it to OutEmp.
        4. Read next employee's salary data.
        5. Compute next employee's salary.
        6. Write next employee's salary to OutEmp and add it to payroll total.
    end

Figure 8.5 Structure Chart for Writing the Payroll File

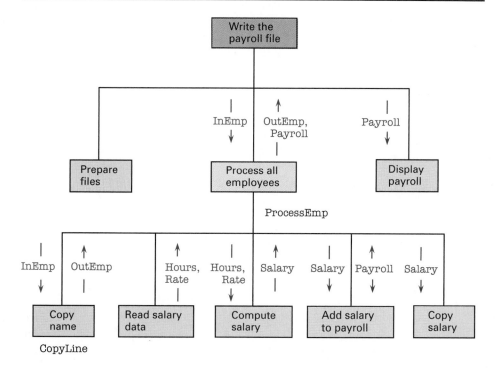

Case Study: Preparing a Payroll File, continued

Implementation

Figure 8.6 shows the complete program. The program uses three text files: Output, InEmp, and OutEmp. Besides InEmp and OutEmp, the only variable declared in the main program is Payroll. We declare variables Hours, Rate, and Salary in ProcessEmp and NextCh in CopyLine. This is consistent with our policy of declaring a variable in the highest-level module that processes it.

Figure 8.6 Writing a Payroll File

Directory: CHAP8
File: WRITEPAY.PAS

```
program WritePayroll (Output, InEmp, OutEmp);
{
  Writes each employee's name and gross salary to an
  output file and computes total payroll amount
}
  var
    InEmp,                  {data file}
    OutEmp : Text;          {output file}
    Payroll : Real;         {output - total payroll}

{Insert procedure CopyLine (see Fig. 8.3) here.}

  procedure ProcessEmp (var InEmp {input file},
                            OutEmp {output file} : Text;
                            var Payroll {output} : Real);
  {
    Processes all employees and computes payroll total.
    Pre : InEmp and OutEmp are prepared for input/output.
    Post: All employee data are copied from InEmp to OutEmp and
          the sum of their salaries is returned through Payroll.
    Uses: CopyLine
  }
    var
      Hours,                {input - hours worked}
      Rate,                 {input - hourly rate}
      Salary : Real;        {output - gross salary}

  begin  {ProcessEmp}
    Payroll := 0.0;
    While not EOF(InEmp) do
      begin
        CopyLine (InEmp, OutEmp);          {Copy employee name.}
        ReadLn (InEmp, Hours, Rate);       {Get salary data.}
        Salary := Hours * Rate;
        WriteLn (OutEmp, Salary :4:2);
        Payroll := Payroll + Salary
      end   {while}
  end; {ProcessEmp}

begin {WritePayroll}
  {Prepare InEmp and OutEmp}
  Reset (InEmp);
  Rewrite (OutEmp);

  {Process all employees and compute payroll total.}
  ProcessEmp (InEmp, OutEmp, Payroll);
```

```
{Display result}
   WriteLn (Output, 'Total payroll is $', Payroll :4:2)
end. {WritePayroll}
```

```
Total payroll is $20200.00
```

The `while` loop in `ProcessEmp` tests whether the next character is the `<eof>` character. If it is not, procedure `CopyLine` copies an employee's name from its input file (`InEmp`) to its output file (`OutEmp`). `CopyLine` processes every other line of file `InEmp`, starting with the first line.

After `CopyLine` processes the `<eoln>` character that follows an employee's name, the statement

```
   ReadLn (InEmp, Hours, Rate);     {Get salary data.}
```

reads that employee's salary data from `InEmp` and advances the file-position pointer to the first letter of the next employee's name. Next, the statement

```
   WriteLn (OutEmp, Salary :4:2);
```

writes the salary for the current employee to file `OutEmp`. After the current employee's salary is added to the payroll total, the next employee is processed.

The Importance of Advancing Past the <eoln> Character

It is easy to make an error when reading character data mixed with numeric data. Many problems are caused by not advancing past the `<eoln>` character. For example, consider what would happen if we attempted to use the statement

```
   Read (InEmp, Hours, Rate);     {Get salary data.}
```

to read the first employee's salary data instead of the call to `ReadLn`. The difficulty is that the `Read` procedure advances the file-position pointer for file `InEmp` up to the `<eoln>` character but not past it:

```
   40.0 500.00<eoln>
```

When `CopyLine` is called to copy the second employee's name, the `while` loop exit occurs immediately, without reading the name, because the next character is the `<eoln>` character. The `<eoln>` character is processed just before `CopyLine` returns to the main program, and the next character is now the first letter of an employee's name. When

```
   Read (InEmp, Hours, Rate);     {Get salary data.}
```

executes again, a non-digit found while reading number error occurs, and
the program stops.

Exercises for Section 8.4

Self-Check

1. a. What would be the effect, if any, of trailing blanks at the end of data lines
      in the data file for the program in Fig. 8.6?
   b. What would be the effect of blank lines?
2. How would placing the employee names and salary amounts on separate
   data lines in file OutEmp make it easier to write the program that will print
   the payroll checks?

Programming

1. Write a program that reads file OutEmp produced by program WritePayroll
   (Fig. 8.6) and displays a count of the number of employees processed by
   WritePayroll and their average salary.

8.5 Putting It All Together

Besides illustrating many of the Pascal language features introduced in this
chapter, the case study that follows provides a slightly different approach to
problem design. As part of the problem analysis, we will design the format of
the problem output and the format of each line of the data file. This is the first
time that we have been concerned with these issues. Problems of this kind are
often called *data processing* problems to indicate that the emphasis is on transforming data rather than performing extensive computations. Because the program solution is so lengthy, we will carefully develop algorithms for the main
program and all procedures before writing any code. The main point of this
case study is to follow the stepwise design and development of the algorithm
and to understand the modules and their interaction; a thorough understanding
of the code is secondary.

Case Study: Preparing Semester Grade Reports

Problem

The registrar would like a program that can be used to prepare grade reports
for students at the end of a semester. For each student, the program should
write a table that shows each course taken during the semester and the grade
and credits for that course. The program should also compute the student's
semester grade point average and write it on the grade report along with the
number of credits earned toward graduation.

Analysis

This problem is different from most of the others we have studied so far because its main purpose is to write the student data in a particular format. We will assume that we have a great deal of freedom in designing the format of the program input and output. We can decide to have each student's data typed at the keyboard during program execution or in a previously prepared data file. To allow some editing of data beforehand, it would make sense to prepare a data file. It would also be beneficial to write the program output to a file rather than display it on the screen. Once we have written the output file, we can send it to the printer, and the grade reports can then be printed and mailed to the students.

The first step is to determine the format of the grade report we would like prepared for each student. Figure 8.7 shows the report form that we will use. The grade report in Fig. 8.7 displays the student's name, her performance in each course, the number of credits earned toward graduation, and her grade point average (GPA). In this case, the GPA, 1.8, was computed by accumulating the total number of points earned in courses that received a grade of A through F (4 * 3, or 12, for CIS101; 0 for CIS210; 2 * 3, or 6, for HIS356) and dividing by the credits for those courses (10).

Figure 8.7 Grade Report Format

```
Spring Semester Grade Report for: Jane Williams
Course      Grade   Credits
CIS101        A        3
CIS210        F        4
HIS356        C        3
PHI210        P        3
Graduation credits earned: 9
Semester grade point average: 1.8
```

Next, we must decide the contents of the data file and its organization. We can place the data for each student on a separate line in the form shown next for two students:

```
Jane Williams/ CIS101A3  CIS210F4 HIS356C3 PHI210P3
Billy Joe/ PHI025B4 HIS120C3  MAT255
```

The student's name comes first followed by a slash and a list of course data. Each course's data consist of a six-character ID code, a grade, and the number of credit hours; one or more blanks may appear between courses. The first line shows that Jane Williams took four courses and received a grade of A for CIS101, a three-credit course. She received a grade of F in CIS210 (four credits), a C in HIS356 (three credits), and a P in PHI210 (three credits).

If we examine the grade report shown in Fig. 8.7, we see that each data line will generate a multiline table in the output file. Some of the information on the data line will simply be echoed (the student's name, each course ID), and some will be used in the computations (course grade and credits).

In the problem data requirements that follow, we list the input and output files. The variable StuCount will be used to count the students as they are processed. All other problem inputs and outputs will be declared as local variables in procedures.

Data Requirements

Problem Input
```
StuData : Text            {student data file}
```

Problem Outputs
```
GradeReport : Text        {grade report file}
StuCount : Integer        {count of students}
```

Design

In this subsection, we discuss the algorithm for the main program and all procedures. We do not show any code until after we have finished discussing the procedures. The main program must prepare the files for input and output. It calls procedure DoOneStudent (step 5 below) to process each student's data line and print that student's grade report. Figure 8.8 is a structure chart for the program system; the main program algorithm follows.

Algorithm for Main Program
1. Prepare StuData for input and GradeReport for output.
2. Initialize StuCount to 0.
3. while more students do
    begin
        4. Increment StuCount.
        5. Process next student's data line and write the student's grade report.
    end
6. Display the count of students processed.

Figure 8.8   Structure Chart for Student Transcript Program

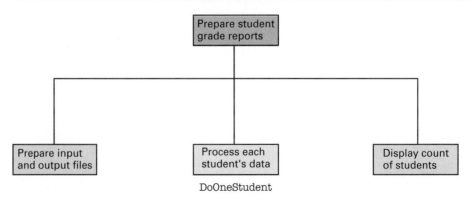

Design of Procedure DoOneStudent

The actual processing of a student's data is done by procedure DoOneStudent. DoOneStudent must write the student's name and each line of the grade report table. It must also compute and write graduation credits earned and GPA. The inputs, outputs, and local variables for DoOneStudent follow.

Data Requirements for DoOneStudent
Input Parameters

```
StuData : Text              {student data file}
StuCount : Integer          {count of students}
```

Output Parameter

```
GradeReport : Text          {grade report file}
```

Local Variables

```
GradCredits : Integer       {total graduation credits earned}
GPA : Real                  {grade point average}
GPAPoints : Integer         {total points earned toward GPA}
GPACredits : Integer        {total credits used to compute GPA}
Error : Boolean             {error flag — indicator of data error}
```

Relevant Formula

```
GPA = total points earned for GPA / total credits for GPA
```

The Boolean variable Error is a flag that will be used to indicate whether an error was found in a student's data line. It will be initialized to False and reset to True when a new data error is detected.

Algorithm for DoOneStudent
1. Initialize Error to False.
2. Write the grade report heading (first line of Fig. 8.7).
3. Read and write the student's name.
4. Write the grade table heading (second line of Fig. 8.7).
5. Initialize GradCredits, GPAPoints, and GPACredits to 0.
6. while there are more courses and no errors occurred do
    7. Read the data for the next course, updating total graduation credits, GPA points, GPA credits, and Error if an error occurred. Write the course data on a separate line of the grade report.
8. Compute GPA.
9. if no error occurred then
    10. Write GradCredits and GPA to the output file
  else
    11. Display an error message

We will use level-2 procedures for step 3 (IOName), step 7 (ProcessCourse), step 8 (FindAve), and step 10 (WriteGPA). Figure 8.9 shows the relationship between DoOneStudent and its subordinate modules. Of these, only ProcessCourse has its own subordinate modules, which are discussed next.

Figure 8.9 Structure Chart for DoOneStudent

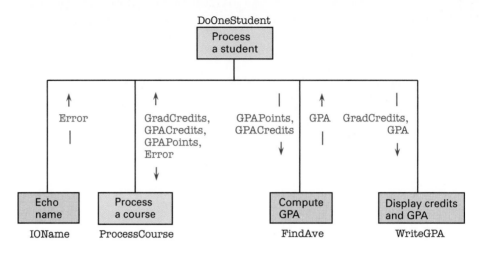

Design of ProcessCourse and Its Subordinate Modules

ProcessCourse must read and process the data for a single course. Each course's data consist of a six-character ID, a letter grade, and a digit character. The data requirements and algorithm for ProcessCourse follow.

Data Requirements for ProcessCourse
Input Parameter

    StuData : Text   {student data file}

Input/Output Parameters

    GradCredits : Integer   {total graduation credits earned}
    GPACredits : Integer   {total credits used to compute GPA}
    GPAPoints   : Integer   {total points earned toward GPA}

Output Parameters

    GradeReport : Text   {grade report file}
    Error : Boolean   {error flag}

Local Variables

    Grade : Char   {the letter grade}
    Credits : Integer   {number of credits}

Algorithm for ProcessCourse
1. Read and write the course ID.
2. Read and write the course grade.
3. Read and write the course credits.
4. Update total graduation credits, GPAPoints, and GPACredits based on the course grade and credits.

We will use level-3 procedures for step 1 (IOCourse), step 3 (IOCredit), and step 4 (UpdateGPA). IOCourse will read and write the six characters of a course ID, ignoring any blanks between course data. IOCredit will read the course credits as a character and convert it to an integer value (stored in Credits). UpdateGPA will use the student's grade to determine the number of graduation and GPA credits earned as well as grade points. Figure 8.10 shows the structure chart for ProcessCourse and its subordinate modules.

Figure 8.10   Structure Chart for ProcessCourse

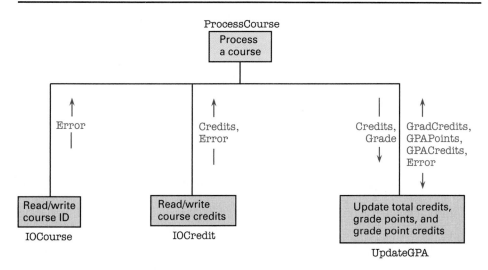

Implementation

Figure 8.11 shows the main program for the transcript problem. The declaration part contains a declaration for the string constant Semester, which is written to file GradeReport by procedure DoOneStudent. The declaration part also shows one sequence for the procedures. The level-3 modules (IOCourse, IOCredit, UpdateGPA) should come before ProcessCourse. The level-2 modules, including ProcessCourse, should come before DoOneStudent. In the program body, the while condition

        not EOF(StuData)

is True as long as there are students left to process.

Figure 8.11   Main Program for Transcript Problem

```
program Transcript (Input, Output);
{Writes a semester grade report for each student}

  const
    Semester = 'Spring Semester';
```

Directory: CHAP8
File: TRANSCRI.PAS

```pascal
var
  StuData,                {input - file of student data}
  GradeReport : Text;     {output - file of grade reports}
  StuCount : Integer;     {count of current student}

{
  Insert level-3 modules here: IOCourse, IOCredit, UpdateGPA.
  Insert level-2 modules here: IOName, ProcessCourse,
    FindAve, WriteGPA
  Insert DoOneStudent here.
}

begin {Transcript}
  {Prepare StuData for input and GradeReport for output.}
  Reset (StuData);
  Rewrite (GradeReport);

  StuCount := 0;
  {Process all students until done.}
  while not EOF(StuData) do
    begin
      StuCount := StuCount + 1;
      DoOneStudent (StuData, GradeReport, StuCount)
    end; {while}

  {Display a count of students.}
  WriteLn (Output, StuCount :1, ' students processed')
end.  {Transcript}
```

Figure 8.12 shows procedure DoOneStudent. The statement

```pascal
    Page (GradeReport);          {Start a new page}
```

will cause each student's grade report to start on a new page when file
GradeReport is sent to the printer. The while condition

```pascal
    (not EOLN(StuData)) and (not Error)
```

is True as long as the <eoln> mark has not been reached and no errors were
detected. When a single error is detected, the statement

```pascal
    ReadLn (StuData);            {skip over <eoln>}
```

executes, moving the file-position pointer to the start of the next student's data.
If we continued processing the current student's data line after an error, it
would be possible to read past the <eoln> and attempt to process the next
student's data as belonging to the current student.

Figure 8.12   Procedure DoOneStudent

```pascal
procedure DoOneStudent (var StuData {input file},
                            GradeReport {output file} : Text;
                        StuCount {Input} : Integer);
{
  Processes the data line for one student.
```

```
Pre : StuCount is the number of the student being processed.
      The file-position pointer for StuData is at the start of a data
      line.
Post: A grade report for one student is written to the output
      file.  The file-position pointer for StuData has been
      advanced to the start of the next line.  If an error occurs,
      the grade report is terminated and an error message is
      written to the screen.
}
  var
    Credits,                   {course credits}
    GradCredits : Integer;  {total graduation credits earned}
    GPA : Real;                {grade point average}
    GPAPoints,                 {total points earned toward GPA}
    GPACredits : Integer;   {total credits used to compute GPA}
    Error : Boolean;           {flag - set True for data error}

begin {DoOneStudent}
  {Perform initialization}
  Error := False;                       {Assume no errors.}
  Page (GradeReport);                   {Start a new page.}
  Write (GradeReport, Semester, ' grade report for: ');
  IOName (StuData, GradeReport, Error);  {Write student name.}
  WriteLn (GradeReport);                       {Terminate line.}
  WriteLn (GradeReport, 'Course', 'Grade' :10, 'Credits' :10);
  GradCredits := 0;
  GPAPoints := 0;
  GPACredits := 0;

  {Process all course data for a student.}
  while (not EOLN(StuData)) and (not Error) do
    ProcessCourse (StuData, GradeReport, GradCredits,
                   GPAPoints, GPACredits, Error);
  ReadLn (StuData);                     {skip over <eoln>}

  {Compute GPA}
  GPA := FindAve(GPAPoints, GPACredits);

  {Write graduation credits and GPA or display an error message.}
  if not Error then
    WriteGPA (GradeReport, GradCredits, GPA)
  else
    WriteLn (Output, 'Grade report for student ',
             StuCount : 1, ' invalid -- data error')
end; {DoOneStudent}
```

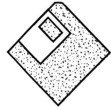

Directory: CHAP8
File: TRANSCRI.PAS

Figure 8.13 shows the subordinate modules for DoOneStudent except for
ProcessCourse, which will be discussed next, and FindAve (see Fig. 6.26). In
IOName, the while condition

```
(NameCh <> NameSentinel) and (not EOLN (StuData))
```

is True as long as the sentinel character ('/') has not been read and the end
of the line has not been reached. The end-of-line test was included to detect a
missing sentinel character. The if statement following the while loop sets Error
to True if the sentinel character is missing.

Figure 8.13   Procedures IOName and WriteGPA

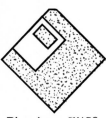

Directory: CHAP8
File: TRANSCRI.PAS

```
procedure IOName (var StuData {input},
                      GradeReport {output} : Text;
                  var Error {output} : Boolean);
{
 Writes the student name to the output file.
 Pre : The pointer for StuData is at the start of a data line.
 Post: The pointer for StuData is just past the sentinel character
       or is at <eoln>.  Each data character read is written to
       file GradeReport except for the sentinel.  If the file position
       pointer is at <eoln>, Error is set to True.
}
  const
    NameSentinel = '/';

  var
    NameCh : Char;              {each character of the name}

begin {IOName}
  {Read and write student name.}
  Read (StuData, NameCh);
  while (NameCh <> NameSentinel) and (not EOLN(StuData)) do
    begin
      Write (GradeReport, NameCh);
      Read (StuData, NameCh)
    end; {while}

  {If end of line reached, set error flag.}
  if EOLN(StuData) then
    Error := True
end; {IOName}


procedure WriteGPA (var GradeReport {output file} : Text;
                    GradCredits {input} : Integer;
                    GPA {input} : Real);
{
 Writes the graduation credits earned and GPA to the output file.
 Pre : GradeReport is opened for output.
 Post: GradCredits and GPA are written to the output file.
}
begin {WriteGPA}
  WriteLn (GradeReport, 'Graduation credits earned: ',
           GradCredits :1);
  WriteLn (GradeReport, 'Semester GPA: ', GPA :3:1)
end; {WriteGPA}
```

Figure 8.14 shows ProcessCourse (near the end of the figure) and its subordinate procedures. Procedure IOCourse begins by calling procedure SkipBlanks (see programming exercise 1) to skip over blanks and read the first character of the course ID. The while condition

```
while (I < IDSize) and (not EOLN(StuData)) do
```

is True as long as fewer than six nonblank characters have been read and the end of the data line has not been reached. In IOCredits, the if statement assigns an integer value to Credits when CreditCh is a digit character; otherwise, Error is set to True.

In UpdateGPA, the if statement guards the case statement by using a set membership test to validate Grade. The case statement increments Grad-Credits by Credits for a grade of A through D or P (Pass). It increments GPACredits by Credits for a grade of A through D or F (Fail). It increments GPAPoints by the product of Credits and a number between 1 (for D) and 4 (for A) for a grade of A through D. For example, the expression

```
(4 - (Ord(Grade) - Ord('A')))
```

evaluates to 4 − 1, or 3, when Grade is 'B'.

Figure 8.14 ProcessCourse and Subordinate Procedures

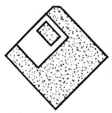

Directory: CHAP8
File: TRANSCRI.PAS

```
{Insert procedure SkipBlanks here.}

procedure IOCourse (var StuData {input},
                        GradeReport {output} : Text;
                    var Error {output} : Boolean);
{
 Writes the course ID to the output file.
 Pre : None
 Post: Writes the next six nonblank characters to the output file.
       Sets Error to True if <eoln> is reached first.
 Uses: Procedure SkipBlanks
}
  const
    IDSize = 6;

  var
    I : Integer;                     {count of characters read}
    CourseCh : Char;                 {each character of course ID}

begin {IOCourse}
  {Skip over blanks and read the first character of the course ID.}
  SkipBlanks (StuData, CourseCh);

  {Display each character of ID.}
  Write (GradeReport, CourseCh);
  I := 1;                            {first character displayed}
  while (I < IDSize) and (not EOLN(StuData)) do
    begin
      Read (StuData, CourseCh);
      Write (GradeReport, CourseCh);
      I := I + 1
    end; {while}

  {If end of line reached, set error flag.}
  if EOLN(StuData) then
    Error := True
end; {IOCourse}
```

```
procedure IOCredit (var StuData {input},
                         GradeReport {output} : Text;
                     var Credits {output} : Integer;
                     var Error {output} : Boolean);
{
Reads a digit character, converts it to an integer, and
writes it to the output file.
Pre : None
Post: Returns the numeric value of the digit character read
      through Credits.  Sets Error to True if the character
      is not a digit.
}
  var
    CreditCh : Char;               {digit character read}


begin {IOCredit}
  {Read and write credit character.}
  Read (StuData, CreditCh);
  Write (GradeReport, CreditCh :10);

  {Convert digit character to integer value.}
  if ('0' <= CreditCh) and (CreditCh <= '9') then
    Credits := Ord(CreditCh) - Ord('0')
  else
    Error := True
end; {IOCredit}




procedure UpDateGPA (Grade {input} : Char;
                     Credits {input} : Integer;
                     var GradCredits, GPAPoints,
                         GPACredits {input/output} : Integer;
                     var Error {output} : Boolean);
{
Updates graduation credits, GPA credits, and graduation points
based on the value of Grade and Credits.
Pre : None
Post: If Grade is valid, returns new values for GradCredits,
      GPAPoints, GPACredits.  Sets Error to True if
      Grade is not valid.
}
begin {UpdateGPA}
  if Grade is ['A'..'D','F','P','I','W'] then
    case Grade of
      'A','B','C','D' : begin
                          GradCredits := GradCredits + Credits;
                          GPACredits := GPACredits + Credits;
                          GPAPoints := GPAPoints + Credits *
                                      (4 - (Ord(Grade) - Ord('A')))
                        end;
      'F'             : GPACredits := GPACredits + Credits;
      'P'             : GradCredits := GradCredits + Credits;
      'I','W'         : {do nothing}
    end {case}
  else
    Error := True
end; {UpdateGPA}
```

```
procedure ProcessCourse (var StuData {input},
                             GradeReport {output} : Text;
                         var GradCredits, GPAPoints,
                             GPACredits {input/output} : Integer;
                         var Error {output} : Boolean);
{
 Processes the data for one course.
 Pre : None
 Post: Reads all the data for one course and writes it to
       the output file.  Returns the updated values of
       graduation credits, GPA credits, and GPA points.
       Sets Error to true if a data error occurs.
}
  var
   Grade : Char;          {course grade}
   Credits : Integer;     {number of credits for the course}

 begin {ProcessCourse}
   IOCourse (StuData, GradeReport, Error);
   Read (StuData, Grade);
   Write (GradeReport, Grade :10);
   IOCredit (StuData, GradeReport, Credits, Error);
   WriteLn (GradeReport);
   UpdateGPA (Grade, Credits, GradCredits,
              GPAPoints, GPACredits, Error)
end; {ProcessCourse}
```

Testing the Transcript Program

When you run the transcript program with some sample student data, you should generate grade reports in the form shown earlier. Verify that the error tests included in the program work and that an error in one student's data does not propagate, preventing you from processing another student's correct data. Test for the effect of a missing sentinel character, missing blanks between course data, an incorrect grade, or an invalid number of credits. Also, make sure that the GPA computed and the graduation credits earned are accurate for a variety of different grades.

Exercises for Section 8.5

Self-Check

1. How is EOLN(StuData) used to test for different program states in procedures DoOneStudent (Fig. 8.12), IOCourse (Fig. 8.14), and IOName (Fig. 8.13)?
2. Would it be easy to modify program Transcript so that bad input data are written to a separate report file? Why or why not?

Programming

1. Write procedure SkipBlanks, which skips over any blanks. The procedure should return through its second parameter the first nonblank read from a data file (its first parameter).

8.6 Common Programming Errors

File processing in any programming language tends to be difficult to master, and Pascal is no exception. Remember to include in the program heading the name of each file you want to process. This name, which will be used as a file variable in the program, may differ from the actual directory name of the associated disk file. All file names must be declared as variables (type Text) except for system files Input and Output.

Remember to prepare a file for input or output using the Reset or Rewrite procedure (except for system files Input and Output). If you rewrite an existing file, the data on that file may be lost. Make sure that you do not inadvertently place the Reset or Rewrite statement in a loop. If you do, a Read operation in the loop will repeatedly read the first file component; a Write operation in the loop will repeatedly write the first file component.

The Read (ReadLn) procedure can be used only after a file has been prepared for input. Similarly, the Write (WriteLn) procedure can be used only after a file has been prepared for output. Be sure to specify the file name as the first procedure parameter; otherwise, the system file Input or Output will be assumed. An attempt to read beyond end of file error occurs if a Read operation is performed after all data characters have been processed.

When using function EOLN or EOF to control data entry, don't forget to include the data file name as the function argument. Remember to skip over the <eoln> character, using ReadLn, after you have reached the end of a data line.

If you press the Return key an extra time when you have finished creating a data file, you may place an extra empty line at the end of the data file. The following file contains one number per line and an empty line at the end.

```
500<eoln>
37<eoln>
<eoln><eof>
```

Although the empty line may seem harmless, if we use the while condition

```
while not EOF(InData) do
```

to control a loop that reads and processes one number per line, the empty line will cause the loop to execute one extra time. Because there are no data to read, an attempt to read beyond end of file error will occur.

CHAPTER REVIEW

In this chapter, you learned how to instruct a program to read its data from a data file rather than from the keyboard, and how to save the output generated by a program as a file on disk. Both features use files of characters (data type `Text`).

The `<eoln>` character breaks a text file into lines. The `EOLN` function can test for an `<eoln>` character, and the `WriteLn` statement places an `<eoln>` character in a text file. An `<eoln>` character that is read into a type `Char` variable is stored as a blank character.

When text files are processed, sequences of characters are transferred between main memory and disk storage. The data type of a variable used in an input list must be `Char` or `Integer` (or a subrange of `Char` or `Integer`) or `Real`. The data type of an expression used in an output list must be `Char` or `Integer` (or a subrange of `Char` or `Integer`), `Boolean`, `Real`, or a character string.

Use the `Reset` procedure to move the file position pointer for an input file to the first character in the file. Use the `Rewrite` procedure to prepare an output file before writing to it. While a file is being read, the `EOF` function can test whether the end of the file has been reached.

New Pascal Constructs

The Pascal constructs introduced in this chapter are described in Table 8.3.

Table 8.3 Summary of New Pascal Constructs

Construct	Effect

File Declaration
`var`
  `MoreChars,`
  `MoreDigits : Text;`
  `I : Integer;`
  `NextCh : Char;`
	`MoreChars` and `MoreDigits` are text files.

Reset and Rewrite Procedures
`Reset (More Digits);`
`Rewrite (MoreChars);`
	`MoreDigits` is prepared for input, and `MoreChars` is prepared for output.

Read and Write Procedures
`Read (MoreDigits, I);`
`WriteLn (MoreChars, 'number: ', I);`
	The next integer is read from file `MoreDigits` into variable `I`. The string `'number: '` is written to More-Chars followed by the value of `I`.

Table 8.3, *continued*

Construct	Effect

EOF Function
 	
```Reset (MoreDigits);```
```Rewrite (MoreChars);```
```while not EOF(MoreDigits) do```
  ```begin```
    ```ReadLn (MoreDigits, I);```
    ```WriteLn (MoreChars, I)```
  ```end; {while}```
	File MoreDigits is prepared for input and file MoreChars for output. The first integer value on each line of file MoreDigits is written to a separate line of file MoreChars.

EOLN Function
 	
```Reset (MoreDigits);```
```while not EOLN(MoreDigits) do```
  ```begin```
    ```Read (MoreDigits, NextCh);```
    ```Write (Output, NextCh)```
  ```end;   {while}```
```ReadLn (MoreDigits)```
	File MoreDigits is prepared for input. Each character on the first line is read into NextCh and displayed on the terminal screen. The file-position pointer for MoreDigits is advanced to the first character of the second line.

✓ Quick-Check Exercises

1. The _____ operation prepares a file for input, and the _____ operation prepares it for output.
2. The _____ character separates a _____ file into lines, and the _____ character appears at the end of a file.
3. What data types can be read or written to a text file?
4. Is it ever permissible to pass a file as a value parameter to a procedure?
5. Where are files stored?
6. Is is possible for EOLN to be False if EOF is True?
7. Can a text file be used for both input and output by the same program?
8. Correct the following segment:

   ```
   Reset(Number);
   while not EOF do
     Read (InFile, Number);
   ```

Answers to Quick-Check Exercises

1. Reset, Rewrite
2. <eoln>, Text, <eof>
3. Any of the standard data types (or a subrange thereof) except Boolean can be read; any of the standard types (or a subrange thereof) of a string literal can be written.
4. no
5. secondary storage or disk
6. no
7. Yes, but it may not be open for both input and output at the same time.
8. Reset (InFile);
   while not EOF(InFile) do
     Read (InFile, Number);

Review Questions

1. List three advantages to using files for input and output as opposed to the standard input and output you have used thus far in this course.
2. a. Explain why a file may have two distinct names.
   b. What conventions are followed for choosing each name?
   c. Which name appears in the program heading?
   d. Which name appears in the file variable declaration?
   e. Which name appears in an operating system command?
3. Explain how `Read` and `ReadLn` differ in reading data items from a text file.
4. Let X be type `Real`, N type `Integer`, and Ch type `Char`. Indicate the contents of each variable after each input operation is performed, assuming the file consists of the following lines and that the `Reset (InData)` operation occurs before each sequence of statements.

   ```
   23 53.2 ABC<eoln>
   145 Z<eoln>
   ```

   a. `Read (InData, N, X);`
      `ReadLn (InData, Ch);`
   b. `ReadLn (InData, Ch, N);`
   c. `ReadLn (Indata);`
      `Read (Indata, X, Ch);`
5. Write a loop that reads up to 10 integer values from a data file and displays them on the screen. If there are not 10 integers in the file, the message `That's all folks` should be displayed after the last number.
6. Write a procedure that copies several data lines typed at the keyboard to a text file. The copy process should be terminated when the user enters a null line.

Programming Projects

1. Write a procedure that reads the data for one employee from file `OutEmp` produced by program `WritePayroll` (see Section 8.4) and writes a payroll check to an output file. The format of the check should be similar to the one shown below:

   ```
   Temple University              Check No.      12372
   Philadelphia, PA                 Date:      03-17-92

   Pay to the
   Order of:  Peter Liacouras          $   20000.00

                                       Jane Smith
   ```

Directory: CHAP8
File: PROJ8_1.PAS

2. Write a program that reads the initial check number and the data from the keyboard and then writes checks using the procedure from programming project 1 and a data file generated by running program `WritePayroll`. Write a separator line consisting of 80 underscore characters between checks.
3. Each year the state legislature rates the productivity of the faculty of each of the state-supported colleges and universities. The rating is based on reports submitted by the faculty members that indicate the average number of hours worked per week during the school year. Each faculty member is rated, and the university receives an overall rating.

The faculty productivity ratings are computed as follows:

a. "Highly productive" means over 55 hours per week reported.
b. "Satisfactory" means reported hours per week are between 35 and 55.
c. "Overpaid" means reported hours per week are less than 35.

Read the following data from a data file (assuming all names are padded with blanks to 10 characters):

Name	Hours
Herm	63
Flo	37
Jake	20
Maureen	55
Saul	72
Tony	40
Al	12

As part of your solution, your program should include procedures that correspond to the procedure headers shown next:

```
procedure PrintHeader;
{Displays table heading}

procedure DisplayProductivity (Hours {input} : Real);
{Displays productivity ranking based on value of Hours}

procedure ProcessName (var FacHours {input} : Text);
{Reads and displays one faculty name from file FacHours}

procedure ProcessData (var FacHours {input} : Text;
                           var Count {input/output} : Integer;
                           var Sum {input/output} : Real);
{
 Reads all data lines from file FacHours and displays body of
 table and returns number of faculty (Count) and the sum of
 their hours worked (Sum).
 Uses: ProcessName and DisplayProductivity.
}
```

4. Write a program that reads several lines from a data file and prints each word of the file on a separate line of an output file followed by the number of letters in that word. Also print a count of words in the file on the screen when done. Assume that words are separated by one or more blanks.

5. Compute the monthly payment and the total payment for a bank loan, given
   a. the amount of the loan
   b. the duration of the loan in months
   c. the interest rate for the loan
   Your program should read in one loan at a time, perform the required computation, and print the values of the monthly payment and the total payment.

   Test your program with at least the following data (and more if you want).

Directory: CHAP8
File: PROJ8_5.PAS

Loan	Months	Rate
16000	300	12.50
24000	360	13.50
30000	300	15.50

42000	360	14.50
22000	300	15.50
300000	240	15.25

Hints:

a. The formula for computing a monthly payment is

$$monthpay = \frac{ratem \times expm^{months} \times loan}{expm - 1.0}$$

where

$$ratem = rate/1200.00$$
$$expm = (1.0 + ratem)$$

and you will need a loop to multiply *expm* by itself *months* times.

b. The formula for computing the total payment is

$$total = monthpay \times months$$

6. Use your solution to programming project 5 as the basis for writing a program that will write a data file containing a table of the following form:

```
              Loan Amount: $1000
Interest      Duration        Monthly        Total
Rate          (years)         Payment        Payment
10.00            20           --------       --------
10.00            25           --------       --------
10.00            30           --------       --------
10.25            20           --------       --------
                     .
                     .
                     .
```

The output file produced by your program should contain payment information on a $1000 loan for interest rates from 10% to 14% with increments of 0.25%. The loan durations should be 20, 25, and 30 years.

7. Whatsamata U. offers a service to its faculty in computing grades at the end of each semester. A program processes three weighted test scores and calculates a student's average and letter grade (based on an A as 90–100, a B as 80–89, etc.). Read the student data from a file and write each student's name, test score, average, and grade to an output file.

   Write a program to provide this valuable service. The data will consist of the three test weights followed by three test scores and a student ID number (four digits) for each student. Calculate the weighted average for each student and the corresponding letter grade. This information should be printed along with the initial three test scores. The weighted average for each student is equal to

   $$weight_1 \times score_1 + weight_2 \times score_2 + weight_3 \times score_3$$

   For summary statistics, print the highest average, lowest average, average of the averages, and total number of students processed.

   Sample data:

0.35	0.25	0.40		*test weights*
100	76	88	1014	*test scores and ID*

8. Write a program that reads in a string of characters that represent a Roman numeral and then converts it to Arabic form (an integer). The character values for Roman numerals are as follows:

M	1000
D	500
C	100
L	50
X	10
V	5
I	1

Test your program with the following data: LXXXVII (87), CCXIX (219), MCCCLIV (1354), MMDCLXXIII (2673), MCDLXXVI (1476).

Watts S. Humphrey founded the Software Process Program of the Software Engineering Institute at Carnegie Mellon University and is an SEI fellow. The Software Process Program provides leadership in establishing advanced software engineering processes, metrics, methods, and quality programs for the U.S. government and its contractors. Humphrey was previously associated with IBM Corporation in various capacities including responsibility for commercial software development.

How did your interest in computer science, and especially software engineering, develop?

I started as an engineer in the 1940s when there was a lot of interest in how to make machines do complex tasks. I did some early work in analog computers and cryptographics and found the challenge of building intricate things was fascinating. What is interesting to me in looking back is that the excitement of making complex functions perform in a system very quickly moved into software. And while the challenge of building machines that work continues to be interesting, I find the really intriguing puzzles in software. It's still great fun getting things to work in software.

What are the important influences on your thinking about software methodology today?

There are several. Because I was trained as a research scientist, I approach projects as controlled experiments. One of the key questions in software development—and it's a tricky problem because the human element is so strong in software—is what works and what doesn't. I have found that there are a large number of things that you can actually measure and that things are in fact more predictable than people generally expect. By experimenting with one parameter at a time and measuring results, you can better understand what works and what doesn't.

The second influence on my thinking is quality. I don't think laymen realize how difficult it is to get a complex software product to work. As the phone company demonstrated recently, a minor error way down in some remote part of the system can, if it's encountered under the right circumstances, disable a major activity. The point I like to emphasize is that the quality of a complex software system is basically governed by the quality of its worst piece. As a consequence, the software community needs to focus on how to make every software element of very high quality. Then you can make high quality systems.

The third is the concept of process itself. There's a lot of research activity in this area today, looking at process development and process management and how you couple that with people management and technology improvements to improve software engineering. It's a subject that we are really just exploring today and it's a very exciting field.

Peter J. Denning wrote in a recent article for *The American Scientist* ("Beyond Formalism") that "much practice for software design . . . ignores communication between designers and users." Do you think that's true?

I certainly agree with what he said, and communication is important across the board. But the issue we are struggling with is that no one really has the answer. The implication in a lot of discussion is "If you would only do it my way everything would be okay," and that is far from the truth. The challenge is to be able to live with the uncertainty that you really don't know the answer and put together an approach that is much more experimental. What one needs to focus on is not what we want to do, but how we should go about discovering what we want to do. If you treat it as a learning problem, you say, "Here are the steps we must take to define a piece; once we get that piece to where we really understand it, we'll build it." Some of the things being done now in incremental development, for example, are moving in this direction. So it's not a communication problem as much as it is a problem with the way we deal with software development. And it's true for almost any kind of complex system.

What do you think is the proper role for management in organizations that develop large software projects?

I think management has multiple roles. One is to define the goals of the project and make sure they are understood and communicated throughout the organization. Second is to provide the disciplines of planning, tracking, controlling, and reporting. SEI has developed five levels of process maturity for software organizations and they start at level 1, where organizations are operating out of control, typically blowing schedules, costs, and having severe quality problems. We have found that more than 70 percent of U.S. software organizations are at level 1. What they need to do to get to level 2 is put these very rudimentary management disciplines in place—estimating, scheduling, reporting, and basic controls. The third responsibility is to build and support the technical team in doing their work. The people doing software development are working inside a system, performing according to a process. Management's job is to work on the process. And by that I mean to focus on how it's working and how it could be improved. Very often management is not doing that. They are following the people doing the work and goading them along instead of focusing on the process and helping to build smoothly operating teams. That is the basic thrust of SEI's level 3, where the process gets defined and people start to understand what their various roles are and how the work is done using appropriate methods.

Is the reason for success, or failure, of large systems due chiefly to technical reasons or to management, or to both?

The success of a large system has many elements and a failure only needs one. It's like trying to find the most critical part of an automobile. You can argue that the wheels are crucial, but the same thing is true of the spark plugs, and so on. That is equally true of the success of a software project. You need appropriate requirements, good design, a well-managed project, a good quality system, and a whole host of other things. A project can fail for any of a large number of reasons but what is the most prevalent kind of failure today? The bulk of software organizations that fail do so for management reasons. They have resource problems, get overcommitted, and have tremendous pressure put on them. These things may result in technical problems, but they are caused by management problems. That is not to say people never fail for technical reasons, but it's not as common as management problems.

9

Software Engineering

Until this point in your study of programming, you have been concerned primarily with writing relatively short programs that solve particular programming problems but that otherwise have little general use. In this chapter you will begin to consider issues related to writing larger, more complex programs, called *programming in the large*.

Software engineering is a term used to denote a collection of tools and techniques that professional programmers in industry use to facilitate the design, coding, and maintenance (upkeep) of large-scale programs. Our discussion focuses on some principles of software engineering that have proved useful for designing large program systems.

In this chapter we describe the different phases of a software project and elaborate on the software engineering method for problem solving and programming first discussed in Section 2.1. We discuss how to modularize a large project so that individual pieces can be implemented by different programmers and at different times. We also discuss how to write software modules to simplify their reuse in other projects.

We then consider the task of testing a program and verifying that it works correctly. We discuss the limitations of program testing and describe formal methods for proving that a program is correct.

Because this chapter introduces many concepts that are used by software professionals, the chapter ends with a discussion of professional behavior, ethics, and responsibilities. There are also important warnings about computer viruses and plagiarism, which apply to student programmers as well as to industrial programmers.

9.1 The Software Challenge

Programming in college, especially at the introductory level, is somewhat different from programming in the real world. In college, an instructor generally gives you the problem specification. In many cases, the specification is ambiguous or incomplete, and interaction between the instructor and the class is necessary so the students can pin down the details.

In the real world, the impetus for a software project comes from users of an existing software product or potential users of a new software product. The users see a need for improving an existing product or for computerizing an operation that is currently done without the use of computers. This need is communicated to the individuals responsible for providing software support in the organization (normally called *systems analysts*).

Because the users are often naive as to the capabilities of a computer, the initial specification for a software product may be incomplete. The specification is clarified through extensive interaction between the users of the software and the systems analysts. Through this interaction, the systems analysts determine precisely what the users want the proposed software to do, and the users learn what to expect from the software product. This way there are fewer surprises in the end.

Although it may seem like common sense to proceed in this manner, very often a software product does not perform as expected. The reason is usually a communication gap between those responsible for the product's design and its eventual users; generally, both parties are at fault when the software fails to meet expectations. To avoid that possibility, a complete, written description of the requirements specification for a new software product must be generated at the beginning of the project, and both users and designers should sign the document.

Programming Teams

Another major difference between programming in college and in industry is that in industry it is rare for a large software project to be implemented by a single programmer. Most often, a large project is assigned to a team of programmers. It is important for team members to coordinate beforehand the overall organization of the project, and to meet on a regular basis to exchange information and report progress.

Each team member is responsible for a set of procedures, some of which may be accessed by other team members. After the initial organizational meeting, each team member should provide the other members with a specification for each procedure that he or she is implementing. Such a specification is similar to the documentation provided for each procedure in this text. It consists of a brief statement of the purpose of the procedure, its pre- and postconditions, and its formal parameter list. This information is all that a potential user of the procedure needs to know in order to call the procedure correctly.

Normally one team member will act as "librarian" by assuming responsibility for determining the status of each procedure in the system. Initially, the library of procedures consists of a stub for each procedure. As a new procedure is completed and tested, its updated version replaces the version currently in the library. The librarian keeps track of the date that each version of a procedure is inserted into the library and makes sure that all programmers are using the latest version of any procedure.

Exercises for Section 9.1

Self-Check

1. How does the role of the systems analyst differ from that of the librarian during the development of a large software system?
2. Explain how a programming team has the potential to complete a large software project more quickly than a single programmer working independently.

9.2 The System/Software Life Cycle

The steps involved in the initial development and continued operation of a software system make up the *system/software life cycle* (SLC), as described next.

1. Requirements specification
   - Prepare a complete and unambiguous problem statement.
   - Users and analysts sign the requirements document.
2. Analysis
   - Understand the problem; determine problem outputs and required inputs.
   - Evaluate alternative solutions.
   - Choose the preferred solution.
3. Design
   - Perform a top-down design of the system.
   - For each module, identify key data elements and subordinate procedures using structure charts.
4. Implementation
   - Write algorithms and pseudocode descriptions of individual procedures.
   - Code the solution.
   - Debug the code.
5. Testing and validation
   - Test the code, validating that it is correct.
   - Involve users and special testing teams in all system tests.
6. Operation, follow-up, and maintenance
   - Run the completed system.
   - Evaluate its performance.
   - Remove new bugs as they are detected.
   - Make required changes to keep the system up to date.
   - Validate that changes are correct and that they do not adversely affect the system's operation.

The engineering and scientific method for solving problems specifies that problem analysis should always precede problem solution (synthesis). The first two stages of the SLC (requirements specification and analysis) are the analysis part, and the next two stages (design and implementation) are the synthesis part. Program users take the lead in developing the requirements specification. System analysts work closely with program users to understand more thoroughly the problem requirements and to evaluate possible alternative solutions.

The SLC is iterative. During the design phase (step 3), problems may arise that make it necessary to modify the requirements specification. Similarly, during implementation (step 4) it may become necessary to reconsider decisions made in the design phase. All changes must be approved by both the systems analysts and the users.

Once the system is implemented, it must be thoroughly tested before it enters its final stage (operation and maintenance). It is possible that system changes identified in these stages will require repetition of earlier stages of the SLC. These changes may be necessary to correct errors found during testing or to accommodate changes required by external sources (for example, a change in federal or state tax regulations).

Estimates will vary as to the amount of time necessary for each stage. For example, a typical system may require a year to proceed through the first four stages, three months of testing, then four or more years of operation and maintenance. With these figures in mind, you can see why it is so important to design and document software in such a way that it can be easily maintained. This is especially important because the persons who maintain the program may not have been involved in the original program design or implementation.

Prototyping

Before we present an in-depth discussion of the SLC, we should mention that there is an alternative approach to traditional system development, called prototyping. In *prototyping*, systems analysts work closely with system users to develop a prototype, or model, of the actual system. Initially a prototype has few working features and just mimics the input/output interaction of the users with the system. At each stage, the users and the analysts decide what changes should be made and what new features should be added; these changes are then incorporated into the prototype. The process continues until a complete prototype is available that performs all the functions of the final system. The analysts and the users can then decide whether to use the prototype as the final system or as the basis of the design for a new system, which will perform the same operations as the prototype but which will be more efficient.

Requirements Specification

Although we have illustrated most of the phases of the SLC in solving all the case studies thus far, we have not really had the opportunity to examine the requirements specification process. Each case study was preceded by a brief statement of the problem, and we began our solutions with the analysis phase. The next case study focuses on issues that are dealt with during each stage of the SLC, beginning with the requirements specification.

Case Study: Telephone Directory Program

Problem
Write an interactive telephone directory program that contains a collection of names and telephone numbers. You should be able to insert a new entry into the directory, retrieve an entry in the directory, change a directory entry, and delete a directory entry.

Data Requirements
In the real world, systems analysts work with software users to clarify detailed system requirements. Some questions that need to be answered deal with the format of the input data, the desired form of any output screens or printed forms, and the need for data validation. In college you follow this process by

interrogating your instructor or teaching assistant to determine the precise details of a programming assignment.

For example, let's say that your instructor has given you the preceding incomplete problem specification for the design of a telephone directory program. Some of the questions that might come to mind and require clarification are the following:

- Is an initial list of names and numbers to be stored in the directory beforehand, or are all entries to be inserted at the same time?
- If there is an initial list, is it stored in a data file or will it be entered interactively?
- If the file is a text file, what are the formatting conventions (for example, will the name start in position 1 and the phone number in position 20)? Are the name and number on the same data line or on separate lines?
- Is the final directory stored in main memory or as a file in secondary memory?
- Can more than one number be associated with a particular name? If so, should the first number, the last number, or all numbers be retrieved?
- Is there a limit on the length of a name? How are the names stored (for example, *last, first* or *first last*)?
- Are phone numbers stored as numbers or as strings of characters? Do they contain area codes? Are there any special characters, such as hyphens and parentheses, in a phone number? Should you check for illegal characters in a number or for numbers that are too short or too long?
- Should the names be stored in alphabetical order or in the sequence in which they were entered into the directory?
- Do you need a printed list of names and phone numbers for the directory? How should that list be formatted?
- Is it possible to change names as well as phone numbers?
- What information is needed to retrieve a directory entry?
- When an entry is retrieved, should both the name and number be displayed or just the number? What form should the display take?
- What action should be taken if a new entry has the same name as a person already in the directory? Should this entry be flagged as an error?

As you can see, plenty of questions are left unanswered by the initial problem statement. To complete the requirements specification, you should answer these questions and more. Many of the questions deal with details of input data, the handling of potential errors in input data, and formats of input data and output lists.

Analysis

Once the system requirements have been specified, the analysis stage begins. Before you embark on the design of a program solution, make sure you completely understand the problem. If the requirements specification has been carefully done, this will be easy. Any remaining questions should be cleared up at this time.

The next step is to evaluate different approaches to the program design.

As part of this investigation, the systems analysts and the users may consider whether any existing commercial software packages can satisfy their requirements. They must also determine the impact of the new software product on existing computer systems and what new hardware or software will be needed to develop and run the new system. The feasibility of each approach is determined by estimating its cost and anticipated benefits. The analysis stage culminates with the selection of what appears to be the best design approach.

Your choices will be more constrained in your coursework. Some decisions you will often need to make are whether to use a personal computer or a mainframe, what programming language to use for implementation, and how to structure and organize internal data and external data files. Other factors to consider in evaluating design approaches are the main memory requirements for a program and its data and the requirements for secondary storage of files.

Design

Once you understand the problem and have selected an overall approach to the design, it is time to develop a high-level design of the system. The top-down design approach instructs us to start at the top level and divide the original problem into subproblems. For each subproblem, we identify a subsystem that solves the subproblem. As we have done before, we can use a structure chart to indicate the relationships among the subproblems (and the subsystems). A structure chart for our telephone directory problem is shown in Fig. 9.1.

Figure 9.1   Structure Chart for Telephone Directory Problem

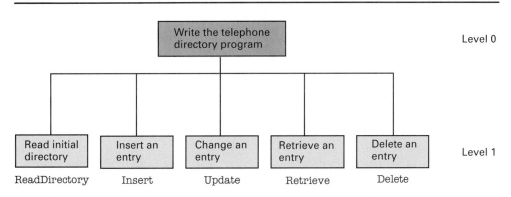

Figure 9.1 shows the top two levels of the structure chart—the original problem and its major subproblems. Each major subproblem should be implemented as a separate subsystem of modules. The modules are determined by refining and subdividing the major subproblems into still smaller subproblems. Figure 9.2 shows that to solve the subproblem "Retrieve an entry" we must be able to "Read a name," "Find a name in the directory," and "Get entry information from the directory."

Figure 9.2 Structure Chart for Retrieve an Entry

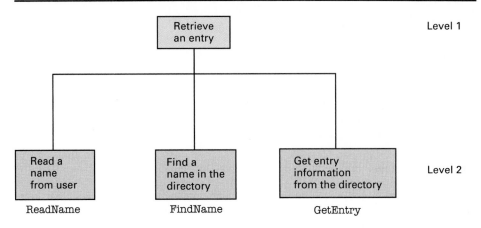

The second part of the design step of the SLC is to identify the major data elements and procedures for each module. We will use procedural and data abstraction to accomplish this step, as described in the next section.

Exercises for Section 9.2

Self-Check

1. List the six phases of the software life cycle. Which phase is the longest?
2. Draw a structure chart that shows a refinement for the subproblem "Change an entry."

9.3 Procedural Abstraction Revisited

Abstraction is a powerful technique that helps programmers (and problem solvers) deal with complex issues in a piecemeal fashion. The dictionary defines *abstraction* as the process of separating the inherent qualities or properties of something from the actual physical object to which they belong. One example of the use of abstraction is the representation of a program variable (for example, `Name` and `TelNumber`) by a storage location in memory. We don't have to know anything about the physical structure of memory to use variables in programming.

So far you have practiced *procedural abstraction,* which is the philosophy that procedure development should separate the concern of *what* is to be achieved by a procedure from the details of *how* it is to be achieved. In other words, you can specify what you expect a procedure to do, then use that procedure in the design of a problem solution before you know how to implement the procedure.

For example, we can use procedural abstraction to outline a program fragment to retrieve an entry from the directory:

```
ReadName (   );            {read the name that we are seeking}
FindName (   );            {locate the name in the directory}
if the name was found then
   GetEntry (   );         {retrieve entry from directory}
```

This fragment calls three procedures that were first shown in Fig. 9.2. We can fill in the parameter lists after the data flow information is added to the structure chart.

Procedure Libraries

As you progress through this course, you will write many Pascal programs and procedures. You should try to keep each new procedure as general as possible so you can reuse it in other applications. Eventually you will build a sizable library of your own procedures. Reusing tried and tested procedures is always more efficient than starting from scratch; each new procedure that you write will have to be thoroughly tested and debugged, requiring a lot of startup time in every case. The procedures in your personal library already will have been tested, so you will save time if you use procedures over and over again.

As an example, it would be helpful to have available a set of procedures for performing common data entry operations. Since procedure Read cannot be used to read Boolean values, your own procedure for this purpose would be useful. Procedure ReadLnBool, shown earlier (see Fig. 7.5), reads a character value and returns either True or False based on the data character. ReadLnBool should certainly be included in a programmer's library.

In many situations we would like a data value to lie within a specific subrange of values. For example, we might like to read in a character that is an uppercase letter or an integer in the range −10 to +10. Procedure EnterInt (see Fig. 9.3) accomplishes the latter operation. You easily could write similar procedures, called EnterChar and EnterReal, for other standard data types of Pascal. These procedures would also be useful additions to a programmer's library.

Figure 9.3 Procedure EnterInt

```
procedure EnterInt (MinN, MaxN {input} : Integer;
                    var N {output} : Integer);
{
 Reads an integer between MinN and MaxN into N.
 Pre : MinN and MaxN are assigned values.
 Post: Returns in N the first data value between MinN and MaxN
       if MinN <= MaxN is true; otherwise, N is not defined.
}
  var
    InRange : Boolean;          {program flag — loop control}
```

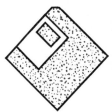

Directory: CHAP9
File: ENTERINT.PRO

```
begin {EnterInt}
  {Check for non-empty range.}
  if MinN <= MaxN then
    InRange := False              {no valid value in N as yet}
  else
    begin
      WriteLn ('Error - empty range for EnterInt');
      InRange := True              {Skip data entry loop.}
    end; {if}

  {Keep reading until a valid number is read into N.}
  while not InRange do
    begin
      Write ('Enter an integer between ');
      Write (MinN :1, ' and ', MaxN :1, '> ');
      ReadLn (N);
      InRange := (MinN <= N) and (N <= MaxN)    {Is N in range?}
    end {while}

end; {EnterInt}
```

It would also be practical to have a function named UpCase (see Fig. 9.4) that returns the uppercase form of an argument that is a lowercase letter. We will use function UpCase later in this chapter.

Figure 9.4 Function UpCase

Directory: CHAP9
File: UPCASE.FUN

```
function UpCase (Ch : Char) : Char;
{
 Returns the uppercase letter corresponding to Ch.
 Pre : Ch is defined.
 Post: If Ch is lowercase, returns the corresponding uppercase
       letter; otherwise, returns Ch.
}
begin {UpCase}
  if Ch in ['a'..'z'] then
    UpCase := Chr(Ord(Ch) - Ord('a') + Ord('A'))
  else
    UpCase := Ch
end; {UpCase}
```

PROGRAM
STYLE

Validating a Library Procedure's Parameters

Procedure EnterInt begins by checking whether its user correctly entered its input parameters, MinN and MaxN. If the parameters define an empty range, an error message is displayed and the Read operation is skipped. Make sure you carefully validate input parameters for procedures that are candidates for inclusion in a library. Since library procedures may be reused many times by many different programmers, this extra effort can pay valuable dividends.

Exercises for Section 9.3

Self-Check

1. What two pieces of information must you know about a library procedure before you can call it?
2. Why is the validation of procedure parameters more critical for a library procedure than for a procedure that is used in only a single program?

Programming

1. Write procedure `EnterChar` that returns a data character that lies within a specified range of characters. Your procedure should display an error message if the specified range is invalid.
2. Redo programming exercise 1 for a procedure that reads a real data value between a specified range of real numbers.

9.4 Data Abstraction and Abstract Data Types

From this point on in the course, we will begin to make extensive use of another type of abstraction, data abstraction. Through *data abstraction*, we specify the data objects for a problem and the operations to be performed on those data objects without being overly concerned with how the data objects will be represented and stored in memory, or how the operations will be implemented. We can describe *what* information is stored in the data object without being specific as to *how* the information is organized and represented. This is the *logical view* of the data object as opposed to its *physical view*, which is the actual internal representation in memory. Once we understand the logical view, we can use the data object and its operators in our programs; however, we (or someone else) will eventually have to implement the data object and its operators before we can run any program that uses them.

One simple example of data abstraction is the use of the Pascal data type `Real`, which is an abstraction for the set of real numbers. The computer hardware limits the range of real numbers that can be represented, and not all real numbers within a specified range can be represented. Also, the results of manipulating real numbers are often approximations to the actual result. However, we can generally use the data type `Real` and its Pascal operators (+,–,*, /,:=,<=,<, etc.) without being concerned with the details of its implementation.

Information Hiding

One advantage of procedural abstraction and data abstraction is that they enable a designer to make implementation decisions in a step-by-step manner. The designer can postpone making decisions regarding the actual internal representation of the data objects and the implementation of its operators. At the top levels of the design, the designer focuses on how to use a data object and its operators; at the lower levels of design, the designer works out the implementation details. In that way, the designer can control or reduce the overall complexity of the problem.

If the details of a data object's implementation are not known when a higher-level module is implemented, the higher-level module can access the data object only through its operators. From a software engineering viewpoint, this constraint is an advantage rather than a limitation. It allows the designer to change his or her mind at a later date and possibly choose a more efficient method of internal representation or implementation. If the higher-level modules reference a data object only through its operators, the higher-level module will not have to be rewritten and may not even need to be recompiled. The process of "hiding" the details of a low-level module's implementation from a higher-level module is called *information hiding*. We will explain how information hiding works later.

Abstract Data Types

One of the goals of software engineering is to write *reusable code,* that is, code that can be reused in many different applications, preferably without having to be altered and recompiled. One way we can write reusable code is to *encapsulate,* or combine, a data object together with its operators in a separate program module. As we discussed earlier, we can manipulate the data object in new programs by calling the operator procedures and functions contained in the module. We need not be concerned with the details of the data object's representation in memory or the details of the operators' implementation. The combination of a data object with its operators is called an *abstract data type* (ADT).

A primary goal of this book is to show you how to write and use ADTs in programming. As you progress through this course, you will create a large collection of ADTs in your own program library. Since the ADTs in your library already will have been coded, debugged, tested, and maybe even compiled, their use will make it much easier for you to design and implement new applications programs.

Normally an abstract data type consists of two parts: its specification and its implementation. The *specification part* describes the structure of the data object and the capabilities of its operators. The specification part contains all the information needed by Pascal to link the abstract data type with another program. It also contains the information that a potential user of the ADT needs to know. The *implementation part* contains the actual implementation of the operators, which may be hidden from users of the ADT.

Although standard Pascal does not support separate compilation, many extended versions of Pascal provide the capability to separately compile modules that contain ADTs. If you compile an ADT, then you can link its executable code with other programs that use it. If you are careful to include a fairly complete set of operator procedures in the ADT, the module containing the ADT will not have to be recompiled for each new application.

Self-Check

1. List the Pascal operators and standard functions that should be considered part of the complete specifications for the following built-in data types:
   a. `Real`   b. `Integer`   c. `Char`   d. `Boolean`
2. What is information hiding? Why is it important to a software designer?

9.5 Abstract Data Type DayADT

An ADT usually declares the form of a *data structure,* which can be used to store an actual data object. You will see how to do this in later chapters. However, we can illustrate the fundamental concepts now by developing a simpler ADT, DayADT, that declares an enumerated type Day whose values represent the days of the week. As part of DayADT, we provide operator procedures for reading and writing the days of the week. DayADT would be a useful addition to your library because Pascal does not allow you to directly read and write enumerated type values.

Figure 9.5 shows a possible form for ADT DayADT. Figure 9.5 is separated into two sections: *specification* and *implementation.* The *specification* (the section in color) is one long comment that should be read by a programmer who wants to use DayADT because it contains all the information the programmer needs to know.

Figure 9.5   Abstract Data Type DayADT

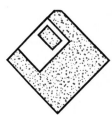

Directory: CHAP9
File: DAYADT.ADT

```
{
  Specification of DayADT

  Structure:    Day is an enumerated data type whose values
                represent the days of the week.

  Operators:    The following descriptions assume these
                parameters:

                    ADay is type Day.
                    ValidDay is type Boolean.

  ReadDay (var ADay, var ValidDay) : Reads two data characters
  and stores the value represented by the data in ADay.  Sets
  ValidDay to indicate whether the data are valid.

  WriteDay (ADay) : Displays the value of ADay.
}


{
  Implementation of DayADT
}
```

```
type
   Day = (Sunday, Monday, Tuesday, Wednesday,
          Thursday, Friday, Saturday);

{Insert function UpCase here (see Fig. 9.4)}

procedure ReadLnDay (var ADay {output} : Day;
                     var ValidDay {output} : Boolean);
{
 Reads two data characters and stores the value represented by
 the data in ADay.  Sets ValidDay to indicate whether the data
 are valid.
 Pre : None
 Post: ADay is assigned a value if the
       two characters read are SU, MO, TU, WE, TH, FR, or SA;
       otherwise, ADay is undefined.
       ValidDay is set to True if ADay is defined;
       otherwise, ValidDay is set to False.
 Uses: UpCase
}
   var
     DayCh1,                          {input - first letter in day}
     DayCh2 : Char;                   {input - second letter in day}

begin {ReadLnDay}
   Write ('Enter first two letters of the day name> ');
   Read (DayCh1, DayCh2);
   {Convert to uppercase}
   DayCh1 := UpCase(DayCh1);
   DayCh2 := UpCase(DayCh2);

   {Convert to day of week}
   ValidDay := True;                          {Assume valid day}
   if (DayCh1 = 'S') and (DayCh2 = 'U') then
     ADay := Sunday
   else if (DayCh1 = 'M') and (DayCh2 = 'O') then
     ADay := Monday
   else if (DayCh1 = 'T') and (DayCh2 = 'U') then
     ADay := Tuesday
   else if (DayCh1 = 'W') and (DayCh2 = 'E') then
     ADay := Wednesday
   else if (DayCh1 = 'T') and (DayCh2 = 'H') then
     ADay := Thursday
   else if (DayCh1 = 'F') and (DayCh2 = 'R') then
     ADay := Friday
   else if (DayCh1 = 'S') and (DayCh2 = 'A') then
     ADay := Saturday
   else
     ValidDay := False                  {day is not valid}
end; {ReadLnDay}


procedure WriteDay (ADay {input} : Day);
{
 Displays the value of ADay.
 Pre : ADay is defined.
 Post: Displays a string corresponding to the value of ADay.
}
begin {WriteDay}
   case ADay of
     Sunday    : Write ('Sunday');
     Monday    : Write ('Monday');
     Tuesday   : Write ('Tuesday');
```

```
         Wednesday : Write ('Wednesday');
          Thursday : Write ('Thursday');
            Friday : Write ('Friday');
          Saturday : Write ('Saturday')
       end {case}
    end; {WriteDay}
```

The specification describes the structure of the data type encapsulated in the ADT and lists any other modules needed by the ADT. For each operator, there is a list of parameters and a summary of the operation performed. Variable parameters are preceded by the reserved word var.

The specification is followed by the implementation section, which contains declarations for the encapsulated data type and its operator procedures. The procedure declarations are preceded by a comment that reminds the user of the ADT to insert function UpCase, which is called by procedure ReadLnDay.

Using Abstract Type Day

You should save the complete ADT shown in Fig. 9.5 as a file on disk. (Insert function UpCase where indicated in the implementation section first.) When you use DayADT in a new program, this file can be read from disk and inserted in the declaration part of the new program. You should place the declaration for type Day so that it appears with the other type declarations in the new program and precedes the declaration of any variable of type Day. The declarations for procedures ReadLnDay and WriteDay should appear with the other procedure declarations. If your compiler allows procedures to be declared before variables, you could insert the entire ADT right after the last type declaration in the new program. This is non-standard, however, and would not be possible on all Pascal compilers.

Some Pascal compilers have *compiler directives,* which are special lines inserted in the program file that provide instructions to the compiler. Often a compiler directive instructs the compiler to include a previously saved file into another file that is being compiled. For example, the line on the left (for VAX Pascal) or the comment on the right (for Turbo Pascal)

```
%Include 'DayADT.PAS'
```

instructs the compiler to include file DayADT.ADT at the point where this appears in the program being compiled. The lines in file DayADT.ADT would be inserted and translated, and any syntax errors would be displayed.

Alternatively, some compilers allow you to compile source files that are not complete Pascal programs as separate program modules (for example, VAX Pascal modules or Turbo Pascal units). In this case, a file containing Pascal code similar to that shown in Fig. 9.5 could be compiled as a separate program module, resulting in an object file that would be saved on disk. You could then write a new program that uses ADT DayADT without including this code in your new program (called a *client* of DayADT). After compiling the client program, you could instruct the linker to link its object code with that of module DayADT.

You could then load the resulting object code file for the client program into memory and run it. How to create and use separate module files is discussed in Appendix D for VAX Pascal and in Appendix E for Turbo Pascal.

For our purposes, we will assume that the disk file for DayADT must be inserted directly in the source file of any new program that uses it. We will use comments such as

```
{Insert data type Day from DayADT.}
{Insert procedures ReadLnDay and WriteDay from DayADT.}
```

to remind you to do this; you should perform the insertion manually or by using a compiler directive if one is available on your system.

■ Example 9.1

Figure 9.6 uses DayADT. It reads and displays one day of the week and a message if the day read is the first day of the week.   ■

Figure 9.6   Testing DayADT

Directory: CHAP9
File: TESTDAY.PAS

```
program TestDay (Input, Output);
{
  Tests abstract data type DayADT.

  Modules needed:  Uses Day, ReadLnDay, WriteDay from
      DayADT (see Fig. 9.5)
}

  {Insert data type Day from DayADT.}

  var
    Today : Day;                {input – day being read}
    GoodDay : Boolean;          {program flag for valid data}

  {Insert procedures ReadLnDay and WriteDay from DayADT.}

begin {TestDay}
  WriteLn ('What day is today?');
  ReadLnDay (Today, GoodDay);
  WriteLn;
  if not GoodDay then
    WriteLn ('Error – no day read')
  else
    begin
      Write ('Today is ');
      WriteDay (Today);
      WriteLn;
      if Today = Sunday then
        WriteLn ('Today is the first day of the week')
    end {if}
end.  {TestDay}


What day is today?
Enter first two letters of the day name> SU
Today is Sunday
Today is the first day of the week
```

The *module dependency diagram* in Fig. 9.7 summarizes the interaction between modules. It shows that program TestDay uses DayADT and that DayADT uses function UpCase. A module dependency diagram resembles a system structure chart. The difference is that a system structure chart shows control flow and data flow between the procedures of a single module or program system, whereas a module dependency diagram shows control flow between modules.

Figure 9.7   Module Dependency Diagram

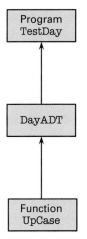

Exercises for Section 9.5

Self-Check

1. Describe the contents of the specification and implementation sections of an ADT.
2. Draw a structure chart for program TestDay that shows the data flow information between program procedures.

Programming

1. Write an ADT MonthADT that contains the declaration for an enumerated type Month, procedures ReadMonth and WriteMonth, and function Month-Equivalent. Function MonthEquivalent has an integer argument of 1 through 12 and returns an appropriate enumerated constant as its value.
2. Write a client program that tests your MonthADT.

9.6 Software Testing

Whether a program is designed carefully and runs efficiently does not really matter if the program does not do what it is supposed to do. One way to show that a program is correct is through testing. It is very difficult, however, to determine just how much testing should be done. Very often errors will appear in a software product after it is delivered. Some notable software errors in operational programs have caused power brownouts, telephone network saturation, and space flight delays. In some situations, it is impossible to test a software product in advance of its use. Examples would be software that controls a missile or that prevents a nuclear disaster in the event of a nuclear power plant malfunction.

Preparing a Test Plan Early

It is best to develop a plan for testing early in the design stage of a new system. Some aspects of a test plan include deciding how the software will be tested, when the tests will occur, and who will do the testing. Normally testing is done by the programmer, by other members of the software team who did not code the module being tested, and by users of the software product. Some companies have special testing groups that are expert at finding bugs in other programmers' code. If the test plan is developed early in the design stage, testing can take place concurrently with the design and coding. The earlier an error is detected, the easier and less expensive it is to correct.

Another advantage of deciding on a test plan early is that programmers are encouraged to prepare for testing as they write their code. A good programmer will practice *defensive programming* and include code that detects unexpected or invalid data values. For example, if a procedure has the precondition

```
pre : N greater than zero
```

it would be a good idea to place the `if` statement

```
if N <= 0 then
   WriteLn ('Invalid value for parameter N -- ', N :1);
```

at the beginning of the procedure. This `if` statement will provide a diagnostic message in the event that the parameter passed to the procedure is invalid.

Similarly, if a data value being read from the keyboard is supposed to be between 0 and 40, a defensive programmer would use procedure `EnterInt` (see Fig. 9.3), as shown next:

```
WriteLn ('Enter number of hours worked>');
EnterInt (Hours, 0, 40)
```

The second and third parameters of `EnterInt` define the range of acceptable values for its first parameter.

Structured Walkthroughs

One important testing technique is called a structured walkthrough. In a *structured walkthrough,* the programmer describes, or "walks through," the logic of a new module as part of a presentation to other members of the software team. The purpose of the walkthrough is for team members to identify design errors or bugs that may have been overlooked by the programmer because he or she is too close to the problem. The goal is to detect errors in logic before they become part of the code.

Black Box versus White Box Testing

There are two basic ways to test a completed module or system: *black box,* or *specification-based,* testing and *white box* testing, also known as *glass box* testing. In black box testing, we assume that the program tester has no idea of the code inside the module or system. The tester's job is to verify that the module does what its specification says it does. For a procedure, this means ensuring that the procedure's postconditions are satisfied whenever its preconditions are met. For a system or subsystem, this means ensuring that the system does indeed satisfy its original requirements specification. Because the tester cannot look inside the module or system, he or she must prepare sufficient sets of test data to ensure that the system outputs are correct for all valid system inputs. The tester should especially check the *boundaries* of the system, that is, particular values for the program variables where the system performance changes. For example, a boundary for a payroll program would be the value of hours worked that triggers overtime pay. Also, the module or system should not crash when presented with invalid inputs. Black box testing is most often done by a special testing team or by program users.

In white box testing, the tester has full knowledge of the code for the module or system and must ensure that each and every section of code has been thoroughly tested. For a selection statement (`if` or `case`), this means checking all possible paths through the selection statement. The tester must determine that the correct path is chosen for all possible values of the selection variable, taking special care at the boundary values where the path changes.

For a loop, the tester must make sure that the loop always performs the correct number of iterations and that the number of iterations is not off by one. Also, the tester must verify that the computations inside the loop are correct at the boundaries, that is, for the initial and final values of the loop-control variable. Finally, the tester must make sure that the module or system still meets its specification when a loop executes zero times and that there are no circumstances under which the loop could execute forever.

Integration Testing

Section 6.9 discussed the differences between top-down and bottom-up testing of a single system. Another aspect of testing is called integration testing. In *integration testing,* the program tester must determine whether the individual components of a system that have been separately tested (using top-down or bottom-up testing or some combination) can be integrated with other like components. Each phase of integration testing will deal with larger units, progressing from individual modules, through subsystems, and ending with the entire system. For example, after two subsystems are completed, integration testing must determine whether the two subsystems can work together. Once the entire system is completed, integration testing must determine whether that system is compatible with other systems in the computing environment in which it will be used.

Exercises for Section 9.6

Self-Check

1. Explain why a procedure interface error would not be discovered through white box testing.
2. Devise a set of data to test procedure EnterInt (Fig. 9.3) using
   a. white box testing
   b. black box testing

9.7 Formal Methods of Program Verification[1]

Section 9.6 described some aspects of program and system testing. We stated that testing should begin as early as possible in the design phase and continue through system implementation. Even though testing is an extremely valuable tool for providing evidence that a program is correct and meets its specification, it is difficult to know how much testing is enough. For example, how do we know that we have tried enough different sets of test data or that all possible paths through the program have been executed?

For these reasons, computer scientists have developed a second method of demonstrating the correctness of a program. This method, called *formal verification,* involves the application of formal rules to show that a program meets its specification. By carefully applying formal rules, we can determine that a program meets its specification just as a mathematician proves a theorem using definitions, axioms, and previously proved theorems. Formal verification works well on small programs, but there is some question as to whether this method can be used effectively on very large programs or program systems.

A thorough discussion of formal verification is beyond the scope of this book. However, we will introduce two key concepts, assertion and loop invariant, and use them to help document and clarify some modules.

Assertions

An important part of formal verification is the documenting of a program through *assertions*—logical statements about the program that are "asserted" to be true. An assertion is written as a comment and describes what is supposed to be true about the program variables at that point.

---

[1] The material in this section was adapted from an outline prepared by James C. Pleasant, Department of Computer and Information Sciences, Tennessee State University, Johnson City, Tennessee.

Example 9.2

407

9.7 Formal Methods
of Program
Verification

Example 9.2

The next program fragment contains a sequence of assignment statements, each followed by an assertion.

```
A := 5;            {assert: A is 5}
X := A;            {assert: X is 5}
Y := X + A;        {assert: Y is 10}
```

The truth of the first assertion, {A is 5}, follows from executing the first statement with the knowledge that 5 is a constant. The truth of the second assertion, {X is 5}, follows from executing X := A with the knowledge that A is 5. The truth of the third assertion, {Y is 10}, follows from executing Y := X + A with the knowledge that X is 5 and A is 5. In this fragment, we used assertions as comments to document the change in a program variable after each assignment statement executes.

The task of using formal verification is to prove that a program fragment meets its specification. For the preceding fragment, this means proving that the final assertion, or *postcondition* (in this case, {Y is 10}), follows from the initial presumption, or *precondition* (in this case, {5 is a constant}), after the program fragment executes. The assignment rule (described next) is critical to this process. If we know that {A is 5} is true, the assignment rule allows us to make the assertion {X is 5} after executing the statement X := A.

The Assignment Rule

```
{P(A)}
X := A;
{P(X)}
```

Explanation: If P(A) is a logical statement (assertion) about A, the same statement will be true of X after the assignment statement X := A executes. ■

For our purposes, it will suffice to use assertions as a documentation tool to improve our understanding of programs rather than as a means of formally proving them correct. Our assertions will be written in informal English, not in a formal language for logical statements. We have already used assertions to document the effect of executing a procedure.

Preconditions and Postconditions

A procedure's precondition is a logical statement about its input parameters. A procedure's postcondition may be a logical statement about its output parameters, or it may be a logical statement that describes the change in *program state* caused by the procedure's execution. Any of the following activities represents a change in program state: changing the value of a variable, writing additional program output, reading new input data.

Example 9.3

The precondition and the postcondition for procedure EnterInt (see Fig. 9.3) are repeated next.

```
procedure EnterInt (MinN, MaxN {input} : Integer;
                        var N {output} : Integer);
{
 Reads an integer between MinN and MaxN into N.
 Pre : MinN and MaxN are assigned values.
 Post: Returns in N the first data value between MinN and MaxN
       if MinN <= MaxN is true; otherwise, N is not defined.
}
```

The precondition tells us that input parameters MinN and MaxN are defined before the procedure begins execution. The postcondition tells us that the procedure's execution assigns the first data value between MinN and MaxN to the output parameter N whenever MinN <= MaxN is true. ∎

Loop Invariant

We stated earlier that loops are a common source of program errors. It is often difficult to determine that a loop body executes exactly the right number of times or that loop execution causes the desired change in program variables. A special type of assertion, a *loop invariant,* is used to help prove that a loop meets its specification. A loop invariant is a logical statement involving program variables that is true before the loop is entered and after each execution of the loop body. It must, therefore, be true just after the loop is exited. An invariant is called such because it is a relationship that remains true as loop execution progresses.

As an example of a loop invariant, let's examine the following loop, which accumulates the sum of the integers 1, 2, . . . , N, where N is a positive integer and Sum, I, and N are type Integer.

```
{
 Accumulate the sum of integers 1 through N in Sum.

 assert: N >= 1
}
Sum := 0;
I := 1;
while I <= N do
  begin
    Sum := Sum + I;
    I := I + 1
  end; {while}

{assert: Sum is 1 + 2 + 3 + ... + N-1 + N}
```

The first assertion, {N >= 1}, is the precondition for the loop, and the last assertion is its postcondition.

We stated previously that the loop invariant must be true before the loop begins execution and after each loop repetition. Since it traces the loop's progress, the loop invariant should be a logical statement about the loop-control variable I and the accumulating sum.

Figure 9.8 sketches the loop's progress for the first three iterations of the loop. At the end of the third iteration, I is 4 and Sum is 6—the sum of all integers less than 4 (1 + 2 + 3). When loop repetition finishes, I will be N+1 and Sum will contain the desired result (1 + 2 + 3 + ... + N). Therefore, we propose the invariant

```
{invariant: I <= N+1 and Sum is 1 + 2 + ... + I-1}
```

In English this means that I must be less than or equal to N+1 and that after each loop repetition, Sum is equal to the sum of all positive integers less than I.

Figure 9.8   Sketch of Summation Loop

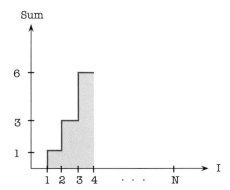

You may be wondering why the first part of the invariant is I <= N+1 instead of I <= N. This is because the loop invariant must be true after the last iteration of the loop. Since the last step taken in the loop body is to increment I, the last value assigned to I just prior to loop exit is N+1.

The loop invariant must also be true before loop execution begins. At this point, I is 1 and 1 <= N+1 is true for N >= 1 (the precondition). Also, the invariant requires that the value of Sum be equal to the summation of all positive integers less than 1. Because Sum is initialized to 0, this is also the case.

In program verification, the loop invariant is used to prove that the loop meets its specification. For our purposes, we will use the loop invariant to document what we know about the loop's behavior, and we will place it just before the loop body, as shown next.

```
{
  Accumulate the sum of integers 1 through N in Sum.

  assert: N >= 1
}
Sum := 0;
I := 1;
while I <= N do
  {invariant: I <= N+1 and Sum is 1 + 2 + ... + I-1}
  begin
    Sum := Sum + I;
    I := I + 1
  end; {while}

{assert: Sum is 1 + 2 + 3 + ... + N-1 + N}
```

Loop Invariants as a Design Tool

Some computer scientists recommend writing the loop invariant as a preliminary step before coding the loop. The invariant serves as a specification for the loop, and it can be used as a guide to help determine the loop initialization, the loop repetition condition, and the loop body. For example, we can write the following loop invariant to describe a summation loop that adds N data items:

```
{invariant:
   Count <= N and
   Sum is the sum of all data read so far
}
```

From the loop invariant, we can infer the following:

• the loop initialization is:

```
Sum := 0.0;
Count := 0;
```

• the loop repetition test is:

```
Count < N
```

• the loop body is

```
Read (Next);
Sum := Sum + Next;
Count := Count + 1;
```

Given all this information, it becomes a simple task to write the summation loop (see programming exercise 2).

Invariants and the for Statement

Since the loop invariant states what we know to be true about a loop after each iteration, we should be able to write an invariant for a for statement as well as a while statement. However, the loop-control variable in a for statement is undefined after loop exit occurs. So that the loop invariant will remain true, we will assume that the loop-control variable in a for statement is incremented just before loop exit and retains its final value. This assumption allows us to use a loop invariant to document the following for loop:

```
{assert: N >= 1}

Sum := 0;
for I := 1 to N do
  {invariant: I <= N+1 and Sum is 1 + 2 + ... + I-1}
  Sum := Sum + I;

{assert: Sum is 1 + 2 + 3 + ... + N-1 + N}
```

More Loop Invariants

This subsection provides another example of the use of a loop invariant and assertions to document a loop.

■ Example 9.4

Figure 9.9 shows a sentinel-controlled `while` loop that computes the product of a collection of data values. Loop exit occurs after the sentinel value (value of `Sentinel`) is read. The loop invariant indicates that `Product` is the product of all values read before the current one and that none of these values was the sentinel. The preconditions and postconditions for the loop are written as assertions.   ■

Figure 9.9 Sentinel-Controlled Loop with Invariant

```
{
  Compute the product of a sequence of data values.

  assert: Sentinel is a constant
}
Product := 1;
WriteLn ('When done, enter ', Sentinel :1, ' to stop.');
WriteLn ('Enter the first number> ');
ReadLn (Num);
while Num <> Sentinel do
  {invariant:
     Product is the product of all prior values read into Num
     and no prior value of Num was the sentinel
  }
  begin
    Product := Product * Num;
    WriteLn ('Enter the next number> ');
    ReadLn (Num)
  end; {while}

{assert:
   Product is the product of all numbers
   read into Num before the sentinel
}
```

Exercises for Section 9.7

Self-Check

1. a. Write the loop invariant and the assertion following the loop for the `while` loop in procedure `EnterInt` (Fig. 9.3).
   b. What other assertions should be added to procedure `EnterInt` to facilitate its verification?
2. If the sentinel-controlled loop in Fig. 9.9 were rewritten as a flag-controlled loop, what would the new loop invariant look like? The flag `NoZero` should remain true until a zero value is read.
3. Write the loop invariant and the assertion following the loop for the loop in procedure `IOName` of Fig. 8.13.

Programming

1. Wrte a function that returns the count (`N`) of the number of nonzero digits in an arbitrary integer (`Number`). Your solution should include a `while` loop for which the following loop invariant is valid:

```
{invariant:
    0 <= Count <= N and Number has been
    divided by 10 Count times.
}
```

and this assertion would be valid following the loop:

```
{assert: Count is N}
```

2. Write a program fragment that implements the loop whose invariant is described in the subsection entitled "Loop Invariants as a Design Tool."

9.8 Professional Ethics and Responsibilities

Software engineers and computer programmers are professionals and should always act that way. As part of their jobs, computer programmers may be able to access large data banks that contain sensitive personnel information, information that is classified "secret" or "top secret," or financial transaction data. Programmers should always behave in a socially responsible manner and not retrieve information they are not entitled to see. They should not use any information that they access for their own personal gain or do anything that would be considered illegal, unethical, or harmful to others.

You may have heard stories about "computer hackers" who have broken into secure data banks by using their own computers to call by telephone the computer that controls access to a data bank. Some hackers have sold classified information retrieved in this way to intelligence agencies of other countries. Others retrieve similar information for their own amusement, as a prank, or just to demonstrate that they can. Regardless of the intent, such activity is illegal and subject to government prosecution.

Another illegal activity sometimes practiced by hackers is the insertion of special code, called a *virus,* in a computer's disk memory. A virus will cause sporadic activities to occur that disrupt the operation of the host computer. For example, unusual messages may appear on the screen at certain times. Viruses can also cause the host computer to erase portions of its own disk memory, thereby destroying valuable information and programs. Viruses are spread from one computer to another when data are copied from the infected disk and processed by a different computer. Certainly these kinds of activities should not be considered harmless pranks; they are illegal and often cause irreparable damage.

A programmer who changes information in a data base containing financial records is guilty of *computer theft* or *computer fraud.* This is a felony, which can lead to fines and imprisonment.

Another example of unprofessional behavior is using someone else's program or code without permission. While it is certainly permissible to use procedures in libraries that have been developed for reuse by your own company's programmers, you should not use another programmer's personal code or code from another company without permission. Failure to do so could lead to an expensive lawsuit against you and/or your company.

Another fraudulent practice is submitting another student's code as your own. This, of course, is plagiarism, and is no different from copying material from a book or paper and calling it your own work. Most universities have severe penalties for plagiarism, ranging from a failing grade for the course to dismissal from the university. Even if you modify the code slightly or substitute your own comments or different variable names, you are still guilty of plagiarism if you use another person's ideas and code. To avoid any question of plagiarism, find out beforehand your instructor's rules with respect to working with others on a project. If group efforts are not allowed, make sure that you work independently and submit only your own code.

Many commercial software packages are protected by copyright laws and cannot be copied or duplicated. It is illegal to make additional copies of protected software that you may be using at work for use on your home computer. Besides the fact that this is against the law, using software copied from another computer increases the possibility that your computer will receive a virus. You should act ethically and honor any copyright agreements that pertain to a particular software package.

9.9 Common Programming Errors

When using a procedure from a library, you must know the name of the library in which the procedure is found and you must have a description of the procedure interface. Specifically, you must know the Number, Order, and Type (NOT) of the procedure's parameters. Make sure that all variable formal parameters correspond to actual parameters that are variables of the same type. Also, make sure that all preconditions for a procedure's parameters (as listed in the procedure interface) are satisfied before the procedure call statement executes. Finally, the library containing the procedure you are using must be linked to your program before you attempt to run it.

The rules for using an abstract data type (ADT) are different on each Pascal system. In Turbo Pascal, you can encapsulate an ADT in a unit; in VAX Pascal, you can encapsulate an ADT in a module. The client program must communicate to the Pascal compiler the names of any ADTs used. You must also compile the ADT before you compile the Pascal program. In Turbo Pascal, the ADT is automatically linked to the object code; in VAX Pascal, you must do this during the link step.

If your system does not support separate compilation of ADTs, you must insert the data type and procedure declarations directly in the main program or the client of the ADT. Make sure that each declaration from the ADT is inserted before its first reference.

CHAPTER REVIEW

This chapter discussed programming in the large and the software engineering process. It introduced the system/software life cycle (SLC) and described the phases of the SLC:

1. Requirements specification
2. Analysis
3. Design
4. Implementation
5. Testing and validation
6. Operation, follow-up, and maintenance

Special emphasis was placed on discussion of two phases of the software life cycle which had not yet been covered in depth: requirements specification and testing and validation. We discussed planning for testing, selection of test teams, structured walkthroughs, black box testing, white box testing, and integration testing.

We also introduced program verification as an alternative to testing and described the use of assertions and loop invariants. In this course, we will use informal logical statements about programs and loops to document our programs so that we can better understand them.

We also reviewed procedural abstraction and introduced data abstraction. We described the use of procedure libraries and special modules called abstract data types (ADTs), which encapsulate a data object together with its operators. We showed how to write in standard Pascal an ADT consisting of an enumerated type together with operators that read and write values of that type.

You saw that there were many advantages to creating and using your own procedure libraries. Procedures are the building blocks of larger program systems. The use of procedures makes it easier to assign pieces of a large project to different members of a programming team. Once a procedure is completed and tested, it can be included in a library of procedures to simplify its reuse in other programs and by other programmers.

Finally, since we have geared the discussion in this chapter to techniques practiced by software professionals, we discussed ethics and professional behavior. We described the special responsibilities that programmers have because of their ability to access sensitive information. We discussed computer viruses and how they are spread. We also described how using another programmer's code or ideas is plagiarism and carries severe penalties in industry as well as in the classroom.

✓ Quick-Check Exercises

1. The six phases of the software life cycle are listed below in arbitrary order. Place them in their correct order.

   testing and validation, design, requirements specification, operation and maintenance, implementation, analysis

2. In which phases are the users of a software product likely to be involved?
3. In which phases are the programmers and analysts likely to be involved?
4. Which phase lasts the longest?

5. Name the two sections of an abstract data type. Where is the data type declaration found? Where are the procedure declarations found?

6. _____ testing requires the use of test data that exercise each statement in a module.

7. _____ testing focuses on testing the functional characteristics of a module.

8. Which of the following may be false?

   loop invariant, `while` condition, assertion?

9. The use of loop invariants is useful for which of the following?

   loop control, loop design, and loop verification.

10. Write a loop invariant for the following code segment:

```
Product := 1;
Counter := 2;
while Counter < 5 do
  begin
    Product := Product * Counter;
    Counter := Counter + 1
  end;
```

Answers to Quick-Check Exercises

1. requirements specification, analysis, design, implementation, testing and validation, operation and maintenance
2. requirements specification, testing and validation, operation and maintenance
3. all phases
4. operation and maintenance
5. specification and implementation sections; specification; implementation
6. white box
7. black box
8. `while` condition
9. loop design, loop verification
10. {invariant:
       Counter <= 6 and
       Product contains product of all integers < Counter
    }

Review Questions

1. Explain why the principle of information hiding is important to the software designer.
2. Define the terms *procedural abstraction* and *data abstraction*.
3. Which of the following are likely to occur in a programmer's library of procedures? Explain your answers.
   a. a procedure that raises a number to a specified power
   b. a procedure that writes the user instructions for a particular program
   c. a procedure that displays the message HI MOM in block letters
   d. a procedure that displays the block letter M
4. Write an abstract data type for the positions on a baseball team (pitcher, catcher, infield, outfield) and operators to read and write those positions.
5. Write an abstract data type Money that allows you to do basic arithmetic operations (addition, subtraction, multiplication, and division) on real numbers having exactly two digits to the right of the decimal point.

6. Which of the following statements is incorrect?
   a. Loop invariants are used in loop verification.
   b. Loop invariants are used in loop design.
   c. A loop invariant is always an assertion.
   d. An assertion is always a loop invariant.
7. Briefly describe a test plan for the telephone directory program described in Section 9.2. Assume that integration testing is used.
8. Write a procedure that computes the average number of characters found on the lines of a text file. Include loop invariants and any other assertions necessary to verify that the procedure is correct.

Programming Projects

1. Write an abstract data type that consists of data type `ColorType` and operators for reading and writing the colors (red, yellow, green, blue, black, brown, orange, purple, and white).
2. Write a set of library procedures (or functions) that may be used to determine the following information for an integer input parameter:
   a. Is it a multiple of 7, 11, or 13?
   b. Is the sum of the digits odd or even?
   c. What is the square root value?
   d. Is it a prime number?
   Write a client program that tests your library procedures using the following input values: 104 3773 13 121 77 3075.
3. Each month, a bank customer deposits $50 into a savings account. Assume that the interest rate is fixed and is a problem input. The interest is calculated on a quarterly basis. For example, if the account earns 6.5 percent annually, it earns one-fourth of 6.5 percent every three months. Write a program to compute the total investment, the total amount in the account, and the interest accrued for each of the 120 months of a 10-year period. Assume that the rate is applied to all funds in the account at the end of a quarter, regardless of when the deposits were made.

    Print all values accurate to two decimal places. The table printed by your program when the annual interest rate is 6.5 percent should begin as follows:

Directory: CHAP9
File: PROJ9_3.PAS

MONTH	INVESTMENT	NEW AMOUNT	INTEREST	TOTAL SAVINGS
1	50.00	50.00	0.00	50.00
2	100.00	100.00	0.00	100.00
3	150.00	150.00	2.44	152.44
4	200.00	202.44	0.00	202.44
5	250.00	252.44	0.00	252.44
6	300.00	302.44	4.91	307.35
7	350.00	357.35	0.00	357.35

4. Redo programming project 3, adding columns to allow comparison of interest compounded monthly (one-twelfth of annual rate every month) with continuously compounded interest. The formula for continuously compounded interest is

$$amount = principle \times e^{rate * time}$$

where *rate* is the annual interest rate and *time* is expressed in years.
5. An employee time card is represented as one long string of characters. Write a program that processes a collection of these strings stored in a data file and writes the results to an output file.

The data string for each employee has the form

Positions	Data
1–10	Employee last name
11–20	Employee first name
21	Contains C for city office or S for suburban office
22	Contains U (union) or N (nonunion)
23–26	Employee identification number
27	blank
28–29	Number of regular hours (a whole number)
30	blank
31–36	Hourly rate (dollars and cents)
37	blank
38–39	Number of dependents
40	blank
41–42	Number of overtime hours (a whole number)

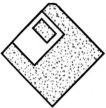

Directory: CHAP9
File: PROJ9_5.PAS

a. Compute gross pay using the formula

$$gross = regular\ hours \times rate + overtime\ hours \times 1.5 \times rate$$

b. Compute net pay by subtracting the following deductions:

$federal\ tax = .14 \times (gross - 13 \times dependents)$
$social\ security = 0.052 \times gross$
$city\ tax = 4\%$ of $gross$ if employee works in the city
$union\ dues = 6.75\%$ of $gross$ for union member

6. Write a menu-driven program that contains options for creating a data file to be processed by the payroll program described in programming project 5 (the user should be prompted to enter several time cards from the keyboard), displaying the time cards in the file on a printer, adding new time cards to the end of an existing file, and deleting time cards from an existing file based on their ordinal position within the file (e.g., deleting the seventh time card), and quitting the program.

   To add or delete lines from a text file requires copying the original data file to a *scratch*, or temporary, file and then back to the original file. During the copy process, time cards to be deleted are simply not copied to the scratch file. Adding new time cards to the end of the file takes place after all the time cards from the original file have been copied to the scratch file.

INTERVIEW
Robert Sedgewick

Robert Sedgewick is Professor of Computer Science at Princeton University. He has held visiting research positions at Xerox PARC, Institute for Defense Analyses, and INRIA. Sedgewick is a widely published author, whose research interests include mathematical analysis of algorithms, structures and algorithms, and program visualization.

What was the major influence on your choosing computer science as a profession?

I like to program. I think that's a primary reason why most people are in the profession. In ancient times (the early 1960s), quite a bit of effort was required to get near a computer, and you would be crazy to even try to do it if you didn't like it. Getting a one hundred-line program to work was something that might require a week's work, since one-day turnaround was common. You turned in your card deck one day and got your printout the next day. Under those circumstances, you were strongly motivated to outsmart the system, and it was quite satisfying to be able to actually do so.

Why are algorithms and data structures fundamental to computer science?

Algorithms and data structures represent an abstraction of the notion of a particular program running on a particular machine. This abstraction has served us well, because algorithms and data structures have been remarkably robust, across generations of machines. The best available sorting method today is the same as the best available sorting method 30 years ago, and the same goes for data structures and algorithms for searching and many other problems. Thus, though one might think that new technology would make old methods obsolete, it has turned out that algorithms and data structures can be thought of as representative of the knowledge built up over the years in all the programs that have been written. When you develop a program for sorting, or searching, or some other classical problem, then either you are inventing something that has eluded others over the years, or you are reinventing some classical algorithm. The former happens sufficiently often to make the field still exciting, even for newcomers, and the latter happens sufficiently often that it is worthwhile to study the best classical methods and take advantage of others' experience.

Is there a connection between famous classical problems like Towers of Hanoi, dining philosophers, or traveling salesman and the study of areas like software engineering or computer graphics?

Most of the "classical problems" in computer science are not too old and not too far removed from practical problems. Anyone involved in a serious endeavor solving a practical problem with a computer is very likely to encounter recursion (as typified by Towers of Hanoi), synchronization (as typified by dining philosophers), and NP-completeness (as typified by the traveling salesman problem). An educated computer scientist will have a better chance to cope, having studied the classical problems.

Universal models of computation, Turing machines and the like, seem like games theoreticians play that aren't that important for computing professionals making a living in the real world. What is the link between computational models and applications?

Sometimes there are direct links. Often, the very best way to solve a problem is to invent an abstract machine (computational model) suited to the problem, then write a simple simulator for the machine. Other times, the links are indirect, but also very important. For example, intensive study of computational models related to problems like the traveling salesman problem have led to the development of the theory of "NP-completeness," which tells the practicing programmer not to expect to easily find a tricky way to solve the traveling salesman problem efficiently, and that there are a vast number of similar "NP-complete" problems. By studying the theory, one can perhaps learn to more easily recognize (and perhaps avoid) the onset of NP-completeness in practice. This is a very significant advance over the situation faced by practicing programmers even in 1975.

What major events do you foresee in research in algorithms and data structures in the 1990s?

Serendipity is one of the most attractive aspects of working in research. No one can know where the real breakthroughs will come, so I'll pass on this question.

Among the goals of studying algorithms is the design of more efficient programs. Efficiency of a similar kind is also a goal for those who build computers—the architects. In what ways do hardware and software designers share information to achieve common goals?

Given a specific program, a good hardware designer can build a machine that will do an outstanding job executing that program, but a great hardware designer will come up with a machine that is fast for a large class of similar programs. Conversely, given a specific machine, a good software designer can write a program that will come up with a program that will run fast on a large class of similar machines. The best way to generalize, in both cases, is through abstraction: settle on a specific set of operations that the hardware should be built to perform and that should be used to build the software. Common goals are best served when both sides agree on the same set of operations. Actually, this is frequently the case in successful machine designs. Note that this goes back to your earlier question on the value of models of computation.

10

Arrays

I n the programs we have written so far, each variable was associated with a single memory cell. These variables are called simple variables, and their data types are simple ones. The only exceptions were file variables, which were associated with a collection of characters stored on disk.

In this chapter, you will study *structured variables*, or data structures. A structured variable represents a grouping of related data items in main memory. The items in a structured variable can be processed individually, although some operations can be performed on the structure as a whole.

Pascal provides *type constructors*, which can be used to form new data types from simpler objects. The type constructor array is described in this chapter. The type constructors record and set are discussed in later chapters.

The *array* is a data structure in which we store a collection of data items of the same type (for example, all the exam scores for a class). By using an array, we can associate a single variable name (for example, Scores) with the entire collection of data. This association enables us to save the entire collection of data in main memory (one item per memory cell) and to reference individual items easily. To process an individual item, we specify the array name and indicate the array element being manipulated (for example, Scores[3] references the third item in the array Scores).

Because each score is saved in a separate cell in main memory, we can process the individual items more than once and in any order. In previous programs, we reused the same cell to store each exam score. Consequently, we could not access the third score after the fourth score was read.

The use of arrays of characters makes it easier to store character strings in memory. String variables or strings are introduced for that purpose, and you will see how to read textual data into strings.

10.1 The Array Data Type

This section illustrates the basic operations that can be performed on an array. We begin by showing how to allocate memory space for an array in Pascal.

Array Type Declaration

Normally, we first describe the structure of an array in an *array type declaration*. Then we can allocate storage for one or more arrays of that type. The array type RealArray, declared next, is followed by the declaration of array X of type RealArray.

```
type
   IndexRange = 1..8;
   RealArray = array [IndexRange] of Real;

var
   X : RealArray;
```

Pascal associates eight memory cells with the name X. Each element of array X can contain a single real value. So a total of eight real values can be stored and referenced using the array name X.

Array X

X[1]	X[2]	X[3]	X[4]	X[5]	X[6]	X[7]	X[8]
16.0	12.0	6.0	8.0	2.5	12.0	14.0	– 54.5

First   Second   Third   Eighth
element   element   element   element

To process the data stored in an array, we must be able to reference each individual element. The *array subscript* differentiates among elements of the same array. For example, if X is the array with eight elements, we can refer to the elements of array X as shown in Fig. 10.1.

The *subscripted variable* X[1] (read as "X sub 1") references the first element of the array X, X[2] the second element, and X[8] the eighth element. The number enclosed in brackets is the array subscript. Later, you will see that the subscript can be an expression of any ordinal type.

■ Example 10.1

Let X be the array shown in Fig. 10.1. Some statements that manipulate this array are shown in Table 10.1.

Table 10.1   Statements That Manipulate Array X

Statement	Explanation
WriteLn (X[1])	Displays the value of X[1], or 16.0.
X[4] := 25.0	Stores the value 25.0 in X[4].
Sum := X[1] + X[2]	Stores the sum of X[1] and X[2], or 28.0, in the variable Sum.
Sum := Sum + X[3]	Adds X[3] to Sum. The new Sum is 34.0.
X[4] := X[4] + 1.0	Adds 1.0 to X[4]. The new X[4] is 26.0.
X[3] := X[1] + X[2]	Stores the sum of X[1] and X[2] in X[3]. The new X[3] is 28.0.

The contents of array X after execution of these statements are shown next. Notice that only X[3] and X[4] have changed.   ■

Array X

X[1]	X[2]	X[3]	X[4]	X[5]	X[6]	X[7]	X[8]
16.0	12.0	28.0	26.0	2.5	12.0	14.0	– 54.5

First   Second   Third   Eighth
element   element   element   element

■ Example 10.2

The declaration section for a plant operations program is shown next. The type declaration declares two simple types, EmpRange and Day, and two array types, EmpArray and DayArray. Two arrays, Vacation and PlantHours, are declared in the variable declaration section.

```
const
   NumEmp = 10;                         {number of employees}

type
   EmpRange = 1..NumEmp;                {subscript range}
   EmpArray = array [EmpRange] of Boolean;
   Day = (Sunday, Monday, Tuesday, Wednesday,
           Thursday, Friday, Saturday);
   DayArray = array [Day] of Real;

var
   Vacation : EmpArray;
   PlantHours : DayArray;
```

The array Vacation has ten elements (subscripts 1 through NumEmp); each element of array Vacation can store a Boolean value. The contents of this array could indicate which employees are on vacation (Vacation[I] is True if employee I is on vacation). If employees 1, 3, 5, 7, and 9 are on vacation, the array would have the values shown in Fig. 10.2.

The array PlantHours has seven elements (subscripts Sunday through Saturday). The array element PlantHours[Sunday] could indicate how many hours the plant was operating on Sunday of the past week. The array shown in Fig. 10.3 indicates that the plant was closed on the weekend and operated a single shift on Monday and Thursday, double shifts on Tuesday and Friday, and a triple shift on Wednesday.   ■

It is possible to eliminate the declarations for the constant NumEmp and data types EmpRange and EmpArray and just declare the array Vacation, as shown next.

```
var
   Vacation : array [1..10] of Boolean;
```

Figure 10.2 Array Vacation

Vacation[1]	True
Vacation[2]	False
Vacation[3]	True
Vacation[4]	False
Vacation[5]	True
Vacation[6]	False
Vacation[7]	True
Vacation[8]	False
Vacation[9]	True
Vacation[10]	False

Figure 10.3 Array PlantHours

425

10.1 The Array Data
Type

PlantHours[Sunday]	0.0
PlantHours[Monday]	8.0
PlantHours[Tuesday]	16.0
PlantHours[Wednesday]	24.0
PlantHours[Thursday]	8.0
PlantHours[Friday]	16.0
PlantHours[Saturday]	0.0

There are three advantages to the original set of declarations. First, it is easy to change the declared size of array Vacation. By simply redefining the constant NumEmp, we change the array size. Second, the data types EmpArray and Day-Array can be used as type identifiers elsewhere in the program. And third, the constant NumEmp can be referenced in the program body.

Because a type identifier is not used in the revised declaration of array Vacation, its type is said to be *anonymous*. In general, you should avoid using anonymous (unnamed types).

Array Type Declaration

Form: type
             array type = array [*subscript type*] of *element type;*
Example: type
             IndexRange = 1..5;
             SmallArray = array [IndexRange] of Char;
Interpretation: The identifier *array type* describes a collection of array elements; each element can store an item of type *element type*. The *subscript type* can be either of the standard ordinal types Boolean or Char, an enumerated type, or a subrange type. There is one array element for each value in the *subscript type*.

The *element type* describes the type of each element in the array. All elements of an array are the same type.
Note 1: The standard types Real and Integer cannot be used as a *subscript type*; however, a subrange of the integers may be a *subscript type*.
Note 2: The *element type* can be any standard or user-defined type.

Note 1 in the preceding display states that the standard types Integer and Real cannot be used as subscript types. Type Integer is not allowed because an array of type Integer would have an excessive number of elements. Type Real is not allowed because it is not an ordinal type.

It is important to realize that an array type declaration does not require allocation of storage space in memory. The array type describes only the structure of an array. Only variables actually store information and require storage. Storage space is not allocated until a variable of this type is declared.

Abstract Array

We can summarize what we have discussed so far about arrays in the following specification for an abstract array.

Specification for an Abstract Array

Structure: An array is a collection of elements of the same data type. For each array, an ordinal subscript type is specified. There is an array element that corresponds to each value in the ordinal type. The ordinal type Integer cannot be a subscript type; however, a subrange of type Integer can be a subscript type.

Operators: Two basic operations act on the elements of an array: *store* and *retrieve*. The store operation inserts a value into the array. If A is an array and C is a variable that is assignment compatible (defined in Section 7.7) with the element type of A, the statement

```
A[I] := C
```

stores the contents of C in element I of array A. If the element type of A is assignment compatible with the type of variable D, the statement

```
D := A[I]
```

retrieves element I of array A and copies its value into D. For both of these statements, the value of subscript I must be in the range of the array subscript type; otherwise, a run-time error occurs.

The assignment operator can also be used to copy the contents of one array to another of the same type. If arrays A and B are the same type, the statement

```
A := B
```

copies all values associated with array B to array A.

The preceding display summarizes all the information you need to know to use an array. You do not need to know how Pascal stores the elements of an array in memory or how it implements the retrieve and store operators.

Exercises for Section 10.1

Self-Check

1. What is the difference between the expressions X3 and X[3]?
2. For the following declarations, how many memory cells are reserved for data and what type of data can be stored there? Is the memory allocated after the type declaration or after the variable declaration?

```
type
   IndexRange = 1..5;
   AnArray = array [IndexRange] of Char;
```

```
      var
         Grades : AnArray;
```

3. Write the variable and type declarations for the valid array descriptions that
   follow.
   a. subscript type `Boolean`, element type `Real`
   b. subscript type `'A'..'F'`, element type `Integer`
   c. subscript type `Char`, element type `Boolean`
   d. subscript type `Integer`, element type `Real`
   e. subscript type `Char`, element type `Real`
   f. subscript type `Real`, element type `Char`
   g. subscript type `Day` (enumerated type), element type `Real`

10.2 Selecting Array Elements for Processing

Using a Subscript as an Index to an Array

Each array reference includes the array name and a subscript enclosed in
brackets; the subscript determines which array element is processed. The subscript (sometimes called an *index*) used in an array reference must be an expression that is assignment compatible with the subscript type specified in the
array declaration. Very often, the subscript type is a subrange whose host type
is `Integer`. In this case, the subscript must be an integer expression whose
value is in the range specified by the subscript type. For the array `Vacation`
declared in Example 10.2, the allowable subscript values are the integers 1
through 10.

■ Example 10.3

Table 10.2 shows some sample statements involving the array X shown in Fig.
10.1. I is assumed to be a type `Integer` variable with value 6. Make sure you
understand each statement.

Table 10.2 Some Sample Statements for Array X in Figure 10.1

Statement	Effect
`Write (4, X[4])`	Displays 4 and 8.0 (value of X[4])
`Write (I, X[I])`	Displays 6 and 12.0 (value of X[6])
`Write (X[I] + 1)`	Displays 13.0 (value of 12.0 + 1)
`Write (X[I] + I)`	Displays 18.0 (value of 12.0 + 6)
`Write (X[I+1])`	Displays 14.0 (value of X[7])
`Write (X[I+I])`	Illegal attempt to display X[12]
`Write (X[2*I])`	Illegal attempt to display X[12]
`Write (X[2*I-4])`	Displays −54.5 (value of X[8])
`Write (X[Trunc(X[5])])`	Displays 12.0 (value of X[2])

Table 10.2, *continued*

Statement	Effect
X[I] := X[I+1]	Assigns 14.0 (value of X[7]) to X[6]
X[I–1] := X[I]	Assigns 14.0 (new value of X[6]) to X[5]
X[I] – 1 := X[I–1]	Illegal assignment statement

You can see two attempts to display element X[12], which is not in the array. These attempts result in an `index expression out of bounds` run-time error. This means there is no array element with the current subscript, or index, value.

The last `Write` statement in Table 10.2 uses `Trunc(X[5])` as a subscript expression. Because this evaluates to 2, the value of X[2] (and not X[5]) is printed. If the value of `Trunc(X[5])` is outside the range 1 through 8, a run-time error occurs.

Two different subscripts are used in the last three assignment statements in the table. The first assignment statement copies the value of X[7] to X[6] (subscripts I+1 and I); the second assignment statement copies the value of X[6] to X[5] (subscripts I and I–1). The last assignment statement causes a syntax error because there is an expression to the left of the assignment operator. ∎

SYNTAX
DISPLAY

Array Reference

Form: *name*[*subscript*]

Example: X[3 * I – 2]

Interpretation: The *subscript* must be an expression that is assignment compatible with the subscript type specified in the declaration for array *name*. If the expression is the wrong data type, the syntax error `index type is not compatible with declaration` is detected. If the expression value is not in range, the run-time error `index expression out of bounds` occurs.

Using for Loops with Arrays

Frequently, we want to process the elements of an array in sequence, starting with the first element, for example, entering data into the array or printing its contents. We can accomplish this sequential processing using a for loop whose loop-control variable (I) is also the array subscript (X[I]). Increasing the value of the loop-control variable by 1 causes the next array element to be processed.

■ Example 10.4

The array Cube, declared as follows, stores the cubes of the first 10 integers (for example Cube[1] is 1, Cube[10] is 1000).

```
type
  IndexRange = 1..10;
  IntArray = array [IndexRange] of Integer;
```

```
var
  Cube : IntArray;                    {array of cubes}
  I : Integer:                        {loop-control variable}
```

The for statement

```
for I := 1 to 10 do
  Cube[I] := I * I * I
```

initializes this array as follows.

10.2 Selecting Array Elements for Processing

Array Cube

[1]	[2]	[3]	[4]	[5]	[6]	[7]	[8]	[9]	[10]
1	8	27	64	125	216	343	512	729	1000

■ Example 10.5

For array PlantHours (see Example 10.2), the enumerated type Day is the declared subscript type. The assignment statements

```
PlantHours[Sunday]    := 0.0;
PlantHours[Monday]    := 8.0;
PlantHours[Tuesday]   := 16.0;
PlantHours[Wednesday] := 24.0
```

assign the values shown in Fig. 10.3 to the first four elements of PlantHours. Assuming that Today is type Day, the following statements have the same effect.

```
PlantHours[Sunday] := 0.0;
for Today := Monday to Wednesday do
  PlantHours[Today] := PlantHours[Pred(Today)] + 8.0
```

The assignment statement in the for loop executes for three values of Today (Monday through Wednesday). Table 10.3 shows the effect of the assignment statement for each value of Today. ■

Table 10.3 Assigning Values to Array PlantHours

Today	Pred(Today)	**Effect**
Monday	Sunday	Assigns 8.0 to PlantHours[Monday]
Tuesday	Monday	Assigns 16.0 to PlantHours[Tuesday]
Wednesday	Tuesday	Assigns 24.0 to PlantHours[Wednesday]

■ Example 10.6

In Fig. 10.4, the declarations

```
const
  MaxItems = 8;                       {number of data items}

type
  IndexRange = 1..MaxItems;
  RealArray = array [IndexRange] of Real;
```

```
var
  X : RealArray;                     {array of data}
  I : IndexRange;                    {loop-control variable}
```

allocate storage for an array X of Real elements with subscripts in the range 1..8. The program uses three for loops to process the array X. The loop-control variable I ($1 <= I <= 8$) is also the array subscript in each loop. The first for loop

```
for I := 1 to MaxItems do
  Read (X[I]);
```

reads one data value into each array element (the first item is stored in X[1], the second item in X[2], and so on). The Read statement is repeated for each value of I from 1 to 8; each repetition causes a new data value to be read and stored in X[I]. The subscript I determines the array element that receives the next data value. The data line shown in the sample run causes the array to be initialized, as in Fig. 10.1.

The second for loop accumulates (in Sum) the sum of all values stored in the array. (We trace this loop later.) The last for loop

```
for I := 1 to MaxItems do
  WriteLn (I :4, X[I] :8:2, X[I]-Average :14:2)
```

displays a table that shows each array element, X[I], and the difference between that element and the average value, X[I]-Average.

Figure 10.4 Table of Differences

Directory: CHAP10
File: SHOWDIFF.PAS

```
program ShowDiff (Input, Output);
{
  Computes the average value of an array of data and
  prints the difference between each value and the average
}
  const
    MaxItems = 8;                         {number of data items}

  type
    IndexRange = 1..MaxItems;
    RealArray = array [IndexRange] of Real;

  var
    X : RealArray;                        {array of data}
    I : IndexRange;                       {loop-control variable}
    Average,                              {average value of data}
    Sum      : Real;                      {sum of the data}

begin   {ShowDiff}
  {Enter the data.}
  Write ('Enter ', MaxItems :1, ' numbers> ');
  for I := 1 to MaxItems do
    Read (X[I]);

  {Compute the average value.}
  Sum := 0.0;                                       {Initialize Sum.}
  for I := 1 to MaxItems do
    Sum := Sum + X[I];                      {Add each element to Sum.}
  Average := Sum / MaxItems;                    {Get average value.}
```

```
WriteLn ('The average value is ', Average :3:1); WriteLn;
{Display the difference between each item and the average.}
WriteLn ('Table of differences between X[I] and the average');
WriteLn ('I' :4, 'X[I]' :8, 'Difference' : 14);
for I := 1 to MaxItems do
   WriteLn (I :4, X[I] :8:1, X[I]-Average :14:1)
end. {ShowDiff}
```

```
Enter 8 numbers> 16.0  12.0  6.0  8.0  2.5  12.0  14.0  -54.5
The average value is 2.0

Table of differences between X[I] and the average
   I    X[I]    Difference
   1    16.0        14.0
   2    12.0        10.0
   3     6.0         4.0
   4     8.0         6.0
   5     2.5         0.5
   6    12.0        10.0
   7    14.0        12.0
   8   -54.5       -56.5
```

The program fragment

```
Sum := 0.0;                           {Initialize Sum.}
for I := 1 to MaxItems do
   Sum := Sum + X[I];       {Add each element to Sum.}
```

accumulates the sum of all eight elements of array X in the variable Sum. Each
time the for loop is repeated, the next element of array X is added to Sum. The
execution of this program fragment is traced in Table 10.4 for the first three
repetitions of the loop. ∎

Table 10.4 Partial Trace of for Loop

Statement Part	I	X[I]	Sum	**Effect**
Sum:= 0.0;			0.0	Initializes Sum.
for I := 1 to MaxItems do	1	16.0		Initializes I to 1;
Sum := Sum + X[I]			16.0	add X[1] to Sum.
increment and test I	2	12.0		2 <= 8 is true;
Sum := Sum + X[I]			28.0	add X[2] to Sum.
increment and test I	3	6.0		3 <= 8 is true;
Sum := Sum + X[I]			34.0	add X[3] to Sum.

In Fig. 10.4, the subscripted variable X[I] is an actual parameter for the
standard Pascal Read or WriteLn procedure. You always have to read data into

an array one element at a time, as shown in this example. In most instances, you also have to display one array element at a time; however, this requirement may be waived when you are dealing with strings and packed arrays of characters (see Section 10.7).

Exercises for Section 10.2

Self-Check

1. If an array is declared to have 10 elements, must the program use all 10 of them?
2. The following sequence of statements changes the initial contents of array X displayed in Fig. 10.4. Describe what each statement does to the array and show the final contents of array X after all statements execute.

```
I := 3;
X[I] := X[I] + 10.0;
X[I - 1] := X[2 * I - 1];
X[I + 1] := X[2 * I] + X[2 * I + 1];
for I := 5 to 7 do
  X[I] := X[I + 1];
for I := 3 downto 1 do
  X[I + 1] := X[I]
```

3. Write program statements that will do the following to array X shown in Fig. 10.4:
   a. replace the third element with 7.0
   b. copy the element in the first location into the first one
   c. subtract the first element from the fourth and store the result in the fifth element
   d. increase the sixth element by 2
   e. find the sum of the first five elements
   f. multiply each of the first six elements by 2 and place each product in an element of the array AnswerArray
   g. display all even-numbered elements on one line

10.3 Using Arrays

This section illustrates the use of an array. It demonstrates two different methods for array access: sequential access and random access. We discuss their differences after the case study.

Case Study: Home Budget Problem

Problem
Your parents want a program that keeps track of their monthly expenses in each of several categories. The program should read each expense amount, add it to the appropriate category total, and print the total expenditure by category.

The input data consist of the category and the amount of each purchase made during the past month.

Analysis

Your parents have selected these budget categories: entertainment, food, clothing, rent, tuition, insurance, and miscellaneous. Seven separate totals must be accumulated; each total can be associated with a different element of a seven-element array. The program must read each expenditure, determine to which category it belongs, and then add that expenditure to the appropriate array element. When finished with all expenditures, the program should print a table that shows each category and its accumulated total. As in all programs that accumulate a sum, each total must be initialized to zero.

We could simply use an array with subscripts 1 through 7; however, the program would be more readable if we declare a data type `BudgetCat` and use this data type as the array subscript type.

Data Requirements

Data Type
```
BudgetCat = (Entertainment, Food, Clothing, Rent,
             Tuition, Insurance, Miscellaneous);
```

Problem Inputs
Each expenditure and its category

Problem Output
The array of seven expenditure totals (`Budget`)

Design

Initial Algorithm
1. Initialize all category totals to zero.
2. Read each expenditure and add it to the appropriate total.
3. Print the accumulated total for each category.

Structure Chart and Refinements
The structure chart in Fig. 10.5 shows the relationships among the three steps. The array `Budget` is manipulated by all three procedures in the program solution. Procedures `Initialize` and `Post` store information in this array; this information is displayed by procedure `Report`.

Implementation

Coding the Main Program
Figure 10.6 shows the program. The main program contains declarations for the data type `BudgetCat` and the array `Budget`. The array `Budget` (type `BudgetArray`) appears in each parameter list and is passed between each procedure and the main program. When an entire array is passed, no subscript is used.

Case Study: Home Budget Problem, continued

Figure 10.5 Structure Chart for Home Budget Problem

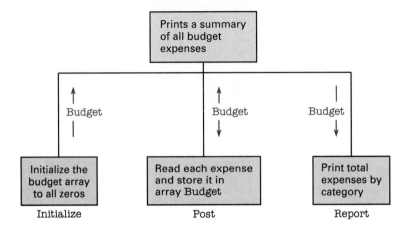

Figure 10.6 Home Budget Program

Directory: CHAP10
File: HOMEBUDG.PAS

```
program HomeBudget (Input, Output);

{Prints a summary of all expenses by budget category}

   type
      BudgetCat = (Entertainment, Food, Clothing, Rent,
                   Tuition, Insurance, Miscellaneous);
      BudgetArray = array [BudgetCat] of Real;    {array type}

   var
      Budget : BudgetArray;              {output – array of totals}


   procedure Initialize (var Budget {output} : BudgetArray);
   {
      Initializes array Budget to all zeros.
      Pre : None
      Post: Each element of Budget is 0.0.
   }
      var
        NextCat : BudgetCat;            {loop–control variable,
                                            array subscript}
   begin  {Initialize}
     for NextCat := Entertainment to Miscellaneous do
       Budget[NextCat] := 0.0
   end;  {Initialize}


   procedure Post (var Budget {input/output} : BudgetArray);
   {
      Reads each expenditure amount and adds it to the appropriate
      element of array Budget.
```

```
      Pre : Each array element Budget[i] is 0.0.
      Post: Each array element Budget[i] is the sum of expense
            amounts for category i.
    }
  begin  {Poststub}
    WriteLn ('Procedure Post entered')
  end;  {Poststub}


  procedure Report (Budget {input} : BudgetArray);
  {
    Prints the expenditures in each budget category.}
    Pre : Array Budget is defined.
    Post: Displays each budget category name and amount.
  }
    var
      NextCat : BudgetCat;                    {loop-control variable,
                                               array subscript}

    procedure PrintCat (NextCat {input} : BudgetCat);
    {
      Displays budget category.
      Pre : NextCat is a budget category.
      Post: Displays NextCat as a string.
    }
    begin  {PrintCat}
      case NextCat of
        Entertainment : Write ('Entertainment' :15);
        Food          : Write ('Food          ' :15);
        Clothing      : Write ('Clothing      ' :15);
        Rent          : Write ('Rent          ' :15);
        Tuition       : Write ('Tuition       ' :15);
        Insurance     : Write ('Insurance     ' :15);
        Miscellaneous : Write ('Miscellaneous' :15)
      end  {case}
    end; {PrintCat}


  begin  {Report}
    WriteLn;
    WriteLn ('Category       ' :15,  'Expenses' :15:2);  {heading}
    {Print each category name and the total.}
    for NextCat := Entertainment to Miscellaneous do
      begin
        PrintCat (NextCat);
        WriteLn (Budget[NextCat] :15:2)
      end {for}
  end;  {Report}

begin  {HomeBudget}
  {Initialize array Budget to all zeros.}
  Initialize (Budget);

  {Read and process each expenditure.}
  Post (Budget);

  {Print the expenditures in each category.}
  Report (Budget)
end. {HomeBudget}
```

The loop-control variable NextCat (type BudgetCat) is declared as a local variable in each procedure. In procedure Initialize, the assignment statement

```
Budget[NextCat] := 0.0
```

is repeated once for each value of NextCat and sets each element of Budget to zero. In procedure Report, the statements

```
PrintCat (NextCat);
WriteLn (Budget[NextCat] :15:2)
```

call PrintCat to display a budget category name and WriteLn to display the category total.

Procedure Post must read each expenditure and add it to the appropriate array element. The total of all entertainment expenditures is accumulated in Budget[Entertainment], all food expenditures are accumulated in Budget[Food], and so forth.

Coding Procedure Post

Procedure Post is shown in Fig. 10.7; it uses procedure EnterCat to read the budget category as an integer value and function ConvertCat to convert this value to type BudgetCat.

Figure 10.7 Procedure Post for Home Budget Problem

Directory: CHAP10
File: HOMEBUDG.PAS

```
procedure Post (var Budget {input/output} : BudgetArray);
{
  Reads each expenditure amount and adds it to the appropriate
  element of array Budget.
  Pre : Each array element Budget[i] is 0.0
  Post: Each array element Budget[i] is the sum of expense
        amounts for category i.
}
  const
    Quit = 0;                          {sentinel category number}
    MaxCategory = 7;                   {number of budget categories}

  var
    Choice  : Integer;                 {next category as an integer}
    NextCat : BudgetCat;               {next category as type BudgetCat}
    Expense : Real;                    {expenditure amount}


  procedure EnterCat (var Choice {output} : Integer);
  {
    Reads the budget category as an integer value.
    Pre : None
    Post: Choice is an integer from 0 to 7.
  }
  begin
    repeat
      WriteLn ('0 — Quit program');
      WriteLn ('1 — Entertainment');
      WriteLn ('2 — Food');
      WriteLn ('3 — Clothing');
```

```
      WriteLn ('4 - Rent');
      WriteLn ('5 - Tuition');
      WriteLn ('6 - Insurance');
      WriteLn ('7 - Miscellaneous');
      WriteLn ('Enter the category number> ');
      ReadLn (Choice)
    until Choice in [Quit..MaxCategory]
  end; {EnterCat}


  function ConvertCat (Choice : Integer) : BudgetCat;
  {
    Converts from an integer value to a value of type BudgetCat.
    Pre : Choice is between 1 and 7.
    Post: Returns a value from Entertainment to Miscellaneous.
  }
  begin {ConvertCat stub}
    ConvertCat := Rent
  end; {ConvertCat}


begin {Post}
  {Read each budget category and expense and add it to Budget.}
  EnterCat (Choice);
  while Choice <> Quit do
    {invariant:
        no prior value of Choice is Quit
        and Budget[NextCat] is the sum of prior budget entries
        for category NextCat.
    }
    begin
      NextCat := ConvertCat(Choice);   {Convert to type BudgetCat}
      Write ('Enter the expenditure amount $');
      ReadLn (Expense); WriteLn;
      Budget[NextCat] := Budget[NextCat] + Expense;
      EnterCat (Choice)
    end {while}
end; {Post}
```

Procedure `Post` begins by calling `EnterCat` to read an integer representing the category into `Choice`. The `while` loop body is executed for each value of `Choice` that is not zero. Function `ConvertCat` assigns a value to `NextCat` (type `BudgetCat`) based on the value of `Choice`. The assignment statement

```
Budget[NextCat] := Budget[NextCat] + Expense;
```

adds the expense amount to whatever element of array `Budget` is selected by `NextCat`.

Testing

A sample run of the home budget program is shown in Fig. 10.8. For the sake of brevity, we display the list of categories just once. As indicated in this run, it is not necessary for the input data to be in order by category. You should verify that all budget categories without purchases remain zero. Also, verify that out-of-range category values do not cause the program to terminate prematurely.

Figure 10.8   Sample Run of Home Budget Program

```
0 - Quit program
1 - Entertainment
2 - Food
3 - Clothing
4 - Rent
5 - Tuition
6 - Insurance
7 - Miscellaneous
Enter the category number> 3
Enter the expenditure amount $25.00

Enter the category number> 7
Enter the expenditure amount $25.00

Enter the category number> 3
Enter the expenditure amount $15.00

Enter the category number> 1
Enter the expenditure amount $675.00

Enter the category number> 0

    Category      Expenses
    Entertainment   675.00
    Food              0.00
    Clothing         40.00
    Rent              0.00
    Tuition           0.00
    Insurance         0.00
    Miscellaneous    25.00
```

Sequential versus Random Access to Arrays

The home budget program illustrates two common ways of selecting array elements for processing. Often, we need to manipulate all elements of an array in some uniform manner (for instance, we might want to initialize them all to zero). In such situations, it makes sense to process the array elements in sequence (*sequential access*), starting with the first and ending with the last. In procedures `Initialize` and `Report`, we accomplish that by using a `for` loop whose loop-control variable is also the array subscript.

In procedure `Post`, the order in which the array elements are accessed depends completely on the order of the data. The value assigned to `NextCat` determines the element to be incremented. This approach is called *random access* because the order is not predictable.

Self-Check

1. What happens if the user of the budget program enters the category −1 by mistake?
2. Write function ConvertCat. Integer values from 1 to 7 should be converted to values of type BudgetCat from Entertainment to Miscellaneous. Use a case statement.

Programming

1. Write a procedure that copies each value stored in one array to the corresponding element of another array. (For example, if the arrays are InArray and OutArray, copy InArray[1] to OutArray[1], then copy InArray[2] to OutArray[2], and so on.)
2. Write a procedure that reverses the values stored in an array. If array X has N elements, then X[1] becomes X[N], X[2] becomes X[N−1], and so forth. Hint: Make a local copy of the array before you start to reverse the elements.

10.4 Arrays as Operands and Parameters

The Pascal operators (for example, <, =, >, +, and −) can manipulate only one array element at a time (provided the element type is an appropriate simple type). Consequently, an array name in an expression is generally followed by its subscript.

Copying an Array

One exception to the preceding rule is the *array copy* operation. It is possible to copy the contents of one array to another array, provided the arrays are the same array type. Given the declarations

```
const
  MaxSize = 100;

type
  Index = 1..MaxSize;
  TestArray = array [Index] of Real;

var
  W, X, Y : TestArray;
  Z : array [Index] of Real;
```

the assignment statements

```
X := Y;               {valid array copy}
W := Y;               {valid array copy}
```

copy each value in array Y to the corresponding element of arrays X and W (that is, Y[1] is copied to X[1] and W[1], Y[2] to X[2] and W[2], and so forth.)

It is important to realize that the assignments

```
Z := Y;                    {invalid array copy}
X := Z;                    {invalid array copy}
```

are invalid. Even though array Z has the same structure as arrays W, X, and Y, the type of array Z is anonymous and is not considered the same as the named type TestArray. Therefore, you must either declare array Z as type TestArray or use a loop to copy each element individually. This is another reason to avoid the use of anonymous or unnamed types (see Section 10.1).

Arrays as Parameters

If several elements of an array are being manipulated by a procedure, it is generally better to pass the entire array of data instead of individual array elements. In Fig. 10.6, the procedure call statements

```
Initialize (Budget);
Post (Budget);
Report (Budget)
```

pass the entire array Budget to each procedure. Budget is declared as a variable parameter in procedures Initialize and Post and as a value parameter in procedure Report.

In all three procedures, the formal parameter is declared as type BudgetArray. This is necessary because the formal and the actual parameter must be the same array type. The procedure heading

```
procedure Initialize (var Budget : array [BudgetCat] of Real);
```

is invalid because the parameter type must be an identifier.

When an array is used as a variable parameter, Pascal passes the address of the first actual array element into the procedure data area. Because the array elements are stored in adjacent memory cells, the entire array of data can be accessed. The procedure directly manipulates the actual array.

When an array is used as a value parameter, a local copy of the array is made when the procedure is called. The local array is initialized so that it contains the same values as the corresponding actual array. The procedure manipulates the local array, and any changes made to the local array are not reflected in the actual array.

The next two examples illustrate the use of arrays as parameters, assuming the following declarations.

```
const
  MaxSize = 5;

type
  IndexType = 1..MaxSize;
  TestArray = array [IndexType] of Real;

var
  X, Y, Z : TestArray;
```

Although it is possible to use a single assignment statement to copy one array to another, the assignment statement

```
Z := X + Y        {illegal addition of arrays}
```

is invalid because the operator + cannot have an array as an operand. You might use procedure AddArray (Fig. 10.9) to add two arrays of type TestArray.

Figure 10.9   Procedure AddArray

```
procedure AddArray (A, B  {input}  : TestArray;
                    var C {output} : TestArray);
{
  Stores the sum of A[i] and B[i] in C[i]. Array elements
  with subscripts 1..MaxSize are summed, element by element.
  Pre : A[i] and B[i] (1 <= i <= MaxSize) are assigned values
  Post: C[i] := A[i] + B[i] (1 <= i <= MaxSize).
}
  var
    I : IndexType;          {loop control and array subscript}
begin  {AddArray}
  {Add corresponding elements of each array.}
  for I := 1 to MaxSize do
    C[I] := A[I] + B[I]
end;  {AddArray}
```

Directory: CHAP10
File: ADDARRAY.PRO

The parameter correspondence for arrays established by the procedure call statement

```
AddArray (X, Y, Z)
```

is shown in Fig. 10.10. Arrays A and B in the procedure data area are local copies of arrays X and Y. As indicated by the solid arrow, the address of the first element of array Z is stored in parameter C. The procedure results are stored directly in array Z. After execution of the procedure, Z[1] will contain the sum of X[1] and Y[1], or 3.5; Z[2] will contain 6.7; and so on. Arrays X and Y will be unchanged.   ■

■ Example 10.8

Function SameArray in Fig. 10.11 determines whether two arrays (of type TestArray) are identical. Two arrays are considered identical if the first element of one is the same as the first element of the other, the second element of one is the same as the second element of the other, and so forth.

We can determine that the arrays are not identical by finding a single pair of unequal elements. Consequently, the while loop may be executed anywhere from one time (first elements unequal) to MaxSize − 1 times. Loop exit occurs when a pair of unequal elements is found or just before the last pair is tested.

Figure 10.10 Parameter Correspondence for AddArray (X, Y, Z)

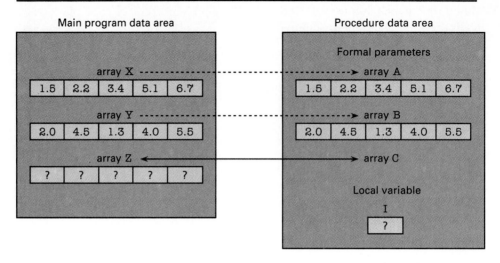

Figure 10.11 Function SameArray

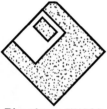

Directory: CHAP10
File: SAMEARRA.FUN

```
function SameArray (A, B : TestArray) : Boolean;
{
  Returns a value of True if the arrays A, B are identical;
  otherwise, returns a value of False.
  Pre : A[i] and B[i] (1 <= i <= MaxSize) are assigned values.
  Post: Returns True if A[i] = B[i] for all i in range
          1..MaxSize; otherwise, returns False.
}
  var
    I : Integer;                      {array subscript}

begin
  I := 1;                            {Start with first pair.}

  {Test corresponding elements of arrays A and B.}
  while (I < MaxSize) and (A[I] = B[I]) do
    {invariant:
       1 <= I <= MaxSize and
       A[I] = B[I] for all prior values of I
    }
    I := I + 1;                      {Advance to next pair.}

  {assert:
    an unequal pair was found or all but the
    last pair were compared
  }
  SameArray := A[I] = B[I]           {Define result.}
end;  {SameArray}
```

After loop exit, the Boolean assignment statement

```
SameArray := A[I] = B[I]     {Define result.}
```

defines the function result. If loop exit occurs because the pair of elements with subscript I is unequal, the function result is False. If loop exit occurs because the last pair of elements is reached, the function result is True if this pair is equal; otherwise, the function result is False.

As an example of how you might use function SameArray, the if statement

```
if SameArray(X, Y) then
   Z := X
else
   AddArray (X, Y, Z)
```

either copies array X to array Z (when X and Y are identical) or stores the sum of arrays X and Y in array Z (when X and Y are not identical).

Because the arrays have MaxSize elements, a common error is to use the condition

```
(I <= MaxSize) and (A[I] = B[I])
```

as the while condition in Fig. 10.11, which causes all element pairs to be tested by the while condition if the arrays are equal. When I is MaxSize + 1, the first part of this condition evaluates to False; however, the second part must still be evaluated unless short-circuit evaluation is used. This leads to an index expression out of bounds run-time error because array element A[MaxSize+1] does not exist. ∎

Efficiency of Variable Parameters versus Protection of Value Parameters

Parameters A and B in Fig. 10.11 are declared as value parameters because they only store data passed into procedure AddArray and their values should not be changed by AddArray. Pascal must create a local copy of these two arrays each time procedure AddArray is called. This copying uses valuable computer time and memory space. If the arrays being copied are very large, the program may terminate with an error because all its memory space has been used.

To conserve time and memory space, experienced programmers sometimes declare arrays that are used only for input as variable parameters rather than as value parameters. This means, however, that the corresponding actual array is directly manipulated by the procedure and is no longer protected from accidental modification by the procedure. Any changes (either by accident or by design) made to the actual array are an undesirable side effect of the function's execution. If an array corresponds to a value parameter, the changes are made to a local copy, and the actual array is unaffected.

Finding the Minimum or Maximum Value in an Array

A common operation is to determine the minimum or maximum value stored in an array. In Chapter 4, we wrote a program to find the smallest of three characters (see Fig. 4.15). The approach taken to finding the minimum or maximum value in an array is similar. The algorithm for finding the maximum value follows.

Algorithm for Finding the Maximum Value in an Array

1. Assume that the first element is the largest so far and save its subscript as the subscript of the largest so far.
2. for each array element do
    3. if the current element is > than the largest so far then
        4. Save the subscript of the current element as the subscript of the largest so far.

Function MaxBudget in Fig. 10.12 implements this algorithm for the array Budget displayed in Fig. 10.8. The function returns the subscript (type Category) of the largest value in array Budget.

Figure 10.12   Function MaxBudget

Directory: CHAP10
File: MAXBUDGE.FUN

```
function MaxBudget (Budget {input} : BudgetArray) : BudgetCat;
{
  Returns the subscript of the largest element in array Budget.
  Pre : Array Budget is defined.
  Post: Budget[MaxIndex] is the largest value in the array.
}
  var
    MaxIndex,                     {index of largest so far}
    NextIndex : BudgetCat;   {index of current element}

begin {MaxBudget}
  MaxIndex := Entertainment;   {Assume first element is largest.}
  for NextIndex := Entertainment to Miscellaneous do
    if Budget[NextIndex] > Budget[MaxIndex] then
      MaxIndex := NextIndex;

  {assert:
     All elements are examined and
     MaxIndex is the index of the largest element
  }
  MaxBudget := MaxIndex                 {Define result.}
end; {MaxBudget}
```

It is important to realize that function MaxBudget returns the subscript (or index) of the largest value, not the largest value itself. Assuming NextCat is type BudgetCat, the following statements display the largest value.

```
NextCat := MaxBudget(Budget);
WriteLn ('The largest expenditure is $', Budget[NextCat] :4:2)
```

Although not as easy to read, the single statement that follows is equivalent; it uses the function designator as the subscript expression.

```
WriteLn ('The largest expenditure is $',
         Budget[MaxBudget(Budget)] :4:2)
```

Individual Array Elements as Parameters

It is acceptable practice to use a single array element as an actual parameter. For example, the expression

```
Round(Budget[5])
```

rounds the value stored in the fifth element of array `Budget`, where the subscripted variable `Budget[5]` is the actual parameter passed to function `Round`.

■ Example 10.9

Procedure `Exchange` in Fig. 10.13 exchanges the values of its two type `Real` parameters.

Figure 10.13   Procedure Exchange

```
procedure Exchange (var P, Q {input/output} : Real);
{
  Exchanges the values of P and Q.
  Pre : P and Q are assigned values.
  Post: P has the value passed into Q and vice-versa.
}
  var
    Temp : Real;              {temporary variable for the exchange}

begin {Exchange}
  Temp := P;   P := Q;   Q := Temp
end; {Exchange}
```

Directory: CHAP10
File: EXCHANGE.PRO

The procedure call statement

```
Exchange (X[2], X[1])
```

uses this procedure to exchange the contents of the first two elements (type `Real`) of array `X`. The identifier `X` is the name of an array in the calling program. The actual parameter `X[2]` corresponds to formal parameter `P`; the actual parameter `X[1]` corresponds to formal parameter `Q`. This correspondence is shown in Fig. 10.14 for a particular array `X`.   ■

Figure 10.14   Parameter Correspondence for Exchange (X[2], X[1])

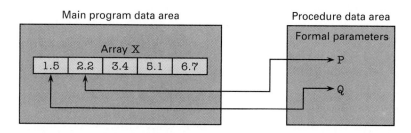

It is illegal to use a subscripted variable as a formal parameter. For example, the procedure declaration

```
procedure Exchange (var X[i], X[j] {input/output} : Real);
```

would cause a syntax error.

Exercises for Section 10.4

Self-Check

1. When is it better to pass an entire array of data to a procedure rather than individual elements?
2. When is a copy of an entire array made for an array that is a procedure parameter? What happens to the copy after the procedure executes?
3. In function SameArray, what will be the value of I when the statement

   ```
   SameArray := A[I] = B[I]
   ```

   executes if array A is equal to array B? If the third elements do not match?
4. Describe how to modify function MaxBudget to get a new function, MinBudget, that returns the smallest array element.

Programming

1. Write a procedure that assigns a value of True to element I of the output array if element I of one input array has the same value as element I of the other input array; otherwise, assign a value of False. If the input arrays have subscript type IndexType, the output array should have the following type:

   ```
   type
      BoolArray = array [IndexType] of Boolean;
   ```

10.5 Reading Part of an Array

Usually, we don't know in advance exactly how many elements will be stored in an array. For example, if a professor is processing exam scores, there might be 150 students in one class, 200 in the next, and so on. In this situation, we should declare an array that can accommodate the largest class. Only part of this array will actually be processed for a smaller class.

■ Example 10.10

The array Scores, declared as follows, can accommodate a class of up to 250 students. Each array element can contain an integer value between 0 and 100.

```
const
   MaxSize = 250;
   MaxScore = 100;

type
   ClassIndex = 1..MaxSize;
   ScoreRange = 0..MaxScore;
```

```
    ScoreArray = array [ClassIndex] of ScoreRange;
    ClassRange = 0..MaxSize;

  var
    Scores : ScoreArray;
    ClassSize : ClassRange;
```

Procedure ReadScores in Fig. 10.15 reads up to 250 exam scores and prints a warning message when the array is filled. The actual number of scores read is returned as the value of ClassSize. It calls EnterInt (see Fig. 9.3) to read each exam score.

Figure 10.15   Reading Part of an Array

Directory: CHAP10
File: READSCOR.PRO

```
procedure ReadScores (var Scores {output} : ScoreArray;
                      var ClassSize {output} : ClassRange);

{
  Reads an array of exam scores (Scores)
  for a class of up to MaxSize students.
  Pre : None
  Post: The data values are stored in array Scores.
        The number of values read is stored in
        ClassSize (0 <= ClassSize <= MaxSize).
  Uses: Procedure EnterInt (see Fig. 9.3)
}
  const
    Sentinel = -1;                    {sentinel value}

  var
    TempScore : Integer;              {temporary storage for a score}

begin
  Write ('Enter next score after the prompt or enter ');
  WriteLn (Sentinel :1, ' to stop.');

  {Read each array element until done.}
  ClassSize := 0;                             {initial class size}
  EnterInt (Sentinel, MaxScore, TempScore);
  while (TempScore <> Sentinel) and (ClassSize < MaxSize) do
    {invariant:
       No prior value of TempScore is Sentinel and
       ClassSize <= MaxSize
    }
      begin
        ClassSize := ClassSize + 1;          {Increment ClassSize.}
        Scores[ClassSize] := TempScore;      {Save the score.}
        EnterInt (Sentinel, MaxScore, TempScore);
      end; {while}

  {Assert:  Sentinel was read or array is filled.}
  if ClassSize = MaxSize then
    WriteLn ('Array is filled.')
end;  {ReadScores}
```

In any subsequent processing of array Scores, use the variable ClassSize to limit the number of array elements processed. Only the subarray with subscripts 1..ClassSize contains meaningful data; consequently, array elements with subscripts larger than ClassSize should not be manipulated. ClassSize should be passed as a parameter to any procedure that processes the partially filled array. ■

Exercises for Section 10.5

Self-Check

1. In procedure ReadScores, what prevents the user from entering more than MaxSize scores?
2. What is the range of data values that can be entered? What is the range of data values that can be stored in the array?
3. Rewrite the while loop in ReadScores as a repeat-until loop. Why is the while loop better? Why can't we use a for loop?

10.6 More Examples of Array Processing

Many of the arrays processed so far had subscript types that were subranges of the integers. This, of course, is not required in Pascal, because a subscript type can be any ordinal type (except Integer). A number of different array types are described in Table 10.5.

Table 10.5 Some Array Types and Applications

Array Type	Application

`type NameArray =`
`    array [1..10] of Char;`
`var Name : NameArray;`
	`Name[1] := 'A';` stores a person's name (up to 10 letters).

`type Temperatures =`
`    array [-10..10] of Real;`
`var Fahrenheit : Temperatures;`
	`Fahrenheit[0] := 32.0;` stores Fahrenheit temperatures corresponding to -10 through 10 degrees Celsius.

`type Counters =`
`    array ['A'..'Z'] of Integer;`
`var LetterCount : Counters;`
	`LetterCount['A'] := 0;` stores the number of times each uppercase letter occurs.

`type Flags =`
`    array ['A'..'Z'] of Boolean;`
`var LetterFound : Flags;`
	`LetterFound['X'] := False;` stores a set of flags indicating which letters occur and which do not.

`type BoolCounts =`
`    array [Boolean] of Integer;`
`var Answers : BoolCounts;`
	`Answers[True] := 15;` stores the number of true answers and false answers to a quiz.

The array Name has ten elements and can store the letters of a person's name. The array Fahrenheit, with twenty-one elements, can store the Fahrenheit temperature corresponding to each Celsius temperature in the range −10 through +10 degrees Celsius. For example, Fahrenheit[0] would be the Fahrenheit temperature, 32.0, corresponding to 0 degrees Celsius. Arrays LetterCount and LetterFound have the same subscript type (that is, the uppercase letters) and are discussed in the next section. The array Answers has only two elements, with subscript values True and False.

Arrays with Subscripts of Type Char

An array with subscript type Char (or a subrange of Char) is a useful data structure, as shown in the next example.

■ Example 10.11

The arrays LetterCount and LetterFound described in Table 10.5 have the subscript type ['A'..'Z']. Thus, there is an array element for each uppercase letter. The program in Fig. 10.16 displays the number of occurrences of each letter in a line of text. It uses LetterCount['A'] to store the number of occurrences of the letter 'A'. If the letter A occurs, LetterFound['A'] is True; otherwise, LetterFound['A'] is False. Function UpCase (see Fig. 9.4) converts the case of each letter read into NextChar to uppercase so that both t and T cause the count for letter T to be incremented.

Figure 10.16   Counting Letters in a Line

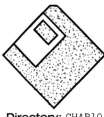

Directory: CHAP10
File: CONCORDA.PAS

```
program Concordance (Input, Output);
{
  Finds and prints the number of occurrences of each letter.
  The case of each letter is immaterial. Letters with counts
  of zero are not displayed.
}
  const
    Sentinel = '*';                 {sentinel character}

  type
    Letter = 'A'..'Z';
    CountArray = array [Letter] of Integer;
    FoundArray = array [Letter] of Boolean;

  var
    LetterCount : CountArray;       {output - array of counts}
    LetterFound : FoundArray;       {array of flags}
    NextChar : Char;                {input - each input character}

  {Insert function UpCase (see Fig. 9.4) here.}

begin  {Concordance}
  {Initialize LetterCount and LetterFound.}
  for NextChar := 'A' to 'Z' do
    begin
      LetterCount[NextChar] := 0;      {Initialize counts.}
      LetterFound[NextChar] := False   {Initialize flags.}
    end; {for}
```

```
{Count the letters in a line.}
WriteLn ('Type in a line of text ending with ', Sentinel);
repeat
  Read (NextChar);                    {Get next character.}
  NextChar := UpCase(NextChar);       {Convert to uppercase.}
  if NextChar in ['A'..'Z'] then
    begin  {letter}
      LetterCount[NextChar] := LetterCount[NextChar] + 1;
      LetterFound[NextChar] := True        {Set letter flag.}
    end  {letter}
until NextChar = Sentinel;

{Print counts of letters that are in the line.}
WriteLn;
WriteLn ('Letter', 'Occurrences' :16);
for NextChar := 'A' to 'Z' do
  if LetterFound[NextChar] then
    WriteLn (NextChar :6, LetterCount[NextChar] :16)
end. {Concordance}


Type in a line ending with *
This is it!*

Letter      Occurrences
   H                  1
   I                  3
   S                  2
   T                  2
```

In the last `if` statement, the condition

```
LetterFound[NextChar]
```

is true if there are one or more occurrences of the letter `NextChar`. This `if` statement ensures that only counts greater than zero are printed. This condition can also be written as

```
LetterCount[NextChar] > 0
```

Doing this is more efficient, because it allows us to eliminate the array `LetterFound`. ■

Case Study: Cryptogram Generator Problem

Problem

Your local intelligence agency needs a program to encode messages. One approach is to use a program that generates cryptograms. A cryptogram is a coded message that is formed by substituting a code character for each letter of the original message. The substitution is performed uniformly throughout the original message—for instance, every A is replaced by an S, every B is replaced by a P, and so forth. All punctuation (including spaces between words) remains unchanged.

Analysis

The program must examine each character in the message and replace each character that is a letter by its code symbol. We can store the code symbols in an array `Code` with subscript type `'A'..'Z'` and element type `Char`. The character stored in `Code['A']` will be the code symbol for the letter `'A'`. This enables us to simply look up the code symbol for a letter by using that letter as an index to the array `Code`.

Data Requirements

Problem Inputs
```
Code : array ['A'..'Z'] of Char    {array of code symbols}
Each message character
```

Problem Outputs
```
Each character of the cryptogram
```

Design

Initial Algorithm

1. Read in the code symbol for each letter.
2. Read each message character and display the cryptogram.

Algorithm Refinements and Structure Chart
As shown in the structure chart (see Fig. 10.17), procedure `ReadCode` performs step 1, and procedure `Encrypt` performs step 2. The data requirements and algorithms for these procedures follow the structure chart.

Local Variable for ReadCode
```
NextLetter : 'A'..'Z'   {Loop control variable and array subscript}
```

Figure 10.17 Structure Chart for Cryptogram Generator

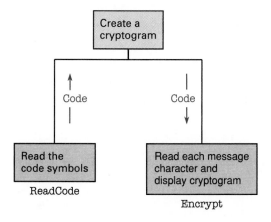

Algorithm for ReadCode
1. Display the alphabet.
2. `for` each letter `do`
> 3. Read in the code symbol and store it in array `Code`.

Local Constant for Encrypt
```
Sentinel = '#'   {sentinel character for the message}
```

Local Variable for Encrypt
```
NextChar : Char    {each message character}
```

Algorithm for Encrypt
1. `repeat`
> 2. Read the next message character.
> 3. Display the message character or its code symbol.

> `until` the message is complete

Implementation

The program in Fig. 10.18 assumes that the uppercase letters are consecutive characters, as they are in the ASCII character set. This program must be modified slightly for computers that use the EBCDIC character set, which contains some special characters between the letters I and J and between the letters R and S. One possible modification would be to replace the `for` statement in procedure ReadCode with

```
for NextLetter := 'A' to 'Z' do
  if NextLetter in ['A'..'I', 'J'..'R', 'S'..'Z'] then
    Read (Code[NextLetter]);
```

The `if` statement causes the Read statement to be skipped when `NextLetter` is a special character.

Figure 10.18 Cryptogram Generator

Directory: CHAP10
File: CRYPTOGR.PAS

```
program Crytogram (Input, Output);

{Generates cryptograms corresponding to input messages}

  type
    Letter = 'A'..'Z';
    CodeArray = array [Letter] of Char;

  var
    Code : CodeArray;               {input — array of code symbols}

  {Insert function UpCase (see Fig. 9.4) here.}

  procedure ReadCode (var Code {output} : CodeArray);
  {
    Reads in the code symbol for each letter.
    Pre : None
    Post: 26 data values are read into array Code.
```

```
      }
      var
        NextLetter : Letter;              {each letter}

   begin {ReadCode}
     WriteLn ('First specify the code.');
     WriteLn ('Enter a code symbol under each letter.');
     WriteLn ('ABCDEFGHIJKLMNOPQRSTUVWXYZ');
     {Read each code symbol into array Code.}
     for NextLetter := 'A' to 'Z' do
       Read (Code[NextLetter]);
     ReadLn;                              {Terminate input line.}
     WriteLn                              {Skip a line.}
   end;   {ReadCode}


   procedure Encrypt (Code {input} : CodeArray);
   {
     Reads each character and prints it or its code symbol.
     Pre : Array Code is defined.
     Post: Each character read was printed or its code
           symbol was printed and the sentinel was just read.
     Uses: UpCase (see Fig. 9.4)
   }
     const
       Sentinel = '#';                    {sentinel character}

     var
       NextChar : Char;         {input – each message character}

   begin   {Encrypt}
     WriteLn ('Enter each character of your message;');
     WriteLn ('terminate it with the symbol ', Sentinel);
     repeat
       Read (NextChar);
       NextChar := UpCase(NextChar);      {Convert to uppercase.}
       if NextChar in ['A'..'Z'] then
         WriteLn (Code[NextChar] :5)         {Print code symbol.}
       else
         WriteLn (NextChar :5)               {Print non–letter.}
     until NextChar = Sentinel
   end;   {Encrypt}


begin   {Cryptogram}
  {Read in the code symbol for each letter.}
  ReadCode (Code);

  {Read each character and print it or its code symbol.}
  Encrypt (Code)
end.  {Cryptogram}

First specify the code you wish to use.
Enter a code symbol under each letter.
ABCDEFGHIJKLMNOPQRSTUVWXYZ
BCDEFGHIJKLMNOPQRSTUVWXYZA

Enter each character of your message;
terminate it with the symbol #
A     B
```

```
t    U
i    J
n    O
y    Z

o    P
n    O
e    F
!    !
#    #
```

Testing

In the preceding sample run, the code symbol for each letter is entered directly beneath that letter and read by procedure ReadCode. The sample run ends with two output columns: the first contains the message; the second contains its cryptogram. For a simple test, try using each letter as its own code symbol. In that case, both columns should be the same. Make sure the program encodes lowercase letters as well as uppercase letters. Characters that are not letters should not be changed.

Exercises for Section 10.6

Self-Check

1. Describe the following array types:
   a. array [1..20] of Char
   b. array ['0'..'9'] of Boolean
   c. array [-5..5] of Real
   d. array [Boolean] of Char

2. Provide array type declarations for representing the following:
   a. a group of rooms (living room, dining room, kitchen, etc.) that have a given area
   b. elementary school grade levels with a given number of students per grade
   c. a group of colors with letter values assigned according to the first letter of their name (for example, 'B' for blue)

3. Why is it that spaces and commas are not encoded in the cryptogram program?

Programming

1. Make changes to the cryptogram program to encode the blank character and the punctuation symbols , ; : ? ! . . Hint: Use subscript type Char.

10.7 Strings and Packed Arrays of Characters

Until now, our use of character data has been quite limited. We have used variables of type Char to hold single character values. This section discusses the manipulation of character arrays.

The variable declaration statement

```
const
  Size = 10;

type
  IndexRange = 1..Size;
  CharArray = array [IndexRange] of Char;

var
  Name : CharArray;
  I : Integer;
```

declares a character array Name with 10 elements; a single character can be stored in each array element.

The program in Fig. 10.19 first reads a sequence of characters into the array Name, then prints the characters stored in Name. For the data shown in Fig. 10.19, the array Name would be defined as shown below. Name[9] contains the blank character.

Array Name

[1]	[2]	[3]	[4]	[5]	[6]	[7]	[8]	[9]	[10]
J	o	n	a	t	h	a	n	□	B

Figure 10.19 Program StoreChars

```
program StoreChars (Input, Output);

{Reads a string of characters into an array}

  const
    Size = 10;

  type
    IndexRange = 1..Size;
    CharArray = array [IndexRange] of Char;

  var
    Name : CharArray;
    I : Integer;

begin {StoreChars}
  Write ('Enter your first name and an initial ');
  WriteLn ('using 10 characters> ');
  for I := 1 to Size do
    Read (Name[I]);
  ReadLn;
  WriteLn;
  Write ('Hello ');
```

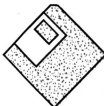

Directory: CHAP10
File: STORECHA.PAS

```
    for I := 1 to Size do
      Write (Name[I]);
    WriteLn ('!')
  end. {StoreChars}
```

```
Enter your first name and initial using 10 characters> Jonathan B
Hello Jonathan B!
```

As with any other array, a loop must be used to print all the data stored in a character array. The next section introduces a special type of array that simplifies operations on strings.

Declaring String Variables

You can use a *packed array* to facilitate the manipulation of character strings. When an array is *packed,* some compilers can store more than one character in each computer memory cell. This means that less storage space is required for storing a character string in a packed array. Another important benefit is that Pascal makes it easier for the programmer to manipulate character strings that are stored in packed arrays.

The declaration of two packed arrays, FirstName and LastName, follow.

```
const
  StringLength = 10;

type
  StringIndex = 1..StringLength;
  String10 = packed array [StringIndex] of Char;

var
  FirstName, LastName : String10;
```

Variables FirstName and LastName are called *string variables,* or *strings,* of length 10 (value of StringLength), because they can each store a character string consisting of exactly 10 characters.

The statement

```
FirstName := 'A.C. Jones';   {Assign a string to FirstName.}
```

stores the string value 'A.C. Jones' in the string variable FirstName, as follows.

Array FirstName

[1]	[2]	[3]	[4]	[5]	[6]	[7]	[8]	[9]	[10]
A	.	C	.	□	J	o	n	e	s

if FirstName is not a string variable, this statement causes a syntax error. Because FirstName and LastName are both the same array type, the assignment statement

```
LastName := FirstName;          {copy FirstName to LastName}
```

copies the string value stored in FirstName to LastName.

Each string value stored in a string variable must have the same length as the string variable receiving it. The string assignments

```
FirstName := 'Jones';        {invalid - string too short}
FirstName := 'A.C. Johnson'; {invalid - string too long}
```

would cause a `type conflict of operands` syntax error because they violate this rule.

457

10.7 Strings and
Packed Arrays of
Characters

SYNTAX
DISPLAY

String Variable Declaration

Form: type *string type* = packed array [1.. *size*] of Char;
Example: type String10 = packed array [1..10] of Char;
Interpretation: The identifier *string type* denotes an array type that can store a string value consisting of *size* characters.
Note: The subscript type for *string type* must begin with 1.

Referencing Individual Characters in a String

For the most part, we can manipulate individual characters of a string just like any type `Char` variable. If `FirstName` contains the string `'A.C. Jones'`, the statements

```
FirstName[1] := 'D';
FirstName[6] := 'B';
```

change the value of `FirstName` to the string `'D.C. Bones'`. If `NextChar` is type `Char`, the statement

```
NextChar := FirstName[2];
```

stores a period in `NextChar`. Also, the following `if` condition is true when the value of `I` is 2 or 4.

```
if FirstName[I] = '.' then
  WriteLn ('Period at position ', I :1)
```

The only thing we can't do is pass an element of a string as a variable parameter to a procedure declared in a program system. However, it is permissible to read individual characters directly into a string variable. The statement

```
Read (FirstName[1])
```

replaces the first character in string `FirstName` with the next data character.

Displaying String Variables

The statements

```
Write ('Hello ', FirstName);
WriteLn ('. Good to see you.')
```

display the line

```
Hello D.C. Bones. Good to see you.
```

when `FirstName` contains the string `'D.C. Bones'`. As shown, a string variable can appear without a subscript as a parameter in a `Write` or `WriteLn` statement. When this is done, the variable's contents are printed as a single string.

A format specification can be used with a string variable. The statements

```
Write ('Hello ', FirstName :4);
WriteLn ('! Good to see you.')
```

display the line

```
Hello D.C.! Good to see you.
```

Because the field width (4) is less than the length (10) of string `FirstName`, only the first four characters of `FirstName` are displayed. If the field width is larger than the length of the string, leading blanks are displayed before the string value. Table 10.6 provides some examples.

Table 10.6 Displaying a Formatted String

Statement	Effect
Write (FirstName : 10)	D.C. Bones
Write (FirstName : 6)	D.C. B
Write (FirstName : 12)	D.C. Bones

Abstract Data Type StringADT

Because operations with strings are common, it would be desirable to have an abstract data type `StringADT` that contains a declaration for data type `StringType` and a procedure (`ReadLnString`) for reading a string from either the keyboard or a data file. There is no need to provide a procedure for displaying a string, because the standard Pascal `Write(Ln)` procedures can be used for this purpose.

Before writing procedure `ReadLnString`, let's consider its specification. We will assume that each data string appears at the end of a line, followed by `<eoln>`. The number of characters actually read and stored in a string variable is limited by its declared length (say, `StringLength`). If the `<eoln>` comes before `StringLength` characters are read, the blank character should be stored in the array elements that did not receive data (called *padding a string with blanks*). If there are more than `StringLength` characters before the `<eoln>`, only the first `StringLength` characters should be stored in the string variable; the remaining characters will be ignored. For example, if `StringLength` is 10 and the data string is `Hello<eoln>`, the last five elements of the string variable receiving data would contain the blank character. If the data string is `Hello Class<eoln>`, the second s (the eleventh character) would not be stored.

Figure 10.20 shows the specification for StringADT; Figure 10.21 shows its implementation, including procedure ReadLnString. In Fig. 10.21, the constant StringLength has a value of 20.

Figure 10.20   Specification for StringADT

```
{
  Specification of abstract data type StringADT

Structure:    StringType is a data type that represents a string
              value consisting of StringLength characters.

Operators:    The following description assumes these
              parameters:

                  InFile is type Text.
                  InString is type StringType.
                  CurLength is type Integer.

  ReadLnString (var InFile, var InString, var CurLength) :
  Reads a data string of up to StringLength characters from
  file InFile into InString and returns the number of
  characters read through CurLength.
}
```

Figure 10.21   Implementation of StringADT

```
{
  Implementation of StringADT
}

    const
      StringLength = 20;                    {maximum string length}

    type
      StringIndex = 1..StringLength;
      StringType = packed array [StringIndex] of Char;

procedure ReadLnString (var InFile {input} : Text;
                        var InString {output} : StringType;
                        var CurLength {output} : Integer);
{
  Reads a data string from file InFile into InString and returns the
  number of characters read through CurLength.
  Pre : StringLength is the length of a string
        variable of type StringType and file InFile
        is opened for input.
  Post: Reads up to StringLength characters from file InFile into
        InString and advances to the next data line.
        Stops reading characters if <eoln>
        is reached before InString is filled and pads
        the rest of the string with blanks. The
        number of characters read is saved in CurLength
        (0 <= CurLength <= StringLength).
}
  const
    Pad = ' ';                              {character used for padding}
```

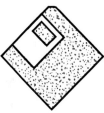

Directory: CHAP10
File: STRINGAD.ADT

```
      var
        I : Integer;                    {loop-control character}

    begin {ReadLnString}
      {Read each character and store it in the next array element.}
      CurLength := 0;              {no characters read}
      while (not EOLN(InFile)) and (CurLength < StringLength) do
        {invariant:
           InString[1..CurLength] contains characters read so far
           and CurLength <= StringLength and the <eoln> was not read
        }
        begin
          CurLength := CurLength + 1;         {Increment subscript.}
          Read (InFile, InString[CurLength])   {Read next character.}
        end;  {while}

      {assert: at end of line or string is filled}
      ReadLn (InFile);                       {Advance to next line.}
      {Pad rest of string with blanks}
      for I := CurLength + 1 to StringLength do
        InString[I] := Pad
    end;  {ReadLnString}
```

The while loop in Fig. 10.21 reads each data character and stores it in the next element of InString, as determined by subscript CurLength. The loop invariant

```
{invariant:
    InString[1..CurLength] contains characters read so far
    and CurLength <= StringLength and the <eoln> was not read
}
```

indicates that, at the end of each loop iteration, the subarray In-String[1..CurLength] contains the data characters read so far. In the sketch of array InString that follows, the array elements containing data characters are shown under the color screen. During each iteration of the loop, the value of CurLength increases by 1, and the portion of the array under the color screen grows by one element.

Array InString

[1] [2] · · · [CurLength]	· · · [StringLength]
elements containing data	

Loop exit will occur when the <eoln> is the next data character or after StringLength characters are read. After loop exit, the statement

```
ReadLn (InFile);                   {Advance to next line.}
```

advances to the next line of file InFile, skipping over any extra characters at the end of the data line.

If the data line contains less than StringLength characters, then a blank character should be stored in all array elements that did not receive data. This is done by the for statement in Fig. 10.21. If CurLength is equal to String-

Length, the string is already filled with data, so the `for` loop body is not executed.

Table 10.7 shows the values returned through `InString` and `CurLength` for three calls to procedure `ReadLnString` when `StringLength` is 5. For the last call, only the uppercase letters are read; the lowercase letters are skipped.

Table 10.7 Results of Calls to ReadLnString

StringLength	**Data String**	InString	CurLength
5	ABC<eoln>	'ABC '	3
5	ABCDE<eoln>	'ABCDE'	5
5	ABCDEfg<eoln>	'ABCDE'	5

The only reason for returning the number of characters actually read through `CurLength` is to enable the client program to display the data string without "printing" the blank padding. If `AString` is type `StringType` and `ALength` is type `Integer`, the statements

```
ReadLnString (Input, AString, ALength);
WriteLn ('*', AString :ALength, '*')
```

would read a data string into `AString` and display it between asterisks. So if `StringLength` is 20 and the data string is

```
a short one<eoln>
```

the following line would be displayed:

```
*a short one*
```

If you use `Input` as the first parameter in a call to `ReadLnString`, the data string is read from the keyboard. Because of differences in the way Pascal systems perform interactive input, `ReadLnString` may not always read data from the keyboard as expected.

Comparing Strings

Function `SameArray` in Fig. 10.11 determines whether two arrays of real numbers are identical. It is much easier to make this determination for strings because Pascal allows them to be operands of the relational operators. Assuming the declarations

```
type
  IndexRange = 1..3;
  String3 = packed array [IndexRange] of Char;

var
  AlphaStr, BetaStr : String3;          {strings being compared}
  Same, Differ : Boolean;               {Boolean flags}
```

the statement

```
Same := AlphaStr = BetaStr          {Are strings identical?}
```

assigns the value True to Same when AlphaStr and BetaStr contain the same string. The assignment statement

```
Differ := AlphaStr <> BetaStr        {Are strings different?}
```

assigns the value True to Differ when AlphaStr and BetaStr contain different strings. Finally, the assignment statement

```
Same := AlphaStr = 'Rob'
```

assigns the value True to Same when AlphaStr contains the string 'Rob'.

Using the relational operators, <, <=, >, and >=, it is also possible to compare equal-length strings for *lexicographic,* or alphabetical, order. The result of such a comparison is based on the collating sequence (order of characters) for your computer.

For example, the condition

```
AlphaStr < BetaStr
```

is true if the string stored in AlphaStr is considered less than the string stored in BetaStr. This is determined by comparing corresponding characters in both strings starting with the first pair. If the characters are the same, the next pair is checked. If the characters in position i are the first different pair, then AlphaStr is less than BetaStr if AlphaStr[i] is less than BetaStr[i].

The conditions shown in Table 10.8 are true for all character codes shown in Appendix C. The reason each condition is true is explained in the last column.

Table 10.8 Some True String Comparisons

AlphaStr	**Operator**	BetaStr	**Reason Condition Is True**
'AAA'	<	'ZZZ'	'A' < 'Z'
'AZZ'	<	'ZZZ'	'A' < 'Z'
'ZAZ'	<	'ZZA'	'A' < 'Z'
'AZZ	<	'BAA'	'A' < 'B'
'B11'	>	'A99'	'B' > 'A'
'B11'	<	'B12'	'1' < '2'
'ACE'	<	'AID'	'C' < 'I'
'123'	>	'103'	'2' > '0'
'123'	>=	'123'	All characters equal
'30 '	>=	'123'	'3' > '1'

The last line of Table 10.8 shows the curious result that '30 ' >= '123' is true. It is true, because the condition result is based solely on the relationship between the first pair of different characters, '3' and '1'. To avoid these funny results, replace any blanks in numeric strings with zeros. The condition

```
'300' >= '123'
```

is true while the condition

```
'030' >= '123'
```

is false, as expected.

In summary, the following statements are true for string variables where `AlphaStr` is the string variable declared previously.

- A string literal can be assigned to a string variable of the same length (for example, `AlphaStr := 'ABC'`).
- A string variable can be written without using a loop [for example, `Write ('Alpha is ', AlphaStr)`].
- A string variable can be compared to a string variable or a string literal of the same length (for example, `AlphaStr <> 'ZZZ'`).

Exercises for Section 10.7

Self-Check

1. What would be returned by `ReadLnString` through `InString` and `Cur-Length` for the data string

   ```
   The quick fox jumped<eoln>
   ```

   when `StringLength` is 10, 20, and 25?
2. If an assignment statement is used to store a string into a packed array, what must be true about the length of the string? What can be done if this is not the case?
3. What is the difference between determining whether two arrays of real numbers are the same and determining if two packed arrays of characters are the same? What, if any, are the restrictions on the subscript types of the two packed arrays being compared?

Programming

1. Write a procedure that finds the actual length of a string that is padded with blanks. Do not include the blank padding in the actual length.
2. Write a procedure that stores the reverse of an input string parameter in its output parameter (for example, if the input string is `'happy     '`, the output string should be `'yppah     '`). The actual length of the string being reversed (excluding blank padding) should also be an input parameter.
3. Write a program that uses the procedure in the preceding exercise to determine whether a string is a palindrome. (A palindrome is a string that reads the same left to right as it does right to left, for example, `'level'`.)

10.8 Using Strings

Now that we have a way to store character strings in memory, we can improve our capability to manipulate textual data. Suppose that during the spring semester you begin thinking about a summer job. One thing you might want to do is write a program that prints form letters so you can do a mass mailing to inquire about summer job opportunities in a variety of fields.

Case Study: Printing a Form Letter

Problem

You want a program that can help you write job application letters. Each letter will be sent to an output file for printing.

Analysis

A letter consists of a heading, a salutation, the body, and a closing. The heading, the salutation, and the first line of the body will be different for each letter, but the body and the closing will be the same. First, you'll use an editor to create the letter body and the closing and save them as a text file (BodyFile). To individualize each letter, you want to enter data for the first part of the letter at the keyboard and then write the first part of the letter to the output file (Letter). Next, you can write the rest of the letter from file BodyFile to the output file.

An example of the data entry process for the first part of the letter follows. The information you'll enter is in color.

```
Today's date             > July 27, 1992
Employer name            > Peter Liacouras
Company name             > Temple University
Address                  > Broad and Montgomery Streets
City, state, and zip> Philadelphia, PA 19122
```

This data would be inserted in the first several lines written to the output file, as shown in Fig. 10.22.

Figure 10.22   First Lines of File Letter

```
                                              July 27, 1992

Peter Liacouras
Temple University
Broad and Montgomery Streets
Philadelphia, PA 19122

Dear Peter Liacouras:

    I am interested in applying for a job at Temple University.
```

Data Requirements

Problem Inputs

```
BodyFile : Text              {body of the letter}
Date : StringType            {today's date}
Employer : StringType        {employer's name}
Company : StringType         {company name}
Address : StringType         {company address}
CityStZip : StringType       {city, state, and zip}
```

Problem Output

```
Letter : Text                {complete letter}
```

Design

Initial Algorithm
1. Read the preamble data from the keyboard and write it to Letter.
2. Copy the letter body to Letter.

Algorithm Refinement and Structure Chart
From the structure chart in Fig. 10.23, you can see that procedures Preamble and WriteBody perform steps 1 and 2, respectively.

Figure 10.23   Structure Chart for Form Letter Program

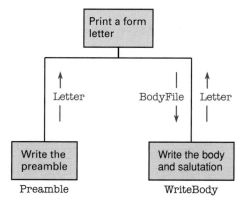

Implementation

Coding the Main Program
The main program body, shown in Fig. 10.24, prepares both text files and calls procedures Preamble and WriteBody. They, in turn, call procedure ReadLnString declared in StringADT (see Fig. 10.21). The main program displays a message before data entry begins and a message after the letter is completed.

Figure 10.24   Form Letter Writing Program

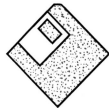

Directory: CHAP10
File: FORMLETT.PAS

```
program FormLetter (Input, Output, BodyFile, Letter);
{
   Writes a job application letter to an output file. The data
   for the letter preamble is read from the keyboard; the letter
   body is copied from a data file to the output file.
   Module needed: StringADT (see Fig. 10.21) with
                         StringLength = 80
}
   {Insert declaration for StringType from StringADT.}
   {Insert procedure ReadLnString from StringADT here.}
   {Insert procedures Preamble and WriteBody here.}

begin {FormLetter}
   Reset (BodyFile);
   Rewrite (Letter);
```

```
    WriteLn (Output, 'Writing job application letter.');
    Preamble (Letter);
    WriteBody (BodyFile, Letter);
    WriteLn (Output, 'Letter copied to output file.')
end. {FormLetter}
```

Coding the Procedures

Procedure `Preamble` (see Fig. 10.25) reads from the keyboard the strings needed for the letter heading and the salutation. After data entry, the strings read into `DateString`, `Employer`, `Company`, `Address`, `CityStZip` are written to file `Letter`.

Figure 10.25 Procedure Preamble

Directory: CHAP10
File: FORMLETT.PAS

```
procedure Preamble (var Letter {output} : Text);
{
  Writes a preamble for a job application letter to an output file.
  Pre : The output file is opened.
  Post: Writes the heading, salutation, and first sentence of a
        job application letter using data entered at the keyboard.
  Uses: ReadLnString
}
  const
    PageWidth = 50;                            {padding for date}

  var
    DateString,                                {input - data strings}
    Employer, Company,                         {           "          }
    Address, CityStZip : StringType;           {           "          }
    DateLen,  EmpLen, CompLen,
    AddLen, CityLen    : Integer;              {length of each string}

begin {Preamble}
  {Enter all data}
  Write ('Today''s date        > ');
  ReadLnString (Input, DateString, DateLen);
  Write ('Employer name       > ');
  ReadLnString (Input, Employer, EmpLen);
  Write ('Company name        > ');
  ReadLnString (Input, Company, CompLen);
  Write ('Address             > ');
  ReadLnString (Input, Address, AddLen);
  Write ('City, state, and zip> ');
  ReadLnString (Input, CityStZip, CityLen);

  {Write letter preamble.}
  WriteLn (Letter, ' ' :PageWidth, DateString :DateLen);
  WriteLn (Letter);
  WriteLn (Letter, Employer);
  WriteLn (Letter, Company);
  WriteLn (Letter, CityStZip);
  WriteLn (Letter);
  WriteLn (Letter, 'Dear ', Employer :EmpLen, ':');
  WriteLn (Letter);
```

```
   Write (Letter, '     I am interested in applying for a job at ');
   WriteLn (Letter, Company :CompLen, '.');
   WriteLn (Letter)
end; {Preamble}
```

Procedure `WriteBody` copies the body of the letter (not shown) from the input file to the output file. Procedure `WriteBody` is shown in Fig. 10.26. The `while` loop copies each line of the data file to the output file.

Figure 10.26   Procedure WriteBody

```
procedure WriteBody (var BodyFile {input},
                         Letter    {output} : Text);
{
   Copies the body of a job application letter from a data file
   to an output file.
   Pre : The input file and output file are opened.
   Post: Writes the letter body to the output file.
   Uses: ReadLnString
}
   var
      OneLine : StringType;          {next data line}
      LineLength : Integer;          {length of line read}

begin {WriteBody}
   {Copy each line until done.}
   while not EOF(BodyFile) do
      begin
         ReadLnString (BodyFile, OneLine, LineLength);
         WriteLn (Letter, OneLine :LineLength)
      end {while}
end; {WriteBody}
```

Directory: CHAP10
File: FORMLETT.PAS

Testing

Test procedure `ReadLnString` using a driver program before you run the form letter program. Try to read strings from the keyboard as well as from a data file. See what happens when the data lines are longer than the length of the receiving string variable and when the data line is exactly the same length as the string variable. When you run the form letter program, try using an empty file `BodyFile`.

Exercises for Section 10.8

Self-Check

1. Procedure `Preamble` displays several character strings. What method is used so that the blank padding is not displayed?

Programming

1. Assume that the technique used in procedure Preamble to keep the blank padding from being displayed does not work on your computer. Write a procedure WriteString that displays characters 1 through CurLen of a string where the string and CurLen are passed as parameters.

10.9 Searching and Sorting an Array

This section discusses two common problems in processing arrays: *searching* an array to determine the location of a particular value and *sorting* an array to rearrange the array elements in sequence. As an example of an array search, we might want to search the array of exam scores read in by procedure ReadScores (see Fig. 10.15) to determine which student, if any, got a particular score. An example of an array sort would be rearranging the array elements so that they are in increasing (or decreasing) order by score. This would be helpful if we want to display the list in order by score or if we need to locate several different scores in the array.

Array Search

We can search an array for a particular score (called the search *target*) by examining each array element, starting with the first, and testing to see whether it matches the target score. If a match occurs, we have found the target and can return its subscript as the search result. If a match does not occur, we should continue searching until we either get a match or test all array elements without success. The data requirements and the algorithm for a search function follow.

Data Requirements for Search

Input Parameters
```
Scores: ScoreArray        {array to be searched}
ClassSize : ClassRange    {number of elements in Scores}
Target : Integer          {score being searched for}
```

Function Output
The subscript of the first element containing Target or zero if Target was not found

Program Variables
```
Next : Integer      {subscript of next score to test}
NotFound: Boolean   {program flag — true if target has not
                     been found in elements tested so far}
```

Algorithm for Search

1. Start with the first array element.
2. Set NotFound to True.

3. while the target is not found and there are more elements do
   4. if the current element matches the target then
      Set NotFound to False.
      else
         Try the next element.
5. if the target was not found then
      Return zero.
   else
      Return its subscript.

The while loop in step 3 executes until it finds the target in the array or it has tested all array elements without success. Step 4 compares the current array element (selected by subscript Next) to the target and sets NotFound to False if they match. If they do not match, the subscript Next is increased by 1. After loop exit, the if statement defines the function result as 0 (target was not found) or as the value assigned to Next when the match occurred. Figure 10.27 shows function Search.

Figure 10.27 Function Search

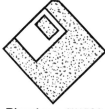

Directory: CHAP10
File: SEARCH.FUN

```
function Search (Scores : ScoreArray;
                 ClassSize : ClassRange;
                 Target : Integer)        : Integer;
{
  Searches for Target in array Scores.
  Pre : 1 <= ClassSize <= MaxSize and
        subarray Scores[1..ClassSize] is defined.
  Post: Returns the subscript of Target if found;
        otherwise, returns zero.
}
  var
    Next : Integer;         {index of the current score}
    NotFound : Boolean;     {program flag — true if target has not
                            been found in elements tested so far}

begin  {Search}
  {Compare each value in Scores to Target until done.}
  Next := 1;                        {Start with the first score.}
  NotFound := True;                 {Target is not found.}
  while NotFound and (Next <= ClassSize) do
    {invariant:
      Target was not found in subarray Scores[1..Next-1]
      and Next is <= ClassSize+1
    }
    if Scores[Next] = Target then
      NotFound := False             {Target is found.}
    else
      Next := Next + 1;             {Advance to next score.}

  {assert:
    Target was found or all elements were tested without success.
  }
  if NotFound then
    Search := 0                     {Target was not found.}
```

```
        else
            Search := Next                      {Target found at Scores[Next].}

end; {Search}
```

The program flag `NotFound` is used to control loop repetition and to communicate the results of the search loop to the `if` statement that follows the loop. `NotFound` is set to `True` before entering the search loop. `NotFound` is reset to `False` as soon as an element is tested that matches the target. The only way `NotFound` can remain true throughout the entire array search is if no array element matches the target. The `if` statement returns 0 when `NotFound` remains true; otherwise, it returns the value of subscript `Next` that caused `NotFound` to be changed to `False`.

The loop invariant is

```
{invariant:
    Target was not found in subarray Scores[1..Next-1]
    and Next <= ClassSize+1
}
```

This means that for each value of `Next` (starting with 1), the target was not found in an array element with a smaller subscript than `Next`. Because `Next <= ClassSize+1` must also be true after loop exit, `Scores[ClassSize]` is the last array element that can be compared to the target.

In the following sketch of array `Scores`

Array Scores

[1] [2]	· · ·	[Next-1] [Next] · · · [ClassSize]
elements tested without success		

the elements under the color screen are the ones that have already been tested, and the element with subscript `Next` will be tested in the current loop iteration. If `Scores[Next]` does not match the target, the portion of the array under the color screen will grow by one element, and the value of `Next` will increase by 1.

The invariant is true before the first iteration (`Next` is 1) because there are no array elements that precede the element with subscript 1. If the current element matches the target, loop exit will occur without changing `Next`, so the invariant will still be true. If `Next` becomes `ClassSize+1`, all array elements will have been tested without success (the entire array will be under the color screen) and loop exit will occur.

Sorting an Array

In Section 6.3 we discussed a simple sort operation involving three numbers. We performed the sort by examining pairs of numbers and exchanging them if they were out of order. There are many times when we would like to be able to sort the elements in an array, for example, to print a grade report in order by score.

This section discusses a fairly intuitive (but not very efficient) algorithm called the *selection sort*. To perform a selection sort of an array with N elements (subscripts 1..N), we locate the smallest element in the array and then switch the smallest element with the element at subscript 1, thereby placing the smallest element at position 1. Then we locate the smallest element remaining in the subarray with subscripts 2..N and switch it with the element at subscript 2, thereby placing the second smallest element at position 2. Then we locate the smallest element remaining in subarray 3..N and switch it with the element at subscript 3, and so on.

Figure 10.28 traces the operation of the selection sort algorithm. The column on the left shows the original array. Each subsequent column shows the array after the next smallest element is moved to its final position in the array. The subarray under the color screen represents the portion of the array that is sorted after each exchange occurs. Note that, at most, N–1 exchanges will be required to sort an array with N elements. The algorithm follows.

Algorithm for Selection Sort

1. for Fill := 1 to N–1 do
      2. Find the position of the smallest element
         in subarray Fill..N.
      3. if Fill is not the position of the smallest element then
            4. Switch the smallest element with the one at
               position Fill.

Figure 10.28 Trace of Selection Sort

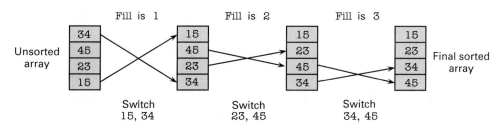

To refine step 2 of the selection sort algorithm, we need a loop that "searches" for the smallest element in the subarray with subscripts Fill..N. This loop must save the index of the smallest element found so far and compare each new element to the smallest element so far. If a new element is smaller than the smallest so far, the index of the new element is saved.

Step 2 Refinement
2.1 Initialize the position of the smallest so far to Fill.
2.2 for Next := Fill+1 to N do

2.3 if the element at Next < the smallest so far then

2.4 Reset the position of the smallest so far to Next.

Procedure SelectSort in Fig. 10.29 implements the selection sort algorithm for the array Scores with ClassSize elements. Local variable IndexOfMin holds the index of the smallest exam score found so far in the current subarray. After each execution of the inner for loop, procedure Switch is called to exchange the elements with subscripts IndexOfMin and Fill, provided that IndexOfMin and Fill are different. After the execution of procedure SelectSort, the exam scores will be in increasing order by exam score.

Figure 10.29   Selection Sort Procedure

```
procedure Switch (var Num1, Num2 {input/output} : Integer);
{Switches values of Num1 and Num2.
 Pre : none
 Post: Num1 is old Num2, and Num2 is old Num1.
}
   var
      Temp : Integer;              {temporary value}

begin  {Switch}
   Temp := Num1;
   Num1 := Num2;
   Num2 := Temp
end; {Switch}


procedure SelectSort (var Scores {input/output} : ScoreArray;
                          ClassSize {input} : Integer);
{
 Sorts the data in array Scores.
 Pre : 1 <= ClassSize <= MaxSize and
       subarray Scores[1..ClassSize] is defined.
 Post: The values in Scores[1..ClassSize] are in increasing order.
}
   var
      Fill,          {index of element being filled with next smallest score}
      Next,                    {element being compared to smallest so far}
      IndexOfMin : Integer;                     {index of smallest so far}

begin {SelectSort}
   for Fill := 1 to ClassSize-1 do
      begin
         {invariant:
            The elements in Scores[1..Fill-1] are in
            their proper place and Fill <= ClassSize.
         }
         {Find the position of smallest element in Scores[Fill..ClassSize].}
         IndexOfMin := Fill;
         for Next := Fill+1 to ClassSize do
            {invariant:
               The element at IndexOfMin is the smallest
               in Scores[Fill..Next-1] and Next <= ClassSize+1.
            }
            if Scores[Next] < Scores[IndexOfMin] then
               IndexOfMin := Next;
```

```
{assert: Element at IndexOfMin is smallest in Scores[Fill..ClassSize].}
{Exchange elements with subscripts Fill and IndexOfMin.}
   if IndexOfMin <> Fill then
      Switch (Scores[Fill], Scores[IndexOfMin])
   end {for Fill}
end; {SelectSort}
```

The loop invariant for the outer loop

```
{invariant:
   The elements in Scores[1..Fill-1] are in
   their proper place and Fill <= ClassSize.
}
```

summarizes the progress of the selection sort. The subarray whose elements are in their proper place is shown under the color screen in the sketch of array Scores below. The remaining elements are not yet in place and are all larger than Scores[Fill-1].

Array Scores	
[1] [2] . . . [Fill-1] [Fill] . . . [ClassSize]	
elements in their proper place	elements larger than Scores[Fill-1]

During each pass, the portion of the array under the color screen grows by one element, and Fill is incremented to reflect this. When Fill is equal to ClassSize, the first ClassSize-1 elements will be in their proper place, so Scores[ClassSize] must also be in its proper place.

Exercises for Section 10.9

Self-Check

1. Explain the loop invariant for the inner for loop and sketch its meaning.
2. For the Search function in Fig. 10.27, what happens if:
   a. the last student score matches the target?
   b. several scores match the target?
3. Trace the execution of the selection sort on the following list:

   10 55 34 56 76 5

   Show the array after each exchange occurs. How many exchanges are required? How many comparisons?
4. How could you modify the selection sort algorithm to get the scores in descending order (largest score first)?

Programming

1. Write a procedure to count the number of students with a passing grade on the exam (60 or higher).

2. Another method of performing the selection sort is to place the largest value in position N, the next largest in position N−1, and so on. Write this version.

3. A technique for implementing an array search without introducing a program flag is to use a `while` loop that increments `Next` as long as both of the following statements are true: the target does not match the current element, and `Next` is less than `ClassSize`. After loop exit, the element at position `Next` can be tested again to determine the function result. If the element matches the target, the result is `Next`; otherwise, the result is `0`. Write the function body.

10.10 Analysis of Algorithms: Big-O Notation (Optional)

There are many algorithms for searching and sorting arrays. Since arrays can have a very large number of elements, the time required to process all the elements of an array can be significant. Therefore, it is important to have some idea of the relative efficiency of different algorithms. It is difficult to get a precise measure of the performance of an algorithm or program. For this reason, we normally try to approximate the effect on an algorithm of a change in the number of items, N, that the algorithm processes. In this way, we can see how an algorithm's execution time increases with N, so we can compare two algorithms by examining their growth rates.

For example, if we determine that the expression

$$2N^2 + N - 5$$

expresses the relationship between processing time and N, we say that the algorithm is an $O(N^2)$ algorithm, where O is an abbreviation for order of magnitude. This notation is known as *Big-O notation*. The reason that this is an $O(N^2)$ algorithm instead of an $O(2N^2)$ algorithm or an $O(2N^2 + N - 5)$ algorithm is that the fastest growing term (the one with the largest exponent) is dominent for large N and we ignore constants.

To search an array of N elements for a target using our `Search` function, we have to examine all N elements if the target is not present in the array. If the target is in the array, then we have to search only until we find it. However, the target could be anywhere in the array—it is equally likely to be at the beginning of the array as at the end. So on average, we have to examine $N/2$ array elements to locate a target value in an array. This means that an array search is an $O(N)$ process, so the growth rate is linear.

To determine the efficiency of a sorting algorithm, we normally focus on the number of array element comparisons and exchanges that it requires. Performing a selection sort on an array with N elements requires $N - 1$ comparisons during the first pass through the array, $N - 2$ comparisons during the second pass, and so on. Therefore, the total number of comparisons is represented by the series

$$1 + 2 + 3 + \ldots + (N - 2) + (N - 1)$$

The value of this series is expressed in the closed form

$$\frac{N \times (N - 1)}{2} = N^2/2 - N/2$$

The number of comparisons performed in sorting an array of N elements using selection sort is always the same; however, the number of array element exchanges varies, depending on the initial ordering of the array elements. During the search for the kth smallest element, the inner `for` loop sets `IndexOfMin` to the index of the kth smallest element in the array. If `IndexOfMin` is set to k, then the kth smallest element is already in its correct place, so no exchange takes place. If this never happens, there will be one exchange at the end of each iteration of the outer loop, or a total of $N - 1$ exchanges (*worst-case situation*). If the array happens to be sorted before procedure `SelectSort` is called, all its elements will be in their proper place, so there will be zero exchanges (*best-case situation*). Therefore, the number of array element exchanges for an arbitrary initial ordering is between zero and $N - 1$, which is $O(N)$.

Because the dominant term in the expression for the number of comparisons shown earlier is $N^2/2$, selection sort is considered an $O(N^2)$ process, and the growth rate is quadratic (proportional to the square of the number of elements). What difference does it make whether an algorithm is an $O(N)$ process or an $O(N^2)$ process? Table 10.9 evaluates N and N^2 for different values of N. A doubling of N causes N^2 to increase by a factor of 4. Since N^2 increases much more quickly than N, the performance of an $O(N)$ algorithm is not as adversely affected by an increase in array size as is an $O(N^2)$ algorithm. For large values of N (say, 100 or more), the differences in performance for an $O(N)$ and an $O(N^2)$ algorithm are significant. (See the last three lines of Table 10.9.)

Table 10.9 Table of Values of N and N²

N	N^2
2	4
4	16
8	64
16	256
32	1024
64	4096
128	16384
256	65536
512	262144

Other factors besides the number of comparisons and exchanges affect an algorithm's performance. For example, one algorithm may take more time preparing for each exchange or comparison than another. Also, one algorithm might exchange subscripts, whereas another algorithm might exchange the array elements themselves. The latter process can be more time-consuming. Another measure of efficiency is the amount of memory required by an algorithm. Chapter 19 discusses additional techniques for searching and sorting that are considerably more efficient than the simple ones discussed so far.

Exercises for Section 10.10

Self-Check

1. Determine how many times the WriteLn statement is displayed in each of the following fragments. Indicate whether the algorithm is $O(N)$ or $O(N^2)$.

   a. ```
for I := 1 to N do
    for J := 1 to N do
        WriteLn (I, J)
```
   b. ```
for I := 1 to N do
    for J := 1 to 2 do
        WriteLn (I, J)
```
   c. ```
for I := 1 to N do
    for J := N downto I do
        WriteLn (I, J)
```

**Programming**

1. Write a program fragment that compares the values of *Y1* and *Y2* below for *N* up to 100 in increments of 10. Does the result surprise you?

$$Y1 = 100N + 10$$
$$Y2 = 5N^2 + 2$$

# 10.11 Common Programming Errors

The most common error in the use of arrays is an index expression out of bounds run-time error. This error occurs when the subscript value is outside the allowable range for the array being processed. Most often, this error is caused by an incorrect subscript expression, a loop parameter error, or a nonterminating loop. Before you spend considerable time debugging, carefully check all suspect subscript calculations for out-of-range errors. You can do that most easily by inserting diagnostic output statements in your program to print subscript values that might be out of range.

If the subscript whose value is out-of-range is type Integer, make its type the same as the array subscript type. This will cause a run-time error to occur as soon as the subscript is assigned an incorrect value.

If an out-of-range subscript occurs inside a loop, make sure the loop is terminating properly. If the loop-control variable is not being updated as expected, the loop may be repeated more often than required. This could happen, for example, if the update step comes after the loop end statement, or if the loop begin and end are erroneously omitted.

Also doublecheck the subscript values at the loop boundaries. If these values
```

are in range, it is likely that all other subscript references in the loop are in range as well.

As with all Pascal data types, make sure there are no type inconsistencies. The subscript type and the element type used in all array references must correspond to the types specified in the array declaration.

Similarly, the types of two arrays used in an array copy statement or as corresponding parameters must be the same. Remember to use only identifiers without subscripts as formal array parameters and to specify the types of all array parameters using identifiers.

A variable of type `packed array [1..N] of Char` is a string variable of length N (a constant). A string variable of length N can be assigned a string value consisting of exactly N characters. An `incompatible type` syntax error is detected if a string value that is too short or too long is assigned to a string variable. If one string variable is assigned to another, they both must be the same length. If `InString` is a string variable, remember that `InString[I]` cannot correspond to a variable parameter of type `Char`.

CHAPTER REVIEW

This chapter introduced a data structure called an array, which is a convenient facility for naming and referencing a collection of like items. We discussed how to declare an array type and how to reference an individual array element by placing a subscript in brackets following the array name.

The `for` statement enables us to easily reference the elements of an array in sequence. We can use `for` statements to initialize arrays, to read and print arrays, and to control the manipulation of individual array elements in sequence.

We also examined how to allocate storage for a string variable and how to store a string value in a string variable. You saw that operations such as comparison, assignment, and display are performed more easily on a string variable because the entire string can be processed as a unit rather than element by element.

Two common operations involving arrays were discussed: searching an array and sorting an array. We wrote a function for searching an array and also described the selection sort procedure. Finally, we discussed how to use Big-O notation as a measure of an algorithm's efficiency.

New Pascal Constructs

Table 10.10 describes the Pascal constructs introduced in this chapter.

Table 10.10 Summary of New Pascal Constructs

Construct	Effect
Array Declaration	
`type` `IndexRange = 1..10;`	The data type `IntArray` describes an array with 10

Table 10.10, *continued*

Construct	Effect

`IntArray = array [IndexRange] of Integer;`
 	
`var`
`  Cube, Count : IntArray;`
	type `Integer` elements. `Cube` and `Count` are arrays with this structure.

Packed Array Declaration

`type`
`  Index = 1..10;`
`  String10 = packed array [Index] of Char;`
 	
`var`
`  Name : String10;`
	The data type `String10` describes a packed array of 10 characters. `Name` is a string variable of length 10.

Array References

`for I := 1 to 10 do` `  Cube [I] := I * I * I`	Saves `I` cubed in the `I`th element of array `Cube`.
`if Cube[5] > 100 then`	Compares `Cube[5]` to 100.
`Write (Cube[1], Cube[2])`	Displays the first two cubes.

Array Copy

`Count := Cube`	Copies contents of array `Cube` to array `Count`.

Operations on Strings

`Name := 'R. Koffman'`	Saves `'R. Koffman'` in `Name`.
`WriteLn (Name)`	Displays `'R Koffman'`.
`if Name > 'Daffy Duck' then`	Compares `Name` to `'Daffy Duck'`.

✓ Quick-Check Exercises

1. What is a data structure?
2. Which standard types cannot be array subscript types? Array element types?
3. Can values of different types be stored in an array?
4. If an array is declared to have ten elements, must the program use all ten?
5. When can the assignment operator be used with array operands? Answer the same question for the equality operator.
6. The two methods of array access are _____ and _____.
7. The _____ loop allows us to access the elements of an array in _____ order.

8. Can the variable declared as follows be used to store a string of length 5 using an assignment statement? If not, why not?

```
var
   AString : packed array [6..10] of Char;
```

9. Explain why variable parameters are a more efficient use of memory when passing arrays to a procedure.

10. Declare variables `First` and `Last` that can be used to save a person's first name and last name (maximum of 20 characters each) in separate strings. Under what circumstances can the Pascal `Read` procedure be used to read a data string into `First` or `Last`?

Answers to Quick-Check Exercises

1. A data structure is a grouping of related values in main memory.
2. `Real` and `Integer`; all can be element types.
3. no
4. no
5. if the arrays are the same type; if the arrays are packed arrays of characters with a subscript type of the form `1..N`
6. random and sequential
7. `for`, sequential
8. No, the subscript type must be the subrange type `1..5`.
9. A local copy of each array used as a value parameter is made when a procedure is called.
10.
```
type
   AString = packed array [1..20] of Char;

var
   First, Last : AString;
```

No circumstances; a loop must always be used.

Review Questions

1. Identify the error in the following code segment. When will the error be detected?

```
program Test;
   type
      AnArray = array [1..8] of Integer;

   var
      X : AnArray;
      I : Integer;

begin {Test}
   for I := 1 to 9 do
      X[I] := I
end. {Test}
```

2. Declare an array of reals called `Week` that can be referenced by using any day of the week as a subscript, where Sunday is the first subscript.

3. Identify the error in the following Pascal fragment.

```
type
  AnArray = array [Char] of Real;

var
  X : AnArray;
  I : Integer;

begin
  I := 1;
  X[I] := 8.384
end.
```

4. Is the last statement in the following Pascal fragment a valid Pascal statement?

```
type
  RealArray = array [1,,8] of Real;

var
  X : RealArray;
  I : Integer;

begin
  I := 1;
  X(I) := 8.384
end.
```

5. What are two common ways of selecting array elements for processing?

6. Write a Pascal program segment to print out the index of the smallest and the largest numbers in an array X of 20 integers with values from 0 to 100. Assume array X already has values assigned to each element.

7. The parameters for a procedure are two arrays (type `RealArray`) and an integer that represents the length of the arrays. The procedure copies the first array in the parameter list to the other array in reverse order using a loop structure. Write the procedure.

8. List three advantages to using packed character arrays.

9. What would be a valid reason for not passing an array that provides input to a procedure as a value parameter?

10. How many exchanges are required to sort the following list of integers using selection sort? How many comparisons?

> 20   30   40   25   60   80

Programming Projects

1. Write a program for the following problem. You are given a file that contains a collection of scores (type `Integer`) for the last exam in your computer course. You are to compute the average of these scores and assign grades to each student according to the following rule.

   If a student's score is within 10 points (above or below) of the average, assign a grade of `Satisfactory`. If a student's score is more than 10 points higher than the average, assign a grade of `Outstanding`. If a student's score is more than 10 points below the average, assign a grade of `Unsatisfactory`.

   The output from your program should consist of a labeled two-column list that shows each score and its corresponding grade. As part of the solution, your program should include functions and procedures that correspond to the function and procedure headers that follow.

```
procedure ReadStuData (var RawScores {input} : Text;
                       var Score {output} : ArrayType;
                       var Count {output} : Integer;
                       var TooMany {output} : Boolean);
{
  Reads exam scores from file RawScores into array Scores.
  Count contains number of students read. TooMany is set to
  True if RawScores contains more than MaxSize scores.
}

procedure PrintGrade (OneScore {input} : Integer;
                      Average {input} : Real);
{Prints student grade after comparing OneScore to Average}

function Mean (Score : ArrayType; Count : Integer) : Real;
{Computes average of Count student scores}

procedure PrintTable (Score {input} : ArrayType;
                      Count {input} : Integer);
{
  Prints a table showing each student's score and grade
  on a separate line.
  Uses: PrintGrade.
}
```

Directory: CHAP10
File: PROJ10_1.PAS

2. Redo programming project 1 assuming that each line of file RawScores contains a student's ID number (an integer) and an exam score. Modify procedure Read–StuData to read the ID number and the score from the Ith data line into array elements ID[I] and Score[I], respectively. Modify procedure PrintTable to display a three-column table with the following headings:

   ID   Score   Grade

3. Write a program to read N data items into two arrays, X and Y, of size 20. Store the product of corresponding elements of X and Y in a third array Z, also of size 20. Print a three-column table displaying the arrays X, Y, and Z. Then compute and print the square root of the sum of the items in Z. Make up your own data, with N less than 20.

4. Another approach to sorting an array is to create an *index* to the array, where the index is an array whose element values represent array subscripts. An index allows us to access the elements of a second array in sequential order without rearranging the second array's element values. After "sorting," the first element of the index array will contain the subscript of the smallest array element, the second element of the index array will contain the subscript of the second smallest element, and so on. For example, if the array Scores contains the exam scores 60, 90, 50, 100, 75, the array ScoresIndex should contain the subscripts 3, 1, 5, 2, 4. ScoresIndex[1] is 3 because Scores[3] is the smallest score (50); ScoresIndex[2] is 1 because Scores[1] is the second smallest score (60), and so on. Write procedure IndexSort which creates an index array for its input array parameters.

5. The results of a true-false exam given to a computer science class have been coded for input to a program. The information available for each student consists of a student identification number and the student's answers to 10 true-or-false questions. The available data are as follows:

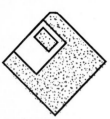

Student Identification	Answer String
0080	FTTFTFTTFT
0340	FTFTFTTTFF
0341	FTTFTTTTTT
0401	TTFFTFFTTT
0462	TTFTTTFFTF
0463	TTTTTTTTTT
0464	FTFFTFFTFT
0512	TFTFTFTFTF
0618	TTTFFTTFTF
0619	FFFFFFFFFF
0687	TFTTFTTFTF
0700	FTFFTTFFFT
0712	FTFTFTFTFT
0837	TFTFTTFTFT

Write a program that first reads in the answer string representing the 10 correct answers (use FTFFTFFTFT as data). Next, read each student's data and compute and store the number of correct answers for each student in one array and store the student ID number in the corresponding element of another array. Determine the best score, Best. Then print a three-column table that displays the ID number, the score, and the grade for each student. The grade should be determined as follows: if the score is equal to Best or Best–1, give an A; if it is Best–2 or Best–3, give a C. Otherwise, give an F.

6. Modify the test scoring program developed for programming project 5 to allow for multiple-choice questions having answers 'A' through 'E'. Compute the average number of correct answers, the range of the scores (that is, largest number correct to smallest number correct), and the average of the grades assigned (use the grade point equivalencies A = 4.0, C = 2.0, and F = 0.0).

7. The results of a survey of the households in your township are available for public scrutiny. Each record contains data for one household, including a four-digit integer identification number, the annual income for the household, and the number of household members. Write a program to read the survey results into three arrays and perform the following analyses:

   a. Count the number of households included in the survey and print a three-column table displaying the data. (Assume that no more than 25 households were surveyed.)

   b. Calculate the average household income and list the identification number and income of each household that exceeds the average.

   c. Determine the percentage of households that have incomes below the poverty level. Compute the poverty level income using the formula

   $$p = \$6500.00 + \$750.00 * (m - 2)$$

   where m is the number of members of each household. This formula shows that the poverty level depends on the number of family members, m, and that the poverty level income increases as m gets larger.

   Test your program on the following data.

Identification Number	Annual Income	Household Members
1041	12,180	4
1062	13,240	3
1327	19,800	2
1483	22,458	8
1900	17,000	2
2112	18,125	7
2345	15,623	2
3210	3,200	6
3600	6,500	5
3601	11,970	2
4725	8,900	3
6217	10,000	2
9280	6,200	1

8. Assume that your computer has the very limited capability of being able to read and write only single integer digits and to add together two integers consisting of one decimal digit each. Write a program that can read in two integers of up to 30 digits each, add these digits together, and display the result. Test your program using pairs of numbers of varying lengths.

   Hints: Store the two numbers in two integer arrays of size 30, one digit per array element. If the number is less than 30 digits in length, enter enough leading zeros (to the left of the number) to make the number 30 digits long.

   You will need a loop to add the digits in corresponding array elements starting with subscript 30. Don't forget to handle the carry digit if there is one! Use a Boolean variable to indicate whether the sum of the last pair of digits is greater than 9.

9. Assume that a set of sentences is to be processed. Each sentence consists of a sequence of words, separated by one or more blank spaces. Write a program that will read these sentences and count the number of words with one letter, the number of words with two letters, and so on, up to 10 letters.

10. Write an interactive program that plays the game of Hangman. Read the word to be guessed into string Word. The player must guess the letters belonging to Word. The program should terminate when either all letters have been guessed correctly (player wins) or a specified number of incorrect guesses have been made (computer wins).

   Hint: Use a string Solution to keep track of the solution so far. Initialize Solution to a string of symbols '*'. Each time a letter in Word is guessed, replace the corresponding '*' in Solution with that letter.

11
Records

The preceding chapter introduced the array, a data structure that is fundamental to programming and included in almost every high-level programming language. This chapter examines another data structure, the record (available in Pascal but not in all other high-level languages). Records make it easier to organize and represent information in Pascal, a major reason for the popularity of the Pascal language.

Like an array, a record is a collection of related data items. Unlike an array, however, the individual components of a record can contain data of different types. We can use a record to store a variety of information about a person, such as name, marital status, age, and date of birth. Each data item is stored in a separate record field; we can reference each data item scored in a record through its field name.

In this chapter, we revisit abstract data types. We develop an abstract data type consisting of a record type and associated operators.

11.1 The Record Data Type

A *data base* is a collection of information stored in computer memory or in a disk file. A data base is subdivided into records, which normally contain information regarding particular data objects. For example, the description of a person, place, or thing would be stored as a record.

Record Type Declaration

Before a record can be created or saved, the record format must be specified through a record type declaration.

■ Example 11.1

The staff of our small software firm is growing rapidly. To keep the records more accessible and organized, we decide to store relevant data, such as the following descriptive information, in an employee data base.

```
ID: 1234
Name: Caryn Jackson
Gender: Female
Number of Dependents: 2
Hourly Rate: 6.00
Total wages: 240.00
```

We can declare a record type Employee to store this information. There must be six *fields* in the record type, one for each data item. We must specify the name of each field and the type of information stored in each field. We choose the names in the same way we choose all other identifiers: the names describe the nature of the information represented. The contents of each field determine the appropriate data type. For example, the employee's name should be stored in a string field.

The record type Employee has six distinct fields. One is a string type, two are type Real, one is type Integer, one is a subrange type, and one is type Char.

```
const
  StringLength = 20;

type
  IDRange = 1111..9999;
  StringIndex = 1..StringLength;
  StringType = packed array [StringIndex] of Char;

  Employee = record
              ID : IDRange;
              Name : StringType;
              Gender : Char;
              NumDepend : Integer;
              Rate, TotWages : Real
           end; {Employee}
```

The record type is a template that describes the format of each record and the name of each data element. A variable declaration is required to allocate storage space for a record. The record variables Clerk and Janitor are declared next.

```
var
  Clerk, Janitor : Employee;
```

The record variables Clerk and Janitor both have the structure specified in the declaration for record type Employee. Thus, the memory allocated for each consists of storage space for six distinct values. The record variable Clerk is pictured as follows, assuming the values shown earlier are stored in memory. ■

Record variable Clerk

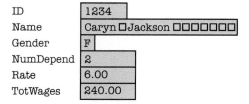

As illustrated in the type declaration for Employee, each field of a record can be a standard data type or a user-defined simple or structured data type. The record type declaration is described in the next display.

Record Type Declaration

Form: type
  rec type = record
                id list$_1$: *type*$_1$;
                id list$_2$: *type*$_2$;

```
                         .
                         .
                         .
              id list_n : type_n
          end;
Example: type
         Complex = record
                      RealPart, ImaginaryPart : Real
                  end;
```

Interpretation: The identifier *rec type* is the name of the record structure being described. Each *id list_i* is a list of one or more field names separated by commas; the data type of each field in *id list_i* is specified by *type_i*.
Note: *type_i* can be any standard or user-defined data type, including a structured type. If *type_i* is a user-defined data type, it can be defined either before the record or as part of the record description.

Manipulating Individual Fields of a Record

We can reference a record field by using a *field selector*, which consists of the record variable name followed by the field name. A period separates the field name and the record name.

■ Example 11.2
Figure 11.1 is an example of the record variable Clerk. The data shown earlier could be stored in Clerk through the sequence of assignment statements in the figure.

Figure 11.1 Record Variable Clerk

```
Clerk.ID := 1234;
Clerk.Name := 'Caryn Jackson        ';
Clerk.Gender := 'F';
Clerk.NumDepend := 2;
Clerk.Rate := 6.00;
Clerk.TotWages := Clerk.TotWages + Clerk.Rate * 40.0
```

Once data are stored in a record, they can be manipulated the same as other data in memory. For example, the last assignment in Fig. 11.1 computes the clerk's new total wages by adding this week's wages to her previous total wages. The computed result is saved in the record field Clerk.TotWages.

The statements

```
Write ('The clerk is ');
case Clerk.Gender of
  'F', 'f' : Write ('Ms. ');
  'M', 'm' : Write ('Mr. ')
end; {case}
Write (Clerk.Name)
```

display the clerk's name after an appropriate title ('Ms.' or 'Mr.'); the output line follows. ∎

```
The clerk is Ms. Caryn Jackson
```

Abstract Record

We can summarize what we have discussed about records in the following specification for an abstract record.

Specification for Abstract Records

Structure: A record is a collection of related data values of different types. Each data value is stored in a separate field of the record.

Operators: Two basic operators act on fields of a record: *store* and *retrieve*. The store operator inserts a value into the record field. If A is a record with a field named B, and C is an expression that is assignment compatible with the type of field B, the statement

```
A.B := C
```

stores the contents of C in field B of record A. If field B of record A is assignment compatible with the type of variable C, the statement

```
C := A.B
```

retrieves the value in field B of record A and copies it into C.

The assignment operator can also be used to copy the contents of one record to another record of the same type. If A and D are record variables of the same type, the statement

```
A := D
```

copies all values associated with record D to record A.

Exercises for Section 11.1

Self-Check

1. Each part in an inventory is represented by its part number, a descriptive name, the quantity on hand, and the price. Define a record type Part.
2. A catalog listing for a textbook consists of the author's name, the title, the publisher, and the year of publication. Declare a record type CatalogEntry

and variable Book and write assignment statements that store the relevant data for this textbook in Book.

11.2 The with Statement

It is tedious to write the complete field selector each time you reference a field of a record. You can use the with statement to shorten the field selector.

```
with Clerk do
  begin
    Write ('The clerk is ');
    case Gender of
      'F', 'f' : Write ('Ms. ');
      'M', 'm' : Write ('Mr. ')
    end;  {case}
    WriteLn (Name);

    TotWages := TotWages + 40.0 * Rate;
    WriteLn ('The clerk''s total wages are $', TotWages :4:2)
  end; {with}
```

As you can see, you don't need to specify both the record variable and the field names inside a with statement. The record variable Clerk is identified in the with statement header; consequently, only the field name is needed, not the complete field selector (for example, Rate instead of Clerk.Rate). The with statement is particularly useful when you are manipulating several fields of the same record variable, as in this example.

SYNTAX
DISPLAY

---

with Statement

Form: with *record var* do
                        statement

Example: with Clerk do
                        if NumDepend > 3 then
                            Rate := 1.5 * Rate

Interpretation: *statement* can be a single statement or a compound statement. *record var* is the name of a record variable. Anywhere within *statement*, you can reference a field of *record var* by specifying only its field name.

■ Example 11.3

The program in Fig. 11.2 computes the distance from an arbitrary point on the *x-y* plane to the origin (intersection of the *x*-axis and the *y*-axis). The values of the *x*-coordinate and the *y*-coordinate are entered as data and stored in the fields X and Y of the record variable Point1. The formula used to compute the distance, *d*, from the origin to an arbitrary point (X, Y) is

$$d = \sqrt{X^2 + Y^2}$$

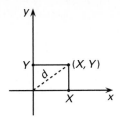

   Because the record variable `Point1` is specified in the `with` statement header, we need only the field names `X` and `Y` to reference the coordinates of the data point. Each coordinate is read separately, because it is illegal to use a record variable as a parameter of a `ReadLn` or `WriteLn` procedure (i.e., only individual fields of a record variable may be read or displayed at a terminal, not the entire record). ∎

Figure 11.2 Distance from Point to Origin

```pascal
program DistOrigin (Input, Output);

{Finds the distance from a point to the origin}

   type
     Point = record
               X, Y : Real
             end;   {Point}

   var
     Point1 : Point;        {input - the data point}
     Distance : Real;       {output - its distance from the origin}

begin
   with Point1 do
     begin
       Write ('X> ');
       ReadLn (X);
       Write ('Y> ');
       ReadLn (Y);
       Distance := Sqrt(Sqr(X) + Sqr(Y));
       WriteLn ('Distance to origin is ', Distance :4:2)
     end {with}
end.   {DistOrigin}


X> 3.00
Y> 4.00
Distance to origin is 5.00
```

Directory: CHAP11
File: DISTORIG.PAS

PROGRAM
STYLE

A Word of Caution About the with Statement

Although the `with` statement is helpful in reducing the length of program statements that manipulate record components, it also can reduce the clarity of those statements. For example, in Fig. 11.2 it is not obvious that the statement

```
Distance := Sqrt(Sqr(X) + Sqr(Y));
```

is passing to the function Sqr two record fields (Point.X and Point.Y) and not two variables.

The possibility of confusion and error increases when you are manipulating two record variables (say, Point1 and Point2). In that case, if the field name X is referenced by itself, it is not apparent whether we mean Point1.X or Point2.X. Pascal uses the record variable specified in the closest with statement header.

Exercises for Section 11.2

Self-Check

1. Write the Pascal statements, using a with statement, required to print the values stored in Clerk in the form shown in Fig. 11.1.

Programming

1. Modify program DistOrigin to find the distance between two points. Use the formula

$$distance = \sqrt{(X_1 - X_2)^2 + (Y_1 - Y_2)^2}$$

Store the points in two record variables of type Point.

11.3 Records as Operands and Parameters

Because arithmetic and logical operations can be performed only on individual memory cells, record variables cannot be used as the operands of arithmetic and relational operators. Arithmetic and logical operators must be used with individual fields of a record, as shown in the previous section. This is also true at this point for the standard procedures Read/ReadLn and Write/WriteLn. (Chapter 15 examines how to read and write entire record variables to certain types of files.)

Record Assignment

We can copy all the fields of one record variable to another record variable of the same type using a record copy (assignment) statement. If Clerk and Janitor are both record variables of type Employee, the statement

```
Clerk := Janitor     {copy Janitor to Clerk}
```

copies each field of Janitor into the corresponding field of Clerk.

Records as Parameters

A record can be passed as a parameter to a function or procedure, provided the actual parameter is the same type as its corresponding formal parameter. The use of records as parameters can shorten parameter lists considerably, because one parameter (the record variable) can be passed instead of several related parameters.

■ Example 11.4

In a grading program, the summary statistics for an exam might consist of the average score, the highest and lowest scores, and the standard deviation. In previous problems, we would have stored these data in separate variables; now, however, it makes sense to group them together as a record.

```
type
  ExamStats = record
                Low, High : 0..100;
                Average, StandardDev : Real
              end;  {ExamStats}

var
  Exam : ExamStats;
```

A procedure that computes one of these results (for example, `Average`) could be passed a single record field (for example, `Exam.Average`). A procedure that manipulates more than one field could be passed the entire record. An example is procedure `PrintStat`, shown in Fig. 11.3. ■

Figure 11.3 Procedure PrintStat

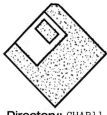

Directory: CHAP11
File: PRINTSTA.PRO

```
procedure PrintStat (Exam {input} : ExamStats);
{
  Prints the exam statistics.
  Pre : The fields of record variable Exam are assigned values.
  Post: Each field of Exam is displayed.
}
begin {PrintStat}
  with Exam do
    begin
      WriteLn ('High score: ', High :1);
      WriteLn ('Low score: ', Low :1);
      WriteLn ('Average: ', Average :3:1);
      WriteLn ('Standard deviation: ', StandardDev :3:1)
    end  {with}
end;  {PrintStat}
```

■ Example 11.5

Before performing a potentially dangerous or costly experiment in the laboratory, we can often use a computer program to simulate the experiment. In computer simulations, we need to keep track of the time of day as the experiment progresses. Normally, the time of day is updated after a certain period has elapsed. The record type `Time` is declared as follows, assuming a twenty-four-hour clock.

```
type
  Time = record
    Hour : 0..23;
    Minute, Second : 0..59
  end;  {Time}
```

Procedure `ChangeTime` in Fig. 11.4 updates the time of day, `TimeOfDay` (type `Time`), after a time interval, `ElapsedTime`, which is expressed in seconds. Each statement that uses the `mod` operator updates a particular field of the record represented by `TimeOfDay`. The `mod` operator ensures that each updated value is within the required range; the `div` operator converts multiples of sixty seconds to minutes and multiples of sixty minutes to hours. ∎

Figure 11.4 Procedure ChangeTime

Directory: CHAP11
File: CHANGETI.PAS

```
procedure ChangeTime (ElapsedTime {input} : Integer;
                      var TimeOfDay {input/output} : Time);
{
  Updates the time of day, TimeOfDay, assuming a 24-hour clock
  and an elapsed time of ElapsedTime in seconds.
  Pre : ElapsedTime and record TimeOfDay are assigned values.
  Post: TimeOfDay is incremented by ElapsedTime.
}

var
  NewHour, NewMin, NewSec : Integer; {temporary values}

begin {ChangeTime}
  with TimeOfDay do
    begin
      NewSec := Second + ElapsedTime;        {total seconds}
      Second := NewSec mod 60;               {seconds mod 60}
      NewMin := Minute + (NewSec div 60);    {total minutes}
      Minute := NewMin mod 60;               {minutes mod 60}
      NewHour := Hour + (NewMin div 60);     {total hours}
      Hour := NewHour mod 24                 {hours mod 24}
    end {with}
end;  {ChangeTime}
```

Reading a Record

Normally, we use a procedure to read data into a record. Procedure Read-Employee in Fig. 11.5 could be used to read data into the first five fields of a record variable of type `Employee`. Because we are passing a record variable to `ReadEmployee`, only one parameter is needed, not five. The procedure call statement

```
ReadEmployee (Clerk)
```

causes the data read to be stored in record variable `Clerk`.

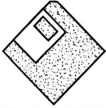

```
procedure ReadEmployee (var OneClerk {output} : Employee);
{
  Reads one employee record into OneClerk.
  Pre : None
  Post: Data are read into record OneClerk.
  Uses: procedure ReadLnString (see Fig. 10.21)

  var
    NameLen : Integer;              {actual length of Name}

begin {ReadEmployee}
  with OneClerk do
    begin
      Write ('ID> ');
      ReadLn (ID);
      Write ('Name> ');
      ReadLnString (Input, Name, NameLen);
      Write ('Sex (F or M)> ');
      ReadLn (Gender);
      Write ('Number of dependents> ');
      ReadLn (NumDepend);
      Write ('Hourly rate> ');
      ReadLn (Rate);
      WriteLn ('Total wages to date> ');
      ReadLn (TotWages)
  end   {with}
end; {ReadEmployee}
```

The procedure call statement

```
ReadLnString (Input, Name, NameLen);
```

calls procedure ReadLnString (see Fig. 10.21) to enter a data string. ReadLn–
String returns a character string (Name) and an integer value (NameLen) that
indicates the number of characters read into Name. The latter value is not saved
in the employee's record.

Exercises for Section 11.3

Self-Check

1. What does the following program segment do? Provide the declarations for
   variables Exam1 and Exam2.

   ```
   PrintStat (Exam1);
   Exam2 := Exam1;
   Exam2.High := Exam2.High - 5.0;
   PrintStat (Exam2)
   ```

2. If all fields of variable Now (type Time) are initially 0, how is Now changed by
   the execution of the following program segment?

   ```
   ChangeTime (3600, Now);
   ChangeTime (7125, Now)
   ```

Programming

1. Write a procedure that initializes all fields of a variable of type Time to 0.
2. Write a procedure to read in the data for a record variable of type CatalogEntry. (See exercise 2 at the end of Section 11.1).
3. Write a procedure that reads in the coordinates of a point (type Point) on the *x-y* plane.

11.4 Abstract Data Types Revisited

Abstraction is a powerful tool in programming. Procedural abstraction enables us to focus on the operations that we want to perform without having to provide immediately the details of how each operation will be implemented.

Data abstraction is the technique of focusing on the data and the operations to be performed without being concerned about how the data are actually represented in memory. Chapter 9 showed you how to implement an abstract data type (ADT) consisting of a data type and its relevant operators. An ADT can be saved as a separate file and inserted into a Pascal program as needed.

The program that uses an ADT is called the *client program*. A client program can declare and manipulate objects of this data type and use the data type's operators without knowing the details of the internal representation of the data type or the implementation of its operators; the details are hidden from the client program (called *information hiding*). In this way, we separate the use of the data and the operators (by the client program) from the representation and the implementation (by the ADT).

Data abstraction provides several advantages. It allows us to implement the client program and the ADT relatively independent of each other. If we decide to change the implementation of an operator (procedure) in the ADT, we can do so without affecting the client program. Finally, because the internal representation of a data type is hidden from its client program, we can even change the internal representation at a later time without modifying the client program.

Abstract Data Type EmpRecADT

Whenever we declare a new record type, we should determine what operators are needed to process a record variable of that type and consider encapsulating the new type and its operators in an ADT. At the very least, we should provide operators for reading and writing a record. We should also provide operators that set and retrieve individual field values. We may also want to provide an operator that compares two record variables for equality. Figure 11.6 shows the specification for ADT EmpRecADT, which stores and processes employee records.

{
    Specification of EmpRecADT

    Structure: A record variable of type Employee contains
                  storage space for a collection of data items that
                  describe a single employee, such as the employee's
                  ID number, name, gender, number of dependents,
                  hourly rate, and total accumulated wages.

    Operators: The operator descriptions that follow assume these
                  parameters:

        Empl and Emp2 are type Employee.
        EmpName is type StringType (declared in StringADT.)
        EmpID is type IDRange (a subrange of Integer).
        Depend is type Integer.
        EmpRate, EmpWages are type Real.
        EmpGender is type Char.

        CreateEmp (var Empl) : Initializes a new employee record by
        setting its ID field to 9999, its name and gender field to blank,
        and all other fields to zero

        PutID (var Empl, EmpID) : Stores EmpID, the employee's ID,
        in record Empl

        PutName (var Empl, EmpName) : Stores EmpName, the employee's
        name, in Empl

        PutGender (var Empl, EmpGender) : Stores EmpGender, the
        employee's gender, in record Empl

        PutDepend (var Empl, EmpDepend) : Stores EmpDepend, the
        number of dependents, in record Empl

        PutRate (var Empl, EmpRate) : Stores EmpRate, the employee's
        hourly rate, in record Empl

        PutTotWages (var Empl, EmpWages) : Stores EmpWages, the
        employee's total wages, in record Empl

        GetID (Empl) : (function) Returns the ID of Empl

        GetName (Empl, var EmpName) : Returns the name of Empl
        through EmpName

        GetGender (Empl) : (function) Returns the gender of Empl

        GetDepend (Empl) : (function) Returns the number of
        dependents for Empl

        GetRate (Empl) : (function) Returns the hourly rate for
        Empl

        GetTotWages (Empl) : (function) Returns the total wages for
        Empl

        ReadEmpRec (var Empl) : Enters the data for Empl from the
        keyboard

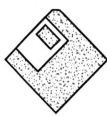

Directory: CHAP11
File: EMPRECAD.ADT

```
WriteEmpRec (Empl) : Displays employee Empl

SameEmpRec (Empl, Emp2) : (function) Returns True if
     employee Empl and Emp2 are identical (that is, corresponding
     fields are equal)
}
```

In the specification for EmpRecADT, operators, such as GetID and GetName, that retrieve a value from an employee record are sometimes called *accessor* operators. GetName is implemented as a procedure instead of a function because it returns a string type.

Using Abstract Data Type EmpRecADT

We can use ADT EmpRecADT to create employee records and process those records without knowing much about record type Employee. We can use the ADT operators as building blocks to create new client programs and procedures, as shown in the next examples.

■ Example 11.6
The following program fragment creates a new employee, Clerk, and defines each field of Clerk to match his record, first shown in Example 11.1.

```
CreateEmp (Clerk);
PutID (Clerk, 1234);
PutName (Clerk, 'Caryn Jackson      ');
PutGender (Clerk, 'F');
PutDepend (Clerk, 2);
PutRate (Clerk, 6.00);
PutTotWages (Clerk, 240.00);
```

The first statement initializes variable Clerk. Each of the remaining statements stores the data item passed as its second parameter in Clerk. Using the operator procedures enables us to do this without knowing the exact structure of data type Employee or its field names.   ■

■ Example 11.7
Figure 11.7 shows procedure UpdateTotWages, which computes weekly wages earned and updates the total wages for the employee record represented by Emp. The weekly wages computation uses the hourly rate, which is stored in the employee record.

Figure 11.7   Procedure UpdateTotWages

Directory: CHAP11
File: UPDATETO.PRO

```
procedure UpdateTotWages (var Emp {input/output} : Employee;
                              Hours {input} : Real);
{
 Adds the weekly wages earned to the total wages for Emp.
 Pre : The hourly rate and total wages for Emp are defined.
 Post: The total wages for Emp are increased by hours
       worked (Hours) times the hourly rate.
}
```

```
var
  WeekWages,                          {weekly wages}
  NewTotal   : Real;                  {new total wages}

begin {UpdateTotWages}
  WeekWages := Hours * GetRate(Emp);
  NewTotal := GetTotWages(Emp) + WeekWages;
  PutTotWages (Emp, NewTotal)
end; {UpdateTotWages}
```

Procedure UpdateTotWages uses operators GetRate and GetTotWages to retrieve the employee's hourly rate and previous total wages. After the new total is computed, it uses procedure PutTotWages to store that value in the employee record. ∎

∎ Example 11.8

Boolean function SameIDName (see Fig. 11.8) returns True if the employee record passed as its first argument (type Employee) contains the ID and name values passed as its second and third arguments, respectively. Operator GetName retrieves the employee's name and stores it in TempName before the comparison is performed.

Figure 11.8   Function SameIDName

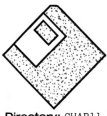

Directory: CHAP11
File: SAMEIDNA.FUN

```
function SameIDName (Emp : Employee;
                     EmpID : IDRange;
                     EmpName : StringType) : Boolean;
{
 Determines whether the ID and name fields of Emp are matched.
 Pre : ID and Name fields of Emp are defined.
 Post: Returns True if there is a match; otherwise, returns
       False.
}
  var
    TempName : StringType;            {the name of Emp}

begin {SameIDName}
  GetName (Emp, TempName);            {Get the name.}
  SameIDName := (GetID(Emp) = EmpID) and (TempName = EmpName)
end; {SameIDName}
```

The following if statement calls SameIDName to determine whether the values of AnID (type Integer) and AName (type StringType) match the ID and name of employee Clerk.

```
    if SameIDName(Clerk, AnID, AName) then
      WriteLn ('Employee ', Aname, ' has ',
               GetDepend(Clerk) :1, ' dependents.')
    else
      begin
        WriteLn ('Employee''s ID and name do not match');
        WriteLn ('ID is ', GetID(Clerk) :4);
```

```
GetName (Clerk, CName);
    WriteLn ('Name is ', CName)
end; {if}
```

If both fields match, the `if` statement displays the employee's name and number of dependents; otherwise, it displays the employee's ID and name. ∎

Initializing an Abstract Data Type

In Example 11.6, we called procedure `CreateEmp` to initialize a variable of type `Employee` before storing data in that variable. We do not really need to do this; however, it is common practice to call an initialization procedure (sometimes called a *constructor* operator) before using a variable whose type declaration is encapsulated in an ADT.

Software Engineering: Hiding a Record's Internal Representation

In the `if` statement shown in Example 11.8, we used the statements

```
WriteLn ('ID is ', GetID(Clerk) :4);
GetName (Clerk, CName);
WriteLn ('Name is ', CName)
```

to retrieve and display the name and ID of employee `Clerk`. If we knew that `Clerk` is a record with fields called `ID` and `Name`, we could use the following statement pair instead

```
WriteLn ('ID is ', Clerk.ID :4);
WriteLn ('Name is ', Clerk.Name)
```

However, this would be bad programming practice because the qualified identifiers `Clerk.ID` and `Clerk.Name` depend on a particular internal representation for data type `Employee`. If we later decided to change the structure of this data type or rename its fields, the client program that contains this statement would be incorrect. However, if we always use operators `GetID` and `GetName` in client programs to retrieve the employee ID and name, then all client programs will still be correct. (We may, however, need to modify and recompile these operators if the internal representation of the record changes.)

Implementing the Abstract Data Type

Figure 11.9 shows the implementation part for ADT `EmpRecADT`. Ideally, the implementation part would be hidden from the user of the ADT. The specification part, shown earlier, contains all the information that a user needs to know. Because of space limitations, we have omitted operators `PutGender`,

PutDepend, PutRate, and PutSal, which are all similar to PutID. We have also omitted operators GetGender, GetDepend, GetRate, and GetSal, which are all similar to GetId (see programming exercise 1 at the end of this section).

Figure 11.9   Implementation Part for EmpRecADT

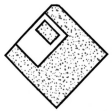

Directory: CHAP11
File: EMPRECAD.ADT

```
{
   Implementation of EmpRecADT

   Module needed: StringADT (see Fig. 10.21)
}

   {Insert declaration for StringType from StringADT.}

   type
     IDRange = 1111..9999;

     Employee = record
                   ID = IDRange;
                   Name : StringType;
                   Gender : Char;
                   NumDepend : Integer;
                   Rate, TotWages : Real
                 end; {Employee}

   {Insert operator ReadLnString from StringADT.}

   procedure CreateEmp (var Empl {output} : Employee);
   {
    Initializes the ID field of a new employee record to 9999,
    the name and gender fields to blank, and all other fields to 0.
    Pre : None
    Post: The ID of Empl is 9999, the name and gender fields are blank,
          and all other fields are 0.
   }
   begin {CreateEmp}
     Empl.ID := 9999;
     Empl.Name := '                   ';
     Empl.Gender := ' ';
     Empl.NumDepend := 0;
     Empl.Rate := 0.0;
     Empl.TotWages := 0.0
   end; {CreateEmp}

   procedure PutID (var Empl {output} : Employee;
                    EmpID {input} : IDRange);
   {Stores EmpID as the ID of Empl.}
   begin {GetID}
     Empl.ID := EmpID
   end; {PutID}

   procedure PutName (var Empl {output} : Employee;
                      EmpName {input} : StringType);
   {Stores EmpName as the name of Empl.}
   begin {PutName}
     Empl.Name := EmpName
   end; {PutName}

   {Insert operators PutGender, PutDepend, PutRate, PutTotWages here.}
```

```
function GetID (Empl : Employee) : IDRange;
{Returns the ID of Empl.}
begin {GetID}
  GetID := Empl.ID
end; {GetID}


procedure GetName (Empl {input} : Employee;
                   var EmpName {output} : StringType);
{Returns the name of Empl through EmpName.}
begin {GetName}
  EmpName := Empl.Name
end; {GetName}

{Insert operators GetGender, GetDepend, GetRate, GetTotWages here.}


procedure ReadEmp (var Empl {output} : Employee);
{
 Reads one employee record into Empl.
 Pre : None
 Post: Data are read into record Empl.
 Uses: procedure ReadLnString (see Fig. 10.21)
}
  var
    NameLen : Integer;              {actual length of Name}

begin {ReadEmp}
  with Empl do
    begin
      Write ('ID> ');
      ReadLn (ID);
      Write ('Name> ');
      ReadLnString (Input, Name, NameLen);
      Write ('Gender (F or M)> ');
      ReadLn (Gender);
      Write ('Number of dependents> ');
      ReadLn (NumDepend);
      Write ('Hourly rate> ');
      ReadLn (Rate);
      WriteLn ('Total Wages> ');
      ReadLn (TotWages)
    end {with}
end; {ReadEmp}


procedure WriteEmp (Empl {input} : Employee);
{
 Displays record Empl.
 Pre : Empl is defined.
 Post: Displays all fields of record OneEmp along a data line.
}
begin {WriteEmp}
  with Empl do
    begin
      Write (ID, '' :5);
      Write (Name, '' :5);
      Write (Gender :5);
      Write (NumDepend :5);
      Write (Rate :10:2);
      WriteLn (TotWages :10:2)
    end {with}
end; {WriteEmp}
```

```
function SameEmp (Empl, Emp2 {input} : Employee) : Boolean;
{
  Compares records Empl and Emp2 for equality.
  Pre : Empl and Emp2 are initialized.
  Post: Returns True if records Empl and Emp2 are identical.
}
begin {SameEmp}
  SameEmp := (Empl.ID = Emp2.ID) and
             (Empl.Name = Emp2.Name) and
             (Empl.Gender = Emp2.Gender) and
             (Empl.NumDepend = Emp2.NumDepend) and
             (Empl.Rate = Emp2.Rate) and
             (Empl.TotWages = Emp2.TotWages)
end; {SameEmp}
```

The body of function SameEmp contains a Boolean expression that returns True only when all fields of Empl match their corresponding fields in Emp2. It returns False if any pair of values does not match.

Exercises for Section 10.4

Self-Check

1. What does the following program segment do? What does it display for the two records shown? What data types are required for MyEmp, YourEmp, Name1, and Name2?

```
CreateEmp (MyEmp);
PutID (MyEmp, 1233);
PutName (MyEmp, 'Jennie Moss          ');
CreateEmp (YourEmp);
PutID (YourEmp, 1234);
PutName (YourEmp, 'Jackie Moss          ');
if SameEmp(MyEmp, YourEmp) then
  WriteLn ('Duplicate record for employee # ', GetID(MyEmp) :1)
else if GetID(YourEmp) = GetID(MyEmp) then
  WriteLn ('Error - two records with same ID')
else
  begin
    GetName (MyEmp, Name1);
    GetName (YourEmp, Name2);
    WriteLn (Name1, '***** ', Name2)
  end; {if}
```

Programming

1. Write the following operators:
   a. GetGender, GetDepend, GetRate, and GetTotWages
   b. PutGender, PutDepend, PutRate, and PutTotWages
2. Write an operator ReduceDepend that reduces the number of dependents of its first parameter (type Employee) by the value of its second parameter (type Integer).

11.5 Hierarchical Records

To solve any programming problem, we must select data structures that enable us to efficiently represent a variety of information. The selection of data structures is an important part of the problem-solving process. The data structures we use can profoundly affect the efficiency and the simplicity of the completed program.

The data-structuring facilities in Pascal are powerful and general. In the previous examples, all record fields were simple types or strings. It is possible to declare a record type with fields that are other structured types. We call a record type with one or more fields that are record types a *hierarchical record*.

We began our study of records by introducing the record type Employee. In this section, we modify that record by adding new fields for storage of the employee's address, starting date, and date of birth. The record type New-Employee is declared in Fig. 11.10, along with two additional record types, Date and Address.

Figure 11.10 Declaration of a Hierarchical Record

```
const
   StringLength = 20;       {length of all strings except zipcode}
   ZipStringSize = 5;       {length of zipcode string}

type
   IDRange = 1111..9999;
   StringIndex = 1..StringLength;
   ZipIndex = 1..ZipStringSize;
   StringType = packed array [StringIndex] of Char;
   ZipString = packed array [ZipIndex] of '0'..'9';
   Month = (January, February, March, April, May, June,
            July, August, September, October, November, December);

   Employee = record
                ID : IDRange;
                Name : StringType;
                Gender : Char;
                NumDepend : Integer;
                Rate, TotWages : Real
              end; {Employee}

   Address = record
                Street, City, State : StringType;
                ZipCode : ZipString
             end; {Address}

   Date = record
             ThisMonth : Month;
             Day : 1..31;
             Year : 1900..1999
          end;  {Date}
```

```
NewEmployee = record
                PayData : Employee;
                Home : Address;
                StartDate, BirthDate : Date
            end;   {NewEmployee}

var
   Programmer : NewEmployee;
```

Figure 11.11   Record Variable Programmer (Type NewEmployee)

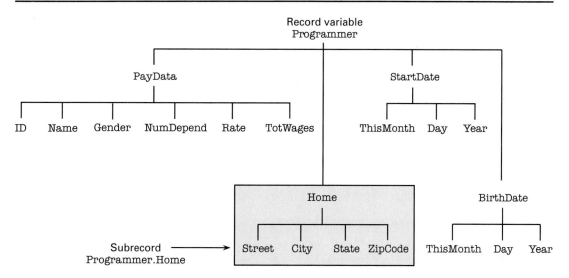

If `Programmer` is a record variable of type `NewEmployee`, the hierarchical structure of `Programmer` can be sketched as shown in Fig. 11.11. This diagram provides a graphic display of the record form.

The diagram in Fig. 11.11 shows that `Programmer` is a record with fields `PayData`, `Home`, `StartDate`, and `BirthDate`. Each of these fields is itself a record (called a *subrecord* of `Programmer`). The fields of each subrecord are indicated under that subrecord.

To reference a field in this diagram, we must trace a complete path to it starting from the top of the diagram. For example, the field selector

```
Programmer.StartDate
```

references the subrecord `StartDate` (type `Date`) of the variable `Programmer`. The field selector references the Year field of the subrecord `Programmer.StartDate`. The field selector

```
Programmer.Year
```

is incomplete (which `Year` field?) and would cause a syntax error.

The record copy statement

```
Programmer.StartDate := DayOfYear
```

is valid if `DayOfYear` is a record variable of type `Date`. This statement copies each field of `DayOfYear` into the corresponding field of the subrecord `Programmer.StartDate`.

In many situations, we can use the `with` statement to shorten the field selector. The statement

```
with Programmer.StartDate do
   WriteLn ('Year started: ', Year:4, ', day started: ', Day:1)
```

displays two fields of the subrecord `Programmer.StartDate`. The computation for updating total wages could be written as

```
with Programmer.PayData do
   TotWages := TotWages + Rate * 40.0
```

The `with` statement

```
with Programmer do
   WriteLn (PayData.Name, ' started work in ', StartDate.Year :4)
```

displays an output line of the form

```
Caryn Jackson       started work in 1976
```

It is also possible to nest `with` statements. The following nested `with` statement also displays the preceding output line.

```
with Programmer do
  with PayData do
    with StartDate do
      WriteLn (Name, ' started work in ', Year :4)
```

The record variable name (`Programmer`) must precede the subrecord names, as shown. The order of the field names `PayData` and `StartDate` is not important.

We can also use a list of record variable names and field names in a `with` statement. The statement

```
with Programmer, PayData, StartDate do
   WriteLn (Name, ' started work in ', Year :4)
```

is equivalent to the ones just discussed.

Procedure `ReadNewEmp` in Fig. 11.12 could be used to read in a record of type `NewEmployee`. It calls procedures `ReadEmployee` (see Fig. 11.5), `ReadAddress`, and `ReadDate` (see the programming exercise at the end of this section).

Figure 11.12   Procedure ReadNewEmp

507

11.6 Variant Records
(Optional)

```
procedure ReadNewEmp (var NewEmp {output} : NewEmployee);
{
   Reads a record into record variable NewEmp.
   Pre : None
   Post: Reads data into all fields of record NewEmp.
   Uses: Procedures ReadEmployee (see Fig. 11.5),
         ReadAddress, and ReadDate (see programming exercise)
}
begin{ReadNewEmp}
  with NewEmp do
    begin
      ReadEmployee (PayData);
      ReadAddress (Home);
      ReadDate (StartDate);
      ReadDate (BirthDate)
    end {with}
end; {ReadNewEmp}
```

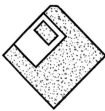

Directory: CHAP11
File: READNEWE.PRO

Exercises for Section 11.5

Self-Check

1. What must be the type of NewAddress if the following statement is correct?

   ```
   Programmer.Home := NewAddress
   ```

2. Write the field selector needed to reference each of the following fields.
   a. the programmer's salary
   b. the programmer's street address
   c. the programmer's month of birth
   d. The month the programmer started working

Programming

1. Write procedures ReadAddress and ReadDate.

11.6 Variant Records (Optional)

All record variables of type NewEmployee have the same form and structure. It is possible, however, to define record types that have some fields that are the same for all variables of that type (fixed part) and some fields that may be different (variant part).

For example, we might want to include additional information about an employee based on the employee's marital status. For all married employees, we might want to know the spouse's name and the number of children. For all divorced employees, we might want to know the date of the divorce. For all single employees, we might want to know whether the employee lives alone.

This new employee type, Executive, is declared in Fig. 11.13 and uses several data types declared earlier in Fig. 11.10.

Figure 11.13 Record Type Executive and Record Variable Boss

```
const
    StringLength = 20;      {length of all strings except zipcode}
    ZipStringSize = 5;      {length of zipcode string}

type
    IDRange = 1111..9999;
    StringIndex = 1..StringLength;
    ZipIndex = 1..ZipStringSize;
    StringType = packed array [StringIndex] of Char;
    ZipString = packed array [ZipIndex] of '0'..'9';
    Month = (January, February, March, April, May, June,
             July, August, September, October, November, December);

    Employee = record
                 ID : IDRange;
                 Name : StringType;
                 Gender : Char;
                 NumDepend : Integer;
                 Rate, TotWages : Real
               end; {Employee}

    Address = record
                 Street, City, State : StringType;
                 ZipCode : ZipString
              end; {Address}

    Date = record
             ThisMonth : Month;
             Day : 1..31;
             Year : 1900..1999
           end;  {Date}

    NewEmployee = record
                    PayData : Employee;
                    Home : Address;
                    StartDate, BirthDate : Date
                  end;  {NewEmployee}

    MaritalStatus = (Married, Divorced, Single);
    Executive = record
                  PayData : Employee;
                  Home : Address;
                  StartDate, BirthDate : Date;
                  case MS : MaritalStatus of
                  Married  : (SpouseName : StringType;
                                  NumberKids : Integer);
                  Divorced : (DivorceDate : Date);
                  Single   : (LivesAlone : Boolean)
                end; {Executive}

var
    Boss : Executive;
```

The fixed part of a record always precedes the variant part. The fixed part of record type Executive has the form of record type NewEmployee. The variant part begins with the *tag field*

```
case MS : MaritalStatus of
```

which defines a special field MS, of type MaritalStatus. The value of the tag field MS (Married, Divorced, or Single) indicates the form of the remainder of the record. If the value of the tag field is Married, there are two additional fields, SpouseName (type StringType) and NumberKids (type Integer); otherwise, there is only one additional field, DivorceDate (type Date) or LivesAlone (type Boolean).

Figure 11.14 shows three variants of record variable Boss, starting with the tag field. The fixed parts of all these records (not shown) have the same form.

For each variable of type Executive, the compiler allocates sufficient storage space to accommodate the largest of the record variants. However, only one variant is defined at any given time, and that particular variant is determined by the tag field value.

The amount of storage required for each variant depends on how many bytes are used to store integer values and enumerated type values on a particular computer. The first variant in Fig. 11.14 requires more than 20 bytes of storage (one byte per character of the spouse's name) and should be the largest.

Figure 11.14   Three Variants of Record Variable Boss

Boss.MS	Married
Boss.SpouseName	Elliot□Koffman□□□□□□
Boss.NumberKids	3

Boss.MS	Divorced
Boss.DivorceDate.ThisMonth	May
Boss.DivorceDate.Day	20
Boss.DivorceDate.Year	1989

| Boss.MS | Single |
| Boss.LivesAlone | True |

■ Example 11.9

If the value of Boss.MS is Married, then only the variant fields SpouseName and NumberKids can be correctly referenced; all other variant fields are undefined. Assuming the first variant shown in Fig. 11.15 is stored in record Boss, the program fragment

```
with Boss do
   begin
      WriteLn ('The spouse''s name is ', SpouseName, '.');
      WriteLn ('They have ', NumberKids :1, ' children.')
   end {with}
```

displays the line

```
The spouse's name is Elliot Koffman.
They have 3 children.
```

We must ensure that the variant fields that are referenced are consistent with the current tag field value. The compiler and the run-time system do not normally check this. If the value of Boss.MS is not Married when the preceding fragment is executed, the information displayed will be meaningless. For that reason, a case statement is often used to process the variant part of a record. By using the tag field as the case selector, we can ensure that only the currently defined variant is manipulated. ∎

∎ Example 11.10
The fragment in Fig. 11.15 displays the data stored in the variant part of record Boss. The value of Boss.MS determines what information is displayed. ∎

Figure 11.15   Displaying a Variant Record

```
{Display the variant part.}
with Boss do
   case MS of
      Married :
         begin
            WriteLn ('The spouse''s name is ', SpouseName, '.');
            WriteLn ('They have ', NumberKids :1, ' children.')
         end; {Married}
      Divorced :
         with DivorceDate do
            WriteLn ('Divorced on ', Ord(ThisMonth) + 1 :2,
                     '/', Day :2, '/', Year :4);
      Single :
         if LivesAlone then
            WriteLn ('Lives alone')
         else
            WriteLn ('Does not live alone')
end {case}
```

The syntax for a record with fixed and variant parts is described in the following syntax display.

Record Type with Variant Part

Form: type

$rec\ type$ = record

$id\ list_1$: $type_1$;
$id\ list_2$: $type_2$;
$\quad$.
$\quad$.   } *fixed part*
$\quad$.
$id\ list_n$: $type_n$;

case tag: $tag\ type$ of
$label_1$: ($field\ list_1$);
$label_2$: ($field\ list_2$);
$\quad$.
$\quad$.   } *variant part*
$\quad$.

$label_k$: ($field\ list_k$)
end;

Example: type
```
        Face = record
                Eyes : Color;
                case Bald : Boolean of
                True  : (WearsWig  : Boolean);
                False : (HairColor : Color)
                end;
```

Interpretation: The *field list* for the fixed part is declared first. The variant part starts with the reserved word case. The identifier *tag* is the name of the tag field of the record; the tag field name is separated by a colon from its type (*tag type*), which must be type Boolean, an enumerated type, or a subrange of an ordinal type.

The case labels (*label₁*, *label₂* ,..., *label_k*) are lists of values of the tag field as defined by *tag type*. *Field list_i* describes the record fields associated with *label_i*. Each element of *field list_i* specifies a field name and its type; the elements in *field list_i* are separated by semicolons. *Field list_i* is enclosed in parentheses.

Note 1: All field names must be unique. The same field name may not appear in the fixed and variant parts or in two field lists of the variant part.

Note 2: An empty field list (no variant part for that case label) is indicated by an empty pair of parentheses, ( ).

Note 3: It is possible for a field list to also have a variant part. If it does, the variant part must follow the fixed part of the field list.

Note 4: There is only one end for the record type declaration; there is no separate end for the case.

When you initially store data in a record with a variant part, the tag field value should be read first. Once the value of the tag field is defined, data can be read into the variant fields associated with that value.

Case Study: Areas and Perimeters of Different Figures

Problem
We want to write a program that determines the area and the perimeter for a variety of geometric figures.

Analysis
To solve this problem, we will declare a record type that represents a geometric figure and provide procedures for entering the figure's characteristics, computing its perimeter, computing its area, and displaying its characteristics. Because the characteristics for a figure are related, we want to save them in a record. However, the characteristics for each figure shape are different, so we must use a record with a variant part. The record declared next has two fixed fields for storing the figure's area and perimeter; the variant part is used for storing the figure's characteristics.

Data Requirements

Data Types
```
FigKind = (Circle, Rectangle, Square, Other);
Figure = record
            Area, Perimeter : Real;
         case Shape : FigKind of
            Circle    : (Radius : Real);
            Rectangle : (Width, Height : Real);
            Square    : (Side : Real);
            Other     : ()
         end; {Figure}
```

Problem Inputs
A letter representing the kind of figure
The relevant characteristics for the figure selected

Problem Outputs
{figure area}
{figure perimeter}

Design

Initial Algorithm
1. Determine the type of the figure.
2. Read in the figure characteristics.

3. Compute the area of the figure.
4. Compute the perimeter of the figure.
5. Display the complete record for the figure.

Implementation

Coding the Main Program

We will write a procedure to perform each algorithm step. The main program (Fig. 11.16) consists of a sequence of calls to these procedures.

Figure 11.16   Program Geometry

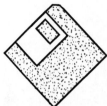

Directory: CHAP11
File: GEOMETRY.PAS

```
program Geometry (Input, Output);
{Finds perimeters and areas of various kinds of figures}

   const
     Pi = 3.14159;

   type
     FigKind = (Circle, Rectangle, Square, Other);
     Figure = record
                 Area, Perimeter : Real;
               case Shape : FigKind of
                 Circle    : (Radius : Real);
                 Rectangle : (Width, Height : Real);
                 Square    : (Side : Real);
                 Other     : ()
               end; {Figure}

   var
     MyFig : Figure;                    {a figure}

   {
    Insert procedures GetFigure, ReadFigure, DisplayFigure,
    ComputeArea, and ComputePerim.
   }

begin {Geometry}
   GetFigure (MyFig);
   ReadFigure (MyFig);
   ComputeArea (MyFig);
   ComputePerim (MyFig);
   DisplayFig (MyFig)
end. {Geometry}


Enter the object's shape.
Enter C (Circle), R (Rectangle), S (Square)> R
Enter width > 5.0
Enter height> 6.5

Figure shape is Rectangle
Width is 5.00
Height is 6.50
Area is 32.50
Perimeter is 23.00
```

Coding the Procedures

Procedure GetFigure reads in the character that denotes the kind of figure and saves the corresponding value of type FigKind in the tag field Shape. If the character entered is not one of the letters (C, R, or S), the value Other is stored in the tag field. ReadFigure must read the data required for the kind of figure indicated by the tag field. The other operator procedures are straightforward and are shown in Fig. 11.17.

Figure 11.17   Operator Procedures for Data Type Figure

Directory: CHAP11
File: GEOMETRY.PAS

```
procedure GetFigure (var OneFig {output} : Figure);
{
  Defines tag field of OneFig.
  Pre : None
  Post: The tag field value corresponds to the next data character.
}
  var
    FigChar : Char;        {input - data character for figure shape}

begin {GetFigure}
  WriteLn ('Enter the kind of object');
  Write ('Enter C (Circle), R (Rectangle), or S (Square)> ');
  Read (FigChar);
  if FigChar in ['c', 'C', 'r', 'R', 's', 'S'] then
    case FigChar of
      'c', 'C' : OneFig.Shape := Circle;
      'r', 'R' : OneFig.Shape := Rectangle;
      's', 'S' : OneFig.Shape := Square
    end {case}
  else
    OneFig.Shape := Other
end; {GetFigure}


procedure ReadFigure (var OneFig {input/output} : Figure);
{
  Enters data into OneFig.
  Pre : The tag field of OneFig is defined.
  Post: The characteristics of OneFig are defined.
}
begin  {ReadFigure}
  with OneFig do
    {Select the proper variant and read pertinent data}
    case Shape of
      Circle    : begin
                    Write ('Enter radius> ');
                    ReadLn (Radius)
                  end; {Circle}
      Rectangle : begin
                    Write ('Enter width > ');
                    ReadLn (Width);
                    Write ('Enter height> ');
                    ReadLn (Height)
                  end; {Rectangle}
      Square    : begin
                    Write ('Enter length of side> ');
                    ReadLn (Side)
                  end; {Square}
```

```
            Other      : WriteLn ('Characteristics are unknown')
          end {case}
end; {ReadFigure}


procedure ComputePerim (var OneFig {input/output} : Figure);
{
   Defines Perimeter field of OneFig.
   Pre : The tag field and chracteristics of OneFig are defined.
   Post: Assigns value to Perimeter field.
}
begin {ComputePerim}
  with OneFig do
    case Shape of
      Circle    : Perimeter := 2.0 * Pi * Radius;
      Rectangle : Perimeter := 2.0 * (Width + Height);
      Square    : Perimeter := 4.0 * Side;
      Other     : Perimeter := 0.0
    end {case}
end; {ComputePerim}


procedure ComputeArea (var OneFig {input/output} : Figure);
{
   Defines Area field of OneFig.
   Pre : The tag field and characteristics of OneFig are defined.
   Post: Assigns value to Area field.
}
begin {ComputeArea}
  with OneFig do
    case Shape of
      Circle    : Area := Pi * Radius * Radius;
      Rectangle : Area := Width * Height;
      Square    : Area := Side * Side;
      Other     : Area := 0.0
    end {case}
end; {ComputeArea}


procedure DisplayFig (OneFig {input} : Figure);
{
   Displays the characteristics of OneFig.
   Pre : All fields of OneFig are defined.
   Post: Displays each field of OneFig.
}
begin {DisplayFig}
  with OneFig do
    {Display shape and characteristics.}
    begin
      Write ('Figure shape is ');
      case FigShape of
        Circle    : begin
                      WriteLn ('Circle');
                      WriteLn ('Radius is ', Radius :4:2)
                    end; {Circle}
        Rectangle : begin
                      WriteLn ('Rectangle');
                      WriteLn ('Height is ', Height :4:2);
                      WriteLn ('Width is ', Width :4:2)
                    end; {Rectangle}
```

```
      Square      : begin
                      WriteLn ('Square');
                      WriteLn ('Side is ', Side :4:2)
                    end; {Square}
        Other     : WriteLn ('No characteristics for figure')
      end; {case}

    {Display area and perimeter}
    WriteLn ('Area is ', Area :4:2);
    WriteLn ('Perimeter is ', Perimeter :4:2)
  end {with}
end; {DisplayFig}
```

In each procedure, a `case` statement controls the processing of the data in the variant part. Procedures `ComputePerim` and `ComputeArea` define their respective fields in the data structure.

Exercises for Section 11.6

Self-Check

1. Determine how many bytes are needed to store each variant for a record of type `Executive`, assuming two bytes for an integer or an enumerated type value and one byte for a character or a Boolean value. Don't include the tag field in your calculations.
2. Write a statement that displays `Boss.SpouseName` if defined or the message `Not married`.

Programming

1. Write a procedure to display a record of type `Face` as declared in the syntax display in this section.
2. Add the variant

   ```
   RightTriangle : (Base, Height : Real);
   ```

   to `Figure` and modify the operator procedures to include triangles. Use the formulas

   $$area = \tfrac{1}{2}\, base \times height$$
   $$hypotenuse = \sqrt{base^2 + height^2}$$

   where *base* and *height* are the two sides that form the right angle and *hypotenuse* is the side opposite the right angle.

11.7 Common Programming Errors

When programmers use records, their most common error is incorrectly specifying the record field to be manipulated. The full field selector (record variable and field name) must be used unless the record reference is nested inside a with statement or the entire record is to be manipulated. So far, we have discussed the latter option only for record copy statements and for records passed as parameters. When reading or writing records at the terminal, you must process each field separately.

If a record variable name is listed in a with statement header, only the field name is required to reference fields of that record inside the with statement. You must still use the full field selector to reference fields of any other record variable.

For variant records, remember that the value of the tag field determines the form of the variant part that is currently defined. Manipulating any other variant will cause unpredictable results. You must ensure that the correct variant is being processed—the computer does not check this. So always manipulate a variant record in a case statement with the tag field as the case selector to ensure that the proper variant part is being manipulated.

CHAPTER REVIEW

This chapter examined the record data structure. Records were shown to be useful for organizing a collection of related data items of different types. Using hierarchical records and variant records, we created some very general data structures to model our "real world" data organization.

In processing records, we discussed how to reference each individual component through the use of a field selector consisting of the record variable name and the field name separated by a period. We introduced the with statement as a means of shortening the field selector. If a record variable name is specified in a with statement header, then the field name may be used by itself inside the with statement.

Each individual component of a record must be manipulated separately in an input or an output operation or in an arithmetic expression. However, it is permissible to assign one record variable to another record variable of the same type (record copy statement) or to pass a record as a parameter to a procedure or function.

New Pascal Constructs

The Pascal constructs introduced in this chapter are described in Table 11.1.

Table 11.1 Summary of New Pascal Constructs

Construct	Effect

Record Declaration

```
type
  Part = record
           ID : 1111..9999;
           Quantity : Integer;
           Price : Real
         end; {Part}
var
  Nuts, Bolts : Part;
```

A record type Part is declared with fields that can store two integers and a real number. Nuts and Bolts are record variables of type Part.

Record Variant Declaration

```
type
  ChildKind = (Girl, Boy);
  Child = record
            First, Last : Char;
            Age : Integer;
            case Sex : ChildKind of
            Girl : (Sugar, Spice :
                      Real):
            Boy : (Snakes, Snails,
                     Tails : Integer)
          end; {Child}
var
  Kid : Child;
```

A record type with a variant part is declared. Each record variable can store two characters and an integer. One variant part can store two real numbers, and the other can store three integers. The record variable Kid is type Child.

Record Reference

```
TotalCost := Nuts.Quantity
               * Nuts.Price
```

Multiplies two fields of Nuts.

```
WriteLn (Bolts.ID :4)
```

Prints ID field of Bolts.

Record Copy

```
Bolts := Nuts
```

Copies record Nuts to Bolts.

with Statement

```
with Bolts do
  Write (ID :4, Price :8:2)
```

Prints two fields of Bolts.

Referencing a Record Variant

```
with Kid do
  case Sex of
    Girl :
      begin
        Write (Pounds of sugar> ');
        ReadLn (Sugar)
      end; {Girl}
      Boy :
      begin
        Write ('Number of snakes> ');
        ReadLn (Snakes)
      end {boy}
  end; {case}
```

Uses a case statement to read data into the variant part of record variable Kid. If tag field Sex is Girl, reads a value into the field Sugar. If tag field Sex is Boy, reads a value into the field Snakes.

1. What is the primary difference between a record and an array? Which would you use to store the catalog description of a course? Which would you use to store the names of the students in the course?
2. What is a field selector?
3. Why do we use a `with` statement? What is a disadvantage of using the `with` statement?
4. If you use nested `with` statements to reference fields of a hierarchical record, what identifier should appear in the outermost `with` statement header?
5. When can you use the assignment operator with record operands? When can you use the equality operator?
6. For `AStudent` declared as follows, provide a statement that displays the initials of `AStudent`.

```
type
   StringIndex = 1..StringLength;
   StringType = packed array [StringIndex] of Char;
   Student = record
               First, Last : StringType;
               Age, Score : Integer;
               Grade : Char
            end; {Student}

var
   AStudent : Student;
```

7. How many fields are there in a record of type `Student`?
8. If an `Integer` uses two bytes of storage, a character one, and `StringLength` is 20, how many bytes of storage are occupied by `AStudent`?
9. Write a procedure that displays a variable of type `Student`.
10. When should you use a record variant?

Answers to Quick-Check Exercises

1. The values stored in an array must all be the same type; the values stored in a record do not have to be the same type. Record for catalog item; array for list of names.
2. A field selector is used to select a particular record field for processing.
3. A `with` statement allows us to abbreviate field selectors. It is helpful when we must reference several fields of the same record. Its disadvantage is that it makes the program less readable because it separates the record variable name from the field name. It is particularly confusing when there are multiple records of the same type or when a record has nested subrecords.
4. the record variable name
5. when the records are the same type; never
6. `WriteLn (AStudent.First[1], AStudent.Last[1])`
7. five
8. 45
9. ```
procedure WriteStudent (OneStu {input} : Student);
begin
   WriteLn ('Student is ', OneStu.FirstName,
              ' ', OneStu.LastName);
   WriteLn ('Age is ', OneStu.Age :1);
```
```

```
        WriteLn ('Score is ', OneStu.Score :1);
        WriteLn ('Grade is ', OneStu.Grade)
      end;
```

10. when an object has some fields that are always the same and some fields that may be different

Review Questions

1. Declare a record called Subscriber that contains the fields Name, StreetAddress, MonthlyBill (how much the subscriber owes), and which paper the subscriber receives (Morning, Evening, or Both).

2. Write a Pascal program to enter and then print out the data in record Competition declared as follows:

```
const
   StringLength = 20;

type
   StringIndex = 1..StringLength;
   StringType = packed array [StringIndex] of Char;
   OlympicEvent= record
                    Event,
                    Entrant,
                    Country : StringType;
                    Place : Integer
                 end; {OlypmicEvent}

var
   Competition: OlympicEvent;
```

3. Explain the use of the with statement.

4. Identify and correct the errors in the following program.

```
program Report (Input, Output);

   type
      String15 = packed array [1..15] of Char;
      SummerHelp = record
                      Name : String15;
                      StartDate : String15;
                      HoursWorked : Real
                   end; {SummerHelp}
   var
      Operator : SummerHelp;

begin {Report}
   with SummerHelp do
      begin
         Name := 'Stoney Viceroy ';
         StartDate := 'June 1, 1984    ';
         HoursWorked := 29.3
      end; {with}
   WriteLn (Operator)
end.   {Report}
```

5. Declare the proper data structure to store the following student data: GPA, Major, and Address (consisting of StreetAddress, City, State, ZipCode). Use whatever data types are most appropriate for each field.

6. Write the variant declaration for Supplies, which consists of Paper, Ribbon, or Labels. For Paper, the information needed is the number of sheets per box and the size of the paper. For Ribbon, the size, color, and kind (Carbon or Cloth) are needed. For Labels, the size and number per box are needed. For each supply, the cost, the number on hand, and the reorder point must also be stored. Use whatever data types are appropriate for each field.

7. Write the declaration for Vehicle. If the vehicle is a Truck, then BedSize and CabSize are needed. If the vehicle is a wagon, then third seat or not is needed (Boolean). If the vehicle is a Sedan, then the information needed is TwoDoor or FourDoor. For all vehicles, you need to know whether the transmission is Manual or Automatic; if it has AirConditioning, PowerSteering, or PowerBrakes (all Boolean); and the GasMileage. Use whatever data types are appropriate for each field.

Programming Projects

1. Represent an article of clothing using a record that consists of the article's description (a string), color (enumerated type ColorType), and price. Write a new abstract data type ClothingADT with operators that read and display a single article of clothing. ClothingADT should use StringADT (see Fig. 10.21) and the ADT developed for programming project 1 in Chapter 9. Use ClothingADT in a client program that reads and displays the data for each clothing item from a text file in which each item's data takes up three lines: description, color, price. Read each item's data into the same program variable.

Directory: CHAP11
File: PROJ11_1.PAS

2. Modify programming project 1 to display a summary table that indicates the count of items read in each color. Also, display the total value of all items. You should use an array of integers with subscript type ColorType to keep track of the count of items in each color.

3. Write FractionADT that includes the type declaration shown next and includes operators for adding, subtracting, multiplying, and dividing two fractions.

```
type
  Fraction = record
               Num, Denom : Integer;
             end;
```

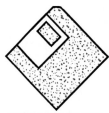

Directory: CHAP11
File: PROJ11_3.PAS

4. Add operators to FractionADT in programming project 3 that reduce a fraction and compute its decimal equivalent. Also, add operators that test whether two fractions are identical (same numerator and denominator) or equivalent (same decimal value).

5. Implement an abstract data type that consists of the data structure described in review question 5 and procedures for reading and displaying an object of that type.

6. A number expressed in scientific notation is represented by its mantissa (a fraction) and its exponent. Write a procedure that reads two character strings that represent numbers in Pascal scientific notation and stores each number in a record with two fields. Write a procedure that prints the contents of each record as a real value. Also write a procedure that computes the sum, the product, the difference, and the quotient of the two numbers. *Hint:* The string -0.1234E20 represents a number in scientific notation. The fraction -0.1234 is the mantissa and the number 20 is the exponent.

7. At a grocery store, the food has been categorized, and those categories are to be computerized. Write a procedure to read and store information into a variant record with appropriate data types.

The first letter read will be M, F, or V (indicating meat, fruit, or vegetable, respectively). The second item will be the name of the food (maximum of 20 letters). The third item read will be the unit cost. The fourth item read will be the unit (O for ounces, or P for pounds).

The last field read will be one character that indicates information based on the M, F, or V read earlier. For meat, the valid input values are R for red meat, P for poultry, and F for fish. For fruit, the valid input values are T for tropical and N for nontropical. For vegetables, the valid input values are B for beans, P for potatoes, O for other.

The procedure should check that each data item is valid before assigning a value to the record parameter. Also write a procedure to print the data stored for a food object.

8. Add a fourth category, J (junk food), to the variant record defined in programming project 7. The store sells two types of junk food, pop (P) and chips (C). Modify the procedures written for project 7 to take the junk food category into account and to allow the user to read and write the food records to a text file. Write a program to test these procedures and a new procedure SearchFile that has an input parameter whose value is one of the food codes (M, F, V, or J) and displays the contents of all records for that food type.

9. Implement an abstract data type that consists of the data structure described in review question 6 and procedures for reading and displaying an object of that type.

10. Implement an abstract data type that consists of the data structure described in review question 7 and procedures for reading and displaying an object of that type.

C. J. Date is an independent author, lecturer, and consultant specializing in relational database systems. He is best known for his books, especially An Introduction to Database Systems, Vol. I *(5th Edition, Addison-Wesley, 1990). He is a co-founder, with Dr. E. F. Codd (the originator of the relational model), of the consulting company Codd and Date International. He was previously a database specialist for IBM where he was involved in technical planning for the IBM relational products SQL/DS and DB2.*

INTERVIEW
C. J. Date

The study of databases has grown substantially over the past few years. Do you think that's a true statement? Why?

Yes, it certainly is true, and I think there are two main reasons. First, the *practical* significance of the subject has grown by leaps and bounds—so much so, that these days almost all commercial applications of computers are in fact database applications. Second, the spread of relational database ideas in the early 1970s provided a solid *theoretical* basis for the field, a theoretical basis that previously was all too conspicuous by its absence.

What is a database? Has the definition changed over the years?

Fundamentally, a database is just a collection of data that is organized in a way that facilitates subsequent use of that data—especially unanticipated use (what is usually called "ad hoc query"). For example, we might have a database contain-

ing information about classical music, and a typical ad hoc query might be "How many string quartets did Sibelius write?" A database doesn't have to be stored on a computer, although these days it usually will be. If it is, then all access to the data will be via a software system called the database management system (DBMS). The DBMS provides the ad hoc query support just mentioned, together with a large number of auxiliary services that have come to be taken for granted—such things as protecting the data against unauthorized access, recovering the data in the event of a failure, and so on. Nowadays, therefore, all of these extra capabilities are usually taken as part of what we mean in general terms when we talk about a "database." So yes, the definition has changed—perhaps I should say expanded—over the years.

What do you see as the major research accomplishments in database technology? In what commercial areas have those accomplishments been realized?

Without any doubt *the* major research accomplishment was the creation of the relational model as a foundation for database technology. That work in turn paved the way for numerous other accomplishments in such areas as database design theory, query optimization, data integrity, recovery and concurrency, higher-level interfaces, and distributed databases. All of this work has had—and continues to have—a significant impact on commercial products, although of course the research is always a few years ahead of its commercialization.

Where do you think database technology has failed to meet expectations?

Let me distinguish between actual failure, on the one hand, and lack of success on the other! The biggest *failure*, it seems to me, has been in the commercial realization of relational ideas; most of the current products have failed in all too many ways to deliver on the full potential of relational technology. As for *lack of success*, there are certainly a number of problems that we might reasonably have expected to solve by now and yet have not done so, but that doesn't mean we will never succeed in solving them. One specific example might be the problem of missing information. A more general example might be the semantic modeling problem.

What do you see as the exciting developments in database technology today? Do you think databases will look radically different by the year 2000?

There is still a considerable amount of research to be done at a fairly fundamental level: the current work in logic-based systems is an example of that. There is also a great deal of activity in so-called "next-generation" systems, which is likely to have some pretty far-reaching effects, both on the internal architecture of database systems and on their externals. Yes, I do think databases will look rather different in a few years. They will certainly be bigger and faster. They will have intercommunication capabilities, so that a user in San Francisco will be able to access data in Sydney, Australia, for example, without even having to know that the data is somewhere else. Perhaps the most obvious difference will be that we will routinely mix all kinds of different data—formatted records (as in the databases of today), unstructured text, pictures (e.g., photographs, x-rays, maps), audio data, etc.—within a single system. Interactive video interfaces are a possibility. The end is not in sight.

What got you interested in the field of databases?

I got into database technology somewhat by chance, but once I was in I found it fascinating for a number of reasons. Perhaps the overriding one was that, for the first time since I had entered the computing field, I had found an application for the mathematics and logic I had studied at college. Database technology was appealing both on an intellectual level (because there were serious logical problems to be solved) and on a pragmatic level (because there were clear practical applications). Also, the field was comparatively new, and my early involvement almost inevitably led me into the teaching and writing role that occupies so much of my time now and that I really enjoy.

For someone considering a concentration in databases, what are the key prerequisites for a successful start?

Database technology is going to be based for a very long time to come on the relational model, and the relational model in turn is based on elementary set theory and predicate logic. Thus, an essential ingredient for success in the database field is a willingness to learn a little bit about sets and logic (or a prior knowledge of those topics, of course). I hasten to say, however, that the level of knowledge required is not very deep; the basics of the relational model can be learned in less than a day. On the other hand, fully understanding and appreciating all of the implications of the model can take many years, as I know from personal experience—very satisfying years too, let me add.

12

Arrays with Structured Elements

S o far, you have seen programs that use arrays with many different sub-script and element types. All the arrays we have discussed to this point have had elements that were simple types. These arrays are called *linear arrays* or *one-dimensional arrays*. This chapter examines arrays whose elements are structured types, including arrays of arrays (multidimensional arrays) and arrays of records.

We begin by examining arrays with elements that are themselves arrays. These arrays of arrays are called *multidimensional arrays* and are often used to store tables of data or to represent multidimensional objects.

We also examine arrays with elements that are records. Arrays of records are useful data structures that can represent many real-world objects. For example, it is convenient to use an array of records to represent a class of students or the members of a baseball team.

Finally, we show you how to perform some common operations on arrays of records. These operations include searching for a particular record in an array and ordering the array elements according to the values in a particular field (sorting the array).

12.1 Arrays of Arrays: Multidimensional Arrays

Two-dimensional arrays, the most common multidimensional arrays, are used to store information that we normally represent in table form. Examples would be a seating plan for a room (organized by row and column) or a monthly budget (organized by category and month). We give some examples of both two- and three-dimensional arrays in this section.

■ Example 12.1

A two-dimensional object we are all familiar with is a tic-tac-toe board. The declarations

```
type
  MoveRange = 1..3;
  BoardRow = array [MoveRange] of Char;
  BoardArray = array [MoveRange] of BoardRow;

var
  TicTacToe : BoardArray;
```

allocate storage for the array TicTacToe. This array has nine storage cells arranged in three rows and three columns. A single character value can be stored in each cell.

In the preceding declarations, BoardRow is declared as an array type with three elements of type Char, and BoardArray is declared as an array type with three elements of type BoardRow. Consequently, the variable TicTacToe (type BoardArray) is an array of arrays, or a two-dimensional array, as pictured in Fig. 12.1.

It is generally clearer to use a single array type declaration to declare a multidimensional-array type. The declarations

```
type
  MoveRange = 1..3;
  BoardArray = array [MoveRange, MoveRange] of Char;

var
  TicTacToe : BoardArray;
```

are equivalent to the ones at the beginning of this example in that they allocate storage for a two-dimensional array (TicTacToe) with three rows and three columns. This array has nine elements, each of which must be referenced by specifying a row subscript (1, 2, or 3) and a column subscript (1, 2, or 3). Each array element contains a character value. The array element TicTacToe[2,3] (or TicTacToe[2][3]) pointed to in Fig. 12.1 is in row 2, column 3 of the array; it contains the character 0. The diagonal line consisting of array elements TicTacToe[1,1], TicTacToe[2,2], and TicTacToe[3,3] represents a win for player X, because each cell contains the character X. ■

Array Type Declaration (Multidimensional)

Form: type
          multidim = array [*subscript*$_1$] of array [*subscript*$_2$] ...
               of array [*subscript*$_n$] of *element type*;

or

          type
          multidim = array [*subscript*$_1$, *subscript*$_2$. ... , *subscript*$_n$]
                    of *element type*;

Example: type
          YearByMonth = array [1900..1999, Month] of Real;
          Election = array [Candidate] of array [Precinct]
                    of Integer;

Interpretation: *Subscript*$_i$ represents the subscript type of dimension *i* of array type *multidim*. The subscript type can be Boolean, Char, an enumerated type, or a subrange type with host type Integer or any other ordinal type. The *element type* can be any standard data type or a previously defined simple or structured data type.

Although we are focusing our discussion on arrays with two and three dimensions, there is no limit on the number of dimensions allowed in Pascal. There may, however, be a limit imposed by the particular compiler you are using. Be aware that the amount of memory space allocated for storage of a multidimensional array can be quite large. For this reason, avoid passing multidimensional arrays as value parameters.

■ Example 12.2

The declarations

```
type
    BudgetCat = (Entertainment, Food, Clothing, Rent,
                 Tuition, Insurance, Miscellaneous);
    BudgetArray = array [BudgetCat] of Real;
    Month = (January, February, March, April, May, June, July,
             August, September, October, November, December);
    MonthBudget = array [Month] of BudgetArray;

var
    Budget : MonthBudget;
```

allocate storage space for a two-dimensional array of real numbers called `Budget`. The first dimension is type `Month`; the second dimension is type `BudgetCat`. The array element `Budget[January, Entertainment]` stores the amount budgeted for entertainment in the first month.

`MonthBudget` is an array type with 12 elements of type `BudgetArray`. An alternate declaration for `MonthBudget` is

```
type
    BudgetCat = (Entertainment, Food, Clothing, Rent,
                 Tuition, Insurance, Miscellaneous);
    Month = (January, February, March, April, May, June, July,
             August, September, October, November, December);
    MonthBudget = array [Month, BudgetCat] of Real;
```

■

■ Example 12.3

Your instructor wants you to store the seating plan (see Fig. 12.2) for your class on a computer. The declarations

```
const
    RowMax = 11;            {number of rows in the room}
    SeatsPerRow = 9;        {number of seats in a row}
    StringSize = 10;        {characters in a string}

type
    RowRange = 1..RowMax;
    SeatRange = 1..SeatsPerRow;
    StringRange = 1..StringSize;
    StringType = packed array [StringRange] of Char;
    SeatPlan = array [RowRange, SeatRange] of StringType;

var
    MyClass : SeatPlan;     {seating plan for MyClass}
    Row : RowRange;         {row subscript}
    Seat : SeatRange;       {column subscript}
```

allocate storage for a two-dimensional array of strings called `MyClass`. Array `MyClass` could be used to hold the names of the students seated in a classroom with 11 rows and 9 seats in each row. Because each string is 10 characters long, the array requires 990 bytes of storage ($11 \times 9 \times 10$). The statements

```
Row := RowMax div 2 + 1;        {the middle row}
Seat := SeatsPerRow div 2 + 1;  {the middle seat}
MyClass[Row, Seat] := 'Marilyn   '
```

place a student named Marilyn in row 6, seat 5, the center of the classroom. ■

Figure 12.2 Seating Plan for a Class

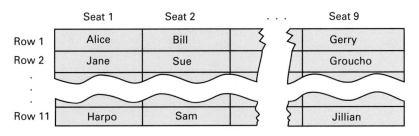

■ Example 12.4

The array `Table` declared as

```
var
   Table : array [1..7, 1..5, 1..6] of Real;
```

consists of three dimensions: the first subscript can take on values from 1 to 7; the second, from 1 to 5; and the third, from 1 to 6. A total of $7 \times 5 \times 6$, or 210, real numbers can be stored in the array `Table`. All three subscripts must be specified in each reference to array `Table` (for example, `Table[2,3,4]`). ■

■ Example 12.5

Your job is to computerize a small office. The first step is to store the information in your boss's two file cabinets, which are labeled "Business" and "Personal." Each file cabinet contains 2 drawers, and each drawer has 26 folders labeled A through Z (see Fig. 12.3). Each folder contains a memo of up to 512 characters. The following declarations allocate storage for an array `Office` that will hold all the information in the two filing cabinets.

```
const
   MemoLength = 512;

type
   CabinetType = (Business, Personal);
   DrawerType = (Top, Bottom);
   FolderType = 'A'..'Z';
   MemoRange = 1..MemoLength;
   Memo = packed array [MemoRange] of Char;
   FileCabinet = array [CabinetType, DrawerType, FolderType] of Memo;

var
   Office : FileCabinet;
```
■

Figure 12.3   Office Files to Be Computerized

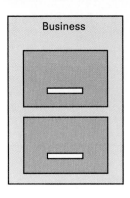
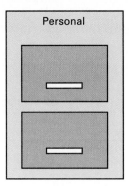

The array Office would occupy a large amount of storage space. Using 1K bytes to mean 1024 bytes, the array would require 52K bytes of storage (2 × 2 × 26 × 512). The subscripted variable Office[Business, Bottom, 'A'] references the first folder (label A) in the bottom drawer of the file cabinet labeled "Business." The statement

```
Write (MemoFile, Office[Business, Bottom, 'A'])
```

copies the memo in this folder to output file MemoFile (type Text).

Storage of Multidimensional Arrays

Most Pascal compilers store multidimensional arrays in adjacent memory cells to simplify accessing the individual elements. The elements of a two-dimensional array are normally stored in order by row (i.e., first row 1, then row 2, and so on). This is called *row-major order.* To access a particular array element, the compiler computes the *offset* of that element from the first element stored. To perform this computation, the compiler must know the size of each element in bytes and the number of elements per row. Both values are available from the array type declaration.

For example, the array TicTacToe would be stored as shown in Fig. 12.4. There are three elements per row, and each element occupies one byte of storage. The offset for element TicTacToe$[i, j]$ is computed from the formula

$$offset = (i - 1) \times 3 + (j - 1)$$

This formula gives a value of 0 as the offset for element TicTacToe[1,1] and a value of 5 as the offset for element TicTacToe[2,3].

Exercises for Section 12.1

Self-Check

1. Declare a three-dimensional array type in which the first subscript consists of letters from 'A' to 'F', the second subscript consists of integers from 1

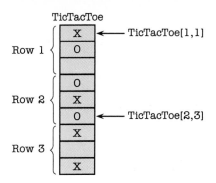

to 10, and the third consists of the user-defined type Day. Real numbers will be stored in the array. How many elements can be stored in an array with this type?

2. Assuming the following declarations,

```
type
   RowRange = 1..5;
   ColRange = 1..4;
   MatrixType = array [RowRange, ColRange] of Real;
var
   Matrix : MatrixType;
```

answer these questions:

a. How many elements in array Matrix?
b. Write a statement to display the element in row 3, column 4.
c. What is the offset for this element?
d. What formula is used to compute the offset for Matrix[i, j]?

12.2 Processing Multidimensional Arrays

We must specify a row subscript and a column subscript to reference an element of a two-dimensional array. The type of each subscript must be compatible with the corresponding subscript type specified in the array declaration.

If I is type Integer, the statement

```
for I := 1 to 3 do
   Write (TicTacToe[1,I])
```

displays the first row of array TicTacToe (TicTacToe[1,1], TicTacToe[1,2], and TicTacToe[1,3]) on the current output line. The statement

```
for I := 1 to 3 do
   WriteLn (TicTacToe[I,2])
```

displays the second column of TicTacToe (TicTacToe[1,2], TicTacToe[2,2], and TicTacToe[3,2]) in a vertical line.

We can use nested loops to access all elements in a multidimensional array in a predetermined order. In the next three examples, the outer loop-control variable determines the row being accessed, and the inner loop-control variable selects each element in that row.

■ Example 12.6

Procedure PrintBoard in Fig. 12.5 displays the current status of a tic-tac-toe board. A sample output of this procedure is also shown.   ■

Figure 12.5   Procedure PrintBoard with Sample Output

Directory: CHAP12
File: PRINTBOA.PRO

```
procedure PrintBoard (TicTacToe {input} : BoardArray);
{
  Displays the status of a tic-tac-toe board.
  Pre : Array TicTacToe is defined.
  Post: Displays each element of array TicTacToe.
}
  var
    Row, Column : MoveRange;

begin {PrintBoard}
  WriteLn ('-------');
  for Row := 1 to 3 do
    begin
      {Print all columns of current row.}
      for Column := 1 to 3 do
        Write ('|', TicTacToe[Row,Column]);
      WriteLn ('|');
      WriteLn ('-------')
    end {Row}
end; {PrintBoard}


-------
|X|0| |
-------
|0|X|0|
-------
|X| |X|
-------
```

■ Example 12.7

Function IsFilled in Fig. 12.6 returns a value of True if a tic-tac-toe board is all filled up; it returns a value of False if there is at least one cell that contains the constant Empty. Assume that all cells are initialized to Empty before the game begins. To move to a particular cell, a player replaces the constant Empty in that cell with an X or an 0. A player can call function IsFilled before making a move to determine if there are any possible moves left. The if statement

```
if IsFilled(TicTacToe) then
  WriteLn ('Game is a draw!')
```

prints an appropriate message when there are no moves.   ■

```
function IsFilled (TicTacToe : BoardArray) : Boolean;
{
  Tests whether the array TicTacToe is filled.
  Pre : All elements of array TicTacToe are assigned values.
  Post: Returns False if any cell contains the constant
        Empty; otherwise, returns True (array is filled).
}
  const
    Empty = ' ';

  var
    Row, Column : MoveRange;    {row and column subscripts}

begin {IsFilled}
  IsFilled := True;                    {Assume the array is filled.}
  {Reset IsFilled to False if any cell is empty.}
  for Row := 1 to 3 do
    for Column := 1 to 3 do
      if TicTacToe[Row,Column] = Empty then
        IsFilled := False                {Array is not filled.}
end; {IsFilled}
```

Directory: CHAP12
File: ISFILLED.FUN

■ Example 12.8

Procedure EnterMove in Fig. 12.7 is used to enter a move into the array
TicTacToe. EnterMove calls procedure EnterInt (see Fig. 9.3) twice to enter a
pair of values into the move coordinates, MoveRow and MoveColumn. If the cell
selected by these coordinates is empty, its value is reset to the character stored
in Player (X or 0). ■

Figure 12.7 Procedure EnterMove

```
procedure EnterMove (Player {input} : Char;
                     var TicTacToe {input/output} : BoardArray);
{
  Stores an X or 0 (identity of Player) in the array TicTacToe.
  Pre : Player is X or 0 and array TicTacToe has at least
        one empty cell.
  Post: The value of Player is stored in the empty cell of
        TicTacToe whose coordinates are read in; the rest
        of array TicTacToe is unchanged.
  Uses: Procedure EnterInt (see Fig. 9.3)
}
  const
    Empty = ' ';                 {contents of an empty cell}

  var
    MoveRow, MoveColumn : Integer;    {coordinates of
                                       selected cell}

  {Insert procedure EnterInt (see Fig. 9.3).}

begin {EnterMove}
  repeat
    WriteLn ('Enter your move row and then the column');
    EnterInt (1, 3, MoveRow);
```

Directory: CHAP12
File: ENTERMOV.PRO

```
      EnterInt (1, 3, MoveColumn);
      if TicTacToe[MoveRow, MoveColumn] <> Empty then
        WriteLn ('Cell is occupied - try again')
    until TicTacToe[MoveRow, MoveColumn] = Empty;

    {assertion: A valid move is entered}
    TicTacToe[MoveRow, MoveColumn] := Player        {Define cell}
  end; {EnterMove}
```

■ Example 12.9

A university offers 50 courses at each of five campuses. The registrar's office can conveniently store the enrollments of these courses in the array Enroll, declared as follows:

```
const
  MaxCourse = 50;                        {maximum number of courses}

type
  Campus = (Main, Ambler, Center, Delaware, Montco);
  ClassArray = array [1..MaxCourse, Campus] of Integer;

var
  Enroll : ClassArray;
```

This array consists of 250 elements, as shown in Fig. 12.8. En‐roll[1,Center] represents the number of students in course 1 at Center campus.

Figure 12.8 Two-Dimensional Array Enroll

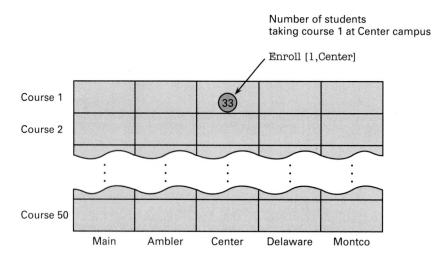

If the registrar wants to break down enrollment information according to student rank, it would require a three-dimensional array with 1,000 elements. This array is declared as follows and is shown in Fig. 12.9.

```
const
  MaxCourse = 50;              {maximum number of courses}

type
  Campus = (Main, Ambler, Center, Delaware, Montco);
  Rank = (Freshman, Sophomore, Junior, Senior);
  BigClassArray = array [1..MaxCourse, Campus, Rank] of Integer;

var
  ClassEnroll : BigClassArray;            {class enrollment}
  CurCampus : Campus;                     {current campus}
  ClassRank : Rank;                       {current rank}
  Total : Integer;                        {student totals}
```

The subscripted variable `ClassEnroll[1, Center, Senior]` represents the number of seniors taking course 1 at Center campus. ∎

Figure 12.9 Three-Dimensional Array ClassEnroll

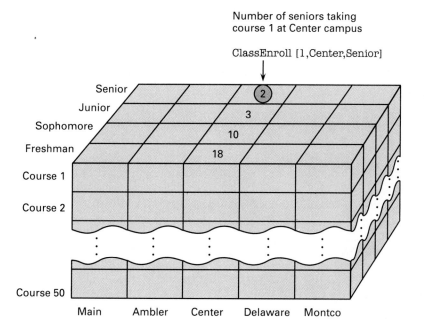

∎ Example 12.10

The program segment

```
Total := 0;
for ClassRank := Freshman to Senior do
  Total := Total + ClassEnroll[1, Center, ClassRank]
```

computes the total number of students of all ranks in course 1 at Center campus.

The program segment

```
Total := 0;
for CurCampus := Main to Montco do
    for ClassRank := Freshman to Senior do
        Total := Total + ClassEnroll[1, CurCampus, ClassRank]
```

computes the total number of students in course 1 (regardless of rank or campus). ■

Exercises for Section 12.2

Self-Check

1. Declare a three-dimensional array that can keep track of the number of students in the math classes (Math1, Algebra, Geometry, Algebra2, Trigonometry, Calculus) at your old high school according to the grade level and the sex of the students. How many elements are in this array?

2. Extend row-major order to three dimensions and show how the array ClassEnroll might be stored. What would be the offset for the array element ClassEnroll[1, Center, Senior] and the general formula for ClassEnroll[i, j, k]?

Programming

1. For the array Matrix declared in self-check exercise 2 in Section 12.1, answer the following:
   a. Write a loop that computes the sum of the elements in row 5.
   b. Write a loop that computes the sum of the elements in column 4.
   c. Write nested loops that compute the sum of all the array elements.
   d. Write nested loops that display the array elements in the following order: display column 4 as the first output line, column 3 as the second output line, column 2 as the third output line, and column 1 as the fourth output line.

2. Write a function that determines who has won a game of tic-tac-toe. The function should first check all rows to see if one player occupies all the cells in that row, then check all columns, and then check the two diagonals. The function should return a value from the enumerated type (NoWinner, XWins, OWins).

3. Redefine MaxCourse as 5 and write program segments that perform the following operations:
   a. Enter the enrollment data.
   b. Find the number of juniors in all classes at all campuses. Count students once for each course in which they are enrolled.
   c. Find the number of sophomores on all campuses who are enrolled in course 2.
   d. Compute and print the number of students at Main campus enrolled in each course and the total number of students at Main campus in all courses. Count students once for each course in which they are enrolled.
   e. Compute and print the number of upperclass students in all courses at each campus, as well as the total number of upperclass students enrolled. (Upperclass students are juniors and seniors.) Again, count students once for each course in which they are enrolled.

12.3 Data Abstraction Illustrated

By this time, you have learned quite a lot about Pascal and programming. Your knowledge of arrays and records will enable you to write fairly sophisticated programs. This section develops a general program that might be used by a company to analyze sales figures. We will use data abstraction, focusing on the data structure and its operators, to solve this problem.

Case Study: Sales Analysis Problem

Problem

The HighRisk Software Company has employed us to develop a general sales analysis program that they can market to a number of different companies. This program will be used to enter monthly sales figures for a specified range of years and display these values in a variety of formats. The program will be *menu driven,* which means that the user will be given a choice of different options to perform.

Analysis

Figure 12.10 shows a sample interaction with a program user, beginning with a display of the menu. To save space, the menu is displayed only once.

Figure 12.10   Sample Run of the Sales Analysis Program

```
Menu for Sales Analysis Program

0.  Get help.
1.  Initialize the sales table.
2.  Enter data into the sales table.
3.  Display sales data as a two-dimensional table.
4.  Compute annual sales totals.
5.  Display annual sales totals.
6.  Display largest monthly sales amount for a given year.
7.  Graph monthly sales data for a given year.
8.  Exit the program.

Choose an option - Enter a number between 0 and 8> 1
Sales table initialized.

Choose an option - Enter a number between 0 and 8> 2
First year - Enter a number between 1900 and 1999> 1991
Last year - Enter a number between 1991 and 1999> 1992

For year 1991, enter sales amount for each month or 0.0:
   January $1000.00
  February $600.00
     March $700.00
        .
        .
        .
```

```
For year 1992, enter sales amount for each month or 0.0:
   January $500.00
  February $400.00
     March $400.00

           .
           .
           .


Choose an option - Enter a number between 0 and 8> 3
Table of Sales Volume by Year and Month:

Year    January  February    March    April      May     June
1991    1000.00    600.00   700.00   800.00   950.00  1000.00
1992     500.00    400.00   400.00   900.00  1000.00    55.00

Year       July   August September  October  November December
1991     500.00   500.00    900.00   600.00    950.50  1000.00
1992     300.00   800.00    750.00   900.00    600.00   300.00

Choose an option - Enter a number between 0 and 8> 4
Annual sums computed.

Choose an option - Enter a number between 0 and 8> 5
Make sure you compute annual sums first!

Annual Sales Totals:
Year          Sales
1991        9500.50
1992        6905.00

Choose an option - Enter a number between 0 and 8> 6
Find largest monthly sales for a given year:
Enter a number between 1991 and 1992 > 1992
The largest monthly sales amount was $1000.00 occurring in May

Choose an option - Enter a number between 0 and 8> 7
Graph monthly sales data for a given year:
Enter a number between 1991 and 1992 > 1992
```

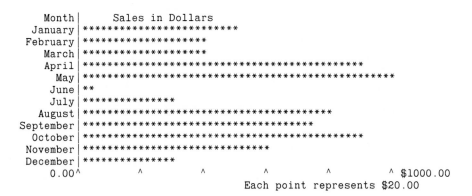

```
Choose an option - Enter a number between 0 and 8> 8
Exit program?  Enter Y (Yes) or N (No)> Y
Sales analysis completed.
```

The operations to be performed are listed in the menu and illustrated in Fig. 12.10. The main program will repeatedly display the menu and then perform each choice selected by the user.

Data Requirements

Problem Inputs
table of sales data
each option selected by the user

Problem Outputs
sales table displayed as a matrix
annual sales totals displayed in a table
largest monthly sales amount for a particular year
graph of the monthly sales amounts for a particular year

Abstract Data Type Specification
We can encapsulate the sales table and its associated operators in an abstract data type (ADT). Figure 12.11 shows the specification for SalesTableADT.

Figure 12.11 Specification of SalesTableADT

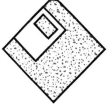

Directory: CHAP12
File: SALESTAB.ADT

```
{
   Specification of abstract data type SalesTableADT
   Structure:    The sales table consists of a collection of Real
                 values organized by year and month; there is one value
                 for each month in the range of years covered.  The
                 range of years covered is represented by a pair of
                 integer values.

   Operators:    The following descriptions assume these parameters:
                    Sales represents the sales table.
                    Year is type Integer.
                    AMonth and MaxMonth are type Month (from MonthADT).
                    Amount and MaxAmount are type Real.

      Initialize (var Sales):  Initializes all sales amounts to zero
      and all annual totals to zero

      EnterSales (var Sales):  Reads from the keyboard the range of
      years covered and a sales amount for each month of the year
      range

      GetSales (Sales, Year, AMonth) : (function) Retrieves the sales
      amount for a particular year and month

      PutSales (var Sales, Year, AMonth, Amount) : Stores the sales
      amount for a particular year and month

      GetFirst (Sales) : (function) Returns the first year in the
      range of years covered by the sales table

      GetLast (Sales) : (function) Returns the last year in the range
      of years covered by the sales table

      DisplaySales (Sales):  Displays the data in the sales table
```

Case Study: Sales Analysis Problem, continued

```
ComputeAnnual (var Sales):  Computes the annual sales totals

DisplayAnnual (Sales):  Displays the annual sales totals

LargestMonth (Sales, Year, var MaxAmount, var MaxMonth):  Finds
the largest monthly sales amount (MaxAmount) and its
corresponding month (MaxMonth) for a particular year (Year)

GraphYear (Sales, Year):  Displays the monthly sales figures in a
bar graph for a particular year
}
```

The specification in Fig. 12.11 references data type Month declared in ADT MonthADT. ADT MonthADT will also provide operators that read and write values of type Month. MonthADT will be based on DayADT (see Fig. 9.5) and is left as a programming exercise. Figure 12.12 shows the module interaction for a client program of SalesTableADT.

Figure 12.12 Module Interaction for a Client of SalesTableADT

Design
The main program for our sales analysis solution uses the sales table and operators from SalesTableADT. The main program must first create an initially empty sales table. It then reads and processes each user request.

Algorithm for Main Program
1. Create an initially empty sales table.
2. repeat
      3. Display the menu.
      4. Read the user's choice.
      5. Perform the user's choice.
   until the user is done

Procedure `DoChoice` will be used to implement step 5. `DoChoice` calls the sales table operators that perform the choice selected by the user.

Implementation

Coding the Main Program and Procedure DoChoice

Figure 12.13 shows the main program. Variable `Sales` (type `SalesTable`) represents the sales table.

Figure 12.13   Program SalesAnalysis

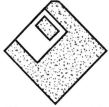

Directory: CHAP12
File: SALESANA.PAS

```
program SalesAnalysis (Input, Output);
{
  Analyzes data provided for a sales table organized by year
  and month.  Tabulates, displays, and graphs sales data
  as directed by the program user.

  Modules needed:  MonthADT, SalesTableADT, and procedure EnterInt
}
  const
     ExitChoice = 8;                 {option for exiting program}

  {
   Insert type declarations for Month (from MonthADT) and
   SalesTable (from SalesTableADT)
  }

  var
    Sales : SalesTable;             {table of sales data}
    Choice : Integer;               {option selected}

  {
   Insert procedure EnterInt (see Fig. 9.3).

   Insert SalesTableADT operators:
      Initialize, EnterSales, DisplaySales, ComputeAnnual, DisplayAnnual,
      LargestMonth, GraphYear, GetFirst, GetLast, PutSales, GetSales.

   Insert operator WriteMonth from MonthADT.

   Insert procedures DisplayMenu, DisplayHelp,
      ShowLargest, DrawGraph, and Validate.
  }

  procedure DoChoice (var Choice {input/output} : Integer;
                      var Sales {input/output} : SalesTable);
  {
   Performs the option selected by Choice on sales table.
   Pre : Choice is defined.
   Post: Performs option selected by Choice on Sales.  Changes
         Choice to zero if user entered ExitChoice by mistake.
   Uses: DisplayHelp, DisplayMenu, ShowLargest, DrawGraph, Validate;
         SalesTableADT operators; WriteMonth from MonthADT;
         procedure EnterInt (see Fig. 9.3).
  }
```

```
begin {DoChoice}
  case Choice of
    0 : DisplayHelp;
    1 : Initialize (Sales);
    2 : EnterSales (Sales);
    3 : DisplaySales (Sales);
    4 : ComputeAnnual (Sales);
    5 : DisplayAnnual (Sales);
    6 : ShowLargest (Sales);
    7 : DrawGraph (Sales);
    8 : Validate (Choice)
  end {case}
end; {DoChoice}

begin {SalesAnalysis}
  Initialize (Sales);               {Create an empty sales table.}
  {Perform user's choice until done.}
  repeat
    DisplayMenu;
    EnterInt (0, ExitChoice, Choice);
    DoChoice (Choice, Sales)
  until Choice = ExitChoice
end. {SalesAnalysis}
```

The case statement in Fig. 12.13 calls five procedures that are not operators of SalesTableADT or MonthADT. They are procedures DisplayMenu, DisplayHelp, ShowLargest, DrawGraph, and Validate. DisplayMenu and DisplayHelp are left as programming exercises at the end of this section. We showed the menu printed by DisplayMenu earlier during the problem analysis. Procedure DisplayHelp should provide additional explanation about how to perform a particular operation and what data should be entered by the user.

Procedure ShowLargest (see Fig. 12.14) is called when Choice is 6 (Display largest monthly sales amount for a given year). It first reads in the desired year, calls operator LargestMonth to find the largest sales amount and month, and then displays the results returned by LargestMonth.

Figure 12.14   Procedure ShowLargest

Directory: CHAP12
File: SALESANA.PAS

```
procedure ShowLargest (var Sales {input} : SalesRecord);
{
 Displays the largest monthly sales amount for a given year.
 Pre : Choice is 6.
 Post: Reads in a year and displays the largest sales amount
       for that year and the month in which it was sold.
 Uses: GetFirst, GetLast, EnterInt, LargestMonth, WriteMonth.
}
  var
    Year : Integer;          {year entered by user}
    MaxAmount : Real;        {largest sales amount}
    MaxMonth : Month;        {month of largest sales}
```

```
begin {ShowLargest}
  WriteLn ('Find largest monthly sales for a given year:');
  Write ('For year - ');
  EnterInt (GetFirst(Sales), GetLast(Sales), Year);
  LargestMonth (Sales, Year, MaxAmount, MaxMonth);
  Write ('The largest monthly sales amount was $',
         MaxAmount :4:2, ' occurring in ');
  WriteMonth (MaxMonth);              {display month string}
  WriteLn
end; {ShowLargest}
```

In procedure `ShowLargest` and the operators that follow, we declare `Sales` as a variable parameter even though it is used only for input. We have done this to save the time and memory space that would be needed to make a local copy of this rather sizable data structure.

Procedure `DrawGraph` (see Fig. 12.15) is called when `Choice` is 7 (Graph monthly sales data for a given year). It reads in the year selected by the user and then calls operator `GraphYear` to draw the graph for that year.

Figure 12.15 Procedure DrawGraph

```
procedure DrawGraph (var Sales {input} : SalesRecord);
{
 Graphs monthly sales data for a given year.
 Pre : Choice is 7.
 Post: Reads in a year and graphs its monthly sales figures.
 Uses: EnterInt, GetFirst, GetLast, GraphYear.
}
  var
    Year : Integer;               {year entered by user}

begin {DrawGraph}
  WriteLn ('Graph monthly sales data for a given year:');
  Write ('For year - ');
  EnterInt (GetFirst(Sales), GetLast(Sales), Year);
  GraphYear (Sales, Year)
end; {DrawGraph}
```

Directory: CHAP12
File: SALESANA.PAS

Procedure `Validate` (see Fig. 12.16) is the last procedure called by the main program (`Choice` is `ExitChoice`). Its purpose is to verify that the user really wants to exit the program. The style box following the figure discusses why it is desirable to do this.

Figure 12.16 Procedure Validate

```
procedure Validate (var Choice {input/output} : Integer);
{
 Validates the user's request to exit the program.
 Pre : Choice is ExitChoice.
 Post: Changes Choice to 0 if the user does not want
       to exit the program.
}
```

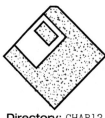

Directory: CHAP12
File: SALESANA.PRO

```
var
   ExitChar : Char;                {used to validate exit request}

begin {Validate}
   Write ('Exit program?  Enter Y (Yes) or N (No)> ');
   Read (ExitChar);
   if (ExitChar = 'Y') or (ExitChar = 'y') then
      WriteLn ('Sales analysis completed.')
   else
      Choice := 0                 {cancel exit request}
end; {Validate}
```

PROGRAM
STYLE

Verifying an Exit Request

Program users must verify that they want to exit the sales analysis program when `Choice` is `ExitChoice`. Without this verification step, all data entry and analysis performed so far may have to be repeated if the program user selects the exit option by mistake.

Choosing the Representation for SalesTable

The first step in implementing abstract data type `SalesTableADT` is to choose an internal representation for the data structure. We can use a two-dimensional array (first dimension is year, second dimension is month) of real values to store the sales data.

Besides the sales data, we also need to specify the first and last years of the range covered. We can store these values as separate fields in a record along with the sales data.

The last implementation decision is whether we should store the annual sales totals in this record. We could recompute these totals each time we need them or compute them once and save them in the sales table record. It makes more sense to save them rather than recompute them, so we will need an array of 12 real values for storing the annual sales totals as a separate record field.

Figure 12.17 sketches record variables `Sales` (type `SalesTable`), assuming the sales data are stored in array `Sales.Data` and the annual totals are stored in array `Sales.AnnualTotal`. We have shown only the sections of these arrays that would be defined when `Sales.First` is 1986 and `Sales.Last` is 1992.

Figure 12.18 shows the type declarations for record `SalesTable` that would appear at the beginning of the implementation part of `SalesTableADT`. The specification part was shown earlier in Fig. 12.11.

Figure 12.17   Record Variable Sales

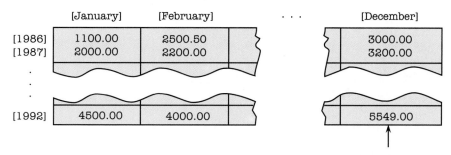

Sales.First 1986
Sales.Last   1992

Array Sales.Data

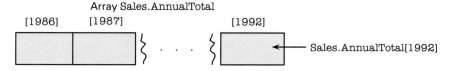

Sales. Data [1992, December]

Array Sales.AnnualTotal

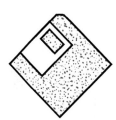

[1986]   [1987]   [1992]

Sales.AnnualTotal[1992]

Figure 12.18   Declaration of Data Type SalesTable

```
{
 Implementation of SalesTableADT

 Modules needed:  MonthADT and procedure EnterInt (see Fig. 9.3).
}

  const
    MinYear = 1900;                   {minimum year covered}
    MaxYear = 1999;                   {maximum year covered}

{Insert declaration for Month from MonthADT.}

type
  YearRange = MinYear..MaxYear;
  SalesArray = array [YearRange, Month] of Real;
  TotalArray = array [YearRange] of Real;
  SalesTable = record
                First, Last : YearRange;   {year range}
                Data : SalesArray;         {sales data}
                AnnualTotal : TotalArray   {annual totals}
              end; {SalesTable}
```

Directory: CHAP12
File: SALESTAB.ADT

Coding the Operators: Initialize and EnterSales

The next step is to implement the sales table operators. Figure 12.19 shows procedures Initialize and EnterSales.

Figure 12.19   Procedures Initialize and EnterSales

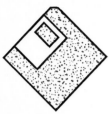

```
{Insert EnterInt and WriteMonth from MonthADT.}

procedure Initialize (var Sales {output} : SalesTable);
{
 Initializes all sales data to zero, all sales totals to zero,
 and the range of years covered to MinYear through MaxYear.
 Pre : MinYear <= MaxYear
 Post: All sales data and annual totals contain zero and
       the year range is MinYear..MaxYear.
}
  var
    CurMonth : Month;              {current month}
    CurYear : YearRange;           {current year}

begin {Initialize}
  {Store zeros in array Sales.Data.}
  Sales.First := MinYear;
  Sales.Last := MaxYear;
  for CurYear := MinYear to MaxYear do
    for CurMonth := January to December do
      Sales.Data[CurYear, CurMonth] := 0.0;

  {Store zeros in array Sales.AnnualTotal.}
  for CurYear := MinYear to MaxYear do
    Sales.AnnualTotal[CurYear] := 0.0;

  WriteLn ('Sales table initialized.')
end; {Initialize}


procedure EnterSales (var Sales {input/output} : SalesTable);
{
 Reads the range of years covered and enter a sales amount
 for each month of the year range.
 Pre : Record Sales has been initialized.
 Post: The first and last years of the year range are read in and
       data values are read for each month and year in the range.
       MinYear <= first year <= last year <= MaxYear
 Uses: EnterInt and WriteMonth
}
  var
    CurMonth : Month;              {current month}
    CurYear : YearRange;           {current year}
    TempYear : Integer;            {holds data value for year}

begin {EnterSales}
  {Enter first and last years of year range.}
  Write ('First year - ');
  EnterInt (MinYear, MaxYear, TempYear);
  Sales.First := TempYear;
  Write ('Last year - ');
  EnterInt (Sales.First, MaxYear, TempYear);
  Sales.Last := TempYear;

  {Enter sales table data.}
  for CurYear := Sales.First to Sales.Last do
    begin
      WriteLn;
```

```
            Write ('For year ', CurYear :4);
            WriteLn (', enter sales amount for each month or 0.0:');
            for CurMonth := January to December do
              begin
                WriteMonth (CurMonth);
                Write (' $');
                ReadLn (Sales.Data[CurYear, CurMonth])
              end {for CurMonth}
        end {for CurYear}
end; {EnterSales}
```

Both procedures `Initialize` and `EnterSales` use a pair of nested `for` loops to access a block of elements in the array `Sales.Data`. `Initialize` sets all elements of arrays `Sales.Data` and `Sales.AnnualTotal` to 0.

Procedure `EnterSales` calls `EnterInt` twice to read in the range of years covered. Next, procedure `EnterSales` reads the sales data into rows `Sales.First` through `Sales.Last` of array `Sales.Data`. Procedure `EnterSales` calls `WriteMonth` to display each month name as a prompt.

PROGRAM
STYLE

External versus Internal Reference to a Field of an ADT

Because procedure `EnterSales` is part of the abstract data type `SalesTableADT`, it is perfectly all right for `EnterSales` to use the qualified identifiers `Sales.First` and `Sales.Last`. However, functions `GetFirst` and `GetLast` should be used outside `SalesTableADT` to retrieve the first and last years covered by the sales table data. For example, the procedure call statement

```
    EnterInt (GetFirst(Sales), GetLast(Sales), Year);
```

is used in both `ShowLargest` and `DrawGraph` (see Figs. 12.14 and 12.15) for this purpose.

Operators GetSales, PutSales, GetFirst, and GetLast

Next, we will implement four relatively simple operators (see Fig. 12.20). `GetSales` and `PutSales` are used to retrieve and store sales data for a particular year and month. These operators could be used to build a client procedure that edits incorrect sales data (see programming exercise 3 at the end of this section). `GetFirst` and `GetLast` are used to retrieve the first and last years of the range covered by the current sales table.

Figure 12.20 GetSales, PutSales, GetFirst, and GetLast

```
function GetSales (var Sales : SalesTable;
                   Year : YearRange;
                   AMonth : Month) : Real;
{
```

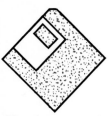

```
Retrieves the sales amount for a particular year and month.
Pre : The sales table is defined and
      MinYear <= Year <= MaxYear
Post: Returns the sales entry for month AMonth and year Year.
}
begin {GetSales}
  GetSales := Sales.Data[Year, AMonth]
end; {GetSales}


procedure PutSales (var Sales {input/output} : SalesTable;
                        Year {input} : YearRange;
                        AMonth {input} : Month;
                        Amount {input} : Real);
{
 Stores the sales amount for a particular year and month.
 Pre : MinYear <= Year <= MaxYear
 Post; The sales entry for month AMonth and year Year
       is Amount.
}
begin {PutSales}
  Sales.Data[Year, AMonth] := Amount
end; {PutSales}


function GetFirst (var Sales : SalesTable) : Integer;
{Returns the first year of the range covered.}
begin {GetFirst}
  GetFirst := Sales.First
end; {GetFirst}


function GetLast (var Sales : SalesTable) : Integer;
{Returns the last year of the range covered.}
begin {GetLast}
  GetLast := Sales.Last
end; {GetLast}
```

Procedure DisplaySales

Most screens are not wide enough to display the sales data for all twelve months
of a year. Consequently, `DisplaySales` calls `ShowHalf` twice: first to print the
sales figures for the first six months and then to print the last six months.
`ShowHalf` begins by displaying the six months covered as column headings.
Next, a pair of nexted `for` loops displays the sales figures for those six months
of each year. (See Fig. 12.21.)

Figure 12.21   Procedure DisplaySales

```
procedure ShowHalf (var Sales {input} : SalesTable;
                    FirstMonth, LastMonth {input} : Month);
{
 Displays the sales amounts by year for each of the months from
 FirstMonth to LastMonth.
 Pre : Record Sales is defined and FirstMonth < LastMonth.
```

```
  Post: Displays the sales volumes in a table whose rows are
        the years covered and whose columns are
        FirstMonth..LastMonth.
  Uses: WriteMonth
}
  var
    CurMonth : Month;                {loop-control variable}
    CurYear : YearRange;             {loop-control variable}

begin {ShowHalf}
  {Print table headings for the months displayed.}
  Write ('Year');
  for CurMonth := FirstMonth to LastMonth do
    begin
      Write (' ');                   {Leave a space.}
      WriteMonth (CurMonth)          {Print month name.}
    end; {for}
  WriteLn;                           {End the heading.}

  {Print sales figures for each month of each year.}
  for CurYear := Sales.First to Sales.Last do
    begin
      Write (CurYear :4);
      for CurMonth := FirstMonth to LastMonth do
        Write (Sales.Data[CurYear, CurMonth] :10:2);
      WriteLn
    end {for CurYear}
end; {ShowHalf}


procedure DisplaySales (var Sales {input} : SalesTable);
{
 Displays the data in the sales table.
 Pre : Record Sales is defined.
 Post: All entries of the sales table for years First
       through Last are displayed.
 Uses: ShowHalf.
}

begin {DisplaySales}
  {Display first 6 months and last 6 months of array Sales.}
  ShowHalf (Sales, January, June);    WriteLn;
  ShowHalf (Sales, July, December);   WriteLn
end; {DisplaySales}
```

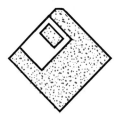

Directory: CHAP12
File: SALESTAB.ADT

Procedures ComputeAnnual and DisplayAnnual

Procedure ComputeAnnual (Fig. 12.22) accumulates the sum of each row of the
sales table and stores it in the appropriate element of array Sales.AnnualTotal.
Procedure DisplayAnnual simply displays the values stored in this array.

Figure 12.22   Procedures ComputeAnnual and DisplayAnnual

```
procedure ComputeAnnual (var Sales {input/output} : SalesTable);
{
  Computes and stores the annual sales totals.
  Pre : Record Sales has been defined.
```

```
  Post: Annual totals for years First through Last
        are computed and stored in Sales.
}
   var
     CurMonth : Month;                     {loop-control variable}
     CurYear : YearRange;                  {loop-control variable}
     Sum : Real;                           {sum for each year}

begin {ComputeAnnual}
  {Find each annual total.}
  for CurYear := Sales.First to Sales.Last do
    begin
      {Accumulate sum for 12 months}
      Sum := 0.0;
      for CurMonth := January to December do
        Sum := Sum + Sales.Data[CurYear, CurMonth];
      Sales.AnnualTotal[CurYear] := Sum    {Store sales total.}
    end; {for CurYear}

  WriteLn ('Annual sums computed.')
end; {ComputeAnnual}


procedure DisplayAnnual (var Sales {input} : SalesTable);
{
 Displays the annual sales totals.
 Pre : Record Sales is defined.
 Post: Each annual total is displayed.
}
   var
     CurYear : YearRange;                      {loop-control variable}

begin {DisplayAnnual}
  WriteLn ('Make sure you compute annual sums first!');
  WriteLn; WriteLn ('Annual Sales Totals:');
  WriteLn ('Year' :4, 'Total Sales' : 15);
  for CurYear := Sales.First to Sales.Last do
    WriteLn (CurYear :4, Sales.AnnualTotal[CurYear] :15:2)
end; {Display Annual}
```

Procedures LargestMonth and GraphYear

Figure 12.23 shows procedures LargestMonth and GraphYear. Procedure LargestMonth returns through MaxAmount the largest value in row Year of the array Sales.Data. It does this by saving the largest value found so far (starting with Sales.Data[Year, January]) in parameter MaxAmount. Each time an array element containing a larger value is found, its value is stored in MaxAmount and its month subscript is stored in MaxMonth.

Figure 12.23 Procedures LargestMonth and GraphYear

```
procedure LargestMonth (var Sales {input} : SalesTable;
                            Year {input} : YearRange;
                            var MaxAmount {output} : Real;
                            var MaxMonth {output} : Month);
```

```
{
 Finds the largest monthly sales amount (MaxAmount) and its
 month (MaxMonth) for a particular year (Year).
 Pre : Record Sales is defined and MinYear <= Year <= MaxYear.
 Post: The largest value for year Year is returned in MaxAmount;
       the corresponding month is returned in MaxMonth.
}
   var
      CurMonth : Month;                {loop-control variable}

begin {LargestMonth}
  {Find the largest value in row Year of array Sales.Data.}
  MaxAmount := Sales.Data[Year, January];
  MaxMonth := January;          {Assume first month was largest.}

  {Examine rest of array for largest value.}
  for CurMonth := February to December do
    {invariant:
      MaxAmount contains largest amount so far and
      Sales.Data[Year, MaxMonth] is equal to MaxAmount.
    }
    if Sales.Data[Year, CurMonth] > MaxAmount then
      begin
        {Save new largest amount so far.}
        MaxAmount := Sales.Data[Year, CurMonth];
        MaxMonth := CurMonth
      end {if}
end; {LargestMonth}



procedure GraphYear (var Sales {input} : SalesTable;
                         Year {input} : YearRange);
{
 Displays the monthly sales figures in a bar graph for a particular year.
 Pre : Record Sales is defined and MinYear <= Year <= MaxYear.
 Post: Displays a bar graph showing the relative size of each
       monthly sales amount for a particular year (Year).
}
   const
      Star = '*';                  {symbol plotted}
      ScreenWidth = 50;            {longest bar length}

   var
      MaxAmount,             {the largest value plotted}
      Increment,             {the amount represented by each point}
      PlotVal    : Real;     {the amount plotted so far}
      MaxMonth,              {and its month}
      CurMonth : Month;      {loop-control variable}

begin  {GraphYear}
  {Define the scale for the horizontal axis.}
  LargestMonth (Sales, Year, MaxAmount, MaxMonth);
  Increment := Round(MaxAmount / ScreenWidth);
  if Increment = 0.0 then
    Increment := 1.0;                      {Prevent infinite loop.}

  {Plot the bar graph.}
  WriteLn;
  WriteLn ('Month' :9, '|     Sales in Dollars'); {Print heading}
```

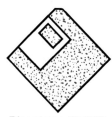

Directory: CHAP12
File: SALESTAB.ADT

```
{Print a bar for each month of the year.}
for CurMonth := January to December do
  begin
    WriteMonth (CurMonth);                        {Print the month.}
    Write ('|');
    {Plot points until value plotted exceeds element value.}
    PlotVal := Increment;             {Initialize sum plotted.}
    while PlotVal <= Sales.Data[Year, CurMonth] do
      begin
        Write (Star);                          {Plot a new point.}
        PlotVal := PlotVal + Increment  {Add to sum plotted.}
      end; {while}
    WriteLn
  end; {for}

{Draw horizontal scale}
WriteLn (0.0 :9:2, '^          ^         ^          ^',
                   '          ^         ^ $', MaxAmount :4:2);
WriteLn ('Each point represents $' :45, Increment :4:2)
end;  {GraphYear}
```

Procedure `GraphYear` draws a bar chart showing the monthly sales amounts for a particular year of array `Sales.Data`. Each row of the bar graph represents a different month, and each bar consists of a sequence of asterisks. To normalize the bar graph, procedure `GraphYear` first calls procedure `LargestMonth` to find the largest monthly sales amount for that year. Next, this amount is divided by the constant `PlotWidth` (value is 50) to get the value represented by each point plotted. For each month being displayed, the `while` loop in `GraphYear` continues to plot points until the value plotted exceeds the sales amount for that month. Hence, the largest sales amount will be plotted as a bar of length `PlotWidth`; all other bars will be smaller.

Testing the Sales Analysis Program

A sample run of the sales analysis program was shown in Fig. 12.10. To test this program, you must first implement `MonthADT` and procedure `DisplayMenu`. During testing, you should see what happens when you enter unusual data. For example, what is the effect of entering year values outside the subrange defined by `YearRange`? Also, see what happens when operators are selected in an unnatural order. For example, does the program crash or print strange values if the sales table is displayed before it is read? Does printing the annual sales totals before they are computed cause a problem? You should also provide procedure `DisplayHelp` and verify that it performs its intended operation.

Exercises for Section 12.3

Self-Check

1. Explain why the variable `TempYear` is needed in procedure `EnterSales`.
2. Why is it necessary for `DisplaySales` to call `ShowHalf` twice?

1. Write procedures `DisplayMenu` and `DisplayHelp`.
2. Write abstract data type `MonthADT`.
3. Develop a new procedure (not an operator) that edits an incorrect sales table entry. The user should enter the year and month of the incorrect entry and the correct sales amount. Use operators `GetSales` and `PutSales` to display the current entry and store a revised value if needed.
4. Write a new operator that reads the sales data from an external file rather than from the keyboard. The file variable should be a parameter of this procedure. Explain how the main program would have to be modified to use this operator.

12.4 Parallel Arrays and Arrays of Records

Often a data collection contains items of different types. For example, the data that represent the performance of a class of students on an exam consist of the students' names, their exam scores, and their grades.

Parallel Arrays

One approach to organizing these data would be to declare separate arrays with identical subscript types for the names, scores, and grades, as follows:

```
const
  MaxClass = 200;
  StringLength = 20;

type
  ClassIndex = 1..MaxClass;
  StringIndex = 1..StringLength;
  StringType = packed array [StringIndex] of Char;
  NameArray = array [ClassIndex] of StringType;
  ScoreArray = array [ClassIndex] of Integer;
  GradeArray = array [ClassIndex] of Char;

var
  Names  : NameArray;
  Scores : ScoreArray;
  Grades : GradeArray;
```

These three arrays are called *parallel arrays*, because all the data items with the same subscript (say, *I*) pertain to a particular student (the *I*th student). Related data items are in the same shade of color in Fig. 12.24. The data for the first student are stored in `Names[1]`, `Scores[1]`, and `Grades[1]`. A better way to organize the student data is shown next.

Figure 12.24 Three Parallel Arrays

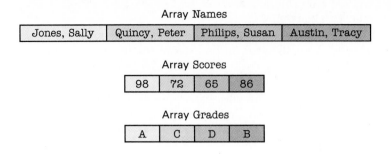

Declaring an Array of Student Records

A more natural and more convenient organization of the class performance data is to group all the information pertaining to a particular student in a record. The data structure declared next represents the class data as a single array of records named Class. A sample array Class is shown in Fig. 12.25.

```
const
   MaxClass = 200;
   StringLength = 20;

type
   ClassIndex = 1..MaxClass;
   StringIndex = 1..StringLength;
   StringType = packed array [StringIndex] of Char;
   Student = record
               Name  : StringType;
               Score : Integer;
               Grade : Char
            end; {Student}
   StudentArray = array [ClassIndex] of Student;

var
   Class : StudentArray;
```

Figure 12.25 Array of Records

Array Class

	Name	Score	Grade
Class[1]	Jones, Sally	98	A ◄——— Class[1].Grade
Class[2]	Quincy, Peter	72	C
Class[3]	Philips, Susan	65	D
Class[4]	Austin, Tracy	86	B

In Fig. 12.25, the data for the first student are stored in record Class[1]. The individual data items are Class[1].Name, Class[1].Score, and Class[1].Grade. As shown, Class[1].Grade is A.

If procedure ReadOneStudent is available to read a single student record, the following for statement can be used to fill the entire array Class with data.

```
for I := 1 to MaxClass do
  ReadOneStudent (Class[I]);
```

Each time ReadOneStudent is called, the record returned will be stored as the Ith element (1 <= I <= MaxClass) of array Class. The following for statement can be used to display all the names read.

```
for I := 1 to MaxClass do
  WriteLn (Class[I].Name)
```

Using the with Statement with an Array of Records

Be careful when you use a with statement to process an array of records. For example, the with statement that begins

```
with Class[I] do
```

uses the subscripted variable Class[I] as its record variable. The particular array element referenced depends on the value of I. If I is undefined or is out of range, a run-time error will result.

If I is updated inside the with statement, the array element referenced will not change. For example, the following statements display the first student's name MaxClassSize times. Because I is 1 when the with statement is reached, Class[1] is the record referenced in the with statement body. Even though the for loop changes the value of I, Class[1] is still the record referenced, so Class[1].Name will be displayed repeatedly.

```
I := 1;
{incorrect attempt to display all student names}
with Class[I] do
  for I := 1 to MaxClass do
    WriteLn (Name)
```

The correct way to sequence these statements is shown next.

```
{Display all student names.}
for I := 1 to MaxClass do
  with Class[I] do
    WriteLn (Name)
```

Now all student names will be printed, because I is changed by the for statement external to the with statement. Each time the with statement is reached, it references a new record. Whenever a for statement accesses an array of records in sequential order, the with statement should be nested inside the for statement and not vice versa.

Exercises for Section 12.4

Self-Check

1. For the array of records Class, what value is displayed by each valid statement? Which are invalid?

   a. WriteLn (Class[3].Name[4]);
   b. WriteLn (Class[3].Grade[4]);
   c. WriteLn (Class.Grade[3]);
   d. WriteLn (Class[4].Name);
   e. WriteLn (Class[4].Name[4].Grade)
   f. WriteLn (Class[3].Grade)
   g. WriteLn (Class[3]);
   h. WriteLn (Class.Name[4]);

2. Write a for loop that could be used to read data into the three parallel arrays declared in this section. Assume that the number of students, NumStu, is known before loop execution begins.

3. Does storage of an array of records require more or less memory space than storage of parallel arrays?

Programming

1. Write procedure ReadOneStudent. Read each student's name and score; leave the grade field undefined.

12.5 Processing an Array of Records

In the next problem, we will process the array of student records described in the previous section. This array will be part of a larger data structure that stores all the information needed to analyze student performance on an exam.

Case Study: Grading an Exam

Problem

Your computer science professor wants a program that will assist her in assigning grades for an exam. The program should read and display each student's name and exam score, compute and display all exam statistics (i.e., number of students who took the exam, lowest score, highest score, average score, median score, and standard deviation), and assign letter grades based on the class average and standard deviation.

Analysis

Currently your professor stores the information for her classes in a gradebook. Each gradebook page lists the students on the left and has a column on the right for storing the exam scores and the corresponding letter grades. The exam statistics appear at the bottom of the page. A sample entry for one exam is shown in Fig. 12.26. The student names and numeric scores are provided as input data; the letter grades, the number of students, and the exam statistics are all undefined initially.

Figure 12.26 Sample Gradebook Entry

```
Name                    Score/Grade
Sally Adams                 80     ?
Robert Baker                70     ?
Jane Cohen                  60     ?
William Dooley              73     ?
     .
     .
     .

Number of Students          ?

Lowest Score                ?
Highest Score               ?
Median Score                ?
Average Score               ?
Standard Deviation          ?
```

Figure 12.27 shows a sample run of the grading program. The program begins by reading the names and the scores of three students. Next, the exam statistics are computed and displayed, grades are assigned, and the final student records are displayed.

Figure 12.27 Sample Run of Grading Program

```
Enter the data requested for each student.
Enter a blank for an unknown grade.
Press RETURN after prompt "Name >" when done.

Name > Joe Costa
Score> 80
Grade>

Name > Lee Hayes
Score> 70
Grade>

Name > Bill Titcomb
Score> 60
Grade>

Name >
3 student records were read.
```

Case Study: Grading an Exam, continued

```
The exam statistics follow:
Low   High   Median   Average   Standard deviation
 60    80      70       70.0          10.0

The student names, scores, and grades follow:
Joe Costa                80         A
Lee Hayes                70         C
Bill Titcomb             60         D
```

Data Requirements

Problem Inputs
name of each student taking the exam
score of each student taking the exam

Problem Outputs
each student's name, score, and letter grade
count of students taking the exam
exam statistics, including low score, high score, median score, average, and
standard deviation

Specification for GradeBookADT
We will use a single data structure to store all the information needed for
one exam in the gradebook. We will encapsulate the data structure and its
operators in ADT GradeBookADT. Figure 12.28 shows its specification.

Figure 12.28 Specification for GradeBookADT

Directory: CHAP12
File: GRADEBOO.ADT

```
{
   Specification of abstract data type GradeBookADT

   Structure:   Contains the name, score, and grade for each student
                who took the exam and a count of students.  Also
                contains a collection of values representing the exam
                statistics.

   Operators:   The following descriptions assume that Test is type
                GradeBook.

     CreateBook (var Test):  Creates a gradebook page that is
     initially empty

     ReadBook (var Test):  Reads the student names and exam scores,
     and counts the number of students who took the exam

     DisplayStudents (Test):  Displays the name, numeric score, and
     letter grade for each student who took the exam

     ComputeStats (var Test):  Computes the exam statistics

     DisplayStats (Test):  Displays the exam statistics

     AssignGrades (var Test):  Assigns a letter grade to each student
}
```

In addition to the ADT shown in Fig. 12.28, we will use another ADT called StudentADT, which will be specified later. StudentADT will allow us to store and process a single student (data type Student). We will use operators ReadStudent (read a student record) and WriteStudent (write a student record). Figure 12.29 shows the interaction between modules.

Figure 12.29   Module Interaction for Grading Program System

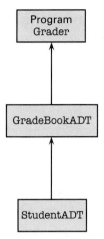

Design
The main program for our student grading program uses the data structure and operators described in GradeBookADT. The main program algorithm is shown next.

Algorithm for Main Program
1. Read the student data.
2. Compute the exam statistics.
3. Print the exam statistics.
4. Assign letter grades to each student.
5. Print each student's final record.

Coding the Main Program
Figure 12.30 shows the main program. The main program body consists of calls to the operator procedures declared in GradeBookADT.

Figure 12.30   Student Grading Program

```
program Grader (Input, Output);
{
   Computes and displays the exam statistics, assigns letter
   grades, and displays each student's record.

   Module needed: GradeBookADT
}
```

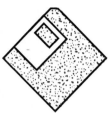

Case Study: Grading an Exam, continued

```
{Insert constant and type declarations from GradeBookADT.}

var
  Test  : GradeBook;                    {data for one test}

{
  Insert GradeBookADT operators:
    CreateBook, ReadBook, DisplayStudents, AssignGrades,
    ComputeStats, DisplayStats
}

begin {Grader}
  CreateBook (Test);
  ReadBook (Test);
  ComputeStats (Test);
  DisplayStats (Test);
  AssignGrades (Test);
  DisplayStudents (Test)
end. {Grader}
```

Choosing the Representation for GradeBookADT

The first step in implementing ADT GradeBookADT is to choose an internal
representation for the data structure. In Section 12.4, we used an array of
records to store student data. We can store all the exam statistics in a record.
The student array and the statistics record could be separate fields of a com-
posite record. Figure 12.31 sketches record variable Test (type GradeBook),
assuming the student data are stored in array Test.Class and the statistics are
stored in record Test.Stats. The number of students who took the exam will
be stored in Test.NumStu. Figure 12.32 shows the type declarations for record
GradeBook that would appear at the beginning of the implementation part of
GradeBookADT.

Figure 12.31 Record Variable Test

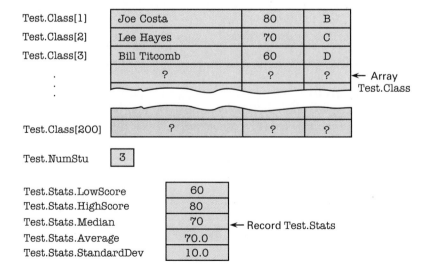

Figure 12.32   Declaration of Data Type GradeBook

```
{
 Implementation of GradeBookADT

 Module needed:  StudentADT
}

  const
    MaxClass = 200;                     {maximum number of students}

  {Insert type declaration for Student from StudentADT.}

  type
    ClassRange = 0..MaxClass;
    StudentArray = array [ClassRange] of Student; {array of
                                                   records}

    Statistics = record                 {statistics record}
                   LowScore,
                   HighScore,
                   Median      : Integer;
                   Average,
                   StandardDev : Real
                 end; {Statistics}

  GradeBook = record
                Class : StudentArray;     {student data}
                NumStu : ClassRange;      {count of students}
                Stats : Statistics        {exam statistics}
              end; {GradeBook}
```

Directory: CHAP12
File: GRADEBOO.ADT

Coding the Operators: CreateBook and ReadBook

The next step is to implement the operators described in the specification for
GradeBookADT (see Fig. 12.28). Figure 12.33 shows the first two operators,
CreateBook and ReadBook.

Figure 12.33   Procedures CreateBook and ReadBook

```
{Insert ReadStudent and WriteStudent from StudentADT.}

procedure CreateBook (var Test {output} : GradeBook);
{
 Initializes record Test so that it is considered empty.
 Pre : None
 Post: Sets count of students to zero.
}
begin {CreateBook}
  Test.NumStu := 0
end; {CreateBook}


procedure ReadBook (var Test {output} : GradeBook);
{
 Reads student names and exam scores.  Also counts the number
 of students who took the exam.
 Pre : None
```

Directory: CHAP12
File: GRADEBOO.ADT

Case Study: Grading an Exam, continued

```
    Post: Student names and exam scores are stored along with a count of
          students.
    Uses: Procedure ReadStudent from StudentADT.
    }
      const
        Sentinel = '                      ';      {sentinel name}

      var
        NextStudent : Student;                    {next student record}

    begin {ReadBook}
      WriteLn ('Enter the data requested for each student.');
      WriteLn ('Enter a blank for an unknown grade.');
      WriteLn ('Press RETURN after prompt "Name >" when done.');
      repeat
        ReadStudent (NextStudent);                {Read next student.}
        if NextStudent.Name <> Sentinel then
          begin
            Test.NumStu := Test.NumStu + 1;       {Increase count.}
            Test.Class[Test.NumStu] := NextStudent  {Store student.}
          end {if}
      until (NextStudent.Name = Sentinel) or
            (Test.NumStu = MaxClass);

      {assert:  no more students or array is filled}
      WriteLn (Test.NumStu :1, ' student records were read.')
    end; {ReadBook}
```

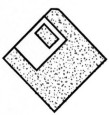

Directory: CHAP12
File: GRADEBOO.ADT

Procedure `CreateBook` simply sets `Test.NumStu` to 0. Procedure `ReadBook` calls procedure `ReadStudent` (part of `StudentADT`) to enter the data for each student who took the exam. `ReadStudent` returns the next student's data through its parameter `NextStudent`. The program user can indicate that there are no more students by pressing the Return key after the prompt for a student's name. If a nonblank name is read, the count of students processed (`Test.NumStu`) is incremented by 1, and the statement

```
      Test.Class[Test.NumStu] := NextStudent {Store student.}
```

copies the data just read into the next element of the array `Test.Class`. The final count of students is stored in `Test.NumStu` when the procedure finishes execution.

Procedure DisplayStudents
Procedure `DisplayStudents` (see Fig. 12.34) displays the count of students and a table of student records. Procedure `WriteStudent` (part of `StudentADT`) determines the actual form of each record displayed.

Figure 12.34   Procedure DisplayStudents

```
procedure DisplayStudents (Test {input} : GradeBook);
{
```

```
 Displays the number of students and the name, numeric score,
 and letter grade for each student who took the exam.
 Pre : The student names and scores are defined and
       0 <= count of students <= MaxClass.
 Post: All student records are displayed.
 Uses: Procedure WriteStudent from StudentADT.
}
   var
     I : ClassRange;                {loop-control variable}

begin {DisplayStudents}
   WriteLn ('The count of students is ', Test.NumStu :1);
   WriteLn;
   WriteLn ('The student names, scores, and grades follow:');
   for I := 1 to Test.NumStu do
     WriteStudent (Test.Class[I])
end; {DisplayStudents}
```

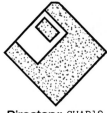

Directory: CHAP12
File: GRADEBOO.ADT

Procedure AssignGrades

Procedure AssignGrades (see Fig. 12.35) assigns a letter grade to each student. The grade can be determined by comparing the student's score to the class average and the standard deviation. Decision Table 12.1 describes the desired grade assignment.

Figure 12.35 Procedure AssignGrades

```
procedure AssignGrades (var Test {input/output} : GradeBook);
{
 Assigns letter grade to each student.
 Pre : All exam scores are defined and
       the average and standard deviation are defined.
 Post: The grade for each student is defined.
}
   var
     I : ClassRange;                {loop-control variable}

begin  {AssignGrades}
   with Test, Stats do
     for I := 1 to NumStu do
       with Class[I] do
         if Score >= Average + 1.0 * StandardDev then
           Grade := 'A'
         else if Score >= Average + 0.5 * StandardDev then
           Grade := 'B'
         else if Score >= Average - 0.5 * StandardDev then
           Grade := 'C'
         else if Score >= Average - 1.0 * StandardDev then
           Grade := 'D'
         else
           Grade := 'F'
end; {AssignGrades}
```

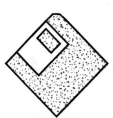

Directory: CHAP12
File: GRADEBOO.ADT

Case Study: Grading an Exam, continued

Table 12.1 Decision Table for Assigning Letter Grades

Score Range	Grade
`>= Average + 1.0 * StandardDev`	A
`>= Average + 0.5 * StandardDev`	B
`>= Average - 0.5 * StandardDev`	C
`>= Average - 1.0 * StandardDev`	D
`< Average - 1.0 * StandardDev`	F

The `if` statement in procedure `AssignGrades` implements the decision table. The `for` loop causes this `if` statement to be repeated once for each student. Because the `if` statement is nested inside the `with` statement, the fields `Score` and `Grade` reference fields of the record variable `Test.Class[I]` (i.e., the current student record).

Procedure ComputeStats

Procedure `ComputeStats` computes the exam statistics and stores the results in the subrecord `Test.Stats`. `ComputeStats` calls a different function to compute each statistic. Function `FindAverage` returns the average score and is shown in Fig. 12.36. Function `FindStandardDev` and `FindMedian` are discussed later. The rest of the statistical functions are left as exercises at the end of this section. Procedure `DisplayStats` displays the contents of record `Stats` and is also left as an exercise.

Figure 12.36 Function FindAverage and Procedure ComputeStats

Directory: CHAP12
File: GRADEBOO.ADT

```
{Insert FindLow, FindHigh, FindMedian, and FindStandardDev}

function FindAverage (Test : GradeBook) : Real;
{
 Defines the average of the scores in array Test.Class.
 Pre : Student Scores are stored in Test.Class.
 Post: Returns the average in Test.Stats.Average.
}
  var
    Sum : Real;            {the accumulating sum of scores}
    I : ClassRange;        {loop-control variable and subscript}

begin {FindAverage}
  {Accumulate the sum of all scores}
  Sum := 0;
  for I := 1 to Test.NumStu do
    Sum := Sum + Test.Class[I].Score;

  {Return the average score or 0.0}
  if Test.NumStu <> 0 then
    FindAverage := Sum / Test.NumStu
  else
    FindAverage := 0.0
end; {FindAverage}
```

```
procedure ComputeStats (var Test {input/output} : GradeBook);
{
 Computes the exam statistics.
 Pre : Array Test.Class and Test.NumStu are defined.
 Post: Each exam statistic is computed and stored.
}
begin {ComputeStats}
  with Test.Stats do
    begin
      Average := FindAverage(Test);
      LowScore := FindLow(Test);
      HighScore := FindHigh(Test);
      Median := FindMedian(Test);
      StandardDev :  FindStandardDev(Test)
    end {with}
end; {ComputeStats}
```

Function FindStandardDev

The *standard deviation* of the exam scores

$$\text{standard deviation} = \sqrt{\frac{\sum_{i=1}^{N}(score_i - average)^2}{N-1}}$$

which measures the spread, or dispersion, of the grades around the average grade. Statistical theory states that for a bell curve, 68.34 percent of the grades will lie within one standard deviation of the average grade. Function Find−StandardDev in Fig. 12.37 implements the formula for standard deviation. The function declaration must precede procedure ComputeStats.

Figure 12.37 Function FindStandardDev

```
function FindStandardDev (Test : GradeBook) : Real;
{
 Returns the standard deviation of the exam scores.
 Pre : The exam scores and their average are defined.
 Post: Returns the standard deviation if defined;
       otherwise, returns zero.
}
  var
    SumSquares : Real;           {sum of squares}
    I : ClassRange;              {loop-control variable and subscript}

begin {FindStandardDev}
  SumSquares := 0;
  with Test do
    for I := 1 to NumStu do
      SumSquares := SumSquares +
                  Sqr(Class[I].Score − Stats.Average);
```

Directory: CHAP12
File: GRADEBOO.ADT

Case Study: Grading an Exam, continued

```
if Test.NumStu > 1 then
   FindStandardDev := Sqrt(SumSquares / (Test.NumStu - 1))
else
   FindStandardDev := 0.0
end; {FindStandardDev}
```

Function FindMedian

Procedure `ComputeStats` (see Fig. 12.36) calls function `FindMedian` to compute the median score on an exam. It is relatively easy to determine the median score once the student records are in order by score. If there is an odd number of records, the median score is found in the middle element of array `Test.Class` where the expression `(Test.NumStu div 2) + 1` computes the subscript of the middle element. For example, if there are five student records, the middle element would be the third score (5 `div` 2 + 1 is 3). If there is an even number of scores, the median score is the average of the two middle scores. For example, if there are four student records, the median is the average of the second and third scores.

Function `FindMedian` is shown in Fig. 12.38. `FindMedian` first calls procedure `SortStudents` to sort the records in array `Test.Class`. Notice that record `Test` is declared as a value parameter in `FindMedian` so that only the local copy of array `Test.Class` will be sorted, not the actual array. `SortStudents` sorts the array of student records and is a modification of procedure `SelectSort` (see Fig. 10.29), which sorts an array of integers. In `SortStudents`, procedure `Switch` is used to switch a pair of array records instead of a pair of integer values.

Figure 12.38   Procedures Switch and SortStudents and Function FindMedian

```
procedure Switch (var Stu1, Stu2 {input/output} : Student);
{Switches student records Stu1 and Stu2.
 Pre : None
 Post: Stu1 is old Stu2, and Stu2 is old Stu1.
}
   var
      Temp : Student;            {temporary student}

begin  {Switch}
   Temp := Stu1;
   Stu1 := Stu2;
   Stu2 := Temp
end; {Switch}


procedure SortStudents (var Test {input/output} : GradeBook);
{
 Orders the student records in sequence by exam score.
 Pre : Student data are defined and the count of students
       is between 1 and MaxClass.
```

```
  Post: The student records are in increasing order by score.
}
  var
    Fill,      {index of element being filled with next smallest score}
    Next,                  {element being compared to smallest so far}
    IndexOfMin : ClassRange;         {index of smallest so far}

begin {SelectSort}
  with Test do
    {Sort array field Class based on exam scores.}
    for Fill := 1 to NumStu-1 do
      begin
        {invariant:
          The elements in Class[1..Fill-1] are in their
          proper place and Fill <= NumStu.
        }
        {Find index of element with smallest score in Class[Fill..N].}
        IndexOfMin := Fill;
        for Next := Fill+1 to NumStu do
          {invariant:
            IndexOfMin is the index of the element with smallest
            score in Class[Fill..Next-1] and Next <= NumStu+1.
          }
          if Class[Next].Score < Class[IndexOfMin].Score then
            IndexOfMin := Next;

      {assert: Element at IndexOfMin is next smallest.}
      {Exchange elements with subscripts Fill and IndexOfMin}
      if IndexOfMin <> Fill then
        Switch (Class[Fill], Class[IndexOfMin])
    end {for Fill}
end; {SelectSort}
```

Directory: CHAP12
File: GRADEBOO.ADT

```
function FindMedian (Test : GradeBook) : Integer;
{
 Returns the median score for the exam.
 Pre : Student data are defined and
       the count of students is between 1 and MaxClass.
 Post: Returns the middle score if there is an odd number
       of scores; otherwise, returns the average of the
       middle two scores.
 Uses: SortStudents
}
  var
    Middle : ClassRange;     {index to middle element}

begin {FindMedian}
  SortStudents (Test);          {Sort the local array.}
  with Test do
    begin
      Middle := (NumStu div 2) + 1;
      if Odd(NumStu) then
        FindMedian := Class[Middle].Score     {Use middle score.}
      else                          {Average 2 middle scores.}
        FindMedian := (Class[Middle - 1].Score +
                       Class[Middle].Score) div 2
  end {with}
end; {FindMedian}
```

Case Study: Grading an Exam, continued

Abstract Data Type StudentADT

Before we can run the program, we must implement ADT StudentADT. Figure 12.39 shows the specification for ADT StudentADT; Figure 12.40 shows its implementation. StudentADT uses module StringADT (see Fig. 10.21).

Figure 12.39   Specification of StudentADT

```
{
  Specification of abstract data type StudentADT

  Structure:   Student contains descriptive information about one
               student such as the student's name, exam score, and
               grade.

  Operators:   The following descriptions assume this parameter:

                   AStudent is type Student.

    ReadStudent (var AStudent) : Reads a student record from the
    keyboard into AStudent

    WriteStudent (AStudent) : Displays student record AStudent
}
```

Figure 12.40   Implementation of StudentADT

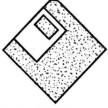

Directory: CHAP12
File: STUDENTA.ADT

```
{
  Implementation of StudentADT

  Module needed: StringADT (see Fig. 10.21)
}

{Insert type declaration for StringType from StringADT.}

type
  Student = record
              Name : StringType;
              Score : Integer;
              Grade : Char
            end; {Student}

{Insert ReadLnString from StringADT here.}


procedure ReadStudent (var AStudent {output} : Student);
  {
  Reads the data for one student from the keyboard into AStudent.
  Pre : None
  Post: The data read is returned through AStudent.  The grade field
        may contain a letter grade (A through F) or a blank if the
        grade is unknown.  The score and grade are not read if the
        name is blank.
```

```
  Uses: Procedure ReadLnString
  }
     var
        NameLength : Integer;                 {length of name string}

  begin {ReadStudent}
    with AStudent do
      begin
        WriteLn;
        Write ('Name > ');
        ReadLnString (Input, Name, NameLength);
        if NameLength <> 0 then
          begin
            Write ('Score> ');
            ReadLn (Score);
            Write ('Grade> ');
            ReadLn (Grade)
          end {if}
      end {with}
  end; {ReadStudent}


  procedure WriteStudent (AStudent {input} : Student);
  {
   Displays student record AStudent.
   Pre : Record AStudent is defined.
   Post: The fields of AStudent are displayed across an output line.
  }
  begin {WriteStudent}
    WriteLn (AStudent.Name :20, AStudent.Score :10,
             AStudent.Grade :10)
  end; {WriteStudent}
```

Testing the Grading Program

A sample run of the grading program was shown in Fig. 12.27. We should
verify that the program works correctly when the array Test.Class is empty
(no student records) and when the array is completely filled (MaxClass students
took the exam). Use a small value of MaxClass for the latter case.

Exercises for Section 12.5

Self-Check

1. For the data in Fig. 12.27, what value is displayed by each valid statement?
   Which are invalid?
   a. WriteLn (Test.Class.NumStu);
   b. WriteLn (Exam.NumStu);
   c. with Test, Class[1] do
        WriteLn (Score, Grade, Name);

```
d. WriteLn (Test.NumStu);
e. WriteLn (Class.NumStu);
f. WriteLn (Test.Class.Name[2]);
g. WriteLn (Test[1].Class.Name[2]);
h. WriteLn (Test.Class[1].Name[2]);
i. WriteLn (Test.Class[1].Name);
j. WriteLn (Statistics.Average);
```

2. How could you get the scores in descending order (largest score first)? What changes would be needed to sort the array Class by student name instead of by score?

3. Since we are ordering the array by Score field, we propose changing procedure Switch to exchange only the Score fields. Describe the effect of this proposal.

Programming

1. Write procedure DisplayStats.
2. Write functions FindLow and FindHigh.

12.6 Common Programming Errors

When you use multidimensional arrays, make sure the subscript for each dimension is consistent with its declared type. If any subscript value is out of range, a run-time error will be detected.

If you use nested for loops to process the array elements, make sure that loop-control variables used as array subscripts are in the correct order. The order of the loop-control variables determines the sequence in which the array elements are processed.

When an array of records is processed, the array name and the subscript must be included as part of the field selector (for example, X[I].Key references field Key of the Ith record). If you use a for statement to process all array elements in sequence, then you must nest any with statement that references the array records inside the for statement, as shown next.

```
for I := 1 to N do
  with X[I] do
    ...
```

As the loop-control variable I changes, the next array record is processed by the with statement. If the nesting order is reversed, as in

```
with X[I] do
  for I := 1 to N do
    ...
```

then the same array record is processed N times. The record that is processed is determined by the value of I when the with statement is first reached. Changing the value of I inside the with statement has no effect.

CHAPTER REVIEW

In this chapter, arrays of arrays, or multidimensional arrays, were used to represent tables of information and game boards. We used nested loops to manipulate the elements of a multidimensional array in a systematic way. The correspondence between the loop-control variables and the array subscripts determines the order in which the array elements are processed.

You also saw how to manipulate arrays of records. Arrays of records can be used to represent many real-world data collections. We used the process of data abstraction to develop abstract data types that were used in the solution of two rather large applications programs.

New Pascal Constructs

The Pascal constructs introduced in this chapter are described in Table 12.2.

Table 12.2 Summary of New Pascal Constructs

Construct	Effect

Declaring Multidimensional Arrays
```type```
  ```Day = (Sunday,Monday,Tuesday,Wednesday,```
       ```Thursday,Friday,Saturday);```
  ```Matrix = array [1..52, Day] of Real;```
 	
```var```
  ```Sales : Matrix;```
	Matrix describes a two-dimensional array with 7 rows (days of the week) and 52 columns. Sales is an array of this type and can store 364 real numbers.

Array References ```Write (Sales[3, Monday])```	Displays the element of Sales for Monday of week 3.

```for Week := 1 to 52 do```
  ```for Today := Sunday to Saturday do```
    ```Sales[Week, Today] := 0.0```
	Initializes each element of Sales to 0.

```ReadLn (Sales[1, Sunday])```	Reads the value for the first Sunday into Sales.

Declaring Arrays of Records
```type```
  ```AElement = record```
          ```Data : Real;```
          ```Key : Integer```
        ```end; {AElement}```
  ```DataArray = array [1..10] of AElement;```
 	
```var```
  ```MyData : DataArray```
	DataArray is an array type with 10 elements of type AElement (a record). Each element has fields named Data and Key.
	
	MyData is a variable of type DataArray.

Table 12.2, *continued*

Construct	Effect

Referencing an Array of Records
`MyData[1].Data := 3.14159;`
`MyData[10].Key  := 9999;`
	The real value 3.14159 is stored in the first `Data` field of array `MyData`; the value 9999 is stored in the last `Key` field.

✓ Quick-Check Exercises

1. In Pascal, how many subscripts can an array have?
2. What is the difference between row-major and column-major order? Which does Pascal use?
3. What does row-major order mean when an array has more than two subscripts?
4. What control structure is used to process all the elements in a multidimensional array?
5. Write a program segment to display the sum of the values (type `Real`) in each column of a two-dimensional array `Table` with data type `array [1..5, 1..3] of Real`. How many column sums will be displayed? How many elements are included in each sum?
6. Write the type declaration for an array that stores the batting averages by position (`Catcher`, `Pitcher`, `FirstBase`, etc.) for each of 10 baseball teams in two leagues (`American` and `National`).
7. Write the type declaration for a data structure that stores a player's name, salary, position, batting average, fielding percentage, and number of hits, runs, runs batted in, and errors.
8. Write the type declaration for a data structure that stores the information in exercise 7 for a team of 25 players.
9. If the array `Team` has the structure described in exercise 8, write a program segment that displays the first two categories of information for the first five players.

Answers to Quick-Check Exercises

1. There is no specific limit; however, the size of the array is limited by the memory space available, and multidimensional arrays can require considerable memory.
2. In row-major order, the first row of the array is placed at the beginning of the memory area allocated to the array. It is followed by the second row, and so on. In column-major order, the first column is placed at the beginning of the array memory area. Pascal uses row-major order.
3. If an array `Table` has `N` subscripts, the array elements are placed in memory in the order `Table[1,1,...,1,1]`, `Table[1,1,...,1,2]`, `Table[1,1,...,1,3]`, and so on. Then the next-to-last subscript is changed, and the elements `Table[1,1,...,2,1]`, `Table[1,1,...,2,2]`, `Table[1,1,...,2,3]` ... are placed. The first subscript will be the last one that changes.
4. nested `for` loops
5. ```
for Column := 1 to 3 do
  begin
    ColumnSum := 0.0;
      for Row := 1 to 5 do
        ColumnSum := ColumnSum + Table[Row,Column];
```
```

```
        WriteLn ('Sum for column ', Column :1, ' is ', ColumnSum)
     end {for Column}
```

three column sums; five elements added per column

6. type
```
     Position = (Pitcher, Catcher, FirstBase, SecondBase, ThirdBase,
                   ShortStop, LeftField, CenterField, RightField);
     League = (American, National);
     BAArray = array [League, 1..10, Position] of Real;
```

7. type
```
     StringType = packed array [1..20] of Char;
     Player = record
                 Name : StringType;
                 Salary : Real;
                 Place : Position;
                 BatAve, FieldPct : Real;
                 Hits, Runs, RBIs, Errors : Integer
              end; {Player}
```

8. type
```
     StringType = ...
     Player = ...
     TeamArray = array [1..25] of Player;
```

9. for I := 1 to 5 do
```
     WriteLn (Team[I].Name, Team[I].Salary)
```

Review Questions

1. Define row-major order.
2. Declare an array that can be used to store each title of the Top40 hits for each week of the year given that the TitleLength will be 20 characters.
3. Write the declaration of the array YearlyHours to store the hours each of five employees works each day of the week, each week of the year.
4. Write the declarations for the array CPUArray that will hold 20 records of type CPU. The record CPU has the following fields: IDNumber (11 characters in length), Make (5 characters), Location (15 characters), and Ports (integer).
5. Use the following declarations for this exercise and exercises 6 through 9.

```
const
   TotalEmployees = 20;

type
   Employee = record
                 ID : Integer;
                 Rate,
                 Hours : Real
              end; {Employee}
   EmpArray = array [1..TotalEmployees] of Employee;

var
   Employees : EmpArray;
```

   Write the function TotalGross that will return the total gross pay given the data stored in array Employees.

6. Explain what is wrong with the following fragment and fix it.

```
I := 1;
with Employees[I] do
   while I <= TotalEmployees do
```

```
begin
    WriteLn (Hours :12:2);
    I := I + 1
end {while}
```

7. Explain what is wrong with the following fragment and fix it.

```
I := 1;
while (Employees[I].ID <> 999) and (I <= MaxEmployees) do
    I := I + 1;
```

8. Write a fragment that displays the ID number of each employee who works between 10 and 20 hours per week.
9. Write a fragment that displays the ID number of the employee who works the most hours.
10. Procedure SortStudents in Fig. 12.38 placed the elements of an array in order by Score field. Change the condition in the procedure so that records with the same Score value are ordered by name (smallest name first). The field Score is called the *primary key*, and the field Name is called the *secondary key*.

Programming Projects

1. Write a program that generates the Morse code for a sentence that ends in a period and contains no other characters except letters and blanks. After reading the Morse code into an array of strings, your program should read each word of the sentence and display its Morse equivalent on a separate line. The Morse code is as follows:

A .-   B -...   C -.-.   D -..   E .   F ..-.   G --.   H ....   I ..   J .---   K -.-   L .-..   M --
N -.   O ---   P .--.   Q --.-   R .-.   S ...   T -   U ..-   V ...-   W .--   X -..-   Y -.--   Z --..

Your program should make use of StringADT (Fig. 10.21) and include procedures corresponding to the procedure headers shown next.

```
procedure ReadCode (var CodeFile {input} : Text;
                    var Code {output} : CodeArray);
{Stores Morse codes read from CodeFile in array Code}

procedure SkipBlanks (Sentence {input} : StringType;
                      var I {input/output} : StringIndex);
{If Sentence[I] is blank, advances I to next nonblank
 in Sentence.}

procedure WriteCode (Code {input} : CodeArray;
                     Letter : Char);
{Writes Morse equivalent for a letter.}
```

2. Write a set of procedures to manipulate a pair of matrices. Provide procedures for addition, subtraction, and multiplication. Each procedure should validate its input parameters (i.e., check all matrix dimensions) before performing the required data manipulation.
3. Write a program that uses ADT TallyADT to store election results in an appropriate data structure. The ADT should contain the following operators:

Procedure Initialize (var Tally): Reads in the number of precincts (up to 10) and the letter (up to J) corresponding to the last candidate; initializes all vote totals to zero

Procedure ReadTally (var Tally): Reads in the votes by precinct for each candidate.

Procedure WriteTable (Tally): Displays the election results in the form shown

Procedure CountBallot (var Tally): Determines the count of votes received by each candidate and the corresponding percentage of the total votes cast

Procedure FindWinner (Tally, var Cand1, var Cand2, var Over50): Determines the letters of the highest-scoring candidate (Cand1) and the second-highest-scoring candidate (Cand2) and sets Over50 to True if the highest scoring candidate receives more than 50 percent of the vote

Procedure DisplayWinner (Cand1, Cand2, Over50): Displays the name of Cand1 and the message Won the election if Over50 is true; otherwise, displays the message Runoff election between 2 highest-scoring candidates and Cand1 and Cand2.

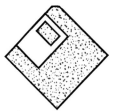

Directory: CHAP12
File: PROJ12_3.PAS

Write a main program that uses this ADT and run the program for the data shown below and also when candidate C receives only 108 votes in precinct 4.

Precinct	Candidate A	Candidate B	Candidate C	Candidate D
1	192	48	206	37
2	147	90	312	21
3	186	12	121	38
4	114	21	408	39
5	267	13	382	29

4. Modify programming project 3 to make it an interactive menu-drive program. Menu options should include initializing the vote table (prompt the user for the number of candidates, their names, and the number of precincts), displaying the vote table with row and column totals, displaying the precinct totals, displaying the candidates' names and votes received (raw count and percentage of votes cast), displaying winner's name (or names in the event of a tie), and exiting the program.

5. For the sales analysis problem (see Section 12.3), provide these operators:

GetFileData (var InFile, var Sales): Reads the sales data from file InFile

EditData (var Sales): Prompts the user to determine the year, month, and new amount for a sales entry to be changed and then calls PutSales to change that entry

Add these options to the menu and test them.

6. For the student grading program (see Section 12.5), provide the following operators:

ReadBookFile (var InFile, var Test): Reads in the student exam data from data file InFile

AddStudent (var Test, ExamData): Reads a student record from the keyboard into ExamData and adds it to the collection of student records

GetStudent (Test, StudentName, var ExamData): Returns through ExamData the record for the student specified by StudentName

PutStudent (var Test, StudentName, ExamData): Stores new exam data (passed through ExamData) in the record for the student specified by StudentName

EditStudent (var Test): Prompts the user for the name of a student whose score and/or grade may be changed; reads in the new score and grade and calls PutStudent to make the change

Change the program to a menu-driven program and test these new operators.

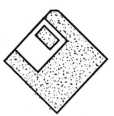

7. Implement an ADT that represents a telephone directory for a company. The telephone directory should contain space for up to 100 names, phone numbers, and room numbers. You should have operators to create an empty directory (all names blank), read in the telephone directory from a file, retrieve the entry corresponding to a given name, display the telephone directory, and add a new entry to the directory. You will also need an abstract data type for an individual telephone entry that contains operators to read and write a single entry.

8. Write a menu-driven program that tests the operators in programming project 7.

9. Use a three-dimensional array to represent a building (floors 1 to 3, wings A and B, and rooms 1 to 5). Each entry in the array will be a record containing a person's name and phone number. Provide operators to create an initially empty building (all names are blank), read data into the building, display the entire building, display a particular floor of the building, retrieve the entry for a particular room, and store a new entry in a particular room. To designate a particular room, the program user must enter the floor number, wing letter, and room number as data. You will also need an abstract data type to represent, read, and display a single entry.

10. Many supermarkets use computer equipment that allows the checkout clerk to drag an item across a sensor that reads the bar code on the product container. After the computer reads the bar code, the store inventory data base is examined, the item's price and product description are located, counts are reduced, and a receipt is printed. Your task is to write a program that simulates this process.

    Your program will need to read the inventory information from the data file on disk into an array of records. The data in the inventory file is written one item per line, beginning with a 2-digit product code, followed by a 30-character product description, its price, and the quantity of that item in stock. Your program will need to copy the revised version of the inventory to a new data file after all purchases are processed.

    Processing customers' orders involves reading a series of product codes representing each person's purchases from a second data file. A zero product code is used to mark the end of each customer order. As each product code is read, the inventory list is searched to find a matching product code. Once located, the product price and description are printed on the receipt, and the quantity on hand is reduced by 1. At the bottom of the receipt, you are to print the total for the goods purchased by the customer.

11. Write a program that simulates the movement of radioactive particles in a 20-by-20 foot two-dimensional shield around a reactor. Particles enter the shield at some random position in the shield coordinate space. Once a particle enters the shield, it moves 1 foot/second in one of four directions. The direction for the next second of travel is determined by a random number between 1 and 4 (forward, backward, left, right). A change in direction is interpreted as a collison with another particle, which results in a dissipation of energy. Each particle can have only a limited number of collisions before it dies. A particle exits the shield if its position places it outside the shield coordinate space before K collisions occur. Determine the percentage of particles that exit the shield, where K and the number of particles are input as data items. Also compute the average number of times a particle's path crosses itself during travel time within the shield. *Hint:* Mark each array position occupied by a particle before it dies or exits the shield.

Patrick H. Winston is Professor of Computer Science at the Massachusetts Institute of Technology and Director of the interdepartmental Artificial Intelligence Laboratory there. He is also author of Artificial Intelligence *and co-author of* Lisp, *two of the most widely used texts on these subjects. He is currently involved in the study of learning, precedent-based reasoning, common-sense problem solving, problem solving via abstraction, and applications of Artificial Intelligence to database mining, scheduling, and dynamic resource allocation.*

People often seem confused about what artificial intelligence is and is not. In your text, *Artificial Intelligence,* **you define the goals of AI as "[attempting] to make computers more useful [and] to understand the principles that make intelligence possible." Has your thinking about the goals of AI changed since that was written nine years or so ago?**

I would say my sense of the goals of AI is more precise perhaps, but not fundamentally changed. Now I tend to say that the engineering goal of Artificial Intelligence is to solve real-world problems using Artificial Intelligence as an armamentarium of ideas about representing knowledge, using knowledge, and assembling systems. The scientific goal, on the other hand, is to determine which ideas about representing knowledge, using knowledge, and assembling systems account for various sorts of intelligence.

Of all the choices you could have made, why did you choose AI? What influenced you most in that decision?

Well, I have always wanted to understand what thinking is all about. When I was a graduate student, I looked for answers, as many do, by taking subjects offered in psychology and neuroanatomy. But even though I learned a lot, I felt that something was missing. Luckily, that was about the time I heard that the students of Marvin Minsky and Seymour Papert were not only trying to understand intelligence, they were trying to *produce* it. I resolved instantly to be one of those students. And when I did, I learned that what was missing was the idea that you can study the computations that make intelligence possible without concerning yourself too much with the particular computer that happens to be performing those computations, be it natural or made of silicon.

What comes to mind when you think of the major achievements in AI over the past decade? Who do you think has benefited the most from the accomplishments of AI?

Lots. Especially in the last half of the decade, which has been especially exciting because so much conventional wisdom has been overturned. For example, we now know that the memory required to do visual recognition need not involve any explicit three dimensional models—an idea that used to seem ridiculous ten years ago. But this is just one example; similar stories can be told for just about every subfield of AI. I've taken to telling my students that the exams stay the same from year to year, but all the answers change.

One sometimes hears of the MIT or Carnegie-Mellon or some other institutional view of artificial intelligence, suggesting that several views of AI are extant. Do you think such diversity of viewpoints exists in the field and, if so, do you think it's healthy?

Certainly there are lots of approaches, and many are championed by advocates with almost religious zeal. And on the whole, this is a good thing because AI, like most fields, benefits from diverse ideas and excited people. And besides, any adequate account of intelligence, from a computational point of view, is unlikely to rest on just a few elegant laws like electromagnetism rests on Maxwell's equations. There is room for lots of approaches to be right with respect to some part of the total picture.

What significant achievements can we look forward to in AI in the 1990s?

Making predictions in AI is always dangerous because there are critics who take failure to meet some claimed objective at a predicted time to mean *never* instead of *not yet*. Also, we still need breakthroughs in AI, and it is hard to predict when someone will have a breakthrough idea. But if you force me, nevertheless, to hazard something, I would claim that the results of the past few years suggest that the next decade will be the decade of learning. Ten years from now, we will know a great deal about how to learn using a combination of already known facts and a little observation, and conversely, we will know a great deal about how to dig regularities out of lots of data with no background knowledge. Some of this is bound to change the world, at least in a minor way, and maybe in a major way, especially if the technology can be harnessed, for example, to individually tailored product marketing or to, say, pharmaceutical development.

13
Recursion

A recursive procedure or function is one that calls itself. This ability enables a recursive procedure to be repeated with different parameter values. You can use recursion as an alternative to iteration (looping). Generally, a recursive solution is less efficient, in terms of computer time, than an iterative one because of the overhead for the extra procedure calls. In many instances, however, the use of recursion enables us to specify a natural, simple solution to a problem that would otherwise be difficult to solve. For this reason, recursion is an important and powerful tool in problem solving and programming.

13.1 The Nature of Recursion

Problems that lend themselves to a recursive solution have the following characteristics:

- One or more simple cases of the problem (called *stopping cases*) have a simple, nonrecursive solution.
- The other cases of the problem can be reduced (using recursion) to problems that are closer to stopping cases.
- Eventually the problem can be reduced to stopping cases only, which are relatively easy to solve.

The recursive algorithms that we write generally consist of an `if` statement with this form:

> `if` the stopping case is reached `then`
>   Solve it.
> `else`
>   Reduce the problem using recursion.

Figure 13.1 illustrates this approach. Let's assume that for a particular problem of size N, we can split the problem into a problem of size 1, which we can solve (a stopping case), and a problem of size $N - 1$. We can split the problem of size $N - 1$ into another problem of size 1 and a problem of size $N - 2$, which we can split further. If we split the problem N times, we end up with N problems of size 1, all of which we can solve.

Figure 13.1 Splitting a Problem into Smaller Problems

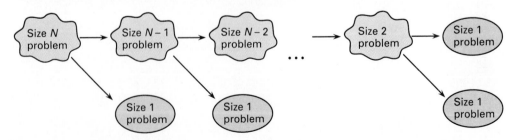

■ Example 13.1

Consider how we might solve the problem of multiplying 6 by 3, assuming that we know the addition tables but not the multiplication tables. The problem of multiplying 6 by 3 can be split into the two problems:

1. Multiply 6 by 2.
2. Add 6 to the result of problem 1.

Because we know the addition tables, we can solve problem 2 but not problem 1. Problem 1, however, is simpler than the original problem. We can split it into two problems, 1.1 and 1.2, leaving us three problems to solve, two of which are additions.

1.1 Multiply 6 by 1.
1.2 Add 6 to the result.

Even though we don't know the multiplication tables, we are familiar with the simple rule that, for any M, $M \times 1$ is M. By solving problem 1.1 (the answer is 6) and problem 1.2, we get the solution to problem 1 (the answer is 12). Solving problem 2 gives us the final answer, 18.

Figure 13.2 implements this approach to doing multiplication as the recursive Pascal function `Multiply`, which returns the product, $M \times N$, of its two arguments. The body of function `Multiply` implements the general form of a recursive algorithm, shown earlier. The stopping case is reached when the condition `N = 1` is true. In this case, the statement

```
Multiply := M                    {stopping case}
```

executes, so the answer is `M`. If `N` is greater than 1, the statement

```
Multiply := M + Multiply(M, N-1)    {recursive step}
```

executes, splitting the original problem into the two simpler problems:

1. Multiply `M` by `N-1`.
2. Add `M` to the result.

Figure 13.2 Recursive Function Multiply

```
function Multiply (M, N : Integer) : Integer;
{
  Performs multiplication using + operator.
  Pre : M and N are defined and N > 0.
  Post: Returns M * N.
}
begin {Multiply}
  if N = 1 then
    Multiply := M                        {stopping case}
  else
    Multiply := M + Multiply(M, N-1)     {recursive step}
end; {Multiply}
```

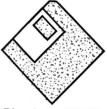

Directory: CHAP13
File: MULTIPLY.FUN

The first of these problems is solved by calling `Multiply` again with `N−1` as its second argument. If the new second argument is greater than 1, there will be additional calls to function `Multiply`.

Note the two different uses of the identifier `Multiply` in the recursive step in Fig. 13.2. The first one assigns a value to `Multiply` representing the function result, while the second calls the function recursively. ∎

For now, you will have to take our word that function `Multiply` performs as desired. You will see how to trace the execution of a recursive function or procedure in the next section.

The next example illustrates how we might solve a difficult problem just by splitting it into smaller problems. You will see how to solve this problem after you have had more experience using recursion.

■ Example 13.2

The Towers of Hanoi problem involves moving a specified number of disks that are all different sizes from one tower (or peg) to another. Legend has it that the world will come to an end when the problem is solved for sixty-four disks. In the version of the problem shown in Fig. 13.3, there are five disks (numbered 1 through 5) and three towers or pegs (lettered A, B, and C). The goal is to move the five disks from peg A to peg C subject to the following rules:

1. Only one disk may be moved at a time, and this disk must be the top disk on a peg.
2. A larger disk can never be placed on top of a smaller disk.

The stopping cases of the problem involve moving only one disk (for example, "move disk 2 from peg A to peg C"). Simpler problems than the original would be to move four disks subject to the conditions above, to move three disks, and so on. Therefore, we want to split the original five-disk problem into one or more problems involving fewer disks. Let's consider splitting the original problem into three problems:

1. Move four disks from peg A to peg B.
2. Move disk 5 from peg A to peg C.
3. Move four disks from peg B to peg C.

Step 1 moves all disks but the largest to tower B, an auxiliary tower. Step 2 moves the largest disk to the goal tower, tower C. Step 3 then moves the remaining disks from B to the goal tower, where they will be placed on top of the largest disk. Let's assume that we can perform step 1 and step 2 (a stopping case); Figure 13.4 shows the status of the three towers after completion of these steps. At this point, it should be clear that we can solve the original five-disk problem if we can complete step 3.

Unfortunately, we still don't know how to perform step 1 or step 3. Both steps, however, involve four disks instead of five, so they are easier than the original problem. We should be able to split them into even simpler problems. Step 3 involves moving four disks from tower B to tower C, so we can split it into two three-disk problems and one one-disk problem:

Figure 13.3 Towers of Hanoi

583

13.1 The Nature of Recursion

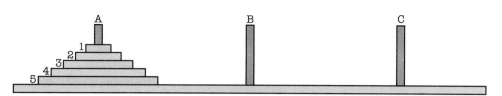

Figure 13.4 Towers of Hanoi After Steps 1 and 2

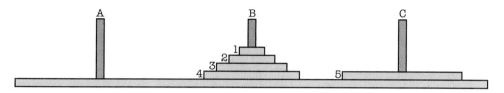

3.1 Move three disks from peg B to peg A.
3.2 Move disk 4 from peg B to peg C.
3.3 Move three disks from peg A to peg C.

Figure 13.5 shows the towers after completion of steps 3.1 and 3.2. The two largest disks are now on peg C. Once we complete step 3.3, all five disks will be on peg C. Although we still do not know how to solve steps 3.1 and 3.3, they are at least simpler problems than the four-disk problem from which they are derived.

By splitting each N-disk problem into two problems involving N-1 disks and a one-disk problem, we eventually reach the point where all the cases involve only one disk, cases that we know how to solve. Later we will write a Pascal program that solves the Towers of Hanoi problem. ■

Figure 13.5 Towers of Hanoi After Steps 1, 2, 3.1, and 3.2

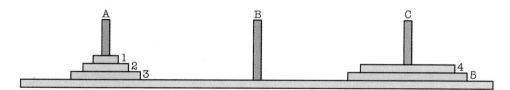

Exercises for Section 13.1

Self-Check

1. Show the problems that are generated by the function designator `Multiply(5, 4)`. Use a diagram similar to Fig. 13.1.
2. Show the problems that are generated when you attempt to solve the problem "Move three disks from peg A to peg C." Answer the same question for the problem "Move three disks from peg A to peg C." Draw a diagram similar to Fig. 13.1.

13.2 Tracing a Recursive Procedure or Function

Hand-tracing an algorithm's execution provides us with valuable insight as to how that algorithm works. We can also trace the execution of a recursive procedure or function. We illustrate how to do this with a recursive function and procedure.

Tracing a Recursive Function

In the last section, we wrote the recursive function `Multiply`. We can trace the execution of the function designator `Multiply(6, 3)` by drawing an *activation frame* that corresponds to each call of the function. An activation frame shows the parameter values for each call and summarizes its execution.

The three activation frames generated to solve the problem of multiplying 6 by 3 are shown in Fig. 13.6. The part of each activation frame that executes before the next recursive call is in color; the part that executes after the return from the next call is in gray. The darker the color of an activation frame, the greater the depth of recursion.

The value returned from each call is shown alongside each black arrow. The return arrow from each function call points to the operator **+**, because the addition is performed just after the return.

Figure 13.6 Trace of Function Multiply

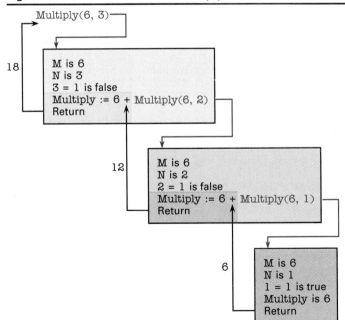

The figure shows that there are three calls to function `Multiply`. Parameter M has the value 6 for all three calls; parameter N has the values 3, 2, and finally 1. Because N is 1 in the third call, the value of M (6) is returned as the result of the third and last call. After the return to the second activation frame, the value of M is added to this result, and the sum (12) is returned as the result of the second call. After the return to the first activation frame, the value of M is added to this result, and the sum (18) is returned as the result of the original call to function `Multiply`.

Tracing a Recursive Procedure

■ Example 13.3

Procedure `Palindrome` in Fig. 13.7 is a recursive procedure that reads in a string of length N and prints it out backward. (A *palindrome* is a string of characters that reads the same backward and forward.) If the procedure call statement

```
Palindrome (5)
```

is executed, the five characters entered at the screen are printed in reverse order. If the characters abcde are entered when this procedure is called, the line

```
abcdeedcba
```

appears on the screen. The letters in color are entered as data and the letters in black are printed. If the procedure call statement

```
Palindrome (3)
```

is executed instead, only three characters are read, and the line

```
abccba
```

appears on the screen.

Figure 13.7   Procedure Palindrome

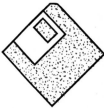

Directory: CHAP13
File: PALINDRO.PRO

```
procedure Palindrome (N : Integer);
{
  Displays a string of length N in
  reverse of the order in which it is entered.
  Pre : N is greater than or equal to one.
  Post: Displays N characters.
}
  var
    Next : Char;    {next data character}

begin {Palindrome}
  if N <= 1 then
    begin {stopping case}
      Read (Next);
      Write (Next)
    end {stopping case}
```

```
    else
      begin {recursion}
        Read (Next);
        Palindrome (N-1);
        Write (Next)
      end {recursion}
end; {Palindrome}
```

Like most recursive procedures, the body of procedure `Palindrome` consists of an `if` statement that evaluates a *terminating condition*, `N <= 1`. When the terminating condition is true, the problem has reached a stopping case: a data string of length 1. If `N <= 1` is true, the `Read` and `Write` statements are executed.

If the terminating condition is false (`N > 1`), the recursive step (following `else`) is executed. The `Read` statement enters the next data character. The procedure call statement

```
    Palindrome (N-1);
```

calls the procedure recursively, with the parameter value decreased by 1. The character just read is not displayed until later. This is because the `Write` statement comes after the recursive procedure call; consequently, the `Write` statement cannot be performed until after the procedure execution is completed and control is returned back to the `Write` statement. For example, the character that is read when `N` is 3 is not displayed until after the procedure execution for `N` equal to 2 is done. Hence, this character is displayed after the characters that are read when `N` is 2 and `N` is 1.

To fully understand this, trace the execution of the procedure call statement

```
    Palindrome (3)
```

The trace shown in Fig. 13.8 assumes the letters `abc` have been entered as data.

The trace shows three separate activation frames for procedure `Palindrome`. Each activation frame begins with a list of the initial values of `N` and `Next` for that frame. The value of `N` is passed into the procedure when it is called, because `N` is a value parameter; the value of `Next` is initially undefined, because `Next` is a local variable.

Figure 13.8 Trace of Palindrome (3)

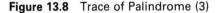
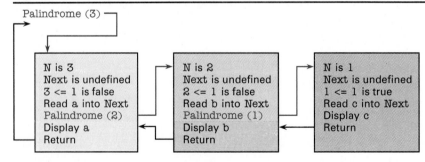

The statements that are executed for each frame are shown next. The statements in color are recursive procedure calls and result in a new activation frame, as indicated by the colored arrows. A procedure return occurs when the procedure end statement is reached. This is indicated by the word Return and a black arrow that points to the statement in the calling frame to which the procedure returns. Tracing the colored arrows and then the black arrows in Fig. 13.8 gives us the sequence of events listed in Fig. 13.9. To help you understand this list, all the statements for a particular activation frame are indented to the same column.

Figure 13.9 Sequence of Events for Trace of Palindrome (3)

Call Palindrome with N equal to 3.
  Read the first character (a) into Next.
  Call Palindrome with N equal to 2.
    Read the second character (b) into Next.
    Call Palindrome with N equal to 1.
      Read the third character (c) into Next.
      Display the third character (c).
      Return from third call.
    Display the second character (b).
    Return from second call.
  Display the first character (a).
  Return from original call.

As shown, there are three calls to procedure Palindrome, each with a different parameter value. The procedure returns always occur in the reverse order of the procedure calls; that is, we return from the last call first, then we return from the next to last call, and so on. After we return from a particular execution of the procedure, we display the character that was read into Next just prior to that procedure call. ∎

Parameter and Local Variable Stacks

You may be wondering how Pascal keeps track of the values of N and Next at any given point. Pascal uses a special data structure called a *stack*, which is analogous to a stack of dishes or trays. Think of the countless times you have stood in line in a cafeteria. Recall that clean dishes are always placed on top of a stack of dishes. When we need a dish, we always remove the one most recently placed on the stack. This causes the next to last dish placed on the stack to move to the top of the stack. (The stack data structure is discussed further in Chapter 16.)

Similarly, whenever a new procedure call occurs, the parameter value associated with that call is placed on the top of the parameter stack. Also, a new cell whose value is initially undefined is placed on top of the stack that is maintained for the local variable Next. Whenever N or Next is referenced, the value at the top of the corresponding stack is always used. When a procedure return occurs, the value currently at the top of each stack is removed, and the value just below it moves to the top.

As an example, let's look at the two stacks right after the first call to Palindrome. There is one cell on each stack, as follows.

After first call to Palindrome

```
   N        Next
| 3 |      | ? |
```

The letter a is read into Next just before the second call to Palindrome.

```
   N        Next
| 3 |      | a |
```

After the second call to Palindrome, the number 2 is placed on top of the stack for N, and the top of the stack for Next becomes undefined again, as shown next. The value in color is at the top of each stack.

After second call to Palindrome

```
   N        Next
| 2 |      | ? |
| 3 |      | a |
```

The letter b is read into Next just before the third call to Palindrome.

```
   N        Next
| 2 |      | b |
| 3 |      | a |
```

However, Next becomes undefined again right after the third call.

After third call to Palindrome

```
   N        Next
| 1 |      | ? |
| 2 |      | b |
| 3 |      | a |
```

During this execution of the procedure, the letter c is read into Next, and c is echo printed immediately because N is 1 (the stopping case).

```
   N        Next
| 1 |      | c |
| 2 |      | b |
| 3 |      | a |
```

The procedure return causes the values at the top of the stack to be removed, as shown next.

N		Next	
2		b	
3		a	

Because control is returned to a `Write` statement, the value of `Next` (b) at the top of the stack is then displayed. Another return occurs, causing the values currently at the top of the stack to be removed.

After second return

N	Next
3	a

Again, control is returned to a `Write` statement, and the value of `Next` (a) at the top of the stack is displayed. The third and last return removes the last pair of values from the stack, and N and `Next` both become undefined.

After third return

N	Next
?	?

Chapter 16 shows you how to declare and manipulate stacks yourself. Because these steps are all done automatically by Pascal, we can write recursive procedures without worrying about the stacks.

Implementation of Parameter Stacks in Pascal

For illustrative purposes, we have used separate stacks for N and `Next` in our discussion; the compiler, however, actually maintains a single stack. Each time a call to a procedure or function occurs, all its parameters and local variables are pushed onto the stack along with the memory address of the calling statement. The latter gives the computer the return point after execution of the procedure or function. Although multiple copies of a procedure's parameters may be saved on the stack, only one copy of the procedure body is in memory.

Exercises for Section 13.2

Self-Check

1. Why is N a value parameter in Fig. 13.7?
2. Assume the characters `*+-/` are entered for the procedure call statement

   ```
   Palindrome (4)
   ```

   What output line would appear on the screen? Show the contents of the stacks immediately after each procedure call and return.
3. Trace the execution of `Multiply(5, 4)` and show the stacks after each recursive call.

13.3 Recursive Mathematical Functions

Many mathematical functions are defined recursively. An example is the factorial of a number n ($n!$).

- 0! is 1
- $n!$ is $n \times (n - 1)!$, for $n > 0$

Thus, $4! = 4 \times 3! = 4 \times 3 \times 2!$, and so on. It is easy to implement this definition as a recursive function in Pascal.

■ Example 13.4

Function Factor in Fig. 13.10 computes the factorial of its argument N. The recursive step

```
Factor := N * Factor(N-1)
```

implements the second line of the factorial definition. This means that the result of the current call (argument N) is determined by multiplying the result of the next call (argument N–1) by N.

Figure 13.10 Recursive Function Factor

Directory: CHAP13
File: FACTOR.FUN

```
function Factor (N : Integer) : Integer;
{
  Computes the factorial of N (N!).
  Pre : N is defined and N >= 0.
  Post: Returns N!
}
begin {Factor}
  if N = 0 then
    Factor := 1
  else
    Factor := N * Factor(N-1)
end;  {Factor}
```

A trace of

```
Fact := Factor(3)
```

is shown in Fig. 13.11. The value returned from the original call, Factor(3), is 6, and this value is assigned to Fact. Be careful when you use the factorial function; its value increases rapidly and could lead to an integer-overflow error (for example, 10! is 24320). ■

Although the recursive implementation of function Factor follows naturally from its definition, this function can be implemented easily using iteration. The iterative version is shown in Fig. 13.12.

Figure 13.11 Trace of Fact := Factor(3)

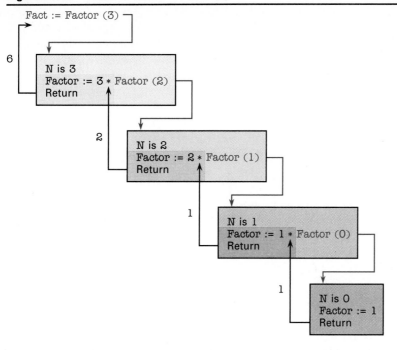

Figure 13.12 Iterative Function Factor

```
function Factor (N : Integer) : Integer;
{
  Computes the factorial of N (N!).
  Pre : N is defined and N >= 0.
  Post: Returns N!
}
  var
    I,                      {loop-control variable}
    Factorial : Integer;    {storage for accumulating product}

begin {Factor}
  Factorial := 1;
  for I := 2 to N do
    Factorial := Factorial * I;

  Factor := Factorial        {Define result}
end; {Factor}
```

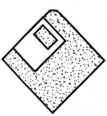

Directory: CHAP13
File: FACTORIT.FUN

Notice that the iterative version contains a loop as its major control structure, whereas the recursive version contains an if statement. Also, a local variable, Factorial, is needed in the iterative version to hold the accumulating product.

■ **Example 13.5**

The Fibonacci numbers are a sequence of numbers that have many varied uses. They were originally intended to model the growth of a rabbit colony. We will not go into details of the model here, but you can see that the Fibonacci sequence 1, 1, 2, 3, 5, 8, 13, 21, 34, ... increases rapidly. The fifteenth number in the sequence is 610 (that's a lot of rabbits!). The Fibonacci sequence is defined as follows:

- Fib_1 is 1.
- Fib_2 is 1.
- Fib_n is $Fib_{n-2} + Fib_{n-1}$, for $n > 2$.

Verify for yourself that the sequence of numbers shown in the preceding paragraph is correct.

A recursive function that computes the Nth Fibonacci number is shown in Fig. 13.13. Although easy to write, the Fibonacci function is not very efficient, because each recursive step generates two calls to function Fibonacci. ■

Figure 13.13 Recursive Function Fibonacci

Directory: CHAP13
File: FIBONACC.FUN

```
function Fibonacci (N : Integer) : Integer;
{
  Computes the Nth Fibonacci number.
  Pre : N is defined and N > 0.
  Post: Returns the Nth Fibonacci number.
}
begin  {Fibonacci}
  if (N = 1) or (N = 2) then
    Fibonacci := 1
  else
    Fibonacci := Fibonacci(N-2) + Fibonacci(N-1)
end;  {Fibonacci}
```

■ **Example 13.6**

Euclid's algorithm for finding the greatest common divisor (GCD) of two positive integers, M and N, is defined recursively as follows. The *greatest common divisor* of two integers is the largest integer that divides them both.

- GCD(M,N) is N if N <= M and N divides M.
- GCD(M,N) is GCD(N,M) if M < N.
- GCD(M,N) is GCD(N, remainder of M divided by N).

This algorithm states that the GCD is N if N is the smaller number and N divides M. If M is the smaller number, then the GCD determination should be performed with the arguments transposed. If N does not divide M, the answer is obtained by finding the GCD of N and the remainder of M divided by N. The declaration and use of the Pascal function GCD is shown in Fig. 13.14. ■

Figure 13.14 Function GCD

593

13.3 Recursive
Mathematical
Functions

```
program FindGCD (Input, Output);

{Prints the greatest common divisor of two integers}
  var
    M, N : Integer;                {two input items}

  function GCD (M, N : Integer) : Integer;
  {
    Finds the greatest common divisor of M and N.
    Pre : M and N are defined and both are > 0.
    Post: Returns the greatest common divisor of M and N.
  }
  begin {GCD}
    if (N <= M) and (M mod N = 0) then
      GCD := N
    else if M < N then
      GCD := GCD(N, M)
    else
      GCD := GCD(N, M mod N)
  end; {GCD}

begin {FindGCD}
  Write ('Enter two positive integers separated by a space: ');
  ReadLn (M, N);
  WriteLn ('Their greatest common divisor is ', GCD (M, N) :1)
end. {FindGCD}


Enter two positive integers separated by a space: 24 84
Their greatest common divisor is 12
```

Directory: CHAP13
File: FINDGCD.PAS

Exercises for Section 13.3

Self-Check

1. Complete the following recursive function, which calculates the value of a number (Base) raised to a power (Power). Assume that Power is positive.

```
function PowerRaiser (Base, Power : Integer) : Integer;
begin
  if Power = _____ then
    PowerRaiser := _____
  else
    PowerRaiser := _____ * _____
end;
```

2. What is the output of the following program? What does function Strange compute?

```
program TestStrange (Output);

  function Strange (N : Integer) : Integer;
  begin  {Strange}
    if N = 1 then
      Strange := 0
    else
      Strange := 1 + Strange (N div 2)
  end;  {Strange}
```

```
begin {TestStrange}
  WriteLn (Strange(8))
end. {TestStrange}
```

3. What would happen if the terminating condition for function `Fibonacci` is just `N = 1`?

Programming

1. Write a recursive function, `FindSum`, that calculates the sum of successive integers starting at `1` and ending at `N` (for example, `FindSum(N) = 1 + 2 + ... + (N–1) + N`).
2. Write an iterative version of the Fibonacci function.
3. Write an iterative function for the greatest common divisor.

13.4 Recursive Procedures with Array Parameters

This section examines three familiar problems and implements recursive procedures to solve them. All three problems involve processing an array.

Case Study: Printing an Array Backward

Problem
Provide a recursive solution to the problem of printing the elements of an array in reverse order.

Analysis
If the array `X` has elements with subscripts `1..N`, then the element values should be printed in the sequence `X[N]`, `X[N–1]`, `X[N–2]`, ... , `X[2]`, `X[1]`. The stopping case is printing an array with one element (`N` is `1`); the solution is to print that element. For larger arrays, the recursive step is to print the last array element (`X[N]`) and then print the subarray with subscripts `1..N–1` backward.

Data Requirements

Problem Inputs
```
X : IntArray      {array of integer values}
N : Integer       {number of elements in the array}
```

Problem Outputs
The array values in reverse order (`X[N]`, `X[N–1]`, ... , `X[2]`, `X[1]`)

Design

Initial Algorithm

1. if N is 1 then
    2. Print X[1].
  else
    begin
      3. Print X[N].
      4. Print the subarray with subscripts 1..N−1.
    end

Implementation

Procedure PrintBack in Fig. 13.15 implements the recursive algorithm.

Figure 13.15 Procedure PrintBack

```
procedure PrintBack (var X {input} : IntArray;
                         N {input} : Integer);
{
  Prints an array of integers (X) with subscripts 1..N in reverse order.
  Pre : Array X and N are defined and N > 0.
  Post: Displays X[N], X[N−1], ... , X[2], X[1].
}
begin {PrintBack }
  if N = 1 then
    WriteLn (X[1])                      {stopping case}
  else
    begin {recursive step}
      WriteLn (X[N]);
      PrintBack (X, N−1)
    end {recursive step}
end;  {PrintBack }
```

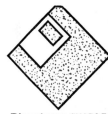

Directory: CHAP13
File: PRINTBAC.PRO

Testing

Given the declarations

```
type
  IndexRange = 1..20;
  IntArray = array [IndexRange] of Integer;

var
  Test : IntArray;
```

and the procedure call statement

```
PrintBack (Test, 3)
```

three WriteLn statements will be executed in the following order, and the elements of Test will be printed backward.

```
WriteLn (Test[3]);
WriteLn (Test[2]);
WriteLn (Test[1])
```

Case Study: Printing an Array Backward, continued

To verify this, in Fig. 13.16 we trace the execution of the original call to PrintBack. Tracing the colored arrows and then the black arrows leads to the sequence of events listed in Fig. 13.17.

Figure 13.16 Trace of PrintBack (Test, 3)

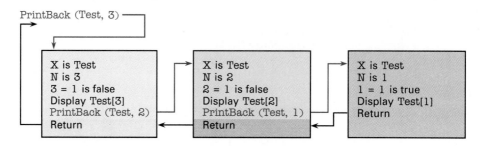

Figure 13.17 Sequence of Events for Trace of PrintBack (Test, 3)

Call PrintBack with parameters Test and 3.
    Print Test[3].
    Call PrintBack with parameters Test and 2.
        Print Test[2].
        Call PrintBack with parameters Test and 1.
            Print Test[1].
            Return from third call.
        Return from second call.
Return from original call.

As shown in Fig. 13.17, there are three calls to procedure PrintBack, each with different parameters. This time, there are no statements left to execute after the returns, because the recursive call

    PrintBack (X, N–1)

occurs at the end of the recursive step.

Case Study: Printing an Array in Normal Order

Problem

Provide a recursive procedure that prints the elements of an array in normal order.

Analysis

We can use the approach we just followed in the preceding problem to print the elements of an array in normal order. Again, the stopping case is an array with just one element.

Data Requirements

Problem Inputs

```
X : IntArray        {array of integer values}
N : Integer         {number of elements in the array}
```

Problem Output

The array values in normal order (X[1], X[2], . . . , X[N−1], X[N])

Design

Initial Algorithm

```
1. if N is 1 then
      2. Print X[1].
   else
     begin
        3. Print the subarray with subscripts 1..N−1.
        4. Print X[N].
     end
```

The only difference between this algorithm and the one shown earlier is that steps 3 and 4 are transposed.

Implementation

Procedure PrintNormal is shown in Fig. 13.18.

Figure 13.18 Procedure PrintNormal

```
procedure PrintNormal (var X {input} : IntArray;
                           N {input} : Integer);
{
  Prints an array of integers (X) with subscripts 1..N.
  Pre : Array X and N are defined and N > 0.
  Post: Displays X[1], ... , X[N−1], X[N].
}
begin {PrintNormal}
  if N = 1 then
    WriteLn (X[1])                        {stopping case}
  else
    begin {recursive step}
      PrintNormal (X, N−1);
      WriteLn (X[N])
    end  {recursive step}
end;  {PrintNormal}
```

Case Study: Printing an Array in Normal Order, continued

Testing

The trace of PrintNormal (Test, 3) is shown in Fig. 13.19. Following the colored arrows and then the black arrows results in the sequence of events listed in Fig. 13.20. This time, there are no statements that precede the recursive calls; a display operation is performed after each return.

Figure 13.19   Trace of PrintNormal (Test, 3)

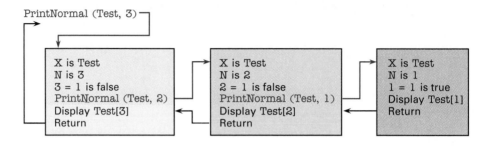

Figure 13.20   Sequence of Events for Trace of PrintNormal (Test, 3)

Call PrintNormal with parameters Test and 3.
   Call PrintNormal with parameters Test and 2.
      Call PrintNormal with parameters Test and 1.
         Print Test[1].
         Return from third call.
      Print Test[2].
      Return from second call.
   Print Test[3].
   Return from original call.

PROGRAM
STYLE

Avoiding Value Array Parameters in Recursive Procedures

X is declared as a variable parameter in procedures PrintBack and PrintNormal, even though it is used for input only. If X was a value parameter instead, each recursive call would generate a local copy of the actual array corresponding to X in each activation frame. This could result in a tremendous waste of time and memory space. For example, if X corresponds to an array with 10 elements and we want to print the entire array (N is 10), there will be 10 activation frames and storage space will be needed for 100 integer values. If N is 100, then storage space will be needed for 100×100, or 10,000, integer values.

Case Study: Recursive Selection Sort

Problem

We have discussed selection sort and implemented an iterative selection sort procedure (see Fig. 10.29). An alternative version of selection sort first finds the largest element in an array and places it where it belongs, then finds and places the next largest element, and so on. This version is a good candidate for a recursive solution.

Analysis

The selection sort algorithm follows from the preceding description. The stopping case is an array of length 1, which is sorted by definition. Review Fig. 10.29 to see how the elements of an array are placed in their final positions by a selection sort.

Design

Recursive Algorithm for Selection Sort

1. if N is 1 then
      2. The array is sorted.
   else
      begin
         3. Place the largest array element in X[N].
         4. Sort the subarray with subscripts 1..N-1.
      end

Implementation

The algorithm is implemented as a recursive procedure at the end of Fig. 13.21. Procedure PlaceLargest performs step 3 of the algorithm. The recursive procedure SelectSort is simpler to understand than the one shown in Fig. 10.29 because it contains a single if statement instead of nested for loops. The recursive procedure executes more slowly, however, because of the extra overhead due to the recursive procedure calls.

Figure 13.21 PlaceLargest and Recursive SelectSort

```
procedure PlaceLargest (var X {input/output} : IntArray;
                        N {input} : Integer);
{
  Finds the largest element in array X[1]..X[N] and exchanges
  it with the element at X[N].
  Pre : Array X and N are defined and N > 0.
  Post: X[N] contains the largest value.
}
  var
    Temp : Integer;        {temporary copy for exchange}
    J,                     {array subscript and loop control}
    MaxIndex : Integer;    {index of largest so far}
```

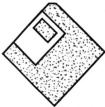

Directory: CHAP13
File: PLACELAR.PRO

Case Study: Recursive Selection Sort, continued

```
begin {PlaceLargest}
  {Save subscript of largest element in MaxIndex.}
  MaxIndex := N;                        {Assume X[N] is largest.}
  for J := N-1 downto 1 do
    if X[J] > X[MaxIndex] then
      MaxIndex := J;                    {X[J] is largest so far.}

  {assertion: MaxIndex is subscript of largest element.}
  if MaxIndex <> N then
    begin {exchange X[N] and X[MaxIndex]}
      Temp := X[N];  X[N] := X[MaxIndex];  X[MaxIndex] := Temp
    end {if}
end; {PlaceLargest}
```

Directory: CHAP13
File: SELECTSO.PRO

```
procedure SelectSort (var X {input/output} : IntArray;
                          N {input} : Integer);
{
  Sorts an array of integers (X) with subscripts 1..N.
  Pre : Array X and N are defined and N > 0.
  Post: The array elements are in numerical order.
}
begin {SelectSort}
  if N > 1 then
    begin {recursive step}
      {Place largest value in X[N] and sort subarray 1..N-1.}
      PlaceLargest (X, N);
      SelectSort (X, N-1)
    end {recursive step}
end; {SelectSort}
```

If N = 1, procedure SelectSort returns without doing anything. This behavior is correct because a one-element array is always sorted.

Exercises for Section 13.4

Self-Check

1. Trace the execution of SelectSort on an array that has the integers 5, 8, 10, and 1 stored in consecutive elements.
2. For the array in exercise 1, trace the execution of PrintNormal and PrintBack.

Programming

1. Provide an iterative procedure that is equivalent to PrintBack in Fig. 13.15.
2. Write a recursive procedure that reverses the elements in an array X[1..N]. The recursive step should shift the subarray X[2..N] down one element into the subarray X[1..N-1] (for example, X[1] gets X[2], X[2] gets X[3], ... X[N-1] gets X[N]), store the old X[1] in X[N], and then reverse the subarray X[1..N-1].

The next case study is considerably more complicated than the preceding ones. It leads to a recursive procedure that solves the Towers of Hanoi problem you encountered in Section 13.1.

Case Study: Towers of Hanoi Problem

Problem
Solve the Towers of Hanoi problem for N disks, where N is a parameter.

Analysis
The solution to the Towers of Hanoi problem consists of a printed list of individual disk moves. We need a recursive procedure that can be used to move any number of disks from one peg to another, using the third peg as an auxiliary.

Data Requirements

Problem Inputs
```
N : Integer                {number of disks to be moved}
FromPeg : 'A'..'C'         {the from peg}
ToPeg : 'A'..'C'           {the to peg}
AuxPeg : 'A'..'C'          {the auxiliary peg}
```

Problem Output
A list of individual disk moves

Design

Initial Algorithm
1. if N is 1 then
    2. Move disk 1 from the *from* peg to the *to* peg.
   else
     begin
       3. Move N–1 disks from the *from* peg to the *auxiliary* peg using the *to* peg.
       4. Move disk N from the *from* peg to the *to* peg.
       5. Move N–1 disks from the *auxiliary* peg to the *to* peg using the *from* peg.
     end

   If N is 1, a stopping case is reached. If N is greater than 1, the recursive step (following else) splits the original problem into three smaller subproblems, one of which is a stopping case. Each stopping case displays a move instruction.

Verify that the recursive step generates the three problems listed before Fig. 13.3 when N is 5, the *from* peg is A, and the *to* peg is C.

Implementation

The implementation of this algorithm is shown as procedure Tower in Fig. 13.22. Procedure Tower has four parameters. The procedure call statement

```
Tower ('A', 'C', 'B', 5)
```

solves the problem posed earlier of moving five disks from tower A to tower C using B as an auxiliary.

In Fig. 13.22, the stopping case (move disk 1) is implemented as a call to procedure WriteLn. Each recursive step consists of two recursive calls to Tower, with a call to WriteLn sandwiched between them. The first recursive call solves the problem of moving N−1 disks to the *auxiliary* peg. The call to WriteLn displays a message to move disk N to the *to* peg. The second recursive call solves the problem of moving the N−1 disks back from the *auxiliary* peg to the *to* peg.

Figure 13.22 Recursive Procedure Tower

Directory: CHAP13
File: TOWER.PRO

```
procedure Tower (FromPeg,
                 ToPeg,
                 AuxPeg {input} : Char;
                 N       {input} : Integer);
{
  Moves N disks from FromPeg to ToPeg
  using AuxPeg as an auxiliary.
  Pre : FromPeg, ToPeg, AuxPeg, and N are defined.
  Post: Displays a list of move instructions that transfer
        the disks.
}
begin  {Tower}
  if N = 1 then
    WriteLn ('Move disk 1 from peg ', FromPeg,
             ' to peg ', ToPeg)
  else
    begin {recursive step}
      Tower (FromPeg, AuxPeg, ToPeg, N−1);
      WriteLn ('Move disk ', N :1, ' from peg ', FromPeg,
               ' to peg ', ToPeg);
      Tower (AuxPeg, ToPeg, FromPeg, N−1)
    end {recursive step}
end;  {Tower}
```

Testing

The procedure call statement

```
Tower ('A', 'C', 'B', 3)
```

solves a simpler three-disk problem: move three disks from peg A to peg C. Its execution is traced in Fig. 13.23; the output generated is shown in Fig. 13.24. Verify for yourself that this list of steps does indeed solve the three-disk problem.

Figure 13.23   Trace of Tower ('A', 'C', 'B', 3)

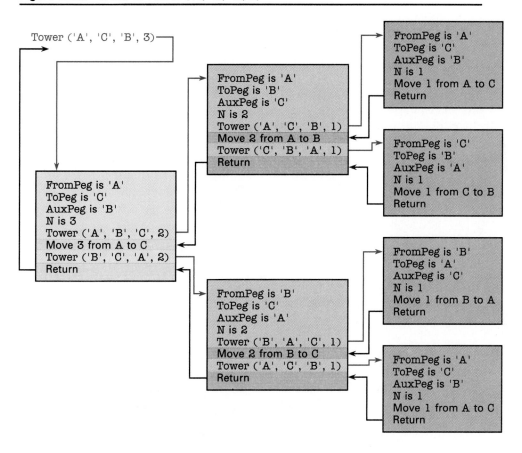

Figure 13.24   Output Generated by Tower ('A', 'C', 'B', 3)

Move disk 1 from A to C
Move disk 2 from A to B
Move disk 1 from C to B
Move disk 3 from A to C
Move disk 1 from B to A
Move disk 2 from B to C
Move disk 1 from A to C

Comparison of Iterative and Recursive Procedures

It is interesting to consider that procedure Tower in Fig. 13.22 will solve the Towers of Hanoi problem for any number of disks. The three-disk problem results in a total of seven calls to procedure Tower and is solved by seven disk moves. The five-disk problem would result in a total of 31 calls to procedure Tower and is solved in 31 moves. In general, the number of moves required to solve the n-disk problem is $2^n - 1$. Because each procedure call requires the allocation and initialization of a local data area in memory, the computer time increases exponentially with the problem size. For this reason, be careful about running the program with a value of N larger than 10.

The dramatic increase in processing time for larger towers is a function of the problem, not of recursion. In general, however, if there are recursive and iterative solutions to the same problem, the recursive solution requires more time and space because of the extra procedure calls. We discuss algorithm efficiency later.

Although recursion was not really needed to solve the simpler problems in this section, it was extremely useful in formulating an algorithm for the Towers of Hanoi. For certain problems, recursion leads naturally to solutions that are much easier to read and understand than their iterative counterparts. In those cases, the benefits gained from increased clarity far outweigh the extra cost in time and memory of running a recursive program.

Exercises for Section 13.5

Self-Check

1. How many moves are needed to solve the six-disk problem?
2. Write a main program that reads in a data value for N (the number of disks) and calls procedure Tower to move N disks from A to B.

13.6 Recursive Functions with Array Parameters

We can follow the process described in the previous sections to write recursive functions with array parameters. That process involves identifying the stopping cases of a problem. For other cases, we must be able to reduce the problem to one that is closer to a stopping case.

Case Study: Summing the Values in an Array

Problem

We want to write a recursive function that finds the sum of the values in an array X with subscripts 1..N.

Analysis

The stopping case occurs when N is 1, that is, the sum is X[1]. If N is not 1, then we must add X[N] to the sum we get when we add the values in the subarray with subscripts 1..N-1.

Data Requirements

Problem Inputs
```
X : IntArray      {array of integer values}
N : Integer       {number of elements in the array}
```

Problem Output
The sum of the array values

Design

Initial Algorithm

1. if N is 1 then
      2. The sum is X[1].
   else
   begin
      3. Add X[N] to the sum of values in the subarray with
          subscripts 1..N-1.
   end

Implementation

Function FindSum in Fig. 13.25 implements this algorithm. The result of calling FindSum for a small array (N is 3) is also shown.

Figure 13.25   Using Recursive Function FindSum

```
program TestFindSum (Input, Output);

{Tests function FindSum.}

  type
    IntArray = array [1..20] of Integer;

  var
    N : Integer;
    X : IntArray;


  function FindSum (var X : IntArray;
                        N : Integer) : Integer;
  {
    Finds the sum of the values in elements 1..N of array X.
    Pre : Array X and N are defined and N > 0.
    Post: Returns sum of first N elements of X.
  }
  begin {FindSum}
    if N = 1 then
      FindSum := X[1]
    else
```

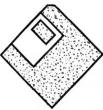

Directory: CHAP13
File: TESTFIND.PRO

```
        FindSum := X[N] + FindSum(X, N-1)
  end;  {FindSum}

begin {TestFindSum}
  N := 3;
  X[1] := 5;  X[2] := 10;  X[3] := -7;
  WriteLn ('The array sum is ', FindSum(X, 3) :3)
end. {TestFindSum}
```

```
The array sum is 8
```

Testing

Figure 13.26 shows a trace of the function call `FindSum(X, 3)`. As before, the colored part of each activation frame executes before the next recursive function call, and each colored arrow points to a new activation frame. The gray part of each activation frame executes after the return from a recursive call, and each black arrow indicates the return point (the operator +) after a function execution. The value returned is indicated alongside the arrow. The value returned for the original call, `FindSum(X, 3)`, is 8, which is printed.

Figure 13.26　Trace of FindSum(X, 3)

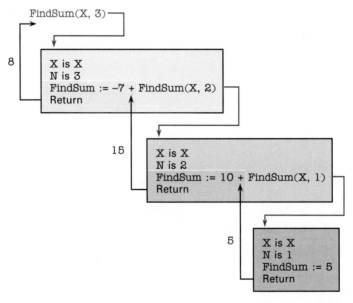

Functions that return Boolean values (`True` or `False`) can also be written recursively. These functions do not perform a computation; however, the function result is still determined by evaluating an expression (type Boolean) containing a recursive call. We will write recursive functions that search an array and compare two arrays next.

The Boolean function Member in Fig. 13.27 returns the value True if the argument Target is in the array X with subscripts 1..N; otherwise, it returns the value False. If N is 1 (the stopping case), the result is determined by comparing X[1] and Target. If N is not 1 (the recursive step), then the result is true if either X[N] is Target or Target occurs in the subarray with subscripts 1..N–1. The recursive step is implemented as the assignment statement

```
Member := (X[N] = Target) or Member(X, Target, N-1)
```

in Fig. 13.27.

Figure 13.27 Recursive Function Member

```
function Member (var X : IntArray;
                     Target,
                     N        : Integer) : Boolean;
{
  Searches for Target in array X with subscripts 1..N.
  Pre : Target, N, and array X are defined and N > 0.
  Post: Returns True if Target is located in array X; otherwise,
        returns False.
}
begin {Member}
  if N = 1 then
    Member := (X[1] = Target)
  else
    Member := (X[N] = Target) or Member(X, Target, N-1)
end; {Member}
```

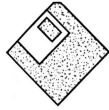

Directory: CHAP13
File: MEMBER.FUN

The function designator Member(X, 10, 3) is traced in Fig. 13.28 for the array X defined in Fig. 13.25. The value returned is True, because the expression X[N] = Target is true when N is 2 (the second activation frame). ■

■ **Example 13.8**

The Boolean function Equal returns the value True if two arrays, say X and Y, of N elements are the same (e.g., X[1] = Y[1], X[2] = Y[2],..., X[N] = Y[N]). This function (see Fig. 13.29) looks similar to function Member. For the stopping case, single-element arrays, the function result depends on whether X[1] = Y[1]. For larger arrays, the result is True if X[N] = Y[N] and the subarrays with subscripts 1..N–1 are equal. ■

Comparison of Iterative and Recursive Functions

Consider the iterative version of function Member shown in Fig. 13.30. A for loop is needed to examine each array element. Without recursion, it is not possible to use the function name in an expression, so a local variable, Found, is needed to represent the result so far. Before returning from the function, the final value of Found is assigned as the function result.

Figure 13.28 Trace of Function Member

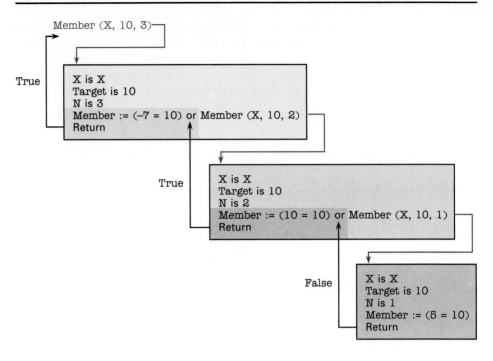

Figure 13.29 Recursive Function Equal

Directory: CHAP13
File: EQUAL.FUN

```
function Equal (var X, Y : IntArray;
               N : Integer) : Boolean;
{
   Compares arrays X and Y with elements 1..N.
   Pre : Arrays X and Y are defined and N > 0.
   Post: Returns True if arrays X and Y are equal; otherwise,
         returns False.
}
begin {Equal}
  if N = 1 then
     Equal := X[1] = Y[1]
  else
     Equal := (X[N] = Y[N]) and Equal(X, Y, N-1)
end;  {Equal}
```

Figure 13.30 Iterative Function Member

```
function Member (var X : IntArray;
                 Target,
                 N       : Integer) : Boolean;
{
   Compares arrays X and Y with elements 1..N.
   Pre : Arrays X and Y are defined and N > 0.
   Post: Returns True if arrays X and Y are equal; otherwise,
         returns False.
```

```
        }
     var
        Found : Boolean;            {local flag}
        I : Integer;                {loop-control variable}

    begin {Member}
       Found := False;              {Assume Target not found.}
       {Search array X for Target.}
       for I := 1 to N do
         Found := Found or (X[I] = Target);

       Member := Found             {Define result.}
    end;  {Member}
```

Directory: CHAP13
File: MEMBERIT.FUN

This is a little different from the iterative array search shown in Chapter 10 (see Fig. 10.27). We could make it more efficient by using a `while` loop and exiting from the loop when Found becomes True; however, the version shown in Fig. 13.30 would still execute faster than the recursive version.

Many programmers would argue that the recursive version is esthetically more pleasing. It is certainly more compact (a single `if` statement) and requires no local variables. Once you are accustomed to thinking recursively, the recursive form is somewhat easier to read and understand than the iterative form.

Some programmers like to use recursion as a conceptual tool. Once they have written the recursive form of a function or procedure, they can always translate it into an iterative version if run-time efficiency is a major concern.

Exercises for Section 13.6

Self-Check

1. Trace the execution of recursive function Equal for the three-element arrays X (element values 1, 15, 10) and Y (element values 1, 5, 7). Write out completely in one equivalent Boolean expression the values that function Equal is assigned through all three recursive calls for array X. Spell out all the values that are being compared.
2. Answer exercise 1 for the recursive function Member and array X.
3. What does the following recursive function do? Trace its execution on array X in exercise 1.

```
    function Mystery (X : IntArray;
                      N : Integer) : Integer;
       var
          Temp : Integer;
    begin {Mystery}
       if N = 1 then
         Mystery := X[1]
       else
         begin
           Temp := Mystery(X, N-1);
           if X[N] > Temp then
             Mystery := X[N]
           else
             Mystery := Temp
         end {if}
    end; {Mystery}
```

Programming

1. Write a recursive function that finds the product of the elements in an array X of N elements.
2. Write a recursive function that finds the index of the smallest element in an array.

13.7 Picture Processing with Recursion

Case Study: Counting Cells in a Blob

This problem illustrates the power of recursion. The problem would be much more difficult without using recursion, but its solution is relatively easy to write recursively.

Problem

We have a two-dimensional grid of cells, each of which may be empty or filled. The filled cells that are connected form a blob. There may be several blobs on the grid. We want a function that accepts as input the coordinates of a particular cell and returns the size of the blob containing that cell.

There are three blobs in the sample grid in Fig. 13.31. If the function parameters represent the X and Y coordinates of a cell, the result of BlobCount (3, 4) is 5; the result of BlobCount(1, 2) is 2; the result of BlobCount(5, 5) is 0; the result of BlobCount(5, 1) is 4.

Figure 13.31 Grid with Three Blobs

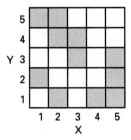

Analysis

Function BlobCount must test the cell specified by its arguments to see if it is filled. There are two stopping cases; the cell (X, Y) is not on the grid, or the cell (X, Y) is empty; in either case, the value returned by BlobCount is 0. If the cell is on the grid and is filled, the value returned is 1 plus the size of the blobs containing each of its neighbors. To avoid counting a filled cell more than once, we mark it as empty once we have visited it.

Data Requirements

Problem Inputs
```
Grid : BlobArray        {the grid}
X, Y : Integer          {X and Y coordinates of the point being visited}
```

Problem Output
The number of the cells in the blob containing point (X, Y)

Design

Algorithm
1. if cell (X, Y) is not in the array then
      2. Return a count of 0.
  else if cell (X, Y) is empty then
      3. Return a count of 0.
  else
    begin
      4. Mark cell (X, Y) as empty.
      5. Add 1 and see whether the blob contains any of
           the eight neighbors of cell (X, Y).
    end

Implementation
Function `BlobCount` is shown in Fig. 13.32. The array type `BlobArray` has element value `Filled` or `Empty`. The following declarations must precede function `BlobCount`. The constants `MaxX` and `MaxY` represent the largest X and Y coordinate, respectively.

```
const
  MaxX = 100;
  MaxY = 100;

type
  RowIndex = 1..MaxX;
  ColIndex = 1..MaxY;
  BlobArray = array [RowIndex ColIndex] of (Filled, Empty);
```

Figure 13.32 Functions BlobCount and StartBlob

```
function BlobCount (var Grid {input/output} : BlobArray;
                        X, Y : Integer) : Integer;
{
 Performs counting operation for StartBlob.
 Pre : Array Grid and point (X, Y) are defined.
 Post: Returns the size of the blob containing the point (X, Y).
       Resets the status of each cell in the blob to Empty.
```

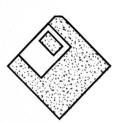

Directory: CHAP13
File: BLOBCOUN.FUN

```
}
begin {BlobCount}
   if (X < 1) or (X > MaxX) or (Y < 1) or (Y > MaxY) then
      BlobCount := 0                    {Cell not in grid.}
   else if Grid[X, Y] = Empty then
      BlobCount :- 0                     {Cell is empty.}
   else {cell is filled}
      begin {recursive step}
         Grid[X, Y] := Empty;
         BlobCount := 1 + BlobCount(Grid, X-1, Y+1) + BlobCount(Grid, X, Y+1) +
               BlobCount(Grid, X+1, Y+1) + BlobCount(Grid, X+1, Y) +
               BlobCount(Grid, X+1, Y-1) + BlobCount(Grid, X, Y-1) +
               BlobCount(Grid, X-1, Y-1) + BlobCount(Grid, X-1, Y)
      end {recursive step}
end; {BlobCount}


function StartBlob (Grid : BlobArray:
                    X, Y : Integer) : Integer;
{
   Counts the number of filled cells in the blob containing
   point (X, Y).
   Pre : Array Grid and point (X, Y) are defined.
   Post: Returns the size of the blob containing the point (X, Y).
   Uses: BlobCount to perform the counting operation.
}
begin {StartBlob}
   {Call BlobCount and return its result.}
   StartBlob := BlobCount(Grid, X, Y)
end; {StartBlob}
```

Function `BlobCount` in Fig. 13.32 implements the counting algorithm; function `StartBlob` simply calls the recursive function `BlobCount`, passes on its arguments, and returns the count computed by function `BlobCount` as its own result. The reason we use two functions instead of one is to protect the actual array from being modified when filled cells are reset to empty by function `BlobCount`. We will come back to this point shortly.

If the cell being visited is off the grid or is empty, `BlobCount` returns a value of zero immediately. Otherwise, the recursive step executes, causing function `BlobCount` to call itself eight times; each time, a different neighbor of the current cell is visited. The cells are visited in a clockwise manner, starting with the neighbor above and to the left. The function result is the sum of all values returned from these recursive calls plus 1 (for the current cell).

The sequence of operations performed in function `BlobCount` is important. The `if` statement tests whether the cell (X, Y) is on the grid before testing whether (X, Y) is empty. If the order was reversed, an `index out of bounds` run-time error would occur whenever (X, Y) was off the grid.

Also, the recursive step resets `Grid[X, Y]` to `Empty` before visting the neighbors of point (X, Y). If this was not done first, then cell (X, Y) would be counted more than once, because it is a neighbor of all its neighbors. A worse problem is that the recursion would not terminate. When each neighbor of the current cell is visited, `BlobCount` is called again with the coordinates of the current cell as arguments. If the current cell is `Empty`, an immediate return occurs. If the current cell was still `Filled`, the recursive step would be executed erroneously. Eventually the program would run out of time or memory space (the latter is often indicated by a `stack overflow` run-time error).

A side effect of the execution of function `BlobCount` is that all cells that are part of the blob being processed are reset to `Empty`. This is the reason for using two functions. Because the array is passed as a value parameter to function `StartBlob`, a local copy is saved when `StartBlob` is called. Only this local array, not the actual array, is changed by function `BlobCount`. If the counting operation was performed in function `StartBlob` instead of function `BlobCount`, eight copies of this array would be made each time the recursive step was executed, and we would soon run out of memory.

Exercises for Section 13.7

Self-Check

1. Trace the execution of function `BlobCount` for the coordinate pairs (1, 1) and (1, 2) in the sample grid.
2. Is the order of the two tests performed in function `BlobCount` critical? What happens if we reverse them or combine them into a single condition?

Programming

1. Write the recursive function `FindMin` that finds the smallest value in an integer array X with subscripts 1..N.

13.8 Common Programming Errors

The most common problem with a recursive procedure is that it may not terminate properly. For example, if the terminating condition is not correct or is incomplete, then the procedure may call itself indefinitely or until all available memory is used up. Normally, a `stack overflow` run-time error indicates that a recursive procedure is not terminating. Make sure you identify all stopping cases and provide a terminating condition for each one. Also be sure that each recursive step leads to a situation that is closer to a stopping case and that repeated recursive calls eventually lead to stopping cases only.

The use of large arrays or other data structures as value parameters can quickly consume all available memory. Unless absolutely essential for data protection, arrays should be passed as variable parameters. Any expression such as N-1 must be passed as a value parameter.

Sometimes it is difficult to observe the result of a recursive procedure execution. If each recursive call generates a large number of output lines and there are many recursive calls, the output will scroll down the screen more quickly than you can read it. On most systems, it is possible to stop the screen temporarily by pressing a control character sequence (for example, control-S). If this cannot be done on your system, you can cause your output to stop temporarily by printing a prompting message followed by a Read (NextChar) operation. Your program then resumes execution when you enter a data character.

CHAPTER REVIEW

This chapter provides several examples of recursive procedures and functions. Studying them should give you some appreciation of the power of recursion as a problem-solving and programming tool and provide you with valuable insight regarding its use. It may take you some time to feel comfortable thinking in this new way, but it is certainly worth the effort.

✓ Quick-Check Exercises

1. Explain the use of a stack in recursion.
2. Which is generally more efficient, recursion or iteration?
3. Which control statement is always in a recursive procedure or function?
4. What are the two uses of the function name in a recursive function?
5. How many times does the function name appear in a recursive function? In a recursive procedure?
6. Why would a programmer use recursion to conceptualize a problem solution but use iteration to implement it?
7. What is the problem with value array parameters in recursion?
8. In a recursive problem involving N items, why must N be a value parameter?
9. What causes a stack overflow error?
10. What can you say about a recursive algorithm that has the following form?

   if *condition* then
       Perform recursive step.

Answers to Quick-Check Exercises
1. The stack is used to hold all parameter and local variable values and the return point for each execution of a recursive procedure.
2. iteration
3. if statement
4. to assign a value to the function and to call it recursively.
5. At least three or more times in a function: once to assign a value for the stopping case, once to assign a value for the recursive step, and once to call the function

recursively. There may be more than one recursive call, as in function Fibonacci. At least once in a procedure.

6. when its solution is much easier to conceptualize using recursion but its implementation would be too inefficient
7. A copy of the array must be pushed onto the stack each time a call occurs. All available stack memory could be exhausted.
8. If N was a variable parameter, it would not be possible to use the expression N–1 as an actual parameter in a recursive call.
9. too many recursive calls
10. Nothing is done when the stopping case is reached.

Review Questions

1. Explain the nature of a recursive problem.
2. Discuss the efficiency of recursive procedures.
3. Differentiate between stopping cases and a terminating condition.
4. Write a recursive procedure that prints the accumulating sum of ordinal values corresponding to each character in a packed array. For example, if the string value is 'a boy', the first value printed would be the ordinal number of a, then the sum of ordinals for a and the space character, then the sum of ordinals for a, space, b, and so on.
5. Write a recursive function that returns the sum of ordinal values corresponding to the string stored in a packed array of characters; however, this time exclude any space characters from the sum.
6. Convert the following program from an iterative process to a recursive function that calculates an approximate value for e, the base of the natural logarithms, by summing the series

$$1 + 1/1! + 1/2! + ...1/N!$$

until additional terms do not affect the approximation.

```
program ELog (Output);

  var
    ENL, Delta, Fact : Real;
    N : Integer;

begin {ELog}
  ENL := 1.0;
  N := 1;
  Fact := 1.0;
  Delta := 1.0;
  repeat
    ENL := ENL + Delta;
    N := N + 1;
    Fact := Fact * N;
    Delta := 1.0 / Fact;
  until ENL = (ENL + Delta);
  Write ('The value of e is ', E :18:15)
end. {ELog}
```

7. Write a recursive function that returns the actual length of a character string stored left-justified in a packed array. Exclude any blank padding from the length returned.

Programming Projects

1. Write a procedure that reads each row of an array as a string and converts it to a row of Grid (see Fig. 13.31). The first character in row 1 corresponds to Grid[1,1], the second character to Grid[1,2], and so on. Set the element value to Empty if the character is blank; otherwise, set it to Filled. The number of rows in the array should be read first. Use this procedure in a program that reads in cell coordinates and prints the number of cells in the blob containing each coordinate pair.

2. The expression for computing $C(n,r)$, the number of combinations of n items taken r at a time is

$$c(n,r) = \frac{n!}{r!(n-r)!}$$

Write and test a function for computing $c(n,r)$, given that $n!$ is the factorial of n.

3. A palindrome is a word that is spelled exactly the same when the letters are reversed, for example, level, deed, and mom. Write a recursive function that returns the Boolean value True if a word, passed as a parameter, is a palindrome.

4. Write a recursive function that returns the value of the following recursive definition:

```
F(X,Y) = X - Y, if X or Y < 0
F(X,Y) = F(X-1,Y) + F(X,Y-1), otherwise
```

5. Write a recursive procedure that lists all the pairs of subsets for a given set of letters. For example:

```
['A', 'C', 'E', 'G',] => ['A', 'C'], ['A', 'E'], ['A', 'G'],
                         ['C', 'E'], ['C', 'G'], ['E', 'G']
```

6. Write a procedure that accepts an 8-by-8 array of characters that represent a maze. Each position can contain either an 'X' or a blank. Starting at position [1,1], list any path through the maze to get to location [8,8]. Only horizontal and vertical moves are allowed (no diagonal moves). If no path exists, write a message indicating this.

   Moves can be made only to locations that contain a blank. If an 'X' is encountered, that path is blocked and another must be chosen. Use recursion.

7. Programming project 6 in Chapter 7 described the bisection method, which finds an approximate root for the equation f(X) = 0 on the interval XLeft to XRight, inclusive (assuming the function is continuous on this interval). The interval endpoints (XLeft and XRight) and the tolerance for the approximation (Epsilon) are input by the user.

   One stopping criterion for the bisection method is the identification of an interval [XLeft, XRight] that is less than Epsilon in length over which f(X) changes sign (from positive to negative or vice versa). The midpoint [XMid = (XLeft + XRight)/2.0)] of the interval will be an approximation to the root of the equation when f(XMid) is very close to zero. Of course, if you find a value of XMid such that f(XMid) = 0, you have found a very good approximation of the root, and the algorithm should also stop.

   To perform the recursive step, replace either XLeft or XRight with XMid, depending on which one has the same sign as XMid. Write a program that uses the bisection method to determine an approximation to the equation

$$5x^3 - 2x^2 + 3 = 0$$

over the interval [-1, 1] using Epsilon = 0.0001.

8. The Eight Queens problem is a famous chess problem that has as its goal the placement of eight queens on a single chessboard so that no queen will be able to attack any other queen. A queen may move any number of squares vertically, horizontally, or diagonally. A chessboard can be represented by a two-dimensional array with eight rows and eight columns. Write a program that contains a recursive routine that solves the Eight Queens problem.

Hint: Arbitrarily choose a location for the first queen, then attempt to place a second queen in the next available open row. This process continues as long as it is possible to place queens. If a dead end is reached, the last-placed queen is removed from the board and repositioned. To do this, the algorithm would need to backtrack to a previous activation of the recursive routine and attempt to place the queen in a different location.

14
Sets and Strings

In this chapter, we complete the study of the set data type. We first looked at sets in Chapter 7; since then, we have used sets and the set membership operator in to simplify conditions. In this chapter, you will learn how to perform the operations of set union, set intersection, and set difference in Pascal and how to test for subsets, supersets, and set equality. These operations make it easier to use sets in programming.

Variable-length strings are the second topic covered in this chapter. Strings are used in programs that process textual data (for example, word processors, text editors, and business data-processing applications). The string data type is in many programming languages, but it is missing in standard Pascal. In standard Pascal, we store fixed-length strings in packed arrays of characters, and we can only display and compare strings.

A data type for variable-length strings, together with several string operators, is an extension found in many Pascal compilers. We will design and implement our own string data type whose operators are based on those commonly found in Pascal compilers. If your version of Pascal supports variable-length strings, you may want to skip Section 14.5, which implements the string operators.

14.1 Set Data Type

Chapter 7 discussed set values in conditional statements. Until now, we have used the set membership operator in only with set values. This section examines the other set operators and shows you how to declare and manipulate set variables.

■ Example 14.1

The following statements define a set type Digit and two set variables, Odds and Evens. Each set variable of type Digit can contain between zero and 10 elements chosen from the integers in the subrange 0..9. The set variables Odds and Evens represent the set of odd digits and even digits in the range 0 through 9. ■

```
type
    Digit = set of 0..9;

var
    Odds, Evens : Digit;

begin
    Odds := [1, 3, 5, 7, 9];
    Evens := [0, 2, 4, 6, 8];
```

The set type declaration is described in the following display.

Set Type Declaration

Form: `type`
              set type = `set of` *base type*;

Example: `type`
              `Uppercase = set of 'A'..'Z';`

Interpretation: The identifier *set type* is defined over the values specified in *base type*. A variable declared to be of type *set type* is a set whose elements are chosen from the values in *base type*. The *base type* must be an ordinal type.

Notes: Most implementations impose a limit on the number of values in the *base type* of a set. In many implementations, this limit is the same as the number of values in the data type `Char` (64, 128, or 256). This allows you to declare `set of Char` as a set type. Given this limitation, you may not use the data type `Integer` as a *base type*; however, a suitable subrange of type `Integer` is allowed.

Set Assignment, Empty Set, and Universal Set

You can modify an existing set by using the set operators discussed in the next section. Before you can manipulate a set, however, you must define its initial elements with a set assignment statement, as shown in the next example.

■ Example 14.2

The following statements specify three set variables defined over the base type `Cars`.

```
type
   Cars = (Dodge, Ford, Lincoln, Cadillac, Fiesta, Pontiac,
           Corvette, Buick, Chevrolet, Mercury, Mustang);
   CarSet = set of Cars;

var
   Avis, Hertz, Merger : CarSet;

begin
   Avis := [Dodge, Lincoln, Fiesta];
   Hertz := [Dodge..Cadillac, Mercury];
```

Each assignment statement consists of a set variable on the left and a set value on the right. A pair of brackets and a list of values from the base type of the set being defined indicate a set value. As shown in the assignment statement for `Hertz`, a list of consecutive values can be denoted as a subrange (see Section 7.6). The set `Avis` consists the three elements listed; the set `Hertz` consists of five elements (what are they?).

It is also possible to have a set variable on the right of the assignment statement, provided both set variables have compatible base types. The value of the set variable on the right would be assigned to the set variable on the left.

```
Merger := Hertz;
```

Often, we want to denote that a set is empty or has no elements. An *empty set* is indicated by an empty pair of brackets([ ]).

```
Merger := [];
```

A set variable must always be initialized before it can be used with any of the set operators. A set variable often is initialized to the empty set or to the *universal set*, which is the set that consists of all values of the base type. For instance, the universal set for a set of type CarSet would be denoted as [Dodge..Mustang]. ∎

The set-assignment statement is shown in the following display. As the display indicates, it is possible to write set expressions that involve set manipulation operators. These operators are described in the next section.

Set Assignment

Form: *set var* := *set expression*

Example: Uppercase := ['A'..'Z']   {set of uppercase letters}

Interpretation: The variable, *set var,* is defined as the set whose elements are determined by the value of *set expression*. The *set expression* may be a set value or another set variable. Alternatively, a *set expression* may specify the manipulation of two or more sets using the set operators. The base type of *set var* and *set expression* must be type compatible, and all the elements in *set expression* must be included in the base type of *set var*.

Set Union, Intersection, and Difference

The set operators union, intersection, and difference require as operands two sets of the same type. The *union* of two sets (set operator +) is the set of elements that are contained in either set or both sets.

```
[1,3,4] + [1,2,4] is [1,2,3,4]
[1,3] + [2,4] is [1,2,3,4]
['A','C','F'] + ['B','C','D','F'] is ['A','B','C','D','F']
['A','C','F'] + ['A','C','D','F'] is ['A','C','D','F']
Avis + Hertz is [Dodge, Ford, Lincoln, Cadillac, Fiesta, Mercury]
```

The *intersection* of two sets (set operator *) is the set of all elements that are common to both sets.

```
[1,3,4] * [1,2,4] is [1,4]
[1,3] * [2,4] is []
['A','C','F'] * ['B','C','D','F'] is ['C','F']
['A','C','F'] * ['A','C','D','F'] is ['A','C','F']
Avis * Hertz is [Dodge, Lincoln]
```

The *difference* of set A and set B (set operator –) is the set of elements that are in set A but not in set B.

```
[1,3,4] - [1,2,4] is [3]
[1,3] - [2,4] is [1,3]
['A','C','F'] - ['B','C','D','F'] is ['A']
['A','C','F'] - ['A','C','D','F'] is []
['A','C','D','F'] - ['A','C','F'] is ['D']
Avis - Hertz is [Fiesta]
Hertz - Avis is [Ford, Cadillac, Mercury]
```

The set operator – is not *commutative*. This means that A – B and B – A can have different values. The set operators + and *, however, are commutative.

The operators +, *, and – are treated as set operators when their operands are sets. The compiler determines which operation is intended from its context (this is called *operator overloading*). You can use these operators to combine two sets to form a third set. If more than one set operator appears in an expression, the normal precedence rules for the operators +, *, and – apply (see Table 4.5). When in doubt, use parentheses to specify the intended order of evaluation.

Often, we need to insert a new element into an existing set. You perform the insertion by forming the union of the existing set and the *unit set,* which contains only the new element. The set [2], which follows, is a unit set.

```
[1,3,4,5] + [2] is [1,2,3,4,5]
```

It makes no difference how many times we insert an element into a set:

```
[1,2,3,4,5] + [2] is [1,2,3,4,5]
```

Avoid the common error of omitting the brackets around a unit set. For example, the expressions

```
[1,3,4,5] + 2
Avis + Cadillac
```

are invalid because one operand is a set and the other is a constant. The correct forms of these expressions follow.

```
[1,3,4,5] + [2]
Avis + [Cadillac]
```

Likewise, the expression

```
[Avis] + [Cadillac]
```

is invalid; the brackets around Avis are not needed because Avis is a set.

■ Example 14.3

Procedure BuildSets in Fig. 14.1 returns a set of odd numbers (Odds) and a set of even numbers (Evens) in the range 0 to MaxNum. Procedure BuildSets uses the set operators + (union) and – (difference). Given the declarations

```
const
  MaxNum = 60;
```

```
type
   IntSet = set of 0..MaxNum;

var
   OneSet, TwoSet : IntSet;
```

the procedure call statement

```
BuildSets (OneSet, TwoSet)
```

stores the set [1, 3, 5, ... , 57, 59] in OneSet and the set [0, 2, 4, 6, ... , 58, 60] in TwoSet. ∎

Figure 14.1 Procedure BuildSets

Directory: CHAP14
File: BUILDSET.PRO

```
procedure BuildSets (var Odds, Evens {output} : IntSet);
{
  Builds a set of odd integers (Odds) and a set of even
  integers (Evens) in the range 0 to MaxNum.
  Pre : None
  Post: Odds contains the odd integers <= MaxNum and
        Evens contains the even integers <= MaxNum.
}
  var
    I : Integer;                     {loop-control variable}

begin  {BuildSets}
  Odds := [];                 {Initialize Odds to the empty set.}

  {Build a set of odd integers.}
  I := 1;                 {Initialize I to first odd integer.}
  while I <= MaxNum do
    {invariant:
        All prior values of I are <= MaxNum and
        Odds contains each prior value of I that is an odd number.
    }
    begin
      Odds := Odds + [I];       {union next odd integer to Odds}
      I := I + 2                 {get next odd integer}
    end; {while}

  {assertion:
      I is greater than MaxNum and Odds contains all
      odd numbers <= MaxNum.
  }
  {Define set Evens.}
  Evens := [0..MaxNum] - Odds
end;   {BuildSets}
```

Set Relational Operators

You can also compare sets through the use of the relational operators =, <>, <=, and >=. Both operands of a set relational operator must have the same base type. The operators = and <> test whether two sets contain the same elements.

```
[1,3] = [1,3] is   True       [1,3] <> [1,3] is False
[1,3] = [2,4] is False        [1,3] <> [2,4] is True
[1,3] = [3,1] is   True       [1,3] <> [3,1] is False
[]    = [1] is False          []    <> [1] is True
```

As indicated by the next-to-last line, the order in which the elements of a set are listed is not important ([1,3] and [3,1] denote the same set). However, we normally list the elements of a set in increasing ordinal sequence.

Other relational operators determine subset and superset relationships.

- Set A is a *subset* of set B (A <= B) if every element of A is also an element of B.

```
[1,3]       <= [1,2,3,4] is True
[1,3]       <= [1,3]     is True
[1,2,3,4] <= [1,3]       is False
[1,3]       <= []        is False
[]          <= [1,3]     is True
```

As indicated in the last line, the empty set, [ ], is a subset of every set.

- Set A is a *superset* of set B (A >= B) if every element of B is also an element of A.

```
[1,3]       >= [1,2,3,4] is False
[1,3]       >= [1,3]     is True
[1,2,3,4] >= [1,3]       is True
[1,3]       >= []        is True
[]          >= [1,3]     is False
```

The set relations A >= B and B <= A are equivalent for any two sets A and B.

The set operators are summarized in Table 14.1.

Table 14.1 Set Operators

Operator	Meaning	Example
+	Set union	['A'] + ['B'] is ['A', 'B']
−	Set difference	['A', 'B'] − ['A'] is ['B']
*	Set intersection	['A', 'B'] * ['A'] is ['A']
=	Set equality	['A', 'B'] = ['B', 'A'] is True
<>	Set inequality	['A', 'B'] <> ['A'] is True
<=	Subset	['A', 'B'] <= ['A'] is False
>=	Superset	['A', 'B'] >= ['B'] is True

Reading and Writing Sets

Like most other data structures, a set cannot be a parameter of the standard Read or Write procedures. Data items to be stored in a set must be read individually and inserted in an initially empty set using the set union operator.

■ **Example 14.4**

Procedure ReadSet in Fig. 14.2 reads a sequence of uppercase letters terminated by * and inserts them in the set represented by parameter Letters (set type LetterSet). Given the declarations

```
type
   LetterSet = set of 'A'..'Z';

var
   MyLetters : LetterSet;
```

you could use the procedure call statement

```
ReadSet (MyLetters)
```

to enter data in the set MyLetters.   ■

Figure 14.2 Procedure ReadSet

Directory: CHAP14
File: READSET.PRO

```
procedure ReadSet (var Letters {output} : LetterSet);
{
  Reads a set of uppercase letters terminated by *
  and stores them in Letters.
  Pre : None
  Post: Returns through Letters all the uppercase letters read
        before the character *.
}
  const
    Sentinel = '*';                              {sentinel character}

  var
    NextChar : Char;                             {next input character}

begin  {ReadSet}
  Letters := [];                                 {Initialize Letters.}
  Write ('Enter a set of uppercase letters');
  WriteLn (' ending with the symbol ', Sentinel);
  Read (NextChar);                               {Read first data item.}
  while NextChar <> Sentinel do
    {invariant:
       No prior value of NextChar is the sentinel and
       Letters contains each uppercase letter read so far.
    }
    begin
      if NextChar in ['A'..'Z'] then
        Letters := Letters + [NextChar];    {Insert next letter.}
      Read (NextChar)                          {Read next character.}
    end  {while}

  {assert: Last character read was the sentinel.}
end;  {ReadSet}
```

To print a set, you need to test every value in the base type to see whether it is a set element. Only values that are set elements should be printed.

Procedure `PrintSet` in Fig. 14.3 prints the uppercase letters in the set represented by its parameter `Letters`.

■

Figure 14.3 Procedure PrintSet

```
procedure PrintSet (Letters {input} : LetterSet);
{
  Prints the uppercase letters in set Letters.
  Pre : Letters is defined.
  Post: Each uppercase letter in Letters is displayed.
}
  var
    NextLetter : 'A'..'Z';             {loop-control variable}

begin {PrintSet}
  for NextLetter := 'A' to 'Z' do
    if NextLetter in Letters then
      Write (NextLetter)               {Print a set member.}
end;  {PrintSet}
```

Directory: CHAP14
File: PRINTSET.PRO

Exercises for Section 14.1

Self-Check

1. Given that `A` is the set `[1,3,5,7]`, `B` is the set `[2,4,6]`, and `C` is the set
`[1,2,3]`, evaluate the following set expressions.

    a. `A + (B - C)`   g. `C + (A - C)`
    b. `A + (B * C)`   h. `C - (A - B)`
    c. `A + B + C`   i. `(C - A) - B`
    d. `(C - A) <= B`   j. `(B + C) = (A + C)`
    e. `[] <= A * B * C`   k. `A - C - [5,7] = []`
    f. `A + B <> [1..7]`   l. `A + B >= [1..7]`

Programming

1. Modify `PrintSet` to print a set of type `Digit`.

14.2 Sets in Computer Graphics

In picture processing, we want to write programs that can find and analyze
patterns of characters that appear in a picture that is displayed on a screen.
Each screen position is called a *pixel*, or picture element. A pixel has a grey level
associated with it that determines whether it is considered dark or light.

One approach to representing the screen is to store it as a two-dimensional
array of pixel values; another approach is to store it as an array of sets. In the
latter representation, each array element is the set of darkened pixels for a line,
and there is one set for each line of the screen.

Figure 14.4 shows a section (called a *window*) of a monitor screen. There is a diagonal line on the left and a vertical bar on the right.

The type declarations for a picture displayed on a screen window consisting of 10 rows and 20 columns follow.

```
const
   ScreenHeight = 10;        {# of rows}
   ScreenWidth = 20;         {# of columns}

type
   PixelValue = (Dark, Light);
   HeightIndex = 1..ScreenHeight;
   Line = set of 1..ScreenWidth;
   Screen = array [HeightIndex] of Line;

var
   Picture : Screen;
```

For the picture in Fig. 14.4, Picture[1] represents the set of darkened elements in the first line and is the set [1, 2, 18, 19, 20]. Picture[2] is the set [2, 3, 18, 19, 20], and Picture[3] is the set [3, 4, 18, 19, 20]. The intersection of these three sets is [18, 19, 20]. This implies that there is a vertical bar on the right. The union of these three sets is [1, 2, 3, 4, 18, 19, 20]. This implies that there is a diagonal bar on the left as well as a vertical bar on the right.

Figure 14.4   Monitor Screen with Window

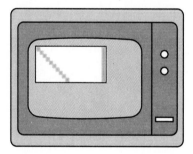

■ Example 14.6

Procedure SetPicture (Fig. 14.5) is called by a picture-processing program to define array Picture. For each pixel, the procedure reads an integer value that represents the grey level (darkness) of that pixel. If the grey level value is greater than Threshold (a parameter), that pixel is inserted in the appropriate set of darkened pixels. As an example, if the value passed to Threshold is 6, the dialogue that follows defines Picture[1] as [1, 2, 18, 19, 20].   ■

```
Enter the grey level (0 – 9) for row 1
Enter 20 values starting with column 1.
7 8 6 5 4 3 3 4 3 4 5 3 4 4 5 5 6 7 8 9
```

Figure 14.5   Procedure SetPicture

629

14.2 Sets in
Computer Graphics

```
procedure SetPicture (Threshold {input} : Integer;
                          var Picture {output} : Screen);
{
  Defines the array Picture representing a computer image by
  reading in the grey level value for each pixel.
  Pre : Threshold is defined.
  Post: Picture[i] is the set of columns in row i with
        grey level value greater than Threshold
        (1 <= i <= ScreenHeight).
}
  var
    Row : HeightIndex;
    Column : 1..ScreenWidth;
    GreyLevel : 0..9;

begin {SetPicture}
  {Define array Picture.}
  for Row := 1 to ScreenHeight do
    begin
      WriteLn ('Enter the grey level (0 − 9) for row ', Row :1);
      Write ('Enter ', ScreenWidth :1);
      WriteLn (' values starting with column 1.');
      Picture[Row] := [];                    {Initialize row set.}
      for Column := 1 to ScreenWidth do
        begin
          Read (GreyLevel);
          if GreyLevel > Threshold then
            Picture[Row] := Picture[Row] + [Column]
        end; {for Column}
      ReadLn;
      WriteLn
    end {for Row}
end; {SetPicture}
```

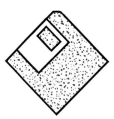

Directory: CHAP14
File: SETPICTU.PRO

Exercises for Section 14.2

Self-Check

1. What is the purpose of the ReadLn and WriteLn statements in procedure SetPicture?
2. Assuming MyPic is type Screen, what is the value of MyPic[1] for the procedure call statement

   SetPicture (5, MyPic)

   when the first data line is: 3 4 5 6 7 8 9 8 7 6 5 4 9 8 7 3 4 9 7 5?

Programming

1. Write procedure ShowPicture that displays the picture on a screen by writing the character @ in each pixel that is considered dark.

14.3 Variable-Length Strings

Many computer applications are concerned with the manipulation of character strings or textual data rather than numerical data. For example, a word processor was used in writing this text; computerized typesetters are used extensively in the publishing of books and newspapers; "personalized" junk mail is computer generated; and computers are used to analyze great works of literature. Basically, a Pascal program is a sequence of words and symbols that are interpreted by a compiler.

If you have ever used a word processor, you are familiar with the kinds of operations we might want to perform on string data. For example, we frequently want to insert one or more characters into an existing string, delete a portion of a string (called a *substring*), overwrite or replace one substring of a string with another, search for a target substring, or join two strings together to form a longer string.

Although standard Pascal does not directly support string manipulation, many extensions to Pascal provide special operators for string manipulation. In this section and sections 14.4–14.5, we discuss an ADT written in standard Pascal which encapsulates string operators that are similar to those found in Pascal extensions.

Fixed-Length and Variable-Length Strings

An important characteristic of a string is its length. Standard Pascal allows us to store fixed-length strings in packed arrays of characters. If S is a variable whose type is packed array [1..n] of Char, there must always be exactly n characters stored in S. If we want to store a shorter string in S, we must pad it with blanks; those extra blank characters are treated as part of the string. This means that the blank characters will appear when we display a fixed-length string or when we join one fixed-length string to another.

To use strings effectively, the length of a string should be *variable* and should depend on its contents. This length must be between zero and some predefined maximum (the string *capacity*). An abstract data type for variable-length strings is described next.

```
{

   Specification for Abstract Data Type VarStringADT

   Structure:   A string is a sequence of characters. The
                length of a string is variable and is based on
                its contents. This length must be between zero
                and some predefined maximum (string capacity).
```

The assignment operator can be used with
string operands.

Operators:

Length (S): (function) Returns the length of its argument
string.

MakeString (S1, var S2): Initializes string S2 to string
value S1, where S1 is a fixed-length string or a packed-
character array whose length is the same as the capacity
of S2. Trailing blanks at the end of string S1 are not
considered part of the string stored in S2.

ReadLnVarStr (var F, var S): Reads characters from text
file F into string S beginning with the character
selected by the file position pointer for file F. If F is
Input, the data is taken from the keyboard. Data entry
stops when either an <eoln> is reached or the number of
characters read equals the string capacity. In any event,
the file-position pointer is advanced past the <eoln>.
The length of S is defined as the number of characters
read.

WriteString (var F, S): Copies the characters stored in
string S to file F. If F is Output, procedure WriteString
displays string S on the screen.

GetChar (S, Index): (function) Retrieves the character at
position Index in string S without changing string S.

PutChar (var S, Index, Ch): Places character Ch into
string S at position Index.

Copy (S1, Index, Size, var S2): Returns in string S2 the
substring of string S1 that consists of Size characters
and begins at position Index. If Index > Length(S1), the
null string is stored in S2.

Concat (S1, S2, var S3): Returns in S3 the string formed
by joining string S2 to the end of string S1. If the new
string is too long, the extra characters at the end of
string S2 are not stored.

Pos (S1, S2): (function) If string S1 is a substring of
string S2, Pos returns the location in S2 of the first

occurrence of string S1. The value returned is the
position in S2 of the first character of S1. If string S1
is not found, function Pos returns 0. If string S1 is the
null string, function Pos returns 1.

Delete (var S, Index, Size): Removes Size characters from
string S beginning at position Index. If Size is too big,
all characters from Index to the end of string S are
removed.

Insert (S1, var S2, Index): Inserts string S1 into string
S2; the substring that formerly began at Index follows
the string inserted. If the new string is too big, the
extra characters at the right end are removed. If Index >
Length (S2) is True before the insertion, string S1 is
joined to the end of old string S2.

}

The specifications for procedures Copy and Pos refer to the null string.
The *null string* is a string of length zero, that is, a string that contains no
characters.

Internal Representation of Data Type VarString

From the preceding specification, we see that a variable-length string has two
components: a sequence of characters (its contents) and the length of that
sequence. Although it is not really necessary to settle on an internal representation at this time, it may help your understanding if we refer to a particular
representation. The record shown in Fig. 14.6 is an obvious choice for representing and storing a string in memory. It consists of a packed array of characters (field Contents) and an integer value that indicates the actual string
length (field Len). The constant Capacity determines the number of characters
that can be stored in field Contents.

Figure 14.6   Declarations for Data Type VarString

```
const
  Capacity = 20;        {predefined maximum length}

type
  StringIndex = 1..Capacity;
  StringType = packed array [String Index] of Char;
VarString = record
            Contents : StringType;
            Len : Integer
          end; {String}
```

The record `SampleStr` (type `VarString`) contains the string value `'xyz'`. Because the string capacity is 20 characters, array `SampleStr.Contents` has 17 elements that are undefined (indicated by `?`).

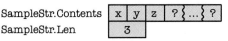

An operator for data type `VarString` processes the array field `Contents`, the integer field `Len`, or both. The operators are illustrated next and implemented in Section 14.5.

ReadLnVarStr, MakeString, Length, and WriteString

`ReadLnVarStr` and `MakeString` define a string's contents. `ReadLnVarStr` accomplishes this by reading data into a string. `ReadLnVarStr` reads and stores characters until it reaches an `<eoln>` or fills the string to its capacity. If you enter the data line

```
xyz<eoln>
```

when

```
ReadLnVarStr (Input, SampleStr)
```

executes, `SampleStr` will be defined as shown earlier.

`MakeString` assigns a fixed-length string to a variable-length string. In figuring the length of the variable-length string, any trailing blanks at the end of the fixed-length string are not counted. If `Sl` is type `StringType`, the statements

```
Sl := 'xyz         ';
MakeString (Sl, SampleStr);
```

also define `SampleStr` as shown earlier.

The function `Length` determines the *actual length* of a string, which is variable and depends on the data stored in it (for example, `Length(SampleStr)` is 3).

Procedure `WriteString` displays a string. The number of characters displayed is determined by the string's actual length.

The statements

```
WriteString (Output, SampleStr);
WriteLn ('*')
```

display the output line

```
xyz*
```

■ Example 14.7

Assume that `Name` is a variable length string whose capacity is 11 characters. The statement

```
ReadLnVarStr (Input, Name);
```

reads up to 11 data characters from the keyboard and stores them in string
Name. If the characters Jane <eoln> are typed at the keyboard, the string
'Jane ' is stored in Name and the length of Name is 5 (trailing blanks count
when they are read by ReadLnVarStr). ■

■ Example 14.8

For the string Name described above, the statements

```
MakeString ('abcde              ', Name);
Write ('Length of ');
WriteString (Output, Name);
Write (' is ', Length(Name) :1)
```

store 'abcde' in Name (length is 5) and display the output line

```
Length of abcde is 5
```

The statement

```
MakeString ('Leonardo           ', Name)
```

stores 'Leonardo' in Name (length is 8). (Notice that trailing blanks do not count
when they are stored by MakeString.) ■

GetChar and PutChar

Function GetChar and procedure PutChar are used to retrieve and insert individual characters of a string. Each call must specify the position in the string
of the character being processed.

■ Example 14.9

The following statements use GetChar and PutChar to replace one character in
a string with another.

```
Ch := GetChar(Expression, 1);
if Ch = '+' then
   PutChar (Expression, 1, '-')
```

The if statement tests whether the string Expression begins with a plus sign;
if so, the plus sign in position one is replaced by a minus sign. If the contents
of Expression are '+4*Y', the value of Ch is '+' and the new contents of
Expression are '-4*Y'; the length of Expression is unchanged (value is 4).■

Substrings and Procedure Copy

It is often necessary to manipulate segments, or *substrings,* of a larger character
string. For example, we might want to examine the three components (month,
day, year) of the string 'Jun 25, 1992'. Procedure copy can be used to do
this, as shown next.

■ Example 14.10

Assume that a date string (stored in Date) always has the form `'MMM DD, YYYY'`, where the characters represented by MMM are the month name, DD the day of the month, and YYYY the year. Assuming Date, MonthStr, Day, and Year are variable-length strings, the procedure call statement

```
Copy (Date, 1, 3, MonthStr)
```

returns (in MonthStr) the substring of Date starting at position 1 and consisting of the first three characters. The procedure call statement

```
Copy (Date, 5, 2, Day)
```

returns (in Day) the two characters that represent the day of the month (positions five and six). Finally, the procedure call statement

```
Copy (Date, 9, 4, Year)
```

returns the four characters that represent the year (positions 9 through 12). If the contents of Date are `'Jun 25, 1992'`, the contents of the variable length strings MonthStr, Day, and Year become `'Jun'`, `'25'`, and `'1992'`, respectively.

■

■ Example 14.11

Procedure PrintWords in Fig. 14.7 displays each word found in its parameter Sentence on a separate line. It assumes that there is always a single blank character between words.

The variable First always points to the start of the current word and is initialized to 1. During each execution of the for loop, the Boolean expression

```
GetChar(Sentence, Next) = WordSeparator
```

tests whether the next character is the symbol `' '`. If so, the substring occupying positions First through Next-1 in Sentence is copied to Word and displayed on the next line by the statements

```
Copy (Sentence, First, Next-First, Word);   {Get word.}
WriteString (Output, Word);
WriteLn;
```

The values of First and Next are shown below just before the fourth word of a string stored in Sentence is displayed. The value of Next-First is 5, so the five-letter word short is displayed.

This is a short example

First: 11 Next: 16

After each word is printed, First is reset to Next + 1, the position of the first character of the next word. After loop exit, the statement

```
Copy (Sentence, First, Length(Sentence)-First+1, Word);
```

stores the last word of Sentence in Word. For the sentence above, the value of First is 17 and the value of the third parameter is 7 (23–17+1), so the last word displayed is the seven-letter word example, which begins at position 17.

■

Figure 14.7 Procedure PrintWords

Directory: CHAP14
File: PRINTWOR.PRO

```
procedure PrintWords (Sentence {input} : VarString);
{
   Displays each word of a sentence on a separate line.
   Pre : Variable length string Sentence is defined.
   Post: Each word in sentence is displayed on a separate line.
   Uses: WriteString, Copy, and GetChar
}
   const
      WordSeparator = ' ';

   var
      Word : VarString;              {each word}
      First,                         {first character in each word}
      Next   : Integer;              {position of next character}

begin {PrintWords}
   {Display each word of Sentence on a separate line.}
   First := 1;            {First word starts at position 1.}
   for Next := 1 to Length(Sentence) do
      begin
         if GetChar(Sentence, Next) = WordSeparator then
            begin
               Copy (Sentence, First, Next-First, Word);   {Get word.}
               WriteString (Output, Word);
               WriteLn;
               First := Next + 1
            end {if}
      end; {for}

   {Display last word.}
   Copy (Sentence, First, Length(Sentence)-First+1, Word);
   WriteString (Output, Word);
   WriteLn
end; {PrintWords}
```

Concatenating Strings

The Copy procedure is used to reference a substring of a longer string. You can use the Concat procedure to combine two or more strings to form a new string.

■ Example 14.12

The following statements join together, or *concatenate*, their string arguments. The string result is stored in Name. For the string contents below (the symbol □ denotes a blank) the statement

```
Concat (Title, Last, Name);
```

stores the string value 'Ms. Peep' in Name. The statements

```
Concat (Title, First, Name);
Concat (Name, Last, Name)
```

store the string 'Ms. Bo Peep' in Name. ■

String Search

In processing string data, we often need to locate a particular substring. For example, we might want to know if the string 'and ' appears in a sentence, and if so, where? If Target is a string of length 4 with contents 'and ', the statement

```
PosAnd := Pos(Target, Sentence)
```

assigns to PosAnd the starting position of the first occurrence of 'and ' in string Sentence. If the string 'Birds and bees fly all day' is stored in Sentence, the value assigned to PosAnd is 7. If the string 'and ' is not in Sentence, the Pos function returns 0.

■ Example 14.13

A compiler can determine the form of many statements by checking whether the statement begins with a reserved word. If leading blanks are removed from Statement and if Target is a string of length 4 with contents 'for ', the condition

```
Pos(Target, Statement) = 1
```

is true when Statement is a for statement.

   Another task of the compiler is to extract the syntactic elements of each statement. A for statement may have the syntactic form

> for *counter* := *initial* to *final* do *statement*

The first two statements that follow use the Pos function to locate the strings 'for ' (contents of Target1) and ':=' (contents of Target2). The if statement copies the substring between these symbols into the string Counter.

```
PosFor := Pos(Target1, Statement);
PosAssign := Pos(Target2, Statement);
if (PosFor > 0) and (PosAssign > PosFor) then
   Copy (Statement, PosFor + 4, PosAssign − PosFor − 4, Counter)
```

Because the string 'for ' has 4 characters, the starting position of the *counter* is at PosFor + 4. The number of characters in the *counter* is determined by the expression PosAssign − PosFor − 4. If the string 'for ID := 1 to N do

X := X + 1' is stored in Statement, then PosFor gets 1, PosAssign gets 8, and the contents of Counter is the string 'ID ' (length is 8 − 1 − 4, or 3). ■

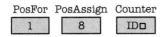

PosFor PosAssign Counter

| 1 | 8 | ID□ |

Procedures Delete and Insert

Besides the string-manipulation functions described so far, there are procedures to insert and delete substrings. They are illustrated next.

■ Example 14.14

Assume that Sentence contains the string 'This is the example.' before the first procedure call. The procedure call statement

```
Delete (Sentence, 1, 5);
```

deletes the first five characters from string Sentence. The new contents of Sentence become 'is the example'.

If Target is the string of length 4 with contents 'the ', the procedure call statement

```
Delete (Sentence, Pos(Target, Sentence), Length(Target));
```

deletes the first occurrence of the string 'the ' from Sentence. The new contents of Sentence become 'is example'. ■

■ Example 14.15

Assume that the contents of Sentence are the string 'is the stuff?' and the contents of NewString are 'Where '. The procedure call statement

```
Insert (NewString, Sentence, 1);
```

inserts the string 'Where ' at the beginning of string Sentence, changing its contents to 'Where is the stuff?'.

If the contents of Target are 'stuff' and the contents of NewString are '*#%! ', the statements

```
PosStuff := Pos(Target, Sentence);
if PosStuff > 0 then
   Insert (NewString, Sentence, PosStuff)
```

insert the string '*#%! ' in front of the string 'stuff' in Sentence. The new contents of Sentence become 'Where is the *#%! stuff'. ■

■ Example 14.16

Procedure Replace in Fig. 14.8 replaces a specified target string (Target) in a source string (Source) with a new string (Pattern). It uses function Pos to locate Target, Delete to delete it, and Insert to insert Pattern in place of Target. The source string is not changed if Target is not found. ■

Figure 14.8 Procedure Replace

639

14.3 Variable-Length
Strings

```
procedure Replace (Target, Pattern : VarString;
                   var Source : VarString);
{
   Replaces first string Target in Source with Pattern if found.
   Pre : Target, Pattern, and Source are defined.
   Post: Source is modified if Target is found.
   Uses: Pos, Length, Delete, Insert, and WriteString
}
   var
      PosTarg : Integer;                {position of Target}

begin {Replace}
   PosTarg := Pos(Target, Source);      {Locate Target.}
   if PosTarg > 0 then
      begin
         Delete (Source, PosTarg, Length(Target));
         Insert (Pattern, Source, PosTarg)
      end {if}
end; {Replace}
```

Directory: CHAP14
File: TEXTEDIT.PAS

Exercises for Section 14.3

Self-Check

1. Determine the results of the following procedure calls and function designators. Assume that all variables are type VarString with a capacity of 20 characters.
   a. MakeString ('Abra   ', Temp1);
   b. MakeString ('cadabra   ', Temp2);
   c. Concat (Temp1, Temp2, Magic)
   d. Length(Magic)
   e. Copy (Magic, 1, 8, HisMagic)
   f. Delete (HisMagic, 4, 3)
   g. Insert (Temp1, HisMagic, 3)
   h. Pos(Temp2, Magic)
   i. GetChar(Magic, 6)
   j. PutChar (Temp1, 1, 'a')
   k. Pos(Temp1, Magic)

2. Explain the difference between ReadLnString (see Fig. 10.21) and Read-LnVarStr, described in this section.

3. Source, Target, and Destin are three variables of type String with capacity 20. Assume that Source begins with a person's last name and has a comma and one space between the last and first names (i.e., *last name, first name*). Use Pos and Copy to store the first name in Destin and the second name in Target.

Programming

1. Write a program that calls PrintWords to read in a sentence and then display each word on a separate line. Insert the necessary declarations and procedure calls.

14.4 String Processing Illustrated

You have been using a text editor to create and edit Pascal programs. This is probably a fairly sophisticated *screen-oriented* editor in which special commands move the cursor around the video screen and specify edit operations. Although you cannot develop such an editor yet, you can write a less sophisticated one.

Case Study: Text Editor

Problem

We need an editor to perform some editing operations on a line of text. The editor should be able to locate a specified target string, delete a substring, insert a substring at a specified location, and replace one substring with another.

Analysis

We can use the string manipulation functions and procedures in StringVar/ADT to perform the editing operations relatively easily. We will write a program that enters a string and then processes a series of edit commands for that string.

Data Requirements

> *Problem Inputs*
> Source : VarString   {the source string}
> Command : Char   {each edit command}
>
> *Problem Output*
> Source : VarString   {modified source string}

Design

Initial Algorithm

1. Read the string to be edited into Source.
2. repeat
   3. Read an edit command.
   4. Perform each edit operation.
   until done

Refinements and Program Structure

Step 4 is performed by procedure DoEdit. DoEdit is responsible for calling the appropriate string operators to read any data strings and to perform the required operations. A portion of the structure chart for the text editor is shown in Fig. 14.9; the local variables and algorithm for procedure DoEdit follow.

Figure 14.9   Structure Chart for Text Editor Program

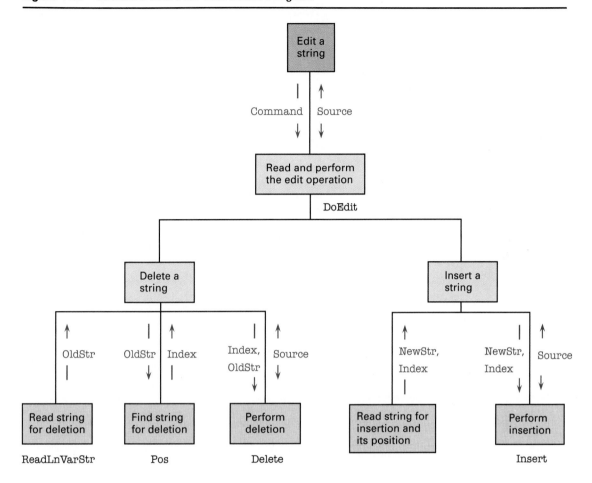

Local Variables

```
OldStr : VarString      {substring to be found, replaced, or deleted}
NewStr : VarString       {substring to be inserted}
Index: Integer           {index to the string Source}
```

Algorithm for DoEdit

1. case Command of
   'D': Read the substring to be deleted and delete it.
   'I': Read the substring to be inserted and its
       position and insert it.
   'F': Read substring to be found and print its position
       if found.
   'R': Read substring to be replaced and replace it
       with a new substring.
   end {case}

Case Study: Text Editor, continued

Implementation
The complete program is shown in Fig. 14.10, along with a sample run.

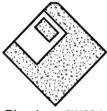

Directory: CHAP14
File: TEXTEDIT.PAS

Figure 14.10   Text Editor Program and Sample Run

```pascal
program TextEdit (Input, Output);
{
  Performs text editing operations on a source string.

  Module needed: VarStringADT, UpCase (see Fig. 9.4), and Replace (see
  Fig. 14.8)
}
  const
    Sentinel = 'Q';       {sentinel command}

  {Insert declaration for VarString from VarStringADT.}
  var
    Source : VarString;             {string being edited}
    Command : Char;                 {each edit command}

    {
      Insert ReadLnVarStr, WriteString, Insert, Delete, Pos,
      Replace, Length from VarStringADT and UpCase and Replace
    }

  procedure DoEdit (Command {input} : Char;
                        var Source : String);
    {
      Performs the edit operation specified by Command.
      Pre : Command and Source are defined.
      Post: One or more data strings are read and
            Source is modified if Command is
            'D','I','F', or 'R'. If Command is 'Q',
            a message is displayed; otherwise, nothing
            is done.
    }
    var
      NewStr,OldStr : VarString;    {auxiliary strings}
      Index : Integer;              {index to string Source}

    begin {DoEdit}
      {Perform the operation.}
      if Command in ['D', 'I', 'F', 'R', 'Q'] then
        case Command of
          'D' : begin {Delete}
                  Write ('Delete what string? ');
                  ReadLnVarStr (Input, OldStr);
                  Index := Pos(OldStr, Source);
                  if Index > 0 then
                    Delete (Source, Index, Length(OldStr))
                  else
                    begin
                      WriteString (Output, OldStr);
                      WriteLn (' not found')
                    end {if}
                end; {delete}
          'I' : begin {Insert}
                  Write ('Insert what string? ');
```

```
                  ReadLnVarStr (Input, NewStr);
                  Write ('At what position? ');
                  ReadLn (Index);
                  Insert (NewStr, Source, Index)
               end; {Insert}
        'F' : begin {Find}
                  Write ('Find what string? ');
                  ReadLnVarStr (Input, OldStr);
                  Index := Pos(OldStr, Source);
                  if Index > 0 then
                     begin
                        WriteString (Output, OldStr);
                        WriteLn (' found at position ', Index :3)
                     end
                  else
                     begin
                        WriteString (Output, OldStr);
                        WriteLn (' not found')
                     end {if}
               end; {Find}
        'R' : begin {Replace}
                  Write ('Replace old string? ')
                  ReadLnVarStr (Input, OldStr);
                  Write ('With new string? ');
                  ReadLnVarStr (Input, NewStr);
                  Replace (OldStr, NewStr, Source)
               end; {Replace}
        'Q' : WriteLn ('Quitting text editor.')
      end {case}
    else
      WriteLn ('Invalid edit character')
  end; {DoEdit}

begin {TextEdit}
  {Read in the string to be edited.}
  WriteLn ('Enter the source string:');
  ReadLnVarStr (Input, Source);

  {Perform each edit operation until done.}
  repeat
    {Get the operation symbol.}
    WriteLn;
    Write ('Enter D (Delete), I (Insert), ');
    Write ('F (Find), R (Replace), Q (Quit): ');
    ReadLn (Command);
    Command := UpCase (Command);      {Convert to uppercase.}

    {Perform operation.}
    DoEdit (Command, Source);

    {Display latest string.}
    Write ('New source: ');
    WriteString (Output, Source);
    WriteLn
  until Command = Sentinel
end. {TextEdit}


Enter the source string:
Mary had a cute little lamb.
```

```
Enter D (Delete), I (Insert), F (Find), R (Replace), Q (Quit): f
Find what string? cute
cute  found at position 12
New source: Mary had a cute little lamb.

Enter D (Delete), I (Insert), F (Find), R (Replace), Q (Quit): i
Insert what string? very
At what position? 12
New source: Mary had a very cute little lamb.

Enter D (Delete), I (Insert), F (Find), R (Replace), Q (Quit): R
Replace old string? lamb
With new string? lamb chop
New source: Mary had a very cute little lamb chop.

Enter D (Delete), I (Insert), F (Find), R (Replace), Q (Quit): D
Delete what string? very cute little
New source: Mary had a lamb chop.

Enter D (Delete), I (Insert), F (Find), R (Replace), Q (Quit): q
Quitting text editor.
New source: Mary had a lamb chop.
```

Exercise for Section 14.4

Self-Check

1. Draw the program structure chart for finding a string and for replacing a string.

14.5 Implementing String Operators (Optional)

This section discusses how to implement ADT VarStringADT. We showed one possible internal representation for a variable length string in Fig. 14.6. This representation is repeated below.

```
{declarations for type VarString}
const
  Capacity = 20;        {predefined maximum length}

type
  StringIndex = 1..Capacity;
  StringType = packed array [StringIndex] of Char;
  VarString = record
                Contents : StringType;
                Len : Integer
              end; {VarString}
```

As stated earlier, an operator for data type `VarString` processes the array field `Contents`, the integer field `Len`, or both. The operations on the array field involve searching an array or copying a portion of the array field that represents a substring. The string operators are implemented in the remainder of this section.

ReadLnVarStr, WriteString, Length, GetChar, and PutChar

Figure 14.11 shows five relatively simple operators in the specification for `VarStringADT`. Procedure `ReadLnVarStr` is similar to procedure `ReadLnString` (see Fig. 10.21) except it does not pad the string read into `InString.Contents` with blanks.

Figure 14.11 ReadLnVarStr, WriteString, PutChar, GetChar, and Length

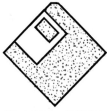

Directory: CHAP14
File: VARSTRIN.ADT

```
procedure ReadLnVarStr (var InFile {input} : Text;
                        var InString {output} : VarString);
{
  Reads a variable length string from InFile into InString.
  Pre : File InFile has been prepared for input.
  Post: Reads up to Capacity characters from file InFile into
        InString and advances to the start of the next data
        line. Stops reading characters if the <eoln>
        character is reached before InString is filled. The
        length of InString is set to the number of characters
        read.
}
  const
    Pad = ' ';                    {character used for padding}

  var
    I : Integer;                  {loop-control variable}

Begin {ReadVarStr}
  {Read each character and store it in the next array element.}
  with InString do
    begin
      Len := 0;                   {no characters read}
      while (not Eoln(InFile)) and (Len < Capacity) do
        {invariant;
            InString.Contents[1..Len] contains characters read so far and
            Len <= Capacity and
            <eoln> was not read.
        }
        begin
          Len := Len + 1;                    {Increment subscript.}
          Read (InFile, Contents[Len])       {Read next character.}
        end;  {while}

      {assert: at end of line or string is filled}
      ReadLn (InFile)                         {Advance to next line.}
    end  {with}
end; {ReadLnVarStr}
```

```
procedure WriteString (var OutFile {output} : Text;
                           OutString {input} : VarString);
{
  Writes the variable length string OutString to OutFile.
  Pre : File OutFile has been prepared for output
        and OutString is defined.
  Post: The characters stored in OutString are written
        to file OutFile.
}
begin {WriteString}
  if OutString.Len > 0 then
    Write (OutFile, OutString.Contents :OutString.Len)
end; {WriteString}


function Length (Str {input} : VarString) : Integer;
{
  Returns the length of string Str.
  Pre : Str is defined.
  Post: The current length of Str is returned as
        the function result.
}
begin {Length}
  Length := Str.Len
end; {Length}

procedure PutChar (var Str {input/output} : VarString;
                       Index : Integer;
                       Ch : Char);
{
  Stores Ch in Str at position Index.
  Pre : Str, Index, and Ch are defined.
  Post: Str.Contents[Index] gets Ch if 1 <= Index <= Str.Len.
}
begin {PutChar}
  if (Index < 1) or (Index > Str.Len) then
    WriteLn ('string index out of range')
  else
    Str.Contents[Index] := Ch
end; {PutChar}


function GetChar (Str : VarString;
                    Index : Integer) : Char;
{
  Retrieves the character at position Index of Str.
  Pre : Str and Index are defined.
  Post: Returns Str.Contents[Index] if 1 <= Index <= Str.Len.
}
begin {GetChar}
  if (Index < 1) or (Index > Str.Len) then
    WriteLn ('string index out of range')
  else
    GetChar := Str.Contents[Index]
end; {GetChar}
```

Procedure MakeString

We can use procedure ReadLnVarStr to read a string value into memory. We can also use the assignment operator to copy one string variable (type Var-

String) to another. It is not possible, however, to directly assign a string value to a string variable. Procedure MakeString accomplishes this task by storing the fixed-length string represented by its first parameter, S1, in the Contents field of its second parameter, S2.

Algorithm for MakeString

1. Assign the fixed length string S1 to S2.Contents.
2. Set S2.Len to the actual length of string S2.Contents; ignore any blank padding at the right end of string S2.Contents.

    The refinement of step 2 follows Fig. 14.12. Step 2 is a loop that searches for the first nonblank character in S2.Contents, starting at the right end of the string. Loop exit occurs after a nonblank character is reached or after the character at position 1 is tested. In procedure MakeString (Fig. 14.12), the Boolean variable InPadding indicates whether the current character is part of the blank padding (InPadding is True).

Figure 14.12 Procedure MakeString

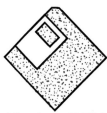

Directory: CHAP14
File: VARSTRIN.ADT

```
procedure MakeString (S1 {input} : StringType;
                      var S2 {output} : VarString);
{
  Stores the fixed length string S1 in the variable length
  string S2.
  Pre : S1 is defined.
  Post: The contents of S2 get S1, and the length of S2 is
        the length of S1 not counting any trailing blanks.
}
  const
    Pad = ' ';                    {blank padding}

  var
    InPadding : Boolean;          {program flag}

begin {MakeString}
  S2.Contents := S1;             {Store all of S1 in S2.}

  {Set S2.Len to position of first nonblank at right end of S1.}
  S2.Len := Capacity;            {Start at right end.}
  InPadding := True;             {Assume in blank padding.}
  while InPadding and (S2.Len > 0) do
    {invariant:
        S2.Len >= 0 and
        S1[S2.Len+1..Capacity] contains all blanks.
    }
    if S1[S2.Len] <> Pad then
      InPadding := False         {out of blank padding}
    else
      S2.Len := S2.Len - 1       {Move to the left.}
end; {MakeString}
```

Refinement of Step 2 of MakeString

2.1 Set S2.Len to Capacity and assume that the character
at position S2.Len is part of the blank padding.
2.2 while still in the blank padding and S2.Len > 0 do
    2.3 if the character at S2.Len is nonblank then
        Found first nonblank, so out of blank padding
    else
        Decrement S2.Len.

Local Variables for MakeString

InPadding : Boolean   {flag indicating whether the current character
                          is in the blank padding}

Procedure Copy

Procedure Copy (Fig. 14.13) copies a portion of its source string (S1) to its destination string (S2). The *substring* copied begins at position Index in the source string and will begin at position 1 in the destination string. The parameter Size represents the length of the substring being copied. Assuming S1 contains the string

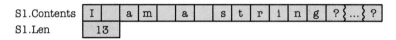

S1.Contents   I   a m a   s t r i n g ?{...}?
S1.Len   13

the procedure call statement

    Copy (S1, 3, 2, S2)

copies the substring of S1 that starts at 3 and whose length is 2 to S2, as shown next.

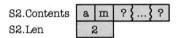

S2.Contents a m ?{...}?
S2.Len   2

Algorithm for Procedure Copy

1. if Size <= 0 or Index is out of range then
    2. Store the null string in S2.
  else
    begin
      3. Define S2.Len.
      4. Copy S2.Len characters from S1 starting with
        the character at position Index.
    end

Step 3 defines S2.Len, the size of the substring copied to S2. S2.Len will be the same as Size unless the last character to be copied from S1, the character at Index + Size − 1, is beyond the end of string S1. In that case, S2.Len should be set to ensure that the character at S1.Len is the last character copied from S1.Contents. Step 4 is a loop that copies individual characters from S1 to S2.

Step 3 Refinement

3.1   if (Index + Size − 1) <= S1.Len then
      Set S2.Len to Size
   else
      Set S2.Len so that the character at position S1.Len
      is the last character copied.

Figure 14.13   Procedure Copy

Directory: CHAP14
File: VARSTRIN.ADT

```
procedure Copy (S1 {input} : VarString
                Index, Size {input} : Integer;
                var S2 {output} : VarString);
{
 Copies a substring of S1 to S2. The substring copied
 starts at position Index of S1. The length of the substring
 to be copied is specified by Size.
 Pre : S1, Index, and Size are defined.
 Post: S2.Contents is the substring copied and S2.Len
       is the size of that substring. if Size <= 0 or
       Index is out of range, the null string is copied.
       If Size is too big, the right end of string S1
       (through position S1.Len) is copied.
}
    var
    I : Integer;                      {loop-control variable}

begin {Copy}
    if (Size <= 0) or (Index < 1) or (Index > S1.Len) then
      S2.Len := 0                     {Store the null string.}
    else
      begin
        {Define S2.Len.}
        if (Index + Size - 1) <= S1.Len then
          S2.Len := Size              {Size is OK.}
        else
          S2.Len := S1.Len - Index + 1; {Size is too big.}

        {
         Copy S2.Len characters from S1 to S2 starting with
         S1.Contents[Index].
        }
        for I := 1 to S2.Len do
          S2.Contents[I] := S1.Contents[Index+I-1]
      end {if}
end; {Copy}
```

Procedure Concat

Procedure Concat *concatenates*, or joins, its two source strings together. The destination string, S3, will contain the string in S1 followed by the string in S2. A result of the procedure call statement follows. A string of length 5 and a string of length 14 are joined together to make a string of length 19.

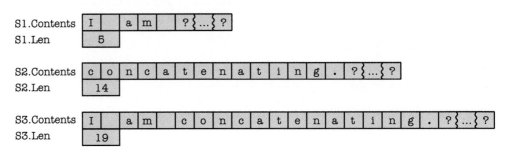

S1.Contents | I | | a | m | | ?{...}? |
S1.Len | | 5 |

S2.Contents | c | o | n | c | a | t | e | n | a | t | i | n | g | . | ?{...}? |
S2.Len | | 14 |

S3.Contents | I | | a | m | | c | o | n | c | a | t | e | n | a | t | i | n | g | . | ?{...}? |
S3.Len | | 19 |

Algorithm for Procedure Concat

1. Store string S1 in S3.
2. Append each character in string S2.Contents to the end of the string being formed in S3.Contents, incrementing S3.Len as each new character is placed in S3.Contents.

Step 1 stores string S1 in string S3, initializing S3.Len to S1.Len. Step 2 is a loop that copies the next character from string S2.Contents to the end of string S3.Contents. In procedure Concat (Fig. 14.14), the variable S2Index selects the next character in string S2.Contents; the current length of string S3 (S3.Len) is incremented before each new character is inserted at S3.Contents[S3.Len].

Figure 14.14 Procedure Concat

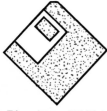

Directory: CHAP14
File: VARSTRIN.ADT

```
procedure Concat (S1, S2 {input} : VarString;
                  var S3 {output} : VarString);
{
  Concatenates the strings in S1 and S2; the resulting
  string is stored in S3.
  Pre : S1 and S2 are defined.
  Post: S3 is string S1 followed by S2.
}
  var
    S2Index : 0..Capacity;     {subscript in S2.Contents}

begin  {Concat}
  S3 := S1;              {Store S1 in S3.}

  {Copy S2 to S3 following S1}
  S2Index := 0;         {Start at beginning of S2.}
  while (S2Index < S2.Len) and (S3.Len < Capacity) do
    {invariant:
       S2Index <= S2.Len and S3.Len <= Capacity
       and S2Index characters from S2 were copied to the end of S3.
    }
    begin
      S2Index := S2Index + 1;
```

```
      S3.Len := S3.Len + 1;
      {Copy next character from string S2 to string S3.}
      S3.Contents[S3.Len] := S2.Contents[S2Index]
    end; {while}

  {assert:
    S3.Contents is S1.Contents followed by
    as much as S2.Contents as will fit and S3.Len
    is the smaller of (S1.Len + S2.Len) and Capacity.
  }
end; {Concat}
```

Function Pos

Finally, function Pos searches a source string for a specified target string. It does this by "sliding" the target string over the source string until each character in the target string matches the source string character under it. For the strings below, there is a match when the target string, S1.Contents, is over positions 3 and 4 of the source string, S2.Contents, so the function result should be 3.

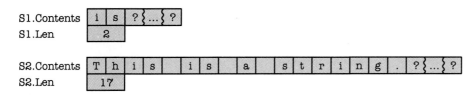

Before searching for the target string, procedure Pos must first check for two special cases: a null target string and a target string that is longer than the source string. If the target string is null, Pos will return the value 1; if the target string is longer than the source string, Pos will return the value 0. The algorithm for Pos follows.

Algorithm for Pos

1. if S1 is the null string then
    2. Return 1.
  else if S1.Len > S2.Len then
    3. Return 0.
  else
    4. Compare S1 to each substring in S2 until a match is found or there are no substrings left to test in S2.

The refinement of step 4 uses a repeat-until loop to perform the slide and match operations. Function Match, a local function in Pos (see Fig. 14.15), compares S1 to the current substring of S2 (step 4.4). Function Match returns False if a nonmatching pair of characters is found; function Match returns True if all pairs match. The Boolean variable Matched stores the result returned by function Match.

Directory: CHAP14
File: VARSTRIN.ADT

Figure 14.15 Functions Match and Pos

```
function Match (S1, S2 : VarString;
                S2Index : Integer) : Boolean;
{
  Attempts to match string S1 with the substring of
  S2 beginning at position S2Index.
  Pre : S1, S2, and S2Index are defined and S1 is not null.
  Post: Returns True if match succeeds; otherwise,
        returns False.
}
  var
    S1Index : 0..Capacity;     {subscript in S1.Contents}

begin {Match}
  if S1.Len > (S2.Len - S2Index + 1) then
    Match := False                    {S2 is too short.}
  else
    begin
      {
      Compare corresponding characters in S1 and S2, starting
      with S1.Contents[1] and S2.Contents[S2Index]
      until an unequal pair is found or the end of S1 is reached.
      }
      S1Index := 0;                    {Start at beginning of S1.}
      repeat
        {invariant:
           all prior pairs of characters tested are equal
           and S1Index <= S1.Len
        }
        S1Index := S1Index + 1          {Advance to next pair.}
      until (S1.Contents[S1Index] <>
        S2.Contents[S2Index+S1Index-1]) or (S1Index >= S1.Len);

      {assert: an unequal pair is found or at end of S1}
      {Define function result based on last pair tested.}
      Match := S1.Contents[S1Index] =
                S2.Contents[S2Index+S1Index-1]
    end {if}
end;   {Match}


function Pos (S1, S2 : VarString) : Integer;
{
  Returns the starting position in S2 of the first occurrence
  of the string S1. Returns 0 if S1 is not a substring of S2.
  Pre : S1 and S2 are defined.
  Post: Returns a value between 1 and S2.Len denoting the
        starting position of the first occurrence of S1 in S2.
        Returns 0 if S1 is not found.
  Uses: Match
}
  var
    S2Index : 0..Capacity;     {subscript in S2.Contents}
    Matched : Boolean;         {program flag}

begin {Pos}
  if S1.Len > S2.Len then
    Pos := 0                    {S1 is longer than S2.}
  else if S1.Len = 0 then
    Pos := 1                    {S1 is the null string.}
  else
```

```
      begin {slide and match}
        {Search for S1 in S2}
        S2Index := 0;                {Start at left end of S2.}
        repeat
          {invariant:
             No prior substring of S2 matches S1 and
             the length of the substring starting
             at S2Index >= S1.Len.
          }
          S2Index := S2Index + 1;      {Slide to right in S2.}
          Matched := Match(S1, S2, S2Index)
        until Matched or (S2.Len - S2Index < S1.Len)

        {assert:
           S1 found at S2.Contents[S2Index] or
           all substrings tested without success
        }
        {Define function result.}
        if Matched then
          Pos := S2Index               {S1 found at S2Index.}
        else
          Pos := 0                     {S1 is not found.}
      end {slide and match}
    end;  {Pos}
```

Step 4 Refinement

4.1 Initialize S2Index to 0.
4.2 repeat
    4.3 Advance S2Index to the next substring in S2.
    4.4 Compare S1 to the substring starting at S2Index.
until there is a match or there are no substrings left.
4.5 if there is a match then
    4.6 Return S2Index.
else
    4.7 Return 0.

Local Declaration in Pos

```
S2Index : Integer    {index in S2.Contents of the current substring}
Matched : Boolean    {flag that holds the result returned by Match}
```

Function Match is a Boolean function that compares S1 to the current substring in S2. The algorithm for function Match follows. A repeat-until loop implements step 3 of Match.

Algorithm for Match

1. if S2 is too short then
    2. Return False.

```
    else
      begin
```
3. Compare corresponding characters in S1 and S2, starting with
   S1.Contents[1] and S2.Contents[S2Index], until an unequal pair
   is found or the end of S1 is reached.
4. if an unequal pair is found then
       Return False.
   else
       Return True.
```
    end
```

Local Variables for Match

```
S1Index : Integer      {index in S1.Contents of the next pair of
                                       characters being compared}
```

Procedures Delete and Insert

Rather than implement procedures Delete and Insert, we leave them as
exercises at the end of this section. Two methods for implementing these
procedures are described in those exercises.

String Comparison

Unfortunately, it is not easy to compare two variable-length strings because
records cannot be used as operands of the relational operators. We can use
relational operators to compare the contents of two strings (for example,
Str1.Contents <> Str2.Contents). The result of such a comparison, however,
is not always meaningful, because the Contents field may not be defined beyond
the string length. One approach would be to pad the Contents field of each
string with blanks before performing the comparison. Programming project 7
deals with the implementation of string-comparison operators.

Exercises for Section 14.5

Self-Check

1. What happens if you call Concat to join two strings whose combined length
   is larger than the string capacity? Is this flagged as an error?
2. Assume that the Write statement in procedure WriteString displays the
   entire string stored in OutString.Contents instead of the substring ending
   at position OutString.Contents[Len]. Show how you could use a loop in
   procedure WriteString to display the substring that is defined.
3. Replace the body of ReadLnVarStr with a call to ReadLnString.

Programming

1. Write a procedure Delete that can be used to delete a substring of a source
   string. The procedure parameters are the source string, the starting position
   of the substring to be deleted, and the length of the substring. The procedure

should move each character that follows the substring being deleted to its new position in the source string.

2. Write a procedure to insert a new string into a source string. The parameters are the two strings and the position in the source string where the new string is to be inserted. First, move the part of the source string that will follow the new substring, to make room for the new string. Next, copy the new string into the space vacated. When you move the old substring, be sure to move the last character first (why?). Also, if the expanded source string is too long, don't move the extra characters at the right end.

3. Programming exercises 1 and 2 can be solved by using procedures `Copy` and `Concat`. Provide alternate solutions that utilize these procedures to extract and concatenate substrings. Hint: To delete, copy the substring following the one to be deleted to a local variable, shorten the original string by changing its length, and then concatenate the modified original string and the local string. To insert, copy the substring following the point of insertion to a local string, shorten the original string by changing its length, and then concatenate the modified original string, the new string, and the local string.

14.6 Strings in Pascal Extensions (Optional)

We have stated that many Pascal compilers provide variable-length strings as an extension. In those compilers, the declaration of a string type takes one of the following forms:

```
type                          type
   String10 = string[10];        String10 = string(10);
```

The variable declaration

```
var
   MyName, YourName : String10;
```

allocates storage for two variable-length strings (`MyName` and `YourName`) of capacity 10.

Many compilers provide functions and procedures similar to the ones discussed in the previous sections. They use the standard Pascal input/output procedures to enter and display strings instead of procedures like `ReadLnVarStr` and `WriteString`.

Instead of using `GetChar` and `PutChar`, we can reference a character in a variable-length string using normal subscript notation (for example, `MyName[1]` references the first character in string `MyName`). Instead of using procedure `MakeString`, we can assign a fixed-length string value to a string variable using the assignment operator. We can also use the relational operators to compare variable-length strings.

Operators `Concat` and `Copy` return a single string as their result and are implemented as functions on most Pascal systems. For example, the statements

```
S2 := Copy (S1, 1, 7);        {instead of Copy (S1, 1, 7, S2)}
S3 := Concat (S2, S1)         {instead of Concat (S2, S1, S3)}
```

copy the first seven characters of string S1 to S2 and then store this substring of S1 followed by S1 itself in S3. If S1 is the string 'double trouble', S3 becomes the string 'double double trouble'. Because standard Pascal functions cannot return strings as values, we implemented these operators as procedures, using the last parameter to return the procedure result.

Finally, you have seen that the operator + can mean addition or set union, depending on its operands. On most extended Pascal systems, it can also mean concatenation. This allows us to write the last line of the preceding example as

```
S3 := S2 + S1
```

Strings in Extended Pascal

In a version of Pascal called Extended Pascal, function Substr is used (instead of Copy) to copy a substring of one string to another string. The *substring variable* S1[3..5] denotes the substring of S1 found in positions 3 through 5, inclusive. A substring variable can be used just like a string variable. The statement

```
S1[3..5] := 'abc'
```

defines this substring of S1, and the statement

```
Write (S1[3..5])
```

displays this substring.

Function Index is used instead of function Pos to search for a substring and the function designator Pos(Target, Source) becomes Index(Source, Target). The function designator Trim(S1) removes any trailing blanks from the end of string S1 and redefines its length accordingly.

14.7 Common Programming Errors

Remember that a set variable, like any variable, must be initialized before it can be manipulated. It is tempting to assume that a set is empty and then to begin processing it without initializing it to the empty set, [ ], through an explicit assignment.

Many of the Pascal operators can be used with sets. The meaning of the operator is, of course, different when its operands are sets and not numbers. Remember to use a unit set (a set of one element) when you insert or delete a set element. The set union operation in the expression

```
['A','E','O','U'] + 'I'              {incorrect set union}
```

is incorrect and should be rewritten as

```
['A','E','O','U'] + ['I']            {correct set union}
```

It is not possible to use a set as an operand of the standard Read or Write procedure. You must read in the elements of a set individually and insert them into an initially empty set using the set union operator. To print a set, you must test each value in the base type of a set for set membership. Only those values that are in the set should be printed.

To perform string manipulation, you can use the operators provided in VarStringADT or extensions to standard Pascal provided by your compiler. In either case, be careful not to mix fixed-length strings and variable-length strings. Fixed-length strings are stored in packed arrays of characters. Also, don't confuse the operators described in this chapter with similar operators provided in your Pascal system. Remember that operators such as Concat and Copy may be implemented as functions (and not procedures) in some versions of Pascal.

CHAPTER REVIEW

The set data type can store a collection of elements of the same type (called the base type). Each value in the base type of a set is either a member of the set or it is not. Unlike an array, a value can be saved only once in a set, and there is no way to determine the sequence in which the values were stored in the set (for example, [1,5,2,4] is the same set as [1,2,4,5]).

String operators can simplify the processing of textual data. Because standard Pascal does not provide a variable-length string data type, we described and implemented VarStringADT in this chapter. Check with your instructor to find what string operators, if any, are provided in your Pascal system.

New Pascal Constructs

The Pascal constructs introduced in this chapter are described in Table 14.2.

Table 14.2 Summary of New Pascal Constructs

Construct	Effect
Set Type Declaration	
```type DigitSet = set of 0...9;```	Declares a set type DigitSet whose base type is the set of digits from 0 through 9.
```var Digits, Primes : DigitSet;```	Digits and Primes are set variables of type DigitSet.
Set Assignment	
Digits := [];	Digits is the empty set.
Primes := [2,3,5] + [7];	Primes is the set [2,3,5,7].
Digits := Digits + [1..3];	Digits is the set [1,2,3].
Digits := [0..9] − [1,3,5,7,9];	Digits is the set [0,2,4,6,8].
Digits := [1,3,5,7,9] * Primes	Digits is the set [3,5,7].

Construct	Effect
Set Relations	
`Primes <= Digits`	True if `Primes` is a subset of `Digits`.
`Primes >= []`	Always True.
`Primes <> []`	True if `Primes` contains any element.
`[1,2,3] = [3,2,1]`	True because order does not matter.
String Declaration	

`const Capacity = 10;`
`type StringType =`
`    packed array [1..Capacity] of Char;`
`  VarString = record`
`                Contents : StringType;`
`                Len : Integer`
`              end; {VarString}`
`var FirstName, LastName, TempName : VarString;`
	`FirstName`, `LastName`, and `TempName` are variable-length strings (string capacity is 10 characters).

String Assignment	

`MakeString ('Daffy     ', FirstName);`
`MakeString ('Duck      ', LastName);`
`TempName := LastName;`
	Saves `'Daffy'` in `FirstName` and `'Duck'` in `LastName` and `TempName`.

String Length	
`Length(FirstName);`	Returns the current length (5) of `FirstName`.
String Copy	
`Copy (FirstName, 1, 3, TempName);`	Copies `'Daf'` to `TempName`.
String Concatenation	
`Concat (FirstName, LastName, TempName);`	Stores `'DaffyDuck'` in `TempName`.
String Search	

`Pos('Du', FirstName);`
`Pos('Du', LastName);`
`Pos('Du', TempName);`
	Returns 0 (`'Du'` not found).
	Returns 1 (`'Du'` found at 1).
	Returns 6 (`'Du'` found at 6).

String Deletion	
`Delete (TempName, 7, 2);`	Changes `TempName` to `'DaffyDk'`.
String Insertion	
`Insert ('uc', TempName, 7);`	Changes `TempName` to `'DaffyDuck'`.

1. What is the universal set?
2. Which can have the most elements: a set union, an intersection, or a difference? Which of these operators is not commutative?
3. Can you have a set whose base type is `Integer` or `Char`? How about a subrange type with host type `Integer` or `Char`?
4. Does it make any difference in which order the elements of a set are inserted? Does it make any difference if an element is inserted more than once into the same set?
5. Given that Set1 is [1..3], what are the contents of the following sets?
   a. `Set2 := Set1 + [4, 5, 6];`
   b. `Set3 := Set1 - Set2;`
   c. `Set4 := Set3 + [4, 7];`
   d. `Set5 := Set4 + [4, 6]`
   e. `Set6 := Set5 * Set2`
6. What is the advantage of storing a string in a variable of type `VarString` instead of using a packed array of characters?
7. Is it easier to compare two strings stored in variables of type `VarString` or in packed arrays of characters? Explain your answer.
8. Assuming S1, S2, and S3 are type `VarString`, what is the effect of the following statements when Pos returns a nonzero value?
   a. `Copy (S1, 1, 6, S3);`
      `Concat (S3, S2, S3);`
   b. `Copy (S2, 1, Pos(S1, S2) - 1, S3);`
   c. `Copy (S2, Pos(S1, S2), Length(S2), S3);`
   d. `Copy (S2, Pos(S1, S2), Length(S1), S3);`
   e. `Delete (S2, Pos(S1, S2), Length(S1));`
   f. `Insert (S2, Pos(S1, S2), Length(S1))`
9. Answer exercise 8 when Pos returns 0.
10. Write procedure `PadString` that pads a variable-length string with blanks.

Answers to Quick-Check Exercises

1. the set containing all the values in the base type
2. The union of two sets. Set difference (operator –) is not commutative.
3. You cannot use `Integer` as a base type, but you probably can use `Char`. A subrange of `Integer` or `Char` can be the base type.
4. no; no
5. a. [1..6] b. [] c. [4,7] d. [4,6,7] e. [4,6]
6. The actual length, excluding blank padding, is also stored. The operators in Var–StringADT can be used to assist in processing the string data.
7. It is easier to compare two packed arrays because you can use the relational operators. The Contents fields of two variables of type `VarString` can be compared, but there may be some problems if the strings are not the same length and are not padded.
8. a. The substring consisting of the first six characters in S1 is concatenated with S2; the result is stored in S3.
   b. The substring of S2 that precedes the first occurrence of S1 in S2 is copied to S3.
   c. The substring of S2 starting at the first occurrence of S1 in S2 is copied to S3.
   d. The substring S1 is copied to S3.

e. The first occurrence of S1 is deleted from S2.

f. The string S1 is inserted in S2 just before its first occurrence.

9. a. not affected

b, c, d. The null string is stored in S3.

e, f. S2 should not be changed.

10.

```
procedure PadString (var AString {input/output} : VarString);
  const
    Pad = ' ';
  var
    I : Integer;

begin {PadString}
  for I := AString.Len + 1 to Capacity do
    AString.Contents[I] := Pad
end; {PadString}
```

Review Questions

1. Why may we be unable to declare a set whose base type is Char?

2. Write the declarations for a set, Oysters, whose values are the months of the year (enumerated type Month). Initialize Oysters to the set of all months that contain the letter r in their name. Write an assignment statement that inserts the month May in this set and deletes the month September.

3. The following for loop prints each member of a set whose elements are values of enumerated type Day. Write the declaration for set TestSet. Rewrite the loop as a while loop whose repetition condition is TestSet <> []. Use the set operator – to delete each set element after it is displayed.

```
for Today := Sunday to Saturday do
  if Today in TestSet then
    WriteDay (Today)
```

4. Provide the declarations for the following two sets. What are the intersection and the union of sets Vowel and Letter? What are the two set differences?

```
Vowel := ['Y', 'U', 'O', 'I'];
Letter := ['A'..'P'];
```

5. What is the difference between the actual length of a string and the capacity of a string? Which does function Length return?

6. If MyString (type VarString) has capacity 10, store the string value 'Hello' in MyString using procedure MakeString. Next, write the assignment statements that would have the same effect.

7. Indicate whether each of the following identifiers is a procedure or function. Describe the type of result returned by each.

```
Length, MakeString, Concat, Pos, Copy, Insert, Delete
```

8. Write the declarations and the statements for a program segment that first reads a data line into a variable of type VarString and stores all the symbols in the subrange '!'..'/' that appear in the string in a set Symbols1. Assume the ASCII character set and test each character in this subrange using function Pos to determine whether it appears in the string. If so, insert it in the set Symbols1. Next, write a new search

loop that scans the string, testing each character in the string for membership in the set ['!'..'/']. Insert each character that qualifies in set Symbols2. When you are done, test whether Symbols1 and Symbols2 are identical sets.

Programming Projects

1. Write a program that removes all the blanks from a character string.
2. Write a program that reads in a sequence of lines and displays a count of the total number of words in those lines and counts the number of words with one letter, two letters, and so on. Your program should make use of VarStringADT and include functions and procedures corresponding to the function and procedure headers shown below. Array element FreqTable[i] keeps track of the counts of words of length i.

```
procedure GetWord (Sentence {input} : VarString;
                   var Index {input/output} : Integer;
                   var Word {output} : VarString);
{Return next word of Sentence found at or after Index.}

procedure TabOneWord (Word {input} : VarString;
                      var FreqTable {input/output} : ArrayType);
{Update FreqTable for cell corresponding to Length(Word).}

procedure TabulateWords (var TestData {input} : Text;
                         var FreqTable {output} : ArrayType);
{
  Read file TestData and tabulate frequency of word lengths in
  array FreqTable.
  Uses: TabOneWord and GetWord.
}

function ArraySum (FreqTable : ArrayType) : Integer;
{Compute sum of word counts stored in FreqTable.}
```

3. Write a program that reads in a sequence of lines and displays each line read with all four-letter words replaced with asterisks.
4. Write a Pascal program to play the game Taxman. In this game a user plays against the computer, and the object is to accumulate the most points. The user selects a number from 1 to 40. If the number is still available, the user is credited with points equal to the number chosen and the computer is credited with points equivalent to the sum of the unclaimed factors of the number chosen. The user may not choose a number that has no factors. After a number is chosen, it and its factors are removed from the set of available numbers. The computer gets all unclaimed numbers added to its score when the game ends.

   For example, consider the game played with the set of numbers 1 to 6. If the user selects 6, the computer gets all factors of 6, namely 3, 2, 1, and the score is tied. Now only 4 and 5 are left to choose from; since the factors of 4 (2 and 1) have been removed from the set of available numbers and 5 has no factors other than itself and 1, the computer wins, 15 to 6. The user should have chosen 5 first, then 4, and then 6. Then the user would have won, 15 to 7.

5. Write a procedure that reads in a list of cards and stores it in an array of sets, one set for each suit. Use an enumerated type for the suits and one for the card face values. The data for each card will be presented in the form of a character

representing the suit and a character representing the card face value ('2'..'9', 'T', 'J', 'Q', 'K', 'A').

6. Consider a card of hands read in project 5 as a bridge hand and evaluate it. Award points for each card according to the following method:

Card Face Value	Points
two..ten	0
jack	1
queen	2
king	3
ace	4

Also add one point for each suit that has only two cards, two points for each suit that has only one card, and three points for each suit that is missing.

7. Provide a group of Boolean functions (LE, LT, EQ, NE, GE, GT) that can be used to compare two variable-length strings (for example, LE(S1, S2) returns True if string S1 <= string S2). Two strings are equal only if they have the same contents and the same length. If one string is a substring of the other, the shorter string is considered less than the longer string.

8. Revise the text editor discussed in Section 14.4 so that it will edit a "page" of text. Store each line of the page in a separate element of an array of strings. Maintain a pointer (index) to the line currently being edited. In addition to the edit commands, include commands that move the index to the top of the page, the bottom of the page, and up or down a specified number of lines. Your program should also be able to delete an entire line, insert a new line preceding the current line, and replace the current line with another. The first two of these new operations will require moving a portion of the array of strings up or down by one element.

9. Write a program to scan a line of characters containing an equation and calculate the result. Assume all operands are integers. Make tests to determine if the equation is valid.

Valid operations are +, −, /, *, and ^, where +, −, /, and * have their typical functions and ^ indicates the left value is raised to the power of the right operand (which must be positive).

Numbers may be negative. All operations are done in left-to-right order (no operator precedence). For example,

Directory: CHAP14
File: PROJ14_9.PAS

2 + 3 ^ 2 + 36 * 1

would be

5 ^ 2 + 36 * 1 = 25 + 36 * 1 = 61 * 1 = 61

Use sets to verify the equations' operations and ignore all blanks. Output should consist of an equal sign (=) and then the answer. If an equation is invalid, display the message ** INVALID **.

10. Rewrite project 9 to allow operands (including exponents) which are either integers or real numbers. You should read the characters of the operands one at a time and convert them to their equivalent numeric value.

15
Binary Files

We covered text files in Chapter 8. Like an array, a file is a collection of elements that are all the same type. Because files are located in secondary memory (that is, on a disk) rather than in main memory, they can be much larger than arrays. The elements of an array can be accessed in arbitrary order, or *random order*; files in standard Pascal can be accessed only in *sequential order*. This means that file component 1, component 2, ..., component $n - 1$ must be accessed before file component n can be accessed.

This chapter reviews text files. We also study other file types whose components are records. Finally, we discuss extensions to Pascal that allow a file to be accessed in random order, just like an array.

15.1 Review of Text Files

This section reviews what you learned about text files in Chapter 8. Files can store large quantities of data on disk. All components of a file are the same type. A text file is a file whose components are characters from the Pascal character set. A special character, the end-of-line mark, separates sequences of adjacent characters into lines. Associated with each file is a file-position pointer, which indicates the next file component to be processed.

You can use a file for input or for output, but not both simultaneously. If you're using a file for input, then its components can be read as data. If you're using a file for output, then new components can be written to the file.

If InFile is the name of a file, the statement

```
Reset (InFile)
```

calls the standard procedure Reset to prepare (*open*) file InFile for input. The file-position pointer is moved to the beginning of file InFile, so that the first file component is read by the next Read operation. The file-position pointer is automatically advanced after each Read operation.

If OutFile is the name of a file, the statement

```
Rewrite (OutFile)
```

calls the standard procedure Rewrite to prepare file OutFile for output. If OutFile is a new file, it is initialized to an empty file. If OutFile is an existing file in disk storage, its file-position pointer is returned to the beginning. In this way, OutFile becomes an empty file, and the data previously associated with the file are lost.

■ Example 15.1

Assume that InFile and OutFile are both text files. The statements

```
Reset (InFile);
Rewrite (OutFile);
```

open InFile for input and OutFile for output, as shown next. If file OutFile is nonempty, the Rewrite operation still returns the file-position pointer to the beginning, causing the existing file data to be lost.   ■

After Reset and Rewrite

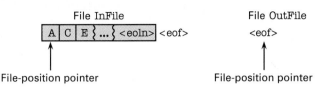

Procedures `Read` and `ReadLn` can be used with system file `Input` (the keyboard) or any other text file that has been opened for input. Similarly, procedures `Write` and `WriteLn` can be used with system file `Output` (the screen) or any other text file that has been opened for output. The file to be processed is determined by the first parameter in a call to any of these procedures. If the first parameter is not a file variable, system file `Input` (for `Read` and `ReadLn`) or system file `Output` (for `Write` and `WriteLn`) is processed.

The `EOF` and `EOLN` functions test for the end of a file and the end of a line of a text file, respectively. The function parameter indicates which input file is being tested. If there is no parameter, system file `Input` is assumed. The function designator `EOF(InFile)` evalutes to `True` when the next character in file `InFile` is the `<eof>`. The function designator `EOLN(InFile)` evaluates to `True` when the next character in file `InFile` is an `<eoln>`.

The specification for the abstract data type text file follows.

Specification for Text File Abstract Data Type

Structure: A text file is an ordered collection of characters stored on disk. A special character, the end-of-line mark, segments the file into lines.

Operators:

`Reset (F)`: Opens file F for input.

`Rewrite (F)`: Opens file F for output.

`Read (F, `*input list*`)`: Reads data from file F into the variables specified in *input list*. If F is missing, it reads data from system file `Input`.

`ReadLn (F, `*input list*`)`: Same as `Read` except that it advances the file-position pointer for file F to the start of the next line after performing the data entry.

`Write (F, `*output list*`)`: Writes data values in *output list* to file F. If F is missing, it writes data to system file `Output`.

`WriteLn (F, `*output list*`)`: Same as `Write` except that it writes an `<eoln>` to file F after all data values.

`EOF (F)`: (function) Returns `True` if the `<eof>` is the next character in file F; otherwise, it returns `False`.

`EOLN (F)`: (function) Returns `True` if an `<eoln>` is the next character in file F; otherwise, it returns `False`.

■ Example 15.2

Procedure CopyFile in Fig. 15.1 reviews the use of the file operators. It copies each character of its input file to its output file. (Procedure CopyFile is based on an earlier program; see Fig. 8.3.)   ■

Figure 15.1 Procedure CopyFile

Directory: CHAP15
File: COPYFILE.PRO

```
procedure CopyFile (var InFile; {input}
                        OutFile {output} : Text);
  {
    Copies file InFile to file OutFile.
    Pre : File InFile is defined.
    Post: File OutFile is a copy of InFile. The file-position
          pointers for both files are advanced to the <eof>
          character.
  }
  var
    NextCh : Char;                {next character}

begin
  Reset (InFile);                {Prepare input file.}
  Rewrite (OutFile);             {Prepare output file.}
  while not EOF(InFile) do
    begin
      While not EOLN(InFile) do
        begin
          Read  (InFile, NextCh);
          Write (OutFile, NextCh)   {Copy character.}
        end; {line}

      {assertion: <eoln> reached}
      ReadLn (InFile);              {Skip <eoln>.}
      WriteLn (OutFile)             {Insert <eoln>.}
    end {file}

  {assertion: <eof> reached}
end; {CopyFile}
```

Exercises for Section 15.1

Self-Check

1. Rewrite procedure CopyFile so that it uses procedure ReadLnString (see Fig. 10.21) to enter a data line instead of the inner while loop.
2. Answer exercise 1 for procedures ReadLnVarStr and WriteString.
3. What does the following program do? What happens if a data line does not contain enough characters to satisfy the input list?

```
program Mystery (InData, Output);
  var
    InData : Text;
    Ch1, Ch2, Ch3 : Char;
begin {Mystery}
  Reset (InData);
  while not EOF(InData) do
    begin
```

```
      ReadLn (InData, Ch1, Ch2, Ch3);
      WriteLn (Ch1, Ch2, Ch3)
   end {while}
end. {Mystery}
```

Programming

1. Write procedure CompressFile that copies all nonblank characters in its
   input file to its output file.

15.2 User-Defined File Types and Binary Files

In a text file, the individual components are characters from the Pascal character
set. We can use the type constructor file to declare new file types whose
components are any type, simple or structured, except for another file type.

■ Example 15.3

Program EchoFile in Fig. 15.2 creates and echo prints a file of integer values
from 1 to 1000. The file type declaration

```
type
   NumberFile = file of Integer;
```

identifies NumberFile as a file type whose components are integer values. The
file that is created, named Numbers, follows.

file Numbers

| 1 | 2 | 3 | 4 | 5 | 6 | … | 999 | 1000 |

Figure 15.2   Program EchoFile

Directory: CHAP15
File: ECHOFILE.PAS

```
program EchoFile (Numbers, Output);

{Creates a file of integer values and echo prints it}

   const
     NumInt = 1000;              {number of integers in the file}

   type
     NumberFile = file of Integer;

   var
     Numbers : NumberFile; {file of integers}
     I,                    {loop-control variable}
     NextInt : Integer;    {each integer read from file Numbers}

begin {EchoFile}
   {Create a file of integers.}
   Rewrite (Numbers);     {Initialize Numbers to an empty file.}
   for I := 1 to NumInt do
     Write (Numbers, I);   {Write each integer to Numbers.}
```

```
{Echo print file Numbers.}
Reset (Numbers);                    {Prepare Numbers for input.}
while not EOF(Numbers) do
   begin
      Read (Numbers, NextInt);   {Read next integer into NextInt.}
      WriteLn (Output, NextInt :4)                    {Display it.}
   end   {while}
end. {EchoFile}
```

EchoFile begins by preparing file Numbers for output (the Rewrite statement). The for loop with loop-control variable I creates a file of integer values. The statement

```
Write (Numbers, I);              {Write each integer to Numbers.}
```

copies each value of I (1 to 1000) to file Numbers.

Next, file Numbers is prepared for input (the Reset statement). The while loop echo prints each value stored in Numbers until the end of file Numbers is reached (EOF(Numbers) is True). Within the loop, the statement

```
Read (Numbers, NextInt);   {Read next integer into NextInt.}
```

reads the next file component (an integer value) into variable NextInt. The statement

```
WriteLn (Output, NextInt :4)                    {Display it.}
```

displays this value on a separate line of the screen (system file Output).   ∎

Comparison of Binary Files and Text Files

File Numbers is called a binary file. A *binary file* is a file that is created by the execution of a program and in which the internal representation of each component is stored directly. It is faster to process a binary file than a text file. For example, if the variable NextInt has the value 244, the statement

```
Write (Numbers, NextInt)
```

copies the internal binary representation of NextInt from memory to file Numbers. If your computer uses two bytes to store an integer value, the byte that stores the highest-order bits would contain all zeros and the byte that stores the lowest-order bits would contain the binary string 11110100 (244 = 128 + 64 + 32 + 16 + 4). Both bytes would be written to disk as the next file component.

Assuming OutFile is a text file, the statement

```
Write (OutFile, NextInt :4)
```

writes the value of NextInt to OutFile using four characters (four bytes). To do this, the computer must first convert the binary number in NextInt to the character string ' 244' and then write the binary code for the characters blank, 2, 4, and 4 to file OutFile. Obviously, it takes more time to do the conversion and copy each character than it does to copy the internal binary representation to disk. It also requires twice as much disk space to store four characters as it does to store the internal binary representation of the integer value (four bytes versus two).

There is another advantage to a binary file. Each time we write a Real value to a text file, the computer must convert this value to a character string, whose precision is determined by the format specification. This may result in a loss of accuracy.

You can use the standard procedures Read and Write with binary files. The file name must be the first parameter. For the Read procedure, all variables in the input list must be the same type as the file components. For the Write procedure, each output expression must be the same type as the file components.

The Pascal system uses an <eof> to denote the end of a binary file; however, we will not show this indicator when we sketch a binary file. We can use the EOF function to test for the end of a binary file in the same way that it tests for the end of a text file. The file name must be passed as a parameter to the EOF function (for example, EOF(Numbers)).

Unlike text files, binary files cannot be segmented into lines. Consequently, the standard procedures ReadLn, WriteLn, and EOLN cannot be used with binary files.

In the next section, you will see that complete data structures (that is, records and arrays) can be read from binary files and written to binary files with a single Read or Write operation. This simplifies input/output considerably and makes it much more efficient. This, of course, is not possible with text files; each array element or record field must be read or written separately. The only exception for text files is writing a packed array of characters.

SYNTAX
DISPLAY

File Type Declaration

Form: type *file type* = file of *component type*;
Example: type
                    Item = record
                                    ID : Integer;
                                    Salary : Real
                            end; {Item}
                    ItemFile = file of Item;

Interpretation: A new type *file type* is declared whose components must be type *component type*. Any standard or previously declared data type, except for another file type or a structured type with a file type as one of its constituents, can be the component type.

SYNTAX
DISPLAY

Read Procedure (for Binary Files)

Form: Read (*infile, input list*)
Example: Read (NumberFile, NextInt)

Interpretation: The Read procedure reads one component of the file *infile* into each variable in *input list* and then advances the file-position pointer to the next unread file component. The type of each variable must correspond to the component type for *infile*. The value of EOF(*infile*) must be False before the Read operation occurs.

Write Procedure (for Binary Files)

Form: Write (*outfile, output list*)
Example: Write (Numbers, NextInt, 500)
Interpretation: The Write procedure appends the value of each expression in *output list* to file *outfile*. The type of each expression must correspond to the component type for *outfile*.

Exercises for Section 15.2

Self-Check

1. Assume your computer uses four bytes to store a type Real value in memory. How many bytes would be required to store six Real numbers in a binary file? Answer the same question for a text file in which each number is written using the format specification :4:2. Are there any circumstances under which either of your answers might change?

2. Complete the following program. What does it do?

```
program Mystery (_____, _____, _____);
   type
      NumberType = file of _____;

   var
      Data : _____;
      OutData : _____;
      Next : Integer;

begin {Mystery}
      _____ (Data);
      _____ (OutData);
   while not EOF(_____) do
      begin
         Read (_____, Next);
         if Next < 50 then
            begin
               Write (_____, Next);
               WriteLn (_____, Next :2, ' Failed')
            end {if}
   end {while}
end. {Mystery}
```

15.3 Files of Records

The components of a binary file can be any type, simple or structured, except for another file type. Often, the components of a binary file are records. This section looks at ways to create a binary file of records.

Creating a Binary File

Unlike a text file, a binary file cannot be created using an editor program. To create a binary file, we must write and run a program that repeats the following steps until the binary file is completed.

1. Read the data for the next file component from a text file (or the keyboard) and save them in memory.
2. Copy the internal binary representation from memory to the binary file.

After the program executes, the binary file is stored on disk and is available for further processing.

The process of creating a binary file with two records is illustrated in Fig.15.3. The text file InData is read by program MakeBinary (see Fig. 15.4), which creates the binary file Employee. The data for each employee, consisting of an ID number, hourly rate, and hours worked, appear on two lines of file InData. After MakeBinary reads an employee's data from InData into record OneEmp, the statement

```
Write (Employee, OneEmp);
```

Figure 15.3 Creating a Binary File with Two Records

File InData (text file)

```
1234<eoln>
3.50  50<eoln>
2335<eoln>
4.35  40<eoln><eof>
```

```
          │
          │
          ▼
  ┌─────────────────┐
  │     Program     │
  │   MakeBinary    │
  └─────────────────┘
          │
          │
          ▼
  ┌────────┬────────┐
  │  1234  │  2335  │
  │  3.50  │  4.35  │
  │   50   │   40   │
  └────────┴────────┘
```

File Employee (binary file)

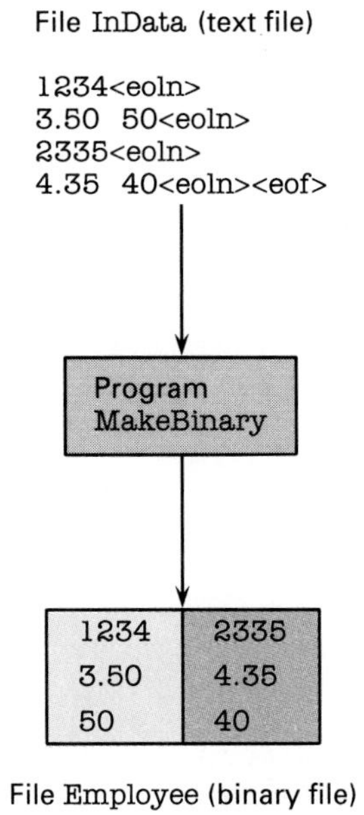

writes the resulting record to file Employee. Because InData is type Text, it has 26 components (all characters) and terminates with an <eof> (not counted). File Employee has only two components; each component is a record with three fields.

Figure 15.4 Program MakeBinary

Directory: CHAP15
File: MAKEBINA.PAS

```
program MakeBinary (InData, Employee);

{Creates a binary file of records}

   type
     Item = record
               ID : Integer;
               Rate : Real;
               Hours : Integer
            end; {Item}
     ItemFile = file of Item;

   var
     InData : Text;              {input - text file}
     Employee : ItemFile;        {output - binary file}
     OneEmp : Item;              {each record}

begin {MakeBinary}
  Reset (InData);
  Rewrite (Employee);
  while not EOF(InData) do
    begin
      {Read next record.}
      with OneEmp do
        begin
          ReadLn (InData, ID);
          ReadLn (InData, Rate, Hours)
        end; {with}
      Write (Employee, OneEmp)        {Write it to Employee.}
    end  {while}
end. {MakeBinary}
```

■ Example 15.4

The program in Fig. 15.5 creates a binary file, Inventory, that represents the inventory of a bookstore. Each file component is a record of type Book, because Inventory is declared as type BookFile (file of Book). The information saved in each component consists of a four-digit stock number, the book's author and title (strings), the price, and the quantity on hand. The program also computes and prints the total value of the inventory.

The main program calls procedure ReadBook to enter the data for each book from the terminal into record variable OneBook. ReadBook first reads the book's stock number. If the stock number is not the sentinel, ReadBook calls procedure ReadLnString (see Fig. 10.21) to read the author and title strings. After OneBook is defined, the statements

```
Write (Inventory, OneBook);    {Copy the book to Inventory}
InvValue := InvValue + OneBook.Price * OneBook.Quantity;
```

copy the internal, binary form of the entire record OneBook to file Inventory and update the inventory value.

Figure 15.5   Creating a BookStore Inventory File

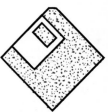

```
program BookInventory (Inventory, Input, Output);
{
 Creates an inventory file, Inventory, from data entered at the
 terminal. Also computes and prints the total inventory value.

 Module needed: StringADT (see Fig. 10.21)
}
  const
    Sentinel = 9999;                            {sentinel stock number}

  {Insert declaration for StringType from StringADT}

  type
    StockRange = 1111..9999;            {range of stock numbers}
    Book = record
              StockNum : StockRange;
              Author,
              Title   : StringType;
              Price : Real;
              Quantity : Integer
           end;  {Book}
    BookFile = file of Book;

  var
    Inventory : BookFile;               {the new inventory file}
    OneBook : Book;                     {each book}
    InvValue : Real;                    {value of inventory}

{Insert ReadLnString from StringADT}

procedure ReadBook (var OneBook {output} : Book);
{
  Reads a book from the keyboard into OneBook.
  Pre : None
  Post: Data are read from the keyboard into each field of the
        record represented by parameter OneBook.
  Uses: ReadLnString
}
  var
    CurLength: Integer;                 {length of a data string}

begin   {ReadBook}
  with OneBook do
    begin
      Write ('Stock number> ');     ReadLn (StockNum);
      if StockNum <> Sentinel then
        begin
          Write ('Author> ');
          ReadLnString (Input, Author, CurLength);
          Write ('Title> ');
          ReadLnString (Input, Title, CurLength);
          Write ('Price $');
          ReadLn (Price);
          Write ('Quantity> ');
          ReadLn (Quantity)
        end {if}
```

```
                             end; {with}
                          WriteLn
                       end;  {ReadBook}


                    begin  {BookInventory}
                       Rewrite (Inventory);          {Prepare Inventory for output.}
                       InvValue := 0.0;              {Initialize inventory value.}

                       {Read and copy each book until done.}
                       WriteLn ('Enter the data requested for each book.');
                       WriteLn ('Enter a stock number of 9999 when done.');
                       ReadBook (OneBook);                       {Read first book.}
                       while OneBook.StockNum <> Sentinel do
                          begin
                             Write (Inventory, OneBook);   {Copy the book to Inventory.}
                             InvValue := InvValue + OneBook.Price * OneBook.Quantity;
                             ReadBook (OneBook)                 {Read next book.}
                          end;  {while}

                       OneBook.StockNum := Sentinel;    {Write sentinel record to file.}
                       Write (Inventory, OneBook);

                       {Print inventory value.}
                       WriteLn ('Inventory value is $', InvValue :4:2)
                    end. {BookInventory}

                    Enter the data requested for each book.
                    Enter a stock number of 9999 when done.
                    Stock Number> 1234
                    Author> Robert Ludlum
                    Title> The Parsifal Mosaic
                    Price $17.95
                    Quantity> 10

                    Stock Number> 7654
                    Author> Blaise Pascal
                    Title> Pascal Made Easy
                    Price $50.00
                    Quantity> 1

                    Stock Number> 9999

                    Inventory value is $229.50
```

The binary file created when the program in Fig. 15.5 is run is shown next. The last record serves as a sentinel. The StockNum field (value is 9999) is the only field of the sentinel record that has its value defined.

File Inventory

1234	7654	9999
Robert Ludlum	Blaise Pascal	?
The Parsifal Mosaic	Pascal Made Easy	?
17.95	50.00	?
10	1	?

Self-Check

1. Assume a real number uses four bytes and an integer uses two bytes. How many bytes are processed when a component of file Inventory is read or written? Answer the same question for file Employee in Fig. 15.3.
2. Why does it not matter that some of the fields of the sentinel record are not defined? Under what circumstances might this present a problem?
3. Write all the declarations necessary for a file whose components are student records, where each record consists of a student ID number and an array of five scores. Write a loop that reads each student's record from the file and displays the student's ID number and first score.
4. Redo exercise 3 assuming that there are 10 students and each student record is an element of the array Class, which is stored as the only component of a binary file.

Programming

1. Write a procedure that resets file Inventory and displays each inventory record on the screen. Call procedure WriteOneRecord to display each record.
2. Write procedure WriteOneRecord.

15.4 File Merge Illustrated

Like most data structures, a file frequently needs to be modified or updated after it has been created. You may want to modify one or more fields of an existing record, delete a record, insert a new record, or simply display the current field values for a record.

Unlike a text file, a binary file cannot be modified with an editor. Instead, we must create a new file whose records are based on the original file. To do this, we must read each existing record, perhaps modify it, and then write it to the new file.

One kind of update operation is a *file merge*. In a file merge, we combine two files of the same type into a third file. If the records in the two original files are ordered according to a key field, the records in the new file must also be in order by key field.

Case Study: Merging Files

Problem

Whenever our bookstore receives a new shipment of books, a file (Update) is prepared that describes the new shipment. To keep our inventory file (Inventory) up to date, we need a program to combine, or merge, the information on these two files, assuming the records on both files are the same type (Book).

Case Study: Merging Files, continued

Analysis

Merging two files is a common data-processing operation. To perform this task efficiently (and most other tasks involving sequential files), we assume that the records on both files are in order by stock number. We also reserve the largest stock number (9999) as a special sentinel record always found at the end of each file.

Our task is to create a third file (NewInven) that contains all data appearing on the two existing files. If a stock number appears on only one of the files, then its corresponding record will be copied directly to NewInven. If a stock number appears on both files, then the data from file Update will be copied to NewInven, because that is the most recent information; however, the Quantity field of the record written to NewInven must be the sum of both Quantity fields (the quantity shipped plus the quantity on hand). The records on the new file must be in order by stock number.

Figure 15.6 illustrates the result of merging two small sample files. For simplicity, only the Stock and Quantity fields of all three files are shown. The only stock numbers appearing on all three files are 4234 and the sentinel stock number (9999). The original inventory file (Inventory) and the update file (Update) each contains four records (including the sentinel); the new inventory file (NewInven) contains six records (including the sentinel), in order by stock number. Records 1111 and 8955 are copied directly from file Inventory; records 6345 and 7789 are copied directly from file Update; and record 4234 is a combination of the data on files Inventory and Update.

The data requirements and the algorithm for a Merge procedure are described next. Because we are writing a procedure, the type declarations, which should appear in the main program, would be similar to those in Fig. 15.5.

Figure 15.6 Sample File Merge Operation

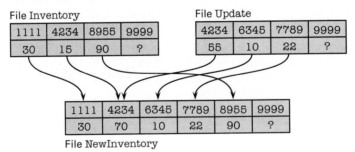

File NewInventory

Data Requirements

Problem Inputs
```
Inventory : BookFile      {current inventory file}
Update : BookFile         {file of new books received}
```

Problem Output
```
NewInven : BookFile       {new inventory file}
```

Local Variables

```
InvenBook : Book        {current record from Inventory}
UpdateBook : Book        {current record from Update}
```

Design

Initial Algorithm

1. Prepare files `Inventory` and `Update` for input and file `NewInven` for output.
2. Read the first record from `Inventory` into `InvenBook` and from `Update` into `UpdateBook`.
3. Copy all records that appear on only one input file to `NewInven`. If a record appears on both input files, sum both `Quantity` values before copying record `UpdateBook` to `NewInven`.

Refinements and Program Structure

Step 3 compares each pair of records stored in `InvenBook` and `UpdateBook`. Because the records on file `NewInven` must be in order by stock number, the record with the smaller stock number is written to `NewInven`. Another record is then read from the file containing the record just written, and the comparison process is repeated. If the stock numbers of `UpdateBook` and `InvenBook` are the same (a record appears on both files), the new value of `Update-Book.Quantity` is computed, the modified record is written to `NewInven`, and the next records are read from both input files.

Step 3 Refinement

3.1 `while` there are more records to copy `do`
    3.2 `if InvenBook.StockNum < UpdateBook.StockNum then`
        3.3 Write `InvenBook` to `NewInven` and read the next record of `Inventory` into `InvenBook`.
    `else if InvenBook.StockNum > UpdateBook.StockNum then`
        3.4 Write `UpdateBook` to `NewInven` and read the next record of `Update` into `UpdateBook`.
    `else`
        3.5 Sum the `Quantity` fields in `UpdateBook`, write `UpdateBook` to `NewInven`, and read the next record from `Inventory` and `Update`.
3.6 Write the sentinel record to `NewInven`.

Let's trace this step, assuming `InvenBook` and `UpdateBook` initially contain the first file records.

InvenBook   UpdateBook

Because 1111 is less than 4234, record InvenBook is copied to file NewInven (step 3.3), and the next record is read into InvenBook.

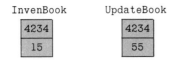

InvenBook   UpdateBook

Now the stock numbers are equal, so the quantity fields are summed (step 3.5), the new record with stock number 4234 is written to file NewInven, and the next records are read into InvenBook and UpdateBook.

InvenBook   UpdateBook

This time the record in UpdateBook is copied to NewInven (step 3.4), the next record is read into UpdateBook, and the merge continues.

What happens when the end of one input file is reached? The stock number for the current record of that file will be 9999 (the maximum), so each record read from the other input file will be copied directly to file NewInven. When the ends of both input files are reached, the while loop is exited and the sentinel record is written to file NewInven (step 3.6).

Procedure CopySmaller implements step 3.2. The structure chart for the Merge procedure is shown in Fig. 15.7.

Figure 15.7   Structure Chart for Procedure Merge

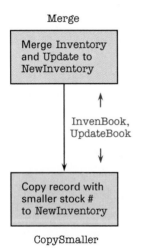

Implementation

Procedure Merge is shown in Fig. 15.8. The only output displayed on the screen as a result of executing procedure Merge is the message File merge completed. After the procedure's execution, you may want to echo print file NewInven. You could do this by resetting file NewInven and then writing individual fields of each record to the screen. Once you are certain file NewInven is correct, you can use an operating system command to rename it Inventory. You could then use the new file Inventory as the input inventory file and merge it with another Update file at a later time.

Figure 15.8 Procedures Merge and CopySmaller

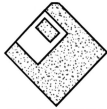

Directory: CHAP15
File: MERGE.PRO

```
procedure CopySmaller (var InvenBook,
                           UpdateBook {input/output} : Book;
                       var Inventory, Update, {input}
                           NewInventory {output} : BookFile);
{
  Writes the next record to file NewInven using data in
  InvenBook and UpdateBook. Also reads a new record from
  Inventory into InvenBook or from Update into UpdateBook or both
  to replace the record(s) that were written.
  Pre : InvenBook and UpdateBook are defined, and files
        Inventory and Update are opened for input and file
        NewInven is opened for output.
  Post: The record with the smaller StockNum field is written to
        NewInven and new data are read into that record. If both
        records have the same StockNum value, the Quantity fields
        are summed in UpdateBook, the modified record is written,
        and new records are read from both input files.
}
begin  {CopySmaller}
  if InvenBook.StockNum < UpdateBook.StockNum then
    begin {<}
      Write (NewInven, InvenBook);          {Copy InvenBook.}
      Read (Inventory, InvenBook)
    end  {<}
  else if InvenBook.StockNum > UpdateBook.StockNum then
    begin {>}
      Write (NewInven, UpdateBook);         {Copy UpdateBook.}
      Read (Update, UpdateBook)
    end {>}
  else
    begin {=}
      UpdateBook.Quantity := UpdateBook.Quantity +
                             InvenBook.Quantity;
      Write (NewInven, UpdateBook);         {Copy new UpdateBook.}
      Read (Inventory, InvenBook);          {Read both records.}
      Read (Update, UpdateBook)
    end  {=}
end;  {CopySmaller}


procedure Merge (var Inventory, Update {input} : BookFile;
                 var NewInven {output} : BookFile);
{
  Merges the data on files Inventory and Update to file NewInven.
```

```
      Pre : Files Inventory and Update are existing files ordered by
            stock number and ending with a sentinel stock number.
      Post: Each record appearing in only Inventory or Update
            is copied to NewInventory. If a stock number appears in
            both files, the Quantity fields are summed and the
            remaining fields are copied from Update. File NewInven
            is in order by stock number and ends with the sentinel.
      Uses: CopySmaller
}
   var
      InvenBook,                {current record of file Inventory}
      UpdateBook : Book;        {current record of file Update}

begin {Merge}
   {Prepare Inventory and Update for input, NewInven for output.}
   Reset (Inventory);  Reset (Update);  Rewrite (NewInven);

   {Read the first record from Inventory and Update.}
   Read (Inventory, InvenBook);  Read(Update, UpdateBook);

   {Copy all records from file Inventory and Update to NewInven.}
   while not EOF(Update) or not EOF(Inventory) do
      CopySmaller (InvenBook, UpdateBook, Inventory,
                   Update, NewInven);

   {Write the sentinel record to NewInven.}
   Write (NewInven, InvenBook);
   WriteLn ('File merge completed')
end;  {Merge}
```

You can adapt the merge procedure to perform other update operations. For example, you could merge a file that represents the daily sales of all books (file Sales) with file Inventory to generate an updated inventory file at the end of each day. If the quantity field of each record in file Sales is subtracted from the quantity field of the corresponding record in file Inventory, the difference would represent the quantity remaining in stock. You could even delete records whose quantity fields became negative or zero by simply not copying such records to NewInven.

PROGRAM STYLE

Analysis of the Merge Procedure

A number of questions arise about the merge procedure shown in Fig. 15.8. For example, what happens if an input file is empty or contains only the sentinel record? Because procedure Merge always reads at least one record, an execution error will occur if either input file is empty. If a file contains only the sentinel record, then only the sentinel record will be read from that file, and all the records in the other file will be copied directly to file NewInven. If both input files contain only the sentinel record, the while loop will be exited immediately, and only the sentinel record will be copied to file NewInven after loop exit.

Finally, we must ask about the efficiency of the merge procedure when the end of one file is reached much sooner than the other. This imbalance would result in the stock number 9999 being repeatedly compared to the stock numbers on the file that is not yet finished. It would be more efficient to exit the `while` loop when the end of one file is reached, then copy all remaining records on the other file directly to file `NewInven`. This modification is left as an exercise at the end of this section.

Testing

To test the merge procedure, provide files that contain only the sentinel record as well as files with one or more actual records. Make sure that the merge procedure works properly regardless of which of the two input files has all its records processed first. Also make sure that there is exactly one sentinel record on the merged file.

Exercises for Section 15.4

Self-Check

1. In procedure `Merge`, what three important assumptions are made about the two files that are merged? Must the two input files have the same number of records?
2. What happens if a record from one input file has the same stock number as a record from the other input file? What happens if one input file has two consecutive records with the same stock number?

Programming

1. Modify procedure `Merge` assuming that its input files do not contain a sentinel record. In this case, there should not be a sentinel record on the merged file. Exit from the merge loop when the end of either file is reached and then copy the remaining records from the unfinished file.

15.5 Searching a Data Base

Computerized matching of data against a file of records is becoming a common practice. For example, many real estate companies maintain a large file of property listings; a realtor can process the file to locate desirable properties for a client. Similarly, computerized dating services maintain a file of clients from which compatible matches can be made.

These large files of data are called *data bases*. In this section we will write a program that searches a data base to find all records that match a proposed set of requirements.

Case Study: Data Base Inquiry

Problem

One reason for storing the bookstore inventory as a computer file is to facilitate answering questions regarding that data base. The following questions might be of interest:

- What books by Robert Ludlum are in stock?
- What books in the price range $5.95 to $8.00 are in stock?
- What is the stock number of the book *Pascal Made Easy* and how many copies are in stock?
- What books costing more than $25 are in stock in quantities greater than 10?

These questions and others can be answered if we know the correct way to ask them.

Analysis

A data base inquiry program has two phases: setting the search parameters and searching for records that satisfy the parameters. In our program, we will assume that all the record fields can be involved in the search. The program user must enter low and high bounds for each field. Let's illustrate how we might set the search parameters to answer this question:

What are the books by Tennyson that cost less than $11 and for which two or more copies are in stock?

Assuming that there are never more than 5,000 copies of a book in stock and that the price of any book does not exceed $1,000, we can use this sample dialogue to set the search parameters.

```
Enter the low bound for stock number or 1111: 1111
Enter the high bound for stock number or 9999: 9999
Enter the low bound for author name or AAA: Tennyson
Enter the high bound for author name or zzz: Tennyson
Enter the low bound for title or AAA: AAA
Enter the high bound for title or zzz: zzz
Enter the low bound for price or $0: $0
Enter the high bound for price or $1000: $10.99
Enter the low bound for quantity or 0: 2
Enter the high bound for quantity or 5000: 5000
```

Data Requirements

Problem Inputs

```
Params : SearchParams      {search parameter bounds}
Inventory : BookFile       {inventory file}
```

Problem Outputs
all books that satisfy the search parameters

Design

Initial Algorithm

1. Prepare file Inventory for input.
2. Enter the search parameters.
3. Display all books that match the parameters.

Refinements and Program Structure
To simplify parameter passing between the procedures that implement steps 1 and 2, we store the search parameters in record variable Params (type SearchParams). The structure chart for the data base inquiry problem is shown in Fig. 15.9.

Figure 15.9   Structure Chart for Data Base Inquiry Problem

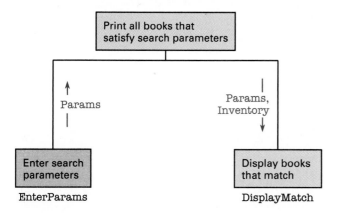

Implementation

Coding the Main Program
The main program is shown in Fig. 15.10.

Figure 15.10   Main Program for Data Base Inquiry Problem

```
program Inquire (Inventory, Input, Output);
{
  Prints all books that satisfy the search parameters specified
  by the program user

  Module needed: StringADT (see Fig. 10.21.)
}
```

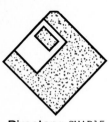

```pascal
const
   MaxQuantity = 5000;                      {maximum quantity}
   MaxPrice = 1000.00;                      {maximum book price}
   MinStock = 1111;                         {minimum stock number}
   MaxStock = 9999;                         {maximum stock number}

{Insert declaration for StringType from StringADT.}


type
   StockRange = MinStock..MaxStock;
   Book = record
            StockNum : StockRange;          {four-digit stock number}
            Author,
            Title    : StringType;
            Price : Real;
            Quantity : Integer
          end;   {Book}

   BookFile = file of Book;

   SearchParams = record                    {search parameter bounds}
                    LowStock, HighStock : StockRange;
                    LowAuthor, HighAuthor,
                    LowTitle, HighTitle    : StringType;
                    LowPrice, HighPrice : Real;
                    LowQuant, HighQuant : Integer
                  end; {SearchParams}
var
   Inventory : BookFile;                    {inventory file}
   Params : SearchParams;                   {search parameters}

{Insert ReadLnString from StringADT.}


procedure EnterParams (var Params {output} : SearchParams);
{
 Enters the search parameters and validates them.
 Pre : None
 Post: Returns the low bound and high bound for each search
       parameter though Params. The low bound for a parameter
       must be <= the high bound and both bounds must be in
       range.
 Uses: ReadLnString
}
begin   {EnterParams stub}
   WriteLn ('Procedure EnterParams entered.')
end;   {EnterParams}




procedure DisplayMatch (var Inventory {input} : BookFile;
                            Params {input} : SearchParams);
{
 Displays all records of Inventory that satisfy search
 parameters.
 Pre : File Inventory is opened for input and Params is defined.
 Post: An inventory record is displayed if its field values are
       within the bounds specified by record Params.
```

```
  }
  begin  {DisplayMatch}
    WriteLn ('Procedure DisplayMatch entered.')
  end;  {DisplayMatch}


begin  {Inquire}
  {Prepare Inventory for input.}
  Reset (Inventory);

  {Enter the search parameters.}
  EnterParams (Params);

  {Display all books that match the search parameters.}
  DisplayMatch (Inventory, Params)
end. {Inquire}
```

Coding the Procedures

Procedure EnterParams is left as an exercise at the end of this section. Procedure DisplayMatch must examine each file record with a stock number between the low and high bounds for stock numbers. If a record satisfies the search parameters, it is displayed. DisplayMatch should also print a message if no matches are found. The local variables and algorithm for procedure DisplayMatch follow.

Local Variables for DisplayMatch

```
NextBook : Book          {current book}
NoMatches : Boolean      {flag indicating whether there are any
                          matches}
```

Algorithm for DisplayMatch

1. Advance to the first record whose stock number is within range.
2. Initialize NoMatches to True.
3. while the current stock number is still in range do
   > begin
   >> 4. if the search parameters match then
   >>> 5. Display the book and set NoMatches to False.
   >>> 6. Read the next book record.
   > end
7. if there are no matches then
   > 8. Print a no books available message.

The structure chart for DisplayMatch is shown in Fig. 15.11. The Boolean function Match implements step 3; procedure Show implements step 4. The procedures are shown in Fig. 15.12.

Figure 15.11 Structure Chart for DisplayMatch

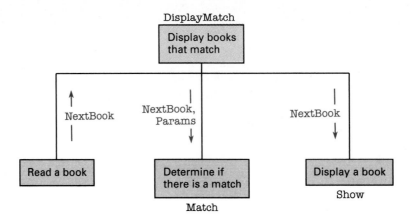

Figure 15.12 Procedures Match, Show, and DisplayMatch

Directory: CHAP15
File: INQUIRE.PAS

```
function Match (NextBook : Book;
                Params : SearchParams) : Boolean;
{
 Determines whether record NextBook satisfies all search
 parameters.
 Pre : NextBook and Params are defined.
 Post: Returns True if all parameters are matched; otherwise,
       returns False.
}
  var
    Matched : Boolean;                        {local Boolean flag}

begin   {Match}
  with Params do
    begin
      Matched := (LowAuthor <= NextBook.Author)
                  and (NextBook.Author <= HighAuthor);
      Matched := Matched and (LowTitle <= NextBook.Title)
                  and (NextBook.Title <= HighTitle);
      Matched := Matched and (LowPrice <= NextBook.Price)
                  and (NextBook.Price <= HighPrice);
      Matched := Matched and (LowQuant <= NextBook.Quantity)
                  and (NextBook.Quantity <= HighQuant)
    end;   {with}

  {Define function result.}
  Match := Matched
end;   {Match}

procedure Show (NextBook {input} : Book);
{
  Displays each field of NextBook at the terminal. Leaves a
  line space after each book.
```

```
  Pre : NextBook is defined.
  Post: All fields of NextBook are displayed.
}
begin  {Show stub}
  WriteLn ('Procedure Show entered.');
  WriteLn ('Stock number is ', NextBook.StockNum :1)
end;  {Show}

procedure DisplayMatch (var Inventory {input} : BookFile;
                            Params {input} : SearchParams);

{
  Displays all records of Inventory that satisfy search
  parameters.
  Pre : File Inventory is opened for input and Params is defined.
  Post: An inventory record is displayed if its field values are
        within the bounds specified by record Params.
  Uses: Match and Show
}
  var
    NextBook : Book;        {the current record}
    NoMatches : Boolean;   {indicates if there were any matches}

begin  {DisplayMatch}
  {
  Advance to first record with a stock number greater than
  or equal to the lower bound.
  }
  Read (Inventory, NextBook);
  while not EOF(Inventory) and
       (Params.LowStock > NextBook.StockNum) do
    Read (Inventory, NextBook);

  {assert: end of file reached or NextBook.StockNum in range}
  {Display each book that satisfies the search parameters.}
  NoMatches := True;            {Assume no matches to start.}
  WriteLn ('Books that satisfy the search parameters follow.');
  while (NextBook.StockNum <= Params.HighStock)
            and not EOF(Inventory) do
    {invariant:
        Each record that matches the parameters is displayed;
        no record with stock number > Params.HighStock was
        processed; and the file position pointer has not passed
        the end of file.
    }
    begin
      if Match(NextBook, Params) then
        begin
          NoMatches := False;        {Signal a match.}
          Show (NextBook)        {Print matched record.}
        end; {if}
      Read (Inventory, NextBook)    {Read the next record.}
    end;  {while}

  {assert: all records in range searched or at end of file}
  if NoMatches then
    WriteLn ('Sorry, no books are available.')
end;  {DisplayMatch}
```

In function `Match`, a local Boolean variable, `Matched`, indicates whether each search parameter is satisfied. Four assignment statements—one for each parameter except stock number—assign a value to `Matched`. If a search parameter is not satisfied, its corresponding assignment statement sets `Matched` to `False`. Because `Matched` is "anded" with the result of each parameter test, once `Matched` is set to `False`, it remains `False`. Consequently, for the function result to be `True`, `NextBook` must satisfy all search parameters.

Testing

Before you can test the data base program, you have to create a binary file using program `BookInventory` (see Fig. 15.5). Make sure you provide search requests that are not satisfied by any file records as well as requests that are. If you specify the maximum range for each search parameter, the program should display all records of the binary file. After a request is satisfied, verify that you can eliminate one or more of the records displayed by narrowing the search parameters.

Exercises for Section 15.5

Self-Check

1. Write the search parameters needed to answer the questions listed at the beginning of this section.
2. Which procedure or function determines whether a particular record matches the search parameters? Which procedure or function displays each record that matches the search parameters?
3. How does Boolean variable `Matched` work in function `Match`? Why is it not necessary to test field `StockNum` in function `Match`?

Programming

1. Write procedures `EnterParams` and `Show` described in the data base inquiry problem.

15.6 File Buffer Variable

Unlike other Pascal data structures, a file is located in secondary storage rather than main memory. For this reason, it is less convenient to access data stored in a file. The file component must first be transferred into main memory (by a `Read` operation) before the data in that component can be manipulated.

To simplify file access, Pascal allocates within main memory a *file-buffer variable* for each file declared in a program. The buffer variable acts as a "window" through which file data can be accessed. The buffer variable for a data file contains a copy of the file component currently selected by the file-position pointer. During a file read, as the file-position pointer moves, the file-buffer variable is automatically updated.

We can access a file's record through its buffer variable. Using the buffer variable is more efficient because it eliminates the need to allocate memory space for a record variable that stores the current file record (for example, record NextBook in Fig. 15.12). It also saves the processing time required to copy the current file record into that record variable.

We denote the file-buffer variable by writing the file name followed by a caret (^). Therefore, Inventory^ represents the file-buffer variable for file Inventory. The field selector Inventory^.Author may look strange, but it correctly references the Author field of the file-buffer variable. The with statement

```
with Inventory^ do
   begin
      WriteLn ('Stock number of book sold is ', StockNum :4);
      Quantity := Quantity − 1;
      SalesTotal := SalesTotal + Price
   end
```

manipulates the StockNum, Price, and Quantity fields of the record currently in the file-buffer variable for file Inventory.

Get and Reset

The Reset operator moves the file-position pointer to the beginning of a file. It also initializes the file-buffer variable for that file. The effect of the statement

```
Reset (Inventory)
```

follows:

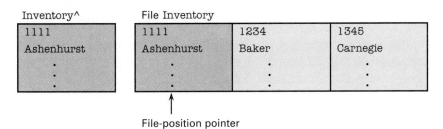

As indicated, the Reset operation moves the file-position pointer to the first file record and copies the data in that record to the file-buffer variable Inventory^. The statement

```
Get (Inventory)
```

advances the file-position pointer to the next file component and automatically updates the file-buffer variable, as shown next.

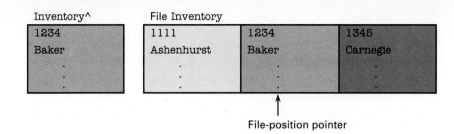

File-position pointer

When the file-position pointer is at the last file component, the next Get operation causes the buffer variable to become undefined, and EOF(Inventory) becomes True.

Reset Procedure (Effect on File-Buffer Variable)

Form: Reset (*infile*)
Example: Reset (Inventory)
Interpretation: The file-position pointer for file *infile* is moved to the beginning of file *infile*. The first file component is stored in the file-buffer variable *infile^*.
Note: The Reset operation is automatically performed on system file Input, so Reset (Input) is not needed and may cause an error on some Pascal systems.

Get Operator

Form: Get (*infile*)
Interpretation: The file-position pointer for file *infile* is advanced, and the next file component is stored in the file-buffer variable *infile^*.
Note: The effect of the Get operation is undefined if EOF(*infile*) is True before or after the Get is executed. The first Get must be preceded by a Reset operation (except for system file Input).

Put and Rewrite

We write a file in Pascal by appending data to the end of the file. Data stored in a file-buffer variable can be appended with the Put operator. Whenever the statement

    Put (*outfile*)

is executed, the current contents of the file-buffer variable *outfile^* are appended to the end of file *outfile*. The data to be transferred must be stored in the file-buffer variable *outfile^* before the Put is executed. The statement must be executed before the first Put operation.

■ Example 15.5

Procedure BuildSmall in Fig. 15.13 creates an abbreviated inventory file, SmallInv, that consists only of the stock number and the quantity of every record in file Inventory. You must declare file types BookFile and Small-BookFile in the calling program. There is no need to declare record variables for storing the current record of each of these files.

Figure 15.13 Procedure BuildSmall

```
procedure BuildSmall (var Inventory {input} : BookFile;
                      var SmallInv {output} : SmallBookFile);
{
  Creates a new inventory file (SmallInv) containing only stock
  numbers and quantities of the records in Inventory.
  Pre : Inventory is defined.
  Post: SmallInv contains a smaller version of each record in
        Inventory.
}
begin {BuildSmall}
  {Initialize buffer variable for Inventory and open SmallInv.}
  Reset (Inventory);
  Rewrite (SmallInv);

  {Copy stock number and quantity from Inventory to SmallInv.}
  while not EOF(Inventory) do
    begin
      {Define buffer variable SmallInv^.}
      SmallInv^.StockNum := Inventory^.StockNum;
      SmallInv^.Quantity := Inventory^.Quantity;
      Put (SmallInv);               {Append data to SmallInv.}
      Get (Inventory)              {Access next record.}
    end  {while}
end;  {BuildSmall}
```

Directory: CHAP15
File: BUILDSMA.PRO

Each assignment statement,

```
SmallInv^.StockNum := Inventory^.StockNum;
SmallInv^.Quantity := Inventory^.Quantity;
```

copies one field from the file-buffer variable for Inventory to the file-buffer variable for SmallInv. The statement

```
Put (SmallInv);                {Append data to SmallInv.}
```

appends the data just copied to file SmallInv; the statement

```
Get (Inventory);               {Access next record.}
```

updates the file-buffer variable for Inventory so that it contains the next record.

■

Rewrite Procedure (Effect on File Buffer Variable)

Form: Rewrite (*outfile*)

Example: Rewrite (SmallInv)

Interpretation: The file-position pointer for file *outfile* is returned to the beginning of file *outfile*, thereby erasing any data that might be stored on the file. The file-buffer variable *outfile*^ becomes undefined. The Rewrite operation is automatically performed on system file Output, so it is not needed, and Rewrite (Output) may cause an error on some Pascal systems.

Put Operator

Form: Put (*outfile*)

Example: Put (SmallInv)

Interpretation: The contents of the file-buffer variable *outfile*^ are appended to the end of file *outfile*. The file-buffer variable must be defined before the Put operation; it becomes undefined after the Put operation. **Note:** The first Put operation must be preceded by a Rewrite operation (except for system file Output).

Get and Put versus Read and Write

Get and Read both can access data stored in a file. The Read procedure enters the current file component into a local variable of the same type. The statement

```
Read (Inventory, NextBook)
```

stores the next component of file Inventory in the variable NextBook and advances the file-position pointer for Inventory.

A local variable is not needed with Get because the data in the file-buffer variable can be accessed directly. However, you can still use Get to store data in a local variable. The statements

```
NextBook := Inventory^;
Get (Inventory)
```

have the same effect as the preceding Read statement; the current file component (stored in Inventory^) is copied into NextBook, and the file-position pointer is advanced.

The statement

```
Write (NewInven, NextBook)
```

writes the data stored in variable NextBook to file NewInven. This can also be accomplished with the statements

```
NewInven^ := NextBook;
Put (NewInven)
```

The assignment statement defines the file-buffer variable `NewInven^`; the `Put` operation appends these data to the end of file `NewInven`.

Exercises for Section 15.6

Self-Check

1. Complete the following program segment. What does it do?

```
program Mystery (_____, _____);
   type
     NumberFile = file of Integer;

   var
     Next : Integer;
     InFile, OutFile : _____;

begin {Mystery}
   Reset (_____);
   Rewrite (_____);
   while not EOF(_____) do
     begin
       _____^ := 2 * _____^;
       Put (_____);
       Get (_____)
     end {while}
end. {Mystery}
```

2. How would you modify procedures `Merge` and `CopySmaller` (see Fig. 15.8) to use `Get` and `Put` instead of `Read` and `Write`? Manipulate the file-buffer variables directly instead of local variables `UpdateBook` and `InvenBook`.

Programming

1. Rewrite procedure `BuildSmall` to copy every other record of file `Inventory` to file `SmallInv`.

15.7 Direct-Access Files (Optional)

The files processed so far in this chapter have been sequential files. This means that each operation is performed on every file record and that the records are processed in order, starting with the first one. Sequential files are perfectly adequate whenever a file-processing operation involves most of the records in a file. However, if we want to modify only a few records in a large file, it is wasteful and time-consuming to have to process every record in the file.

For this reason, several extended versions of Pascal provide operators that enable *direct access* or *random access* to a file. Direct access means that a program can access any file record at any time. A direct-access file is analogous to a large array stored on disk in that the records can be accessed in either sequential order or arbitrary order. With direct access, we can mix Read and Write operations on the same file. With sequential access, we can either read all the records of a file or write all its records.

We cannot use an editor program to create a direct-access file. We must write a program that reads the data for a direct-access file from a text file (or the keyboard), stores this data in memory, and copies the data from memory to the direct-access file. To access a particular file component, we must first move the file-position pointer to that component. Once the file-position pointer has been moved, a Read or Write operation can be performed.

The next few sections detail specifics of direct-access file processing in Turbo Pascal and extended Pascal. You should read only the sections that pertain to the Pascal system you are using. If your Pascal system does not support direct-access files, skip these sections.

Direct-Access Files in Turbo Pascal

In Turbo Pascal, direct access is supported for any binary file but not for text files. If binary file Inventory (see Fig. 15.5) has been opened for input, the procedure call statement

```
Seek (Inventory, 9);
```

advances the file-position pointer for Inventory to record number 9. This is actually the tenth record, because the first record has record number 0. Function FileSize returns the number of records in a binary file. If there are 20 records in file Inventory (record numbers 0 through 19), the function designator FileSize(Inventory) returns 20.

■ Example 15.6

Procedure UpdateBook in Fig. 15.14 updates the record of file Inventory selected by parameter RecNum. The condition

```
(RecNum >= 0) and (RecNum < FileSize(Inventory))
```

is true if RecNum is in range. The statement

```
Seek (Inventory, RecNum);
```

moves the file-position pointer to record number RecNum just before the Read operation and just before the Write operation. It is necessary to execute this statement twice because the Read operation advances the file-position pointer to record RecNum + 1.   ■

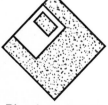

Directory: CHAP15
File: UPDATEBO.PRO

Figure 15.14 Procedure UpdateBook in Turbo Pascal

```
procedure UpdateBook (var Inventory {input/output} : BookFile;
                          RecNum,
                          Sales {input} : Integer);
{
  Updates record RecNum of file Inventory by subtracting the
  amount sold (Sales) from the Quantity field.
```

```
  Pre : Inventory is opened for input (using Reset)
        and RecNum and Sales are defined.
  Post: Quantity field of record RecNum is decremented by Sales.
}
  var
    OneBook : Book;        {record being updated}

begin {UpdateBook}
  if (RecNum >= 0) and (RecNum < FileSize(Inventory)) then
    begin
      Seek (Inventory, RecNum);          {Move to record RecNum.}
      Read (Inventory, OneBook);
      OneBook.Quantity := OneBook.Quantity - Sales;    {Update}
      Seek (Inventory, RecNum);      {Return to record RecNum.}
      Write (Inventory, OneBook)        {Write updated record.}
    end
  else
    WriteLn ('Record number is out of range.')
end; {UpdateBook}
```

Seek Procedure

Form: Seek (*iofile, recnum*)

Example: Seek (Inventory, 10)

Interpretation: The file-position pointer for binary file *iofile* is moved to record number *recnum,* where the first record has record number 0. Unpredictable results will occur if the value of *recnum* is less than 0 or greater than *n* for a file of *n* records. It is not advisable to perform two Seek operations without an intervening Read or Write.

FileSize Function

Form: FileSize(*iofile*)

Example: FileSize(Inventory)

Interpretation: The FileSize function returns the number of records in binary file *iofile*.

Appending a Record in Turbo Pascal

In Turbo Pascal, the function designator FileSize(Inventory) returns the number of records in file Inventory. The statements

```
Seek (Inventory, FileSize(Inventory));
Write (Inventory, NewBook)
```

can be used to append a new record, NewBook, to the end of file Inventory. If there are *n* records in file Inventory, function FileSize returns *n*. Procedure Seek advances the file-position pointer to record number *n* or just past the last record (record number *n* − 1) in the current file. Procedure Write then writes NewBook to the end of the file.

Direct-Access Files in Extended Pascal

In extended Pascal, the file-type declaration for a direct-access file must include an index type. For example, the declarations

```
type
  Book = record
          ....
          end; {Book}

  DABookFile = file [1..100] of Book;

var
  DAInventory : DABookFile;
```

declare a direct-access file type DABookFile. A file of this type can have up to 100 records, indexed by the integers 1 through 100. Any ordinal type can be used as an index type.

You can process the records of file DAInventory in sequential order using any of the standard Pascal procedures and functions discussed earlier. Direct access of selected records of file DAInventory is also permitted with procedure SeekUpdate, which is part of extended Pascal. The procedure call statement

```
SeekUpdate (DAInventory, 10)
```

advances the file-position pointer for file DAInventory to record number 10 (the tenth record) and stores the contents of this record in the file-buffer variable DAInventory^. In extended Pascal, function LastPosition returns the number of records currently in direct-access file DAInventory.

■ Example 15.7

Procedure UpdateBook in Fig. 15.15 updates the record of direct-access file DAInventory selected by parameter RecNum. The condition

```
(RecNum >= 1) and (RecNum <= LastPosition(DAInventory))
```

is true if RecNum is in range. The statement

```
SeekUpdate (DAInventory, RecNum);
```

moves the file-position pointer to record number RecNum and copies that record to the file-buffer variable. After the file-buffer variable is modified, the Put statement replaces record number RecNum with the new contents of the file-buffer variable. ■

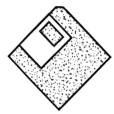

```
procedure UpdateBook (var DAInventory {input/output} : DABookFile;
                          RecNum {input} : Integer;
                          Sales {input} : Integer);
{
  Updates record RecNum of direct access file DAInventory by
  subtracting the amount sold (Sales) from the Quantity field.
  Pre : DAInventory is opened for input and RecNum and Sales
        are defined.
  Post: Quantity field of record RecNum is decremented by Sales.
}
begin {UpdateBook}
  if (RecNum >= 1) and (RecNum <= LastPosition(DAInventory)) then
    begin
      SeekUpdate (DAInventory, RecNum);
      {Modify the file-buffer variable.}
      DAInventory^.Quantity := DAInventory^.Quantity - Sales;
      Put (DAInventory)                {Replace record.}
    end
  else
    WriteLn ('Record number is out of range.')
end; {UpdateBook}
```

Direct-Access-File Type Declaration

Form: type *dafile* = file *index type* of *component type*;
Example: type DAInventory = file [1..MaxSize] of Book;
Interpretation: The identifier *dafile* is associated with a direct-access file type. Each component of a file of type *dafile* has type *component type*. One file record corresponds to each value in *index type*. The first file record corresponds to the minimum value of *index type*; the last file record corresponds to the maximum value of *index type*.

SeekUpdate Procedure

Form: SeekUpdate (*iofile*, *recnum*)
Example: SeekUpdate (DAInventory, 10)
Interpretation: The file-position pointer for direct-access file *iofile* is moved to record number *recnum*, where *recnum* is an expression that is assignment compatible with the index type of file *iofile*. The first record in the file is selected when *recnum* takes on the smallest value in its range. Unpredictable results occur if the value of *recnum* is less than its minimum value or greater than its maximum value. The contents of record *recnum* are copied to the file buffer variable *iofile*^.

LastPosition Function

Form: LastPosition(*iofile*)

Example: LastPosition(DAInventory)

Interpretation: The LastPosition function returns the number of records currently stored in direct-access file *iofile*.

Appending a New Record to the End of a File in Extended Pascal

Use the procedure call statements

```
Extend (Inventory);
Write (Inventory, NewBook)
```

to append a new record, NewBook, to the end of file Inventory.

15.8 Common Programming Errors

Do not forget to prepare a binary file for input or output using the Reset or Rewrite procedure. If you rewrite an existing file, the data on that file will be lost. Make sure you do not inadvertently place the Reset or Rewrite statement in a loop. If you do, a Read operation in the loop will repeatedly read the first file component; a Write operation in the loop will repeatedly write the first file component.

You can perform a number of operations with text files that you cannot perform with binary files, because binary files are not segmented into lines. You cannot use the EOLN function and ReadLn and WriteLn procedures with binary files. Also, you cannot create or modify a binary file using an editor program. A binary file must be created by running a program before it can be used.

You can access the current file component through the file-buffer variable. Avoid the common error of writing the operators that manipulate the file-buffer variable as Get (*infile^*) or Put (*outfile^*). The caret should be deleted and the operators written as Get (*infile*) or Put (*outfile*).

CHAPTER REVIEW

In this chapter, you learned how to declare and manipulate binary files whose components may be any simple or structured type (except for another file type). We created a file of records and merged two files of records into a third file. We also searched a data base to retrieve file records that matched a specified set of search parameters.

Binary files do have an advantage in that an entire record can be transferred between a binary file and a variable in main memory. The variable involved in the data transfer must be the same type as the components of the binary file. Accessing the current file component through the file buffer variable eliminates the need for a separate variable in main memory. The operators `Reset` and `Rewrite` initialize the file-buffer variable. The operator `Get` retrieves the next file component, and the operator `Put` appends the contents of the file-buffer variable to the end of its file.

Finally, we reviewed extensions to Pascal that permit direct access to files. We also showed you how to append a record to the end of a file.

New Pascal Constructs

The Pascal constructs introduced in this chapter are summarized in Table 15.1.

Table 15.1   Summary of New Pascal Constructs

Construct	Effect

File-Type Declaration
`type`
`  DigitFile = file of Integer;`
 	
`var`
`  MoreDigits : DigitFile;`
	Declares a file type `DigitFile` whose components are integers.
	`MoreDigits` is a file of type `DigitFile`.

Get Operator
`Reset (MoreDigits);`
`I := MoreDigits^;`
`Get (MoreDigits);`
`Write (MoreDigits^)`
	The first integer in file `MoreDigits` is placed in the file-buffer variable and assigned to variable `I`. The second integer is displayed.

Put Operator
`Rewrite (MoreDigits);`
`MoreDigits^ := 99;`
`Put (MoreDigits)`
	A new file `MoreDigits` is created whose first component is 99.

✓ Quick-Check Exercises

1. What data types can be read or written to a text file?
2. What data types can be read or written to a binary file?
3. Under what circumstances can a file variable not appear in the program heading? Under what circumstances can a file variable not appear in the variable declarations? Under what circumstances can a file type not appear in the type declarations?
4. When is it appropriate to pass a file as a value parameter to a procedure?
5. Comment on the correctness of this statement: It is more efficient to use a text file because the computer knows that each component is a single character that can be copied into a single byte of main memory; with a binary file, however, the size of the components may vary.
6. What limits the number of records that can be written to a file?

7. What limits the number of records that can be read from a file? How do you know when you have read them all?

8. What happens if the `Reset` operation is performed on a file that has just been created in a program? What happens if the `Rewrite` operation is performed on the same file?

9. How does the Pascal compiler know how big to make the file-buffer variable for a file?

10. The _____ operator stores the first file record in the file-buffer variable. The _____ operator stores the record pointed to by the _____ _____ _____ in the file-buffer variable and advances the _____ _____ _____. The _____ operator copies the record in the file-buffer variable to the file and advances the _____ _____ _____.

Answers to Quick-Check Exercises

1. Any standard data type (or a subrange thereof) except type Boolean can be read; any standard data type (or a subrange thereof) or a string can be written.

2. the file's component type, which is any simple or structured type that does not have a file type as one of its constituents

3. When a file that is being written will not be retained as a permanent file after program execution; when the file is system file `Input` or `Output`; when the file type is type `Text`.

4. never.

5. The statement is not correct. It is true that two binary files may have components of different sizes, but the components of a particular file must all be the same data type and the same size. This size can be determined from the type declarations. Because no data conversions are necessary when you use binary files, binary files are more efficient than text files.

6. The only limit is the available space on disk.

7. The number of records that were written to the file when it was created. Use the EOF function to test for the end-of-file marker.

8. `Reset` prepares the file for input so we can echo print it if we want to check the records that were written. `Rewrite` wipes the file out.

9. The file-buffer variable is the same size as the file components, which can be determined from the type declarations.

10. The `Reset` operator stores the first file record in the file-buffer variable. The `Get` operator stores the record pointed to by the file-position pointer in the file-buffer variable and advances the file-position pointer. The `Put` operator copies the record in the file-buffer variable to the file and advances the file-position pointer.

Review Questions

1. Where are files stored?

2. Modify procedure `CopyFile` to write data to both the file `OutFile` and the system file `Output`.

3. Consider an `EmpStat` file (type Text) that contains records for up to 15 employees. The data for each employee consist of the employee's name (maximum length, 20 characters), social security number (maximum length, 20 characters), gross pay for the week (real), taxes deducted (real), and the net pay (real) for the week. Each data item is on a separate line of file `EmpStat`. Write a program called `PayReport`, which will create a text file `ReportFile` with the heading line

followed by two blank lines, then the pertinent information under each column heading. `ReportFile` should contain up to 18 lines of information after `PayReport` is executed.

4. What are the characteristics of a binary file?

5. Imagine for a moment that you are a college professor who uses a computerized system to maintain student records. Write the type and variable declarations for a file that will consist of multiple records of type `StudentStats`. The statistics kept on each student are the `GPA`, `Major`, `Address` (consisting of `Name`, `StreetAddress`, `City`, `State`, and `ZipCode`), and `ClassSchedule` (consisting of up to six records of `Class`, each containing `Description`, `Time`, and `Days` fields). Use whatever variable types are appropriate for each field.

6. Explain the use and manipulation of a file-buffer variable.

7. What Pascal procedures advance the file-position pointer in a file being used for input?

8. Write a procedure `PlaceLastName` that will accept a file of names of the form *Lastname, Firstname* (example: Drend, Jane) and `Put` only the last name in the file `LastOnly`. Use ADT `VarStringADT` (see Section 14.3) and its operators, two files whose components are type `VarString`, and process their file buffer variables.

Programming Projects

1. Assume you have a file of records, each containing a person's last name, first name, birth date, and sex. Create a new file of records containing only first names and sex. Also print out the complete name of every person whose last name begins with the letter A, C, F, or P through Z and who was born in a month beginning with the letter J.

2. Assume that you have separate text files for the salesmen and the saleswomen in your furniture store. For each employee in these files, include an employee number (four digits), a name, and a salary. Each file should be in order by employee number. Merge these two files into a third file that also has a gender field containing one of the values in the type (`Female, Male`). After the file merge operation, find the average salary for all employees. Then search the new file and print a list of all female employees earning more than the average salary and a separate list of all male employees earning more than the average salary. Hint: You will have to search the new file once for each list. Your program should include procedures corresponding to the following procedure headers.

```
procedure ReadOneRec (var DataFile {input} : Text;
                      Sex {input} : Gender;
                      var EmpRec {output} : EmployeeRec);
{
 Reads one employee record from text file DataFile and assigns
 Sex value to appropriate EmpRec field.
}

procedure MergeFile (var MaleFile, FemaleFile {input} : Text;
                     var OutFile {output} : EmployeeFile);
{
 Merges the records from the two input files, adds gender
 field to the output record.
 Uses: ReadOneRec.
}
```

```
procedure FindAveSalary (var EmpFile {input} : EmployeeFile;
                         var Average {output} : Real);
{Computes average salary using all employee records.}

procedure PrintHigh (Sex {input} : Gender;
                     var EmpFile {input} : EmployeeFile;
                     Average {input} : Real);
{
 Print gender-specific list of persons earning more than
 Average salary.
}
```

3. Write a procedure that will merge the contents of three sorted files by ID number and write the merged data to an output file. The parameters to the procedure will be the three input files and the one output file. Data will be of the form

```
Data = record
         ID : Integer;
         Name : StringType;
         Length : Integer;
         Salary : Real
       end;
```

Assume there is no sentinel record and use procedures Get and Put. Test your procedure with some sample data.

4. Cooking recipes can be stored on a computer and, with the use of files, can be quickly referenced.

a. Write a procedure that will create a text file of recipes from information entered at the terminal. The format of the data to be stored is

   (1) recipe type (Dessert, Meat, etc.)
   (2) subtype (for Dessert, use Cake, Pie, or Brownies)
   (3) name (for cake, German Chocolate)
   (4) number of lines in the recipe to follow
   (5) the actual recipe

   Items 1, 2, 3, and 4 should be on separate lines.

b. Write a procedure that will accept as parameters a file and a record of search parameters that will cause all recipes of a type, all recipes of a subtype, or a specific recipe to be written.

5. College football teams need a service to keep track of records and vital statistics. Write a program that will maintain this information in a file. An update file will be "posted" weekly against the master file of all team statistics to date, and all the records will be updated. All the information in both files will be stored in order by ID number. Each master record will contain the team's ID number; team name; number of games won, lost, and tied; total yards gained by the team's offense; total yards gained by the other teams against this one; total points scored by this team; and total points scored by the other teams against this one.

   For this program, use the master file Teams and update Teams from file Weekly. Write the updated information to a file called NewTeams. In addition, each record of the weekly file should be echo printed. At the completion of processing the files, write a message indicating the number of weekly scores processed, the team that scored the most points, and the team with the most offensive yardage for this week.

6. Write a program that takes a master file of college football information and prints out teams that match a specified set of search parameters. The bounds on the search parameters could be presented in the format described in Section 15.5. Some infor-

mation you might want to print: all teams with a won/lost percentage in a certain range; all teams within a certain range of points scored or scored upon; all teams with a certain range of yardage gained or given up; all teams with a certain number of games won, tied, or lost. (Note: The won/lost percentage is calculated by dividing number of games won by total games played; ties count as half a game won.)

7. Write a program that updates a file of type `Inventory` (see Section 15.3). Your program should be able to modify an existing record, insert a new record, and delete an existing record. Assume that the update requests are in order by stock number and that they have the form

```
type
   ChangeKind = (Delete, Insert, Modify);
   UpdateReq = record
                  case Change : ChangeKind of
                     Delete : (StockNumber : StockRange);
                     Insert : (NewBook : Book);
                     Modify : (ModBook : Book)
               end; {UpdateReq}
```

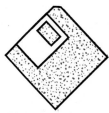

Directory: CHAP15
File: PROJ15_7.PAS

Each update request should be read from a binary file. Only the stock number appears in an update request for a deletion. The new book record is supplied for a request to insert a record or to modify an existing record. Your program should also print an error message for invalid requests, such as an attempt to delete a record that does not exist, an attempt to insert a new record with the same stock number as an existing record, or an attempt to modify a record that does not exist.

8. Redo programming project 7 as a menu-driven program using a direct-access file to save the inventory data. Assume that the `StockNumber` is used as the record number to access the inventory file. The constant `StockRange` should be redefined to be `0..99` (to avoid having 1000 record positions that are never used in the inventory file). Support the following menu options: creating a blank file, inserting records, updating records, deleting records, displaying selected records, and displaying all active records.

Since records cannot be deleted physically from the direct-access inventory file, add a Boolean field (`DeletedRec`) to each inventory record. Deleting a record, then, would simply involve setting field `DeletedRec` to `True` and copying the modified record back to the inventory file. Likewise, adding a record would involve setting the `DeletedRec` field to `False`, in addition to assigning values to each of the other fields.

If your Pascal compiler does not support direct-access files, simply rewrite project 7 as an interactive menu-driven program.

16
Stacks and Queues

Chapter 13 introduced the stack as a useful data structure for storing the actual parameters passed in each call to a recursive procedure or function. A stack is a convenient mechanism for storing information (or dishes in a cafeteria); we can access only the top item in a stack. The first part of this chapter illustrates how to use a stack and how to implement an abstract data type for a stack.

The rest of the chapter discusses a related data structure, the queue. The British people don't "wait in line," they "queue up." We will use a queue to represent a list of airline passengers waiting to see a ticket agent. We will also implement an abstract data type for a queue.

16.1 The Stack Abstract Data Type

In this section, we discuss a data abstraction, the stack, that is useful in computer science applications such as writing compilers. A stack is characterized by the property that at any one time only the top element of the stack is accessible. Some of the operations that we might want to perform on a stack are summarized in the following specification.

```
{

    Specification of Abstract Data Type StackADT

    Elements:    A stack consists of a collection of elements
                 that are all the same data type.
    Structure:   The elements of a stack are ordered according
                 to when they were placed on the stack. Only
                 the element that was last inserted onto the
                 stack can be removed or examined. New elements
                 are inserted at the top of the stack.
    Operators:   The following descriptions assume these
                 parameters:

      S represents the stack.
      X has the same data type as the stack elements.
      Success is type Boolean and indicates whether or not the
      operation succeeds.

      CreateStack (var S): Creates an empty stack.

      Push (var S, X, var Success): If stack S is not full, the
      value in X is placed on the top of the stack and Success
```

```
          is set to True. Otherwise, the top of the stack is not
          changed and Success is set to False.

          Pop (var S, var X, var Success): If stack S is not empty,
          the value at the top of the stack is removed, its value
          is placed in X, and Success is set to True. If the stack
          is empty, X is not defined and Success is set to False.

          Retrieve (S, var X, var Success): If stack S is not
          empty, the value at the top of the stack is copied into
          X, and Success is set to True. If the stack is empty, X
          is not defined and Success is set to False. In either
          case, the stack is not changed.

          IsEmpty(S): (function) Returns True if stack S is empty;
          otherwise, returns False.

          IsFull(S): (function) Returns True if stack S is full;
          otherwise, returns False.
      }
```

We can illustrate how these operators work and use them in a client program without worrying about the details of how the stack is represented in memory. We discuss an internal representation for a stack and implement the stack operators in Section 16.4. Because we want to be able to manipulate different types of data objects using a stack, we use the identifier StackElement to represent the type of each stack element. Each client program must import data types StackElement and Stack from StackADT.

A client program can allocate multiple stacks by declaring several variables of type Stack. Because StackElement can be declared only once in a program, all stacks used in a particular program must have the same type of element.

Procedure CreateStack must be called before a stack can be processed. CreateStack creates a stack that is initially empty. If S is declared as type Stack, the statements

```
CreateStack (S);
if IsEmpty(S) then
   WriteLn ('Stack is empty')
```

display the message Stack is empty.

■ Example 16.1

A stack S of character elements is shown in Fig. 16.1. The stack has four elements; the first element placed on the stack was '2', and the last element placed on the stack was '*'.

Figure 16.1 Stack S

For stack S in Fig. 16.1, the value of IsEmpty(S) is False. The value of IsFull(S) is False if stack S can store more than four elements; otherwise, the value of IsFull(S) is True. The procedure call statement

```
Retrieve (S, X, Success)
```

stores '*' in X (type Char) without changing S. The procedure call statement

```
Pop (S, X, Success)
```

removes '*' from S and stores it in X. The new stack S contains three elements and is shown in Fig. 16.2.

The procedure call statement

```
Push (S, '/', Success)
```

pushes '/' onto the stack; the new stack S contains four elements and is shown in Fig. 16.3. The value of Success (type Boolean) after each operation should be True. ∎

Figure 16.2 Stack S After Pop Operation

Figure 16.3 Stack S After Push Operation

Exercise for Section 16.1

Self-Check

1. Assume that the stack S is defined as in Fig. 16.3. Perform the following sequence of operations. Indicate the result of each operation and the new

stack if it is changed. Rather than draw the stack each time, use the notation |2 + C/ to represent the stack in Fig. 16.3, where the last symbol on the right (/) is at the top of the stack.

```
Push (S, '$', Success);
Push (S, '-', Success);
Pop (S, NextCh, Success);
Retrieve (S, NextCh, Success);
IsEmpty(S);
IsFull(S)
```

16.2 Stack Applications

This section examines some client programs that use stacks. These programs should give you some idea of the importance of the stack data type.

Case Study: Displaying a String in Reverse Order

Problem
A reading instructor is studying dyslexia and wants a program that displays a word or a sentence in reverse order.

Analysis
A stack of characters is a good data structure for such a program. If we first push each data character onto a stack and then pop each character and display it, the characters will be displayed in reverse order. The sequence of characters is displayed in reverse order because the last character pushed onto the stack is the first one popped. For example, the diagram in Fig. 16.4 shows the stack S after the letters in the string 'house' are processed. The first letter popped and displayed is e, the next letter is s, and so on.

Figure 16.4 Pushing 'house' onto a Stack

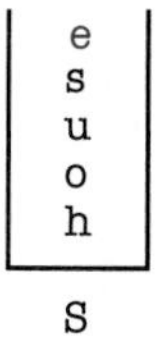

```
  e
  s
  u
  o
  h
S
```

Data Requirements

Problem Input
each data character

Case Study: Displaying a String in Reverse Order, continued

Problem Output
each character on the stack

Program Variable
```
S : Stack      {stack of characters}
```

Design

Initial Algorithm

1. Create an empty stack of characters.
2. Push each data character onto a stack.
3. Pop each character and display it.
4. Indicate whether the stack is empty or full.

Program Structure

The structure chart (Fig. 16.5) shows that procedure `CreateStack` performs step 1, procedure `FillStack` performs step 2, and procedure `DisplayStack` performs step 3. `FillStack` and `DisplayStack` call procedures `Push` and `Pop` from `StackADT`. Functions `IsEmpty` and `IsFull` (from `StackADT`) are called to perform step 4.

Figure 16.5 Structure Chart for PrintReverse

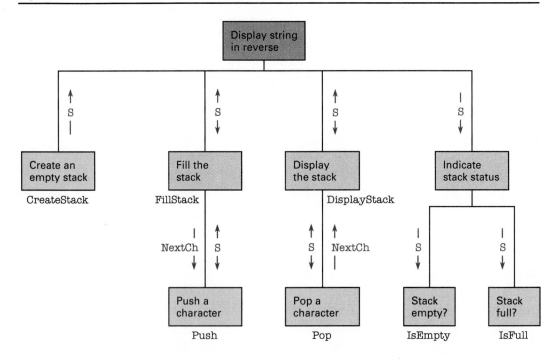

Implementation

Coding the Main Program
The main program and its procedures are shown in Fig. 16.6. The type declarations for StackElement (type is Char) and Stack must be imported from StackADT, along with the stack operators. Procedures FillStack and DisplayStack are described after the program.

Coding the Procedures
The repeat–until loop in procedure FillStack (Fig. 16.7) reads each data character (at least one) into NextCh and pushes it onto the stack. The

Figure 16.6 Program PrintReverse

Directory: CHAP16
File: PRINTREV.PAS

```
program PrintReverse (Input, Output);
{
  Reads a sequence of characters and displays it in reverse
  order.
  Module needed: StackADT
}

  {Insert type declaration for StackElement from StackADT}
  {Insert type declaration for Stack from StackADT}

  var
    S : Stack;                  {the stack of characters}

  {Insert CreateStack, Push, Pop, IsFull, IsEmpty from StackADT}

  {Insert FillStack and DisplayStack.}


begin {PrintReverse}
  CreateStack (S);              {Start with an empty stack.}

  {Fill the stack.}
  FillStack (S);

  {Display the characters in reverse order.}
  DisplayStack (S);

  {Display status of stack S.}
  if IsEmpty(S) then
    WriteLn ('Stack is empty - operation succeeds')
  else if IsFull(S) then
    WriteLn ('Stack is full - reversal failed')
end. {PrintReverse}


Enter a string of one or more characters
Press return when done.
This is a short string.
.gnirts trohs a si sihT
Stack is empty - operation succeeds
```

Case Study: Displaying a String in Reverse Order, continued

`if` statement displays an error message when the input string is too long. This happens when the user enters more characters than the stack capacity before pressing the return key.

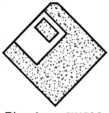

Figure 16.7 Procedure FillStack

```
procedure FillStack (var S {input/output} : Stack};
{
  Reads data characters and pushes them onto the stack.
  Pre : S is a stack.
  Post: Each data character read is pushed onto stack S.
  Uses: Push
}
  var
    NextCh : Char;                  {next character}
    Success : Boolean;              {flag}

begin {FillStack}
  WriteLn ('Enter a string of one or more characters.');
  WriteLn ('Press return when done.');
  repeat
    Read (NextCh);                  {Read next character.}
    Push (S, NextCh, Success)       {Push it onto stack.}
  until EOLN(Input) or not Success;

  {Print an error if stack overflows.}
  if not Success then
    WriteLn ('Stack overflow error - string too long')
end; {FillStack}
```

The `while` loop in procedure `DisplayStack` (Fig. 16.8) pops each character from the stack into `NextCh` and then displays it. The loop is repeated as long as there are characters remaining on the stack (`Success` is `True`). After `DisplayStack` is finished, the stack should be empty.

Figure 16.8 Procedure DisplayStack

```
procedure DisplayStack (var S {input/output} : Stack);
{
  Pops each stack character and displays it.
  Pre : Stack S is defined.
  Post: Each character is displayed and S is empty.
  Uses: Pop
}

  var
    NextCh : Char;                  {next character}
    Success : Boolean;              {flag}

begin {DisplayStack}
  Pop (S, NextCh, Success);
```

```
while Success do
  begin
    Write (NextCh);
    Pop (S, NextCh, Success)
  end; {while}
  WriteLn
end; {DisplayStack}
```

Testing

It is a good idea to see what happens when the stack overflows. This can be done by setting MaxStack to a small value (for example, 10).

Case Study: Checking for Balanced Parentheses

One application of a stack is to determine whether an expression is balanced with respect to parentheses. For example, the expression

```
(a + b * (c / (d - e))) + (d / e)
1         2   3    321   1     1
```

is balanced. We can solve this problem without using a stack by ignoring all characters except the symbols (and). We add 1 to a counter for each open parenthesis that follows another open parenthesis and subtract 1 for each close parenthesis that follows another close parenthesis. Because we are ignoring all other symbols, the parentheses being considered do not have to be consecutive characters. Assuming the initial count is 1, for a balanced expression the count ends at 1, and is never less than 1.

This task becomes more difficult if we use different types of enclosure symbols as parentheses. For example, the expression

```
(a + b * {c / [d - e]}) + (d / e)
```

is balanced, but the expression

```
(a + b * {c / [d - e}]) + (d / e)
```

is not because the subexpression [d - e} is incorrect.

Problem

The set of open parentheses includes {, [, and (. An expression is balanced if each subexpression that starts with the symbol { ends with the symbol }; the same is true for the symbol pairs [,] and (,). Another way of saying this is that the unmatched open parenthesis that is nearest to each close parenthesis must have the correct shape (for example, if } is the close parenthesis in question, the symbol { must be the nearest unmatched open parenthesis.)

Analysis

Without stacks it would be fairly difficult to solve this problem, but with stacks it becomes easy. First, we scan the expression from left to right, ignoring all characters except for parentheses. Then we push each open parenthesis onto a stack of characters. When we reach a close parenthesis, we see if it matches the symbol on the top of the stack. If the characters don't match or the stack is empty, there is an error in the expression. If they do match, we continue the scan.

Data Requirements

Problem Input

```
Expression : VarString     {expression to be checked
                                   for balanced parentheses}
```

Problem Output

the function result indicating whether the parentheses in Expression are balanced

Program Variables

```
ParenStack : Stack {stack of open parentheses}
Balanced : Boolean {flag indicating whether
                                  parentheses are balanced}
NextCh : Char        {next character in Expression}
Index : Integer      {index of the next character}
Open : Char          {open parenthesis at the top of the stack}
Close : Char         {close parenthesis being matched}
```

Design

Initial Algorithm

1. Create an empty stack of characters.
2. Assume that the expression is balanced (Balanced is True).
3. while the expression is balanced and still in the string do
   ```
   begin
   ```
       4. Get the next character in the data string.
       5. if the next character is an open parenthesis then
           6. Push it onto the stack.
       else if the next character is a close parenthesis then
   ```
       begin
   ```
           7. Pop the top of the stack.
           8. if stack was empty or its top was incorrect then
               Set balanced to False.
   ```
           end
   end
   ```

9. `if` the expression is balanced `then`
    10. There is an error if the stack is not empty.

The `if` statement at step 5 tests each character in the expression, ignoring all characters except for open and close parentheses. If the next character is an open parenthesis, it is pushed onto the stack. If the next character is a close parenthesis, the nearest unmatched open parenthesis is retrieved (by popping the stack) and compared to the close parenthesis (steps 7 and 8).

Implementation

Figure 16.9 shows a function that determines whether its input parameter (an expression) is balanced. The `if` statement in the `while` loop tests for open and close parentheses. Each open parenthesis is pushed onto stack `ParenStack`. For each close parenthesis, procedure `Pop` retrieves the nearest unmatched open parenthesis from the `stack`. If the stack was empty, `Pop` sets `Balanced` to `False`, causing the `while` loop exit. Otherwise, the `case` statement sets `Balanced` to indicate whether the character popped matches the current close parenthesis. After loop exit occurs, the function result is defined. It is true only when the expression is balanced and the stack is empty.

Figure 16.9   Function IsBalanced

```
function IsBalanced (Expression {input} : VarString) : Boolean;
{
  Determines whether Expression is balanced with respect
  to parentheses.
  Pre : Expression is defined.
  Post: Returns True if Expression is balanced; otherwise,
        returns False.
  Uses: VarString, Length, and GetChar from VarStringADT
        (see Fig. 14.11)
        Stack, Push, Pop and IsEmpty from StackADT.
}
  var
    ParenStack : Stack;         {stack of open parentheses}
    NextCh,                     {next character in Expression}
    Close,                      {close parenthesis to be matched}
    Open : Char;                {open parenthesis at top of stack}
    Index : Integer;            {index to Expression}
    Balanced : Boolean;         {program flag}

begin {IsBalanced}
  CreateStack (ParenStack);              {Create an empty stack}
  Balanced := True;
  Index := 1;
  while Balanced and (Index <= Length(Expression)) do
    {invariant:
        All closing parentheses so far were matched and
        Index <= Length(Expression) + 1.
    }
```

```
     begin
       NextCh := GetChar(Expression, Index);      {Access next
                                                    character.}
       if NextCh in ['(', '[', '{'] then
         Push (ParenStack, NextCh, Balanced) {stack parenthesis}
       else if NextCh in [')', ']', '}'] then
         begin {close paren}
           Close := NextCh;
           {Get nearest unmatched open parenthesis.}
           Pop (ParenStack, Open, Balanced);
           if Balanced then
             {Check for matching parentheses.}
             case Close of
               ')' : Balanced := Open = '(';
               ']' : Balanced := Open = '[';
               '}' : Balanced := Open = '{'
             end {case}
         end; {close paren}
       Index := Index + 1        {Access next character.}
     end; {while}

   {Define function result}
   if Balanced then
     IsBalanced := IsEmpty(ParenStack)
   else
     IsBalanced := False
end; {IsBalanced}
```

Testing

You have to write a driver program to test function IsBalanced. The driver program has to import type declaration VarString (from VarStringADT) and the type declarations for StackElement (type is Char) and Stack (from StackADT). It also has to import the stack operators and string operators that are called by IsBalanced and ReadLnVarStr to read in the string being tested. Make sure you use a variety of balanced and unbalanced expressions to test IsBalanced, as well as an expression without parentheses.

Exercises for Section 16.2

Self-Check

1. Trace the execution of function IsBalanced for each of the following expressions. Your trace should show the stack after each Push or Pop operation. Also show the values of Balanced, Open, and Close after each parenthesis is processed.

   ```
   (a + b * {c / [d - e]}) + (d / e)
   (a + b * {c / [d - e]}) + (d / e)
   ```

Programming

1. Write a main program to test function IsBalanced.

16.3 Evaluating Expressions

One task of a compiler is to evaluate arithmetic expressions. This section discusses one approach to expression evaluation.

Some of you may use calculators that evaluate postfix expressions. A *postfix expression* is an expression in which each operator follows its operands. We discuss postfix expressions further in Chapter 18; for the time being, however, you can get a pretty good idea of what a postfix expression is by studying the examples in Table 16.1. The grouping marks under each expression should help you visualize the operands for each operator. The more familiar *infix expression* corresponding to each postfix expression is also shown.

The advantage of postfix form is that there is no need to group subexpressions in parentheses or to consider operator precedence. The grouping marks in Table 16.1 are only for our convenience and are not required. Next, we write a program that evaluates a postfix expression.

Table 16.1 Examples of Postfix Expressions

Postfix Expression	Infix Expression	Value
5 6 *	5 * 6	30
5 6 1 + *	5 * (6 + 1)	35
5 6 * 10 –	(5 * 6) – 10	20
4 5 6 * 3 / +	4 + ((5 * 6) / 3)	14

Case Study: Evaluating Postfix Expressions

Problem
Simulate the operation of a calculator by reading an expression in postfix form and displaying its result. Each data character will be a blank, a digit character, or one of the operator characters from the set [+, –, *, /].

Analysis
Using a stack of integer values makes it easy to evaluate the expression. Our program will push each integer operand onto the stack. When an operator is read, the top two operands are popped, the operation is performed on its operands, and the result is pushed back onto the stack. The final result should

be the only value remaining on the stack when the end of the expression is reached.

Data Requirements

Problem Input
```
Expression : VarString   {expression to evaluate}
```

Problem Output
```
Result : Integer      {expression value}
```

Program Variables
```
OpStack : Stack       {stack of integer operands}
Success : Boolean     {flag indicating result of a stack operation}
NextCh : Char         {next character in Expression}
Index : Integer       {index to the next character}
NewOp : Integer       {next integer value in Expression}
Op1, Op2 : Integer    {two operands of an operator}
```

Algorithm

1. Read the expression string.
2. Create an empty stack of integers.
3. Set Success to True.
4. while Success is True and not at the end of the expression do
   begin
   5. Get the next character.
   6. if the character is a digit then
      begin
         7. Get the integer that starts with this digit.
         8. Push the integer onto the stack.
      end
   else if the character is an operator then
      begin
         9. Pop the top two operands.
         10. Evaluate the operation.
         11. Push the result onto the stack.
      end
   end
12. Display the result

Table 16.2 shows the evaluation of the third expression in Table 16.1 using this algorithm. The arrow under the expression points to the character being processed; the stack diagram shows the stack after this character is processed.

Refinements and Program Structure

The stack operators perform algorithm steps 2, 8, 9, 11, and 12. Steps 1 and 5 are performed by procedure ReadLnVarStr and function GetChar (imported

Table 16.2 Evaluating a Postfix Expression

Expression	Action	Stack
5 6 * 10 – ↑	Push 5.	
5 6 * 10 – ↑	Push 6.	
5 6 * 10 – ↑	Pop 6 and 5; evaluate 5 * 6; push 30.	5
5 6 * 10 – ↑	Push 10.	
5 6 * 10 – ↑	Pop 10 and 30; evaluate 30 – 10; push 20.	30
5 6 * 10 – ↑	Pop 20; stack is empty; result is 20.	

from `VarStringADT`). Steps 7 and 10 are the only algorithm steps that require refinement. Step 7 is performed by procedure `GetInteger` and step 10 by function `Eval`. The structure chart in Fig. 16.10 shows the data flow between these two subprograms and the main program.

Figure 16.10 Structure Chart for Program PostFix

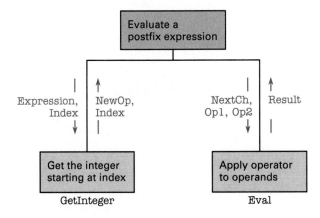

Implementation

Coding the Main Program

The main program is shown in Fig. 16.11. Besides the operators mentioned earlier, data types `StackElement` (type is `Integer`), `Stack`, and `VarString` must all be imported into the main program.

Case Study: Evaluating Postfix Expressions, continued

Each time stack S is manipulated, the Boolean flag Success is set to indicate the success or failure of that operation. If Success is False, the program displays an error message and terminates the expression evaluation. If the final value of Success is True and the stack is empty, the result is displayed.

Figure 16.11 Program PostFix and Sample Run

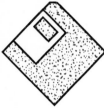

Directory: CHAP16
File: POSTFIX.PAS

```
program PostFix (Input, Output);
{
  Evaluates a postfix expression.

  Modules needed: VarStringADT (see Fig. 14.11) and StackADT (see
                  Section 16.4)
}
  {Insert type declaration for StackElement from StackADT}
  {Insert type declaration for Stack from StackADT}
  {Insert type declaration for VarString from VarStringADT}

  var
    OpStack : Stack;                    {stack of integers}
    Expression : VarString;             {expression to be evaluated}
    NextCh : Char;                      {next data character}
    Index : Integer;                    {index of next character}
    Op1, Op2,                           {operand values from stack}
    NewOp,                              {new operand for the stack}
    Result : Integer;                   {result of operator evaluation}
    Success : Boolean;                  {flag for stack operation}

  {Insert CreateStack, Push, Pop, IsEmpty}
  {Insert ReadLnVarStr, Length, and GetChar}
  {Insert GetInteger and Eval.}

begin {Postfix}
  Write ('Enter your expression> ');
  ReadLnVarStr (Input, Expression);

  CreateStack (Opstack);                         {Create an empty stack.}
  Index := 1;
  Success := True;
  while Success and (Index <= Length(Expression)) do
    {invariant;
        OpStack contains all unprocessed operands and results and
        Index <= Length(Expression) + 1.
    }
    begin
      NextCh := GetChar(Expression, Index);    {Get the next character.}
      if NextCh in ['0'..'9'] then
        begin {digit}
          GetInteger (Expression, Index, NewOp);   {Get integer value.}
          Push (OpStack, NewOp, Success);          {Push integer value.}
          if not Success then
            WriteLn ('Stack overflow error')
        end {digit}
      else if NextCh in ['+','-','*','/'] then
        begin {operator}
          Pop (OpStack, Op2, Success);          {Get last operand.}
          Pop (OpStack, Op1, Success);          {Get first operand.}
          if not Success then
```

```
                 WriteLn ('Invalid expression')
            else
               begin {evaluate operator}
                  Result := Eval(NextCh, Op1, Op2);
                  Push (OpStack, Result, Success);          {Push result.}
                  if not Success then
                     WriteLn ('Stack overflow')
               end {evaluate operator}
         end; {operator}
      Index := Index + 1                         {Go to next character.}
   end; {while}

  if Success then
     Pop (OpStack, Result, Success);                    {Get the result.}
  if Success and IsEmpty(OpStack) then
     WriteLn ('Expression value is ', Result :1)    {Print it.}
  else
     WriteLn ('Invalid expression')
end. {PostFix}

Enter your expression> 5 6 * 10 -

Expression value is 20
```

Coding the Subprograms

Procedure `GetInteger` (Fig. 16.12) accumulates the integer value of a string of consecutive digit characters and returns the value through parameter `NewOp`. The assignment statement

```
    NewOp := (10 * NewOp) + Ord(NextCh) - Ord('0');
```

adds the numeric value of the digit character in `NextCh` to the numeric value being accumulated in `NewOp`. For example, if the current value of `NewOp` is 15 and `NextCh` is `'3'`, `NewOp` gets the value 153. When `GetInteger` returns to the main program, `Index` points to the last digit of the number just processed.

Figure 16.12 Procedure GetInteger

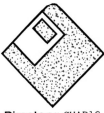

Directory: CHAP16
File: POSTFIX.PAS

```
procedure GetInteger (Expression {input} : VarString;
                      var Index {input/output},
                      NewOp {output} : Integer);
{
  Returns in NewOp the integer whose first digit is at position
  Index.
  Pre : Expression and Index are defined and the character at Index
        is a digit.
  Post: Index points to the last digit of the number whose first digit
        is pointed to by the initial value of Index.
        NewOp is the value of that number.
  Uses: Length and GetChar from VarStringADT
}
begin {GetInteger}
  NewOp := 0;
  NextCh := GetChar(Expression, Index);
```

```
while (NextCh in ['0'..'9']) and (Index <= Length(Expression)) do
   {invariant;
      Every prior character in NextCh was a digit and
      Index <= Length(Expression) + 1 and
      NewOp is the numerical value of all digits processed so far.
   }
   begin
      NewOp := (10 * NewOp) + Ord(NextCh) - Ord('0');
      Index := Index + 1;
      NextCh := GetChar(Expression, Index)
   end; {while}

{assert:
   NewOp is the numerical value of the substring processed and
   Index is at the end of the substring or just past it.
}
if not (NextCh in ['0'..'9']) then
   Index := Index - 1                    {Point to the last digit.}
end; {GetInteger}
```

Whenever an operator is encountered, the main program pops its two operands off the stack and calls function Eval (Fig. 16.13) to compute the result of applying the operator (passed through NextCh) to its operands (passed through Op1, Op2). The case statement in function Eval selects the appropriate operation and performs it.

Figure 16.13 Function Eval

Directory: CHAP16
File: POSTFIX.PAS

```
function Eval (NextCh : Char;
              Op1, Op2 : Integer) : Integer;
{
   Applies operator NextCh to operands Op1, Op2.
   Pre : NextCh is an operator and Op1, Op2 are defined.
   Post: If NextCh is '+', returns Op1 + Op2, and so on.
}
begin {Eval}
   if NextCh in ['+', '-', '*', '/'] then
      case NextCh of
         '+' : Eval := Op1 + Op2;
         '-' : Eval := Op1 - Op2;
         '*' : Eval := Op1 * Op2;
         '/' : Eval := Op1 div Op2      {integer division}
      end {case}
   else
      WriteLn ('Error in operator symbol')
end; {Eval}
```

Testing

You have to import the necessary data types and procedures to test program PostFix. See what happens when the expression is not a valid postfix expression or when it contains characters other than those expected.

Self-Check

1. Trace the evaluation of the last expression in Table 16.1. Show the stack each time it is modified and how the values of NewOp and Result change as the program executes.

Programming

1. Modify program PostFix to handle the exponentiation operator, indicated by the symbol ^. Assume that the first operand is raised to the power indicated by the second operand.

16.4 Implementing a Stack ADT

This section discusses how we might implement a stack in Pascal. We begin with the internal representation for a stack.

Declaration for Type Stack

The data type Stack declared in Fig. 16.14 has two fields, Top and Items. The array field Items provides storage for the stack elements. Top is an index to this array and selects the element at the top of the stack. We can store up to MaxStack (value is 100) elements in an object of type Stack.

Figure 16.14   Declarations for StackADT

```
{
 Implementation of StackADT
}
   const
     MaxStack = 100;

   type
     {Insert declaration for StackElement.}

     Stack = record
               Top : 0..MaxStack;
               Items : array [1..MaxStack] of StackElement
             end; {Stack}
```

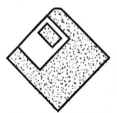

Directory: CHAP16
File: STACKADT.ADT

The comment

```
{Insert declaration for StackElement.}
```

reminds us that we must declare data type StackElement before we can declare record type Stack. If we use the declaration

```
StackElement = Char;
```

a variable of type `Stack` will be able to store up to 100 characters.

As always, storage is not allocated until a variable of type `Stack` is declared. Assuming `StackElement` is type `Char`, the variable declaration

```
var
  S : Stack;
```

allocates storage for a stack, `S`, of up to 100 characters. Notice that the storage space for the entire stack is allocated at one time, even though there will not be any items on the stack initially.

The following abstract stack `S` (on the left) would be represented in memory by the record shown on the right. `S.Top` is 3, and the stack consists of the subarray `S.Items[1..3]`; the subarray `S.Items[4..100]` is currently undefined.

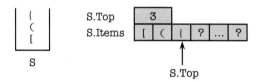

The array element `S.Items[S.Top]` contains the character value `'{'`, which is the value at the top of the stack.

We can change the capacity of a stack by redefining the constant `MaxStack`. Also, we can change the stack elements to another simple type or a structured type by changing the declaration for `StackElement`. If we use the declaration

```
StackElement = Integer;
```

a variable of type `Stack` will be able to store up to 100 integer values.

■ Example 16.2

Figure 16.15 shows the effect of the statement

```
Push (S, '(', Success)
```

where the initial stack `S` is shown on the left. Before `Push` is executed, `S.Top` is 3, so `S.Items[3]` is the element at the top of the stack. Procedure `Push` must

Figure 16.15 Pushing '(' onto Stack S

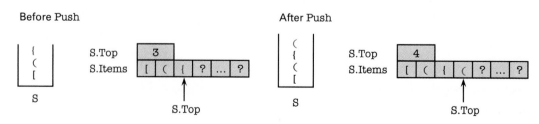

increment S.Top to 4 so the new item ('(') will be stored in S.Items[4], as shown on the right of the figure.

Stack Operators

The stack operators manipulate the array field Items using the Integer field Top as an index to the array. Their implementation is fairly straightforward. You should have little difficulty in reading and understanding the stack operators shown in the implementation section of StackADT (Fig. 16.16).

Figure 16.16 Operators for StackADT

Directory: CHAP16
File: STACKADT.ADT

```
{
  Operators for StackADT
}
  procedure CreateStack (var S {output} : Stack);
  {
    Creates an empty stack.
    Pre : None
    Post: S is an empty stack.
  }
  begin {CreateStack}
    S.Top = 0                {Stack is empty.}
  end; {CreateStack}


  procedure Push (var S {input/output} : Stack;
                  X {input} : StackElement;
                  var Success {output} : Boolean);
  {
    Pushes X onto stack S.
    Pre : X is defined and S is a stack that has been created.
    Post: Sets Success to indicate success (True) or failure (False)
          of push operation.
  }
  begin {Push}
    if S.Top >= MaxStack then
      Success := False       {no room on stack}
    else
      begin
        S.Top := S.Top + 1;      {Increment top-of-stack pointer.}
        S.Items[S.Top] := X;     {Push X onto stack.}
        Success := True
      end {if}
  end; {Push}


  procedure Pop (var S {input/output} : Stack;
                 var X {output} : StackElement;
                 var Success {output} : Boolean);
  {
    Pops the top of stack S into X.
    Pre : S is a stack that has been created.
    Post: Contents of X is character at top of stack S, which is then
          removed from S. Sets Success to indicate success (True)
          or failure (False) of pop operation.
  }
```

```
begin {Pop}
  if S.Top <= 0 then
    Success := False
  else
    begin
      X := S.Items[S.Top];        {Pop top of stack into X.}
      S.Top := S.Top - 1;         {Decrement top-of-stack pointer.}
      Success := True
    end {if}
end; {Pop}


procedure Retrieve (S {input} : Stack;
                    var X {output} : StackElement;
                    var Success {output} : Boolean);
{ Copies the value at the top of the stack into X.
  Pre : S is a stack.
  Post: Contents of X is character at top of stack S; S is
        unchanged. Sets Success to indicate success (True) or
        failure (False).
}
begin {Retrieve}
  if S.Top <= 0 then
    Success := False
  else
    begin
      X := S.Items[S.Top];        {Copy top of stack into X.}
      Success := True
    end {if}
end; {Retrieve}


function IsEmpty (S : Stack) : Boolean;
{
  Pre : S is a stack.
  Post: Returns True if stack S is empty;
        otherwise, returns False.
}
begin {IsEmpty}
  IsEmpty := S.Top <= 0
end; {IsEmpty}


function IsFull (S : Stack) : Boolean;
{
  Pre : S is a stack.
  Post: Returns True if stack S is full;
        otherwise, returns False.
}
begin {IsFull}
  IsFull := S.Top >= MaxStack
end; {IsFull}
```

Procedure `CreateStack` must be called before the stack can be manipulated. In `CreateStack`, the statement

```
S.Top := 0              {stack is empty}
```

initializes a stack by setting its top-of-stack pointer to zero.

Procedure `Push` increments the top-of-stack pointer before it pushes a new value onto the stack. Procedure `Pop` copies the value at the top of the stack (denoted by `S.Items[S.Top]`) into `X` before decrementing the top-of-stack pointer. Procedure `Retrieve` copies the value at the top of the stack into `X` without changing the top-of-stack pointer. Functions `IsFull` and `IsEmpty` test the top-of-stack pointer to determine the stack status.

Efficiency versus Readability

Procedure `Push` in Fig. 16.16 uses the condition `S.Top >= MaxStack` to determine whether the stack represented by `S` is full. It would be more readable, but less efficient, to use the function designator `IsFull(S)` to test whether stack `S` is full. You should use the function designator `Is-Full(S)` for this purpose in any client program that manipulates the stack, because the stack's internal representation may be hidden from a client program. It is perfectly reasonable, however, for another stack operator to directly manipulate internal fields of a stack.

Exercises for Section 16.4

Self-Check

1. Declare a stack of 50 student records, where each record consists of a student's name (packed array of 20 characters), an exam score, and a letter grade. Can you use the stack operators to manipulate this stack?

Programming

1. Write an operator `SizeOfStack` that returns the number of elements currently on the stack.

16.5 The Queue Abstract Data Type

A *queue* is a data abstraction that can be used, for example, to model a line of customers waiting at a checkout counter or a stream of jobs waiting to be printed by a printer in a computer center. A queue differs from a stack in that new elements are inserted at one end (the rear of the queue) and existing elements are removed from the other end (the front of the queue). In this way, the element that has been waiting longest is removed first. In contrast, stack elements are inserted and removed from the same end (the top of the stack). A queue is called a *first-in, first-out* structure (FIFO), while a stack is called a *last-in, first-out* (LIFO) structure.

A queue of three passengers waiting to see an airline ticket agent is shown in Fig. 16.17. The name of the passenger who has been waiting the longest is

McMann (pointed to by Front); the name of the most recent arrival is Carson (pointed to by Rear). Passenger McMann will be the first one removed from the queue when an agent becomes available, and pointer Front will be moved to passenger Watson. Any new passengers will follow passenger Carson in the queue, and pointer Rear will be adjusted accordingly.

The specification for the abstract data type QueueADT follows; compare it with the earlier specification for an abstract stack.

Figure 16.17   A Passenger Queue

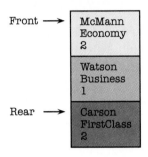

```
{
    Specification of Abstract Data Type QueueADT

    Elements:    A queue consists of a collection of elements
                 that are all the same data type.
    Structure:   The elements of a queue are ordered according
                 to time of arrival. The element that was first
                 inserted into the queue is the only one that
                 may be removed or examined. Elements are
                 removed from the front of the queue and
                 inserted at the rear of the queue.
    Operators:   The following descriptions assume these
                 parameters:

    Q represents the queue.
    El has the same data type as the queue elements.
    Success is type Boolean and indicates whether the
    operation succeeds.

    CreateQueue (var Q); Creates an empty queue Q.
```

```
        Insert (var Q, El, var Success): If queue Q is not full,
        the value in El is inserted at the rear of the queue, and
        Success is set to True. Otherwise, the queue is not
        changed, and Success is set to False.

        Remove (var Q, var El, var Success): If queue Q is not
        empty, the element at the front of the queue is removed and
        copied to El, and Success is set to True. If the queue is
        empty, El is not changed, and Success is set to False.

        Retrieve (Q, var El, var Success): If queue Q is not empty,
        the element at the front of the queue is copied into El,
        and Success is set to True. If the queue is empty, El is
        not defined, and Success is set to False. In either case,
        the queue is not changed.

        IsEmpty(Q): (function) Returns True if queue Q is empty;
        otherwise, returns False.

        IsFull(Q): (function) Returns True if queue Q is full;
        otherwise, returns False.

        SizeOfQueue(Q): (function) Returns the number of elements
        in the queue.
}
```

We implement `QueueADT` in the next section. As before, we assume that the identifier `QueueElement` represents the type of each queue element. Each client program must import the type declarations for `Queue` and `QueueElement`.

Exercise for Section 16.5

Self-Check

1. Draw the queue in Fig. 16.17 after the insertion of first-class passenger `Harris` (3 seats reserved) and the removal of one passenger from the queue. Which passenger is removed? How many passengers are left?

16.6 Queue Application

Our application is a program that processes a queue of airline passengers.

Case Study: Maintaining a Queue of Passengers

Problem

Write a menu-driven program that maintains a queue of passengers waiting to see a ticket agent. The program user should be able to insert a new passenger at the rear of the queue, display the passenger at the front of the queue, and remove the passenger at the front of the queue. Just before it terminates, the program should display the number of passengers left in the queue.

Analysis

We can use the queue abstract data type and operators Insert, Retrieve, and Remove to process the queue. We can simplify the program by using an abstract data type, Passenger, that contains type declarations for an airline passenger and provides its input/output operators (ReadPass and WritePass). We will implement this abstract data type later.

Data Requirements

Problem Inputs
```
Choice : Char                {operation to be performed}
NextPass : Passenger         {next passenger's data}
```

Problem Output
```
FirstPass : Passenger        {passenger at the front of the queue}
```

Program Variables
```
PassQueue : Queue            {queue of passengers}
Success : Boolean            {flag for storing the result
                                 of a queue operation}
```

Design

Initial Algorithm

1. Initialize the queue.
2. repeat
    3. Display the menu.
    4. Read the operation selected.
    5. Perform the operation selected.
   until user is done or a queue operation fails
6. Display the number of passengers left in the queue.

Implementation

Coding the Main Program

The main program (Fig. 16.18) imports the type declarations for Passenger (from PassengerADT) and for QueueElement and Queue (both from QueueADT).

Procedure CreateQueue (from QueueADT) initializes the passenger queue to an empty queue. In the main program body, the statement

```
Write ('Enter I(nsert), R(emove), D(isplay), or Q(uit)> ');
```

displays the menu of choices (step 3). After the selection is read into Choice, the main program calls procedure ModifyQueue to perform step 5. Procedure ModifyQueue is discussed next.

Figure 16.18 Program UseQueue

```
program UseQueue (Input, Output);
{
  Manipulates a queue of airline passengers.
  Modules needed: QueueADT (see Section 16.5) and PassengerADT (see Fig.
  16.21)
}
{
  Insert type declaration for Passenger from PassengerADT
  Insert type declaration for QueueElement from QueueADT
  Insert type declaration for Queue from QueueADT
}
  var
    PassQueue : Queue;          {passenger queue}
    Choice : Char;              {operation request}
    Success : Boolean;          {program flag}
{
    Insert ReadPass, WritePass from PassengerADT
    Insert CreateQueue, Insert, Remove, Retrieve, SizeOfQueue from
    QueueADT

    Insert ModifyQueue (see Fig. 16.19)
}

begin {UseQue}
  CreateQueue (PassQueue);              {Start with an empty queue.}

  {Process all requests until done.}
  repeat
    Write ('Enter I(nsert), R(emove), D(isplay), or Q(uit)> ');
    ReadLn (Choice);
    {Process current request.}
    ModifyQueue (PassQueue, Choice, Success);
    WriteLn
  until (Choice = 'Q') or (not Success)
end. {UseQueue}
```

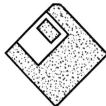

Directory: CHAP16
File: USEQUEUE.PAS

Coding ModifyQueue

For each selection, procedure ModifyQueue (Fig. 16.19) calls the operators required to manipulate the Queue (from QueueADT) and the operators needed to read or display a passenger record (from PassengerADT). The main control structure is a case statement that determines which operators are called.

Figure 16.19   Procedure ModifyQueue

Directory: CHAP16
File: USEQUEUE.PAS

```
procedure ModifyQueue (var Q {input/output} : Queue;
                           Choice {input} : Char;
                           var Success {output} : Boolean);
{
  Performs the operation indicated by Choice on the queue Q.
  Pre : Q has been created.
  Post: Q is modified based on Choice and Success indicates
          whether requested operation was performed.
  Uses: ReadPass, WritePass, Insert, Remove, Retrieve
}
  var
    NextPass,                     {new passenger}
    FirstPass : Passenger;        {passenger at front of queue}

begin {ModifyQueue}
  if Choice in ['I', 'R', 'D', 'Q'] then
    case Choice of
      'I' : begin {insert}
              WriteLn ('Enter passenger data.');
              ReadPass (NextPass);
              Insert (Q, NextPass, Success);
              if not Success then
                WriteLn ('Queue is full — no insertion')
            end; {insert}
      'R' : begin {remove}
              Remove (Q, FirstPass, Success);
              if Success then
                begin
                  WriteLn ('Passenger removed from queue follows.');
                  WritePass (FirstPass)
                end
              else
                WriteLn ('Queue is empty — no deletion')
            end; {remove}
      'D' : begin {display}
              Retrieve (Q, FirstPass, Success);
              if Success then
                begin
                  WriteLn ('Passenger at head of queue follows.');
                  WritePass (FirstPass)
                end
              else
                WriteLn ('Queue is empty — no passenger')
            end; {display}
      'Q' : begin {quit}
              WriteLn ('Leaving passenger queue.');
              WriteLn ('Number of passengers in the queue is ',
                          SizeOfQueue(Q) :1)
            end {quit}
    end {case}
  else
    WriteLn ('Incorrect choice — try again.')
end; {ModifyQueue}
```

Testing

Before you can run program UseQueue, you must insert all the necessary type
declarations and procedures imported from PassengerADT and QueueADT. If

these ADTs import other data types and/or procedures, they also must be inserted in program UseQueue (because PassengerADT includes operators that read and display strings, this is highly likely). We examine PassengerADT next.

You can store the initial passenger list by selecting a sequence of insert operations. In the sample run of program UseQueue, shown in Fig. 16.20, passenger Brown is inserted first, followed by passenger Watson. After passenger Brown is removed from the queue, the new passenger at the front of the queue (Watson) is displayed.

To test the program thoroughly, you have to try to display or remove a passenger after the queue is empty. Either attempt should cause the error message Queue is empty – to be displayed before the program terminates. To check that there is no insertion after the queue is full, it is necessary to redefine the queue capacity (part of the declaration for type Queue) so that the message Queue is full – no insertion appears after a small number of passenger insertions takes place.

Figure 16.20   Sample Run of Program UseQueue

```
Enter I(nsert), R(emove), D(isplay), or Q(uit)> I
Enter passenger data.
Passenger Name> Brown
Class (F, B, E, S)> E
Number of Seats - Enter an integer between 1 and 30> 2

Enter I(nsert), R(emove), D(isplay), or Q(uit)> I
Enter passenger data.
Passenger Name> Watson
Class (F, B, E, S)> B
Number of Seats - Enter an integer between 1 and 30> 1

Enter I(nsert), R(emove), D(isplay), or Q(uit)> I
Enter passenger data.
Passenger Name> Dietz
Class (F, B, E, S)> E
Number of Seats - Enter an integer between 1 and 30> 3

Enter I(nsert), R(emove), D(isplay), or Q(uit)> R
Passenger removed from queue follows.
Brown
Economy Class
   2 Seats

Enter I(nsert), R(emove), D(isplay), or Q(uit)> D
Passenger at head of queue follows.
Watson
Business Class
   1 Seat

Enter I(nsert), R(emove), D(isplay), or Q(uit)> Q
Leaving passenger queue.
Number of passengers in the queue is 2
```

Case Study: Maintaining a Queue of Passengers, continued

Coding the Abstract Data Type PassengerADT

Figure 16.21 shows an ADT that contains a declaration for record type Passenger. Because the Name field is a packed array of characters (type StringType), procedure ReadLnString is needed to read a passenger's name. Procedure ReadPass and WritePass read and write a single passenger's record. (The completion of WritePass is left as an exercise.)

Figure 16.21 Abstract Data Type PassengerADT

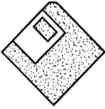

Directory: CHAP16
File: PASSENGE.ADT

```
{
  Specification of abstract data type PassengerADT

  Structure:    A record variable of type Passenger contains
                storage space for a collection of data items that
                describe a single airline passenger, such as the
                passenger's name, flight class, and number of
                seats reserved.

  Operators:    The operator descriptions that follow assume this
                parameter:
                     OnePass is type Passenger.

     ReadPass (var OnePass): Reads one record of type Passenger.

     WritePass (OnePass): Displays one record of type Passenger.
}

{
  Implementation of PassengerADT
  Modules needed: EnterInt (see Fig. 9.3) and StringADT (see Fig. 10.21)
}
  {Insert declaration for StringType from StringADT.}

type
  ClassType = (FirstClass, Business, Economy, StandBy, Undesignated);
  Passenger = record
                Name : StringType;
                Class : ClassType;
                NumSeats : Integer
              end; {Passenger}

  {Insert EnterInt and ReadLnString.}

    function ClassConvert (ClassCh : Char) : ClassType;
    {
      Converts a character to a class type.
    }
    begin {ClassConvert stub}
      ClassConvert := Economy
    end; {ClassConvert}


  procedure ReadPass (var OnePass {output} : Passenger);
  {
    Reads one record of type Passenger.
    Pre : None
    Post: Data are read into all fields of OnePass.
    Uses : ReadLnString, ClassConvert, and EnterInt
```

```
  }
  var
    ClassCh : Char;          {input - character for class type}
    NameLen : Integer;       {input - length of Name}

begin {ReadPass}
  with OnePass do
    begin
      Write ('Passenger name> ');
      ReadLnString (Input, Name, NameLen);
      Write ('Class (F, B, E, S)> ');
      ReadLn (ClassCh);
      Class := ClassConvert(ClassCh);
      Write ('Number of Seats - ');
      EnterInt (1, 30, NumSeats)
    end {with}
end; {ReadPass}


procedure WritePass (OnePass : Passenger);
{
  Displays one record of type Passenger.
}
begin {WritePass stub}
  Write ('Name: ');
  WriteLn (OnePass.Name)
end; {WritePass stub}
```

At this point, we can draw the module-dependency diagram for program
UseQueue (Fig. 16.22). The type declaration for Passenger should appear first
in UseQueue, followed by the type declaration for QueueElement (QueueElement

Figure 16.22   Module-Dependency Diagram for UseQueue

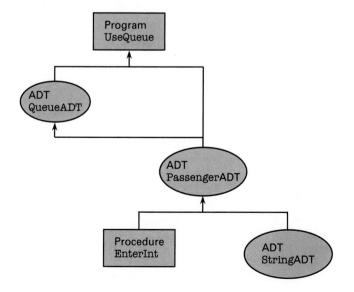

= Passenger) and `Queue`. The first procedures declared should be `EnterInt`
and `ReadLnString`, followed by the operators for `PassengerADT` and the operators for `QueueADT` (implemented next).

Exercises for Section 16.6

Self-Check

1. Draw the queue after the completion of the sample run in Fig. 16.20.

Programming

1. Complete procedure `WritePass`.
2. Complete function `ClassConvert` (in procedure `ReadPass`).

16.7 Implementing a Queue ADT

To represent a queue, we will use a record structure that consists of three
`Integer` fields (`Front`, `Rear`, `NumItems`) and an array field (`Items`) that provides
storage for the queue elements. The declarations for a queue whose capacity is
100 elements is shown in Fig. 16.23.

Figure 16.23   Declarations for QueueADT

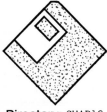

Directory: CHAP16
File: QUEUEADT.ADT

```
{Implementation of QueueADT}
  const
    MaxQueue = 100;

  type
  {Insert declaration for QueueElement.}

  QueueRange = 1..MaxQueue;
  Queue = record
            Front, Rear : QueueRange;
            NumItems : 0..MaxQueue;
            Items : array [QueueRange] of QueueElement
          end; {Queue}
```

The `Integer` fields `Front` and `Rear` are pointers to the queue elements at
the front and the rear of the queue, respectively. The `Integer` field `NumItems`
keeps track of the actual number of items in the queue and allows us to easily
determine if the queue is `Empty` (`NumItems` is 0) or `Full` (`NumItems` is `MaxQueue`).
The comment

```
{Insert declaration for QueueElement.}
```

reminds us that we must declare data type `QueueElement` before we can declare record type `Queue`.

If we use the type declaration

```
type
   QueueElement = Char;
```

a variable of type `Queue` can store up to 100 characters. If we import data type `Passenger` (from `PassengerADT`) and use the declaration

```
type
   QueueElement = Passenger;
```

a variable of type `Queue` can store up to 100 airline passengers.

It makes sense to store the first queue record in element 1, the second queue record in element 2, and so on. After a queue is filled with data, `Front` has a value of 1 and `Rear` points to the last record inserted in the queue (`Rear <= MaxQueue`). Figure 16.24 shows a queue, Q, that is filled to its capacity (`NumItems` is `MaxQueue`). The queue contains the symbols &, *, +, /, and –, in that order.

Because Q is filled to capacity, we cannot insert a new character. We can remove a queue element by decrementing `NumItems` and incrementing `Front` to 2, thereby removing `Q.Items[1]` (the symbol &). However, we still cannot insert a new character, because `Rear` is at its maximum value. One way to solve this problem is to represent the array field `Items` as a circular array. In a *circular array,* the elements wrap around so that the first element actually follows the last. This allows us to "increment" `Rear` to 1 and store a new character in `Q.Items[1]`.

Figure 16.24 A Queue Filled with Characters

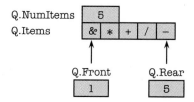

■ Example 16.3

Figure 16.25 shows the effect of inserting a new element in the queue just described. As shown on the left of the figure, three characters are currently in this queue (stored in `Q.Items[3..5]`). The question marks in `Q.Items[1..2]` indicate that the values stored in these elements have been removed from the queue. The two elements that are currently unused are shown in gray.

The right side of Fig. 16.25 shows the queue after insertion of a new character (`'$'`). The value of `Rear` is "incremented" to 1, and the next element is inserted in `Q.Items[1]`. This queue element follows the character `'–'` in `Q.Items[5]`. The value of `Q.Front` is still 3 because the character `'+'` at `Q.Items[3]` has been in the queue the longest. `Q.Items[2]` is now the only

Figure 16.25 A Queue as a Circular Array

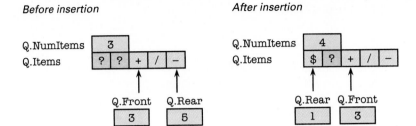

queue element that is unused. The new queue contains the symbols +, /, –, and $, in that order.

Figure 16.26 shows the operators for the queue abstract data type. ∎

Figure 16.26 Operators for QueueADT

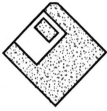

```
procedure CreateQueue (var Q {output} : Queue);
{
   Creates an empty queue.
   Pre : None
   Post: Q is initialized to a queue of zero elements.
}
begin {CreateQueue}
   Q.NumItems := 0;                   {Queue is empty.}
   Q.Front := 1;
   Q.Rear := MaxQueue                 {Queue is circular.}
end; {CreateQueue}


procedure Insert (var Q {input/output} : Queue;
                  El {input} : QueueElement;
                  var Success {output} : Boolean);
{
   Inserts El in queue Q.
   Pre : Q has been created.
   Post: If Q is not full, increments Rear and inserts El.
         Sets Success to indicate success or failure.
}
begin {Insert}
   if Q.NumItems = MaxQueue then
      Success := False        {Queue is full.}
   else
      begin {insert El}
         Q.Rear := (Q.Rear mod MaxQueue) + 1;     {Increment Rear.}
         Q.Items[Q.Rear] := El;
         Q.NumItems := Q.NumItems + 1;
         Success := True
      end {insert El}
end; {Insert}


procedure Remove (var Q {input/output} : Queue;
                  var El {output} : QueueElement;
                  var Success {output} : Boolean);
{
   Removes the element at the front of queue Q and copies it into
   El.
```

```
      Pre : Q has been created.
      Post: Front is decremented,
            If Q is not empty, El contains its first element,
            and Success indicates success or failure.
  }
  begin {Remove}
    if Q.NumItems = 0 then
      Success := False          {Queue is empty.}
    else
      begin
        {Remove the element at the front of the queue.}
        El := Q.Items[Q.Front];
        Q.Front := (Q.Front mod MaxQueue) + 1; {Increment Front.}
        Q.NumItems := Q.NumItems − 1;
        Success := True
      end {if}
  end; {Remove}


  procedure Retrieve (Q {input} : Queue;
                      var El {output} : QueueElement;
                      var Success {output} : Boolean);
  }
    Copies the value at the front of queue Q into El without
    removing it.
    Pre : Q has been created.
    Post: If Q is not empty, El contains its first element
          and Success indicates success or failure.
  }
  begin {Retrieve}
    if Q.NumItems = 0 then
      Success := False          {Queue is empty.}
    else
      begin
        {Retrieve the item at the front of the queue.}
        El := Q.Items[Q.Front];
        Success := True
      end {if}
  end; {Retrieve}

  function IsEmpty (Q : Queue) : Boolean;
  {
      Tests for an empty queue.
      Pre : Q has been created.
      Post: Returns True if queue Q is empty; otherwise, returns False.
  }
  begin {IsEmpty}
    IsEmpty := Q.NumItems = 0
  end; {IsEmpty}

  function IsFull (Q : Queue) : Boolean;
  {
      Test for a full queue.
      Pre : Q has been created.
      Post: Returns True if queue Q is full; otherwise, returns False.
  }
  begin {IsFull}
    IsFull := Q.NumItems = MaxQueue
  end; {IsFull}

  function SizeOfQueue (Q : Queue) : Integer;
  {
      Finds the number of elements in a queue.
```

```
        Pre : Q has been created.
        Post: Returns the number of elements in the queue.
}
begin {SizeOfQueue}
  SizeOfQueue := Q.NumItems
end; {SizeOfQueue}
```

Procedure CreateQueue must be called before any of the other operators. CreateQueue sets Q.NumItems to 0 and Q.Front to 1, because array element Q.Items[1] is considered the front of the empty queue. Q.Rear is initialized to MaxQueue because the queue is circular.

In procedure Insert, the statement

```
Q.Rear := (Q.Rear mod MaxQueue) + 1;          {Increment Rear.}
```

is used to increment the value of Q.Rear. When Q.Rear is less than MaxQueue, this statement simply increments its value by 1. But when Q.Rear is equal to MaxQueue, this statement sets Q.Rear to 1 (MaxQueue mod MaxQueue is 0), thereby wrapping the last element of the queue around to the first element. Because CreateQueue initializes Q.Rear to MaxQueue, the first queue element will be placed in Items[1], as desired.

In procedure Remove, the element currently stored in Items[Front] is copied into El before Q.Front is incremented. In procedure Retrieve, the element at Items[Front] is copied into El, but Q.Front is not changed.

The number of elements in the queue is changed by procedures Insert and Remove, so Q.NumItems must be incremented by 1 in Insert and decremented by 1 in Remove. The value of Q.NumItems is tested in both IsFull and IsEmpty to determine the status of the queue. Function SizeOfQueue simply returns the value of Q.NumItems.

Exercises for Section 16.7

Self-Check

1. What are the final values of Q.Front, Q.Rear, and the Name fields of Q.Items[1..3] after the sample run of UseQueue in Fig. 16.20?
2. Provide the algorithm for the operator in programming exercise 1, which follows. If program UseQueue calls this operator, how does it affect the module dependency diagram in Fig. 16.22?

Programming

1. Write an operator for QueueADT that displays the entire queue contents, from Front to Rear, inclusive.

16.8 Common Programming Errors

In this chapter, we used an array field to store the contents of a stack or a queue. Consequently, all stack and queue operators manipulated an array subscript. The errors you are likely to encounter are the same errors discussed at the end of Chapter 10. The most common error when using arrays is an out-of-range subscript.

The client programs in this chapter all used one or more abstract data types. Make sure that the abstract data types are available in your procedure library and that all necessary type declarations and procedure declarations are inserted where they belong in the client program. Take advantage of any compiler directives provided by your Pascal compiler to perform this insertion automatically. Otherwise, you will have to use an editor to do the insertions yourself.

CHAPTER REVIEW

This chapter introduced two data structures, stacks and queues. Stacks are used to implement recursion and expression translation. A stack is a last-in, first-out data structure. This means that the last item inserted is the first one removed. In contrast, a queue is a first-in, first-out data structure. Queues are used to implement waiting lists.

We showed how to use these abstractions to perform many useful operations. In particular, we used stacks to check for balanced parentheses and to evaluate arithmetic expressions. We also showed how to implement stacks and queues using arrays.

✓ Quick-Check Exercises

1. A stack is a _____ data structure; a queue is a _____ data structure.
2. Would a compiler use a stack or a queue in a program that converts regular arithmetic expressions to postfix form?
3. Would a time-sharing system use a stack or a queue in a program that determines which job should be executed next?
4. Would a compiler use a stack or a queue to keep track of return addresses for procedure calls?
5. Draw the array representation of the following stack. What is S.Items[1]? What is the value of S.Top? What is the value of S.Items[S.Top−1]?

6. Why should the statement S.Top := S.Top − 1 not appear in a client program of StackADT?
7. Write a program segment that removes the element just below the top of the stack from the stack. Use the stack operators.
8. Write a stack operator called PopNextTop that performs the operation in exercise 7. Do not use the stack operators.
9. Assume that a circular queue Q of capacity 6 contains the five characters +, *, −, &, and #, where + is stored in the front of the queue. In the array representation, what

is the value of Q.Front? What is the value of Q.Rear? What is the value of Q.Items[Q.Rear-1]?

10. Delete the character at the front of the queue in exercise 9 and insert the character \ and then %. Draw the new queue. What is the value of Q.Front? What is the value of Q.Rear? What is the value of Q.Items[Q.Rear-1]?

11. Can you have two stacks of real numbers in the same client program? Can you have a stack of integers and a stack of characters in the same client program?

Answers to Quick-Check Exercises

1. last-in, first-out; first-in, first-out
2. stack
3. queue, to give priority to the job waiting the longest to execute
4. stack

S.Top

S.Items

5. &; S.Top is 3; *
6. The client program should not be aware of the internal representation of the stack.
7. Pop (S, X, Success);
   Pop (S, Y, Success);
   Push (S, X, Success)
8. procedure PopNextTop (var S {input/output} : Stack;
                                      var Ch {output} : Char;
                                      var Success {output} : Boolean);
   begin
     S.Items[Top-1] := S.Items[S.Top];
     S.Top := S.Top - 1
   end; {PopNextTop}
9. Q.Front is 1; Q.Rear is 5; &

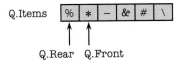

Q.Items

Q.Rear   Q.Front

10. Q.Front is 2; Q.Rear is 1; \
11. yes; no

Review Questions

1. Show the effect of each of the following operations on stack S. Assume that Y (type Char) contains the character '&'. What are the final values of X and Success (type Boolean) and the contents of stack S? Ignore any statements with syntax errors.

```
CreateStack (S);
Push (S, '+', Success);
Pop (S, X, Success);
Pop (S, X, Success);
Push (S, '(', Success);
Push (S, Y, Success);
Pop (S, '&', Success)
```

2. Assuming stack S is implemented in an array, answer question 1 by showing the values of integer field Top and array field Items after each operation.
3. Write a stack operator called PopTwo that removes the top two stack elements and returns them as procedure results. Use procedure Pop.
4. Answer question 3 without using Pop.
5. Answer question 1 for a queue Q of characters. Replace CreateStack with CreateQueue, Push with Insert, and Pop with Remove.
6. Assuming queue Q is implemented in an array with five elements, asnwer question 2 by showing the values of integer fields Front and Rear and array field Items after each operation.
7. Write a queue operator called MoveToRear that moves the element currently at the front of the queue to the rear of the queue. The element that was second in line will be at the front of the queue. Do this using Insert and Remove operators.
8. Answer question 7 without using Insert and Remove operators. Manipulate the internal queue fields directly.
9. Write a queue operator called MoveToFront that moves the element at the rear of the queue to the front of the queue. Do this using Insert and Remove.
10. Answer question 9 without using Insert and Remove.

Programming Projects

1. Write a client program that uses the Queue ADT to simulate a typical session for a bank teller. Change QueueElement to represent a customer at a bank. Store the customer's name, transaction type, and amount in the customer record. After every five customers are processed, display the size of the queue and the names of the customers who are waiting.

Directory: CHAP16
File: PROJ16_1.PAS

As part of your solution, your program should include procedures that correspond to the following procedure headers.

```
procedure WriteCust (OneCust {input} : Customer);
{Displays a single customer record.}

procedure ReadCust (var OneCust {output} : Customer);
{Reads a single customer record from the keyboard.}

procedure Arrive (var WaitingLine {input/output} : Queue;
                  var Success {output} : Boolean;
{
  Simulates the arrival of a single customer.
  Calls: ReadCust
}

procedure Depart (var WaitingLine {input/output} : Queue;
                  var Success {output} : Boolean);
{
  Simulates the departure of a single customer.
  Calls: WriteCust
}

procedure Show (WaitingLine {input} : Queue);
{
  Displays size and contents of the customer queue.
  Calls: WriteCust
}
```

2. Carry out project 1 using a stack instead of a queue.

3. Write a program to monitor the flow of an item into and out of a warehouse. The warehouse will have numerous deliveries and shipments for this item (a widget) during the time period covered. A shipment out is billed at a profit of 50 percent over the cost of a widget. Unfortunately, each shipment received may have a different cost associated with it. The accountants for the firm have instituted a last-in, first-out system for filling orders. This means that the newest widgets are the first ones sent out to fill an order. This method of inventory can be represented using a stack. The Push procedure will insert a shipment received. The Pop procedure will delete a shipment out. Each data record will consist of

> S or O: shipment received or an order to be sent
> #: quantity received or shipped out
> Cost: cost per widget (for a shipment received only)
> Vendor: character string that names company sent to or
> > received from

Write the necessary procedures to store the shipments received and to process orders. The output for an order will consist of the quantity and the total cost for all the widgets in the order. Hint: Each widget price is 50 percent higher than its cost. The widgets used to fill an order may come from multiple shipments with different costs.

4. Redo project 3 assuming the widgets are shipped using a first-in, first-out strategy. Use a queue to store the widget orders.

5. Write a client program for the stack abstract data type that can be used to compile a simple arithmetic expression without parentheses. For example, the expression

```
A + B * C - D
```

should be compiled as the table

Operation	Operand1	Operand2	Result
*	B	C	Z
+	A	Z	Y
−	Y	D	X

The table shows the order in which the operations are performed, (*, +, −) and the operands for each operator. The result column gives the name of an identifier (working backward from Z) chosen to hold each result. Assume the operands are the letters A through F and the operators are (+, −, *, /).

Your program should read each character and process it as follows. If the character is a blank, ignore it. If it is an operand, push it onto the operand stack. If the character is not an operator, display an error message and terminate the program. If it is an operator, compare its precedence with that of the operator on top of the stack (* and / have higher precendence than + and −). If the new operator has higher precedence than the one currently on top (or if the stack is empty), it should be pushed onto the stack.

If the new operator has the same or lower precedence, the operator on the top of the stack must be evaluated next. This is done by popping it off the operator stack along with a pair of operands from the operand stack and writing a new line of the output table. The character selected to hold the result should then be pushed onto the operand stack. Next, the new operator should be compared to the new top of the operator stack. Continue to generate output table lines until the top of the operator stack has lower precedence than the new operator or until the stack is empty. At this point, push the new operator onto the top of the stack and examine the next character in the data string. When the end of the string is reached, pop any remaining operator along with its operand pair as just described. Remember to push the result character onto the operand stack after each table line is generated.

6. A dequeue might be described as a double-ended queue, that is, a structure in which elements can be inserted or removed from either end. Write a Pascal ADT that contains the declarations and operators necessary to implement a dequeue.

17

Dynamic Data Structures

This chapter discusses how Pascal can be used to create *dynamic data structures*. Dynamic data structures are data structures that expand and contract as a program executes. A dynamic data structure is a collection of elements (called *nodes*) that are records. Unlike an array, which always contains storage for a fixed number of elements, the number of records stored in a dynamic data structure changes as the program executes.

Dynamic data structures are extremely flexible. It is relatively easy to add new information by creating a new node and inserting it between two existing nodes. It is also relatively easy to delete a node.

In this chapter, we examine several examples of dynamic data structures. These include lists, stacks, queues, and circular lists. You will learn how to store information in these data structures and how to process that information.

17.1 Pointers and the New Statement

Before discussing dynamic data structures, we will introduce the pointer data type. We can declare variables (called *pointer variables*) whose types are pointer types. We can store the memory address of a data object in a pointer variable and, in this way, reference or access the data object through the pointer variable that points to it.

For example, the type declaration

```
type
  RealPointer = ^Real;

var
  P : RealPointer;
```

identifies RealPointer as the name of a data type. Read ^Real as "pointer to Real." The variable declaration specifies that P is a pointer variable of type RealPointer. This means that we can store the memory address of a type Real variable in P.

The statement

```
New (P):
```

calls the Pascal procedure New, which allocates storage for a type Real value and places the address of this memory cell in pointer variable P. Once storage is allocated for the type Real value pointed to by P, we can store a value in that memory cell and manipulate it. The exact location in memory of this particular cell is immaterial.

We can represent the value of a pointer variable by an arrow drawn to a memory cell. The diagram

shows that pointer variable P points to a memory cell whose contents are unknown. This is the situation that exists just after New(P) is executed.

Notice that the two memory cells shown in the diagram are allocated storage at different times. Storage is allocated for the cell on the left during compilation when the variable declaration is reached. Storage is allocated for the cell on the right during run time when the New statement is executed.

The symbol P^ references the memory cell pointed to by pointer variable P. The ^ (caret) is called the *dereferencing operator*. The assignment statement

        P^ := 15.0

stores the Real value 15.0 in memory cell P^ (the cell pointed to by P), as shown next.

The statement

        Write (P^ :12:1)

displays the value (15.0) stored in memory cell P^.

We are introducing pointer variables and pointer types now because they are used to create and access dynamic data structures. Later in this chapter, you will see how to use a pointer variable to reference a dynamic data structure and how to use pointer fields to connect the nodes of a dynamic data structure.

SYNTAX
DISPLAY

Pointer Type Declaration

Form: type *ptype* = ^*dtype*;
Example: type RealPointer =^Real;
Interpretation: Pointer type *ptype* is a data type whose values are memory cell addresses. A data object whose address is stored in a variable of type *ptype* must be type *dtype*.

SYNTAX
DISPLAY

New Procedure

Form: New (*pvar*)
Example: New (P)
Interpretation: Storage for a new data object is allocated, and the address of this data object is stored in pointer variable *pvar*. If *pvar* is type *ptype*, the internal representation and size of the new data object is determined from the declaration for *ptype*. Use *pvar*^ to reference this data object.

Special Precautions for Pointer Variables

A pointer variable can contain only a memory address. If P is the pointer variable declared in the previous section, the following statements are invalid because you cannot assign a type Integer or type Real value to a pointer variable.

```
P := 1000;      {invalid assignment}
P := 15.5;      {invalid assignment}
```

You cannot display the value (an address) of a pointer variable. Therefore, the statement

```
WriteLn (P);    {invalid attempt to display an address}
```

is also invalid.

Records with Pointer Fields

Pointers can be used to construct dynamic data structures. Because we don't know beforehand how many nodes will be in a dynamic data structure, we cannot allocate storage for a dynamic data structure in the conventional way, that is, through a variable declaration. Instead, we must allocate storage for each node as needed and, somehow, join that node to the rest of the structure.

We can connect two nodes if we include a pointer field in each node. The declarations

```
type
  NodePointer = ^Node;
  Node = record
            Current : packed array [1..2] of Char;
            Volts : Integer;
            Link : NodePointer
         end; {Node}

var
  P, Q, R : NodePointer;
```

identify NodePointer as a pointer type. A pointer variable of type NodePointer points to a record of type Node with three fields: Current, Volts, and Link. The Link field is also type NodePointer. We can use this field to point to the "next" node in a dynamic data structure. We illustrate how to connect two nodes in the next section.

Notice that the type declaration for NodePointer makes reference to the identifier Node, which is not yet declared. The declaration of a pointer type is the only situation in which Pascal allows us to reference an undeclared identifier.

Variables P, Q, and R are pointer variables and can be used to reference records of type Node (denoted by P^, Q^, and R^). An address can be stored in a pointer variable in one of two ways. The statements

```
New (P);  New (Q);
```

allocate storage for two records of type Node. The memory address of the first of these records is stored in P, and the memory address of the second of these records is stored in Q. All three fields of these two nodes are initially undefined.

The assignment statements

```
P^.Current := 'AC';   P^.Volts := 115;
Q^.Current := 'DC';   Q^.Volts := 12;
```

define two fields of these nodes, as shown in Fig. 17.1. The Link fields are still undefined. It makes no difference where the arrow representing the value of a pointer variable touches its node.

Besides using a New statement, we can also use an assignment statement to store an address in a pointer variable. The *pointer assignment statement*

```
R := P;
```

copies the value of pointer variable P into pointer variable R. This means that pointers P and R contain the same memory address and, therefore, point to the same node, as shown in Fig. 17.2.

Figure 17.1   Nodes P^ and Q^

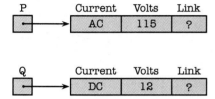

Figure 17.2   Nodes (R^, P^) and Q^

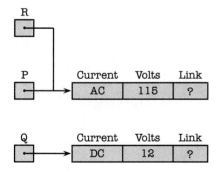

We can compare two pointer variables using the relational operators = and <>. The following conditions are all true for pointer variables P, Q, and R. We cannot use any of the other relational operators with pointer variables.

```
P = R
P <> Q
R <> Q
```

The pointer assignment statements

```
P := Q;   Q := R;
```

would have the effect of exchanging the nodes pointed to by P and Q, as shown in Fig. 17.3.

Figure 17.3 Nodes (R^, Q^) and P^

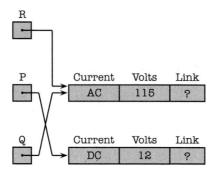

The statement

```
WriteLn (Q^.Current, P^.Current);
```

displays the Current fields of the records pointed to by Q and P. For the situation depicted in Fig. 17.3, the line

```
ACDC
```

would be displayed.

The statement

```
New (Q);
```

changes the value of Q to the address of a new node, thereby disconnecting Q from its previous node. The data fields of the new node pointed to by Q are initially undefined; however, the statement

```
Q^ := R^;
```

copies the contents of node R^ to node Q^. Figure 17.4 shows the three nodes P^, Q^, and R^.

Pointers P, Q, and R are analogous to subscripts in that they select a particular node, or element, of a data structure. Unlike subscripts, however, their

Figure 17.4 Nodes R^, P^, and Q^

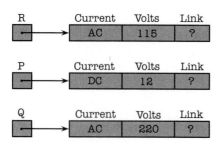

range of values is not declared and their values (memory cell addresses) cannot be printed.

It is important that you understand the difference between using P and P^ in a program. P is a pointer variable (type NodePointer) and is used to store the address of a data structure of type Node. P can be assigned a new value through a pointer assignment or execution of a New statement. P^ is the name of the record pointed to by P and can be manipulated like any other record in Pascal. The field selectors P^.Current and P^.Volts can be used to reference data (a string and an integer) stored in this record.

Connecting Nodes

One purpose of dynamically allocated nodes is to enable us to grow data structures of varying size. We accomplish this by connecting individual nodes. If you look at the nodes allocated in the last section, you will see that their Link fields are undefined. Because the Link fields are type NodePointer, they can be used to store a memory cell address. The pointer assignment statement

```
{1} R^.Link := P;
```

copies the address stored in P into the Link field of node R^, thereby connecting node R^ to node P^. Similarly, the pointer assignment statement

```
{2} P^.Link := Q
```

copies the address stored in pointer variable Q into the Link field of node P^, thereby connecting node P^ to node Q^. The situation after execution of these two assignment statements is shown in Fig. 17.5. The arrows that represent the new values of R^.Link and P^.Link are shown in color. The label next to the arrow denotes one of the pointer assignments.

Figure 17.5 Connecting Nodes

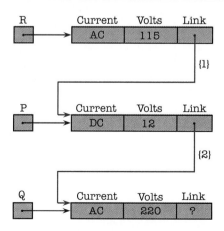

The data structure pointed to by R has now grown to include all three nodes. The first node is referenced by R^. The second node can be referenced by P^ or R^.Link^. Finally, the third node can be referenced by Q^, P^.Link^, or even R^.Link^.Link^.

Exercises for Section 17.1

Self-Check

1. For Fig. 17.5, explain the effect of each valid assignment statement. Which are invalid?

   a. `R^.Current := 'CA'`   e. `R^.Link^.Volts := 0`
   b. `P^ := R^`   f. `P := R`
   c. `P.Current := 'HT'`   g. `R^.Link^.Link^.Current := 'XY'`
   d. `P := 54`   h. `Q^.Volts := R^.Volts`

2. The assignment statements

   ```
   R := P;  P := Q;  Q := R
   ```

   exchange the values of pointer variables P and Q (type NodePointer). What do the following assignment statements do?

   a. `R^.Current := P^.Current;`
   b. `P^.Current := Q^.Current;`
   c. `Q^.Current := R^.Current`

Programming

1. Write a program segment that creates a collection of nodes and stores the musical scale (do, re, mi, fa, so, la, ti) in those nodes. Connect the nodes so that do is stored in the first node, re in the second, and so on.

17.2 Manipulating the Heap

In the last section, you saw that a new record is created whenever the New procedure is executed. You may be wondering where in memory the new record is stored. Pascal maintains a storage pool of available memory cells called a *heap*; memory cells from this pool are allocated whenever procedure New is executed.

Effect of the New Statement on the Heap

If P is a pointer variable of type NodePointer (declared in the last section), the statement

```
New (P)
```

allocates memory space for the storage of two characters, an integer variable, and an address. These cells are originally undefined (they retain whatever data were last stored in them) and the memory address of the first cell allocated is stored in P. Allocated cells are no longer considered part of the heap. The only way to reference allocated cells is through pointer variable P (for example, P^.Current, P^.Volts, or P^.Link).

Figure 17.6 shows the pointer variable P and the heap before and after the execution of New (P). The *before* diagram shows pointer variable P as undefined before the execution of New (P). The *after* diagram shows P pointing to the first of three memory cells allocated for the new record (assuming that three memory cells can accommodate a record of type Node). The cells still considered part of the heap are in the darker color.

Figure 17.6 Heap Before and After New (P)

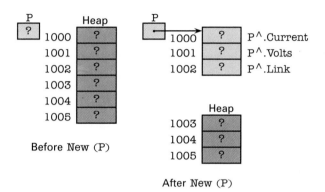

Before New (P)

After New (P)

For example, if the memory cells with addresses 1000 through 1005 were originally in the heap, after the execution of New (P) only the memory cells with addresses 1003 through 1005 would be considered still part of the heap. The address 1000 would be stored in pointer variable P, and that cell would be named P^.Current; memory cells 1001 and 1002 would be named P^.Volts and P^.Link, respectively.

Returning Cells to the Heap

The procedure call statement

```
Dispose (P)
```

returns the memory cells pointed to by P to the heap, restoring the heap to the state shown on the left of Fig. 17.6. The value of pointer variable P becomes undefined, and the data formerly associated with P^ are no longer accessible. The three cells that are returned to the heap can be reused later when another New statement is executed.

Often, more than one pointer points to the same record. For this reason, you must be careful when you return the storage occupied by a record to the heap. If cells are reallocated after they are returned, errors may result if they are later referenced by another pointer that still points to them. Make sure you have no need for a particular record before you return the storage occupied by it.

The Dispose Procedure

Form: Dispose (*pvar*)

Example: Dispose (P)

Interpretation: The memory cells that make up the record whose address is stored in pointer *pvar* are returned to the heap. These cells can be reallocated when procedure New is called.

17.3 Linked Lists

This section introduces an important data structure called a *linked list* or, simply, *list*. You will see how to build and manipulate lists in Pascal.

Abstract Lists

An abstract list is a sequence of nodes in which each node is linked, or connected, to the node following it. An abstract list with three nodes follows.

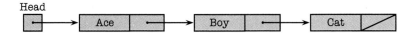

Each node in the list has two fields: the first field contains data; the second field is a pointer (represented by an arrow) to the next list element. A pointer variable (Head) points to the first list element, or *list head*. The last list element always has a diagonal line in its pointer field to indicate the end of the list.

A list is an important data structure because it can be modified easily. For example, a new node containing the string 'Bye' can be inserted between the strings 'Boy' and 'Cat' by changing only one pointer value (the one from 'Boy') and setting the pointer from the new node to point to 'Cat'. This is true regardless of how many elements are in the list. The list shown next is after the insertion; the new pointer values are shown in color.

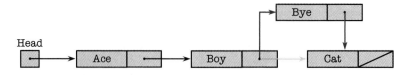

Similarly, it is quite easy to delete a list element. Only one pointer value has to be changed, the pointer that currently points to the element being deleted. The linked list is redrawn as follows after the string 'Boy' is deleted, by changing the pointer from the node 'Ace'. The node containing the string

'Boy' is effectively disconnected from the list and can be returned to the heap. The new list consists of the strings 'Ace', 'Bye', 'Cat'.

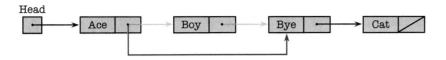

Representing Linked Lists Using Pointers

The preceding abstract list is relatively easy to create in Pascal using pointers and dynamic allocation. In Section 17.1, you saw how to connect three nodes with pointer fields. Although you didn't know it at the time, the data structure shown in Fig. 17.5 could be considered a list of three nodes with pointer variable R as the pointer to its head.

In Pascal, the reserved word nil is a predefined value that can be assigned to any pointer variable. It indicates that the pointer variable does not point to any memory cells on the heap. If Head is a pointer variable, we can use the assignment statement

```
Head := nil
```

to indicate that Head points to an *empty list,* a list with zero nodes.

Head

The pointer value nil is drawn as a diagonal line.

Normally, we assign the value nil to the pointer field of the last node in a list. After the assignment statement

```
Q^.Link := nil
```

is executed, the data structure in Fig. 17.5 implements the following linked list. Each node has two data fields (Current and Volts) and one pointer field (Link).

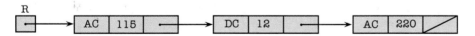

Representing Linked Lists Using Arrays

You can also represent a linked list as an array of records in which an Integer field stores the index of the next list element. Figure 17.7 shows the previous abstract list stored in an array (Nodes) whose elements are records (type Node). The Link field of each record contains the index (subscript) of the next element. The variable R contains the subscript (1) of the first list element (Nodes[1]). The three list nodes happen to be stored in array elements 1, 3, and 2, in that order, although any three elements could be used. Element 2 has a Link field of 0, which indicates the end of the list.

Figure 17.7 Array Representation of a Linked List

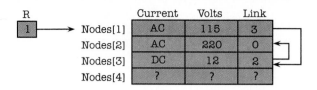

PROGRAM
STYLE

Storage Considerations for List Representations

Lists stored in arrays are just as easy to modify as lists that you create using pointer variables. To insert or delete a list element, it is necessary only to change one or more subscript values. The disadvantage, however, is that memory space for the entire array must be allocated at one time. If you create a list using pointer variables and dynamic allocation, the size of the list in memory will grow and shrink as needed, and the storage allocated to it will change accordingly. For this reason, we recommend using pointers to implement lists.

Exercises for Section 17.3

Self-Check

1. For the array Nodes shown in Fig. 17.7, trace the execution of the following program fragment. What is printed?

```
R := 1;
while R <> 0 do
   begin
      WriteLn (Nodes[R].Current, Nodes[R].Volts);
      R := Nodes[R].Link
   end; {while}
```

Programming

1. Solve programming exercise 1 from Section 17.1, assuming that an array is used to store the scale.

17.4 Linked-List Operators

This section and the ones that follow consider some common list-processing operations and show how to implement them using pointer variables. We assume that the structure of each list node corresponds to type ListNode, declared as follows. Pointer variable Head points to the list head.

```
const
   StringSize = 3;

type
   StringIndex = 1..StringSize;
```

```
StringType = packed array [StringIndex] of Char;
ListPointer = ^ListNode;
ListNode = record
              Word : StringType;
              Link : ListPointer
           end; {ListNode}

var
   Head : ListPointer;          {pointer to list head}
```

Traversing a List

In many list-processing operations, we must process each node in the list in sequence; this is called *traversing* a list. To traverse a list, we must start at the list head and follow the list pointers.

One operation that we must perform on any data structure is to display its contents. To display the contents of a list, we traverse the list and display only the values of the information fields, not the link fields. Procedure PrintList in Fig. 17.8 displays the Word field of each node (type ListNode) in the existing list whose list head is passed as a parameter (type ListPointer). If Head points to the list

Head

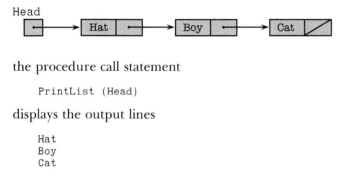

the procedure call statement

```
PrintList (Head)
```

displays the output lines

```
Hat
Boy
Cat
```

Figure 17.8 Procedure PrintList

```
procedure PrintList (Head {input} : ListPointer);
{
  Displays the list pointed to by Head.
  Pre : Head points to a list whose last node has a pointer
        field of nil.
  Post: The Word field of each list node is displayed and
        the last value of Head is nil.
}
begin {PrintList}
  {Traverse the list until the end is reached.}
  while Head <> nil do
    {invariant: No prior value of Head was nil.}
    begin
      WriteLn (Head^.Word);
      Head := Head^.Link              {Advance to next node.}
    end {while}
end; {PrintList}
```

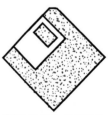

Directory: CHAP17
File: PRINTLIS.PRO

The while condition

```
Head <> nil
```

is common in loops that process lists. If the list to be printed is an empty list, this condition is true initially and the loop body is skipped.

If the list is not empty, the loop body executes and the statement

```
Head := Head^.Link        {advance to next node}
```

advances the pointer Head to the next list element, which is pointed to by the Link field of the current list element. After the last value in the list is printed, the value nil is assigned to Head and the while loop is exited.

Because Head is a value parameter, a local copy of the pointer to the first list element is established when the procedure is entered. This local pointer is advanced, but the corresponding pointer in the calling program remains unchanged. What would happen to our list if Head was a variable parameter?

Warning About Variable Parameters for Pointers

The last line in the preceding paragraph asks you to consider the effect of parameter Head being a variable parameter instead of a value parameter. We know that this would allow the procedure to change the corresponding actual parameter, regardless of our intentions. In PrintList and many similar procedures, the last value assigned to the pointer parameter is nil. If Head is a variable parameter, the corresponding actual parameter would be set to nil, thereby disconnecting it from the list that it pointed to before the procedure call.

Creating a List

Procedure CreateList in Fig. 17.9 creates a linked list by reading in a sequence of data strings that end with a sentinel ('***') and storing each string in a list. If the data lines

```
Hat
Boy
Cat
***
```

are entered, the list shown in the preceding section is created. Notice that the sentinel string is not stored in the list.

Figure 17.9 Procedures FillRest and CreateList

```
procedure FillRest (Last {input} : ListPointer);
{
  Appends new nodes to the end of a list.
  Pre : Last points to the last node in a list of length n.
  Post: Last points to the last node in a list of length >= n.
```

Each data string is stored in a new node in the order
in which it was read. The last node contains the data
string just before the sentinel.
```
      Uses: ReadLnString
  }
     var
        NextWord : StringType;        {next data word}
        NextLen : Integer;            {its length}

  begin {FillRest}
     ReadLnString (Input, NextWord, NextLen);
     while NextWord <> Sentinel do
        {invariant:
           Last points to the last node in a list and
           the last string read is stored in node Last^ and
           no prior data string was the Sentinel.
        }
        begin
           New (Last^.Link);              {Attach a new node to Last^.}
           Last := Last^.Link;           {Reset Last to new list end.}
           Last^.Word := NextWord;          {Store current word.}
           ReadLnString (Input, NextWord, NextLen)
        end; {while}

     {assertion: The last string read was the Sentinel.}
     Last^.Link := nil                    {Mark end of list.}
  end; {FillRest}


procedure CreateList (var Head {output} : ListPointer);
{
   Creates a linked list of strings pointed to by Head.
   Each new string is appended to the end of the list so the
   strings will be stored in the order in which they were read.
   Pre : None
   Post: Head points to the first string entered. Head is
         set to nil if the sentinel string is the first string.
   Uses: ReadLnString (see Fig. 10.21) and FillRest.
}
     const
        Sentinel = '***';

     var
        FirstWord : StringType;        {first data word}
        FirstLen : Integer;            {its length}

  begin {CreateList}
     {Display instructions to user.}
     WriteLn ('Enter each data string on a line.');
     WriteLn ('Enter ', Sentinel, ' when done.');

     {Create and fill the list head with the first word.}
     ReadLnString (Input, FirstWord, FirstLen);
     if FirstWord = Sentinel then
        Head := nil                                 {empty list}
     else
        begin {build list}
           New (Head);                              {Create the list head.}
           Head^.Word := FirstWord;     {Store FirstWord in list head.}
           FillRest (Head)                          {Fill rest of list.}
        end {build list}
  end; {CreateList}
```

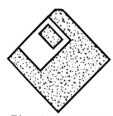

Directory: CHAP17
File: CREATELI.PRO

Procedure `CreateList` first displays the user's instructions and then reads the first data word into `FirstWord`. If `FirstWord` is the sentinel, `Head` is set to `nil` to indicate an empty list. If `FirstWord` is not the sentinel, the statements

```
New (Head);                           {Create the list head.}
Head^.Word := FirstWord;        {Store FirstWord in list head.}
```

allocate a new node `Head^`, into which `FirstWord` (string `'Hat'`) is copied. The procedure call statement

```
FillRest (Head)                       {Fill rest of list.}
```

calls procedure `FillRest` to grow the rest of the list. The value of `Head` is passed into `FillRest` as the initial value of parameter `Last`. Figure 17.10 shows the partial list right after `FillRest` is called.

Figure 17.10 List After Call to FillRest

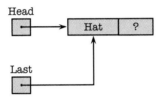

The `while` loop in `FillRest` is repeated until the sentinel is read. Each time the loop is repeated, the statements

```
{1} New (Last^.Link);        {Attach a new node to Last^.}
{2} Last := Last^.Link       {Reset Last to new list end.}
    Last^.Word := NextWord;  {Store last word read.}
```

attach a new node to the current end of the list, reset `Last` to point to the new end of the list, and then store the data word in node `Last^`. The list after the first execution of the loop body is shown in Fig. 17.11. Each new pointer value is shown in color, along with the label of the statement that defines it; the initial value of `Last` is shown in gray.

After loop exit, the statement

```
Last^.Link := nil                     {Mark end of list.}
```

marks the end of the list. If the sentinel string followed `'Boy'`, the `Link` field of the second node in Fig. 17.11 would be set to `nil`.

Figure 17.11 List After First Execution of while Loop Body

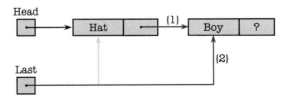

Searching a List for a Target

Another common operation is searching for a target value in a list. A list search is similar to an array search in that we must examine the list elements in sequence until we find the value we are seeking or we examine all list elements without success. The latter is indicated by reaching the list node whose pointer field is nil.

Function Search in Fig. 17.12 returns a pointer to the first list node that contains the target value. If the target value is missing, Search returns a value of nil. Search uses the Boolean flag Found to indicate whether the target value was found. The if statement in the while loop sets Found to True if the current list node contains the target value. The while loop exit occurs right after Found is set to True or the last list node is tested.

Figure 17.12   Function Search

```
function Search (Head : ListPointer;
                 Target : StringType) : ListPointer;
{
  Searches a list for a specified Target string.
  Pre : Head points to a list and Target is defined.
  Post: Returns a pointer to Target if found;
        otherwise, returns nil if Target is not found.
}
  var
    Found : Boolean;       {flag indicating whether Target is found}

begin {Search}
  Found := False;          {Target not found}
  while not Found and (Head <> nil) do
    {invariant:
       no prior list node contained Target and
       no prior value of Head was nil
    }
    if Head^.Word = Target then
      Found := True
    else
      Head := Head^.Link;     {Move down the list.}

  {assertion: Target was found or end of list was reached.}
  if Found then
    Search := Head               {success}
  else
    Search := nil                {failure}
end; {Search}
```

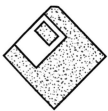

Directory: CHAP17
File: SEARCH.FUN

PROGRAM
STYLE

Avoiding Falling off the End of a List

It is tempting to eliminate the Boolean flag in Fig. 17.12 and to rewrite the while loop as

```
while (Head <> nil) and (Head^.Word <> Target) do
  Head := Head^.Link;
```

The while loop exit occurs if all list elements test without success (Head is nil) or the current node contains the target value. We can then return the value of Head as the search result. If your compiler uses short-circuit evaluation, the while loop will execute as expected. However, if it doesn't use short-circuit evaluation, a run-time error may occur whenever the target value is missing because the condition

```
Head^.Word <> Target
```

is undefined when Head is nil. Because short-circuit evaluation is not required in standard Pascal, you should always precede this condition with a separate test that Head is not nil, as was done in Fig. 17.12.

Exercises for Section 17.4

Self-Check

1. Trace the execution of function Search for the list that contains the three strings 'Hat', 'Boy', 'Cat'. Show the value of pointer Head after each execution of the while loop. Do this for the target strings 'Boy', 'Cap', and 'Dog'.

Programming

1. Write a function that finds the length of a list.
2. Write a recursive version of function Search. Your function should implement the following recursive algorithm:

> if the list is empty then
>   Target is missing—return nil.
> else if Target is in the list head then
>   Return a pointer to the list head.
> else
>   Search the rest of the list.

17.5 Linked-List Representation of a Stack

Chapter 16 introduced stack and queue abstract data types and showed you how to implement them using an array for storage of the individual elements of a stack or a queue. Because the number of elements in a stack or a queue varies, it makes good sense to implement these data structures as dynamically allocated linked lists.

Think of a stack as a linked list in which all insertions and deletions are performed at the list head. A list representation of a stack S is shown on the left of Fig. 17.13. The pointer S.Top points to the top of stack S. If a new node is pushed onto the stack, it should be inserted in front of the node currently pointed to by S.Top. Stack S after the insertion of the symbol '*' is shown at the bottom of the figure.

Figure 17.13 Physical Stack S (left) and Abstract Stack (right)

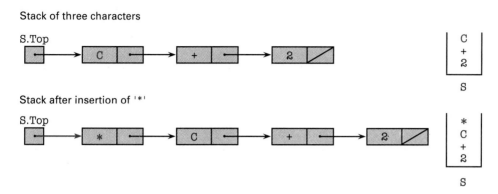

Each element of a stack can be stored in a node with a data field (type StackElement) and a pointer field (type StackNext) that points to the next stack node (type StackNode). These data types are declared as follows:

```
type
   {Insert declaration for StackElement}

   StackNext = ^StackNode;
   StackNode = record
               Item : StackElement;
               Next : StackNext
            end; {StackNode}
```

The stack S can be represented by a record variable with a single pointer field, Top, that points to the top of the stack. The declarations for type Stack and record variable S (type Stack) follow.

```
type
   Stack = record
            Top : StackNext          {top-of-stack pointer}
         end; {Stack}

var
   S : Stack;
   NextCh : Char;
   Success : Boolean;
```

■ Example 17.1

If data type StackElement is the same as Char, the assignment statement

```
   S.Top := nil;
```

initializes stack S to the empty stack, as shown next.

S.Top

S

Assuming procedure Push (see Fig. 16.16) has been modified to handle the new stack declaration, the statements

```
Push (S, '+', Success);
Push (S, 'A', Success);
```

should redefine stack S, as shown next.

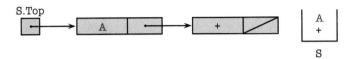

S.Top

A
+

S

Two new nodes must be allocated to create stack S. Assuming Pop has also been modified, the statement

```
Pop (S, NextCh, Success);
```

should return the character value 'A' to NextCh (type Char) and redefine stack S, as shown next. ∎

S.Top

+

S

Stack Operators

Each of the stack operators first shown in Fig. 16.16 is rewritten in this section assuming the previous type declaration for Stack. We begin with CreateStack, shown in Fig. 17.14. CreateStack must be called first; it creates an empty stack by initializing the top-of-stack pointer to nil.

Figure 17.14 Procedure CreateStack

```
procedure CreateStack (var S {output} : Stack);
{
   Creates an empty stack.
   Pre : None
   Post: S is an empty stack.
}
begin {CreateStack}
   S.Top := nil                    {Set top-of-stack pointer to nil.}
end; {CreateStack}
```

Directory: CHAP17
File: STACKLIS.ADT

Procedure Push (Fig. 17.15) must allocate a new node for storing the data item being pushed onto the stack. The node just allocated becomes the new top of the stack.

```
procedure Push (var S {input/output} : Stack;
                    X {input} : Char;
                    var Success {output} : Boolean);
{
  Pushes X onto stack S.
  Pre : X is defined and S is a stack.
  Post: Sets Success to indicate success (True) or failure (False)
        of push operation.
}
  var OldTop : StackNext;         {pointer to old top of stack}

begin {Push}
  if IsFull(S) then
    Success := False
  else
    begin
      OldTop := S.Top;           {Save old top of stack.}
      New (S.Top);               {Allocate new node at top of stack.}
      S.Top^.Next := OldTop;     {Link new node to old stack.}
      S.Top^.Item := X;          {Store X in new node.}
      Success := True
    end {if}
end; {Push}
```

Directory: CHAP17
File: STACKLIS.ADT

Each call to procedure Push places a new node on the stack. The statements

```
{1} OldTop := S.Top;         {Save old top of stack.}
{2} New (S.Top);             {Allocate new node at top of stack.}
{3} S.Top^.Next := OldTop;   {Link new node to old stack.}
```

allocate a new node (pointed to by S.Top) and connect this node to the former top of the stack (pointed to by OldTop). Figure 17.16 shows a stack before and after the letter 'A' is pushed onto it. The original value of S.Top is shown in gray, and the new value is shown in color.

Figure 17.16 Pushing 'A' onto a Stack

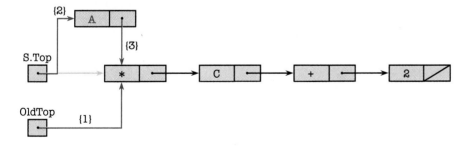

Procedure Pop (Fig. 17.17) retrieves the value at the top of the stack and returns the node in which it is stored to the heap. The node that follows the one just popped becomes the new top of the stack.

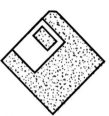

Figure 17.17 Procedure Pop

```
procedure Pop (var S {input/output} : Stack;
               var X {output} : Char;
               var Success {output} : Boolean);
{
  Pops the top of stack S into X.
  Pre : S is a stack.
  Post: Contents of X is character at top of stack S, which is then
        removed from S. Sets Success to indicate success (True)
        or failure (False) of pop operation.
}
  var
    OldTop : StackNext;             {pointer to old top of stack}

begin {Pop}
  if S.Top = nil then
    Success := False
  else
    begin
      X := S.Top^.Item;            {Copy top of stack into X.}
      OldTop := S.Top;             {Save old top of stack.}
      S.Top := S.Top^.Next;        {Reset top of stack.}
      Dispose (OldTop);            {Return top node to the heap.}
      Success := True
    end {if}
end; {Pop}
```

Procedure Pop first copies the value at the top of the stack into X. Next, the statement with label {2}

```
{1} OldTop := S.Top;               {Save old top of stack.}
{2} S.Top := S.Top^.Next;          {Reset top of stack.}
{3} Dispose (OldTop);              {Return top node to the heap.}
```

resets S.Top to point to the node following the current top node. The statement with label {3} returns the former top node to the heap so its memory cells can be reallocated. The effect of popping 'A' from the stack is shown in Fig. 17.18.

Procedure Retrieve accesses the value at the top of the stack but does not pop it off the stack. (Retrieve is left as an exercise at the end of the next section.)

Figure 17.18 Popping the Stack

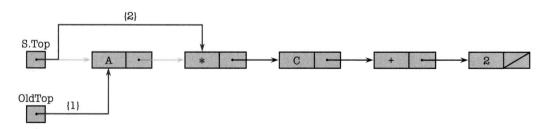

Function IsEmpty tests whether the stack is empty, and function IsFull tests whether the stack is full. The stack is considered full when there are no storage cells left on the heap that can be allocated to the stack. Unfortunately, standard Pascal does not allow us to test the availability of cells on the heap, so we assume that there is always space for one more stack element and that IsFull will always return False. This may eventually lead to a stack overflow error. Functions IsEmpty and IsFull are shown in Fig. 17.19.

Fig. 17.19 Functions IsEmpty and IsFull

```
function IsEmpty (S : Stack) : Boolean;
{
  Pre : S is a stack.
  Post: Returns True if stack S is empty; otherwise, returns False.
}
begin {IsEmpty}
  IsEmpty := S.Top = nil
end; {IsEmpty}

function IsFull (S : Stack) : Boolean;
{
  Pre : S is a stack.
  Post: Returns True if stack S is full; otherwise, returns False.
}
begin {IsFull}
  IsFull := False          {Assume unlimited heap storage.}
end; {IsFull}
```

PROGRAM STYLE

Time and Space Tradeoffs for Stack Implementations

The advantage of using pointer types to implement a stack is that we can increase the size of the stack when we push on a new element and decrease its size when we pop off an element. In this way, the storage space allocated to the stack expands and contracts as needed. In the array implementation shown earlier, the entire array is allocated at once, whether or not it is all needed.

This apparent saving of memory is not without cost. Each stack element requires an additional pointer field that is used for storage of the address of the next stack element. An array implementation does not require this extra field, because the elements of an array are implicitly linked together.

With respect to time, it is usually more costly for a compiler to access elements of a stack stored in an array. This is because the compiler must compute the actual memory address corresponding to a subscript value that represents the top of the stack. If the top of the stack is stored in a pointer field, no computation is required because the address of the first stack node is stored directly.

Exercises for Section 17.5

Self-Check

1. Explain why the field `NumItems` is not needed in the type declaration for `Stack`. What changes would be required to the type declaration and the stack operators if field `NumItems` were included?
2. Provide the algorithm for operator `CopyStack` that makes a copy of an existing stack.
3. What changes would have to be made to program `PrintReverse` (Fig. 16.6) to use the new stack data type and its operators?

Programming

1. Implement `CopyStack`.

17.6 Linked-List Representation of a Queue

We can also implement a queue as a linked list that grows and shrinks as elements are inserted and deleted. We declare queue Q using the following declarations.

```
type
    {Insert declaration for QueueElement}

    QueueNext = ^QueueNode;
    QueueNode = record
                    Item : QueueElement;
                    Next : QueueNext
                end; {QueueNode}

    Queue = record
                Front, Rear : QueueNext;
                NumItems : Integer
            end; {Queue}

var
    Q : Queue;
    NextPass : QueueElement;
    Temp : QueueNext;
```

The declaration for variable Q allocates storage for a record with two pointer fields, `Front` and `Rear`, and one integer field, `NumItems`. As shown in Fig. 17.20, `Front` points to the first record inserted in the queue, `Rear` points to the last record, and `NumItems` is a count of records. Each node of the queue (type `QueueNode`) contains storage for a queue element (type `QueueElement`) and a pointer to the next queue node (type `QueueNext`).

In a linked-list representation of a queue, the queue expands and contracts as queue elements are inserted and removed during program execution. If we store the queue elements in an array, we must allocate storage for the entire queue at compile time.

Figure 17.20   Representing a Queue as a Linked List

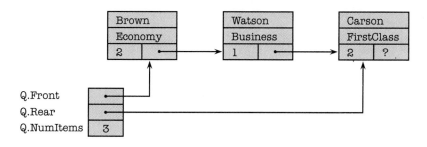

Queue Operators for Linked-List Representation

Queue operator `CreateQueue` is shown in Fig. 17.21 for a linked-list representation of a queue. Procedure `CreateQueue` initializes `NumItems` to `0` and pointers `Front` and `Rear` to `nil`.

Figure 17.21   Procedure CreateQueue

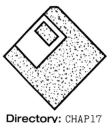

Directory: CHAP17
File: QUEUELIS.ADT

```
procedure CreateQueue (var Q {output} : Queue);
{
   Creates an empty queue.
   Pre : None.
   Post: Q is initialized to a queue of zero elements.
}
begin {CreateQueue}
   Q.NumItems := 0;           {Queue is empty.}
   Q.Front := nil;
   Q.Rear  := nil
end; {CreateQueue}
```

In queue operator `Remove` (see Fig. 17.22), the statements

```
{1}   Temp := Q.Front;              {Point Temp to first node.}
      El := Q.Front^.Item;             {Retrieve passenger.}
{2}   Q.Front := Q.Front^.Next;     {Delete passenger node.}
      Dispose (Temp);                 {Deallocate storage.}
```

remove the first passenger from the front of the queue, storing the passenger data in `El` (type `QueueElement`). Figure 17.23 shows the effect of these statements on the queue shown in Fig. 17.20. The `Dispose` statement returns the queue node containing the deleted passenger data to the heap.

Figure 17.22   Procedure Remove

```
procedure Remove (var Q {input/output} : Queue;
                  var El {output} : QueueElement;
                  var Success {output} : Boolean);
{
    Removes the element at the front of queue Q
    and copies it into El.
    Pre : Q has been created.
    Post: If Q is not empty, El contains its first element,
          Q.Front points to new first element,
          and Success indicates success or failure.
}
  var
     Temp : QueueNext;            {temporary pointer}

begin {Remove}
  if Q.NumItems = 0 then
    Success := False           {Queue is empty.}
  else
    begin
      {Remove the element at the front of the queue.}
      Temp := Q.Front;               {Point Temp to first node.}
      El := Q.Front^.Item;             {Retrieve passenger.}
      Q.Front := Q.Front^.Next;       {Delete passenger node.}
      Dispose (Temp);                  {Deallocate storage.}

      Q.NumItems := Q.NumItems - 1;
      Success := True
    end {if}
end; {Remove}
```

Figure 17.23   Removing Passenger Brown from the Queue

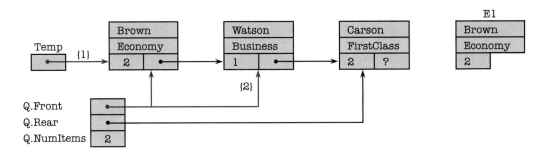

In Operator Insert (see Fig. 17.24), the statements

```
New (Q.Rear);              {Point Rear to first node.}
Q.Front := Q.Rear          {Point Front to first node.}
```

execute when the queue is empty. These statements allocate a single queue node
and point Front and Rear to this node. If the queue is neither empty nor full,
the statements

```
{1} New (Q.Rear^.Next);   {Attach a node at end of queue.}
{2} Q.Rear := Q.Rear^.Next   {Point Rear to new node.}
```

allocate a new node at the end of the queue and point Rear to it. In either case, the statement

```
Q.Rear^.Item := El;            {Define new passenger node.}
```

stores the contents of record El at the new end of the queue. The effect of these statements is shown in Fig. 17.25 for variable El and for the queue in Fig. 17.23. By executing both the Remove and Insert procedures, we shift the element originally at the front of the queue to the rear of the queue.

Figure 17.24 Procedure Insert

```
procedure Insert (var Q {input/output} : Queue;
                  El {input} : QueueElement;
                  var Success {output} : Boolean);
{
   Inserts El in queue Q.
   Pre : Q has been created.
   Post: If Q is not full, inserts El in a new node and
         resets Q.Rear to point to the new node.
         Sets Success to indicate success or failure.
}
begin {Insert}
  if IsFull(Q) then
    Success := False
  else
    begin {insert El}
      if Q.NumItems = 0 then
        begin {empty queue}
          New (Q.Rear);                {Point Rear to first node.}
          Q.Front := Q.Rear            {Point Front to first node.}
        end {empty queue}
      else
        begin {extend queue}
          New (Q.Rear^.Next);   {Attach a node at end of queue.}
          Q.Rear := Q.Rear^.Next       {Point Rear to new node.}
        end; {extend queue}
      Q.Rear^.Item := El;             {Define new passenger node.}
      Q.NumItems := Q.NumItems + 1;
      Success := True
    end  {insert El}
end; {Insert}
```

Directory: CHAP17
File: QUEUELIS.ADT

Figure 17.25 Reinserting Passenger Brown in the Queue

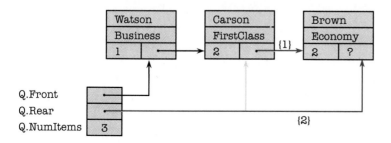

Queue as a Circular List

Section 16.7 demonstrated that a circular array is a convenient data structure for storing the elements of a queue. In this section you will see how to represent and manipulate a queue using a circular list.

Figure 17.26 shows a queue, Q, of three elements represented as a circular list. This is called a *circular list* because the pointer field of the last list element (passenger Carson) is not nil; instead, it points back to the first list element (passenger Brown). Only the pointer Q.Rear is required to access the queue because the pointer Q.Rear^.Next points to the first record in the queue (passenger Brown).

This enables us to eliminate the pointer field Front from the record type Queue.

The statements

```
{1}  New (Temp);
{2}  Temp^.Next := Q.Rear^.Next;
     Temp^.Item := El;
{3}  Q.Rear^.Next := Temp;
{4}  Q.Rear := Temp;
```

insert a new node in a circular queue. Statement {1} allocates a new node, and statements {2} and {3} insert the new node at the rear of the queue. Statement {4} resets Q.Rear to point to the new node. The effect of these statements is shown in Fig. 17.27, assuming the data for passenger McMann are stored in NextPass.

To remove a node, the pointer Q.Rear^.Next should be reset to point to the node following the one that is currently at the front of the queue. The statements

```
     El := Q.Rear^.Next^.Item;
{1}  Q.Rear^.Next := Q.Rear^.Next^.Next;
```

store the data for passenger Brown in El and remove the first queue element. Figure 17.28 shows the effect of statement {1} on the queue above.

The implementation of a queue as a circular list is left as a programming project at the end of this chapter.

Figure 17.26 A Queue as a Circular List

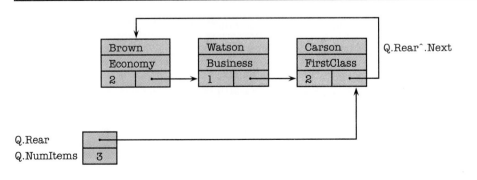

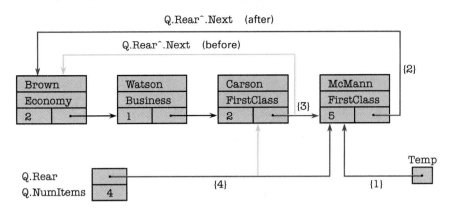

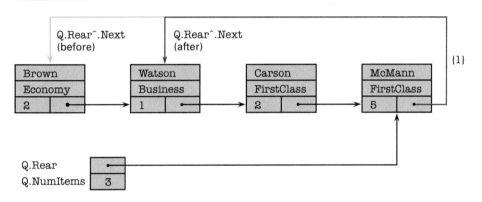

Figure 17.28 Removing Passenger Brown from a Queue

Exercises for Section 17.6

Self-Check

1. What does the following segment do to queue Q shown in Fig. 17.20?

```
New (Q.Rear^.Next);
Q.Rear := Q.Rear^.Next;
Q.Rear^.Item.Name := 'Johnson
Q.Rear^.Item.Class := Economy;
Q.Rear^.Item.NumSeats := 5;
Q.NumItems := Q.NumItems + 1
```

2. What does the following statement do to queue Q shown in Fig. 17.26?

```
Q.Rear := Q.Rear^.Next;
```

3. Insert passenger Billingsly, Business class, 2 seats in the queue of Fig. 17.26.

Programming

1. Write function `SizeOfQueue` for both a linked-list queue and a queue as a circular list.
2. Write procedure `Retrieve` for both a linked-list queue and a queue as a circular list.

17.7 Common Programming Errors

Syntax Errors

Make sure you use the dereferencing operator `^` where it is needed. If `P` is a pointer variable, `P^.X` should be used to reference field `X` of the record pointed to by `P`.

The `New` and `Dispose` procedures allocate and deallocate storage, respectively. Both procedures require a parameter that is a pointer variable. `New (P)` is correct, while `New (P^)` is incorrect.

Run-Time Errors

You should look out for a number of run-time errors when you are traversing linked data structures with pointers. For example, if `Next` is supposed to point to each node in the linked list, the statement

```
while Next <> nil do
   Write (Next^.Word);
   Next := Next^.Link;
```

executes forever. That happens because the pointer assignment statement is not included in the loop body, so `Next` is not advanced down the list.

A run-time error can occur when the pointer `Next` is advanced too far down the list and `Next` takes on the value `nil`, indicating the end of the list. If pointer `Next` has the value `nil`, the `while` condition

```
while (Next <> nil) and (Next^.ID <> 9999) do
```

causes a run-time error on some systems because `Next^.ID` is undefined when `Next` is nil. The `while` condition should be rewritten as

```
while (Next^.Link <> nil) and (Next^.ID <> 9999) do
```

Finally, if pointer `Next` is a procedure parameter that corresponds to a list head pointer, make sure it is a value parameter. Otherwise, the last value assigned to `Next` will be returned as a procedure result. This may cause you to lose some of the elements originally in the linked list.

Problems with heap management can also cause run-time errors. If your program gets stuck in an infinite loop while you are creating a dynamic data structure, it is possible for your program to consume all memory cells on the storage heap. This situation will lead to a `heap overflow` or `stack overflow` run-time error.

Make sure your program does not attempt to reference a list node after the node is returned to the heap. All pointers to a node being returned should be assigned new values so that the node can never be accessed unless it is reallocated.

Debugging Tips

Because the value of a pointer variable cannot be printed, it is difficult to debug programs that manipulate pointers. You have to trace the execution of such a program by printing an information field that uniquely identifies the list element being processed instead of the pointer value itself.

When you are writing driver programs to test and debug list operators, it is often helpful to create a sample linked structure using the technique shown in Section 17.1. Use a sequence of `New` statements and temporary pointer variables to allocate the individual nodes. Next, use assignment statements to define the data and the pointer fields of the structure.

▬ CHAPTER REVIEW

This chapter introduced several dynamic data structures. We discussed the use of pointers to reference and connect elements of a dynamic data structure. The procedure `New` allocates additional elements, or nodes, of a dynamic data structure; the procedure `Dispose` returns memory cells to the storage heap.

We also covered many different aspects of manipulating linked lists. We showed how to build or create a linked list, how to traverse a linked list, and how to insert and delete elements of a linked list.

We revisited stacks and queues and showed you how to implement them as linked data structures. And we wrote new stack operators for the representation of a stack using a linked list.

New Pascal Constructs

The Pascal constructs introduced in this chapter are described in Table 17.1.

Table 17.1 New Pascal Constructs

Construct	Effect
Pointer Type Declaration	

`type`
  `Pointer = ^Node;`
  `Node = record`
       `Info : Integer;`
       `Link : Pointer`
     `end; {Node}`
	The identifier `Pointer` is declared as a pointer to a record of type `Node`, where `Node` is a record type containing a field (`Link`) of type `Pointer`.

Table 17.1, *continued*

Construct	Effect
`var` `Head : Pointer;`	Head is a pointer variable of type `Pointer`.
New Procedure `New (Head)`	A new record of type `Node` is allocated. This record is pointed to by `Head` and is referenced by `Head^`.
Dispose Procedure `Dispose (Head)`	The memory space occupied by the record `Head^` is returned to the storage pool.
Pointer Assignment `Head := Head^.Link`	The pointer `Head` is advanced to the next node in the dynamic data structure pointed to by `Head`.

✓ Quick-Check Exercises

1. Procedure _____ allocates storage space for a data object that is referenced through a _____; procedure _____ returns the storage space to the _____.

2. What is the major advantage of using pointer representations of linked lists instead of array representations?

3. It is just as easy to modify a linked list that is represented as an array as one that is represented using pointers. True or false?

4. When an element is deleted from a linked list represented using pointers, it is automatically returned to the heap. True or false?

5. All pointers to a node that is returned to the heap are automatically reset to `nil` so they cannot reference the node returned to the heap. True or false?

6. Why do you need to be wary of passing a list-head pointer as a variable parameter to a procedure?

7. If a linked list contains three elements with values `'Him'`, `'Her'`, and `'Its'` and H is a pointer to the list head, what is the effect of the following statements? Assume the data field is `Pronoun`, the link field is `Next`, and N and P are pointer variables.

```
N := H^.Next;
N^.Pronoun := 'She';
```

8. Answer exercise 7 for the following segment.

```
P := H^.Next;
N := P^.Next;
P^.Next := N^.Next;
Dispose (N);
```

9. Answer exercise 7 for the following segment.

```
N := H;
New (H);
H^.Pronoun := 'His';
H^.Next := N;
```

10. Write a single statement that will place the value nil in the last node of the three-element list in exercise 7.

Answers to Quick-Check Exercises
1. New; pointer; Dispose; heap
2. Storage space is allocated as needed and not all at once.
3. true
4. false; Dispose must be called.
5. false
6. The actual parameter may be advanced down a list, and in this way part of the list will be lost.
7. replaces 'Her' with 'She'
8. deletes the third list element
9. inserts a new list with value 'His' at the front of the list
10. H^.Next^.Next^.Next := nil;

Review Questions

1. Differentiate between dynamic and nondynamic data structures.
2. Describe a simple linked list. Indicate how the pointers are utilized to establish a link between nodes. Also indicate any other variables that would be needed to reference the linked list.
3. Give the missing type declarations and show the effect of each of the following statements. What does each do?

```
New (P);
P^.Word := 'ABC';
New (P^.Next);
Q := P^.Next;
Q^.Word := 'abc';
Q^.Next := nil;
```

4. Assume the following type declarations for questions 4 through 9.

```
type
  StringType = packed array [1..10] of Char;
  ListPointer = ^Node;
  Node = record
           Name : StringType;
           Link : ListPointer
         end;

  HeadNode = record
               Head : ListPointer;
               NumItems : Integer
             end;

var
  List: HeadNode;
  P, Next : ListPointer;
```

Write a program segment that places the names Washington, Roosevelt, and Kennedy in successive elements of the linked list referenced by record `List`. Define `List.NumItems` accordingly.

5. Write a program segment to insert the name Eisenhower between Roosevelt and Kennedy.

6. Write an operator called `DeleteLast` that removes the last element from any list referenced by record `List`.

7. Write a procedure called `PlaceFirst` that places its second parameter value as the first node of the linked list referenced by record `List`.

8. Write a procedure called `CopyList` that creates a linked list with new nodes that contain the same data as the linked list referenced by `List`.

9. Write a procedure to delete all nodes with `Name` field `Smith` from a linked list referenced by record `List`.

Programming Projects

1. Rewrite the queue operators shown in Section 16.7 for a queue represented as a linked list.

2. Rewrite the queue operators shown in Section 16.7 for a queue represented as a circular list.

3. Do programming project 1 at the end of Chapter 16 using the queue operators from programming project 1 or 2 of this chapter.

4. Do programming project 3 at the end of Chapter 16 using the stack operators implemented in this chapter.

5. Do programming project 4 at the end of Chapter 16 using the queue operators from programming project 1 or 2 of this chapter.

6. A polynomial can be represented as a linked list, where each node contains the coefficient and the exponent of a term of the polynomial. The polynomial $4x^3 + 3x^2 - 5$ would be represented as the following linked list:

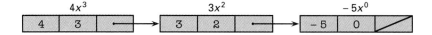

Write an abstract data type `Polynomial` that has operators for creating a polynomial, reading a polynomial, and adding and subtracting a pair of polynomials. Hint: To add or subtract two polynomials, traverse both lists. If a particular exponent value is present in either one, it should also be present in the result polynomial unless its coefficient is zero.

7. Each student in the university takes a different number of courses, so the registrar has decided to use a linked list to store each student's class schedule and an array of records to represent the whole student body. A portion of this data structure follows.

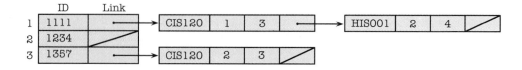

The records show that the first student (ID is 1111) is taking section 1 of CIS120 for 3 credits and section 2 of HIS001 for 4 credits; the second student (ID is 1234) is not enrolled, and so on. Write an abstract data type for this data structure. Provide operators for creating the original array of student ID numbers, inserting a student's initial class schedule, adding a course, and dropping a course. Write a menu-driven program that uses this abstract data type.

8. The Radix sorting algorithm uses an array of queues (numbered 0 through 9) to simulate the operation of the old card sorting machines. The algorithm requires that one pass be made for every digit of the numbers being sorted. For example, a list of three-digit numbers would require three passes through the list. During the first pass, the least significant digit (the ones digit) of each number is examined and the number is added to the rear of the queue whose subscript matches the digit. After all numbers have been processed, the elements of each queue, beginning with Queue[0], are copied one at a time to the end of an eleventh queue prior to beginning the next pass. Then the process is repeated for the nextmost significant digit (the tens digit) using the order of the numbers in the eleventh queue. Repeat the process again using the third most significant digit (the hundreds digit). After the final pass, the eleventh queue will contain the numbers in sorted order. Write a program that implements the Radix sort using QueueADT.

18
Ordered Lists and Trees

Chapter 17 introduced dynamic data structures, including pointers, linked lists, and linked-list implementations of stacks and queues. This chapter discusses dynamic data structures that provide improved search behavior, including ordered lists and binary search trees. We will assume that each record has a *key field*, which uniquely identifies that record (e.g., an ID number). An ordered list is a list in which each node's position is determined by the value of its key field, so that the key values form an increasing sequence as we advance down the list. This is different from a stack or a queue, in which a node's position is determined by when it was inserted in the list.

Each list node you have seen so far has had a single pointer field connecting it to the next node. This chapter introduces data structures that have two pointer fields, which enable each node to be connected to two others. The binary tree, as one such data structure, has wide application in computer science. This chapter shows you how to use binary trees to represent expressions. We discuss traversing a tree and its relationship to expression evaluation. We also show you how to store information in a binary search tree and how to retrieve that information in an efficient manner.

18.1 The Ordered List Abstract Data Type

This section considers the problem of maintaining an ordered list. We want to be able to insert an element and know that the list will still be in order after the insertion. Similarly, after a list element is deleted, the remaining elements should still be in order. As long as we maintain the order of the list elements as we perform each insertion, we will never have to sort the list. It is also easier to search for a particular list element if the elements are in order.

The specification of an abstract data type for an ordered list (type `OrderList`) and its operators follows.

```
{
    Specification of Abstract Data Type OrderListADT

    Structure:    An ordered list is a collection of elements
                  such that each element includes among its data
                  fields a special field that is considered the
                  key field. The key-field values in an ordered
                  list form an increasing sequence. For
                  simplicity, assume that there are no duplicate
                  keys.

    Operators:    For the following descriptions, assume these
                  parameters:
```

```
      List represents the ordered list.
      El has the same data type as the list elements.
      Target is a possible key-field value.
      Success is a Boolean flag indicating success (True) or
      failure (False) of an operation.

   CreateList (var List): Creates an empty ordered list; must
   be called before any other operators.

   SizeOfList(List): (function) Returns the number of elements
   currently in the ordered list.

   Search (List, Target, var Success): Searches a list to find
   the key Target. If Target is found, sets Success to True;
   otherwise, sets Success to False.

   Insert (var List, El, var Success): Inserts item El into
   the list, maintaining the list order, and sets Success to
   True. If there is already an element with the same key
   value as El, Success is set to False and no insertion is
   performed.

   Delete (var List, Target, var Success): Deletes the element
   whose key value is Target, maintaining the list order, and
   sets Success to True. If Target is not located, sets
   Success to False.

   Retrieve (List, Target, var El, var Success): Copies the
   element whose key is Target into El and sets Success to
   True. If there is no element with key Target, El is not
   defined and Success is False.

   Replace (var List, El, var Success): Replaces the element
   whose key value is the same as the key value of El and sets
   Success to True. If there is no element whose key value
   matches the key value of El, sets Success to False.

   DisplayList (List): Displays the list elements in
   sequential order by key.
}
```

As before, we can illustrate how these operators work and use them in a client program without worrying about the details of how the list is represented in memory. In Section 18.3, we discuss one internal representation for an ordered list and implement the ordered list operators. Because we want to be able to manipulate different types of data objects stored in an ordered list, we use the identifier `ListElement` to represent the type of each list element and `KeyType` to indicate the type of the record key. We also need two constants, `MinKey` and `MaxKey` (both type `KeyType`), that bracket the range of allowable values for the key field. Each client program must import constants `MinKey` and `MaxKey` and data types `ListElement`, `KeyType`, and `OrderList` from abstract data type `OrderListADT`.

Examples of Ordered Lists

The top of Fig. 18.1 shows an ordered list that contains three four-digit integer values (1234, 2222, and 5669). The list head (variable `MyList`) contains a pointer field that points to a *dummy list node* with key field 999 (value of `MinKey`). This node and the dummy list node with key field 10000 (value of `MaxKey`) are not considered part of the ordered list; they serve as sentinels and are used to simplify writing the list operators (discussed in Section 18.3). Record variable `MyList` also contains an integer field that indicates the number of actual nodes (3) in the list (the dummy nodes are not counted). The bottom of the figure shows the same list after insertion of a new node with key field 4000.

In Fig. 18.2, record variable `PassList` represents an ordered list of airline passengers. In this list, the key field is the passenger name, so the records are in order by passenger name. The first and last nodes are dummy nodes and are not included in the count (2) of list elements.

Figure 18.1 Insertion into an Ordered List

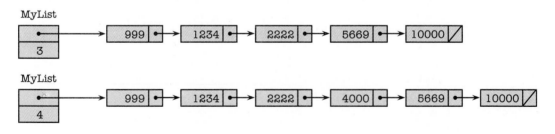

Figure 18.2 Ordered List of Airline Passengers

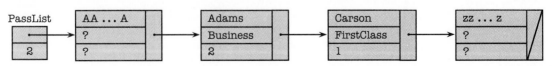

18.2 Using an Ordered List

As you might expect, we can use the ordered list abstract data type to maintain an ordered list of integers, real numbers, or airline passengers. We can modify the menu-driven program in Fig. 16.18 to maintain an ordered list of airline passengers instead of placing the passengers in a queue. As shown in Fig. 18.2, the key field for each passenger record would be the passenger's name. The advantage of using an ordered list is that we can remove or delete any passenger from the list, whereas in a queue only the passenger at the front can be removed. Also, we can easily display the passengers in an ordered list in sequence by key field. Programming project 1 at the end of this chapter asks you to modify the menu-driven program to use an ordered list of passenger data. We solve a simpler problem next.

Case Study: Building an Ordered List of Integers

Problem
To illustrate the ordered-list operators, we will write a short client program that builds and displays an ordered list of integer values.

Analysis
The client program must import all necessary constants and data types from `OrderListADT`. The program begins by creating an empty list. Next, it reads a group of integer values and inserts them in the ordered list. After the ordered list is formed, the program displays the ordered list. Then it performs a list search, a list deletion, and displays the final ordered list.

Data Requirements

Problem Input
```
NextKey : KeyType          {each record key}
```

Problem Output
```
MyList : OrderList         {ordered list}
```

Program Variables
```
NextNode : ListElement     {each list node}
Success : Boolean    {flag indicating the result of a list operation}
```

Design

Algorithm

1. Create an empty ordered list.
2. Read the first key value.

3. while the sentinel is not read do
    begin
        4. Insert the next key in the ordered list.
        5. Read a new key value.
    end
6. Display the ordered list and its size.
7. Perform a search operation.
8. Perform a delete operation.
9. Display the ordered list and its size.

Implementation

The client program is shown in Fig. 18.3. The constants MinKey and MaxKey
and the data types KeyType and ListElement for an ordered list of integers
are imported from OrderListADT. We must also import data type OrderList
and the operators that manipulate the ordered list from OrderListADT.

Figure 18.3 Program UseOrderList

Directory: CHAP18
File: USEORDER.PAS

```
program UseOrderList (Input, Output);
{
  Builds and displays an ordered list using data type OrderList.
  Module needed: Uses OrderListADT
}
  const
    {Insert declarations for MinKey (999) and
     MaxKey (10000) from OrderListADT.}
    Sentinel = MaxKey;

  type
    {Insert declaration KeyType and
     ListElement (both type integer) from OrderListADT.}

    {Insert type declaration for OrderList from OrderListADT.}

  var
    MyList : OrderList;            {ordered list}
    NextNode : ListElement;        {each list node}
    Target : KeyType;              {target key}
    Success : Boolean;             {program flag}


  {Insert CreateList, Insert, Delete, Search, DisplayList, SizeOfList
   from OrderListADT.}

begin {UseOrderList}
  {Initialize the list}
  CreateList (MyList);

  {Read and insert the keys in the ordered list.}
  WriteLn ('Enter ', Sentinel :1, ' to stop.');
  Write ('Enter next key value or ', Sentinel :1, '> ');
  ReadLn (NextNode);
  while NextNode <> Sentinel do
    {invariant:
```

```
          All prior values of NextNode that are not duplicates were
          inserted in MyList and
          no prior value of NextNode was the sentinel.
       }
     begin
       Insert (MyList, NextNode, Success);
       if Success then
         WriteLn (NextNode :1, ' inserted.')
       else
         WriteLn ('Out-of-range or duplicate key - no insertion.');
       Write ('Enter next key value or ', Sentinel :1, '> ');
       ReadLn (NextNode)
     end; {while}

  {assert: Ordered list completed.}
  {Display the ordered list and its size.}
  WriteLn; WriteLn ('The ordered list follows.');
  DisplayList (MyList);
  Write ('The number of nodes in the list is ');
  WriteLn (SizeOfList(MyList) :1);  WriteLn;

  {Perform Search operation.}
  Write ('Find record with key> ');
  ReadLn (Target);
  Search (MyList, Target, Success);
  if Success then
    WriteLn (Target, ' found.')
  else
    WriteLn ('Not in the list.');

  {Perform Delete operation.}
  Write ('Delete record with key> ');
  ReadLn (Target);
  Delete (MyList, Target, Success);
  if Success then
    WriteLn (Target :1, ' deleted.')
  else
    WriteLn ('Key not found - no deletion.');
  WriteLn;

  {Display the ordered list and its size.}
  WriteLn ('The ordered list follows.');
  DisplayList (MyList);
  Write ('The number of nodes in the list is ');
  WriteLn (SizeOfList(MyList) :1)
end. {UseOrderList}
```

The client program begins by calling operator CreateList to create an
empty ordered list. Next, the while loop reads each key value into NextNode
and calls operator Insert to place the new key value in the ordered list. If
ListElement were a structured type instead of a simple type, we would need
to import an operator to read all record data. After loop exit, the program calls
other list operators and displays the result of each operation on the ordered
list.

Case Study: Building an Ordered List of Integers, continued

Testing

Before you can run program UseOrderList, it is necessary to insert the missing type and procedure declarations that are imported from OrderListADT. When testing the program, make sure that the final list is in order by record key, that there are no duplicate keys in the list, and that the nodes with key values MinKey and MaxKey are not displayed or counted. You should test the program using record keys that are outside the range of allowable values and using duplicate keys. Also try to delete an element that is not in the list. A sample run is shown in Fig. 18.4.

Figure 18.4   Sample Run of UseOrderList

```
Enter 10000 to stop.
Enter next key value or 10000> 2345
2345 inserted.
Enter next key value or 10000> 3456
3456 inserted.
Enter next key value or 10000> 1111
1111 inserted.
Enter next key value or 10000> 2345
Out-of-range or duplicate key - no insertion.
Enter next key value or 10000> 10000

The ordered list follows.
1111
2345
3456
The number of nodes in the list is 3

Find record with key> 2345
2345 found.
Delete record with key> 1111
1111 deleted.

The ordered list follows.
2345
3456
The number of nodes in the list is 2
```

Exercises for Section 18.2

Self-Check

1. Replace the body of Fig. 18.3 with the following program fragment. What is the effect? What is displayed?

```
begin
   CreateList (MyList);
   Insert (MyList, 3000, Success);
   Insert (MyList, 5000, Success);
   Insert (MyList, 4000, Success);
   Insert (MyList, 4000, Success);
```

```
  Delete (MyList, 4000, Success);
  if Success then
    WriteLn ('O.K.')
  else
    WriteLn ('Error');
  DisplayList (MyList);
  WriteLn ('Number of elements is ', SizeOfList(MyList) :1)
end.
```

2. Indicate what changes would be necessary to the program in Fig. 18.3 to process an ordered list of passengers instead of integers.

18.3 Implementing OrderListADT

In Chapter 17, you saw many advantages to using pointer variables and dynamic allocation to implement linked lists. We have repeatedly emphasized the ease with which insertions and deletions can be performed on such a list. For these reasons, we will represent each node of an ordered list by a record with a pointer field.

The declarations for OrderListADT are shown in Fig. 18.5. Each node in an ordered list contains a data field, Item, and a pointer field, Link, which connects it to the next node in the list. The data field (type ListElement) must include a record key (type KeyType) and can be a simple type or a structured type. Data types ListElement and KeyType must be declared where shown or imported into OrderListADT if they are declared elsewhere.

The record type OrderList is also declared. A variable of type OrderList represents a header node for an ordered list. The header node contains a pointer to the first node in the list (field Head) and a count of list items (field NumItems).

Figure 18.5 Declarations for OrderListADT

```
{
 Implementation of OrderListADT
 Modules needed: InsertKey, ExtractKey, DisplayOne
}
    const
      {Insert declaration for MinKey}
      {Insert declaration for MaxKey}

    type
      {Insert declaration for KeyType}
      {Insert declaration for ListElement}

      NodePointer = ^ListNode;
      ListNode = record
                   Item : ListElement;      {includes a key field}
                   Link : NodePointer
                 end; {ListNode}
```

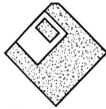

Directory: CHAP18
File: ORDERLIS.ADT

```
OrderList = record
              Head : NodePointer;
              NumItems : Integer
          end; {OrderList}
```

Several declarations must be inserted in Fig. 18.5. The constants `MinKey` and `MaxKey` must be defined as well as data types `ListElement` and `KeyType`. For the ordered list of integers discussed in the previous section, these declarations would be as follows.

```
const
   MinKey = 999;
   MaxKey = 10000;

type
   ListElement = Integer;
   KeyType = Integer;
```

For an ordered list of airline passenger records, we would use the following declarations.

```
const
   MinKey = 'AAAAAAAAAAAAAAAAAAAA';
   MaxKey = 'zzzzzzzzzzzzzzzzzzzz';

type
   ListElement = Passenger;
   KeyType = StringType;
```

We also would have to import data types `StringType` from `StringADT` and `Passenger` from `PassengerADT`.

Procedures InsertKey and ExtractKey

We implement the ordered list operators starting with `CreateList` in the next section. But first, we will examine two procedures, `InsertKey` and `ExtractKey`, that must be imported into `OrderListADT` because they are called by the list operators. They are used to store (`InsertKey`) and retrieve (`ExtractKey`) key-field values. Figure 18.6 shows the form of these procedures for an ordered list of integers.

Figure 18.6 InsertKey and ExtractKey for a List of Integers

```
procedure InsertKey (var El {output} : ListElement;
                         Key {input} : KeyType);
{
  Stores Key in the key field of El.
  Pre : Key is defined and El is an ordered list element.
  Post: The key field of El becomes Key.
}
begin {InsertKey}
  El := Key
end; {InsertKey}
```

```
procedure ExtractKey (El {input} : ListElement;
                      var Key {output} : KeyType);
{
  Retrieves the key field of El.
  Pre : El is an ordered list element.
  Post: Key gets the key field of El.
}
begin {ExtractKey}
  Key := El
end; {ExtractKey}
```

The procedure bodies depend on the structure of `ListElement`. If `ListElement` is type `Passenger`, its key field is `Name` (type `StringType`). In this case, the body of `InsertKey` would be the assignment statement

```
El.Name := Key
```

and the body of `ExtractKey` would be the assignment statement

```
Key := El.Name
```

Procedure CreateList

To simplify the list-processing operations, we assume that an ordered list always begins and ends with a dummy node. The dummy node at the head of the list should have a key value (`MinKey`) that is smaller than all the list keys; the dummy node at the end of the list should have a key value (`MaxKey`) that is larger than all the list keys.

The dummy nodes are analogous to sentinels. The presence of the first dummy node means that we never have to change the pointer to the list head (field `Head`) when a new node is inserted. The presence of the second dummy node keeps us from "falling off" the end of the list when we are searching for a target key. If `MyList` is type `OrderList`, the procedure call statement

```
CreateList (MyList)
```

builds the empty list shown in Fig. 18.7, which contains the two dummy nodes. Procedure `CreateList` is shown in Fig. 18.8; `CreateList` and all the other operators discussed in this section belong in the implementation section of `OrderListADT`.

Figure 18.7 An Empty Ordered List

MyList.Head
MyList.NumItems   0

MinKey { . . . }   MaxKey { . . . }

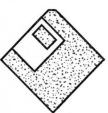

Figure 18.8 Procedure CreateList

```
procedure CreateList (var List {output} : OrderList);
{
   Creates an ordered list containing two dummy nodes whose keys
   are the constants MinKey and MaxKey.
   Pre : None
   Post: List points to the header node for an ordered list.
   Uses: MinKey, MaxKey, InsertKey
}
begin {CreateList}
   New (List.Head);                          {Allocate first dummy node.}
   New (List.Head^.Link);                    {Allocate second dummy node.}
   InsertKey (List.Head^.Item, MinKey);
   InsertKey (List.Head^.Link^.Item, MaxKey);
   List.Head^.Link^.Link := nil;            {Second node is last node.}
   List.NumItems := 0                        {Dummy nodes don't count.}
end; {CreateList}
```

Each call to procedure New allocates storage for a dummy node. The pointer
List.Head points to the first dummy node; the pointer from the first dummy
node, List.Head^.Link, points to the second dummy node. Procedure
InsertKey stores the key values MinKey and MaxKey in the two dummy nodes.
The Link field of the second dummy node is set to nil. The field
List.NumItems is set to 0 because the dummy nodes are not counted as actual
list nodes.

Procedure Locate

Before we can insert an element into an ordered list, we must locate the list
nodes that bracket the element we want to insert. For example, if we want to
insert the key 2345, we must advance the pointer Next to the first node with a
key larger than 2345 and pointer Previous to the node just before that one, as
shown in Fig. 18.9. Then we can execute the statements

```
{1} New (Previous^.Link);              {Join new node to Previous^.}
{2} Previous^.Link^.Link := Next;      {Join new node to Next^.}
```

The effect of these statements is shown in Fig. 18.10. The new pointer values
are in color; the original pointer value is in gray.

Figure 18.9 Previous and Next After Search for 2345 or 3456

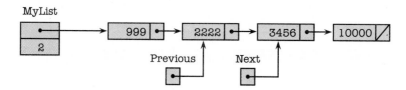

Figure 18.10   Inserting 2345

795

18.3 Implementing
OrderListADT

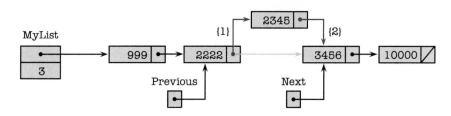

Similarly, before we can delete a list element, we must locate the list node that contains that element and the previous node. For example, if we want to delete the key 3456, we must advance pointer Next to the node with key 3456 and pointer Previous to the node just before it. For the original list shown in Fig. 18.9, pointers Previous and Next should be positioned as shown. Once Next and Previous are positioned as required, we can execute the statement

```
Previous^.Link := Next^.Link;     {Disconnect node Next^.}
```

This statement joins node Previous^ to the node that follows node Next^ (the second dummy node), thereby disconnecting node Next^.

The two pointers Next and Previous appear in each ordered-list operator that we write. Each operator calls procedure Locate to position these pointers as required. Procedure Locate (Fig. 18.11) advances pointer Next to the first list node whose key value is greater than or equal to the Target key. Locate advances pointer Previous to the node preceding node Next^.

Figure 18.11   Procedure Locate

Directory: CHAP18
File: ORDERLIS.ADT

```
procedure Locate (Target {input} : KeyType;
                  var Previous, {input/output}
                      Next       {output} : NodePointer;
                  var SearchSuccess {output} : Boolean);
{
  Attempts to locate a node with key value Target in the
  list whose first node is pointed to by Previous.
  Pre : Target is defined; Previous points to the first dummy node.
  Post: If Target is located, SearchSuccess is set to True;
        otherwise, SearchSuccess is set to False.
        Previous points to the last list node with key < Target;
        Next points to the first list node with key >= Target.
  Uses: ExtractKey
}
  var
    NextKey : KeyType;             {key of node Next^}

begin {Locate}
  {Search for first node with key >= Target.}
  Next := Previous^.Link;          {Start at first actual node.}
  ExtractKey (Next^.Item, NextKey);            {Get first key.}
  while Target > NextKey do
    {invariant:
        Target > key of each node pointed to by Next so far.
    }
```

```
  begin
    Previous := Next;                      {Advance Previous.}
    Next := Next^.Link;                    {Advance Next.}
    ExtractKey (Next^.Item, NextKey)       {Get next key.}
  end; {while}

  {assert: Target is located or NextKey is larger than Target.}
  {Set flag to indicate search results.}
  SearchSuccess := (Target = NextKey)
end; {Locate}
```

The precondition for Locate states that pointer Previous must point to the first dummy node when Locate is called. Locate initializes pointer Next to the first actual list node. The statement

```
    ExtractKey (Next^.Item, NextKey);
```

calls procedure ExtractKey to store the key of node Next^ in NextKey. The while loop moves Next and Previous to their desired positions in the normal way. Loop exit occurs when Next advances to a node whose key is greater than or equal to Target. After loop exit, the Boolean variable SearchSuccess is set to True if NextKey is equal to the Target key.

Procedure Search

Procedure Search (Fig. 18.12) determines whether a particular target key is in the list. Search initializes Previous to point to the first dummy node, calls procedure Locate to perform the actual search, and returns the search result.

Figure 18.12 Procedure Search

```
procedure Search (List {input} : OrderList;
                  Target {input} : KeyType;
                  var Success {output} : Boolean);
{
  Searches an ordered List for Target.
  Pre : List points to the header node for an ordered list.
  Post: Success is True if Target is found; otherwise,
        Success is False.
}
  var
    Previous,                      {pointer to previous node}
    Next       : NodePointer;      {pointer to current node}

begin {Search}
  {Start search at first dummy node.}
  Previous := List.Head;
  {Perform search and define Success}
  Locate (Target, Previous, Next, Success)
end; {Search}
```

Procedure Insert

Procedure `Insert` inserts a node into an ordered list. It first calls `Locate` to search for the key value of the new record and, in this way, determines where the new record should be inserted. If there is already a node with the same key value as the new record, the insertion is not performed. Procedure `Insert` is shown in Fig. 18.13.

Figure 18.13   Procedure Insert

Directory: CHAP18
File: ORDERLIS.ADT

```
procedure Insert (var List {input/output} : OrderList;
                  El {input} : ListElement;
                  var Success {input/output} : Boolean);
{
  Inserts item El into an ordered list.
  Pre : List points to the header node for an ordered list.
  Post: Success is True if insertion is performed; Success is False
        if insertion is not performed because there is already
        an element with the same key as El.
  Uses: ExtractKey

}
  var
     Previous,              {pointer to node preceding El}
     Next : NodePointer;    {pointer to node following El}
     SearchSuccess : Boolean;          {search result}
     ElKey : KeyType;                  {key of record El}

begin {Insert}
  {Validate ElKey and search for a valid key.}
  ExtractKey (El, ElKey);
  if (MinKey > ElKey) or (ElKey > MaxKey) then
     Success := False                  {ElKey is out of range.}
  else
     begin
       {Is ElKey already in the list?}
       Previous := List.Head;          {Start at first dummy node.}
       Locate (ElKey, Previous, Next, SearchSuccess);
       Success := not SearchSuccess    {ElKey is new if search fails.}
     end; {if}

  {Insert if ElKey is in range and is a new key.}
  if Success then
     begin
       New (Previous^.Link);           {Join new node to Previous^.}
       Previous^.Link^.Link := Next;   {Join new node to Next^.}
       Previous^.Link^.Item := El;     {Store El in new node.}
       List.NumItems := List.NumItems + 1
     end {if}
end; {Insert}
```

Procedure `Insert` begins by extracting `ElKey` from `El` and validating it. If `ElKey` is not in the range `MinKey` to `MaxKey`, the Boolean flag `Success` is set to `False`. If `ElKey` is within the allowable range, function `Locate` is called to find `ElKey`, and `Success` is set to `True` if `ElKey` is a new key and is not found. The last `if` statement inserts the new record `El` into the list if its key value is not already there.

Procedure Delete

Procedure `Delete` (Fig. 18.14) calls `Locate` to find the node that contains the `Target` key. If present, this node is deleted and the statement

```
Dispose (Temp);                    {Deallocate storage.}
```

returns its storage cells to the heap.

Directory: CHAP18
File: ORDERLIS.ADT

Figure 18.14 Procedure Delete

```
procedure Delete (var List {input/output} : OrderList;
                      Target {input} : KeyType;
                      var Success {input/output} : Boolean);
{
  Deletes the element with key Target from an ordered list.
  Pre : List points to the header node for an ordered list.
  Post: Success is True if deletion is performed; Success is False
        if deletion is not performed because there is no element
        whose key is Target.
}
  var
    Previous,             {pointer to last list key < ElKey}
    Next,                 {pointer to first list key >= ElKey}
    Temp : NodePointer;   {temporary variable}

begin {Delete}
  {Search the list for the key Target.}
  Previous := List.Head;              {Start at first dummy node.}
  Locate (Target, Previous, Next, Success);

  {If Target is found, delete it.}
  if Success then
    begin
      Temp := Next;        {Point Temp to the node being deleted.}
      Previous^.Link := Next^.Link;        {Disconnect node Next^.}
      Dispose (Temp);                      {Deallocate storage.}
      List.NumItems := List.NumItems - 1
    end {if}
end; {Delete}
```

Procedures `Retrieve` and `Replace` are similar to `Delete` and are left as exercises at the end of this section, along with function `SizeOfList`.

Procedure DisplayList

Procedure `DisplayList` traverses the ordered list, displaying each actual node, but not the dummy nodes. Procedure `DisplayList` calls procedure `DisplayOne` to display each list element. Procedure `DisplayOne` must also be imported into `OrderListADT`. Procedure `DisplayList` is shown in Fig. 18.15.

Figure 18.15 Procedure DisplayList

```
procedure DisplayList (List {input} : OrderList);
{
  Repeatedly calls procedure DisplayOne to display each
```

```
   element of an ordered list.
   Pre : List points to the header node of an ordered list.
   Post: The data fields of each actual element are displayed.
   Uses: ExtractKey and DisplayOne
}
   var
     Next : NodePointer;        {pointer to each list node}
     NextKey : KeyType;         {key of node Next^}

begin {DisplayList}
   Next := List.Head^.Link;              {Start with first actual node.}
   ExtractKey (Next^.Item, NextKey);                    {Get node key.}
   while MaxKey > NextKey do
     {invariant: MaxKey > key of each prior node pointed to by Next}
     begin
       DisplayOne (Next^.Item);             {Display node data.}
       Next := Next^.Link;                  {Advance Next.}
       ExtractKey (Next^.Item, NextKey)
     end {while}
end; {DisplayList}
```

If we are processing an ordered list of integers, procedure DisplayOne displays just one value and has the form shown in Fig. 18.16. If we are processing an ordered list of passengers, procedure DisplayOne is the same as procedure WritePass (see Fig. 16.21).

Figure 18.16   Procedure DisplayOne for a List of Integers

```
procedure DisplayOne (El {input} : ListElement);
{
   Displays element El.
   Pre : El is defined.
   Post: Displays each data field of El.
}
begin {DisplayOne}
   WriteLn (El :1)
end; {DisplayOne}
```

More on InsertKey, ExtractKey, and DisplayOne

Three procedures were imported into abstract data type OrderListADT. These procedures manipulate one or more data fields of a list node. If the data type ListElement is a structured type, these procedures could be part of an abstract data type for that structured type. An example would be an ordered list of passenger data. In this case, we could add new procedures InsertKey and ExtractKey to PassengerADT, shown in Fig. 16.21, and rename procedure WritePass as DisplayOne.

Analysis of Operations on an Ordered List

We have gone through considerable effort to maintain our linked list in ascending order by key value; however, the improvement in search efficiency that results is relatively modest. If we assume that a target key is equally likely to be at the front of a list as at the end of a list, then on the average, we have to examine half of the list elements to find it. This is the same whether or not the target key is in the list. If a list is not ordered, we have to examine all of its elements to determine that a key is not in the list, but only half of its elements, on the average, to find a key that is in the list.

It actually takes longer to insert an item into an ordered list than into an unordered list. In an unordered list, we can arbitrarily insert a new element at the list head. In an ordered list, we must first search for the appropriate position of the new element before we insert it.

The main advantage to using ordered lists occurs when we display the list contents. If the list is unordered, we must find some way to sort it before we can display it. We can always display the elements of an ordered list in ascending order by key without sorting the list.

Exercises for Section 18.3

Self-Check

1. In specifying the ordered list ADT, we assumed that there would be no insertion if the key of a new record was already present in the list. If we decide to allow insertion of duplicate keys, what change to Insert would be required? Would the new record be inserted before or after the existing record with the same key?
2. Two dummy records were placed in the initial list to ensure that there would be no need to insert a record into an empty list or in front of the first list node (that is, all valid keys follow the key MinKey in the first dummy node). How would CreateList, Locate, Insert, and Delete be modified if these nodes were not present?

Programming

1. Write function SizeOfList.
2. Write procedure Retrieve.
3. Write procedure Replace.

18.4 Multiple-Linked Lists and Trees

All the examples you have seen so far have involved elements or nodes with a single pointer field. It is possible to have a list of elements with more than one pointer field. For example, each element in the following list has a forward pointer that points to the next list element and a backward pointer that points to the previous list element. This allows us to traverse the list in the left or the right direction.

This structure is called a *doubly linked list*. The following declarations describe a general node of such a list.

```
type
  MultiLink = ^MultiNode;
  MultiNode = record
                 . . . . .
                 . . . . .  } Data fields
                 . . . . .
                 Left, Right : MultiLink
              end; {MultiNode}
```

Introduction to Trees

A special kind of multiple-linked list that has wide applicability in computer science is a data structure called a *tree*. A sample tree is drawn in Fig. 18.17.

Trees in computer science actually grow from the top down rather than from the ground up. The topmost element is called the *root of the tree*. The pointer variable Root (type Branch) points to the root of the tree in Fig. 18.17. Each tree node has a single data field and two pointer fields called the *left branch* and the *right branch*.

Figure 18.17 Tree

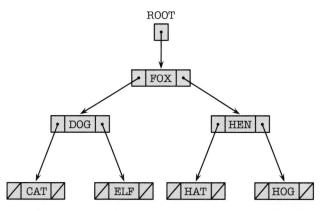

Genealogical terminology is used to describe computer science trees. The node that contains the string 'HEN' is the *parent* of the nodes that contain the strings 'HAT' and 'HOG'. Similarly, the nodes 'HAT' and 'HOG' are *siblings*, because they are both *children* of the same parent node. The root of the tree is an *ancestor* of all other nodes in the tree, and they, in turn, are *descendants* of the root node.

Think of each node in a tree as the root node of its own *subtree*. Because each node has two branches, it spawns two more subtrees, a *left subtree* and a *right subtree*. One or both of these subtrees can be empty (denoted by a branch value of nil). A node with two empty subtrees is called a *leaf node*. The *left (right) child* of a node is the root node of its left (right) subtree. The *depth* of a tree is the length of the longest path from the root node to a leaf node.

The following statements describe the form of a tree node in Fig. 18.17.

Because each node can have at most two children, such a tree is called a *binary tree*.

```
const
  StringSize = 3;

type
  StringRange = 1..3;
  StringType = packed array [StringRange] of Char;
  Branch = ^TreeNode;
  TreeNode = record
               Info : StringType;
               Left, Right : Branch
             end; {TreeNode}
```

Field `Info` contains the data associated with the tree node, a string of three characters.

Trees can be used to represent expressions in memory. For example, the expression

```
(X + Y) * (A − B)
```

could be represented as the tree drawn in Fig. 18.18. This tree has the same shape as the one in Fig. 18.17.

The root node contains the operator (*) that is evaluated last in the expression. Each subtree is also an expression and contains either the subexpression operator (+ or −) in its root or a variable (X, Y, A, or B). There are subtrees for the subexpressions (X + Y) and (A − B).

Figure 18.18 Expression Stored in a Tree

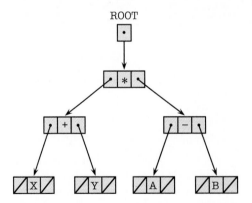

Exercises for Section 18.4

Self-Check

1. For the tree in Fig. 18.17, what statement can be made about the relationship between the word in a node and its left child and right child? What statement can be made regarding the relationship between the word in a node and the words in its left subtree? What about the words in its right subtree?
2. What expression is stored in the following tree?

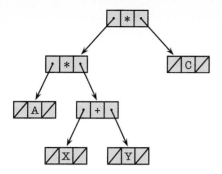

3. Draw the binary-tree representation of the following expressions. Assume the normal rules of expression evaluation.

```
X * Y / (A + B) * C
X * Y / A + B * C
```

18.5 Traversing a Tree

To process the data stored in a tree, we need to be able to traverse the tree, or visit each node in a systematic way. The first approach we illustrate is called an *inorder traversal*. The algorithm for an inorder traversal follows.

Algorithm for Inorder Traversal

1. Traverse the left subtree.
2. Visit the root node.
3. Traverse the right subtree.

You will recall that the left subtree of any node is the part of the tree whose root is the left child of that node. The inorder traversal for the tree shown in Fig. 18.17 would visit the nodes in the sequence

```
'CAT' 'DOG' 'ELF' 'FOX' 'HAT' 'HEN' 'HOG'
```

If we assume that data of each node are printed when the node is visited, the strings are printed in alphabetical order, as shown.

In Fig. 18.19, a numbered circle is drawn around each subtree. The subtrees are numbered in the order that they are traversed. Subtree 1 is the left subtree of the root node. Its left subtree (number 2) has no left subtree (or right subtree); thus, the string 'CAT' would be printed first. The root node for subtree 1 would then be visited and 'DOG' would be printed. Its right subtree consists of the leaf node containing the string 'ELF' (number 3). After 'ELF' is printed, the root node for the complete tree is visited ('FOX' is printed), and the right subtree of the root node (number 4) is traversed in a like manner.

Procedure Traverse in Fig. 18.20 is a recursive procedure that performs an inorder traversal of a tree and displays each node's data. The parameter Root represents the pointer to the root node of the tree being traversed. If the tree is empty (Root = nil), an immediate return occurs. Procedure Traverse, like most procedures that process trees, can be written much more simply with recursion than without it.

Figure 18.19   Subtrees of a Tree

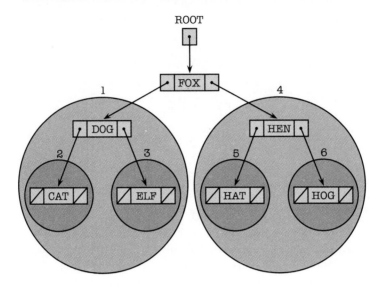

Figure 18.20   Procedure Traverse

```
procedure Traverse (Root {input} : Branch);
{
   Performs an inorder traversal of a binary tree.
   Pre : Root points to a binary tree or is nil.
   Post: Displays each node visited.
}
begin {Traverse}
   if Root <> nil then
      begin {recursive step}
         Traverse (Root^.Left);      {Traverse left subtree.}
         WriteLn (Root^.Info);            {Print root value.}
         Traverse (Root^.Right)     {Traverse right subtree.}
      end {recursive step}
end; {Traverse}
```

The `if` statement in Fig. 18.20 differs from the `if` statements shown in earlier recursive algorithms. Those `if` statements had the form

> if a stopping case is reached then
>   Perform stopping step.
> `else`
>   Perform recursive step.

In a tree traversal, there is nothing to do when a stopping case is reached except unwind from the recursion. Thus, the `if` statement in Fig. 18.20 has the form

```
if a stopping case is not reached then
    Perform recursive step.
```

As you saw earlier, an inorder traversal of the tree shown in Fig. 18.17 would visit the nodes in alphabetical sequence. If we performed an inorder traversal of the expression tree in Fig. 18.18, the nodes would be visited in the sequence

X + Y * A − B

Except for the absence of parentheses, this is the form in which we would normally write the expression. The expression is called an *infix* expression, because each operator is between its operands.

Switching the sequence of the three statements in the `if` statement shown in Fig. 18.20 produces rather different results. The sequence

```
Traverse (Root^.Left);      {Traverse left subtree.}
Traverse (Root^.Right);    {Traverse right subtree.}
WriteLn (Root^.Info)           {Print root value.}
```

displays the root node after traversing each of its subtrees; consequently, each root value will be printed after all the values in its subtrees. This is called a *postorder* traversal. The nodes in Fig. 18.17 would be visited in the sequence

```
CAT     ELF     DOG     HAT     HOG     HEN     FOX
```

The nodes in the expression tree in Fig. 18.18 would be visited in the sequence

X Y + A B − *

The preceding expression is called a postfix expression (see Section 16.3), because each operator follows its operands. The operands of + are X and Y; the operands of − are A and B; the operands of * are the two triples X Y + and A B −.

Finally, the sequence

```
WriteLn (Root^.Info);             {Print root value.}
Traverse (Root^.Left);      {Traverse left subtree.}
Traverse (Root^.Right)      {Traverse right subtree.}
```

displays the root node before traversing its subtrees; consequently, the data field of the root node will be displayed before the data fields of its subtrees. This is called a *preorder* traversal. The nodes in Fig. 18.17 would be visited in the sequence

```
FOX     DOG     CAT     ELF     HEN     HAT     HOG
```

The nodes in the expression tree in Fig. 18.18 would be visited in the sequence

* + X Y − A B

The preceding expression is called a *prefix* expression, because each operator precedes its operands. The operands of + are X and Y; the operands of – are A and B; the operands of * are the two triples + X Y and – A B.

Tracing the Contour of a Tree

An easy way to determine the order in which the nodes of a tree are visited is to outline the contour of the tree, following all indentations, as shown in Fig. 18.21. Move your finger along the tree contour, starting to the left of the root node. As your finger passes under a node (indicated by a colored arrow head), that node is visited in an inorder traversal.

As your finger passes to the right of a node (indicated by a gray arrow head), that node is visited in a postorder traversal. Your finger should be moving in an upward direction when a node is visited in a postorder traversal. As your finger passes to the left of a node (indicated by a black arrow head), that node is visited in a preorder traversal. Your finger should be moving in a downward direction when a node is visited in a preorder traversal.

Figure 18.21   Outlining the Contour of a Tree

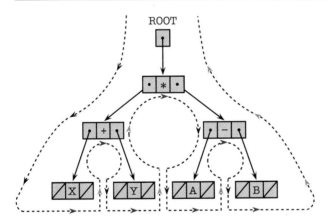

Exercises for Section 18.5

Self-Check

1. Rewrite the expressions shown in exercise 3 for Section 18.4 in prefix and postfix forms.
2. What would be printed by the inorder, preorder, and postorder traversals of the tree in exercise 2 for Section 18.4?
3. What would be printed by the inorder, preorder, and postorder traversals of the tree that follows?

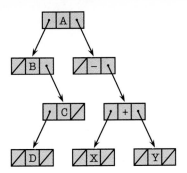

18.6 The Binary Search Tree Abstract Data Type

Trees are also used to organize related data items to facilitate efficient search for and retrieval of an item. For example, the *binary search tree* shown in Fig. 18.17 is arranged so that the left child of each node alphabetically precedes its parent and the right child alphabetically follows its parent.

A binary search tree has the property that for any node all key values less than that node's key value are in its left subtree and all key values greater than that node's key value are in its right subtree. For this reason, searching a binary search tree is a relatively efficient process. To find a particular item (the target key) at any level of the tree, we compare the target key to the key in the subtree root. If the target key is less than the key of the root node, we can eliminate the right subtree and search only the left subtree, thereby cutting the number of nodes to be searched in half. We analyze this process in more detail in Section 18.9.

Binary Search Tree Specification

The binary search tree abstract data type must include operators similar to those provided in the ordered-list abstract data type discussed earlier. The following operations must be performed: create an empty tree, search for a target key, insert a node, delete a node, retrieve a node, replace a node, display the tree, and return its size. The specification for a binary search tree and its operators follows.

```
{
    Specification of Abstract Data Type SearchTreeADT

    Structure:    A binary search tree is a collection of
```

elements such that each element includes among
its data fields a special field called the key
field. Each element of a binary tree has zero,
one, or two subtrees connected to it. The key
field of each element in a binary search tree
is larger than all keys in its left subtree
and smaller than all keys in its right
subtree.

Operators: For the following descriptions, assume these
parameters:

  Tree represents the binary search tree.
  El has the same data type as the tree elements.
  Target is a possible key field value.
  Success is a Boolean flag indicating success (True) or
  failure (False) of an operation.

CreateTree (var Tree): Creates an empty binary search tree;
must be called before any other operators.

SizeOfTree(Tree): (function) Returns the number of elements
currently in the binary search tree.

TreeSearch (Tree, Target, var Success): Searches a tree to
find the key Target. If Target is found, sets Success to
True; otherwise, sets Success to False.

TreeInsert (var Tree, El, var Success): Inserts item El
into the binary search tree and sets Success to True. If
there is already an element with the same key value as El,
Success is set to False and no insertion is performed.

TreeDelete (var Tree, Target, var Success): Deletes the
element whose key value is Target and sets Success to True.
If Target is not located, sets Success to False.

TreeRetrieve (Tree, Target, var El, var Success): Copies
the element whose key is Target into El and sets Success to
True. If there is no element with key Target, El is not
defined and Success is False.

TreeReplace (var Tree, El, var Success): Replaces the
element whose key value is the same as the key value of El

and sets Success to True. If there is no element whose key
value matches the key value of El, sets Success to False.

DisplayTree (Tree): Displays the tree elements in
sequential order by key.
}

Space prevents us from covering the binary search tree abstract data type
with the same thoroughness as we covered the ordered list. We show how to
use the binary search tree next; in Section 18.8, we implement operators
CreateTree, TreeInsert, TreeSearch, and DisplayTree.

18.7 Using a Binary Search Tree

We can use the binary search tree operators in a manner analogous to the way
we use the ordered-list operators. The program in Fig. 18.22 stores a collection
of integer data values in a binary search tree. It does this by repeatedly calling
procedure TreeInsert to insert the node just read at its correct position in the
tree. After the tree is completed, it performs a search for a target key. Finally,
the program displays the keys in sequential order and displays the tree size.
Compare it with program UseOrderList in Fig. 18.3.

Figure 18.22   Using a Binary Search Tree

```
program UseSearchTree (Input, Output);
{
  Builds and displays a binary search tree using SearchTreeADT.
  Module needed: SearchTreeADT
}
  const
    Sentinel = -1;

  type
    {Insert declarations for KeyType and
     TreeElement (both type Integer) from SearchTreeADT.}

    {Insert type declaration for SearchTree from SearchTreeADT.}

  var
    MyTree : SearchTree;          {binary search tree}
    NextNode : TreeElement;       {each tree element}
    Target : KeyType;             {target key}
    Success : Boolean;            {program flag}


  {Insert CreateTree, TreeInsert, TreeSearch, DisplayTree, SizeOfTree
   from SearchTreeADT.}
```

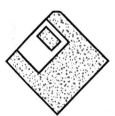

Directory: CHAP18
File: USESEARC.PAS

```
begin {UseSearchTree}
  {Initialize the tree.}
  CreateTree (MyTree);

  {Read and insert the keys in the tree.}
  WriteLn ('Enter ', Sentinel :1, ' to stop.');
  Write ('Enter next key value or ', Sentinel :1, '> ');
  ReadLn (NextNode);
  while NextNode <> Sentinel do
    {invariant:
        All prior values of NextNode that are not duplicates were
        inserted in MyTree and
        no prior value of NextNode was the sentinel.
    }
    begin
      TreeInsert (MyTree, NextNode, Success);
      if Success then
        WriteLn (NextNode :1, ' inserted.')
      else
        WriteLn ('Duplicate key - no insertion.');
      Write ('Enter next key value or ', Sentinel :1, '> ');
      ReadLn (NextNode)
    end; {while}

  {assert: Binary search tree completed.}
  {Perform Search operation.}
  WriteLn;
  Write ('Find record with key> ');
  ReadLn (Target);
  TreeSearch (MyTree, Target, Success);
  if Success then
    WriteLn (Target, ' found.')
  else
    WriteLn ('Not in the tree.');
  WriteLn;

  {Display the binary search tree and its size.}
  WriteLn ('The binary search tree follows.');
  DisplayTree (MyTree);
  Write ('The number of nodes in the tree is ');
  WriteLn (SizeOfTree(MyTree) :1)
end. {UseSearchTree}
```

Building a Binary Search Tree

Figure 18.23 shows a sample run of program UseSearchTree that builds a
binary tree of seven elements with integer-valued keys. The keys are inserted
in the order 4000, 2000, 1000, 5000, 6500, 4500, 3000.

Figure 18.23 Sample Run of Program UseSearchTree

```
Enter -1 to stop.
Enter next key value or -1> 4000
4000 inserted.
Enter next key value or -1> 2000
2000 inserted.
```

```
Enter next key value or -1> 1000
1000 inserted.
Enter next key value or -1> 4000
Duplicate key - no insertion.
Enter next key value or -1> 5000
5000 inserted.
Enter next key value or -1> 6500
6500 inserted.
Enter next key value or -1> 4500
4500 inserted.
Enter next key value or -1> 3000
3000 inserted.
Enter next key value or -1> -1

Find record with key> 2000
2000 found.

The binary search tree follows.
1000
2000
3000
4000
4500
5000
6500
The number of nodes in the tree is 7
```

The keys are inserted one at a time, and each insertion increases the size of the binary tree. To find the insertion point for each new key, compare each new key to the key in the root. If the new key is smaller than the root key, then compare it to the key in the left subtree root; otherwise, compare it to the key in the right subtree root. In this way, move down the tree, branching left or right, until you reach a nil pointer. Attach a new node to the nil pointer and insert the new key in this node.

Figure 18.24 shows the seven partial trees formed by the insertion of each element. We show the branches followed for each key insertion in color. For example, to insert the integer 4500, we first compare 4500 to 4000; 4500 is bigger, so we follow the right branch. Next, we compare 4500 to 5000; 4500 is smaller, so we follow the left branch. Because the left branch from the node with key 5000 is nil, we attach a new node with key 4500 to that pointer. We provide a recursive insertion algorithm in the next section.

The order in which data items are stored in a binary tree has a profound effect on the shape of the binary search tree and, as you will see later, on the efficiency of the search process. The last tree shown in Fig. 18.24 is called a *balanced binary tree*, because the left subtree and the right subtree from each node are the same depth. A tree is also considered balanced if the depth of each node's subtrees differ by at most one.

An entirely different search tree results when the data values arrive in increasing sequence (for example, 1000, 2000, 3000, ...). This unbalanced tree (Fig. 18.25) actually looks more like an ordered list then a tree. Because procedure DisplayTree displays the tree elements in ascending order by key, the program output is the same regardless of the shape of the tree being displayed.

Figure 18.24   Seven Partial Trees

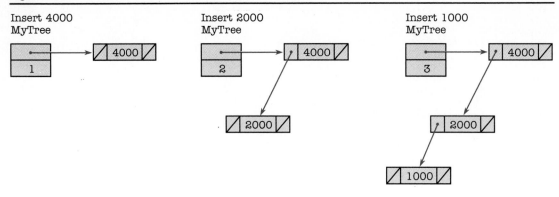

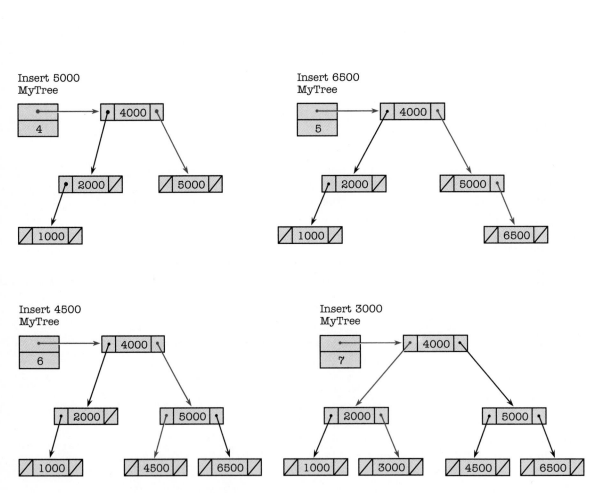

Figure 18.25 Unbalanced Binary Tree

813

18.8 Implementing
SearchTreeADT

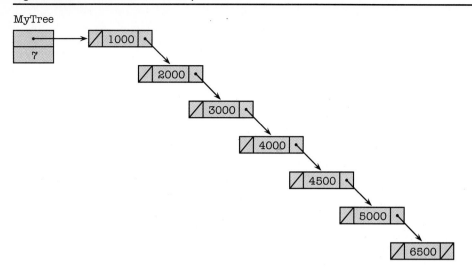

Exercise for Section 18.7

Self-Check

1. Explain the effect of the following program segment. Draw the tree. Is it balanced or unbalanced? If unbalanced, when does it first become unbalanced? What would be displayed by the preorder and postorder tree traversals?

```
begin
  CreateTree (MyTree);
  Insert (MyTree, 3000);
  Insert (MyTree, 2000);
  Insert (MyTree, 4000);
  Insert (MyTree, 5000);
  Insert (MyTree, 2500);
  Insert (MyTree, 6000);
  DisplayTree (MyTree);
  WriteLn ('Number of nodes is ', SizeOfTree(MyTree) :1)
end.
```

18.8 Implementing SearchTreeADT

The declarations for SearchTreeADT are shown in Fig. 18.26. Each node in a binary search tree contains a data field, Item, and two pointers, Left and Right, that connect the node to its children. The data field (type TreeElement) must include a record key (type KeyType) and can be a simple type or a structured type. Data types TreeElement and KeyType must be declared where shown or, if they are declared elsewhere, imported into SearchTreeADT.

The record type `SearchTree` is also declared. A variable of type `Search-Tree` represents a header node for a binary tree. The header node contains a pointer to the root of the tree (field `Root`) and a count of tree items (field `NumItems`).

Figure 18.26   Declarations for SearchTreeADT

```
{
 Implementation of SearchTreeADT
 Modules needed: InsertKey, ExtractKey, DisplayOne
}
  type
    {Insert declaration for KeyType.}
    {Insert declaration for TreeElement.}

    Branch = ^TreeNode;
    TreeNode = record
                 Item : TreeElement;        {includes a key field}
                 Left, Right : Branch
               end; {TreeNode}

    SearchTree = record
                   Root : Branch;
                   NumItems : Integer
                 end; {SearchTree}
```

We implement all the operators called in program `UseSearchTree` in the remainder of this section except for `SizeOfTree`, which is left as a programming exercise. These operators call procedures `InsertKey`, `ExtractKey`, and `DisplayOne`, which were discussed earlier. To use these procedures, change the formal parameter data type `ListElement` to `TreeElement` wherever it appears.

Procedure CreateTree

Procedure `CreateTree` is shown in Fig. 18.27. It simply creates a record of type `SearchTree` with a `Root` field of nil and a count field (`NumItems`) of 0. Assuming `MyTree` is a variable of type `SearchTree`, the tree formed by

```
        CreateTree (MyTree)
```

is shown next.

MyTree.Root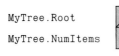

MyTree.NumItems

Figure 18.27   Procedure CreateTree

```
procedure CreateTree (var Tree {output} : SearchTree);
{
  Creates an empty tree. Must be called first.
  Pre : None
```

```
   Post: Tree is the header node for a binary tree.
}
begin {CreateTree}
   Tree.Root := nil;
   Tree.NumItems := 0
end; {CreateTree}
```

Procedure TreeSearch

It is much easier to write a recursive search algorithm than an iterative one. The recursive algorithm for searching a binary tree is shown next.

Algorithm for Binary Tree Search

1. if the tree is empty then
    2. The target key is not in the tree.
  else if the target key matches the root key then
    3. The target key is found in the root node.
  else if the target key is larger than the root key then
    4. Search the right subtree.
  else
    5. Search the left subtree.

Step 2 is an unsuccessful stopping step; step 3 is a successful stopping step. Steps 4 and 5 continue to search the right subtree and the left subtree, respectively.

Procedure TreeSearch is shown in Fig. 18.28. It starts the search at the tree root by calling DoSearch with a parameter of Tree.Root. Procedure Do-Search implements the preceding resursive search algorithm. In DoSearch, we assume that the key field is type KeyType and that procedure ExtractKey is used to extract keys.

Figure 18.28 Procedure DoSearch and TreeSearch

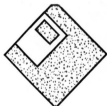

Directory: CHAP18
File: SEARCHTR.ADT

```
procedure DoSearch (Parent {input} : Branch;
                    Target {input} : KeyType;
                    var Success {output} : Boolean);
{
   Searches the subtree pointed to by Parent.
   Pre : Target and Parent are defined.
   Post: If Target is not found, Success is False; otherwise,
         Success is True.
   Uses: ExtractKey
}
   var
      NextKey : KeyType;         {key of node Parent^}

begin {DoSearch}
   if Parent = nil then
      Success := False                    {Tree is empty.}
   else
      begin
         ExtractKey (Parent^.Item, NextKey);
```

```
      if Target = NextKey then
        Success := True                    {Target is found.}
      else if Target > NextKey then
        DoSearch (Parent^.Right, Target, Success)
      else
        DoSearch (Parent^.Left, Target, Success)
    end {if}
end; {DoSearch}


procedure TreeSearch (Tree {input} : SearchTree;
                      Target {input} : KeyType;
                      var Success {output} : Boolean);
{
  Searches for Target in a binary search tree.
  Pre : Tree is the header node of a binary search tree.
  Post: If Target is located, Success is True;
        otherwise, Success is False.
  Uses: DoSearch
}
begin {TreeSearch}
  DoSearch (Tree.Root, Target, Success)
end; {TreeSearch}
```

Procedure TreeInsert

Procedure `TreeInsert` is shown in Fig. 18.29. It stores a tree element (parameter El) in the tree whose header is passed as parameter `Tree`. It begins by storing the key of `El` in `ElKey`. Then it calls `DoInsert` to perform a recursive search for `ElKey`, starting at the tree root. We discussed the insertion process earlier; a recursive insertion algorithm follows.

Figure 18.29   Procedure DoInsert and TreeInsert

Directory: CHAP18
File: SEARCHTR.ADT

```
procedure DoInsert (var Parent {input/output} : Branch;
                    El {input} : TreeElement;
                    ElKey {input} : KeyType;
                    var Success {input/output} : Boolean);
{
  Inserts item El in the subtree with root Parent.
  Pre : Parent, El, and ElKey are defined.
  Post: If a node with key ElKey is found, sets Success to False.
        If a nil pointer is reached, attaches a new node
        containing El to this pointer and sets Success to True.
  Uses: ExtractKey and InsertKey
}
  var
    NextKey : KeyType;            {key of Parent}

begin {DoInsert}
  {Check for empty tree.}
  if Parent = nil then
    begin {Attach new node containing El to Parent.}
      New (Parent);                      {Connect Parent to new node.}
      Parent^.Left := nil;               {Make new node a leaf.}
      Parent^.Right := nil;
      InsertKey (Parent^.Item, El);   {Insert El in node Parent^.}
```

```
          Success := True
        end {Attach}
      else
        begin
          ExtractKey (Parent^.Item, NextKey);
          if ElKey = NextKey then
            Success := False                    {ElKey is in tree.}
          else if ElKey > NextKey then
            DoInsert (Parent^.Right, El, ElKey, Success)
          else
            DoInsert (Parent^.Left, El, ElKey, Success)
        end {if}
end; {DoInsert}


procedure TreeInsert (var Tree {input/output} : SearchTree;
                          El {input} : TreeElement;
                          var Success {input/output} : Boolean);
{
  Inserts item El into a binary tree.
  Pre : El is defined and Tree is the header node of a binary tree.
  Post: Success is True if the insertion is performed. If there is
        a node with the same key value as El, Success is False.
  Uses: ExtractKey and DoInsert
}
var
  ElKey : KeyType:                  {key of record El}

begin {TreeInsert}
  ExtractKey (El, ElKey);                      {Get key.}
  DoInsert (Tree.Root, El, ElKey, Success);
  if Success then
    Tree.NumItems := Tree.NumItems + 1     {New node is in tree.}
end; {TreeInsert}
```

Algorithm for DoInsert

1. `if` the pointer from the last node tested is `nil` `then`
   2. Attach a new node to that pointer, store `El` in this node,
      and set `Success` to `True`.
   `else if` the key of the current node is `ElKey` `then`
   3. Duplicate key; set `Success` to `False`.
   `else if` `ElKey` is greater than the key of the parent node `then`
   4. Insert the node with key `ElKey` in the right subtree of the parent node.
   `else`
   5. Insert the node with key `ElKey` in the left subtree of the
      parent node.

There are two stopping states in the algorithm. If `DoInsert` is passed a
pointer with value `nil` (step 1), it replaces `nil` with the address of a new node,
stores `El` in the new node, and sets `Success` to `True` before returning from the
recursion (step 2). If `DoInsert` finds `ElKey` in the tree, it sets `Success` to `False`
and returns (step 3). Otherwise, `DoInsert` calls itself recursively to process the
left subtree or the right subtree of its current tree. After the return from the

original call to DoInsert, procedure TreeInsert increments the count of tree nodes if the insertion was performed.

Procedure DisplayTree

Procedure DisplayTree (Fig. 18.30) calls procedure Traverse to perform an inorder tree traversal. Traverse then calls procedure DisplayOne to display each tree node.

Figure 18.30 Procedure Traverse and DisplayTree

Directory: CHAP18
File: SEARCHTR.ADT

```
procedure Traverse (Root {input} : Branch);
{
   Performs an inorder traversal of a binary tree.
   Pre : Root points to a binary tree or is nil.
   Post: Displays each node visited.
   Uses: DisplayOne
}
begin {Traverse}
   if Root <> nil then
      begin {recursive step}
         Traverse (Root^.Left);          {Traverse left subtree.}
         DisplayOne (Root^.Item);        {Print root value.}
         Traverse (Root^.Right)          {Traverse right subtree.}
      end {recursive step}
end; {Traverse)


procedure DisplayTree (Tree {input} : SearchTree);
{
   Displays the elements of a binary search tree.
   Pre : Tree is the header node of a binary search tree.
   Post: Each element of the tree is displayed. The elements
         are displayed in ascending order by key.
   Uses: Traverse
}
begin {DisplayTree}
   Traverse (Tree.Root)
end; {DisplayTree}
```

Exercises for Section 18.8

Self-Check

1. Procedure TreeDelete should search for the target key and then delete the node containing it from the tree. Write a recursive algorithm for Tree-Delete, assuming that procedure DeleteNode performs the deletion of the node. DeleteNode has one parameter, which is the pointer from its parent to the node being deleted. Why is DeleteNode a difficult procedure to write?

1. Write function `SizeOfTree`
2. Write procedures `Retrieve` and `Replace` for the search tree abstract data type.

18.9 Analysis of Search Algorithms

This chapter has discussed two techniques for storing data in a systematic way to facilitate searching for a target item and displaying the data in order by key field. The first approach is to store the data in sequence by key field in an ordered list. The second approach is to store the data in a binary search tree. This section discusses the relative merits of each method.

Earlier we showed that we would have to examine $N/2$ items on average to locate an item in an ordered list or to determine that the item is not in the list. Consequently, searching for a data item in an ordered list is an $O(N)$ process, so the growth rate is linear.

Searching a binary search tree is more difficult to analyze. If the tree is balanced, each probe into the tree eliminates one-half of the items. Consequently, we first search a tree with N nodes, then $N/2$ nodes, then $N/4$ nodes, and so on. For example, if N is 1024, 10 more trees (sizes 512, 256, 128, 64, 32, 16, 8, 4, 2, and 1) must be searched to determine that a target is missing. It should require fewer than eleven probes to find a target in the tree. Because 1024 happens to be a power of 2 (1024 is 2 raised to the power 10), the numbers in the preceding list are all powers of 2. Therefore, searching a balanced binary search tree is an $O(\log_2 N)$ process ($\log_2 1024$ is 10). Keep in mind that a binary search tree is not always balanced, so this is really a *best-case analysis*.

What difference does it make whether an algorithm is an $O(N)$ process or an $O(\log_2 N)$ process? Table 18.1 evaluates $\log_2 N$ for different values of N. A doubling of N causes $\log_2 N$ to increase by only 1. Because $\log_2 N$ increases much more slowly with N, the performance of an $O(\log_2 N)$ algorithm is not as adversely affected by an increase in N.

Table 18.1 Table of Values of $\log_2 N$

N	$\log_2 N$
32	5
64	6
128	7
256	8
512	9
1,024	10

Both storage techniques enable us to easily display the data items in sequence by key field. In an ordered list, we simply advance a pointer down the list and display the data fields of the node selected by the pointer. Therefore, displaying the data in an ordered list is an $O(N)$ process.

To display the data in a binary search tree, we must perform an inorder traversal of the tree, displaying the data stored in each node as we visit it. The tree-traversal algorithm is recursive, and the number of procedure calls depends on the size of the tree. The left and the right subtrees of each tree must be traversed, so for a tree of N nodes, there are $2N$ procedure calls. Therefore, a binary search tree display is also an $O(N)$ process. Even though both algorithms are $O(N)$, it takes more time to display a binary search tree, because calling a procedure takes more time than advancing a list pointer.

Another question is the effect on memory of using an ordered list versus a binary search tree. One additional pointer field is needed for each node of a binary search tree, so the storage requirements for a tree versus a list increase linearly with N.

The memory requirements for the algorithms to search and display an ordered list are not affected by N. However, the algorithms to search and display a binary search tree are recursive, so their memory requirements increase with the depth of the tree. If the tree is balanced, its depth is related to $\log_2 N$. The worst case for an inorder traversal occurs for an unbalanced tree with all its nodes in the left subtree (why?). This tree has a depth of N.

18.10 Common Programming Errors

The procedures in this chapter manipulate pointer fields, so review the errors described in Section 17.7. The first and last nodes of an ordered list must be treated as special cases unless you provide dummy or sentinel nodes. Make sure all recursive procedures do, in fact, terminate. Also, be careful when using pointers to list heads as procedure parameters. If the pointer is passed as a variable parameter and is moved down the list, you may disconnect the list head from its list. The same warning applies when you are using pointers to tree roots.

CHAPTER REVIEW

This chapter discussed techniques for maintaining an ordered collection of records and examined two data structures for this purpose. We implemented an abstract data type for an ordered list and one for a binary search tree. These ADTs included operators to search, insert, and delete records.

We also discussed binary trees in general and showed how they can be used to represent expressions in memory. We discussed inorder, preorder, and postorder traversal and related these three methods to infix, prefix, and postfix expressions.

1. Is it more or less efficient to search an ordered list or an unordered list? Is it more or less efficient to insert a new element in an ordered list or in an unordered list?
2. What is the purpose of the dummy nodes in the ordered lists shown in this chapter?
3. Is an ordered list a last-in, last-out structure, a first-in, first-out structure, or neither?
4. In what direction do computer science trees grow?
5. Name the three traversal methods and relate them to the three forms of arithmetic expressions.
6. A node in a tree can have a maximum of two children. True or false?
7. A node in a binary search tree can have a maximum of two children. True or false?
8. What is the relationship between the left child and the right child of a binary search tree? Between the left child and the parent? Between the right child and the parent?
9. When is searching a binary search tree more efficient than searching an ordered list? When isn't it?
10. How do we know if a binary tree is balanced?
11. Traverse the following tree three ways. Is this tree a binary search tree? Is it balanced or unbalanced? If it is unbalanced, why?

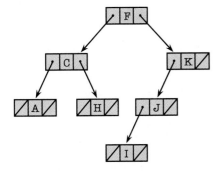

Answers to Quick-Check Exercises
1. Search of an ordered list is more efficient; insertion into an ordered list is less efficient.
2. As sentinel values, they eliminate the need to insert an element at the beginning of a list or to delete the last list element and also help prevent us from searching beyond the last list element.
3. neither
4. from the top down
5. inorder (infix), preorder (prefix), postorder (postfix)
6. false
7. true
8. left child < parent < right child
9. when tree is balanced; when tree is badly unbalanced
10. The depths of the subtrees from every node differ by at most one.
11. Inorder: A C H F I J K
    Preorder: F C A H K J I
    Postorder: A H C I J K F

    It is not a binary search tree, because H is in the wrong subtree of the root. It is not balanced, because the left subtree of K has depth 2, and the right subtree of K has depth zero.

Review Questions

1. Write a procedure to link a node into an existing ordered list. The procedure parameters will be a pointer to the first dummy node and a pointer to the node to be inserted. Asume that dummy sentinel records exist at the beginning and the end of the list and that there are no duplicate records.

    Given the following declarations, insert the new element, preserving ID order:

    ```
    const
      StringLen = 20;

    type
      StringType = packed array [1..StringLen] of Char;
      Ptr = ^Node;
      Node = record
               ID : Integer;
               Name : StringType;
               GPA : Real;
               Link : Ptr
             end; {Node}
    ```

2. Write a procedure to delete a node (parameter `TargetID`) from an ordered list that does not contain a dummy record at the beginning. Assume the declarations above. Let the parameter `Head` (type `Ptr`) point to the first actual list node. Return a Boolean flag.

3. Write a procedure that creates a list of nodes with a GPA of 3.5 or better by copying all qualified records from one linked list into another linked list. The original list is ordered by ID number; the new list should be ordered by GPA. Assume the list nodes are type `Node` as described in question 1. The parameters will be a pointer to the head of the existing list and a pointer to the head of the new linked list (`GPAHead`). Don't remove nodes from the original list, just copy their data.

4. Declare a node for a two-way, or doubly linked, list; indicate how a traversal would be made in reverse order (from the last list element to the list head). Include any variables or fields that are necessary.

5. Discuss the differences between a simple linked list and a binary tree. Consider such things as number of pointer fields per node, search technique, and insertion algorithm.

6. How can you determine if a node is a leaf?

7. Traverse the following tree in inorder, preorder, and postorder.

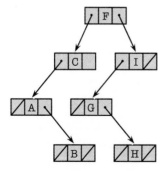

Provide one data sequence that would create this binary search tree. Are there any letters that must occur before other letters?

8. Discuss how you might delete a node from a binary tree. Consider nodes with zero or one child first.

Programming Projects

1. Use an ordered list to maintain an airline passenger list. The main program should be menu driven and allow the user to display the data for a particular passenger, display the entire list, create a list, insert a node, delete a node, and replace the data for a particular passenger.

2. Redo project 1 using a binary search tree for storage of the airline passenger list. When deleting a node, simply change the number of assigned seats to zero and leave the passenger's node in the tree.

3. The set capability is limited in the number of elements that can be stored in a set. A more universal system can be implemented using an ordered list to store a set.

   Write the necessary operators needed to insert and delete integer values from a set. Also write the operators necessary to implement the set difference, intersection, and union operations. To verify the results, display the contents of the sets before and after each operation.

4. In preparing mailing lists, it is often helpful to be able to display them in order either by name or by zip code. This can be done if each list node has a pointer to the next node by name and a pointer to the next node by zip code. The nodes representing each person's data can then be linked in order by both name and zip code; there should be only one copy of each person's data. A header node must be created that contains pointers to the first node in each of the two lists.

   Write a program that reads a record containing a person's name (first and last) and street address (city, state, and zip code); inserts a node containing the information in the two lists; and displays mailing label information in both name and zip code order (after all records have been read). Your solution should make use of StringADT and include procedures corresponding to the following procedure headers.

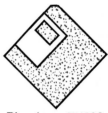

Directory: CHAP18
File: PROJ18_1.PAS

```
procedure WriteOneLabel (A {input} : AddressRec);
{Displays a single address label}

procedure ReadOneLabel (var MailFile {input} : Text;
                        var A {output} : AddressRec);
{Reads a single address from MailFile}

procedure MailCreate (var M {output} : MailingList);
{
   Initializes header node M so that it points to empty Name and
   ZipCode lists
}

procedure MailInsert (var M {input/output} : MailingList;
                      A {input} : AddressRec);
{
   Inserts node containing label information from record A into
   its ordered position in the Name and ZipCode lists pointed to
   by M
}
```

```
procedure DisplayByName (M {input} : MailingList);
{
  Displays labels in Name order.
  Uses: WriteOneLabel
}

procedure DisplayByZipCode (M {input} : MailingList);
{
  Displays labels in ZipCode order.
  Uses: WriteOneLabel
}
```

5. In this chapter, we wrote recursive procedures to perform preorder, inorder, and postorder tree traversals. A tree traversal can be written without using recursion. In that case, it is necessary to push the address of a tree node that is reached during the traversal onto a stack. The node will be popped off later when it is time to traverse the subtree rooted at this node. For example, the algorithm for a nonrecursive preorder traversal follows.

    1. Push `nil` onto the stack.
    2. Assign the root node as the current node.
    3. `while` the current node is not `nil` `do`
       `begin`
          4. Print the current node.
          5. `if` the current node has a right subtree `then`
              Push the right subtree root onto the stack.
          6. `if` the current node has a left subtree `then`
              Make it the current node.
          `else`
              Pop the stack and make the node removed the current node.
       `end`

In this algorithm, each right subtree pointer that is not `nil` is pushed onto the stack; the stack is popped when the current left subtree pointer is `nil`.

Implement and test a nonrecursive procedure for preorder traversal. Write a nonrecursive algorithm for inorder traversal and implement and test it as well.

6. If an arithmetic expression is written in prefix or postfix notation, there is no need to use parentheses to specify the order of operator evaluation. For this reason, some compilers translate infix expressions to postfix notation first and then evaluate the postfix string.

Write a procedure that simulates the operation of a calculator. The input will consist of an expression in postfix notation. The operands will all be single-digit numbers. Your program should print the expression value. For example, if the input string is `'54+3/'`, the result printed should be $((5 + 4) / 3)$, or 3.

To accomplish this, examine each character in the string in left-to-right order. If the character is a digit, push its numeric value onto a stack. If the character is an operator, pop the top two operands, apply the operator to them, and push the result onto the stack. After the string has been completely scanned, there should be only one number on the stack, and that should be the expression value. Besides the operators +, −, *, and /, use ^ to indicate exponentiation.

7. Save each word appearing in a block of text in a binary search tree. Also save the number of occurrences of each word and the line number for each occurrence. Use a stack for the line numbers. After all words have been processed, display each word

in alphabetical order. Along with each word, display the number of occurrences and the line number for each occurrence.

8. Store the Morse code (see programming project 1 for Chapter 12) in a binary tree, as shown. A dot should cause a branch to the left, and a dash should cause a branch to the right. Each node should contain the letter represented by the code symbol formed by tracing a path from the root to that node. For example, following two left branches gives us two dots, which represents the letter I. The first two levels of the Morse-code tree are shown next.

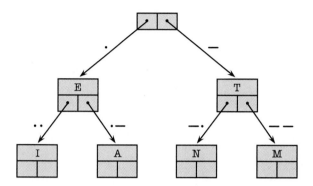

First, build an empty Morse-code tree by constructing a tree of four levels. Then read each letter, followed by its code from a data line, and insert it where it belongs in the tree. After the tree is filled, read in a coded message using a space between each letter of the message and a double space between words. Translate the message into English.

19
Searching and Sorting

C hapter 10 introduced one technique for searching an array for a target key and one technique for sorting an array. Chapter 18 considered other methods of data storage (that is, using ordered lists and binary search trees) that facilitate searching for a target key and eliminate the need for sorting.

Even though alternative methods are available, arrays are frequently used for data storage. Computer scientists have also spent much time and effort to devise efficient algorithms for searching and sorting arrays. This chapter discusses two techniques for searching an array and several techniques for sorting an array and compares these algorithms with respect to their efficiency.

19.1 Binary Search of an Array

We discussed one technique for searching an array in Section 10.9 and wrote a function that returned the index of a target key in an array or the value 0 if the target was not present. To do this, we had to compare array element keys to the target key, starting with the first array element. The comparison process is terminated when the target key is found or the end of the array is reached. We must make N comparisons to determine that a target key is not in an array of N elements. On the average, we must make $N/2$ comparisons to locate a target key that is in the array. Because the constant 2 is ignored, array search is an $O(N)$ process.

Often, we want to search an array whose elements are arranged in order by key field (analogous to an ordered list). We can take advantage of the fact that the array keys are in increasing order and terminate the search when an array key greater than or equal to the target key is reached. There is no need to look any further in the array; all other keys will be larger than the target key.

Both these search techniques are called *sequential searches* because we examine the array elements in sequence. The modified algorithm just discussed is a sequential search of an ordered array. On the average, a sequential search of an ordered array requires $N/2$ comparisons either to locate the target key or to determine that it is not in the array; so we still have an $O(N)$ process.

▬▬▬▬

Case Study: Binary Search

The array searches described here are considered *linear searches,* because their execution time increases linearly with the number of array elements. This can be a problem when we are searching very large arrays (for example, N > 100). Consequently, we often use the *binary-search algorithm* for large sorted arrays.

Problem

Your employer has a directory of customers that she keeps in alphabetical order. Because business has been very good, this list is now too large to search efficiently using a linear search. Write an improved search algorithm that takes advantage of the fact that the array is sorted.

Analysis

The *binary-search algorithm,* like a binary-tree search, takes advantage of the fact that the array is ordered to eliminate half of the array elements with each probe into the array. Consequently, if the array has 1,000 elements, it either locates the target value or eliminates 500 elements with its first probe, 250 elements with its second probe, 125 elements with its third probe, and so on. Therefore, a binary search of an ordered array is an $O(\log_2 N)$ process. You can use the binary search algorithm to find a name in a large metropolitan telephone directory using 30 or fewer probes, so this algorithm should be suitable for your employer.

Because the array is ordered, all we have to do is compare the target value with the middle element of the subarray we are searching. If their values are the same, we are done. If the middle value is larger than the target, we should search the left half of the array next; otherwise, we should search the right half of the array.

The subarray to be searched has subscripts `First..Last`. The variable `Middle` is the subscript of the middle element in this range. The right half of the array (subscripts `Middle..Last`) is eliminated by the first probe, as shown in Fig. 19.1.

`Last` should be reset to `Middle - 1` to define the new subarray to be searched, and `Middle` should be redefined, as shown in Fig. 19.2. The target value, 35, would be found on this probe.

The binary-search algorithm can be stated clearly using recursion. The stopping cases are

* The array bounds are improper (`First > Last`).
* The middle value is the target value.

Figure 19.1   First Probe of Binary Search

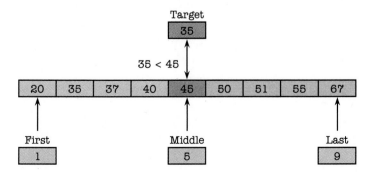

Case Study: Binary Search, continued

Figure 19.2 Second Probe of Binary Search

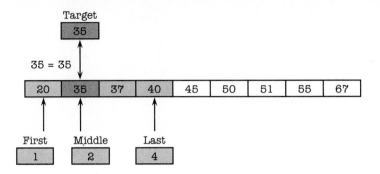

In the first case, the function result is 0; in the second case, the function result is Middle. The recursive step is to search the appropriate subarray.

Data Requirements

Problem Inputs

Table : SearchArray	{array to be searched}
Target : KeyType	{target being searched for}
First : Integer	{first subscript in the subarray}
Last : Integer	{last subscript in the subarray}

Problem Output
Location of Target value or 0 if Target not found

Binary Search Algorithm

1. Compute the subscript of the middle element.
2. if the array bounds are improper then
   3. Return a result of 0.
   else if the target is the middle value then
   4. Return the subscript of the middle element.
   else if the target is less than the middle value then
   5. Search the subarray with subscripts First..Middle−1.
   else
   6. Search the subarray with subscripts Middle+1..Last.

For each of the recursive steps (steps 5 and 6), the bounds of the new subarray must be listed as actual parameters in the recursive call. The actual parameters define the search limits for the next probe into the array.

Implementation
In the initial call to the recursive procedure, First and Last should be defined as the first and last elements of the entire array, respectively. For example, you could use the function designator

```
BinSearch(X, 35, 1, 9)
```

to search an array X with subscripts 1..9 for the target value 35 (assuming X
has type SearchArray and KeyType is Integer). Function BinSearch is shown
in Fig. 19.3.

Figure 19.3 Recursive Binary Search Function

```
function BinSearch (var Table : SearchArray;
                        Target : KeyType;
                        First, Last : Integer) : Integer;
{
  Performs a recursive binary search of an ordered array
  with subscripts First..Last.
  Pre : The elements of Table are in increasing order by
        key field and First and Last are defined.
  Post: Returns the subscript of Target if found in array Table;
        otherwise, returns a value of 0.
}
  var
    Middle : Integer;      {the subscript of the middle element}

begin {BinSearch}
  Middle := (First + Last) div 2;

  {Determine if Target is found or missing or redefine subarray.}
  if First > Last then
    BinSearch := 0                       {Target missing}
  else if Target = Table[Middle] then
    BinSearch := Middle                  {Target found}
  else if Target < Table[Middle] then
    BinSearch := BinSearch(Table, Target, First, Middle-1)
  else
    BinSearch := BinSearch(Table, Target, Middle+1, Last)
end;  {BinSearch}
```

The assignment statement

```
Middle := (First + Last) div 2;
```

computes the subscript of the middle element by finding the average of First
and Last. This value has no meaning when First is greater than Last, but it
does no harm to compute it.

An iterative version of the binary search function is shown in Fig. 19.4. A
Boolean flag, Found, controls repetition of a search loop. Found is set to False
before the while loop is reached. The while loop executes until the Target is
found (Found is True) or the search array is reduced to an array of zero elements
(a *null array*). The if statement in the loop either sets Found to True (Target
= Table[Middle]) or resets index First or index Last. The if statement after
the loop defines the function result.

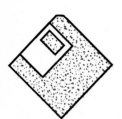

Directory: CHAP19
File: BINARYSE.FUN

Figure 19.4   Iterative Binary Search Function

```
function BinarySearch (var Table : SearchArray;
                           Target : KeyType;
                           First, Last : Integer) : Integer;
{
   Performs an iterative binary search of an ordered array
   with subscripts First..Last.
   Pre : The elements of Table are in ascending order by key field
         and First and Last are defined.
   Post: Returns the subscript of Target if found in array Table;
         otherwise, returns a value of 0.
}
   var
      Middle : Integer;      {the subscript of the middle element}
      Found : Boolean;       {program flag}

begin  {BinarySearch}
   Found := False;                               {Target not found.}
   while (First <= Last) and (not Found) do
      {invariant:
          Last subarray searched was not null and
          Target <> Table[Middle] for all prior values of Middle.
      }
      begin
        Middle := (First + Last) div 2;
        if Target = Table[Middle] then
           Found := True
        else if Target < Table[Middle] then
           Last := Middle - 1            {Search left subarray.}
        else if Target > Table[Middle] then
           First := Middle + 1           {Search right subarray.}
      end; {while}

   {Assert: Target is found or search subarray is null.}
   if Found then
      BinarySearch := Middle              {Target is found.}
   else
      BinarySearch := 0                   {Target is not found.}
end;   {BinarySearch}
```

Testing

You should test both versions of the binary search function carefully. Besides verifying that they locate target values in the array, verify that they also determine when a target value is missing. Use target values within the range of values stored in the array, a target value less than the smallest value in the array, and a target value greater than the largest value in the array. Make sure the binary-search function terminates regardless of whether the target is missing or, if it is not missing, where it is located.

Subarrays with Subscript Zero

The result returned by the binary-search function is inconclusive if 0 is included in the subrange First..Last. For example, if the array being searched has subscript type [-5..5], First is -5 and Last is 5. In this case, it would be better to convert the binary-search function to a procedure with two output parameters: the index of the target if found and a program flag indicating whether the target was found. This modification is left as an exercise.

Exercises for Section 19.1

Self-Check

1. Trace the search of the array Table for a Target of 40. Specify the values of First, Middle, and Last during each recursive call.
2. Provide the algorithm for a recursive procedure that performs binary search and returns a flag as its second output parameter that indicates whether the search was successful.

Programming

1. Write the procedure for self-check exercise 2.

19.2 Searching by Hashing

So far, we have discussed the advantages of using the binary-search technique to retrieve information stored in a large array. Binary search can be used only when the contents of the array are ordered.

Another technique for storing data in an array so that they can be retrieved in an efficient manner is called *hashing*. Hashing consists of implementing a *hash function*, which accepts as its input a designated field of a record (called the *record key*) and returns as its output an integer *hash index*. The hash index selects the particular array element that stores the new data. To retrieve the item later, you need only to recompute the hash index and access the item in that array location. This process is illustrated in the following diagram, where the hash index is 2.

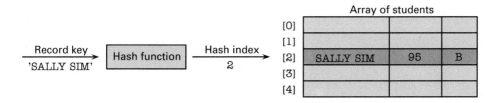

For example, let's assume that we have to maintain a collection of student records. Each record (type Student) has a Name field that is a packed array of characters, an exam score, and a grade. The student data can be stored in an array with subscripts 0..MaxSlots-1. For reasons that will be discussed later, MaxSlots should be a prime number that is at least 20 percent larger than the number of records in the collection. Record types Student and HashArray are declared next.

```
const
  StringLength = 20;                        {length of each name string}
  BlankString = '                    ';     {string of blanks}
  MaxSlots = 97;                            {size of hash table}
  MaxSize = 96;                             {largest subscript in table}

type
  StringIndex = 1..StringLength;
  StringType = packed array [StringIndex] of Char;
  Student = record                          {one student record}
              Name : StringType;
              Score : Integer;
              Grade : Char
            end; {Student}

  HashIndex = 0..MaxSize;
  HashArray = array [HashIndex] of Student;
```

We can use the student's name as the record key. One possible hash function would simply add up the ordinal values of each nonblank character in the student's name, then use the mod function to convert this sum to an integer in the range 0 to MaxSize. Such a function is shown in Fig. 19.5.

Figure 19.5 Function Hash

Directory: CHAP19
File: HASH.FUN

```
function Hash (Key {input} : StringType;
              MaxSlots {input} : Integer) : Integer;
{
  Computes an integer value between 0 and MaxSize.
  Pre : Key, MaxSlots, and StringLength are defined.
  Post: Returns an integer value between 0 and MaxSize
        based on the nonblank characters in Key.
}
const
  Pad = ' ';                     {pad character}

var
  I,                             {loop-control variable}
  HashSum : Integer;             {accumulated hash value}

begin {Hash}
  HashSum := 0;                            {Initialize hash sum.}
  {Add ordinal values for all nonblank characters in Key.}
  for I := 1 to StringLength do
    if Key [I] <> Pad then
      HashSum := HashSum + Ord(Key[I]);

  {Assert:
    HashSum is the sum of ordinal values for all
    nonblank characters in Key
  }
  Hash := HashSum mod MaxSlots              {Define result.}
end; {Hash}
```

Inserting a student record then becomes a matter of passing its key to function Hash and storing the record in the array element selected by Hash. After all records are stored in the array, we can retrieve a particular student's record by passing the student's name to function Hash and accessing the array element selected by Hash. The nice thing about all of this is that it usually takes only one probe into the array to get the record we are seeking. (Sometimes it does take more than one probe, as explained in the next subsection.)

A good hash function disperses the records arbitrarily throughout the hash table. If we display the records starting with the record in position 0 of the table, their keys follow no special order. Empty slots are intermixed with slots that contain actual records. For this reason, do not use hashing when it is important to display frequently the student record in order by key field.

Effect of Collisions

The hashing technique just described works fine as long as Hash never returns the same hash index for two different keys. However, the names 'SILLY SAM' and 'SALLY SIM' would both yield the same hash index because they contain the same letters. It would be an easy matter to improve the hash function so that this does not happen for these two names (see exercise 2 at the end of this section); however, regardless of the hash function used, it is always possible that two different keys will hash to the same index. Such an occurrence is called a *collision*.

One simple way to handle collisions is to insert a new record into the element selected by function Hash only if that slot is currently empty. If that slot is filled, advance to the next empty slot in the array and place the record in that location. The record keys can also be initialized to blank strings to indicate that they are initially empty.

Function LocateSlot (Fig. 19.6) uses this approach to find a desired key, Target, or to determine where in the array a new record with key Target should be placed. To indicate that there is neither a record with key Target nor an empty slot, the function returns MaxSlots, which is 1 more than Max-Size. Function LocateSlot uses the constant BlankString, a string of all blanks, which should be declared earlier.

Algorithm for LocateSlot

1. Start at element selected by Hash function.
2. Initialize number of probes to 1.
3. while Target key not found and
      empty slot not found and
      all elements not examined do
   begin
      4. Advance to next slot.
      5. Increment count of probes.
   end

6. if all table entries were examined without success then
    7. Return MaxSlots
else
    8. Return position of Target or first empty slot.

Figure 19.6 Function LocateSlot

Directory: CHAP19
File: LOCATESL.FUN

```
function LocateSlot (var Class : HashArray;
                         MaxSlots : Integer;
                         Target : StringType) : Integer;
{
   Searches array Class for the student with key field Target.
   Pre : Class, MaxSlots, and Target are defined.
   Post: Returns the index of the student whose name field is
         Target. Returns the location where Target should be
         inserted if missing. Returns MaxSlots if there
         are no empty slots.
   Uses: Hash
}
   var
     Index,                              {index to array}
     Probe : Integer;                    {probe counter}

begin {LocateSlot}
   {Search for student whose name is Target.}
   Index := Hash(Target, MaxSlots); {starting point for search}
   Probe := 1;
   while(Class[Index].Name <> Target) and
        (Class[Index].Name <> BlankString) and
        (Probe <= MaxSlots) do
     {invariant:
         No prior record key matched Target and
         no prior array element was empty and
         number of probes <= MaxSlots + 1.
     }
     begin
       Index := (Index + 1) mod MaxSlots;      {Get next element.}
       Probe := Probe + 1
     end; {while}

   {assert: Target found or empty slot found or array is full}
   if Probe > MaxSlots then
     LocateSlot := MaxSlots                        {Target not found}
   else
     LocateSlot := Index              {Target or empty slot found}
end;  {LocateSlot}
```

The assignment statement

```
Index := (Index + 1) mod MaxSlots      {Get next element.}
```

increments the value of Index. If the current value of Index is MaxSize, the new value will be 0; otherwise, the new value will be one more than the current value.

The local variable Probe counts the number of probes into the array. If Target is missing and the array is completely filled, it would be possible to search forever for an empty slot. The `while` condition (`Probe <= MaxSlots`) prevents this from happening.

We can write procedures to insert and retrieve records in a hash table. Procedure `InsertHash` (Fig. 19.7) inserts a student record into a hash table. The procedure call statement

```
InsertHash (Class, MaxSlots, NextStu, Success)
```

calls `InsertHash` to store record `NextStu` in array `Class`. `InsertHash` uses `LocateSlot` to find the correct slot for the record. If an empty slot is found, the record is inserted and the Boolean flag is set to `True`. If there are no empty slots or there is already a student with the same name in the table, the Boolean flag is set to `False`.

Figure 19.7 Procedure InsertHash

Directory: CHAP19
File: INSERTHA.PRO

```
procedure InsertHash (var Class {input/output} : HashArray;
                          MaxSlots {input} : Integer;
                          NextStu {input} : Student;
                          var Inserted {output} : Boolean);
{
  Inserts a new student record (NextStu) in the array of
  student records Class using hashing.
  Pre : Class, MaxSlots, and NextStu are defined. An empty slot
        in Class is indicated by a record with a blank key field.
  Post: If there is no existing record with the same key as
        NextStu, NextStu is inserted in the first empty array
        element that is nearest to the one selected by Hash.
        Inserted is set to True if the insertion was performed;
        otherwise, Inserted is set to False.
  Uses: LocateSlot
}
  var
    NewIndex : Integer;                      {insertion point}

begin {InsertHash}
    {Locate first empty slot or NextStu.}
    NewIndex := LocateSlot (Class, MaxSlots, NextStu.Name);

    {Perform insertion if slot is empty.}
    if NewIndex = MaxSlots then
       Inserted := False                      {Table is full.}
    else if Class[NewIndex].Name = BlankString then
       begin
          Class[NewIndex] := NextStu;          {Insert new student.}
          Inserted := True
       end
    else
       Inserted := False                       {duplicate entry}
end;   {InsertHash}
```

Procedure `RetrieveHash` (Fig. 19.8) is similar to `InsertHash`. If the target key is in the hash table, the procedure returns the record with that key through its fourth parameter. The procedure returns a Boolean value indicating success or failure through its last parameter.

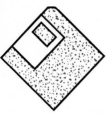

Figure 19.8 Procedure RetrieveHash

```
procedure RetrieveHash (Class {input/output} : HashArray;
                        MaxSlots {input} : Integer;
                        Target {input} : StringType;
                        var NextStu {output} : Student;
                        var Retrieved {output} : Boolean);
{
  Retrieves the record with key Target from the array Class.
  Pre : Class, MaxSlots, and Target are defined. An empty slot
        in Class is indicated by a record with a blank Key field.
  Post: Returns in NextStu the record with key Target.
        Retrieved is set to True if Target is present;
        otherwise, Retrieved is set to false.
  Uses: LocateSlot
}
  var
    NewIndex : Integer;                    {insertion point}

begin {RetrieveHash}
   {Locate first empty slot or NextStu.}
   NewIndex := LocateSlot(Class, MaxSlots, Target);

   {Retrieve record if Target was found.}
   if NewIndex < MaxSlots then
     begin
        NextStu := Class[NewIndex];
        Retrieved := True
     end
   else
      Retrieved := False
end;  {RetrieveHash}
```

Analysis of Hashing

In the best case, it requires just one probe into the hash table to locate a target key or to insert a new record. The more records that are in the array, the greater the chance of one or more collisions and additional probes. To reduce the likelihood of collisions, it is a good idea to leave at least 20 percent extra capacity in the hash table. We can also reduce the chance of multiple collisions by providing better algorithms for resolving a collision than by using the simple approach of advancing to the next slot in the array. Experience shows that the latter approach causes records to be placed in adjacent slots of the hash table, which leads to bands of filled slots and increases the likelihood of multiple collisions.

The hash function should also be constructed so that it distributes the records throughout the hash table. However, we do not want a hash function that is overly complicated, which would require too much computer time to compute the initial hash index. Best results are obtained when the number of table slots is a prime number.

1. Assume that the ordinal number for the letter A is 1, B is 2, and so on; MaxSlots is 10 (array Class has 10 elements). Compute the hash values for the following names and indicate where each name would be stored in the array: 'SAL', 'BIL', 'JIL', 'LIB', 'HAL', 'ROB'

2. A modification to function Hash is proposed in which the ordinal value for each letter is multiplied by its position in the string (for example, for 'SAL', multiply Ord('S') by 1, Ord('A') by 2, and Ord('L') by 3). Why is this a better hash function?

3. An improved way of handling collisions is called quadratic hashing, where 1 (1^2) is added to the initial hash index after probe 1, 4 (2^2) is added after probe 2, 9 (3^2) is added after probe 3, and so on. Modify LocateSlot to use this technique.

19.3 Bubble Sort

So far, we have examined a technique, the selection sort, for sorting an array. Sorting has been widely studied by computer scientists, and many other techniques are available. The remainder of this chapter introduces several sorting algorithms and compares their performance. For each sorting algorithm, we want to see how the array size (N) affects the number of record key comparisons and the number of exchanges performed.

This section discusses a very simple sorting algorithm called the *bubble sort*. The bubble sort compares adjacent array elements and exchanges their values if they are out of order. In this way, the smaller values "bubble" up to the top of the array (toward the first element), while the larger values sink to the bottom of the array. The bubble sort algorithm follows.

Algorithm for Bubble Sort

1. repeat
   2. for each pair of adjacent array elements do
      3. if the values in a pair are out of order then
            Exchange the values.
   until the array is sorted

For example, let's trace through one execution of step 2, or one *pass* through an array being sorted. By scanning the diagrams in Fig. 19.9 from left to right, we can see the effect of each comparison. The pair of array elements being compared is shown in a darker color in each diagram. The first pair of values (M[1] is 60, M[2] is 42) is out of order, so the values are exchanged. The next pair of values (M[2] is now 60, M[3] is 75) is compared in the second array; this pair is in order, and so is the next pair (M[3] is 75, M[4] is 83). The last pair (M[4] is 83, M[5] is 27), is out of order, so the values are exchanged.

Figure 19.9 One Pass of Bubble Sort of Array M

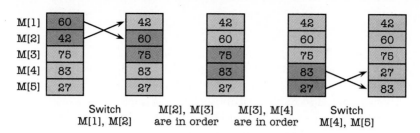

The last array shown in Fig. 19.9 is closer to being sorted than is the original. The only value out of order is the number 27 in M[4]. Unfortunately, it is necessary to complete three more passes through the entire array before this value bubbles up to the top of the array. In each pass, only one pair of values is out of order, so only one exchange is made. The contents of array M after the completion of each pass are shown in Fig. 19.10; the portion that is sorted is shown in the darker color.

We can tell by looking at the contents of the array at the end of pass 4 that the array is now sorted; however, the computer can recognize this only by making one additional pass without doing any exchanges. If no exchanges are made, then all pairs must be in order. This is the reason for the extra pass shown in Fig. 19.10 and for the Boolean flag NoExchanges, described next.

Figure 19.10 Array M After Completion of Each Pass

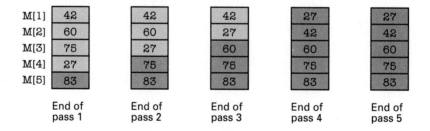

Local Variables for Bubble Sort

NoExchanges : Boolean   {flag to indicate whether any exchanges were made in a pass}
First : Integer   {loop-control variable and subscript}
Pass : Integer   {number of the current pass starting with 1}

Refinement of Step 2 of Bubble Sort

2.1. Initialize NoExchanges to True.
2.2 for each pair of adjacent array elements do

2.3 `if` the values in a pair are out of order `then`
      `begin`
         2.4 Exchange the values.
         2.5 Set `NoExchanges` to `False`.
      `end`

Step 2.2 is the header of a `for` statement. The `for` loop-control variable, `First` is also the subscript of the first element in each pair; consequently, `First+1` is the subscript of the second element in each pair. During each pass, the initial value of `First` is 1. The final value of `First` must be less than the number of array elements so that `First+1` will be in range.

For an array of `N` elements, the final value of `First` can be `N−Pass`, where `Pass` is the number of the current pass, starting with 1 for the first pass. The reason for this is that at the end of pass 1 the last array element must be in its correct place, at the end of pass 2 the last two array elements must be in their correct places, and so on. There is no need to examine array elements that are already in place.

Procedure `BubbleSort` in Fig. 19.11 performs a bubble sort on an array of student records, `Class`. Each record is type `Student`, as declared in Section 19.2. The array `Class` has type `StudentArray`:

```
type
   StuRange = 1..MaxSize;
   StudentArray = array [StuRange] of Student;
```

`MaxSize` is a constant that determines the maximum number of student records that can be stored, and `ClassSize` is a variable that specifies the number of records actually stored (1 <= `ClassSize` <= `MaxSize`).

The array is being sorted on the `Name` field, so `Class[First].Name` is compared to `Class[First+1].Name`. If the student names are out of order, the statement

```
Switch (Class[First], Class[First+1]);   {Switch data.}
```

calls procedure `Switch` to exchange the records of the two array elements listed as actual parameters. Notice that the entire records are switched, not just the names. When `BubbleSort` is done, the array of records will be in alphabetical order by student name.

Figure 19.11   Procedures Switch and BubbleSort

```
procedure Switch (var Stu1, Stu2 {input/output} : Student);
{Switches records Stu1 and Stu2.}

   var
      TempStu : Student;                 {temporary student record}

begin {Switch}
   TempStu := Stu1;  Stu1 := Stu2;  Stu2 := TempStu
end;  {Switch}
```

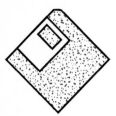

```
procedure BubbleSort (var Class {input/output} : StudentArray;
                          ClassSize {input} : Integer);
{
   Sorts the data in array Class by student name.
   Pre : Class and ClassSize are defined
            (1 <= ClassSize <= MaxSize).
   Post: Array Class is sorted.
}
   var
     NoExchanges : Boolean;          {any exchanges in current pass?}
     First,                          {first element of a pair}
     Pass    : Integer;              {number of current pass}

begin   {BubbleSort}
   Pass := 1;                                 {Start with pass 1.}
   repeat
     {invariant:
        No prior version of array Class was sorted and
        elements following Class[ClassSize-Pass+1] are in place.
     }
     NoExchanges := True;                 {no exchanges yet}

     {Compare student names in each pair of adjacent elements.}
     for First := 1 to ClassSize - Pass do
       if Class[First].Name > Class[First+1].Name then
         begin   {Exchange}
           Switch (Class[First], Class[First+1]); {Switch data.}
           NoExchanges := False                    {Reset flag.}
         end;   {Exchange}

       Pass := Pass + 1                    {Increment pass number.}
   until NoExchanges

   {assert: Array is sorted.}
end; {BubbleSort}
```

Analysis of Bubble Sort

Because the actual number of comparisons and exchanges performed depends on the array being sorted, the bubble-sort algorithm provides excellent performance in some cases and horrible performance in other cases. It works best when an array is nearly sorted to begin with.

Because all adjacent pairs of elements are compared in each pass, the number of comparisons for N passes is represented by the series

$$(N - 1) + (N - 2) + ... 3 + 2 + 1$$

However, if the array becomes sorted early, the later passes and comparisons are not performed. In the worst case, the number of comparisons is $O(N^2)$; in the best case, the number of comparisons is $O(N)$.

Unfortunately, each comparison can lead to an exchange if the array is badly out of order. The worst case occurs when the array is *inverted* (that is, the array elements are in descending order by key) and the number of exchanges is $O(N^2)$. In the best case, only one exchange is made during each pass [($O(N)$ exchanges)], so the number of exchanges also lies between $O(N)$ and $O(N^2)$.

When estimating the performance of a sorting algorithm on a large array whose initial element values are determined arbitrarily, it is best to be pessimistic. For this reason, bubble sort is considered a quadratic sort; its performance is usually worse than selection sort, because the number of exchanges can be $O(N^2)$.

Exercises for Section 19.3

Self-Check

1. How would you modify procedure `BubbleSort` to arrange student records in decreasing sequence by exam score? How about in increasing sequence by letter grade and then alphabetically by name (that is, all A students should be first, listed in alphabetical order; next all B students in alphabetical order; and so on).
2. How many passes of a bubble sort are needed to sort the following array of integers? How many comparisons are performed? How many exchanges? Show the array after each pass.

    40   35   80   75   60   90   70   75

19.4 Insertion Sort

The next sorting algorithm is based on the technique used by a card player to arrange a hand of cards. The player keeps the cards picked up so far in sorted order. After picking up a new card, the player makes room for the new card and inserts it in its proper place in the hand.

The top diagram in Fig. 19.12 shows a hand of cards (ignoring suits) after three cards have been picked up. If the next card is an 8, it should be inserted between the 6 and the 10, maintaining the numerical order. If the card after that is a 7, it should be inserted between the 6 and the 8, as shown in the bottom diagram of the figure. This is also the technique we use to insert new elements into an ordered list.

To adapt this *insertion algorithm* to an array that has been filled with data, we start with a sorted subarray consisting of only the first element. We then insert the second element either before or after the first element, and the sorted subarray has two elements. Next, we insert the third element where it belongs, and the sorted subarray has three elements, and so on. Figure 19.13 illustrates an insertion sort for a five-element array; the sorted portion of the array after each pass is in color.

Figure 19.12   Picking Up a Hand of Cards

Figure 19.13 Insertion Sort

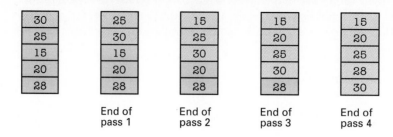

End of pass 1	End of pass 2	End of pass 3	End of pass 4	

Algorithm for Insertion Sort of N-element Array

1. for each value of NextPos from 2 to N do
   begin
   2. Save the element at NextPos in NextVal.
   3. Make room in the sorted subarray (elements 1..NextPos-1) by shifting all values larger than NextVal down one position.
   4. Insert NextVal in the original position of the smallest value moved.
   end

Steps 3 and 4 are illustrated in Fig. 19.14. For the array shown on the left of the figure, the subarray with subscripts 1..3 is sorted, and we want to insert the next element, 20, into its proper place. Because 30 and 25 are greater than 20, both values are shifted down one place (first 30 and then 25). After the shift occurs (middle column), there are temporarily two copies of the value 25 in the array. The first of these is erased when 20 is moved into its correct position, element 2 of the four-element sorted subarray on the right. Steps 2 through 4 should then be repeated to insert the new next value (28) where it belongs.

Procedure InsertSort is shown in Fig. 19.15, where IntArray is an array of Integer values. Procedure ShiftBigger is called to perform the shift operation and to determine the correct position for the array element currently being inserted (NextVal at Table[NextPos]).

Figure 19.14 Inserting the Fourth Array Element

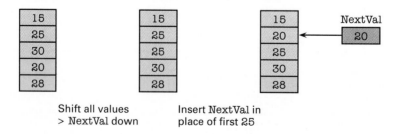

Shift all values > NextVal down	Insert NextVal in place of first 25	

Figure 19.15 Procedure InsertSort

845

19.4 Insertion Sort

```
procedure InsertSort (var Table {input/output} : IntArray;
                          N {input} : Integer);
{
  Performs an insertion sort on array Table with subscripts 1..N.
  Pre : Table and N are defined.
  Post: Table is sorted.
}
  var
    NextPos,       {subscript of the next element to be inserted}
    NewPos,           {subscript of this element after insertion}
    NextVal : Integer;     {temporary storage for next element}

  {Insert ShiftBigger here.}

begin  {InsertSort}
  for NextPos := 2 to N do
    begin
      {invariant: Subarray Table[1..NextPos-1] is sorted.}
      NextVal := Table[NextPos];        {Get next element to insert.}

      {Shift all values > NextVal down one element.}
      ShiftBigger (Table, NextPos, NextVal, NewPos);

      {assert: NewPos is the subscript of smallest value moved.}
      {Insert NextVal in location NewPos.}
      Table[NewPos] := NextVal
    end  {for}
end;  {InsertSort}
```

Directory: CHAP19
File: INSERTSO.PRO

Coding Procedure ShiftBigger

Procedure ShiftBigger must move all array element values larger than NextVal, starting with the array element at position NextPos-1. If NextVal is the smallest value so far, the shift operation terminates after all array elements are moved. If NextVal is not the smallest value so far, the shift operation terminates when a value less than or equal to NextVal is reached. NextVal should be inserted into the position formerly occupied by the last value that was moved. The algorithm for ShiftBigger follows; the procedure is shown in Fig. 19.16.

Algorithm for ShiftBigger

1. Start with the element in position NextPos-1.
2. while first element was not moved and element value > NextVal do
      begin
          3. Move element value down one position.
          4. Advance to next smaller element value.
      end
5. Define NewPos as original position of smallest value moved.

Figure 19.16 Procedure ShiftBigger

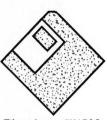

Directory: CHAP19
File: INSERTSO.PRO

```
procedure ShiftBigger (var Table {input/output} : IntArray;
                       NextPos, NextVal {input} : Integer;
                       var NewPos {output} : Integer);
{
  Makes room for NextVal in the subarray Table[1..NextPos]
  and sets NewPos as an index to the correct position of NextVal.
  Pre : Table [1..NextPos−1] is sorted.
  Post: Shifts all values in subarray Table[1..NextPos−1] > NextVal
        by one position and sets NewPos to subscript of last
        element moved.
}
  var
    Done : Boolean;                    {flag}

begin  {ShiftBigger}
  {Shift all values > NextVal. Start with element at NextPos − 1.}
  Done := False;
  while (NextPos > 1) and (not Done) do
    {invariant:
        Table[NextPos] >= NextVal and NextPos >= 1
    }
    if (Table[NextPos−1] > NextVal) then
      begin
        Table[NextPos] := Table[NextPos−1];    {Shift value down.}
        NextPos := NextPos − 1                  {Try next element.}
      end
    else
      Done := True;

  {assert: New position of NextVal is found.}
  NewPos := NextPos
end;  {ShiftBigger}
```

The while statement in Fig. 19.16 compares and shifts all values greater than NextVal in the subarray Table[1..NextPos−1]. We could attempt to eliminate the if statement by using the compound condition

```
(NextPos > 1) and (Table[NextPos−1] > NextVal)
```

as the while condition. However, the second part of this condition causes an array index out of bounds error when NextPos = 1 (NextPos − 1 = 0).

Analysis of Insertion Sort

Procedure ShiftBigger is called $N - 1$ times. In the worst case, ShiftBigger compares all elements in the subarray being processed to NextVal, so the maximum number of record key comparisons is represented by the series

$$1 + 2 + 3 + ... + (N - 1)$$

which is $O(N^2)$. In the best case, only one comparison is required for each call to ShiftBigger [$O(N)$]. The number of record exchanges performed by ShiftBigger is one less than the number of comparisons or, when the new value is the smallest so far, the same as the number of comparisons. Also, each new record is copied into NextVal before the call to ShiftBigger, and NextVal is placed in the array after the return from ShiftBigger (two more exchanges). An "exchange" in insertion sort requires the movement of only one record, whereas in bubble sort or selection sort, an exchange involves a temporary record and requires the movement of three records.

Exercises for Section 19.4

Self-Check

1. Use an insertion sort to sort the following array. How many passes are needed? How many comparisons are performed? How many exchanges? Show the array after each pass.

   40 35 80 75 60 90 70 75

2. Explain how you would modify the insertion sort procedure to sort an array of student records. What changes would be needed to order the array elements as described in exercise 1 of Section 19.3?

19.5 Comparison of Quadratic Sorts

Table 19.1 summarizes the performance of the three quadratic sorts. To give you some idea of what these numbers mean, Table 19.2 shows some values of N and N^2. If N is small (say, 20 or less), it really does not matter which sorting algorithm you use. However, if N is large, avoid using bubble sort unless you are certain that all arrays are nearly sorted to begin with. For most arrays, insertion sort provides better performance than selection sort. Remember that an exchange in insertion sort requires only one record assignment instead of three record assignments, as in the other sorts.

Table 19.1 Comparison of Quadratic Sorts

	Number of Comparisons		Number of Exchanges	
	Best	**Worst**	**Best**	**Worst**
Selection sort	$O(N^2)$	$O(N^2)$	$O(N)$	$O(N)$
Bubble sort	$O(N)$	$O(N^2)$	$O(N)$	$O(N^2)$
Insertion sort	$O(N)$	$O(N^2)$	$O(N)$	$O(N^2)$

Because the time required to sort an array of N elements is proportional to N^2, none of these algorithms is particularly good for large arrays (that is, $N > 100$). The sorting algorithms discussed next provide $N \times \log_2 N$ behavior and are considerably faster for large arrays. You can get a feel for the difference in behavior by comparing the last column of Table 19.2 with the middle column.

Table 19.2 Comparison of Rates of Growth

N	N^2	$N \times \log_2 N$
8	64	24
16	256	64
32	1,024	160
64	4,096	384
128	16,384	896
256	65,536	2,048
512	262,144	4,608

Exercise for Section 19.5

Self-Check

1. Indicate the best method to sort each of the following arrays in ascending order. Explain your choices.

   a. 10 20 30 50 60 80 70
   b. 90 80 70 60 50 40 30
   c. 20 30 40 50 60 70 10
   d. 30 50 10 40 80 90 60

19.6 MergeSort

The next algorithm we consider is called MergeSort. Section 15.4 showed you how to merge two ordered files to generate a third ordered file. MergeSort works in a similar way. The idea is to split the array into two halves, sort each half, and then merge the halves together to get a new sorted array.

We should get an overall improvement in performance, because merging is an $O(N)$ process, and Table 19.1 shows that sorting two smaller arrays takes less effort than sorting one large array. For example, even if we use a quadratic sort to sort each half of the original array, the effort required to sort and merge would be

$$(N/2)^2 + (N/2)^2 + N$$

compared to N^2 to sort the entire array at once. For $N = 100$, the preceding equation evaluates to 5,100, while N^2 is 10,000. You will see that the improvement in performance is even more dramatic. The MergeSort algorithm follows.

Algorithm for MergeSort

1. Split the array into two halves.
2. Sort the left half.
3. Sort the right half.
4. Merge the two arrays together.

Figure 19.17 illustrates this process. An array with subscript type First..Last has been split into a left and a right subarray, both of which are sorted. Middle is the index of the last element in the left subarray. The two subarrays are merged to form a sorted array.

We can reformulate this algorithm using recursion. The stopping case is an array with one element. Because an array with one element is sorted by definition, we do nothing when the stopping condition (First = Last) is True. If the array has more than one element (First < Last), we want to sort subarray Table[First..Middle] and then sort subarray Table[Middle+1..Last] using MergeSort. Next, we merge the sorted subarrays together.

Figure 19.17 Merging Two Sorted Subarrays

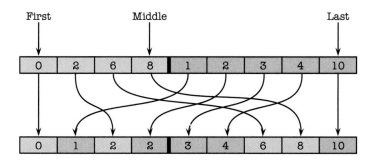

Procedure Inputs

```
Table : IntArray      {original subarray}
First : Integer       {leftmost subscript}
Last : Integer        {rightmost subscript}
```

Procedure Outputs

```
Table : IntArray      {sorted array}
```

Local Variables

```
Middle : Integer      {index of the last element in right subarray}
```

Recursive Algorithm for MergeSort

```
1. if First < Last then
      begin
         2. Set Middle to (First + Last) div 2.
         3. MergeSort Table[First..Middle].
         4. MergeSort Table[Middle+1..Last].
         5. Merge Table[First..Middle] with Table[Middle+1..Last].
      end
```

Procedure MergeSort is shown in Fig. 19.18. When the recursive step executes, MergeSort calls itself first to sort the left subarray and then to sort the right subarray. Next, it calls procedure Merge (discussed next) to merge the two sorted subarrays together. Use the procedure call statement

```
MergeSort (Table, 1, N)
```

to sort the array Table (type IntArray) with subscripts 1..N.

Figure 19.18   Procedure MergeSort

```
procedure MergeSort (var Table {input/output} : IntArray;
                         First, Last {input} : Integer);
{
  Recursive procedure to sort the subarray Table[First..Last].
  Pre : Table, First, and Last are defined.
  Post: Array Table is sorted.
}
  var
    Middle : Integer;    {index of last element in right subarray}

  {Insert procedure Merge.}


begin {MergeSort}
  if First < Last then
    begin
      Middle := (First + Last) div 2;
      MergeSort (Table, First, Middle);
      MergeSort (Table, Middle+1, Last);
      Merge (Table, First, Middle, Last)
    end {if}
end; {MergeSort}
```

The two recursive calls to MergeSort in Fig. 19.18 cause the MergeSort procedure to be applied to two smaller subarrays. If any subarray contains just one element, an immediate return occurs.

Coding Procedure Merge

At the end of MergeSort, the statement

```
Merge (Table, First, Middle, Last)
```

calls procedure Merge to merge the two sorted subarrays. We stated earlier that merging two arrays is analogous to merging two files. In a file merge, two ordered files are merged to form a third file. Procedure Merge must merge two ordered subarrays that are split at Middle into a third array (Temp). The contents of array Temp are copied back into the original array (Table) after the merge. The algorithm for procedure Merge follows.

Local Variables for Merge

```
Temp : IntArray          {result of the merge}
NextLeft : Integer       {index to the left subarray}
NextRight : Integer      {index to the right subarray}
```

1. Start with the first element of each subarray.
2. `while` not finished with either subarray `do`
    3. `if` the current element of the left subarray `<`
        the current element of the right subarray `then`
        4. Copy the current element of the left subarray to the
            merged array and advance to the next element in the
            left subarray and the merged array.
    `else`
        5. Copy the current element of the right subarray to the
            merged array and advance to the next element in the
            right subarray and the merged array.
6. Copy the remaining elements from the unfinished array to the
    merged array.
7. Copy the merged array back to the original array.

Procedure `Merge` is shown in Fig. 19.19. The variables `NextLeft` and
`NextRight` are indexes to the two subarrays being merged; the variable `Index`
is the index to the merged array, `Temp`. `NextLeft` and `Index` are initialized to
`First`; `NextRight` is initialized to `Middle + 1`, which is the first element in the
right subarray.

Figure 19.19 Procedure Merge

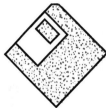

```
procedure Merge (var Table {input/output} : IntArray;
                 First, Middle, Last {input} : Integer);
{
  Merges Table[First..Middle] with Table[Middle+1..Last].
  Pre : Table is defined and First <= Last and
        Middle = (First + Last) div 2.
  Post: Array Table is sorted.
}
  var
    Temp          : IntArray;      {merger of left and right arrays}
    NextLeft,                      {next element in left subarray}
    NextRight,                     {next element in right subarray}
    Index : Integer;               {index to array Temp}

begin {Merge}
  {Start with first element of all three arrays.}
  NextLeft := First;
  NextRight := Middle + 1;
  Index := First;

  {Perform the merge until one subarray is finished.}
  while (NextLeft <= Middle) and (NextRight <= Last) do
      if Table[NextLeft] < Table[NextRight] then
        begin {copy left element}
          Temp[Index] := Table[NextLeft];
          NextLeft := NextLeft + 1;
          Index := Index + 1
        end  {copy left element}
      else
        begin {copy right element}
          Temp[Index] := Table[NextRight];
```

```
                 NextRight := NextRight + 1;
                 Index := Index + 1
              end;  {copy right element}

      {Copy any remaining elements in the left subarray.}
      while NextLeft <= Middle do
        begin
          Temp[Index] := Table[NextLeft];
          NextLeft := NextLeft + 1;
          Index := Index + 1
        end; {while}

      {Copy any remaining elements in the right subarray.}
      while NextRight <= Last do
        begin
          Temp[Index] := Table[NextRight];
          NextRight := NextRight + 1;
          Index := Index + 1
        end; {while}

      {Copy the merged array back into Table.}
      for Index := First to Last do
        Table[Index] := Temp[Index]
  end;  {Merge}
```

Analysis of MergeSort

Our preliminary analysis indicated that MergeSort would be more efficient than a quadratic sort, but how much better is it? Procedure Merge copies data into two N-element arrays (array Temp and then Table). Each array copy is an $O(N)$ process, so procedure Merge is also an $O(N)$ process (remember, we drop the 2 from $2N$).

The remaining question is how many times procedure Merge is called. The answer is that Merge is called once for each execution of the recursive step in MergeSort. The recursive step splits the array into half each time it executes. From earlier splitting processes (for example, binary search), we know that it requires $\log_2 N$ splits to reach the stopping state (N one-element subarrays). Therefore, MergeSort appears to be an $O(N \times \log_2 N)$ process.

Table 19.2 showed that MergeSort provides significant improvement over a quadratic sort for a large array. Bear in mind that this analysis does not provide the whole picture. There is quite a bit of overhead for each recursive call to Merge. Also, MergeSort requires an additional auxiliary array with the same number of elements as the original array. If the array being sorted is truly a very large array, the memory requirements of MergeSort could become a burden. Next, we discuss an $O(N \times \log_2 N)$ sort that moves elements around in the original array and does not require an auxiliary array.

Exercises for Section 19.6

Self-Check

1. Explain why array Temp is needed in Merge.
2. Trace the execution of MergeSort on the following array. Show the values

of First, Last, and Middle for each recursive call and the array elements after returning from each call to Merge. How many times is MergeSort called? How many times is Merge called?

55   50   10   40   80   90   60   100   70   80   20

19.7 QuickSort

The last algorithm we will study is called QuickSort, which works in the following way. Given an array with subscripts First..Last to sort, QuickSort rearranges the array so that all element values smaller than a selected *pivot value* are first, followed by the pivot value, followed by all element values larger than the pivot value. After this rearrangement (called a *partition*), the pivot value is in its proper place. All element values smaller than the pivot value are closer to where they belong, because they precede the pivot value. All element values larger than the pivot value are closer to where they belong, because they follow the pivot value.

An example of this process follows. We assume that the first array element is arbitrarily selected as the pivot. A possible result of the partitioning process is shown beneath the original array.

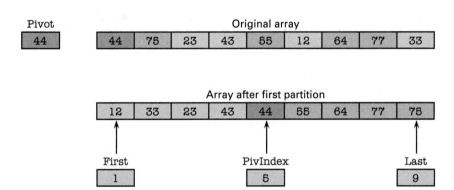

After the partitioning process, PivIndex is 5 and the fifth array element contains the pivot value, 44. All values less than 44 are in the left subarray (color background); all values greater than 44 are in the right subarray (gray background). The next step would be to apply QuickSort recursively to the two subarrays on either side of the pivot value. The algorithm for QuickSort follows. We describe how to do the partitioning later.

Procedure Inputs

```
Table : IntArray      {array being sorted}
First : Integer       {first subscript}
Last : Integer        {last subscript}
```

Procedure Outputs

```
Table : IntArray        {sorted array}
```

Local Variables

```
PivIndex : Integer       {subscript of the pivot value after
                          partitioning}
```

Algorithm for QuickSort

1. if First < Last then
    begin
        2. Partition the elements in the subarray First..Last so
           that the pivot value is in place (subscript is PivIndex).
        3. Apply QuickSort to the subarray First..PivIndex-1.
        4. Apply QuickSort to the subarray PivIndex+1..Last.
    end

A stopping case for QuickSort is an array of one element (First = Last) that is sorted by definition, so nothing is done. If First > Last is true, then the array bounds are improper (also a stopping case). If the array has more than one element, we partition it into two subarrays and sort the subarrays using QuickSort.

The implementation of procedure QuickSort is shown in Fig. 19.20. Use the procedure call statement

```
QuickSort (Table, 1, N)
```

to sort the array Table (type IntArray) with subscripts 1..N.

Figure 19.20 Procedure QuickSort

```
procedure QuickSort (var Table {input/output} : IntArray;
                         First, Last {input} : Integer);
{
  Recursive procedure to sort the subarray Table[First..Last].
  Pre : First, Last, and array Table are defined.
  Post: Table is sorted.
}
  var
    PivIndex : Integer;              {subscript of pivot value -
                                      returned by Partition}

  {Insert Partition here.}


begin  {QuickSort}
  if First < Last then
    begin
      {Split into two subarrays separated by value at PivIndex}
      Partition (Table, First, Last, PivIndex);
      QuickSort (Table, First, PivIndex-1);
      QuickSort (Table, PivIndex+1, Last)
    end  {if}
end;  {QuickSort}
```

The two recursive calls to QuickSort in Fig. 19.20 cause the QuickSort procedure to be applied to the subarrays that are separated by the value at PivIndex. If any subarray contains just one element (or zero elements), an immediate return occurs.

Coding Procedure Partition

Procedure Partition selects the pivot and performs the partitioning operation. If the arrays are randomly ordered to begin with, it does not really matter which element we choose to be the pivot value. For simplicity, we have selected the element with subscript First. We search for the first value at the left end of the subarray that is greater than the pivot value. When we find it, we search for the first value at the right end of the subarray that is less than or equal to the pivot value. These two values are exchanged, and we repeat the search and exchange operations. This is illustrated next, with Up pointing to the first value greater than the pivot and Down pointing to the first value less than or equal to the pivot value.

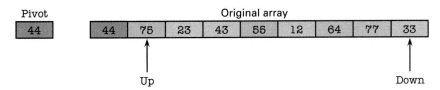

75 is the first value at the left end of the array larger than 44; 33 is the first value at the right end less than or equal to 44, so these two values are exchanged. The pointers Up and Down are then advanced from their current positions to the positions shown next.

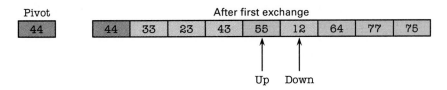

55 is the next value at the left end larger than 44; 12 is the next value at the right end less than or equal to 44, so these two values are exchanged, and Up and Down are advanced again.

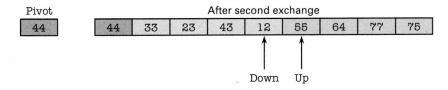

After the second exchange, the first five array elements contain the pivot value and all values less than or equal to the pivot; the last four elements contain all values larger than the pivot. 55 is selected once again by Up as the next element larger than the pivot; 12 is selected by Down as the next element less than or equal to the pivot. Because Up has now "passed" Down, these values are not exchanged. Instead, the pivot value (subscript is First) and the value at position Down are exchanged. This puts the pivot value in its proper position (new subscript is Down), as shown next.

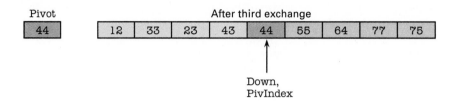

The partitioning process is now complete, and the value of Down is returned as the pivot index (PivIndex). QuickSort is called recursively to sort the left subarray and the right subarray. The algorithm for Partition follows and is implemented in Fig. 19.21.

Local Variables for Partition

Pivot : Integer	{pivot value}
Up : Integer	{index to array elements larger than Pivot}
Down : Integer	{index to array elements less than or equal to Pivot}

Algorithm for Partition

1. Define the pivot value as the contents of Table[First].
2. Initialize Up to First and Down to Last.
3. repeat
    4. Increment Up until Up selects the first element greater than the pivot value.
    5. Decrement Down until Down selects the first element less than or equal to the pivot value.
    6. if Up < Down then
        7. Exchange their values.
    until Up meets or passes Down.
8. Exchange Table[First] and Table[Down].
9. Define PivIndex as Down.

The two while loops in Fig. 19.21 advance pointers Up and Down to the right and the left, respectively. Because Table[First] is equal to Pivot, the second loop stops if Down happens to reach the left end of the array (Down is First). The extra condition (Up < Last) is added to the first while loop to ensure that it also stops if Up happens to reach the right end of the array.

Figure 19.21 Procedures Exchange and Partition

857

19.7 QuickSort

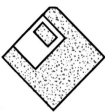

Directory: CHAP19
File: QUICKSOR.PRO

```
procedure Exchange (var X, Y {input/output} : Integer);

{Switches the values in X and Y}

   var
     Temp : Integer;              {temporary cell for exchange}

begin {Exchange}
  Temp := X;          X := Y;          Y := Temp
end;   {Exchange}


procedure Partition (var Table {input/output} : IntArray;
                     First, Last {input}   : Integer;
                     var PivIndex {output} : Integer);
{
  Partitions the subarray of Table with subscripts First..Last
  into two subarrays.
  Pre : First, Last, and array Table are defined.
  Post: PivIndex is defined such that all values
        less than or equal to Table[PivIndex] have
        subscripts <= PivIndex; all values
        greater than Table[PivIndex] have subscripts > PivIndex.
}
   var
     Pivot,                     {pivot value}
     Up,                        {index to values > Pivot}
     Down : Integer;            {index to values <= Pivot}

begin  {Partition}
  Pivot := Table[First];   {Define leftmost element as the pivot.}

  {Find and exchange values that are out of place.}
  Up := First;             {Set Up to point to leftmost element.}
  Down := Last;            {Set Down to point to rightmost element.}

  repeat
    {Move Up to the next value larger than Pivot.}
    while (Table[Up] <= Pivot) and (Up < Last) do
      Up := Up + 1;

    {assertion:  Table[Up] > Pivot or Up is equal to Last.}
    {Move Down to the next value less than or equal to Pivot.}
    while Table[Down] > Pivot do
      Down := Down - 1;

    {assertion:  Table[Down] <= Pivot}
    {Exchange out-of-order values.}
    if Up < Down then
      Exchange (Table[Up], Table[Down])
  until Up >= Down;             {until Up meets or passes Down}
  {assertion:  Values <= Pivot have subscripts <= Down and
               values > Pivot have subscripts > Down.}
  {Put pivot value where it belongs and define PivIndex.}
  Exchange (Table[First], Table[Down]);
  PivIndex := Down
end;   {Partition}
```

Analysis of QuickSort

The QuickSort procedure works better for some arrays than for others. It works best when the partitioning process splits each subarray into two subarrays of almost the same size. The worst behavior results when one of the subarrays has zero elements and the other has all the other elements except for the pivot value. Ironically, this worst-case behavior results when QuickSort is applied to an array that is already sorted. The pivot value remains in position First, and the result of the elements are in the subarray with subscripts First+1..Last.

Procedure Partition compares each array element to the pivot value (an $O(N)$ process). If the array splits are relatively even, the number of calls to partition is $O(\log_2 N)$. Therefore, QuickSort is an $O(N \times \log_2 N)$ process in the best case. In the worst case, there are N calls to Partition, and QuickSort degenerates to an $O(N^2)$ process.

Because data values are normally distributed in random order in an array, QuickSort as presented will work quite well. A possible improvement would be to use the average of two or more array elements as the pivot value. This requires more computation time and also a modification to the algorithm, because the pivot value is no longer an array element value.

Exercises for Section 19.7

Self-Check

1. Complete the trace of QuickSort for the subarrays remaining after the first partition.
2. If an array contains some values that are the same, in which subarray (left or right) will all values that are equal to the pivot value be placed?
3. Trace the execution of QuickSort on the following array. Show the values of First and Last for each recursive call and the array elements after returning from each call. Also, show the value of Pivot during each call and the value returned through PivIndex. How many times is QuickSort called? How many times is Partition called?

   55 50 10 40 80 90 60 100 70 80 20

   Which provides better performance: MergeSort or QuickSort? How would insertion sort do compared to these two?

19.8 Common Programming Errors

One problem with search and sort procedures is the possibility of going beyond the bounds of a subarray. Make sure your Pascal system checks for subscript-range errors. On some systems, the programmer must activate this important check; otherwise, subscript range violations are not detected. If this is the case on your system, make sure you activate this feature when you are debugging any program that manipulates arrays, particularly a search or a sort.

When you are debugging a search or sort procedure, it is best to use relatively small arrays (10 elements or fewer). Make sure you print the new contents of the array after each pass through a sort procedure.

CHAPTER REVIEW

This chapter discussed the binary-search technique, which provides significant improvement over linear search when you are searching large arrays. A linear search is an $O(N)$ process, while a binary search is an $O(\log_2 N)$ process. This means that the time required to perform a binary search increases very slowly. For example, it takes only about twice as long to perform a binary search on an array with 256 elements ($\log_2 256$ is 8) as it takes to perform a binary search on an array with 16 elements ($\log_2 16$ is 4).

We also discussed using a hash table to provide quick access to data stored in an array. The record key is passed to the hash function, which computes an index to the array. In most cases, only one probe is required to access the desired record. If there are collisions (multiple keys with same index value), the array elements following the one selected by the index are examined until the desired key is found or an empty table slot is reached.

We also analyzed several sorting algorithms. Three of these, selection sort, bubble sort, and insertion sort, are $O(N^2)$, or quadratic, sorts. Two of these, MergeSort and QuickSort, are $O(N \times \log_2 N)$. For small arrays, either insertion sort or selection sort should generally be used; bubble sort is a good choice only when the array is likely to be nearly sorted. For large arrays, use MergeSort or QuickSort. Avoid MergeSort when storage space is likely to be limited. Avoid QuickSort when the array is nearly sorted.

✓ Quick-Check Exercises

1. What are three techniques for searching an array?
2. What are two techniques for searching an array whose elements are in order by key field?
3. Rate the three search algorithms in terms of time efficiency for a large array.
4. Rate the three search algorithms in terms of space efficiency for a large array.
5. Define a collision in hashing. What is one technique of resolving collisions?
6. Name three quadratic sorts.
7. Name two sorts with $N \times \log_2 N$ behavior.
8. Which algorithm is particularly good for an array that is already sorted? Which is particularly bad? Explain.
9. What determines whether you should use a quadratic sort or a logarithmic sort?
10. Which quadratic sort's performance is least affected by the ordering of the array elements? Which is most affected?

Answers to Quick-Check Exercises
1. sequential search, binary search, hashing
2. sequential search of an ordered array, binary search
3. hashing, binary search, sequential search
4. sequential search and binary search followed by hashing
5. A collision occurs when two keys have the same hash value. Linear resolution involves scanning consecutive table entries until an empty slot is found or the target is located.

6. selection, insertion, bubble
7. MergeSort, QuickSort
8. Bubble sort and insertion sort: both require $N - 1$ comparisons with no exchanges. QuickSort is bad because the partitioning process always creates one subarray with a single element.
9. array size
10. selection sort; bubble sort

Review Questions

1. Show how the following keys would be stored in a hash table with five slots, assuming the linear method for resolving collisions discussed in the text. The value returned by function Hash is shown after each key.

   'Ace' 3, 'Boy' 4, 'Cat' 5, 'Dog' 3, 'Bye' 1

2. When does QuickSort work best? When does it work worst?
3. Write a function that will recursively search a packed array of 30 characters and return the position of the first comma in the string. If the string does not contain a comma, the function should return 0.
4. What is the purpose of the pivot value in QuickSort? How did we select it in the text? What is wrong with that approach for choosing a pivot value?
5. For the array

   30   40   20   15   60   80   75   4   20

   show the new array after each pass of insertion sort and bubble sort. How many comparisons and exchanges are performed by each?

6. For the array in exercise 5, trace the execution of MergeSort and QuickSort.
7. The shaker sort is an adaptation of the bubble sort that alternates the direction in which the array elements are scanned during each pass. The first pass starts its scan with the first element, moving the larger element in each pair down the array. The second pass starts its scan with the next-to-last element, moving the smaller element in each pair up the array, and so on. Indicate what the advantage of the shaker sort might be. Show how it would sort the array in exercise 5.

Programming Projects

1. Write an abstract data type called HashTable that consists of a declaration for a hash table and the operators in Section 19.2. Write a menu-driven program that maintains a list of passenger records in a hash table (see programming project 1 of Chapter 18). Import the necessary data types and operators.
2. Do programming project 7 in Chapter 18 using ADT HashTable described in project 1 of this chapter.
3. If your Pascal system has a random-number function, use it to store a list of 1000 random integer values in an array. Find out how to access a function or a procedure on your computer system that displays the current or elapsed time during program execution. Test each sorting procedure described in this chapter by timing how long it takes each to sort the same array.

   Your program should include procedures corresponding to the following procedure headers.

```
procedure FillArray (var A {output} : IntArray;
                         Count {input} : Integer);
{
  Fills the first Count positions of A with random integers.
  Uses: System random-number generator.
}

procedure CopyArray (var A {input},
                         B {output} : IntArray;
                         Count {input} : Integer);
{Copies first Count elements of A to B}

procedure StartTime (var Time {output} : Real);
{
  Returns time in seconds prior to beginning a time trial.
  Uses: System clock routine.
}

procedure StopTime (var Time {output} : Real);
{
  Returns time in seconds on completion of a time trial.
  Uses: System clock routine.
}
```

4. One technique for handling collisions in a hash table is to place all records with keys that hash to the same value in a linked list (called a *bucket*). One slot in the hash table is allocated for each hash value, and each slot consists of space for one record and a single pointer field (initially nil). The first record with a particular hash value is placed directly in the hash table. When a second key is encountered with that same hash value, that record is linked to the first record in the table via the pointer field. The third record with that hash value is linked to the second, and so on. Rewrite the operators in ADT HashTable, assuming this technique is used to resolve collisions.

5. The Shell sort is a sorting technique that applies insertion sort to chains of elements in an array where the elements in the chain are chosen by adding an increment value. The increment value decreases with each pass. For example, if an array has 15 elements and the initial increment value is 5, the five chains of elements listed next would be sorted in the "first pass." Each chain would be sorted using insertion sort.

```
X[1], X[6],  X[11]
X[2], X[7],  X[12]
X[3], X[8],  X[13]
X[4], X[9],  X[14]
X[5], X[10], X[15]
```

If the next increment is 3, the following three chains would be sorted. Notice that the chains increase in size as the increment shrinks.

```
X[1], X[4], X[7], X[10], X[13]
X[2], X[5], X[8], X[11], X[14]
X[3], X[6], X[9], X[12], X[15]
```

When the increment shrinks to 1, the whole array is sorted using insertion sort.

The initial insertion sorts involve short chains, so the sorts should be relatively quick. Normally, the performance of insertion sort degrades quickly as the length of the array being sorted increases. However, because the longer chains have had their elements presorted during earlier passes, insertion sort should be able to handle the longer chains more efficiently than would be the case without presorting.

Implement the Shell sort algorithm. Read the increment values for each pass into an array Increments before reading in the elements of the array to be sorted.

6. The binary search is not a useful technique for searching linked lists. Searching linked lists can be done more efficiently when items that are frequently retrieved are stored near the beginning of the list. Two techniques can be used to accomplish this: *move to front* and *transposition*. With the move-to-front technique, every time a target item is located it is removed from its present position in the list and placed in front of the first element in the list. With the transposition technique, after the target item is located, it is moved in front of its predecessor.

Write a Pascal program that stores 30 random integers in a linked list and then computes the average number of comparisons required to search the list 150 times for randomly chosen integers using move-to-front technique and the transposition technique. Be sure to begin with the same list of numbers each time and to include searches for numbers that do not appear in the list.

Appendix A
Reserved Words,
Standard Identifiers,
Operators, Functions, and
Procedures

Reserved Words

and	end	nil	set
array	file	not	then
begin	for	of	to
case	function	or	type
const	goto	packed	until
div	if	procedure	var
do	in	program	while
downto	label	record	with
else	mod	repeat	

Standard Identifiers

Constants:

    False, True, MaxInt

Types:

    Integer, Boolean, Real, Char, Text

Program parameters:

    Input, Output

Functions:

    Abs, ArcTan, Chr, Cos, EOF, EOLN, Exp, Ln, Odd, Ord,
    Pred, Round, Sin, Sqr, Sqrt, Succ, Trunc

Procedures:

    Get, New, Pack, Page, Put, Read, ReadLn, Reset,
    Rewrite, Unpack, Write, WriteLn

Table A.1 Table of Operators

Operator	Operation	Type of Operand(s)	Result Type
:=	Assignment	Any type except file types	—
Arithmetic			
+ (unary)	Identity	Integer or real	Same as operand
– (unary)	Sign inversion		
+	Addition	Integer or real	Integer or real
–	Subtraction		
*	Multiplication		
div	Integer division	Integer	Integer
/	Real division	Integer or real	Real
mod	Modulus	Integer	Integer
Relational			
=	Equality	Ordinal, real, string, set, or pointer	Boolean
<>	Inequality		
<	Less than	Ordinal, real, or string	Boolean
>	Greater than		
<=	Less than or equal	Ordinal, real, or string	Boolean
	or		
	Subset	Set	
>=	Greater than or equal	Ordinal, real, or string	Boolean
	or		
	Superset	Set	
in	Set membership	First operand is any ordinal, second is its set type	Boolean
Logical			
not	Negation		
or	Disjunction	Boolean	Boolean
and	Conjunction		
Set			
+	Union		
–	Set difference	any set type	Same as operand
*	Intersection		

Table A.2   Standard Functions

Name	Description of Computation	Argument	Result
Abs	The absolute value of the argument	Real/integer	Same as argument
Exp	The value of e (2.71828) raised to the power of the argument	Real/integer	Real
Ln	The logarithm (to the base e) of the argument	Real/integer (positive)	Real
Sqr	The square of the argument	Real/integer	Same as
Sqrt	The positive square root of the argument	Real/integer (positive)	argument
Round	The closest integer value to the argument	Real	Integer
Trunc	The integral part of the argument	Real	Integer
ArcTan	The arc tangent of the argument	Real/integer (radians)	Real
Cos	The cosine of the argument	Real/integer (radians)	Real
Sin	The sine of the argument	Real/integer (radians)	Real
Chr	Returns the character whose ordinal number is its argument	Integer	Char
Odd	Returns True if its argument is an odd number; otherwise, returns False	Integer	Boolean
Ord	Returns the ordinal number of its argument	Ordinal	Integer
Pred	Returns the predecessor of its argument	Ordinal	Ordinal
Succ	Returns the successor of its argument	Ordinal	Ordinal

Table A.3 Table of Standard Procedures

Procedure Call	Description
Dispose (P)	Returns the record pointed to by pointer variable P to free storage.
Get (F)	Advances the file-position pointer for file F to its next component and assigns the value of the component to F^.
New (P)	Creates a record of the type pointed to by pointer P and saves its address in P.
Pack (U, I, P)	Copies the elements in unpacked array U, starting with U[I], to packed array P, starting with the first element.
Page (F)	Advances the printer to a new page before printing the next line of file F.
Put (F)	Appends the current contents of F^ to file F.
Read (F, *variables*)	Reads data from file F to satisfy the list of *variables*. If F is not specified, file Input is read.
ReadLn (F, *variables*)	Reads data from text file F to satisfy the list of *variables*. Skips any characters at the end of the last line read.
Reset (F)	Resets the file-position pointer for file F to the beginning. File F can then be read.
Rewrite (F)	Resets the file-position pointer for file F to the beginning; any prior contents are lost. File F can then be written.
Unpack (P, U, I)	Copies the elements in packed array P, starting with the first element, to unpacked array U, starting with U[I].
Write (F, *outputs*)	Writes the data in the order specified by *outputs* to file F. If F is not specified, the data are written to file Output.
WriteLn (F, *outputs*)	Writes the data in the order specified by *outputs* to text file F. Writes an end-of-line mark after the data.

Appendix B
Pascal Syntax Diagrams

program

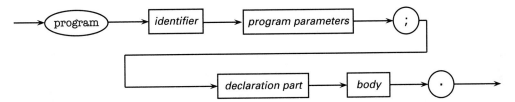

program parameters

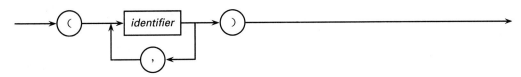

body

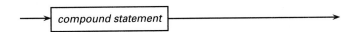

declaration part

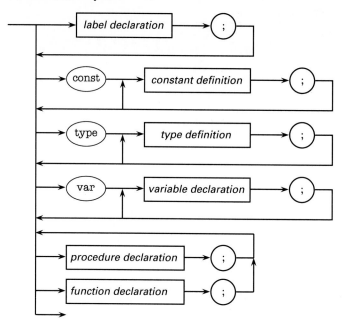

label declaration

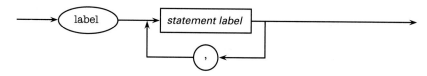

constant definition

type definition

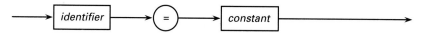

variable declaration

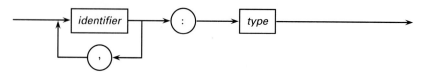

statement label

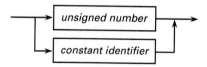

constant

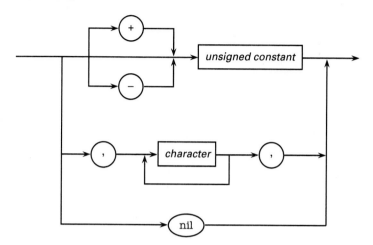

unsigned constant

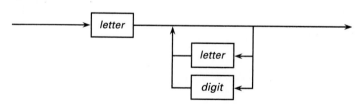

identifier

function declaration

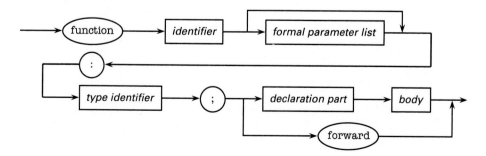

procedure declaration

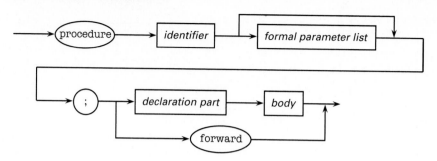

formal parameter list

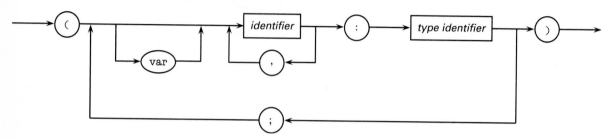

type

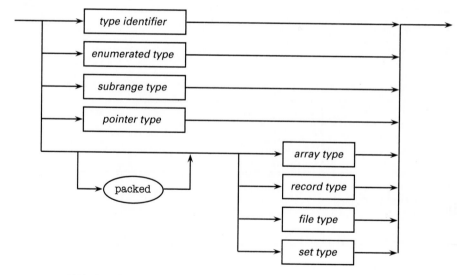

enumerated type

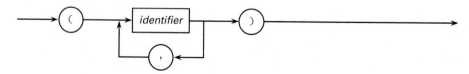

subrange type

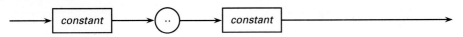

pointer type

array type

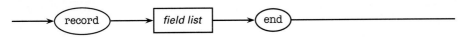

record type

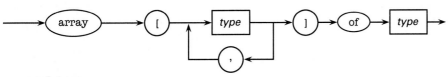

field list

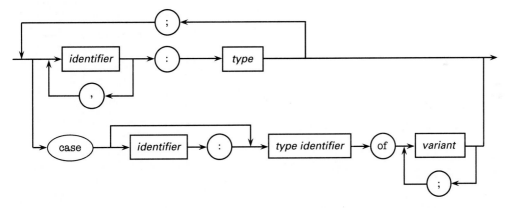

variant

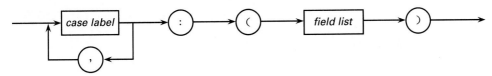

file type

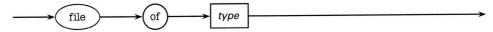

set type

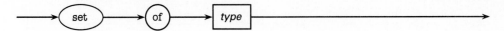

compound statement

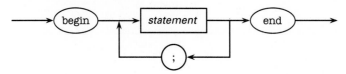

statement

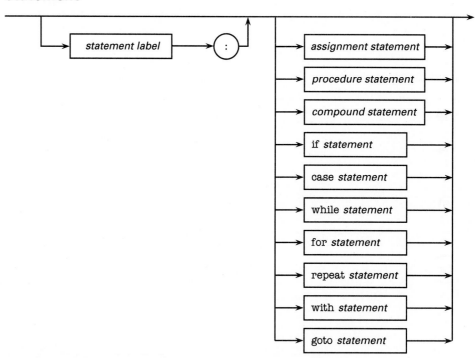

assignment statement

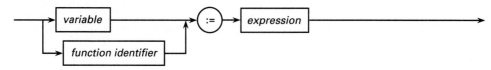

procedure call statement

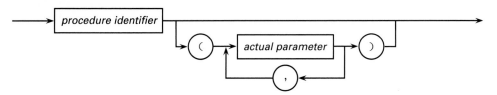

if statement

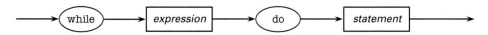

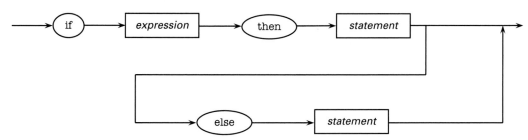

while statement

for statement

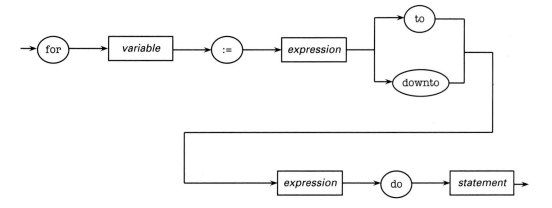

case statement

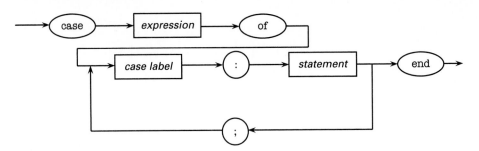

case label

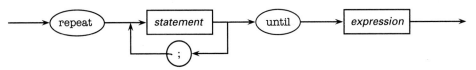

repeat statement

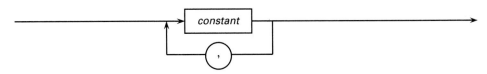

with statement

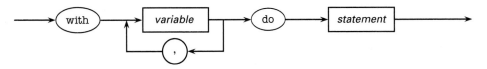

goto statement

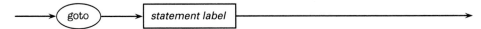

actual parameter

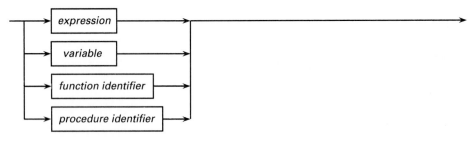

expression

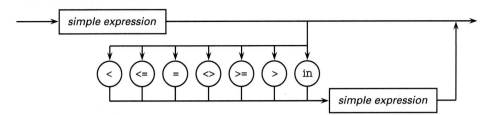

simple expression

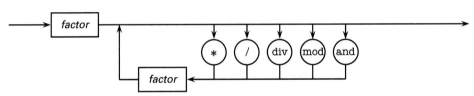

term

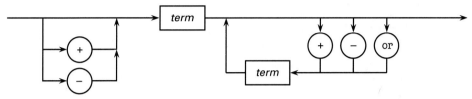

factor

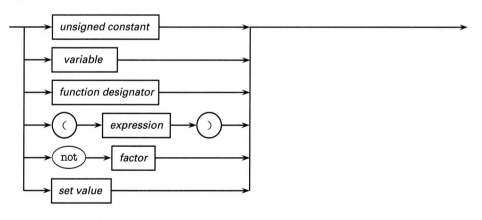

function designator

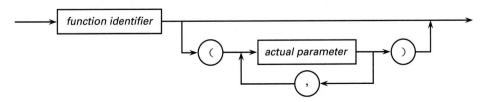

set value

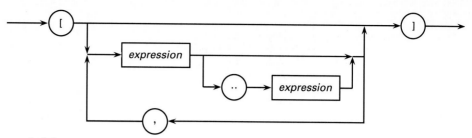

variable

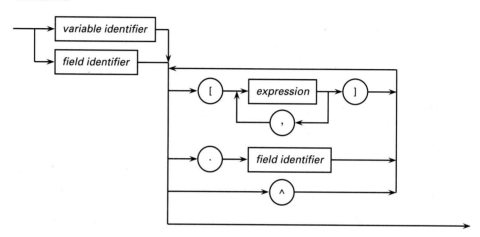

unsigned number

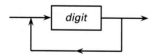

integer

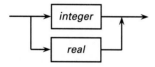

real

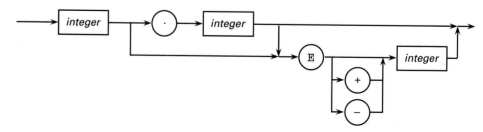

Appendix C
Character Sets

The charts in this appendix show the following character sets: ASCII (American Standard Code for Information Interchange), EBCDIC (Extended Binary Coded Decimal Interchange Code), and CDC* Scientific. Only printable characters are shown. The ordinal number for each character is shown in decimal. For example in ASCII, the ordinal number for 'A' is 65 and the ordinal number for 'z' is 122. The blank character is denoted by a □.

Left Digit(s) \ Right Digit	ASCII									
	0	1	2	3	4	5	6	7	8	9
3			□	!	"	#	$	%	&	'
4	(	)	*	+	,	−	.	/	0	1
5	2	3	4	5	6	7	8	9	:	;
6	<	=	>	?	@	A	B	C	D	E
7	F	G	H	I	J	K	L	M	N	O
8	P	Q	R	S	T	U	V	W	X	Y
9	Z	[	/	]	^	−	'		a	b	c
10	d	e	f	g	h	i	j	k	l	m
11	n	o	p	q	r	s	t	u	v	w
12	x	y	z	{			}	~			

Codes 00–31 and 127 are nonprintable control characters.

*CDC is a trademark of Control Data Corporation.

EBCDIC

Right Digit (across top) · Left Digit(s) (down side)

Left Digit(s)	0	1	2	3	4	5	6	7	8	9
6					□					
7					¢	.	<	(	+	|
8	&									
9	!	$	*	)	;	¬	-	/		
10							^	,	%	—
11	>	?								
12			:	#	@	'	=	"		a
13	b	c	d	e	f	g	h	i		
14						j	k	l	m	n
15	o	p	q	r						
16			s	t	u	v	w	x	y	z
17								\	{	}
18	[	]								
19				A	B	C	D	E	F	G
20	H	I								J
21	K	L	M	N	O	P	Q	R		
22							S	T	U	V
23	W	X	Y	Z						
24	0	1	2	3	4	5	6	7	8	9

Codes 00–63 and 250–255 are nonprintable control characters.

CDC

Right Digit (across top) · Left Digit(s) (down side)

Left Digit(s)	0	1	2	3	4	5	6	7	8	9
0	:	A	B	C	D	E	F	G	H	I
1	J	K	L	M	N	O	P	Q	R	S
2	T	U	V	W	X	Y	Z	0	1	2
3	3	4	5	6	7	8	9	+	−	*
4	/	(	)	$	=	□	,	.	≡	[
5	]	%	≠	→	∨	∧	↑	↓	<	>
6	≤	≥	¬	;						

Appendix D
Vax Pascal Modules

In Vax Pascal, a *module* is a separately compilable program structure. A module heading line contains the reserved word module instead of program. A module does not require a begin line, but its last line is always end.

Figure D.1 shows abstract data type DayADT (see Fig. 9.5) written as a Vax Pascal module. The module begins with the lines

```
[Inherit ('Utility.PEN'), Environment ('DayADT.PEN')]
module DayADT (Input, Output);
```

The Vax Pascal reserved word Inherit precedes the list of files (Utility.PEN) that are needed to compile the current module. If multiple files are needed, a list of their names should appear within the parentheses; each name should be enclosed in apostrophes with a comma between names. The Vax Pascal reserved word Environment precedes the name of the environment file (DayADT.PEN) that will be created by compiling the current module. The module name (DayADT) and its parameters (Input and Output) appear after the Vax Pascal reserved word module.

Figure D.1 Module DayADT

```
[Inherit ('Utility.PEN'), Environment ('DayADT.PEN')]
module DayADT (Input, Output);
{
  Specification of DayADT

  Structure:   Day is an enumerated data type whose values represent
               the days of the week.

  Operators:   ReadLnDay and WriteDay read and display a value of
               type Day.

  Implementation of DayADT
}
  type
    Day = (Sunday, Monday, Tuesday, Wednesday,
           Thursday, Friday, Saturday);


  procedure ReadLnDay (var ADay : Day;
                       var ValidDay : Boolean);
  {
  Reads two data characters and stores the value represented by the
  data in ADay.  Sets ValidDay to indicate whether the data are
  valid.
```

```
      Pre : None
      Post: ADay is assigned a value if the
            two characters read are SU, MO, TU, WE, TH, FR, or SA;
            otherwise, ADay is undefined.
            ValidDay is set to True if ADay is defined;
            otherwise, ValidDay is set to False.
      Uses: UpCase from module Utility.
    }
      var
        DayCh1,                        {input - first letter in day}
        DayCh2 : Char;                 {input - second letter in day}

      begin {ReadLnDay}
        .

        .
      end; {ReadLnDay}

      procedure WriteDay (ADay {input} : Day);
      {
       Displays the value of ADay.
       Pre : ADay is defined.
       Post: Displays a string corresponding to the value of ADay.
      }
      begin
        .

        .
      end; {WriteDay}
    end.  {DayADT}
```

Module DayADT contains declarations for data type Day and its operator procedures, ReadLnDay and WriteDay. (To conserve space, we did not write out the actual procedure bodies.)

Using Module DayADT

The heading for module DayADT indicates that DayADT is a client of another module named Utility, which contains function UpCase (see Fig. 9.4). The lines

```
[Inherit ('Utility.PEN', 'DayADT.PEN')]
program TestDayUtility (Input, Output);
```

indicate that program TestDayUtility is a client program of both modules DayADT and Utility. Notice that the reserved word Environment is not used in a program heading.

Compiling Modules and Client Programs

Module DayADT must be saved in a separate file named DayADT.PAS. This file must be compiled before any of its clients. Because DayADT uses module Utility, you must remember to compile module Utility first. Once DayADT has been compiled, you can compile any client program (or any other module) that uses it.

When you compile module DayADT, Vax Pascal creates its environment file (DayADT.PEN) and saves its object code in file DayADT.OBJ. After compiling a client program but prior to running it, you must link the client's object code file to the object code files for all the modules that it uses.

Appendix E
Turbo Pascal Units

In Turbo Pascal, a *unit* is a separately compilable program structure. The first line of a unit begins with the reserved word `unit` instead of `program`. A unit does not require a begin line, but its last line is always end.

Figure E.1 shows abstract data type `DayADT` (see Fig. 9.5) written as a Turbo Pascal unit. Each unit begins with an interface section, which is followed by an implementation section. The Turbo Pascal reserved words `interface` and `implementation` denote these separate sections. The *interface* section contains declarations for new data types declared in the unit and the procedure or function header for each operator declared in the unit. Each procedure or function header is followed by a comment that describes the operation the module performs and its preconditions and postconditions. The complete procedure and function declarations appear in the implementation section. (To conserve space, we did not write out the actual procedure bodies.)

Figure E.1   Unit DayADT

```
unit DayADT;
{
  Specification of DayADT
    Structure:  Day is an enumerated data type whose values
                represent the days of the week.
}

interface
  type
    Day = (Sunday, Monday, Tuesday, Wednesday,
           Thursday, Friday, Saturday);

  procedure ReadLnDay (var ADay {output} : Day;
                       var ValidDay {output} : Boolean);
  {
  Reads two data characters and stores the value represented by
  the data in ADay.  Sets ValidDay to indicate whether the data are
  valid.
  Pre : None
  Post: ADay is assigned a value if the
        two characters read are SU, MO, TU, WE, TH, FR, or SA;
        otherwise, ADay is undefined.
        ValidDay is set to True if ADay is defined;
        otherwise, ValidDay is set to False.
  Uses: UpCase from unit Utility
  }

  procedure WriteDay (ADay {input} : Day);
  {
  Displays the value of ADay.
```

```
      Pre : ADay is defined.
      Post: Displays a string corresponding to the value of ADay.
      }

implementation
    uses Utility;        {contains function UpCase}

    procedure ReadLnDay (var ADay {output} : Day;
                            var ValidDay {output} : Boolean);
      var
        DayCh1,                          {input – first letter in day}
        DayCh2 : Char;                   {input – second letter in day}

    begin {ReadLnDay}
      .

      .
    end; {ReadLnDay}

    procedure WriteDay (ADay {input} : Day);
    begin {WriteDay}
      .

      .
    end; {WriteDay}
end.   {DayADT}
```

The interface section for unit DayADT contains all the information Turbo Pascal needs to compile a client program that references data type Day or calls operator ReadLnDay or WriteDay. It also contains information a programmer would need to use the unit. The actual implementation of the operators is "hidden" in the implementation section, because the compiler does not need to know those details when it compiles a client program. Similarly, a programmer needs to know only how to call an operator, not how that operator is implemented.

The uses Statement

The uses statement

```
    uses Utility;        {contains function UpCase}
```

indicates that unit DayADT is a client of another unit named Utility, which declares function UpCase (see Fig. 9.4). Similarly, any client of unit DayADT must contain the statement

```
    uses DayADT;
```

A client of both DayADT and Utility needs the statement

```
    uses DayADT, Utility;
```

If the client is a program, the uses statement should follow the program statement. If the client is another unit, the uses statement should come after the interface line or the implementation line of the client. If the client references data type Day in its own interface section, the uses statement must come after the interface line. If the only references to data type Day and operators WriteDay and ReadLnDay appear in the client's implementation section, the uses statement can come after the implementation line.

Compiling Client Programs

Unit DayADT must be saved in a separate file named DayADT.PAS. This file must be compiled before any of its clients and should be compiled to disk. You can accomplish this by changing the destination from memory to disk in the Compile submenu before compiling unit DayADT. Because DayADT uses unit Utility, you must remember to compile unit Utility to disk first. Once DayADT has been compiled, you can compile any client program (or any other unit) that uses it.

When you compile unit DayADT, Turbo Pascal saves its object code in file DayADT.TPU. Prior to running a client program, Turbo Pascal links the client's object code file to the object code files for all the units that the client program uses.

Appendix F
Additional Pascal
Features

This appendix describes additional features of Pascal not covered in the text.

Functions and Procedures as Parameters

A procedure or a function can be passed as a parameter to another procedure or function. For example, say we want to compute the sum below for the integers 1 through N, where f represents a function that is applied to each integer.

$$f(1) + f(2) + f(3) + ... + f(N)$$

If f is the function Sqr (square), then we want to compute the sum

a) $1 + 2^2 + 3^2 + ... + N^2$

If f is the function Sqrt (square root), then we want to compute the sum

b) $\sqrt{1} + \sqrt{2} + \sqrt{3} + ... + \sqrt{N}$

In function SumInt, which follows, the function F is declared as a function parameter. The function designator

```
SumInt(Sqr, 10)
```

computes sum a), above, for N = 10; the function designator

```
SumInt(Sqrt, 10)
```

computes sum b), above, for N = 10.

```
function SumInt (function F(X : Integer) : Real;
                 N : Integer) : Real;
{Computes F(1) + F(2) + . . . + F(N).}
   var
     Sum : Real;                        {the partial sum}
     I : Integer;                       {loop-control variable}
begin {SumInt}
   Sum := 0.0;                          {Initialize Sum.}

   for I := 1 to N do
     Sum := Sum + F(I);

     SumInt := Sum                      {Define result.}
end; {SumInt}
```

The parameter of function F is represented by X (type Integer) in the heading for function SumInt; any identifier may be used. F can also represent a user-defined function with one type Integer parameter.

goto Statements and Labels

The goto statement is used to transfer control from one program statement to another. The label (a positive integer) indicates the statement to which control is transferred. Labels must be declared in label declaration statements at the beginning of a block. In function SameArray, below, the goto statement is used to exit a for loop before the specified number of repetitions (N) are performed.

```
function SAMEARRAY (A, B : RealArray;
                    N : Integer) : Boolean;
{Returns True if arrays A[1..N] and B[1..N] are the same array.}

   label 100;

   var
     I : Integer;                 {loop-control variable}

begin {SameArray}
   SameArray := False;           {Assume arrays are not the same.}

   {Compare elements 1..N until an unequal pair is found.}
   for I := 1 to N do
     if A[I] <> B[I] then
        goto 100;

   {assert: arrays A and B are equal.}
   SameArray := True;

   100: {return from function}
end; {SameArray}
```

The function result is initialized to False, and corresponding array elements are compared in the for loop. If an unequal pair of elements is found, the loop is exited via an immediate transfer of control to label 100. If all pairs are equal, the loop is exited after the Nth pair is tested, and the function result is set to True. This function can easily be implemented without using the goto; computer scientists generally avoid using the goto except when absolutely necessary.

Pack and Unpack

The standard procedures Pack and Unpack are used to transfer data between packed and unpacked arrays. Given the declarations

```
var
  PA : packed array [1..N] of Char;
  UA : array [1..M] of Char;
  I : Integer
```

the procedure call statement

```
Pack (UA, I, PA)
```

copies elements from unpacked array UA (starting with UA[I]) to packed array PA (starting with PA[1]). The procedure (call) statement

```
Unpack (PA, UA, I)
```

copies elements from packed array PA (starting with PA[1]) to unpacked array UA (starting with UA[I]). Arrays PA and UA do not have to be the same size.

Conformant Array Parameters

One of the principal frustrations in using earlier versions of Pascal is that a function or procedure that manipulates an array of one type cannot also manipulate an array of a similar type. For example, a procedure that manipulates array Name declared below cannot manipulate array Flower because the arrays have different types.

```
type
   String1 = packed array [1..20] of Char;
   String2 = packed array [1..8] of Char;

var
   Name : String1;
   Flower : String2;
```

Even though the only difference between these two arrays is their size (number of elements), separate procedures would have to be written to read data into them.

In later versions of Pascal, the *conformant array schema*

```
packed array [U..V : Integer] of Char
```

describes a packed array of characters whose subscript type is a subrange of type Integer. The use of this schema in the following procedure header enables procedure ReadString to read data into a packed array of characters (represented by InString) of any size (represented by Size).

```
procedure ReadString (Size {input} : Integer;
      var InString {output} : packed array [U..V : Integer] of Char);
```

The procedure call statement

```
ReadString (20, Name)
```

could be used to read up to 20 characters into array Name; the procedure call statement

```
ReadString (8, FLOWER)
```

could be used to read up to eight characters into array Flower.

Any identifiers can be used in the declaration of the index-type specification [U..V : Integer] for InString. The data type listed (Integer) must be an ordinal type.

Conformant array schemas can be used with packed and unpacked arrays of any element type, not just Char. Conformant array schemas can also be used with multidimensional arrays. The following two-dimensional conformant array schema is valid if Month is declared as an enumerated type.

```
array [U..V : Integer; J..K : Month] of Real;
```

The corresponding actual parameter must be a two-dimensional array of type Real values. The first subscript type must be a subrange of the integers; the second subscript type must be a subrange of type Month.

Appendix G
Using Turbo Pascal

This appendix describes how to use the Turbo Pascal 6.0 integrated environment on an IBM-compatible personal computer. An *integrated environment* allows you to create, edit, save, compile, run, and debug your programs without having to issue any operating system commands. Turbo Pascal 6.0 is distributed with an interactive tutorial, which you can run by typing `TPTour` after the system prompt.

The Turbo Pascal Menu System

To enter the Turbo Pascal integrated environment, you use the command

```
>Turbo
```

after the system prompt >. Turbo Pascal version 6.0 displays a main menu screen similar to that shown in Fig. G.1. This screen display is organized into three sections. The information displayed in the lines at the top and the bottom of the screen represent tasks that the computer can carry out. The middle area (shown in gray) is the *desktop* area, where you will open the various windows used to create and test your Pascal programs.

Figure G.1 Turbo Pascal 6.0 Main Menu

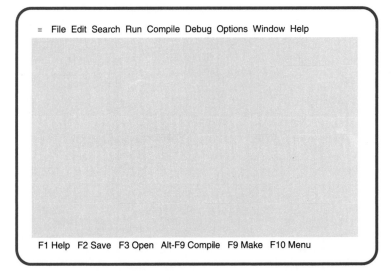

The tasks at the top of the screen are part of Turbo Pascal's *Main menu bar*. You can select any one of these Main menu tasks by pressing and holding the Alt key and then pressing the first letter of the task name (for example, Alt-F for File). You can also select a task by first pressing the F10 key and moving the highlight bar over that task (using the left or right arrow key) and then pressing the Enter key. If your computer has a mouse, you can select a Main menu item by positioning the mouse cursor on the Main menu item and then clicking (pressing) the left mouse button. If you are using a mouse, you do not need to press the F10 key before selecting a Main menu item.

The list of tasks displayed at the bottom of the screen will change as you move from one portion of the Turbo Pascal environment to another. To select a task, press the indicated function key (F1 through F10) on the keyboard. For example, in the Main menu screen (or any screen), to display the Help screen relevant to your current situation within the Turbo Pascal environment, press function key F1. The Help screen provides a description of your current menu screen and its options. Press Esc (Escape) to exit the Help screen and return to your current screen.

Creating a New Program

To create a new Pascal program, you must begin with an empty Edit window on the desktop. Turbo Pascal 6.0 automatically places you in an Edit window called NONAME00.PAS when you enter the environment. However, if you wish to open a new window yourself, select the New option from the File menu, as shown in Fig. G.2. You can do this by typing the letter N, by moving the highlight bar over the word New (using the up and down arrow keys), or by using a mouse.

Once Turbo Pascal places you in the Edit window, you can begin entering your program one line at a time. Press the Enter key after you type each program line. Use the arrow keys to position the cursor (the blinking line on the computer's screen) anywhere on the screen. You can correct typing errors by pressing the backspace key to

Figure G.2   Turbo Pascal File Menu

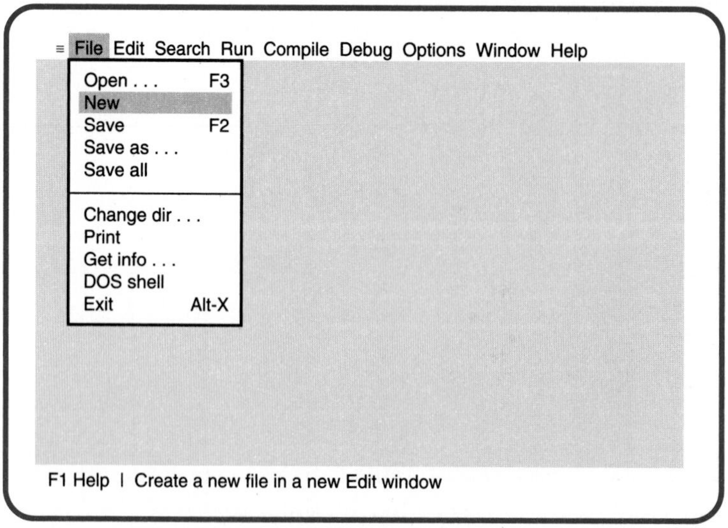

erase all characters from the current cursor position back to the incorrect character. Then you can enter the correct letters in their place. Figure G.3 shows a complete (but incorrect) program in the Edit window NONAME00.PAS.

Figure G.3 Incorrect Program Hello

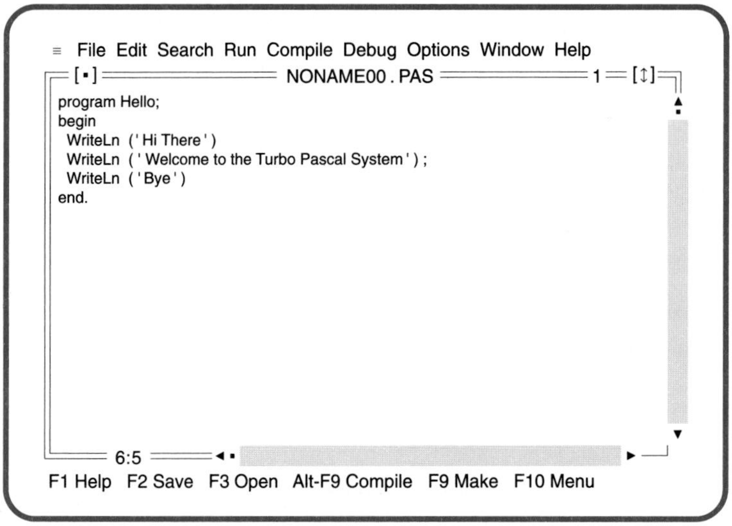

```
 ≡  File  Edit  Search  Run  Compile  Debug  Options  Window  Help
┌─[•]══════════════ NONAME00.PAS ═══════════1═[↕]─┐
│ program Hello;                                           ▲ │
│ begin                                                    ▪ │
│  WriteLn ('Hi There')                                    ▪ │
│  WriteLn ('Welcome to the Turbo Pascal System');           │
│  WriteLn ('Bye')                                           │
│ end.                                                       │
│                                                            │
│                                                            │
│                                                            │
│                                                            │
│                                                            │
│                                                            │
│                                                          ▼ │
│══════ 6:5 ═════◄▪▓▓▓▓▓▓▓▓▓▓▓▓▓▓▓▓▓▓▓▓▓▓▓▓▓▓▓►─┘
   F1 Help  F2 Save  F3 Open  Alt-F9 Compile  F9 Make  F10 Menu
```

After your program is complete, save your program on the disk by pressing the F2 key (Save). Up until this point, your program has been assigned the name NONAME00.PAS by Turbo Pascal. Before saving your program with this name, Turbo Pascal gives you a chance to use a more meaningful name. For example, if you want to use the name FIRST, enter the name FIRST.PAS when prompted by Turbo Pascal, as shown in Fig. G.4. MS-DOS file names may be any combination of eight or fewer letters, digits, or some special characters (no periods or spaces allowed). The .PAS is an extension signifying to Turbo Pascal that this file contains Pascal source code. Now you are ready to exit the Edit window and return to the Main menu (by pressing the F10 key).

Compiling and Running a Program

To compile a program, select the Compile menu from the Main menu bar. Figure G.5 shows the choices contained in the Compile menu. Since you wish to compile your program, select the Compile option. Turbo Pascal begins to compile the program displayed in the Edit window.

When we attempt to compile the program shown in Fig. G.3, Turbo Pascal displays the syntax error message

```
Error 85: ";" expected
```

and returns us to the Edit window. The cursor is positioned at the point in the program where the compilation process stopped (at WriteLn in the fourth line). Error 85 explains

Figure G.4   Saving Program as FIRST.PAS

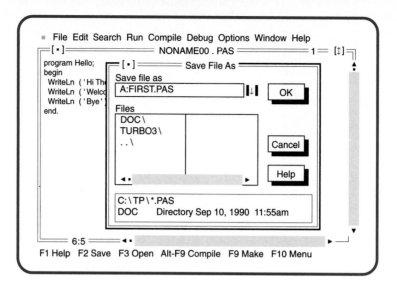

Figure G.5   Turbo Pascal Compile Menu

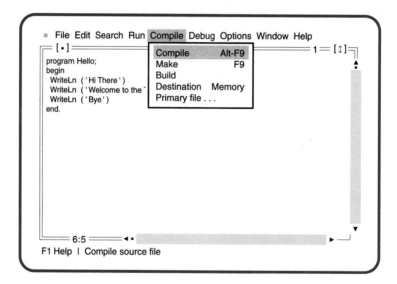

that you forgot to add a semicolon to the end of the third line of program text. Change the line to

```
WriteLn ('Hi There');
```

and save the revised program to disk by pressing the F2 key. Then exit the Edit window and return to the Main menu by pressing the F10 key. From the Main menu, select the Compile menu again and then select the Compile option. This time there are no errors in the program, and a *compilation status window* containing the message `Compile suc-cessful: Press any key` is displayed. Press a key on the keyboard.

To run the program from the Main menu, after it has been compiled, select the Run menu. Figure G.6 shows the choices contained in the Run menu. Since you want to run the program, select the Run option. Turbo Pascal begins executing the program. The main menu screen display is replaced briefly by a *user screen* containing the program output

```
Hi There
Welcome to the Turbo Pascal System
Bye
```

and then the Main menu display returns. To review your program output, type Alt-F5 (i.e., press and hold down the Alt key while pressing the F5 key). The user screen containing the program output reappears and remains visible until you press any key on the keyboard, which returns you to the Main menu screen.

Figure G.6   Turbo Pascal Run Menu

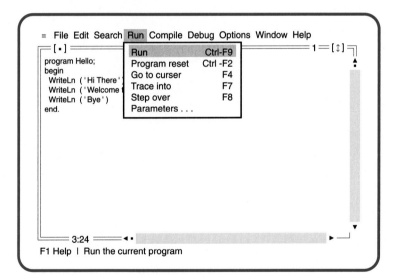

Loading a File

To load a previously saved file into an Edit window, you must get Turbo Pascal to display an Open a File dialog box (see Fig. G.7). You can do this either through the File menu (select option Open) or by pressing function key F3. When the dialog box appears, either type the name of the file into the bar with label Name or select the file name from the list shown under the label Files. If you do not have a mouse, press the Tab key to access the list of files; next, use the up and down arrow keys to select the desired file.

Figure G.7 Loading Program FIRST.PAS from Disk A

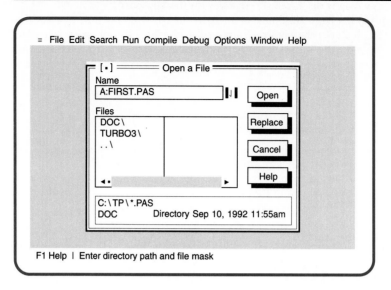

Exiting Turbo Pascal

The File menu Exit option lets you leave Turbo Pascal and return to the operating system. If you choose the Exit option and have made changes to your program in the Edit window but have forgotten to save your revised program, Turbo Pascal gives you one last chance to do so.

Appendix H
Reference Guide to
Pascal Constructs

Construct	Page	Example of Use
program heading	37	`program Guide (Input, Output, Infile, Outfile);`
comment	49	`{`
		`This program shows examples of`
		`Pascal constructs.`
		`}`
constant declaration	37	`const`
integer	51	`StringLength = 20;`
character	60	`Blank = ' ';`
string	297	`School = 'Temple University';`
real	51	`DeansList = 3.5;`
		`Probation = 1.0;`
type declaration		`type`
subrange	314	`StudentIndex = 1..100;`
		`StringIndex = 1..StringLength;`
enumerated	318	`College = (Business, Arts, Science, General);`
string	457	`StringType = packed array [StringIndex] of Char;`
record	487	`StuData = record`
		`Name : StringType;`
		`GPA : Real;`
		`InCollege : College`
		`end; {StuData}`
pointer	749	`ClassPointer = ^Student;`
list node	750	`Student = record`
		`Info : StuData;` `{data field}`
		`Next : ClassPointer` `{pointer}`
		`end; {Student}`
array	425	`MajorArray = array [StudentIndex] of College;`
file	669	`StuFile = file of StuData;`
set	621	`GradeSet = set of 'A'..'Z';`
variable declaration	37	`var`
record	487	`CurStu : StuData;` `{input – student data}`
set	621	`Grades : GradeSet;` `{allowable grades}`
text file	352	`InFile : Text;` `{input – text file}`
binary file	669	`OutFile : StuFile;` `{output – binary file}`
pointer	749	`ClassList : ClassPointer;` `{list of classes}`

Construct	Page	Example of Use
array	425	`Major : MajorArray;` `{array of majors}`
character	60	`NextCh : Char;` `{input - character}`
integer	51	`CountProb : Integer;` `{counter}`
function declaration	234	`function Member (NextCh : Char;`
formal parameters		`                  TestSet : GradeSet) : Boolean;`
		`{Returns True only if NextCh in TestSet}`
		`begin {Member}`
Boolean assignment	127	`  Member := NextCh in TestSet`
set operator in	307	
		`end; {Member}`
procedure declaration	252	`procedure PrintSet (InSet : GradeSet);`
		`{Displays set InSet}`
local variable	98	`  var`
		`    NextCh : Char; {loop control variable}`
		`begin {PrintSet}`
for statement	199	`  for NextCh := 'A' to 'Z' do`
if statement	131	`    if Member(NextCh, InSet) then`
function designator	106	
Write procedure	45	`      Write (NextCh);`
WriteLn procedure	45	`  WriteLn`
end of procedure	98	`end; {PrintSet}`
program body	47	`begin {Guide}`
WriteLn procedure	45	`  WriteLn ('Registration for ', School);`
assignment	40	`  CountProb := 0;` `{initialize counter}`
with statement	490	`  with CurStu do`
compound statement	92	`    begin` `{define fields of CurStu}`
string assignment	456	`      Name := 'Jackson, Michael Bad';`
display prompt	45	`      Write ('Enter GPA> ');`
ReadLn procedure	43	`      ReadLn (GPA);`
enumerated assign	319	`      InCollege := Arts;`
pointer assign	751	`      NextStu := nil`
		`    end; {with}`
case statement with	165	`case CurStu.InCollege of`
field selector as	488	`  Business : WriteLn ('Business major');`
case selector		`  Arts     : WriteLn ('Arts major');`
		`  Science  : WriteLn ('Science major');`
		`  General  : WriteLn ('General major')`
		`end; {case}`
nested if	156	`if CurStu.GPA > DeansList then`
embedded apostrophe	72	`  WriteLn ('  On the Dean''s List')`
		`else if CurStu.GPA > Probation then`
		`  WriteLn ('Satisfactory progress')`
		`else`
		`  begin`
format a string	65	`    WriteLn ('On Probation' :21);`
increment counter	178	`    CountProb := CountProb + 1`
		`  end; {nested if}`

Construct	Page	Example of Use	
array element assign	423	`Major[1] := CurStu.InCollege;`	{save in array}
set assign	622	`Grades := ['A'..'F', 'I', 'W'];`	
set union	622	`Grades := Grades + ['P', 'W'];`	
procedure call	252	`PrintSet (Grades);`	
print a set	627		
open input file	354	`Reset (InFile);`	
repeat statement	203	`repeat`	
file read	360	`  Read (InFile, NextCh);`	{get character}
function designator	235	`  if Member(NextCh, Grades) then`	
		`    WriteLn ('Valid grade')`	
end of line test	351	`until EOLN(InFile);`	
ReadLn with text file	360	`ReadLn (InFile);`	{skip end of line}
while statement	178	`while not EOF(InFile) do`	
end of file test	352	`  begin`	
file read	360	`    Read (InFile, NextCh);`	
echo print	67	`    Write (NextCh)`	
		`  end; {while}`	
open output file	692	`Rewrite (OutFile);`	
file buffer assign	691	`OutFile^ := CurStu;`	{save in file buffer}
Put procedure	692	`Put (OutFile);`	{write buffer to file}
Write to binary file	670	`Write (OutFile, CurStu);`	{write second copy}
Reset binary file	690	`Reset (OutFile);`	
compare strings in		`if OutFile^.Name <> CurStu.Name then`	
buffer and record	461	`  WriteLn ('File I/O error');`	
Get procedure	690	`Get (OutFile);`	{get second copy}
New procedure	749	`New (ClassList);`	{allocate list node}
assign node data	762	`ClassList^.Info := CurStu;`	
allocate second node	762	`New (ClassList^.Next);`	{connect nodes}
assign second node	762	`ClassList^.Next^.Info := OutFile^;`	
list traversal	759	`while ClassList <> nil do`	
		`  begin`	
display node data	754	`    WriteLn (ClassList^.Info.Name);`	
advance pointer	761	`    ClassList := ClassList^.Next`	
		`  end {while}`	
program end	47	`end. {Guide}`	

Answers to Selected Self-Check Exercises

Chapter 1

Section 1.2

1. Contents: −27.2, 75.62
   Memory cells: 998, 2

Section 1.5

1. Add A, B, and C. Store result in X.
   Divide Y by Z. Store result in X.
   Subtract B from C and then add A. Store result in D.
   Add 1 to X. Store result in X.
3. assembly language; machine language

Section 1.6

1. A compiler attempts to translate a source file into machine language. If there are syntax errors, the compiler generates error messages. If there are no errors, it creates an object file. Syntax errors occur when statements do not follow exactly the syntax rules of a language. Syntax errors are found in the source file.

Chapter 2

Section 2.1

1. requirements specification, analysis, design, implementation, testing

Section 2.2

1. It is not a good idea to use a standard identifier as the name of a memory cell because the identifier then cannot be used for its intended purpose.
   The compiler does not allow the use of reserved words as memory cell names.

Section 2.3

1. Because the value of Pi will not change during program execution
3. Reserved words: end, program, begin, const
   Standard identifiers: ReadLn
   Valid identifiers: Bill, Rate, Start, XYZ123, ThisIsALongOne
   Invalid identifiers: Sue's, 123XYZ, Y=Z, Prog#2, 'MaxScores'

Section 2.4

1. Enter two integers:
   M = 10
   N = 21

3. Before execution After execution

Section 2.5

1. The brackets are mismatched. The second example has an embedded comment, which is not allowed in standard Pascal.

3.
```
program Small (Input, Output);
  var
    X, Y, Z : Real;

begin
  Y := 15.0;
  Z := -Y + 3.5;
  X := Y + Z;
  WriteLn (X, Y, Z)
end.
```

The first statement says that the name of the program is Small and that it uses the standard files Input and Output. The reserved word var indicates the start of the variable declarations. The next line declares and reserves space in memory for three variables (X, Y, Z) of type Real. The begin line indicates that executable code follows. The first assignment statement sets the variable Y to the value 15.0. The next statement sets the variable Z to minus the value of Y plus 3.5, which is -11.5. The next statement sets the variable X to the sum of Y and Z, which is 3.5. The next statement prints the values of X, Y, and Z (3.5, 15.0, and -11.5, respectively). The last line indicates the program end.

Section 2.6

1. 15, Integer   'XYZ', Invalid   '*', Char
   $, Invalid   25.123, Real   15., Invalid
   -999, Integer   .123, Invalid   'x', Char
   "X", Invalid   '9', Char   '-5', Invalid
   True, Boolean   'True', Invalid

3. a. 3   b. -3   c. invalid—Real operand
                                                      used with mod

   d. -3.14159   e. invalid—assignment of f. 0.75
                             Real expression to
                             Integer variable

g. invalid—Real operand used with mod h. invalid—division by 0 i. invalid—A mod –10 is undefined

j. 3 k. –3.0 l. invalid—assignment of Real expression to Integer variable

m. invalid—Real operand used with div n. 0 o. 1

p. invalid—division by 0 q. 3

5. a. White is 1.6666.... b. Green is 0.6666.... c. Orange is 0.
   d. Blue is –3.0. e. Lime is 2. f. Purple is 0.6666....

Section 2.7

1. #–99#Bottles
   #–99##–99.00

3.   –15.5640
       –15.564
        –15.56
         –15.6
           –16
     –1.6E+01

Section 2.8

1. WriteLn statements used to display prompts are placed before the ReadLn statements and are used in interactive programs. WriteLn statements that echo data are placed after the ReadLn statements and are used in batch programs.

Chapter 3

Section 3.1

1. Inputs: Hours : Real {number of hours worked}
           Rate : Real {hourly rate of pay}
   Output: Gross : Real {gross salary}
   Algorithm:
      1. Read hours worked and rate of pay.
      2. Compute gross salary.
      3. Print the gross salary.

Section 3.2

1. The algorithm needs to read separately the number of hours to be paid at the normal hourly rate (RegHours) and hours to be paid at overtime rate (OTHours); the formula used to compute gross salary would also need to be modified.

Section 3.3

1. to allow one or more algorithm steps to be executed several times during a single run of the program

Section 3.4

1.

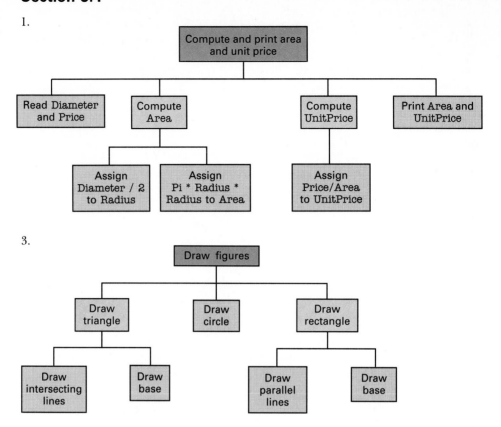

3.

Section 3.5

1. Executing this program would display the message HI MOM vertically with three blank lines between words (first H, then I, and so on)

Section 3.6

1. Displaying user instructions is an example of a subproblem whose detailed implementation should be deferred until the main program is complete. Also, this step is not part of the algorithm for solving the original problem.

Section 3.7

1. Procedure parameters are used to pass information between the separate modules of a program and between the main program and its modules. Parameters make it easier for a procedure to be used by many different calling procedures, or other programs. Procedures with parameters are building blocks for constructing larger programs.

Section 3.8

1. a. `Sqrt(U + V) * Sqr(W)`
   b. `Y * Ln(X)`
   c. `Sqrt(Sqr(X − Y))`
   d. `Abs((X * Y) − (W / Z))`

Chapter 4

Section 4.1

1. true, false, true, true
3.

Section 4.2

1. a. never   b. O.K.

Section 4.3

1. A23B, A1c

Section 4.4

1. ```
If X > Y then
   begin
     X := X + 10.0;
     WriteLn ('X Bigger')
   end
else
   WriteLn ('X Smaller');
WriteLn ('Y is ', Y)
```

3. Y would only be printed when X is not greater than Y.
5. The if statement, expression, simple expression, term, factor, variable, statement, and assignment statement syntax diagrams would be used to validate this if statement.
```

Section 4.5

1.

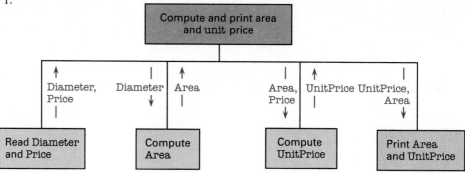

Area is not used by subproblem "Read Diameter and Price," Area is produced as an output from "Compute Area," and Area is used as an input by subproblems "Compute UnitPrice" and "Print Area and UnitPrice."

Section 4.6

1.

a. Case 1 (Both conditions are True. Data: MUD)

Program Statement	Ch1 ?	Ch2 ?	Ch3 ?	AlphaFirst ?	Effect
Write ('Enter three . . .')					Prints prompt.
ReadLn (Ch1, Ch2, Ch3)	M	U	D		Reads data.
if Ch1 < Ch2 then					Is 'M' < 'U'? Value is True.
AlphaFirst := Ch1				M	'M' is first so far.
if Ch3 < AlphaFirst then					Is 'D' < 'M'? Value is True.
AlphaFirst := Ch3				D	'D' is first.
WriteLn (AlphaFirst . . .)					Prints D is the first letter . . ..

b. Case 2 (First condition is True, second is False. Data: COT)

Program Statement	Ch1 ?	Ch2 ?	Ch3 ?	AlphaFirst ?	Effect
Write ('Enter three . . .')					Prints prompt.
ReadLn (Ch1, Ch2, Ch3)	C	O	T		Reads data.
if Ch1 < Ch2 then					Is 'C' < 'O'? Value is True.
AlphaFirst := Ch1				C	'C' is first so far.
if Ch3 < AlphaFirst then					Is 'T' < 'C'? Value is False.

Program Statement	Ch1 ?	Ch2 ?	Ch3 ?	AlphaFirst ?	Effect
WriteLn (AlphaFirst . . .					Prints C is the first letter . . ..

c. Case 3 (Both conditions are False. Data: TOP)

Program Statement	Ch1 ?	Ch2 ?	Ch3 ?	AlphaFirst ?	Effect
Write ('Enter three . . .')					Prints prompt.
ReadLn (Ch1, Ch2, Ch3)	T	0	P		Reads data.
if Ch1 < Ch2 then					Is 'T' < '0'? Value is False.
AlphaFirst := Ch2				0	'0' is first so far.
if Ch3 < AlphaFirst then					Is 'P' < '0'? Value is False.
WriteLn (AlphaFirst . . .					Prints 0 is the first letter . . ..

Both conditions evaluate to False if all three letters are the same.

3. a. (Hours = 30.0, Rate = 5.00)

Program Statement	Hours ?	Rate ?	Gross ?	Net ?	Effect
WriteLn ('This program...')					Print
WriteLn ('A tax amount...')					instructions.
Write ('Hours worked')					Print prompt.
ReadLn (Hours)	30.0				Read Hours.
Write ('Hourly rate')					Print prompt.
ReadLn (Rate)		5.00			Read Rate.
Gross := Hours * Rate			150.0		Gross is 150.
if Gross > TaxBracket then					Is 150 > 125? Value is True.
Net := Gross − Tax				125.0	Net is 125.
WriteLn ('Gross salary...')					Print 150.00.
WriteLn ('Net salary...')					Print 125.00.

b. (Hours = 20.0, Rate = 4.00)

Program Statement	Hours ?	Rate ?	Gross ?	Net ?	Effect
WriteLn ('This program...')					Print
WriteLn ('A tax amount...')					instructions.
Write ('Hours worked')					Print prompt.

Program Statement	Hours ?	Rate ?	Gross ?	Net ?	Effect
ReadLn (Hours)	20.0				Read Hours.
Write ('Hourly rate')					Print prompt.
ReadLn (Rate)		4.00			Read Rate.
Gross := Hours * Rate			80.0		Gross is 80.
if Gross > TaxBracket then					Is 80 > 125?
					Value is False.
Net := Gross				80.0	Net is 80.
WriteLn ('Gross salary...')					Print 80.00.
WriteLn ('Net salary...')					Print 80.00.

Section 4.7

1.

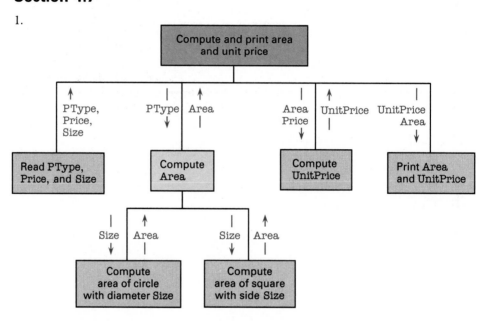

Section 4.8

1.

Statement Part	Salary	Tax	Effect
	13500.00	?	
if Salary < 0.0			13500.00 < 0.00 is False.
else if Salary < 1500.00			13500.00 < 1500.00 is False.
else if Salary < 3000.00			13500.00 < 3000.00 is False.
else if Salary < 5000.00			13500.00 < 5000.00 is False.

Statement Part	Salary	Tax	Effect
else if Salary < 8000.00			13500.00 < 8000.00 is False.
else if Salary <= 15000.00			13500.00 <= 15000.00 is True.
Tax := (Salary − 8000.00)			Evaluates to 5500.00.
* 0.25			Evaluates to 1375.00.
+ 1425.00		2800.00	Tax is 2800.00.

3. a. True with and without short-circuit evaluation.
   b. True with short-circuit evaluation—a division by zero error results without short-circuit evaluation.

Section 4.9

1. ```
if X > Y then
   WriteLn ('X greater')
else
   WriteLn ('Y greater or equal')
```

3. Standard Pascal requires that every possible value of the selector variable must appear as a case label; guarding a case statement prevents a case expression out of range error during program execution and allows the programmer to take corrective actions.

# Chapter 5

## Section 5.1

1. The loop will be executed three times.
   Output: 9
         81
         6561
3. The loop will execute forever if the last statement in the loop body is omitted.

## Section 5.2

1. 5
   25
   125
   625
3. Current output on most systems would display the prompt

   ```
   Next number>
   ```

   read a value for NextNum, and then halt with a run-time error at the statement

   ```
   Sum := Sum + NextNum;
   ```

   since Sum does not have an initial value.
   ```

Corrected program segment:

```
Sum := 0.0;
Count := 0;
while Count <= 5 do
  begin
    Count := Count + 1;
    Write ('Next number> ');
    ReadLn (NextNum);
    Sum := Sum + NextNum
  end;
WriteLn (Count :1, ' numbers were added;');
WriteLn ('their sum is ', Sum :4:2);
```

Section 5.3

1. 0

3. a. Output with data value of 9.45:

```
Enter the initial distance between the worm and apple in inches > 9.45
The distance is 9.45
The distance is 5.95

The last distance before the worm enters the apple is 2.45
```

b. Output with data value of 9.45 and the order of statements in the loop body reversed;

```
Enter the initial distance between the worm and apple in inches > 9.45
The distance is 5.95
The distance is 2.45

The last distance before the worm enters the apple is 2.45
```

Section 5.4

1. This problem is similar to the example in the text. Because the first power of n that is to be displayed is for Power = 0, the initial value of Power should be 1.

Section 5.5

1. ───────────────────────────────────────

a. **Program Statement**	I	J	**Effect**
	?	?	
J := 10		10	Set J to 10.
for I := 1 to 5 do	1		Initialize I to 1.
WriteLn (I, J)			Display 1 and 10.
J := J - 2		8	Assign 10 - 2 to J.
increment and test I	2		2 <= 5 is True.
WriteLn (I, J)			Display 2 and 8.
J := J - 2		6	Assign 8 - 2 to J.

Program Statement	I ?	J ?	Effect
increment and test I	3		3 <= 5 is True.
WriteLn (I, J)			Display 3 and 6.
J := J − 2		4	Assign 6 − 2 to J.
increment and test I	4		4 <= 5 is True.
WriteLn (I, J)			Display 4 and 4.
J := J − 2		2	Assign 4 − 2 to J.
increment and test I	5		5 <= 5 is True.
WriteLn (I, J)			Display 5 and 2.
J := J − 2		0	Assign 2 − 2 to J.
increment and test I	?		Exit loop.

b.
```
J := 10;
for I := 0 to 4 do
   begin
      WriteLn (I + 1, J);
      J := J − 2
   end; {for}
```

3. a. `for Celsius := −10 to 10 do`
   b. `for Celsius := 100 downto 1 do`
   c. `for Celsius := 15 to 50 do`
   d. `for Celsius := 50 downto −75 do`

Section 5.6

1. Output: 10
   20
   30
   40
   50
   60
   70
   80
   90
   100

```
{done as a for statement}
Num := 10;
for Count := 1 to 10 do
   begin
      WriteLn (Num);
      Num := Num + 10
   end;

{done as a repeat statement}
Num := 10;
repeat
   WriteLn (Num);
   Num := Num + 10
until Num > 10;
```

3. A repeat-until loop may be used instead of a while loop when the loop body must be executed at least one time.

Section 5.7

1. a.
```
*
**
***
****
*****
```

   b.
```
***
***
***
***
***
```

Section 5.8

1.
```
Count := 0;
while Count <= N do
  begin
    WriteLn ('Count = ', Count :1);
    Sum := Sum + Count;
    Count := Count + 1;
    WriteLn ('Sum = ', Sum :1)
  end;
```

Chapter 6

Section 6.1

1. Parameters allow information to be exchanged between a procedure and its caller.

3. a.
```
Pre : N contains some initial integer value.
Post: The value of N cubed is displayed.
```

   b.
```
Pre : X and Y contain initial values.
Post: Displays absolute value of the difference of X and Y.
```

Section 6.2

1. a.

b.

Program Statement	Char1	Char2	Result	Effect
	E	A	?	
if Char1 < Char2				Is 'E' < 'A'? Value is False.
GetFirst := Char2			A	Return A as smaller value.

3. Function squares its arguments and returns their sum as its value.

```
C := Hypot(A, B);
```

Section 6.3

1.

Program Statement	ChangeDenom	ChangeNeeded	NumUnits	Effect
	5.0	5.56	?	
NumUnits := Trunc(ChangeNeeded/ChangeDenom)			1	Set NumUnits to 1.
ChangeNeeded := ChangeNeeded − (NumUnits * ChangeDenom)		0.56		Set ChangeNeeded to 0.56.

3. a. Case 1 (Num1 = 8.0, Num2 = 10.0, Num3 = 6.0)

Program Statement	X	Y	Temp	Effect
Order (Num3, Num2) if X > Y then	6.0	10.0	?	Call Order. Is 6.0 > 10.0? Value is False.
Order (Num3, Num1) if X > Y then	6.0	8.0	?	Call Order. Is 6.0 > 8.0? Value is False.
Order (Num2, Num1) if X > Y then	10.0	8.0	?	Call Order. Is 10.0 > 8.0? Value is True.
Temp := X			10.0	Set Temp to 10.0.
X := Y	8.0			Set X(Num2) to 8.0.
Y := Temp		10.0		Set Y(Num1) to 10.0.

b. Effect of this sequence of calls is arrange the values stored in Num1, Num2, and Num3 from largest to smallest.

5. a procedure, because the module must return two output values

Section 6.4

1.

Actual Parameter	Formal Parameter	Description
M	A	Integer, value
MaxInt	B	Integer, value

Actual Parameter	Formal Parameter	Description
Y	C	Real, variable
X	D	Real, variable
Next	E	Char, variable
35	A	Integer, value
M * 10	B	Integer, value
Y	C	Real, variable
X	D	Real, variable
Next	E	Char, variable

3. a. Type Real of Z does not correspond to type Integer of formal parameter X.
   b. Procedure call is correct.
   c. Procedure call is correct.
   d. Type Integer of M does not correspond to type Real of formal parameter A.
   e. 25.0 and 15.0 cannot correspond to variable parameters.
   f. Procedure call is correct.
   g. Parameter names A and B have not been declared in the main program.
   h. Procedure call is correct.
   i. Expressions (X + Y) and (Y − Z) may not correspond to a variable parameter.
   j. Type Real of actual parameter X does not correspond with type Integer of formal parameter X.
   k. Four actual parameters are one too many for three formal parameters.
   l. Procedure call is correct.

Section 6.5

1. FindSum contains calls to ReadLn and Write.
3. Main program data area   PrintSumAve data area

Section 6.6

1. A procedure might be nested inside another to restrict its visibility, so that the only way the nested procedure can be called is from the outer procedure (which should make sure that the nested procedure's preconditions are satisfied before calling it).

Section 6.7

1. The scope of variable N declared in Outer is procedure Outer. The main program body and the procedure Too are not included in the scope of N. Inner is excluded because N is declared as a local variable in Inner.

3. a. Parameter X is set to 5.5; global variable Y is set to 6.6; local variables M and N are set to 2 and 3, respectively; and identifier O is undeclared.
   b. Global variables X and Y are set to 5.5 and 6.6, respectively; identifiers M, N, and O are undeclared.
   c. Global variables X and Y are set to 5.5 and 6.6, respectively; identifiers M, N, and O are undeclared.

Section 6.8

1. Data requirements for DisplayTran:

   Input Parameters
   ```
   TranType : Char        {transaction type}
   Amount : Real          {amount of transaction}
   CurBal : Real          {current balance}
   ```

   Algorithm
   ```
   case TranType of
      'C': display Amount of check and CurBal;
           check for overdraft.
      'D': display Amount of deposit and CurBal.
      'Q': do nothing.
   end
   ```

3. because the precondition for DisplayTran states that it is not appropriate to pass any values for TranType except one of the valid case labels; 'C', 'D', or 'Q'

Section 6.10

1. Mystery(4, 3) → 4 * Mystery(4, 2) → 4 * (4 * Mystery(4, 1))
   → 4 * (4 * (4)) = 64
   Mystery computes the value of M^N.

Chapter 7

Section 7.1

1. Valid constants: MinInt = −MaxInt;
   MaxLetter = 'Z';
   MaxSize = 50;

Section 7.2

1. A cancellation error might occur when a very large number is added to a very small number and the resulting sum contains more significant digits than the computer can store. Representational errors result when the computer cannot represent a number exactly (e.g., the decimal fraction 0.1 is a repeating fraction using base 2 representation).

Section 7.3

1. a. (X > Y) or (X = 15)
   b. ((X > Y) or (X = 15)) and (Z <> 7.5)
   c. (X = 15) and ((Z <> 7.5) or (X > Y))
   d. not Flag and (X <> 15.7)
   e. Flag or (X > 8)

Section 7.4

1. a. valid: 1, 2, 3, 4, 5
   b. valid: '1', '2', '3', '4', '5'
   c. invalid: mixed types
   d. valid: '1', '3', 'A', 'B', 'C'
3. [',', ';', '.', '''', ':', '=', '<', '>', '+', '-', '/',
   '*', '^', '(', ')', '[', ']']

Section 7.5

1. a. 1   b. False   c. True   d. 1
3. Ch := 'A';
   while Ch <= 'Z' do
     begin
       WriteLn (Ch, Ord(Ch));
       Ch := Succ(Ch)
     end;

Section 7.6

1. invalid subranges: e, f, g, h, i, j

Section 7.7

1. a. no constraints   e. not valid, Real result
   b. no way to avoid error   f. J > 0
   c. no constraints   g. not valid, Real expression
   d. J > 0

Section 7.8

1. a. 1   e. Thursday   h. True
   b. 4   f. Friday   i. undefined
   c. False   g. Wednesday   j. 6
   d. Thursday

Section 7.9

1. Output with Epsilon = 0.00001:

   Initial guess for a root > 0.0
   The approximate root is 9.9999237061E-01
   The function value is 5.8207660913E-11
   18 guesses made

Section 8.1

1. The value computed for Count would be the same, even though the period at the end is now processed as data; only blanks are counted in the new loop.

Section 8.2

1. Writing program output to a file allows it to be inspected after the program terminates, to be used as input by another program, or to be sent to the printer if a hard copy is desired.

Section 8.3

	X	N	C
1. a.	3.145	123	'3'
b.	3.145	123	' '
c.	3.145	123	'X'
d.	?	123	'3'
e.	123.0	5	'3'
f.	3.145	23	'3'
g.	3.145	35	'3'
h.	3.145	35	'Z'
i.	3.145	123	'Z'

Section 8.4

1. a. Trailing blanks after a name would be copied as part of the employee's name by procedure CopyLine and would not be encountered by the ReadLn statement in procedure ProcessEmp. Trailing blanks after a value read into Rate would cause CopyLine to read a blank name and would cause the error described next.
   b. Blank lines processed by CopyLine would have the effect of having no name printed if encountered by CopyLine and would potentially cause a runtime error if encountered by the ReadLn statement in ProcessEmp (if a name data line were encountered while looking for a numeric data value to read).

Section 8.5

1. EOLN(StuData) is used as part of an if statement to signal an improperly terminated name line in IOName or an improperly terminated course line in IOCourse; in Do-OneStudent, it is used as part of the while loop condition to process all course data for one student from a single data line.

Chapter 9

Section 9.1

1. The systems analyst interacts with program users to determine the specifications for software that will meet the users' needs. The librarian interacts with the members of the programming team to monitor the status and the location of each module during the software development process.

Section 9.2

1. The six phases of the software life cycle are (1) requirements specification, (2) analysis, (3) design, (4) implementation, (5) testing and validation, and (6) operation and maintenance.

    The last phase, operation and maintenance, lasts the longest.

Section 9.3

1. The procedure's physical location in the computing system must be known, along with a precise description of its interface.

Section 9.4

1. a. type Real operators: +, −, *, /, <=, <, =, <>, >, >=, :=
    standard functions: Abs, Exp, Ln, Sqr, Sqrt, Round, Trunc,
    Arctan, Sin, Cos
    b. type Integer operators: +, −, *, /, div, mod, <=, <, =, <>, >,
    >=, :=
    standard functions: Abs, Sqr, Sqrt, Chr, Ord, Succ, Pred
    c. type Char operators: <=, <, =, <>, >, >=, :=
    standard functions: Ord, Succ, Pred
    d. type Boolean operators: not, and, or, <=, <, =, <>, >, >=,
    :=
    standard functions: Ord, Succ, Pred

Section 9.5

1. In standard Pascal, an ADT specification section might be a long comment that contains a description of the structure of the data type and its operator interfaces. The ADT implementation section would consist of the type and the procedure declarations that must be imported by a client program using the ADT.

Section 9.6

1. Test data used during white box testing are designed to exercise every logic path within a given code segment or procedure. A procedure interface error would not be discovered until after the procedure has become part of a larger module or complete program and has been called at least once.

Section 9.7

1. a. {invariant:
        InRange = False and no N has been read satisfying
        the condition MinN <= N <= MaxN.
    }

    Use the following assertion after the while loop:

        {assert:
            MinN <= N <= MaxN or
            MinN > MaxN and N is not defined.
        }

b. Add the following assertion after the `if-then-else` statement:

```
{assert:
    MinN <= MaxN and an in-range value for N has not been
    entered; or MinN > MaxN and it is not possible to
    enter a value of N in the interval MinN..MaxN.
}
```

3. ```
{invariant:
    T during pass i is equal to DeltaT * (i - 1), for i > 1
    and Height is equal to Tower - 0.5 * G * Sqr(T)
}
```

```
{assert: Height <= 0.0 }
```

Chapter 10

Section 10.1

1. `X3` is a simple variable, whereas `X[3]` refers to the third element of the array named X.

3. a. ```
type
    RealArray = array [Boolean] of Real;
var
    N : RealArray;
```

b. ```
type
    IntArray = array ['A'..'F'] of Integer;

var
    N : IntArray;
```

c. ```
type
    BoolArray = array [Char] of Boolean;

var
    Flags : BoolArray;
```

d. Invalid array

e. ```
type
    RealArray = array [Char] of Real;

var
    X : RealArray;
```

f. Invalid array

g. ```
type
    Day = (Sun, Mon, Tues, Wed, Thurs, Fri, Sat);
    RealArray = array [Day] of Real;

var
    Y : RealArray;
```

Section 10.2

1. No
3. a. `X[3] := 7.0;`
   b. `X[1] := X[5];`
   c. `X[5] := X[4] - X[1];`
   d. `X[6] := X[6] + 2;`
   e.
   ```
   Sum := 0;
   for I := 1 to 5 do
     Sum := Sum + X[I];
   ```

   f.
   ```
   for I := 1 to 6 do
     AnswerArray[I] := X[I] * 2;
   ```

   g.
   ```
   I := 2;
   while I <= 8 do
     begin
       Write (X[I] :8);
       I := I + 2
     end; {while}
   ```

Section 10.3

1. The user will be continually prompted to choose a category until a valid one is entered.

Section 10.4

1. It is better to pass the entire array of data rather than individual elements if several elements of the array are being manipulated by a procedure.
3. `I` is equal to `MaxSize` if both arrays are the same; `I` is equal to 3 if the third elements do not match.

Section 10.5

1. The `while` loop that calls `EnterInt` is exited when `MaxSize` is reached.

3.
```
repeat
  {invariant:
      No prior value read is Sentinel and
      ClassSize <= MaxSize
  }
  EnterInt (Sentinel, MaxScore, TempScore);
  if TempScore <> Sentinel then
    begin
      ClassSize := ClassSize + 1;           {Increment ClassSize.}
      Scores[ClassSize] := TempScore        {Save the score.}
    end {if}
until (TempScore = Sentinel) or (ClassSize = MaxSize);
```

The `repeat-until` loop necessitates that you check twice to see whether the sentinel value has been entered, whereas it is necessary to check only once with the `while` loop. A `for` loop cannot be used in this situation because we do not know in advance how many data items are going to be entered.

Section 10.6

1. a. an array of characters with 20 elements and subscripts of 1 to 20.
   b. an array of Boolean type values with 10 elements and subscripts of the digit characters '0' to '9'
   c. an array of real numbers with 11 elements and subscripts of the integers –5 to 5
   d. an array of characters with two elements and subscripts of False and True
3. Program Cryptogram checks to see that a letter is in the set ['A' .. 'Z'] before encoding it. Because commas and blanks are not members of this set, they are not encoded.

Section 10.7

1. StringLength   InString

   10   'The quick '
   20   'The quick fox jumped'
   25   'The quick fox jumped   '

3. To compare two arrays of Real numbers for equality requires that each array element in the first array be compared one at a time with its corresponding element in the second array. Two packed arrays of characters may be compared directly to one another, as long as they have been declared as having the same subscript range or length.

Section 10.8

1. The number of characters used to display each string is determined by its length (e.g., Company : CompLen); consequently, only the characters actually read in are displayed, not the blank padding.

Section 10.9

1. The inner for loop invariant says that IndexOfMin contains the subscript of the smallest array element found so far in the unsorted portion of the array.

[1] [2] . . .	[Fill–1] [Fill] . . . [Next] . . . [ClassSize]
elements in their proper place	elements larger than Scores[Fill–1]

[IndexOfMin]

3.

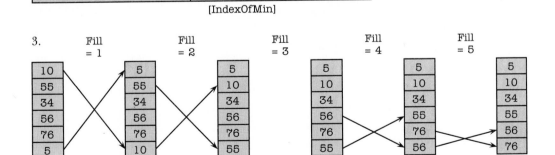

Fifteen comparisons and four exchanges were made.

Section 10.10

1. a. WriteLn executes N * N times; $O(N^2)$
   b. WriteLn executes N * 2 times; $O(N)$
   c. WriteLn executes $(N + (N - 1) + (N - 2) + ... + 2 + 1)$ times; $O(N^2)$

Chapter 11

Section 11.1

```
1. const
     StrLength = 20;

   type
     StringType = packed array [1..StrLength] of Char;
     Part = record
              PartNum : Integer;
              Name : StringType;
              Quantity : Integer;
              Price : Real
            end; {Part}
```

Section 11.2

```
1. with Clerk do
     begin
       WriteLn ('ID: ', ID);
       WriteLn ('Name: ', Name);
       Write ('Gender');
       case Gender of
         'F', 'f' : WriteLn ('Female');
         'M', 'm' : WriteLn ('Male')
       end; {case}
       WriteLn ('Number of Dependents: ', NumDepend);
       WriteLn ('Hourly Rate: ', Rate :4:2);
       WriteLn ('Total Wages: ', TotWages :4:2)
     end; {with}
```

Section 11.3

```
1. type
     ExamStats = record
                   Low, High : 1..100;
                   Average, StandardDev : Real
                 end; {ExamStats}

   var
     Exam1, Exam2 : ExamStats;
```

This program segment prints the statistics for Exam1, copies Exam1 into Exam2, modifies the High field of Exam2, and finally prints new statistics for Exam2.

Section 11.4

1. The program segment initializes two employee records (MyEmp and YourEmp); stores values for ID and Name in each; checks for duplicate Name and ID; checks for different

names with same ID; and stores the Name fields from the two records in string variables if the records are unique. For the two records shown, the output would be

```
Jennie Moss        ***** Jackie Moss
```

MyEmp and YourEmp must be of type Employee; Name1 and Name2 must be of type StringType.

Section 11.5

1. NewAddress must be type Address.

Section 11.6

1. Married: 22 bytes
   Divorced: 6 bytes
   Single: 1 byte

Chapter 12

Section 12.1

1. type
   ```
       Day = (Sun, Mon, Tues, Wed, Thurs, Fri, Sat);
       AnArray = array ['A'..'F', 1..10, Day] of Real;
   ```

   An array of this type can hold 420 elements (6 * 10 * 7).

Section 12.2

1. type
   ```
       Class = (Math1, Algebra, Geometry, Algebra2,
                   Trigonometry, Calculus);
       Sex = (Male, Female);
       MathClassArray = array [Class, 10..12, Sex] of Integer;
   var
       MathInfo : MathClassArray;
   ```

   This array would have 36 elements (6 * 3 * 2).

Section 12.3

1. TempYear is needed in EnterSales to enable use of procedure EnterInt. This is because EnterInt has an Integer as its formal variable argument and Sales.First is type YearRange. A compilation error would result from trying to read Sales.First directly.

Section 12.4

1. a. 1
   d. Austin, Tracy
   f. D

3. It takes the same amount of space to store an array of records as it does to store parallel arrays.

Section 12.5

1. c. 80AJoe Costa
   d. 3
   h. o
   i. Joe Costa

3. The scores will no longer be matched with the correct names.

Chapter 13

Section 13.1

1.

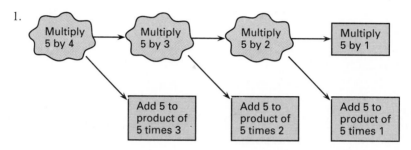

Section 13.2

1. The actual parameter in the recursive call Palindrome (N–1) is an expression and must, therefore, correspond to a formal parameter that is a value parameter.

3.

	M		N		Result
Multiply (5, 4)	M	5	N	4	?
Multiply (5, 3)	M	5,5	N	4,3	?
Multiply (5,2)	M	5,5,5	N	4,3,2	?
Multiply (5, 1)	M	5,5,5,5	N	4,3,2,1	?
return from (5, 1)	M	5,5,5	N	4,3,2	5
return from (5, 2)	M	5,5	N	4,3	10
return from (5, 3)	M	5	N	4	15
return from (5, 4)	M		N		20

Section 13.3

1. ```
   function PowerRaiser (Base, Power : Integer) : Integer;
   begin
      if Power = 1 then
        PowerRaiser := Base
      else
        PowerRaiser := Power * PowerRaiser(Base, Power-1)
   end; {PowerRaiser}
   ```

3. The recursion would go on forever. When N is 2, a recursive call to Fibonacci(0) results. This causes calls to Fibonacci(-1), Fibonacci(-2), and so on.
   ```

Section 13.4

1.
X is 5, 8, 10, 1.   →   X is 5, 8, 1, 10.   →   X is 5, 1, 8, 10.
N is 4.   N is 3.   N is 2.
X becomes 5, 8, 1, 10.   X becomes 5, 1, 8, 10.   X becomes 1, 5, 8, 10.
SelectSort(X, 3)————┘   SelectSort(X, 2)————┘   SelectSort(X, 1)

For the last frame (not shown) N is 1, so an immediate return occurs.

Section 13.5

1. $2^6 - 1$, or 63

Section 13.6

1.

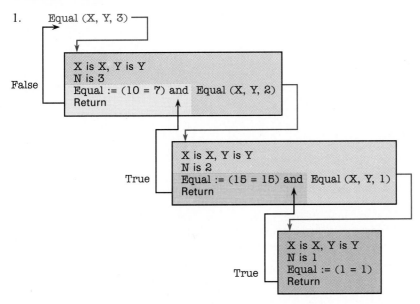

$$\text{Equal} := (X[3] = Y[3]) \text{ and } (X[2] = Y[2]) \text{ and } (X[1] = Y[1])$$

3. Mystery returns the largest value in the array. For the array with element values 10, 15, and 1, the value returned is 25.

Section 13.7

1. BlobCount(1,1) Grid[X, Y] is empty, so 0 is returned.

   BlobCount(1,2) has the value of the expression:

   ```
   1 + BlobCount(0,3) + BlobCount(1,3) + BlobCount(2,3) +
     BlobCount(2,2) + BlobCount(2,1) + BlobCount(1,1) +
     BlobCount(0,1) + BlobCount(0,2)
   ```

   An immediate return occurs with a value of 0 for all function designators except
   BlobCount(2,1).

`BlobCount(2,1)` has the value of the expression:

```
1 + BlobCount(1,2) + BlobCount(2,2) + BlobCount(3,2) +
    BlobCount(3,1) + BlobCount(3,0) + BlobCount(2,0) +
    BlobCount(1,0) + BlobCount(1,1)
```

An immediate return with a value of 0 occurs for each function designator, so `BlobCount(2,1)` returns 1 and `BlobCount(1,2)` returns 1 + 1, or 2.

Chapter 14

Section 14.1

1. a. `[1,3,4,5,6,7]`   e. `True`   i. `[]`
    b. `[1,2,3,5,7]`   f. `False`   j. `False`
    c. `[1,2,3,4,5,6,7]`   g. `[1,2,3,5,7]` k. `True`
    d. `True`   h. `[2]`   l. `True`

Section 14.2

1. The `ReadLn` advances to the start of the next data line after all the values for one picture row have been read. The `WriteLn` advances the cursor to the next screen line.

Section 14.3

1. a. Store `'Abra'` in `Temp1`; current length is 4.
    b. Store `'cadabra'` in `Temp2`; current length is 7.
    c. Store `'Abracadabra'` in `Magic`; current length is 11.
    d. Return 11.
    e. Store `'Abracada'` in `HisMagic`; current length is 8.
    f. Change `HisMagic` to `'Abrda'`; current length is 5.
    g. Change `HisMagic` to `'AbAbrarda'`; current length is 9.
    h. Return 5.
    i. Return `'a'`.
    j. Change `Temp1` to `'abra'`.
    k. Return 8.

3.  ```
    Comma := MakeString (',                    ');
    PosComma := Pos (Comma, Source);
    Copy (Source, 1, PosComma-1, Target);
    Copy (Source, PosComma+2, Capacity-PosComma-1, Destin);
    ```

Section 14.4

1.

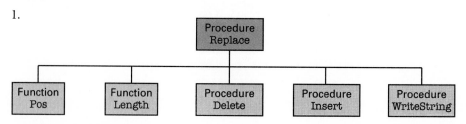
    ```

1. Concat copies as many characters as will fit in the new string. It is not flagged as an error.
3. ReadLnString (InFile, InString.Contents, InString.Len);

Chapter 15

Section 15.1

1. Change the `while` loop body as follows:

```
while not EOF(InData) do
  begin
     ReadLnString (InFile, InString, Len);
     WriteLn (OutFile, InString :Len)
  end; {while}
```

InString is type StringType, and Len is a type Integer variable.
3. It reads in the first three characters of each line of file InData and displays them on a separate output line. If a line contains fewer than three characters, it reads the <eoln> at the end of the line and displays it as a blank. It then skips the next line of data.

Section 15.2

1. It requires 24 bytes to store six numbers in a binary file and 24 bytes in a text file using format specification :4:2. Each number that is larger than 9.99 requires more than 4 bytes and increases the storage requirements for the text file.

Section 15.3

1. 48 bytes for each record of type Book, 8 bytes for an Employee record

3.
```
type
   ScoreArray = array [1..5] of Integer;
   Student = record
               ID : Integer;
               Scores : ScoreArray
             end;
   StudentFile = File of Student;

var
   StuFile : StudentFile;
   NextStu : Student;

begin
  Reset (StuFile);
  while not EOF(StuFile) do
    begin
      Read (StuFile, NextStu);
      WriteLn (Output, NextStu.ID, NextStu.Scores[1])
    end; {while}
```

Section 15.4

1. The file types are the same, all records are in order by stock number in each file, and both files have a sentinel record at the end. They do not need to have the same number of records.

Section 15.5

1.
Question	Stock	Author	Title	Price	Quantity
2	1111..9999	'AAA'..'zzz'	'AAA'...'zzz'	5.95–8.0	1..5000
3	1111..9999	'AAA'..'zzz'	'Pascal ...'	0–1000.00	0..5000
4	1111..9999	'AAA'..'zzz'	'AAA'...'zzz'	25–1000.0	11..5000

3. Only books whose stock numbers qualify are passed to function Match. The Boolean variable Matched has the value of the expression

```
Matched := (LowAuthor <= Author) and (Author <= HighAuthor) and
           (LowTitle <= Title) and (Title <= HighTitle) and ...
```

Section 15.6

1. The following program reads integers one at a time from InFile, doubles them, then writes them to OutFile.

```
program Mystery (InFile, OutFile);
   type
      NumberFile = file of Integer;

   var
      Next : Integer;
      InFile, OutFile : NumberFile;

begin {Mystery}
   Reset (InFile);
   Rewrite (OutFile);
   while not EOF(InFile) do
      begin
         OutFile^ := 2 * InFile^;
         Put (OutFile);
         Get (InFile)
      end {while}
end. {Mystery}
```

Chapter 16

Section 16.1

1. |2+C/$ Success is True.
   |2+C/$−   Success is True.
   |2+C/$ NextCh is '−'; Success is True.
   |2+C/$ NextCh is '$'; Success is True.
   IsEmpty returns False.
   IsFull returns False.

Section 16.2

1. First expression:
```
({
({[
({      Open is '[', Close is ']', Balanced is True.
(       Open is '{'. Close is '}', Balanced is True.
        Open is '(', Close is ')', Balanced is True.
(
        Open is '(', Close is ')', Balanced is True.
```

Second expression:

```
...
({[
({      Open is '[', Close is '}', Balanced is False.
```

Section 16.3

1.

Expression	OpStack	NextCh	NewOp	Result
4 5 6 * 3 / + ^	|4	'4'	4	
4 5 6 * 3 / + ^	|4 5	'5'	5	
4 5 6 * 3 / + ^	|4 5 6	'6'	6	
4 5 6 * 3 / + ^	|4 30	'*'		30
4 5 6 * 3 / + ^	|4 30 3	'3'	3	
4 5 6 * 3 / + ^	|4 10	'/'		10
4 5 6 * 3 / + ^	|14	'+'		14

Section 16.4

```
1. const
     MaxStack = 50;
     StringLen = 20;

   type
     StringType = packed array [1..20] of Char;
     Student = record
                 Name : StringType;
                 Score : Integer;
                 Grade : Char
               end; {Student}

StackElement = Student;
```

Yes, the stack operators can be used.

Section 16.5

1.

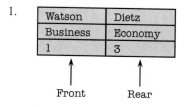

Watson	Carson	Harris
Business	FirstClass	FirstClass
1	2	3

↑ Front   ↑ Rear

Passenger McMahon was removed. There are three passengers left in the queue.

Section 16.6

1.

Watson	Dietz
Business	Economy
1	3

↑ Front   ↑ Rear

Section 16.7

1. Q.Front is 2, Q.Rear is 3, and Q.Items[1..3] are 'Brown', 'Watson', 'Dietz', respectively.

Chapter 17

Section 17.1

1. a. The string 'CA' is stored in the Current field of the record pointed to by R.
   b. The record pointed to by R is copied into the record pointed to by P.
   c. Illegal; P.Current should be written as P^.Current.
   d. Illegal; P cannot be assigned an integer value.
   e. The integer 0 is stored in the Volts field of the record pointed to by the Link field of the record pointed to by R.
   f. Pointer P is reset to point to the same record as pointer R.
   g. The string 'XY' is stored in the Current field of the third record, where the first record is pointed to by R. This is equivalent to Q^.Current := 'XY'.
   h. The Volts field of the record pointed to by R is copied into the Volts field of the record pointed to by Q.

Section 17.3

1. AC   115
   DC   12
   AC   115

Section 17.4

1. When `Target` is `'Boy'`, `Head` points to nodes containing `'Hat'` and `'Boy'`, `Found` is set to `True`, and pointer to `'Boy'` is returned. When `Target` is `'Cap'` or `'Dog'`, `Head` points to nodes containing `'Hat'`, `'Boy'`, `'Cat'`; final value of `Head` is `nil`. This value is returned.

Section 17.5

1. Heap management is performed by the Pascal system, which determines when there are no more cells available on the heap. The revised type declaration would be

```
type
  Stack = record
            Top : StackNext;
            NumItems: Integer
          end;
```

The `Push` operator should increment field `NumItems`, and `Pop` should decrement this field.

3. We should not have to change a client program just because the internal stack representation has changed. These details are hidden from a client program.

Section 17.6

1. It inserts a new queue element (`Johnson`, `Economy`, `5`) at the rear of the queue.

3.
```
New (Temp);
Temp^.Name := 'Billingsly';
Temp^.Class := Business;
Temp^.NumSeats := 2;
Temp^.Next := Q.Rear^.Next;
Q.Rear^.Next := Temp;
Q.Rear := Temp;
Q.NumItems := Q.NumItems + 1;
```

Chapter 18

Section 18.2

1. The first three calls to `Insert` would build the ordered list of integers, `3000`, `4000`, `5000`, pointed to by `MyList`. The second request to insert `4000` returns `False` in `Success`. The call to `Delete` changes `MyList` to the two-element list `3000`, `5000`. The program output is as follows:

```
O.K.
3000
5000
Number of elements is 2
```

Section 18.3

1. We could eliminate the call to Locate, which searches for ElKey, and simply insert ElKey as long as it was in range.

   The node with the duplicate key would be inserted before the first existing list node with that key.

Section 18.4

1. Word in left child < word in tree root < word in right child.

   All words in the left subtree are less than the word in the root, and all words in the right subtree are greater.

3. Inserting parentheses according to the algebraic rules for expression evaluation gives us the following two expressions and trees:

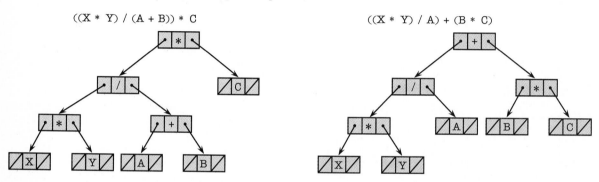

((X * Y) / (A + B)) * C   ((X * Y) / A) + (B * C)

Section 18.5

1. The three forms follow. The parentheses would not appear in the infix forms.

Infix	Prefix	Postfix
X * Y / (A + B) * C	* / * X Y + A B C	X Y * A B + / C *
X * Y / A + B * C	+ / * X Y A * B C	X Y * A / B C * +

3. Inorder: BDCA–X+Y
   Preorder: ABCD–+XY
   Postorder: DCBXY+–A

Section 18.7

1. It builds the following tree, which is unbalanced when the last node (containing key 6000) is inserted, since the right subtree of the node with key 4000 has depth 2 and its left subtree has depth 0.

   Preorder: 3000 2000 2500 4000 5000 6000
   Postorder: 2500 2000 6000 5000 4000 3000

The program output is:

```
2000
2500
3000
4000
5000
6000
Number of nodes is 6
```

```
                3000
               /    \
          2000       4000
              \          \
              2500       5000
                            \
                            6000
```

Section 18.8

1. if Parent is nil then
    Success := False

  else if target key is in node Parent^ then
    begin
      DeleteNode (Parent^);
      Success := True
    end

  else if target key > key of node Parent^ then
    TreeDelete (Parent^.Right, Target, Success)
  else if target Key < key of node Parent^ then
    TreeDelete (Parent^.Left, Target, Success)

Procedure TreeDelete should be called with an initial first parameter of Tree.Root. The problem with DeleteNode is in determining what to do when the node to be deleted has two subtrees—what happens to the subtrees when their parent is removed?

Chapter 19

Section 19.1

1.

First Call			Second Call			Third Call			Fourth Call		
First	Last	Middle	First	Last	Middle	First	Last	Middle	First	Last	Middle
1	9	5	1	4	2	3	4	3	4	4	4

The result is 4.

Section 19.2

1. 'SAL', Hash is (32 + 1) mod 10 = 3, stored at Class[3]
  'BIL', Hash is (23 + 1) mod 10 = 4, stored at Class[4]
  'JIL', Hash is (31 + 1) mod 10 = 2, stored at Class[2]
  'LIB', Hash is (23 + 1) mod 10 = 4, stored at Class[5]
  'HAL', Hash is (21 + 1) mod 10 = 2, stored at Class[6]
  'ROB', Hash is (35 + 1) mod 10 = 6, stored at Class[7]

3. Change the first statement in the while loop body to

```
Index := (Index + Sqr(Probe)) mod MaxSlots
```

Section 19.3

1. Change the if statement to

```
if Class[First].Score < Class[First+1].Score then
   begin {exchange}
```

Change the if statement to

```
if (Class[First].Grade > Class[First+1].Grade)
   or ((Class[First].Grade = Class[First+1].Grade) and
      (Class[First].Name > Class[First+1].Name)) then
      begin {exchange}
```

Section 19.4

1. 40	35	80	75	60	90	70	75	Pass	Comparison	Exchange
35	40							1	1	2
35	40	80						2	1	1
35	40	75	80					3	2	2
35	40	60	75	80				4	3	3
35	40	60	75	80	90			5	1	1
35	40	60	70	75	80	90		6	4	4
35	40	60	70	75	75	80	90	7	3	3
								Total	15	16

Section 19.5

1. a. bubble sort; would be sorted in one pass
   b. selection sort; array is inverted
   c. insertion sort; all elements except the last would be placed with one comparison
   d. insertion sort or selection sort; relatively random order

Section 19.6

1. When doing a merge on two files or two arrays, you need a third file or a third array to store the result.

Section 19.7

1.

```
                              First  Last      PivIndex
[44 75 23 43 55 12 64 77 33]    1     9
[12 33 23 43]44[55 64 77 75]  After partition 5
[12 33 23 43]                   1     4
12[33 23 43]                  After partition 1
                                1     0

    [33 23 43]                  2     4
    [23]33[43]                After partition 3
     23                         2     2

            43                  4     4
```

```
                             First  Last       PivIndex
             [44 55 64 77 75]   5     9
           44[55 64 77 75]    After partition 5
             [55 64 77 75]    6     9
           55[64 77 75]       After partition 6
             [64 77 75]       7     9
           64[77 75]          After partition 7
                              7     6
             [77 75]          8     9
             [75]77           After partition 9
                 75           8     8
                             10     9
```

3.

```
                                     First  Last       PivIndex
   [55 50 10 40 80 90 60 100 70 80 20]   1    11
   [20 50 10 40]55[90 60 100 70 80 80]   After partition 5
   [20 50 10 40]                         1     4
   [10]20[50 40]                         After partition 2
     10                                  1     1
              [50 40]                    3     4
              [40]50                     After partition 4
                 40                      3     3
                                         5     4
                  [90 60 100 70 80 80]   6    11
                  [80 60 80 70]90[100]   After partition 10
                  [80 60 80 70]          6     9
                  [70 60 80]80           After partition 9
                  [70 60 80]             6     8
                  [60]70[80]             After partition 7
                     60                  6     6
                        80               8     8
                           100          11    10
```

There are 12 calls to QuickSort and 6 calls to Partition. QuickSort would probably
beat MergeSort. Because of the small array size, insertion sort would be best.

Index